About This Book

This book teaches you how to use the Java WorkShop software to learn Java programming. You will create applets and applications with Java WorkShop, learning the powerful capabilities of the software as you go, including the Visual Java design tool. By the time you get through with this book, you'll know enough about Java to do just about anything, inside an applet or out. Also, you'll be an expert at using Java WorkShop to program more quickly and efficiently.

Who Should Read This Book

Teach Yourself SunSoft Java WorkShop in 21 Days is for both novice and experienced computer programmers. If you know what variables, loops, and functions are, you should be able to benefit from this book, and veteran programmers will find plenty to learn from here as they are introduced to Java. If any of the following descriptions fits you, you'll definitely want to read this book:

- ☐ You're a real whiz at HTML, are comfortable with the use of CGI programs on your pages, and want to move on to the next level in Web page design.
- ☐ You had some BASIC or Pascal in school and you have a basic grasp of what programming is, and you've heard Java is easy to learn, powerful, and very cool.
- ☐ You've programmed C and C++ for many years, have heard this Java thing is becoming popular, and are wondering what all the fuss is about.
- ☐ You've heard that Java is good for Web-based applets, and you're curious about how good it is for creating more general applications.

What if you know programming, but you don't know object-oriented programming? Fear not. This book assumes no background in object-oriented design. If you know object-oriented programming, the first couple of days will be easy for you.

What if you're a complete beginner? This book might move a little fast for you in the last week, and some of the object-oriented concepts could be intimidating. Java can be a good language to start with, though—take it slow, work through all the examples, and you will be creating your own Java applets in no time at all.

How This Book Is Structured

This book is intended to be read and absorbed over the course of three weeks. During each week, you'll read seven chapters that present concepts related to the Java language, the creation of applets and applications, and Java WorkShop.

Conventions

Text that you type and text that should appear on your screen is presented in `monospace` type

```
It will look like this.
```

to mimic the way text looks on your screen. Variables and placeholders will appear in `monospace italic`.

NOTE

A Note box presents interesting pieces of information related to the surrounding discussion.

TIP

A Tip box offers advice or teaches an easier way to do something.

WARNING

A Warning box advises you about potential problems and helps you steer clear of disaster.

NEW TERM A new term icon indicates where a definition is given. The term appears in italics.

TYPE A type icon identifies some new code that you can type in.

OUTPUT An output icon highlights what the same code looks like when run.

ANALYSIS An analysis icon alerts you to the author's line-by-line analysis.

Teach
Yourself
SUNSOFT
JAVA™
WORKSHOP™

in 21 Days

Teach Yourself
SunSoft Java™
WorkShop™
in 21 Days

Laura Lemay
Charles L. Perkins
Rogers Cadenhead

201 West 103rd Street
Indianapolis, Indiana 46290

Copyright © 1996 by Sams.net Publishing

FIRST EDITION

International Standard Book Number: 1-5721-159-9

Library of Congress Catalog Card Number: 96-68937

99 98 97 96   4 3 2 1

Interpretation of the printing code: the rightmost double-digit number is the year of the book's printing; the rightmost single-digit, the number of the book's printing. For example, a printing code of 96-1 shows that the first printing of the book occurred in 1996.

Composed in AGaramond and MCPdigital by Macmillan Computer Publishing

Printed in the United States of America

Trademarks

President, Sams Publishing   Richard K. Swadley
Publishing Manager   Mark Taber
Managing Editor   Cindy Morrow
Marketing Manager   John Pierce
Assistant Marketing Manager   Kristina Perry

Acquisitions Editor
David Mayhew

Development Editor
Kelly Murdock

Software Development Specialist
Bob Correll

Production/Copy Editor
Heather Stith

Technical Reviewers
Zach Bir, Brad Birnbaum, Alec Plum

Editorial Coordinator
Bill Whitmer

Technical Edit Coordinator
Lorraine Schaffer

Resource Coordinator
Deborah Frisby

Formatter
Frank Sinclair

Editorial Assistants
Carol Ackerman, Andi Richter, Rhonda Tinch-Mize

Technical Assistant
M. C. Moewe

Cover Designer
Tim Amrhein

Book Designer
Gary Adair

Copy Writer
Peter Fuller

Production Team Supervisor
Brad Chinn

Production
Mary Ann Abramson, Debra Bolhuis, Carol Bowers, Jeanne Clark, Bruce Clingaman, Jason Hand, Daniel Harris, Casey Price, Laura Robbins, Bobbi Satterfield, Mark Walchle

Indexer
Tom Dinse

Overview

	Introduction		0
Week 1 at a Glance			**1**
Day 1	Introduction to Java and Java WorkShop		3
2	Object-Oriented Programming		23
3	Java Language Basics		53
4	Working with Objects		79
5	Arrays, Conditionals, and Loops		103
6	Creating Classes and Applications		127
7	More About Methods		149
Week 2 at a Glance			**169**
Day 8	Applet Basics		171
9	Graphics, Fonts, and Color		193
10	Simple Animation and Threads		221
11	More Animation, Images, and Sound		245
12	Simple Events and Interactivity		271
13	Visual Java and the Abstract Windowing Toolkit		293
14	Windows, Networking, and Other Tidbits		347
Week 3 at a Glance			**373**
Day 15	Modifiers		375
16	Packages and Interfaces		393
17	Exceptions		417
18	Multithreading		431
19	Streams		455
20	Native Methods and Libraries		485
21	Advanced Concepts		503
	Graduation		533

Appendixes

A	Language Summary	537
B	Class Hierarchy Diagrams	547
C	The Java Class Library	561
D	How Java Differs from C and C++	571
E	JDK Command-Line Utilities	577
F	Java WorkShop Troubleshooting	583
G	What's on the CD-ROM	587
	Index	591

Contents

Week 1 at a Glance   **1**

Day 1   Introduction to Java and Java WorkShop   **3**

What Is Java? 4
Java's Past, Present, and Future 6
Why Learn Java? 7
    Java Is Platform-Independent 7
    Java Is Object-Oriented 10
    Java Is Easy to Learn 10
Java WorkShop 11
    Obtaining the Software 12
    Installing the Software 13
    Getting Started 13
Creating a Java Applet 14
    Starting a New Project 14
    Entering the Source Code 15
    Compiling the Applet 17
    Testing the Project 18
Summary 19
Q&A 20
Today's Featured Applet 21

Day 2   Object-Oriented Programming   **23**

Thinking in Objects: An Analogy 24
    Objects and Classes 25
Attributes and Behavior 27
    Attributes of an Object 27
    How Objects Behave 28
Creating a Class 29
    Using Portfolio Manager 29
    The Jabberwock Class 30
    Running the Applet 35
Inheritance, Interfaces, and Packages 36
    Inheritance 36
    Creating a Class Hierarchy 37
    How Inheritance Works 39
    Single and Multiple Inheritance 40
    Interfaces 41
    Using Packages 42
Creating a Subclass 42
    Jazzing Up Palindrome 42
    Overriding a Method 44

Importing a Package 44
Using the Source Browser 46
Summary 47
Q&A 48
Today's Featured Applet 49

Day 3   Java Language Basics   **53**

Statements and Expressions 54
Variables and Data Types 54
Declaring Variables 55
Naming Variables 56
Variable Types 57
Assigning Values to Variables 59
Comments 59
Literals 60
Number Literals 60
Boolean Literals 61
Character Literals 61
String Literals 62
Expressions and Operators 63
Arithmetic 63
Creating the Arithmetic Applet 64
More About Assignment 66
Incrementing and Decrementing 67
Creating the PrePost Applet 67
Comparisons 69
Logical Operators 69
Bitwise Operators 70
Operator Precedence 71
String Arithmetic 73
Summary 74
Q&A 75
Today's Featured Applet 76

Day 4   Working with Objects   **79**

Creating New Objects 80
Using new 80
What new Does 82
A Note on Memory Management 82
Introduction to Parameters 83
Using Project Manager 83
Creating the CreateDate2 Applet 84
Project Manager Features 85
Accessing and Setting Class and Instance Variables 86
Getting Values 87
Changing Values 87
Class Variables 88

Calling Methods 89
  Class Methods 91
References to Objects 92
Converting Objects and Primitive Types 93
  Casting Primitive Types 93
  Casting Objects 94
  Casting Primitive Types to Objects and Vice Versa 95
Odds and Ends 96
  Comparing Objects 96
  Determining the Class of an Object 98
The Java Class Library 99
Summary 100
Q&A 100
Today's Featured Applet 101

Day 5 Arrays, Conditionals, and Loops   103

Arrays 104
  Declaring Array Variables 104
  Creating Array Objects 104
  Accessing Array Elements 105
  Changing Array Elements 106
  Multidimensional Arrays 106
Block Statements 107
if Conditionals 107
  The Conditional Operator 108
switch Conditionals 109
for Loops 111
while and do Loops 112
  while Loops 112
  do...while Loops 113
Breaking Out of Loops 114
  Labeled Loops 115
Debugging with Java WorkShop 116
  Creating the Grader Applet 117
  Jumping to Errors 119
  What the Grader Applet Is Supposed to Do 119
Fixing the Errors 120
  The switch Error 121
  Using Breakpoints 122
Summary 124
Q&A 124
Today's Featured Applet 125

Day 6 Creating Classes and Applications   127

Defining Classes 128
Creating Instance and Class Variables 128
  Defining Instance Variables 128
  Constants 129
  Class Variables 130

Creating Methods 131
    Defining Methods 131
    Trying Out Methods 132
    The this Keyword 133
    Variable Scope and Method Definitions 134
    Passing Arguments to Methods 135
    Class and Instance Methods 138
Creating Java Applications 139
    Java Applications and Program Arguments 139
    Passing Arguments to Java Applications 140
    Handling Arguments in Your Java Application 140
    Setting Program Arguments 142
    Converting Arguments 143
Running Applications from the Command Line 144
Summary 145
Q&A 145
Today's Featured Applet 146

Day 7   More About Methods   149

Creating Methods with the Same Name but Different Arguments 150
    Creating the MyRect Class 150
Constructor Methods 154
    Basic Constructor Methods 154
    Calling Another Constructor Method 156
    Overloading Constructor Methods 156
Overriding Methods 159
    Creating Methods that Override Existing Methods 159
    Calling the Original Method 160
    Overriding Constructor Methods 161
Finalizer Methods 162
Java Documentation 163
    Using Source Browser 163
    Inserting Comments into Code 164
    Final Word on Commenting 165
Summary 165
Q&A 166
Today's Featured Applet 166

Week 2 at a Glance   169

Day 8   Applet Basics   171

How Applets and Applications Differ 172
Creating Applets 173
    Major Applet Activities 174
    A Simple Applet 176

Including an Applet on a Web Page 177
    The <APPLET> Tag 178
    Testing the Result 179
    Putting Applets on the Web 180
More About the <APPLET> Tag 180
    ALIGN 181
    HSPACE and VSPACE 183
    CODE and CODEBASE 183
Passing Parameters to Applets 184
    Passing Parameters to BigPalindrome 185
    Changing a Parameter 188
Summary 189
Q&A 190
Today's Featured Applet 191

Day 9   Graphics, Fonts, and Color   193

The Graphics Class 194
    The Graphics Coordinate System 194
Drawing and Filling 195
    Lines 195
    Rectangles 196
    Polygons 199
    Ovals 201
    Arcs 201
    A Simple Graphics Example 206
    Copying and Clearing 207
Text and Fonts 208
    Creating Font Objects 208
    Drawing Characters and Strings 209
    Finding Out Font Information 211
    Using Font Metrics 212
Color 214
    Using Color Objects 214
    Testing and Setting the Current Colors 215
    A Color Example 216
Summary 218
Q&A 218
Today's Featured Applet 219

Day 10 Simple Animation and Threads   221

Creating Animation in Java 222
    Painting and Repainting 222
    Starting and Stopping an Applet's Execution 223
    Putting It Together 223
Introduction to Threads 225
    The Problem with DigitalClock 226
    Writing Applets with Threads 226
    Fixing DigitalClock 228

Reducing Animation Flicker 230
    Avoiding Flicker 230
    How to Override update() 231
    Solution 1: Don't Clear the Screen 231
    Solution 2: Redraw Only What You Have To 234
Summary 241
Q&A 241
Today's Featured Applet 242

Day 11   More Animation, Images, and Sound   245

Retrieving and Using Images 246
    Getting Images 246
    Drawing Images 247
    Modifying Images 251
Creating Animation Using Images 252
    An Example: Pete 252
Retrieving and Using Sounds 260
Sun's Animator Applet 263
Double-Buffering 263
    Creating Applets with Double-Buffering 264
    An Example: Checkers2 Revisited 265
Summary 267
Q&A 268
Today's Featured Applet 268

Day 12   Simple Events and Interactivity   271

Mouse Clicks 272
    mouseDown and mouseUp 272
    An Example: Spots 273
Mouse Movements 277
    mouseDrag and mouseMove 277
    mouseEnter and mouseExit 277
    An Example: Lines 278
Keyboard Events 282
    keyDown and keyUp Methods 282
    Default Keys 283
    An Example: Keys 283
    Testing for Modifier Keys 287
The AWT Event Handler 287
Summary 289
Q&A 290
Today's Featured Applet 291

Day 13   Visual Java and the Abstract Windowing Toolkit   293

An AWT Overview 294
The Basic User Interface Components 296
    Labels 297
    Buttons 298

Check Boxes 299
Radio Buttons 300
Choice Menus 302
Text Fields 303
Panels and Layout 305
Layout Managers 305
Insets 310
Handling User Interface Actions and Events 311
Nesting Panels and Components 314
Nested Panels 314
Events and Nested Panels 315
More User Interface Components 316
Text Areas 316
Scrolling Lists 318
Scrollbars and Sliders 319
Canvases 322
More User Interface Events 322
A Complete Example: RGB to HSB Converter 323
Create the Applet Layout 324
Create the Panel Layout 324
Define the Subpanels 326
Handle the Actions 329
Update the Result 329
The Complete Source Code 331
Introduction to Visual Java 334
Designing an Interface 334
Modifying a Panel Grid 336
Using the Palette Toolbar 336
Stretching a Component 337
Placing Multiple Labels 337
Generating the Interface Code 338
Writing the Program 338
Handling Events 339
Summary 342
Q&A 343
Today's Featured Applet 344

Day 14 Windows, Networking, and Other Tidbits   347
Windows, Menus, and Dialog Boxes 348
Frames 348
Menus 350
Dialog Boxes 353
File Dialog Boxes 355
Window Events 356
Using AWT Windows in Applications 356

Networking in Java 357
    Creating Links Inside Applets 358
    Opening Web Connections 361
    openStream() 361
    The URLconnection Class 364
    Sockets 364
Other Applet Hints 366
    The showStatus() Method 366
    Applet Information 366
    Communicating Between Applets 367
Summary 368
Q&A 368
Today's Featured Applet 370

Week 3 at a Glance   **373**

Day 15   Modifiers   **375**

Method and Variable Access Control 376
    public 377
    Package 377
    protected 378
    private 380
    Conventions for Instance Variable Access 381
Class Variables and Methods 384
The final Modifier 386
    final Classes 386
    final Variables 387
    final Methods 387
abstract Methods and Classes 389
Summary 390
Q&A 390
Today's Featured Applet 391

Day 16   Packages and Interfaces   **393**

Packages 394
    Programming in the Large 394
    Programming in the Small 397
    Hiding Classes 400
Interfaces 401
    Programming in the Large 402
    Programming in the Small 406
Summary 408
Q&A 409
Today's Featured Applet 411

Day 17   Exceptions   **417**

Programming in the Large 418
Programming in the Small 420

Limitations Placed on the Programmer 424
The finally Clause 425
Summary 426
Q&A 426
Today's Featured Applet 428

Day 18 Multithreading   **431**

The Problem with Parallelism 432
Thinking Multithreaded 433
    Synchronization 435
    Protecting a Class Variable 438
Creating and Using Threads 439
    The Runnable Interface 441
    Testing Runnable 441
    Named Threads 443
Knowing When a Thread Has Stopped 444
Thread Scheduling 445
    Preemptive Versus Non-preemptive 446
    Testing Your Scheduler 447
Summary 450
Q&A 450
Today's Featured Applet 452

Day 19 Streams   **455**

Input Streams 456
    The abstract Class InputStream 457
    ByteArrayInputStream 461
    FileInputStream 462
    FilterInputStream 463
    PipedInputStream 469
    SequenceInputStream 469
    StringBufferInputStream 470
Output Streams 471
    The abstract Class OutputStream 471
    ByteArrayOutputStream 472
    FileOutputStream 474
    FilterOutputStream 474
    PipedOutputStream 479
Related Classes 479
Summary 480
Q&A 480
Today's Featured Applet 481

Day 20 Native Methods and Libraries   **485**

Disadvantages of native Methods 486
The Illusion of Required Efficiency 487
    Built-In Optimizations 488
    Simple Optimization Tricks 488

Writing native Methods 489
    The Sample Class 489
    Generating Header and Stub Files 491
    Creating SimpleFileNative.c 494
A Native Library 498
    Linking It All 498
    Using Your Library 498
Summary 499
Q&A 499
Today's Featured Applet 500

Day 21   Advanced Concepts   **503**

The Big Picture 503
    A Powerful Vision 504
The Java Virtual Machine 505
    An Overview 506
    The Fundamental Parts 507
    The Constant Pool 511
    Limitations 512
Bytecodes in More Detail 512
    The Bytecode Interpreter 512
    The Just-in-Time Compiler 513
    Java-to-C Translation 514
The Garbage Collector 515
    The Problem 515
    The Solution 516
    Java's Parallel Garbage Collector 518
The Security Story 519
    Java's Security Model 519
Summary 527
Q&A 528
Today's Featured Applet 528

Graduation   **533**

Other Java Books 533
Web Sites 534
Usenet Newsgroups 535
The Last Word 536

A   Language Summary   **537**

Reserved Words 538
Comments 539
Literals 539
Variable Declaration 540
Variable Assignment 540
Operators 541
Objects 542

Arrays 542
Loops and Conditionals 543
Class Definitions 543
Method and Constructor Definitions 544
Packages, Interfaces, and Importing 545
Exceptions and Guarding 546

B   Class Hierarchy Diagrams   **547**
About These Diagrams 559

C   The Java Class Library   **561**
`java.lang` 562
    Interfaces 562
    Classes 562
`java.util` 563
    Interfaces 563
    Classes 563
`java.io` 564
    Interfaces 564
    Classes 564
                                   565
`java.net` 566
    Interfaces 566
    Classes 566
`java.awt` 566
    Interfaces 566
    Classes 567
`java.awt.image` 568
    Interfaces 568
    Classes 569
`java.awt.peer` 569
`java.applet` 570
    Interfaces 570
    Class 570

D   How Java Differs from C and C++   **571**
Pointers 572
Arrays 572
Strings 573
Memory Management 573
Data Types 573
Operators 574
Control Flow 574
Arguments 574
Other Differences 574

E   JDK Command-Line Utilities   **577**
`javac` 578
`java` 579

     `appletviewer` 580

     `javadoc` 580

     `javah` 581

     `javap` 581

F   **Java WorkShop Troubleshooting**   **583**

     Questions and Answers 584

G   **What's on the CD-ROM**   **587**

     Explorer 588

     HTML Tools 588

     Graphics and Sound Applications 588

     Java 588

     Utilities 589

     About Shareware 589

     Index   **591**

Dedication

To Mary, to Max, and to Mom.
   Rogers

To Eric, for all the usual reasons
(moral support, stupid questions, comfort in dark times).
   LL

For RKJP, ARL, and NMH
the three most important people in my life.
   CLP

Acknowledgments

From Rogers Cadenhead:

To the great folks at Sams, especially Deborah Frisby, David Mayhew, and Mark Taber. They turned a buyer of seven tons of computer books in 1996 into a writer of them. My relationship with the Texas Guaranteed Student Loan Corporation is much better as a result. Thanks also to editors Heather Stith, Kelly Murdock, Zach Bir, Brad Birnbaum, and Alec Plum, who contributed immensely to the book.

From Laura Lemay:

To Sun's Java team, for all their hard work on Java the language and on the browser, and particularly to Jim Graham, who demonstrated Java and HotJava to me on very short notice in May and planted the idea for this book.

To everyone who bought my previous books, and liked them. Buy this one too.

From Charles L. Perkins:

To Patrick Naughton, who first showed me the power and the promise of OAK (Java) in early 1993.

To Mark Taber, who shepherded this lost sheep through his first book.

About the Authors

Laura Lemay is a technical writer and a nerd. After spending six years writing software documentation for various computer companies in Silicon Valley, she decided writing books would be much more fun (but has still not yet made up her mind). In her spare time, she collects computers, e-mail addresses, interesting hair colors, and nonrunning motorcycles. She is also the perpetrator of *Teach Yourself Web Publishing with HTML in 14 Days*.

You can reach her by e-mail at `lemay@lne.com` or visit her home page at `http://www.lne.com/lemay/`.

Charles L. Perkins is the founder of Virtual Rendezvous, a company building a Java-based service that will foster socially focused, computer-mediated, real-time filtered interactions between people's personas in the virtual environments of the near future. In previous lives, he has evangelized NeXTSTEP, Smalltalk, and UNIX and has earned degrees in both physics and computer science. Before attempting this book, he was an amateur columnist and author. He's done research in speech recognition, neural nets, gestural user interfaces, computer graphics, and language theory, but had the most fun working at Thinking Machines and Xerox PARC's Smalltalk group. In his spare time, he reads textbooks for fun.

You can reach him via e-mail at `virtual@rendezvous.com`, or visit his Java page at `http://rendezvous.com/java`.

Rogers Cadenhead is a Web developer, computer programmer, and writer who created the multiuser games *Czarlords* and *Super Video Poker*. Thousands of readers see his work in the *Fort Worth Star-Telegram* question-and-answer column "Ask Ed Brice." He has developed Java applets for Tele-Communications Inc. and other clients.

You can reach him at the e-mail address `rcade@airmail.net`, or visit his Web page for this book at `http://www.spiderbyte.com/java`.

Introduction

At this point, most people with an interest in technology have heard about Java. This language gets the kind of attention normally reserved for multicolor-haired basketball players, Steven Spielberg films, and divorcing British royalty. Java attracts this hype because it's the first 21st century programming language, taking full advantage of the possibilities of the Internet.

Java also is being noticed by people who don't want to program a VCR, much less a computer. It's the language that gave the World Wide Web a brain. The Web started out as a one-way road—information traveling from page to user. This was a remarkable media form (and a great way to look busy at the office), but it was limited in terms of interactivity. Java changed all that. Its programs, called *applets*, can run over the Internet, and they make the Web a more engaging experience. There's animation, sound, games, utilities, and hundreds of other activities now taking place on Web pages—all created with Java.

When Java was introduced, the only way you could write programs was with command-line tools. They were functional, but hard to use in comparison to the development software available for established languages such as C++ and Visual Basic. Java WorkShop, a programming environment designed by the creators of Java, makes it easier to become a better Java programmer. The software has a lot of powerful capabilities that can be used to write applets and applications with the language.

Teach Yourself SunSoft Java WorkShop in 21 Days teaches two things: Java programming and Java WorkShop. As you learn about the Java language, you'll be learning about WorkShop at the same time. You will use the development environment to create not only applets, but also applications, which are more general Java programs that don't need to run inside a Web browser. By the time you finish the book, you'll know enough about Java to do just about anything, inside an applet or out.

How This Book Is Organized

Teach Yourself SunSoft Java WorkShop in 21 Days describes Java in its current state (the 1.0.2 version of the language) and it provides full details on the Java WorkShop development environment. It introduces Visual Java, the graphical tool that makes it easier to develop graphical programs. There are other books that describe only the API prior to 1.0 and older versions of Java WorkShop prior to Visual Java's release.

Java WorkShop is in the last stages of development before its commercial release at the time of this writing, and some features of the software will be expanded or enhanced by the time you read this. Keep this in mind as you work with Java WorkShop to create and compile your Java programs. If things aren't behaving the way you expect, check the Web sites mentioned at the end of this introduction for more information.

Teach Yourself SunSoft Java WorkShop in 21 Days covers Java WorkShop, the Java language, and its class libraries in 21 days, organized as three separate weeks. Each week covers a different broad area.

In the first week, you'll learn about the Java language itself:

- ☐ Day 1 is the basic introduction: what Java is, why it's cool, how to get Java WorkShop, and how to install it. You also will create your first Java applet.
- ☐ On Day 2, you'll explore basic object-oriented programming concepts as they apply to Java. You also will create a jabberwock!
- ☐ On Day 3, you start getting down to details with the basic Java building blocks: data types, variables, and expressions such as arithmetic and comparisons.
- ☐ Day 4 goes into detail about how to deal with objects in Java: how to create them, how to access their variables and call their methods, and how to compare and copy them. You will use the Portfolio Manager and Project Manager features of Java WorkShop.
- ☐ On Day 5, you'll learn more about Java with arrays, conditional statements, and loops.
- ☐ Day 6 is the best one yet. You'll learn how to create classes, the basic building blocks of any Java program, as well as how to put together a Java application (an application being a Java program that can run on its own without a Web browser).
- ☐ Day 7 builds on what you learned on Day 6. On Day 7, you'll learn more about how to create and use methods, including overriding and overloading methods and creating constructors. You also will use the Java WorkShop Source Browser to learn more about methods and classes.

Week 2 is dedicated to applets and the Java class libraries:

- ☐ Day 8 provides the basics of applets—how they're different from applications, how to create them, and the most important parts of an applet's life cycle. You'll also learn how to create HTML pages that contain Java applets.
- ☐ On Day 9, you'll learn about the Java classes for drawing shapes and characters to the screen in black, white, or any other color.
- ☐ On Day 10, you'll start animating those shapes you learned about on Day 9, including learning what threads and their uses are.
- ☐ Day 11 covers more detail about animation, adding bitmap images and audio to the mix.

☐ Day 12 delves into interactivity by explaining how to handle mouse and keyboard clicks from the user in your Java applets.

☐ Day 13 is ambitious; on that day, you'll learn about using Java's Abstract Windowing Toolkit and Java WorkShop Visual Java to create a user interface in your applet including menus, buttons, check boxes, and other elements.

☐ On Day 14, you explore the last of the main Java class libraries for creating applets: windows and dialog boxes, networking, and a few other tidbits.

Week 3 finishes up with advanced topics, for when you start doing larger and more complex Java programs, or when you want to learn more:

☐ On Day 15, you'll learn more about the Java language's modifiers for abstract and final methods and classes as well as for protecting a class' private information from the prying eyes of other classes.

☐ Day 16 covers interfaces and packages, useful for abstracting protocols of methods to aid reuse and for the grouping and categorization of classes.

☐ Day 17 covers exceptions, which are errors, warnings, and other abnormal conditions generated either by the system or by you in your programs.

☐ Day 18 builds on the thread basics you learned on Day 10 to give a broad overview of multithreading and how to use it to allow different parts of your Java programs to run in parallel.

☐ On Day 19, you'll learn all about the input and output streams in Java's input/output library.

☐ Day 20 teaches you about native code and how to link C code into your Java programs to provide missing functionality or to gain performance.

☐ Finally, on Day 21, you'll get an overview of some of the behind-the-scenes technical details of how Java works: the bytecode compiler and interpreter, the techniques Java uses to ensure the integrity and security of your programs, and the Java garbage collector.

The end of each chapter offers common questions asked about that day's subject matter with answers from the authors. It also includes a Featured Applet at the end of each day's lesson from some of the best Java programmers on the World Wide Web. Guidelines are provided for adding each applet easily to Web pages, and all source code is included on the CD-ROM that accompanies this book.

Web Sites for Further Information

Before, while, and after you read this book, there are three Web sites that might be of interest to you as a Java developer.

The official Java Web site is at `http://java.sun.com/`. At this site, you'll find the Java development software, the latest news on Java WorkShop, the new HotJava Web browser, and online documentation for all aspects of the Java language. It has several mirror sites that it lists online, and you should probably use the site closest to you on the Internet for your downloading and Java Web browsing. There is also a site for developer resources and applet users called Gamelan at `http://www.gamelan.com/`.

This book has a companion Web site at `http://www.spiderbyte.com/java`. Information at that site includes examples, more information and background for this book, corrections to this book, and other tidbits that were not included here. Co-author Rogers Cadenhead administers the site, and he welcomes your questions and comments about this book, about Java WorkShop, and about Java itself.

WEEK

1

at a Glance

☐ Introduction to Java and Java WorkShop
Platform-independence
The Java WorkShop environment

☐ Object-Oriented Programming
Objects and classes
Encapsulation
Modularity

☐ Java Language Basics
Java statements and expressions
Variables and data types
Comparisons and logical operators

1

2

3

4

5

6

7

☐ Working with Objects
  Testing and modifying instance variables
  Converting objects

☐ Arrays, Conditionals, and Loops
  Conditional tests
  Iteration
  Block statements

☐ Creating Classes and Applications
  Defining constants
  Defining instance and class variables
  Defining methods

☐ More About Methods
  Overloading methods
  Constructor methods
  Overriding methods

Day 1

Introduction to Java and Java WorkShop

Welcome to the beginning of *Teach Yourself SunSoft Java WorkShop in 21 Days*. For the next three weeks, you will learn about Java programming by using Java WorkShop, SunSoft's new program development software. You will use WorkShop to create two types of programs: applications and applets.

An *applet* is a special kind of Java program that can run over the World Wide Web. Applets are placed on Web pages just like a graphic or a hyperlink and are run by Java-capable browsers such as Netscape Navigator 2.0. Applets are being used to animate graphics, provide dynamically updated information such as sports scores, and accomplish many other tasks.

Applications are every other kind of program. Java, like Visual C++ and other languages, can be used to develop all types of software. Java WorkShop itself was written with Java, and it provides a look at what can be accomplished with the language.

The first day of any class can be intimidating, but today's workload is relatively modest. You will hit the ground running with Java WorkShop, creating your first program with the Java language. The following subjects will be covered:

☐ The story of Java, and why you should learn it

☐ Installing Java WorkShop

☐ Using WorkShop for the first time

You might know some of Java's story already from the many press reports on the language. The rest should be new to readers who are new to Java WorkShop.

What Is Java?

Java is an object-oriented programming language developed by Sun Microsystems, a company known for its UNIX workstations, Internet servers, and network interfaces. Modeled after C++, the Java language was designed to be small, simple, and portable across platforms and operating systems.

Although Java was not created specifically with the Internet in mind, it has proved to be well-suited for it. Sun's language provides an environment where programs can be run safely over the World Wide Web and other Internet services. Java programs can be executed on any system that has a Java interpreter, regardless of the operating system being used, and Java doesn't tax the network because the programs are run on the user's computer. One of the main reasons that so many people are excited by Java is that it gives the Web a brain. Figure 1.1 shows `EarthWeb Chat`, an applet that uses Java to offer America Online-style chat on a Web page. Any browser that can handle Java, such as Netscape Navigator 2.0 for Windows 95 and Internet Explorer 3.0, can run applets.

 NOTE

Visit `http://chat.earthweb.com` with a Java-capable browser to see EarthWeb Chat in action. As of this writing, Netscape Navigator 2.0 is the only popular browser that can run Java applets, and even it only works on some platforms. Future versions of the HotJava and Microsoft Internet Explorer browsers will be Java-capable, according to their developers, and Navigator is being extended so that more versions of its software can handle Java.

To create an applet, you write it in the Java language, compile it using a Java compiler, and refer to that applet with HTML tags in your Web pages. You put the Java files and HTML pages on a Web site in the same way that you normally make HTML and image files available.

Figure 1.1.

The EarthWeb Chat applet.

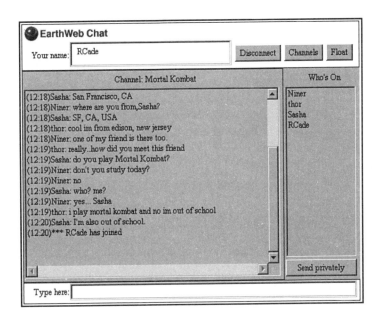

The following is an example of how the `<APPLET>` tag is used to add a Java applet to a Web page:

```
<APPLET CODE="Palindrome.class" WIDTH=150 HEIGHT=25></APPLET>
```

When a user with a Java-capable browser views the page containing the Java applet, the browser downloads the applet to the user's system and executes it. A running Java applet can respond to user input and other data, expanding the sophistication and interactivity of the Web page. People using browsers that cannot handle Java will see text, a static graphic, or nothing at all depending on how the browsing software and the HTML page that includes the applet have been designed.

Applets require a Java-capable browser in order to run, although they also can be tested within Java WorkShop. Later today when you create an applet, you'll learn more about how applets, browsers, and the World Wide Web work together.

A Java program can be an applet, an application, or both depending on how the program is written and the capabilities that it uses. Most of the programs that you will write in this book are applets, but applications also will be covered in detail. If you're a Web developer who is eager to add Java to your bag of tricks, you'll be getting off to a fast start today.

Java's Past, Present, and Future

Before getting to the nitty-gritty of programming, a look at Java's origins is in order. Like most major developments related to the Internet, Java has a history that's only a few years old. When the Java language was developed at Sun Microsystems in 1991, it was supposed to be the brains of a new generation of household appliances—television sets, toasters, VCRs, cable boxes, and the like. At the time, the World Wide Web was still a little-known idea bouncing around the high-energy physics community, in marked contrast to the pervasive phenomenon that it has become today. FirstPerson, the Sun spin-off group, was preparing its new language, which was called Oak, for an expected boom in interactive TVs, 600-channel cable boxes, and other devices.

The goal of Oak was to be small, fast, efficient, and easily portable to a wide range of hardware devices. The language was object-oriented like C++, but it was designed to be easier to learn and to use. However, the slow development of interactive TV as a market left the project on the verge of disbanding in 1993, until Sun executives decided to adapt Oak for use with the World Wide Web.

The original goals for Oak made it an ideal language for distributing executable programs through the Web. It also had benefits as a general-purpose programming language for developing object-oriented programs. When Oak could not be trademarked because of existing products of that name, Sun christened the language as Java in January 1995.

 NOTE

> Contrary to what you might have heard, Java does not stand for Just Another Vague Acronym—it's not an acronym at all. Kim Polese, the one-person marketing team at FirstPerson when Java was named, says that the name was cooked up during a Sun brainstorming session where replacements for Oak were suggested. Java won out over alternatives such as DNA, Silk, Ruby, and WRL (WebRunner Language).

The Java language was used in several projects within Sun, but it did not receive much commercial attention until it was paired with the HotJava Web browser. Sun developed HotJava in late 1994 to showcase both Java applets and the language itself. The browser was a Java application, and it showed developers that complex, windowing software could be produced with the language. The first version of HotJava ran applets that were written with an alpha release of the Java language. In March 1995, a front-page article in the *San Jose Mercury News* sang the praises of Java, describing it as a way to make the Web "as lively as a CD-ROM." Netscape first incorporated Java in version 2.0 of its Navigator browser, and applets are being featured today on several thousand Web pages.

Most of these applets have been developed with the Java Developer's Kit (JDK), released to developers through the World Wide Web and CD-ROMs. The JDK, which has reached version 1.0.2 as of this writing, is a set of command-line development tools used to write Java programs. It is available for Windows 95, Windows NT, MacOS System 7.5, SPARC Solaris (2.3 or later), and Intel x86 Solaris systems.

The future appears promising for the language, and Sun is no longer the only major company making efforts to use it. Several big companies have licensed the Java technology from Sun, including Microsoft, IBM, Novell, Borland, Netscape, and Symantec. Typically, two types of projects are coming out as a result of this licensing: browser-related Java tools and development-related Java tools. Java WorkShop is among several integrated development environments that have come out for Java programming. Others include Symantec Café, Roaster, and Borland C++ 5.0, which comes with Java development tools. There are noteworthy exceptions, however, such as Corel Office JV. This set of productivity applications based on WordPerfect and Quattro Pro is being written entirely with Java.

Why Learn Java?

Now that you know something about the origins of Java, you probably would like to know more about why it has attracted so much interest from software developers, computer companies, and the media. After all, you're embarking on a 21-day effort to learn the language.

A lot of the interest in Java undoubtedly has come from people who want to know if it lives up to the hype. After all, the language has become one of the biggest buzzwords of the Internet, spawning popular magazines, Web sites, training courses, and conferences in a matter of months.

Even if Java had no hype, Java as a language has significant advantages over other languages and programming environments. It is suitable for programming tasks both on and off the Internet because of the following attributes:

- [ ] Java is platform-independent.
- [ ] Java is object-oriented.
- [ ] Java is easy to learn.

Java Is Platform-Independent

For most of the history of computer software development, programs have been developed for a specific operating system. If a software company such as Activision wanted its *Return to Zork* adventure game to run on both Microsoft Windows and Macintosh systems, it had to develop two versions of the software at a significant effort and expense. *Platform independence* is the capability of the same program to work without modification on different operating systems. Java is platform-independent at all levels.

At the source level, Java's primitive data types have consistent sizes across all development platforms. Java's foundation class libraries, which are the building blocks of your Java programs, make it easy to write code that can be moved from platform to platform without rewriting.

NOTE

> *Primitive data types* are used to define the kind of value that variables will hold in a program. Java has primitive data types for integers, floating-point numbers, characters, and boolean values. The primitive data types will be discussed fully on Day 3, "Java Language Basics."

Platform-independence doesn't stop at the source level, however. A compiled Java binary file can run on multiple platforms without the need to recompile the source code because Java binary files are stored in a form called *bytecodes*. Bytecodes are instructions that look a lot like machine code but are not specific to any one processor.

When you compile a program written in C, C++, or most other languages, the compiler translates your program into machine codes, or processor instructions. Those instructions are specific to the processor your computer is running. For example, if you compile your code on an Amiga system, the resulting program will run only on other Amiga systems. If you want to use the same program on another system, you have to go back to your original source, obtain a compiler for that system, and recompile your code. Figure 1.2 shows the result of this system: multiple executable programs for multiple systems.

Things are different when you write code in Java. The Java development environment has both a compiler and an interpreter, and both are needed to run software created with the language. Instead of generating machine codes from source code, the Java compiler generates bytecodes.

Running a Java program requires an extra step from the process shown in Figure 1.3. The compiled bytecodes must be run by a *bytecode interpreter*, as shown in Figure 1.3. For Java applications, the interpreter is run by itself with the name of the Java application as a parameter. For applets, a Java-capable browser such as Netscape Navigator 2.0 has a built-in interpreter that runs the applet.

Figure 1.2.

Traditional compiled programs.

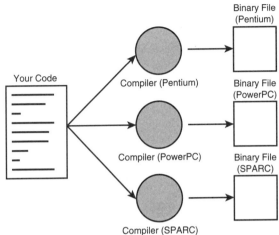

Figure 1.3.

Java programs.

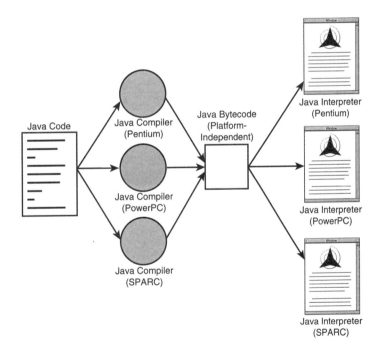

Going through the bytecode interpreter adds an extra step, as you can see by comparing the figures. This step is worthwhile because the bytecodes can be run on any operating system as long as a Java interpreter is available.

The capability to run a single binary file across platforms is crucial to what enables applets to work because the World Wide Web also is platform-independent. Just as HTML files can be read on any platform, applets can be executed on any Java-capable browser.

The disadvantage of using bytecodes is reduced execution speed. System-specific programs run directly on the hardware that they are compiled for, and the speed is significantly faster than interpreted Java bytecodes. For many Java programs, the speed might not be an issue. If you write Java programs that require more execution speed than the interpreter can provide, you have several solutions available to you. You can include native code in your Java programs, which is code written in a language other than Java. You also can use tools to convert your Java bytecodes into native code. However, using native code that is specific to an operating system sacrifices the platform-independent capabilities of Java. This subject will be covered thoroughly on Day 20, "Native Methods and Libraries."

Java Is Object-Oriented

If you do not have experience with object-oriented programming (OOP), you might find it an intimidating subject to tackle, even if you have some experience programming with other languages. To some, object-oriented programming is merely a way to organize programs, and it can be accomplished using any language. Working with a real object-oriented language, however, has great advantages for the creation of flexible, modular programs and code that can be reused elsewhere.

Many of Java's object-oriented concepts are inherited from C++, the language on which it largely is based. It adopts many concepts from other object-oriented languages as well. Like most OOP languages, Java includes a set of class libraries that provide basic data types, system input/output capabilities, and other utility functions. These basic classes are part of the JDK, which also has classes to support networking, common Internet protocols, and user interface toolkit functions. Because these class libraries are written in Java, they are portable across platforms. On Day 2, "Object-Oriented Programming," you will be introduced to the programming style and how it is implemented in Java.

Java Is Easy to Learn

In addition to its portability and object-orientation, one of Java's initial design goals was to be small and simple, and therefore easier to write, easier to compile, easier to debug, and best of all, easier to learn. Keeping the language small also makes it more robust because there are less chances for programmers to make difficult-to-find mistakes.

Java is modeled after C and C++, and much of the syntax and object-oriented structure is borrowed from the latter language. If you are familiar with C++, learning Java will be particularly easy for you because of all the similarities.

Although Java resembles C and C++, most of the more complex parts of those languages have been excluded from Java. The goal was to make the language simpler without sacrificing much of its power. Pointers and pointer arithmetic, two complicated and error-prone features, don't exist in Java. Strings and arrays are real objects in Java, and memory management is automatic. To an experienced programmer, the omissions might be difficult to get used to. Beginners and other programmers should welcome the deviations from C++ because the simplified areas of Java make it easier to learn.

Java WorkShop

Because the JDK uses command-line tools, it is harder to use than programming environments that use windows and other visual features. Java WorkShop enables you to develop Java programs in a graphical environment. It is an integrated development environment that has tools to create, compile, debug, and run Java programs. Once you have mastered all the capabilities of an IDE such as WorkShop, you will be creating Java programs more quickly and efficiently.

NOTE

> An *integrated development environment* (IDE) is a program that consists of several separate development tools—usually a source code editor, compiler, and debugger along with other features. These tools work together throughout the development cycle, making it easier to develop software.

Each feature of Java WorkShop will be covered in detail in the coming days, so you don't need to spend too much time on them right now. The following list is a brief overview of what you can do with each of the program's main features:

- [ ] **Portfolio Manager**   Select a project to edit or begin a new one
- [ ] **Project Manager**   Choose all project settings to determine how programs are compiled, executed, and debugged
- [ ] **Source Editor**   Edit a project's Java source code files and related HTML files
- [ ] **Build Manager**   Compile a project, either as a whole or just the parts that have changed since the last compilation
- [ ] **Visual Java**   Graphically design elements of a project such as menus, dialog boxes, and forms
- [ ] **Source Browser**   Examine the class hierarchy of a project, and search for text in associated files

- ☐ **Debugger**   Debug a project using six different criteria
- ☐ **Project Tester**   Execute a project as a stand-alone application or Web applet linked to an HTML page
- ☐ **Online Help**   Browse pages of general information, context-sensitive help, and a WorkShop tutorial

Each of these features will be used as you create and compile the programs in this book. Today, you will get a chance to try the Portfolio Manager, Project Manager, Source Editor, Build Manager, and Project Tester.

Obtaining the Software

At the time of this writing, Java WorkShop is available to try out for free over the Internet as an "early-access" release. This means that WorkShop still is under development from SunSoft, and a few bugs and performance issues have yet to be dealt with as of "Dev6," the current version. However, this version is a fully capable development evironment. In the course of this book, you'll be advised of any work-arounds that are needed to use beta versions of the software.

NOTE   The training you get with Java WorkShop in this book should be useful regardless of the version of the software you're running. The features of the IDE are explained thoroughly, and are not likely to change greatly between the Dev6 release and the commercial version.

To write the Java programs that are described in this book, you will need to have Java WorkShop installed on your system. The software currently is available for the following systems:

- ☐ Windows 95
- ☐ Windows NT 3.5.1
- ☐ SPARC Solaris (2.4 or later)
- ☐ Intel x86 Solaris systems

Microsoft Windows 95 and NT systems must be running a 90-megahertz Pentium or better with 16M of memory and 45M of hard disk space. Solaris systems must have 32M of memory, 45M of disk space, and an OSF/Motif 1.2.3-compliant windowing system.

The recommended display resolution to use with Java WorkShop is 800 by 600 pixels. Also, the file system of your computer must support long file names, as opposed to the 8-character name, 3-character extension format used by systems such as MS-DOS.

WARNING

> If you have downloaded any version of the Java Developer's Kit previously, you need to uninstall it before installing Java WorkShop. WorkShop comes with its own modified version of the JDK.

If your system meets all the requirements, you're ready to get started with Java WorkShop. The software is available over the World Wide Web at the following URL:

`http://www.sun.com/sunsoft/Developer-products/java/index.html`

If for some reason this URL is not available, visit the Developer's Corner section of the JavaSoft site at `http://java.sun.com`. It will have information on the latest versions of Sun's Java development software and other news of interest to programmers.

After you choose to download Java WorkShop, you will be asked to identify your operating system, review the software licensing agreement, and fill out a questionnaire about yourself. The early-access release of Java WorkShop is sent as a single archive file called `setupws.exe`. Put it in any directory where you normally keep downloaded files.

Installing the Software

After you have finished downloading the archive file, run `setupws.exe` to unpack the archive and install Java WorkShop. (If you have problems downloading the software or getting it to work on your system, see Appendix F, "Java WorkShop Troubleshooting.") You will be asked during the installation where to store Java WorkShop. Accept the default so that a new directory called `Java-WorkShop` is created.

Before you can get started with Java WorkShop, you need to create a directory for the storage of the programs in this book. Go to the `Java-WorkShop` directory and create a subdirectory called `homework`. After you do that, run Java WorkShop if it did not start automatically after it was installed. If you have trouble finding the file to execute in order to run the software, it should be in a subdirectory of the main `Java WorkShop` directory called `Java WorkShop Group`. Once you get the software running, and get through the licensing and registration screens if you're using an early-access version, you're ready to start using the software to create your first Java program.

Getting Started

When you run Java WorkShop, you should be looking at a screen that resembles Figure 1.4. Unlike development environments that you might have used previously, Java WorkShop looks more like a Web site than a software suite because it uses HTML pages, hyperlinks, images, and embedded Java programs in the same manner as a Web site. There even are URL addresses for each part of the program. For example, the opening screen has the URL `doc:/lib/html/jws/splash_page.html`.

Figure 1.4.

The Java WorkShop opening page.

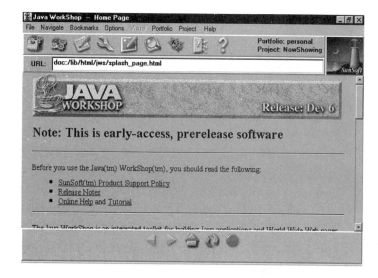

There are two groups of icons on the page: A WorkShop command toolbar with nine icons along the top, and a navigation toolbar with five options along the bottom. The navigation toolbar ought to look familiar; there are, from left to right, arrows to go forward and back, a home icon, a refresh icon, and a stop icon. These commands operate in the same way that they would in a browser such as Netscape Navigator or Microsoft Internet Explorer. You will be introduced to each of the icons on the WorkShop command toolbar as they are used in your first project: a Java applet.

Creating a Java Applet

Your first Java applet will display a palindrome. It could display any line of text ("Hello, World!," for instance), but because this is your rookie attempt at Java programming, it ought to exhibit some panache.

Starting a New Project

The first step in the creation of a new program with Java WorkShop is to create a project where the program can be placed. Like a file directory, a WorkShop project is a place to store related Java programs and HTML files. You create new projects with the Portfolio Manager.

Go to the WorkShop command toolbar on the top edge of the screen and click the icon that looks like an overstuffed suitcase (see Figure 1.5).

Figure 1.5.
The Portfolio Manager icon on the WorkShop command bar.

The Portfolio Manager displays all the projects that are located in the current portfolio. You might see icons for applets and applications that were included in your release of Java WorkShop. You also will see a Portfolio Manager command bar located underneath the WorkShop command bar (see Figure 1.6).

Figure 1.6.
The Create a New Project icon on the Portfolio Manager command bar.

This project is named `Palindrome` because you'll be displaying a palindrome on-screen. Click the icon to create a new project. A set of tabbed dialog boxes appears on-screen, and the Applet dialog box should be visible in front of the other tabbed boxes. If it is not, click the Applet tab and the dialog box will move to the front. In this dialog box, do the following:

1. In the Name field, enter `Palindrome`, and make sure to capitalize it exactly as shown.
2. In the Source Directory field, enter the full path of the `homework` subdirectory that you created earlier today. (On Microsoft Windows systems, it would be `C:/Java-WorkShop/homework` or something similar.)
3. Make sure that the Existing Sources item is set to the No option.
4. Make sure that the Run Page field is blank.
5. Make sure that the Create Using item is set to the Source Editor option.
6. Click the Apply button.

Entering the Source Code

After you click the Apply button to create a new project, Java WorkShop opens up a Source Editor where you can edit a new file called `Palindrome.java`. As with other programming languages, Java source files are created with a text editor. WorkShop comes with its own

Source Editor, and it is used throughout this book. If the Source Editor is not visible on your screen, it is one of the active programs running in the background on your system. Go to the Source Editor (using Alt+Tab on Microsoft Windows systems, for example).

NOTE

> You can create Java programs with any text editor that can save files in plain ASCII text without any formatting characters. On UNIX systems, you can use emacs, pico, and vi. On Windows 95 and NT systems, Notepad and the MS-DOS program Edit are suitable editors. If you use an editor other than WorkShop's Source Editor, you will sacrifice some convenience because Source Editor is the only editor that is integrated into the WorkShop development environment.

When you create a new project, as you have done, WorkShop puts some lines of programming code in the Source Editor to start you off. For the purposes of this exercise, delete all of this starting text. Enter the Java applet shown in Listing 1.1 into the Source Editor. Be sure to include all the parentheses, braces, and quotation marks. The use of spaces and tabs in front of some lines is not as important, as you'll discover later, but for this example, use spaces or tab characters to enter the source code exactly as shown.

WARNING

> The number and colon before each line in Listing 1.1 are part of the listing and not part of the program. They're included so that specific line numbers can be referred to more easily in the text. Don't include them when typing in source files. For example, line 1 in Listing 1.1 should be entered as `import java.awt.Graphics;`, not
> `1: import java.awt.Graphics;`.

TYPE   **Listing 1.1.** `Palindrome.java` **source code.**

```
1: import java.awt.Graphics;
2:
3: public class Palindrome extends java.applet.Applet {
4:
5:     public void paint(Graphics g) {
6:         g.drawString("Are we not drawn onward to new era?", 5, 25);
7:     }
8: }
```

After you enter the listing for `Palindrome.java`, save it by clicking the diskette icon on the Source Editor toolbar or by choosing File | Save from the menu bar. Java source files are given the same name as the class they define. In the preceding example, `Palindrome` is the name of the class that is being defined, so the name of the Java source file should be `Palindrome.java`. After the source code has been saved, exit the Source Editor by choosing File | Close from the menu bar.

It is not important to know what each line of the `Palindrome.java` source code means at this point. However, note the following:

☐ The `import` line at the top of the file is somewhat analogous to an `#include` statement in C. It allows this applet to obtain access to the JDK class used to draw graphics on the screen.

☐ The `paint()` method displays the content of the applet on-screen. Here, the string `Are we not drawn onward to new era?` is drawn.

NOTE

> In case you're unfamiliar with the term, a *palindrome* is a word or phrase that reads the same backwards as it does forwards, if you only consider the letters. For instance, "A man, a plan, a canal, Panama" is a palindrome. So is, "Ah, Satan sees Natasha." That last palindrome came from a Web page devoted to such things, Neil/Fred's Gigantic List of Palindromes, at the following URL:
>
> `http://www.cs.brown.edu/people/nfp/palindrome.html`

Compiling the Applet

After a Java program (application or applet) has been saved, it is not ready to run yet. It must be compiled first. To the right of the WorkShop command toolbar, the names of your current portfolio and project are listed. The project should be `Palindrome` because that is the project you worked on most recently. If a different project is listed, return to the Portfolio Manager by clicking the overstuffed suitcase icon again. All projects are listed, and you can switch to the `Palindrome` project by clicking the icon above its name.

You can compile the current project with the Build Manager. Go to the WorkShop command toolbar on the top edge of the screen and click the wrench icon (see Figure 1.7).

The Build Manager has six commands. The only one you need at present is the Build All Files icon, which looks like two wrenches. It is located on the Build Manager command bar underneath the WorkShop command bar (see Figure 1.8).

Figure 1.7.
The Build Manager icon on the WorkShop command bar.

└─ BUILD MANAGER

Figure 1.8.
The Build All Files icon on the Build Manager command bar.

└─ BUILD ALL FILES

Click the Build All files icon to compile the Palindrome application. You will see the output as WorkShop compiles the Palindrome.java file. If you typed in the file correctly, there should be no error messages, and the word Done should display to show that the program has compiled successfully. If you get errors, you need to make sure that you entered Listing 1.1 exactly as it appears. To correct an error, load the Palindrome.java file back into the Source Editor by clicking the Source Editor icon, make the necessary changes, save the file, and recompile the project with Build Manager.

TIP

The source code of all programs in this book can be found on the accompanying CD-ROM. You can use these as an alternative to typing in the source code, or refer to the CD-ROM if you're having trouble compiling a program successfully. If you are a Windows 95 or NT 4 user, look in the WIN95NT4 directory (which contains long file names) for all the source code and listings. If you are a Windows NT 3.5.1 user, you need to either run the source code install program or manually unzip the source code located in the WINNT351 directory. Palindrome.java is located in the BOOK\SOURCE\DAY01 subdirectory.

When the program compiles without any errors, the class file Palindrome.class is created in the same directory as the source code file Palindrome.java. The class file you have created is the file of bytecodes that can be executed by any system that has a Java interpreter.

Testing the Project

Once an applet has been compiled successfully, it can be viewed on a Web page with the Project Tester. Go to the WorkShop command toolbar on the top edge of the screen and click the light switch icon (see Figure 1.9).

1

Figure 1.9.
*The Project Tester icon
on the WorkShop
command bar.*

PROJECT TESTER

When you click the Project Tester icon, WorkShop creates a sample Web page to put the
Palindrome applet on and then loads the page. You should see a mostly blank Web page with
the words `Are we not drawn onward to new era?` in the upper left corner (see Figure 1.10).

Figure 1.10.
*The Palindrome applet
on a sample Web page.*

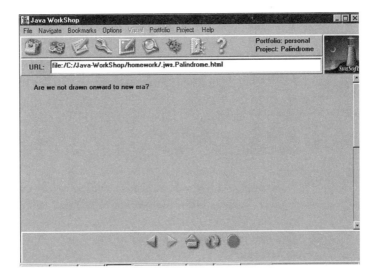

Summary

Today, you received a basic introduction to Java and how Java WorkShop can be used to
develop programs with the language. The story of Java's creation was covered along with the
benefits of programming with the language. Java's strengths are its portability at the source
and binary levels, object-oriented design, and simplicity.

The most common use of Java at present is to create applets for the World Wide Web. Like
C, C++, or other languages, Java also can be used to develop all kinds of software that do not
require the use of a Java-capable browser. WorkShop is a Java application.

To wrap up the day, you created your first Java applet, trying out four different features of
Java WorkShop: the Portfolio Manager, Source Editor, Build Manager, and Project Tester.
Tomorrow, you will learn about object-oriented programming and how it has been
implemented in Java. You also will take a more in-depth look at some of WorkShop's
features.

Q&A

Q Netscape Navigator 2.0 is the only Java-capable browser described in this chapter. Can't I use the HotJava browser to view Java applets?

A The original version of HotJava worked with the alpha release of the Java Developer's Kit. That version of the JDK was replaced by version 1.0, and HotJava was not modified to work with JDK 1.0 or later. At the time of this writing, JavaSoft has made available a "pre-beta" release of HotJava that works with the current JDK. This product could be in official release by the time you read this. For more information, visit the Products and Services section of the JavaSoft Web site at http://java.sun.com.

Q I know a lot about HTML, but not much about computer programming. Can I still write Java programs?

A If you have little or no programming experience, you probably will find this to be a tough 21-day course. However, Java is the simplest object-oriented programming language to learn, and this book emphasizes hands-on experience. If you patiently work through the examples, you should be able to write programs with the language.

Q According to today's lesson, Java applets are downloaded using a Java-enabled browser such as Netscape Navigator 2.0 and run on the user's system. Isn't that an enormous security hole? What stops someone from writing an applet that compromises the security of my system or worse, an applet that damages my system?

A This is an issue to take seriously, and Java implements several security features in regards to applets. The development of Java depends on its capability to be secure. If you could not trust the language and any software that implements it, loading any Java applets with a browser would be foolhardy. The following security measures have been implemented:

☐ Java applets cannot read or write to the disk on the user's system.

☐ Java applets cannot execute any programs on the user's system.

☐ Java applets cannot connect to any machines on the Web, except for the server from which they were originally downloaded.

Some of these restrictions might be disregarded in some browsers or might be removed by the user in the browser configuration, although that would be an unwise thing to do. However, as a Java applet programmer, you cannot expect any of these capabilities to be available.

In addition to those safeguards, the Java compiler and interpreter check both the Java source code and bytecodes to make sure that the Java programmer has not tried any sneaky tricks (for example, overrunning buffers or stack frames).

Although no system can promise to stop every potential security hole, Java's preventive measures significantly reduce the potential for hostile applets. You'll learn more about security issues in Day 21, "Advanced Concepts."

 # Today's Featured Applet

At the end of each day's lesson, a Java applet is featured from the hundreds that have been made available to the public on the World Wide Web. A description of the applet is given, along with brief guidelines on how it can be used on a Web page. The class files used with these applets are included on the CD-ROM that accompanies this book, along with the source code if it has been released by the author.

The first featured applet is `SparkleText` from Kevin J. Jarnot. `SparkleText` displays a line of text with an occasional twinkling effect appearing at different places on the text. Figure 1.11 shows the effect at three different times.

Figure 1.11.
The `SparkleText`
applet in action.

`SparkleText` files are located on the CD-ROM in the `BOOK\3RDPARTY\DAY1\` directory. To use `SparkleText` on a Web page, place these four class files on your Web site: `SparkleText.class`, `SparkleCoordClass.class`, `NervousText.class`, and `Coord.class`. Place the files in the same directory as the Web page, or place them in a subdirectory listed in the `CODEBASE` parameter of the `<APPLET>` tag. The `CODE` tag should be `SparkleText.class`.

Listing 1.2 shows the HTML tags used to run `SparkleText` as it was shown in Figure 1.11.

Listing 1.2. The `<APPLET>` tag for `SparkleText` on a simple HTML page.

```
<HTML>
<BODY>
<APPLET code="SparkleText.class" width=250 height=55 vspace=10>
<PARAM name=text value="SparkleText Applet">
<PARAM name=url value="http://www-cs.canisius.edu/~jarnot/index.html">
<PARAM name=fontname value="Helvetica">
<PARAM name=fontstyle value="BOLD">
<PARAM name=fontsize value="24">
<PARAM name=textcolor value="RED">
<PARAM name=backgroundcolor value="BLACK">
<PARAM name=sparklecolor value="WHITE">
<PARAM name=maxpause value=2000>
<PARAM name=minpause value=20>
<PARAM name=sparklepause value=100>
</APPLET>
</BODY>
</HTML>
```

You can customize `SparkleText` parameters within the `<APPLET>` tag of `SparkleText` as follows:

☐ The `url` parameter is an URL to jump to if the applet is clicked (optional).

☐ The `fontname` parameter specifies the font to use (`Times Roman` is the default).

☐ The `fontstyle` parameter specifies the style of the text (`PLAIN`, `BOLD`, or `ITALIC`).

☐ The `fontsize` parameter specifies the point size of the text (`36` is the default).

☐ The `textcolor` parameter specifies the color of the text (`red` is the default).

☐ The `backgroundcolor` parameter specifies the background color of the text (`gray` is the default).

☐ The `sparklecolor` parameter specifies the color of the sparkle (`yellow` is the default).

☐ The `maxpause` parameter specifies the maximum length of time, in milliseconds, to pause between sparkles (`4000` is the default).

☐ The `minpause` parameter specifies the minimum length of time, in milliseconds, to pause between sparkles (`500` is the default).

☐ The `sparklepause` parameter specifies the length of time, in milliseconds, to pause between the individual frames of the sparkle effect (`150` is the default).

More information on `SparkleText` is available from its author at the following URL:

```
http://www-cs.canisius.edu/~jarnot/sparkletext.html
```

1

Day 2

Object-Oriented Programming

Object-oriented programming (OOP) is one of the biggest programming ideas in recent years, and it's also one of the biggest sources of consternation for programmers unfamiliar with how it works. You might fear that years must be spent learning about OOP and how it makes life easier than other ways to program. The central idea of object-oriented program is simple: Organize programs in ways that echo how things are put together in the real world.

Today, you will get an overview of object-oriented programming concepts in Java and how they relate to the structure of your programs. The following topics will be covered:

- [ ] Classes and objects, and how they relate to each other
- [ ] The two main parts of a class or object: behavior and attributes
- [ ] Class inheritance, and how inheritance affects the way programs are designed
- [ ] Packages and interfaces

As you learn about object-oriented programming in Java, you will explore two features of Java WorkShop: the Portfolio Manager and Source Browser.

If you already are familiar with object-oriented programming, much of today's lesson will be a review for you. Even if you skim over the introductory material, you should create the Java examples so that you get more experience using Java WorkShop.

Thinking in Objects: An Analogy

Consider, if you will, LEGO™ building bricks. LEGO™ bricks, for those of you who do not spend much time with children, are small plastic building blocks in various colors and sizes. They have small round studs on one side that fit snugly into round holes on other bricks to create larger shapes. With different LEGO™ pieces (wheels, engines, hinges, pulleys, and the like), you can make castles, automobiles, giant robots, or just about anything else you can imagine. Each LEGO™ piece is a small object that fits together with other small objects in specific ways to create other, larger objects.

Consider another example. You can walk into a computer store and, with a little expertise and some help, assemble an entire personal computer system from various components: a motherboard, a CPU chip, a video card, a hard disk, a keyboard, and so on. Ideally, when you finish assembling the various self-contained units, you have a system in which all the units work together to create a larger system. You can use this larger system to solve the problems you bought the computer for in the first place.

Internally, each of those computer components might be extremely complicated and engineered by different companies using different methods of design. But you don't need to know how each component works, what every chip on the board does, or how an "A" gets sent to your computer when you press the A key. Each component you use is a self-contained unit, and as the assembler of the overall system, you only are interested in how the units interact with each other. Will this video card fit into a slot on the motherboard? Will this monitor work with this video card? Will each component speak the right commands to the other components it interacts with, so that each part of the computer is understood by every other part? Once you know about the interactions between the components and can match those interactions, putting together the overall system is easy.

What do these examples have to do with programming? Everything. Object-oriented programming is a lot like building structures from LEGO™ bricks or assembling a PC. Using object-oriented programming, your overall program is made up of lots of different self-contained components called objects. Each object has a specific role in the program, and all the objects can talk to each other in defined ways.

Objects and Classes

Object-oriented programming is modeled on the observation that in the real world, objects are made up of many kinds of smaller objects. However, the capability to combine objects is only one general aspect of object-oriented programming. Object-oriented programming provides several other concepts and features to make the creation and use of objects easier and more flexible. The most important of these features is the class.

 A *class* is a template for multiple objects with similar features. Classes embody all the features of a particular set of objects. When you write a program in an object-oriented language, you don't define individual objects. You define classes of objects.

For example, you might have a Tree class that describes the features of all trees (has branches and roots, grows, creates chlorophyll). The Tree class serves as an abstract model for the concept of a tree. To reach out and grab, or interact with, or cut down a tree, you must have a concrete instance of that tree. Of course, once you have a Tree class, you can create lots of different instances of that tree, and each different tree instance can have different features (short, tall, bushy, drops leaves in autumn, and so on), yet still behave like a tree and be immediately recognizable as one (see Figure 2.1).

Figure 2.1.

The Tree *class and* Tree *instances.*

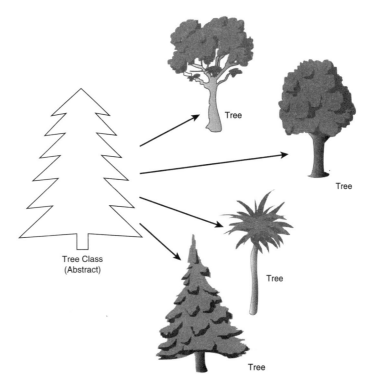

NEW TERM   An *instance* of a class is an actual object of that class. The class is the general, abstract representation of an object, and an instance is its concrete representation. So what, precisely, is the difference between an instance and an object? Nothing, really. Object is the term that is used more generally, but both instances and objects are the concrete representations of a class. In fact, the terms *instance* and *object* often are used interchangeably in OOP terminology. A Tree instance and a Tree object are the same thing.

In an example closer to the kind of thing you might want to do with Java, you could create a class for a button, an item for use on dialog boxes and other windows. The Button class defines the following features of a button:

☐ Its label

☐ Its size

☐ Its appearance

The class also defines how a button behaves, as follows:

☐ Whether it needs a single click or a double-click to be activated

☐ Whether it changes color when clicked

☐ What it does when it's activated

Once you define the Button class, you easily can create instances of that button—in other words, button objects. The instances all take on the basic features of a button as defined by the class, but each one might have different appearances and behavior based on what you want that particular button to do. By creating a Button class, you don't have to keep rewriting the code for each button you want to use in your program. Also, you can reuse the Button class to create different kinds of buttons as you need them—in this program and in other programs.

 TIP

> If you're used to programming in C, you can think of a class as a way to create a new composite data type that is analogous to using struct and typedef in C. Classes, however, can provide much more functionality than just a collection of data, as you'll discover in the rest of today's lesson.

When you write a Java program, you design and construct a set of classes. When your program runs, instances of those classes are created and discarded as needed. Your task, as a Java programmer, is to create the right set of classes to accomplish what your program needs to accomplish.

2

Fortunately, you don't have to start from scratch. The Java environment comes with a library of classes that implement a lot of the basic behavior you need. A *class library* is a set of classes. The Java library has classes to handle basic programming tasks (math functions, arrays, strings, and so on) as well as classes to handle graphics and networking behavior. In many cases, the Java class libraries might be sufficient for your needs; all you would need in your Java program is to create a single class that uses the standard class libraries. For complicated Java programs, however, you might need to create a whole set of classes with defined interactions between them.

Attributes and Behavior

Generally, every class you write in Java is made up of two components: attributes and behavior. In this section, you'll learn about each component as it applies to a theoretical class called `Jabberwock`. To complete this section, you'll create the Java code to implement a representation of a jabberwock—a dragonlike monster from the Lewis Carroll poem *Jabberwocky*.

Attributes of an Object

Attributes are the individual things that differentiate one object from another and determine the appearance, state, or other qualities of that object. Consider how a theoretical class called `Jabberwock` could be created. The attributes of a jabberwock might include the following:

- [ ] **Color:** red, orange, yellow
- [ ] **Sex:** male, female
- [ ] **Appetite:** full, hungry

Attributes of an object also can include other information about its state. For example, you could have features for the jabberwock's attitude (enraged or calm) or its current health (alive or dead).

Attributes are defined by variables; in fact, you can consider them analogous to global variables for the entire object. Because each instance of a class can have different values for its variables, each variable is called an instance variable. *Instance variables* define the attributes of an object. The class defines the type of the attribute, and each instance stores its own value for that attribute.

Each attribute, as the term is used here, has a single corresponding instance variable; changing the value of a variable changes the attribute of that object. Instance variables may be set when an object is created and stay constant throughout the life of the object, or they may be able to change at will as the program runs.

Class variables apply to the class itself and to all of its instances. Unlike instance variables, whose values are stored in the instance, class variable values are stored in the class itself. You will learn about class variables later on this week and will learn more specifics about instance variables tomorrow.

How Objects Behave

Behavior is the only way that objects can do anything to themselves or have anything done to them. The behavior of a class determines what instances of that class do to change their internal state. It also determines what class instances do when asked to do something by another class or object. For example, the Jabberwock class might have some of these behaviors:

- [ ] Get angry
- [ ] Calm down
- [ ] Eat a peasant
- [ ] Skip dinner
- [ ] Recuperate

To define an object's behavior, you create methods. *Methods* are just like functions in other languages, but they are defined inside classes. Methods operate on instances of their class. Java does not have functions of any kind defined outside of classes (unlike C++).

Although methods operate within their own class, methods do not affect only a single object. Objects communicate with each other using methods. A class or object can call methods in another class or object to communicate changes in the environment or to ask that an object change its state.

For example, consider the swordsman in the poem *Jabberwocky*. When he attacked the jabberwock with his vorpal blade, here's what happened:

> "One, two! One, two! And through and through
> The vorpal blade went snicker-snack!
> He left it dead, and with its head
> He went galumphing back."

In Java, the swordsman could be created as a Knight object. When the swordsman chops the head off the jabberwock, it definitely causes a change in the jabberwock's internal state. The Knight object would use a method to tell the Jabberwock object, "I chopped your head off. You're dead."

Just as there are instance and class variables, there are also instance and class methods. Instance methods (which are so common they're usually just called methods) apply and operate on an instance of a class. Class methods apply and operate on a class itself. You'll learn more about class methods later on this week.

Creating a Class

Up to this point, today's lesson has been pretty theoretical. In this section, you'll create a working example of the Jabberwock class so that you can see how instance variables and methods are defined in a class. You also will create a Java applet that creates a new instance of the Jabberwock class, displays its instance variables, and modifies one of its instance variables. Before diving into the Jabberwock example, however, you will get more acquainted with the features of the Portfolio Manager in Java WorkShop.

 NOTE

> The syntax of this example will not be covered in great detail. Don't worry too much if you're not completely sure what's going on. All you need to focus on in this example are the basic parts of the Jabberwock class definition.

Using Portfolio Manager

To start, get into Java WorkShop and click the Portfolio Manager icon on the WorkShop command toolbar. (As a reminder, it's the overstuffed suitcase at far left.) You should see the icons and names of all projects that you have created, which at this point would be Palindrome and perhaps a few projects that were shipped with WorkShop (see Figure 2.2).

Figure 2.2.

The Portfolio Manager.

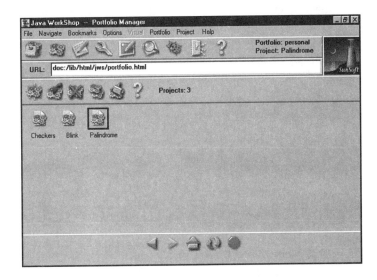

NOTE

Before choosing any options, put your cursor above any of the six icons on the Portfolio Manager toolbar. (It is the toolbar located between the list of current projects and the Java WorkShop command toolbar). On many of the toolbars in Java WorkShop, you can find out about an icon by holding your mouse over it without clicking. A line of text will appear at the lower left corner of the screen describing what the icon does. To see this in action, slowly drag your mouse over each of the icons in the Portfolio Manager toolbar.

The two features of Portfolio Manager that you will use most often are Create a New Project and Remove the Selected Project. One useful command that is not on the Portfolio Manager toolbar is the Choose command on the Portfolio pull-down menu. You can use this command to switch from your personal portfolio to another portfolio.

Two read-only portfolios come with WorkShop: jdk and awt. Use the Choose command to see one of these portfolios. These portfolios contain projects that have an unusual icon—the familiar "puzzle-piece" icon connected to a telephone pole. The telephone pole signifies that the applet is located on an Internet site instead of a directory on your system. You can use the Project Tester to run these applets as if they were stored on your own system. If you currently are connected to the Internet, you can use Project Tester to run these applets as if they were stored on your own system.

In addition to running applets, you can import portfolios and projects from other sites on the Internet. This feature highlights one of the noteworthy features of Java WorkShop: It can use data from Web pages as easily as it uses data from your hard drive. When you're done running the applets available from other portfolios, use the Choose command from the Portfolio pull-down menu to return to your personal portfolio so that you can create a new project.

The Jabberwock **Class**

Your next project will be an applet that creates and uses a Jabberwock class. The applet will be named JabberwockApplet to distinguish it from the Jabberwock class. On the Portfolio Manager toolbar, click the Create a New Project icon. A screen of tabbed dialog boxes will appear with the Applet tab visible in front. (If it isn't visible, click the Applet tab, and it will move forward.) Fill in the dialog box with the following fields:

Name: JabberwockApplet

Source directory: Enter the full path of your homework directory (c:/Java-WorkShop/homework or something similar).

Existing sources: No

Main Class File: You should not be able to change this field because .class will appear in the field as grayed-out text.

Run page: Leave this blank.

Create using: Source Editor

When you're done, click the Apply button. The project will be created, and a Source Editor window will open on your system where you can enter the source code for JabberwockApplet.java. Make the Source Editor the active window on your system and delete all of the starting text that WorkShop has placed in the editing area.

You start by creating a basic class definition. Enter the following:

```
class Jabberwock {

}
```

Congratulations! You now have designed a class. Of course, it doesn't do much at the moment, but that's a Java class at its simplest.

To make Jabberwock more sophisticated, create three instance variables for this class. Just below the class Jabberwock { line, add the following three lines:

```
String color;
String sex;
boolean hungry;
```

These lines create three instance variables. Two, color and sex, can contain String objects. (String is part of that standard class library mentioned earlier.) The third, hungry, is a boolean that refers to whether the jabberwock is hungry (true) or full (false).

NOTE

> In Java, boolean is a real data type that can have the values true or false. Unlike C, booleans are not numbers. You'll hear about this again tomorrow so you won't forget.

You can add some behavior to the class by adding methods. There are all kinds of things a jabberwock can do (claws that bite, jaws that catch, and so on), but to keep things short, just add one method—a method to feed the monster. Add the following lines below the three instance variables in your class definition:

```
void feedJabberwock(Graphics g, int y) {
    if (hungry == true) {
        g.drawString("Yum — a peasant!", 25, y);
        hungry = false;
    } else
```

```
        g.drawString("No, thanks — already ate.", 25, y);
}
// more to come
```

TIP

The last line, `// more to come`, is a comment line. Comments are used for the benefit of programmers looking at source code to figure out what it's doing. Everything from the initial `//` to the end of the line will be ignored by the compiler. In this case, the comment is being used as a placeholder. You'll replace it soon.

The `feedJabberwock` method tests to see whether the jabberwock is hungry (in the line `if (hungry == true) {`. If it is hungry, the jabberwock is fed (much to its delight), and the state of `hungry` is changed to `false`. If the jabberwock is not hungry, a message is displayed that the monster already ate. Here's what your program should look like so far:

```
class Jabberwock {

    String color;
    String sex;
    boolean hungry;

    void feedJabberwock(Graphics g, int y) {
        if (hungry == true) {
            g.drawString("Yum — a peasant!", 25, y);
            hungry = false;
        } else
            g.drawString("No, thanks — already ate.", 25, y);
    }
    // more to come
}
```

TIP

The indentation of each part of the class isn't important to the Java compiler. Using some form of indentation, however, makes your class definition easier to read. This readability pays dividends when you or another programmer tries later on to figure out what the code is doing. The indentation used here, with instance variables and methods indented from the class definition, is the style used throughout this book. The Java class libraries use a similar indentation. You can choose any indentation style that you like.

Before you compile this class, you need to add one more method. The `showAtts` method displays the current values of the instance variables in an instance of your `Jabberwock` class.

In the program, delete the comment line // more to come and replace it with the following:

```
void showAtts(Graphics g, int y) {
    g.drawString("This is a " + sex + " " + color
        + " jabberwock.", 25, y);
    if (hungry == true)
        g.drawString("The jabberwock is hungry.", 25, y+20);
    else
        g.drawString("The jabberwock is full.", 25, y+20);
}
```

The showAtts method displays two lines to the screen: the sex and color of the Jabberwock object, and whether the monster is hungry. Save the source code file by clicking the diskette icon or choosing File | Save.

At this point, you have a Jabberwock class and methods that can be used to modify or display its instance variables. To do something with the class (for example, to create instances of that class and play with them, create the code for a Java applet that uses Jabberwock.

Listing 2.1 shows the full source code for Jabberwock.java. Return to the Source Editor and enter lines 1 through 20 in front of the source code you already have entered. When you're done, save the program.

WARNING

> It is important to note that Java is case-sensitive. In this example, if you enter g.drawstring as a method name instead of g.drawString, it will result as a compiler error because drawstring will not be found in the java.awt.Graphics class.

Listing 2.1. JabberwockApplet.java.

```
 1: import java.awt.Graphics;
 2:
 3: public class JabberwockApplet extends java.applet.Applet {
 4:
 5:     public void paint(Graphics g) {
 6:         Jabberwock j = new Jabberwock();
 7:         j.color = "orange";
 8:         j.sex = "male";
 9:         j.hungry = true;
10:         g.drawString("Calling showAtts ...", 5, 50);
11:         j.showAtts(g, 70);
12:         g.drawString("Feeding the jabberwock ...", 5, 110);
13:         j.feedJabberwock(g, 130);
14:         g.drawString("Calling showAtts ...", 5, 150);
15:         j.showAtts(g, 170);
```

continues

Listing 2.1. continued

```
16:          g.drawString("Feeding the jabberwock ...", 5, 210);
17:          j.feedJabberwock(g, 230);
18:      }
19: }
20:
21: class Jabberwock {
22:     String color;
23:     String sex;
24:     boolean hungry;
25:
26:     void feedJabberwock(Graphics g, int y) {
27:         if (hungry == true) {
28:             g.drawString("Yum — a peasant!", 25, y);
29:             hungry = false;
30:         } else
31:             g.drawString("No, thanks — already ate.", 25, y);
32:     }
33:
34:     void showAtts(Graphics g, int y) {
35:         g.drawString("This is a " + sex + " " + color
36:             + " jabberwock.", 25, y);
37:         if (hungry == true)
38:             g.drawString("The jabberwock is hungry.", 25, y+20);
39:         else
40:             g.drawString("The jabberwock is full.", 25, y+20);
41:     }
42: }
```

Before you can test the applet, you need to compile it with the Build Manager. Return to the main Java WorkShop window. JabberwockApplet should be listed in the current project field in the upper right corner of the screen. (If it isn't, use the Portfolio Manager to make JabberwockApplet the current project). Click the Build Manager icon (the wrench) on the WorkShop command toolbar to bring up the Build Manager options.

To compile JabberwockApplet.java, click the Build All Files icon on the Build Manager toolbar. It's the pair of wrenches side-by-side. If the source code has been entered correctly, you will see the message Done. to show that the compilation was a success.

NOTE

> After this point, you will not receive step-by-step instructions on how to compile and run Java programs unless new commands are being used.

2

Running the Applet

Though most of the code in the Jabberwock class definition has been described, the contents of the JabberwockApplet class in Listing 2.1 are largely new to you. The lines that involve the Jabberwock class will be explained more fully to give you an idea of how classes are used.

ANALYSIS Line 6, Jabberwock j = new Jabberwock(), creates a new instance of the Jabberwock class and stores a reference to it in the variable j. Remember that you usually do not operate directly on classes in your Java programs. Instead, you create objects from those classes and call methods in those objects. Lines 7, 8, and 9 set the instance variables for the Jabberwock object j. The color is set to orange, the sex is set to male, and the hungry boolean instance variable is set to true.

Line 11 calls the showAtts method, defined in your Jabberwock object, with the parameters (g, 70). (The parameters used here and elsewhere in the program determine where text will be displayed in the applet. Disregard them for now.) The showAtts() method displays the values of the instance variables sex and color for the Jabberwock object j. It also displays the value of the instance variable hungry.

Line 13 calls the feedJabberwock() method in Jabberwock to feed object j. Jabberwock object j is hungry when the applet starts because hungry initially is set to true, so the object eats the food. As you saw in the feedJabberwock() method described previously, the instance variable hungry is set to false after the Jabberwock object eats.

Line 15 calls the showAtts() method again, displaying the values of the instance variables for a second time. A change in state for hungry is shown. Line 17 tries to feed the jabberwock again to see what happens. Because Jabberwock object j is no longer hungry, the object refuses to eat the food.

OUTPUT Now that you have become familiar with what the program is doing, click the Project Tester icon on the WorkShop command toolbar to run JabberwockApplet. The output should look like the following:

```
Calling showAtts ...
    This is a male orange jabberwock.
    The jabberwock is hungry.
Feeding the jabberwock ...
    Yum — a peasant!
Calling showAtts ...
    This is a male orange jabberwock.
    The jabberwock is full.
Feeding the jabberwock ...
    No, thanks — already ate.
```

With a basic grasp of classes, objects, methods, and variables, you have put them together successfully in a Java program. But this is only part of the story of object-oriented programming. It's time to learn about the features that make this style of programming so powerful.

Inheritance, Interfaces, and Packages

Inheritance, interfaces, and packages are all mechanisms for organizing classes and class behaviors. The Java class libraries use all of these concepts, and the best class libraries you write for your own programs also will use these concepts.

Inheritance

NEW TERM Inheritance is one of the most crucial concepts in object-oriented programming, and it has a direct effect on how you design and write Java classes. *Inheritance* is a powerful mechanism that allows a class to inherit functionality from an existing class. To create the new class, you only have to specify how that class is different from an existing class, and inheritance gives you automatic access to the existing class. With inheritance, all classes—those you write, those from other class libraries that you use, and those from the standard utility classes as well—are arranged in a strict hierarchy such as the one displayed in Figure 2.3.

Figure 2.3.

A class hierarchy.

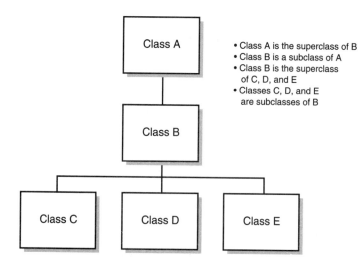

- Class A is the superclass of B
- Class B is a subclass of A
- Class B is the superclass of C, D, and E
- Classes C, D, and E are subclasses of B

NEW TERM Each class has a *superclass* (the class above it in the hierarchy), and each class can have one or more *subclasses* (classes below it in the hierarchy). Classes in the hierarchy inherit from classes above them in the hierarchy.

Subclasses inherit all the methods and variables from their superclasses. In practical terms, this means that if the superclass defines behavior that your class needs, you don't have to redefine that behavior or copy that code from some other class. Your class automatically receives that behavior from its superclass, the superclass gets behavior from its superclass, and so on all the way up the hierarchy. Your class becomes a combination of all the features of the classes above it in the hierarchy, as well as its own features.

At the top of the Java class hierarchy is the class Object—all classes inherit from this one superclass. Object is the most general class in the hierarchy; it defines behavior inherited by all the classes in the Java class hierarchy. Each class further down the hierarchy adds more information and becomes more tailored to a specific purpose. A class hierarchy defines abstract concepts at the top of the hierarchy, and those concepts become more concrete the further down the chain of subclasses that you go.

Most of the time when you create a new class in Java, you will want your class to have all the functionality of an existing class with some new additions or modifications of your own creation. For example, you might want a version of a Button with its own built-in label. To receive all of the Button functionality, all you have to do is define your class as a subclass of Button. Your class automatically has all of the behavior defined in Button, and all of the behavior defined in the superclasses of Button. All you have to worry about are the things that make your new class different from Button itself. The mechanism of defining new classes as the differences between them and their superclasses is called *subclassing*.

NEW TERM *Subclassing* is the creation of a new class that inherits from an existing class in the class hierarchy. Using subclassing, you only need to define the differences between your class and its parent (superclass). The additional behavior all is available to your class through inheritance.

What if your class defines entirely new behavior, and it isn't really a subclass of another class? Your class also can inherit directly from Object, which still allows it to fit neatly into the Java class hierarchy. In fact, if you create a class definition that doesn't indicate its superclass in the first line, Java assumes that the new class is inheriting directly from Object. The Jabberwock class you created in the previous section inherited from Object.

Creating a Class Hierarchy

If you're creating a larger set of classes, it makes sense for your classes not only to inherit from the existing class hierarchy, but also to make up a hierarchy themselves. Creating this hierarchy might take some planning beforehand when you're trying to figure out how to organize your Java code. However, the advantages are significant:

☐ When you develop your classes in a hierarchy, you can put functionality that is common to multiple classes into superclasses. This allows that functionality to be reused repeatedly because each subclass receives that common information from its superclass.

☐ Changing or inserting a class further up in the hierarchy automatically changes the behavior of the lower classes. There is no need to change or recompile any of the lower classes, because they receive the new information through inheritance and not by copying any of the code.

For example, imagine that you have created a Java class to implement all the features of a Jabberwock. It's done, it works, and everything is fine. Now, your next task is to create a Java class called Dragon.

Dragon and Jabberwock have many similar features—both are large monsters that eat peasants. Both have sharp claws, powerful teeth, and fiery breath. Your first impulse might be to open up your Jabberwock class file and copy a lot of the functionality from it into the new class Dragon.

A far better plan is to factor out the common information for Dragon and Jabberwock into a more general class hierarchy. This might be a lot of work just for the classes Jabberwock and Dragon, but when you add Medusa, Yeti, Sasquatch, and so on, having common behavior in a reusable superclass significantly reduces the overall amount of work you have to do.

To design a class hierarchy that might serve this purpose, start at the top with the class Object, the pinnacle of all Java classes. The most general class to which Jabberwock and Dragon both belong might be called Monster. A monster, generally, is defined as a ferocious creature of some kind that terrorizes people. In the Monster class, you define only the behavior that qualifies something as ferocious and terrifying to people, and nothing more.

Below Monster? How about two classes: FlyingMonster and WalkingMonster? FlyingMonster is different from WalkingMonster because it can fly, obviously. The behaviors of flying monsters might include swooping down on prey, carrying people off into the sky, dropping them from great heights, and so on. Walking monsters would behave differently. Figure 2.4 shows what you have so far.

Figure 2.4.
The basic Monster hierarchy.

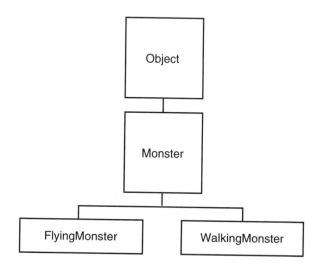

Now, the hierarchy will become even more specific. With FlyingMonster, you might have several classes: Mammal, Reptile, Amphibian, and so on. As an alternative, you could factor out still more behavior and have intermediate classes for TwoLegged and FourLegged monsters, with different behaviors for each (see Figure 2.5).

Finally, the hierarchy is done, and you have a place for Jabberwock. It can be a subclass of reptile, four-legged, flying monsters. (Actually, going all the way up the class hierarchy, Jabberwock would be a subclass of reptile, four-legged, flying monster objects because FlyingMonster is a subclass of Object.)

Where do qualities such as sex, color, or appetite come in? They come in at the place they fit into the class hierarchy most naturally. You can define sex and color as instance variables in Monster, and all subclasses will have those variables as well. Remember that you need to define a feature or a behavior only once in the hierarchy, and it automatically is reused by each subclass.

Figure 2.5.

Two-legged and four-legged flying monsters.

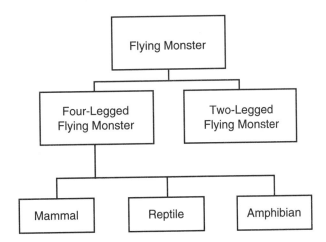

How Inheritance Works

How does inheritance work? How is it that instances of one class automatically receive variables and methods from the classes further up in the hierarchy? For instance variables, when you create a new instance of a class, you get a slot for each variable defined in the current class and a slot for each variable defined in all of its superclasses. In this way, all of the classes combine to form a template for the current object, and each object fills in the information appropriate to its situation.

Methods operate similarly. New objects have access to all the method names of the object's class and its superclasses, but method definitions are chosen dynamically when a method is called. That is, if you call a method of a particular object, Java first checks the object's class for the definition of that method. If the method is not defined in the object's class, Java looks in the superclass of that class, and so on up the chain until the method definition is found (see Figure 2.6).

Figure 2.6.

How methods are located.

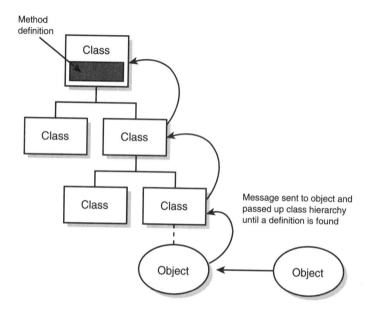

Things get complicated when a subclass defines a method that has the same name, return type, and arguments as a method defined in a superclass. In this case, the method definition that is found first (starting at the bottom of the hierarchy and working upward) is the one that is executed. Because of this, you intentionally can create a new method in a subclass to hide a method in the superclass by defining the new method with the same name, return type, and arguments as the superclass method. This procedure is called *overriding* (see Figure 2.7).

Single and Multiple Inheritance

Java's form of inheritance, as described in the previous sections, is called single inheritance. The rule of *single inheritance* is that each Java class can have only one superclass (although any superclass can have multiple subclasses).

New Term In other object-oriented programming languages, such as C++, classes can have more than one superclass, and they inherit the variables and methods from all those superclasses. This is called *multiple inheritance.* Multiple inheritance provides enormous power (classes can be created that encompass just about any imaginable behavior), but it also significantly complicates class definitions and the code needed to produce them. Java makes inheritance simpler by allowing only single inheritance.

Figure 2.7.
Overriding methods.

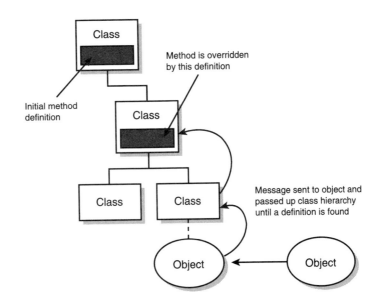

Interfaces

Because of single inheritance, a Java class only has a single superclass. It inherits variables and methods from all superclasses above it in the hierarchy. This makes subclassing easier to implement and design, but it also can be restricting—especially when you have similar behavior that needs to be duplicated across different branches of a class hierarchy. Java solves the problem of shared behavior by using interfaces.

NEW TERM   An *interface* is a collection of method names, without actual definitions, that indicate that a class has a set of behaviors in addition to the behaviors it receives from its superclasses. Although a single Java class only can have one superclass due to single inheritance, that class also can implement any number of interfaces. By implementing an interface, a class provides method definitions for the method names defined by the interface. If two very different classes implement the same interface, they both can respond to the same method calls as defined by that interface. However, what each class does in response to those method calls might be completely different.

You don't need to know much about interfaces right now, so don't panic if this information is confusing. You'll learn more as the book progresses.

Using Packages

 Packages in Java are a way of grouping together related classes and interfaces. Packages enable groups of classes to be available only if they are needed. Packages also eliminate potential conflicts between class names in different groups of classes.

For now, you only need to know the following things about packages:

☐ The class libraries in the JDK are contained in a package called `java`. The classes in the `java` package are guaranteed to be available in any Java implementation and are the only classes guaranteed to be available in any implementation. The `java` package contains other packages for classes that define the language itself, the input and output classes, some basic networking classes, and the windowing toolkit functions. Classes in other packages (for example, those in the `sun` or `netscape` packages) might be available only in specific implementations.

☐ By default, your Java classes have access only to the classes in `java.lang` (the base language package inside the `java` package). To use classes from any other package, you have to either refer to them explicitly by package name or import them in your source file.

☐ To refer to a class within a package, you list all the packages that the class is contained in followed by the class name—each separated by periods. For example, consider the `Color` class. It is contained in the `awt` package, which in turn is contained in the `java` package. To refer to the `Color` class in your program, you use the notation `java.awt.Color`.

Creating a Subclass

As a final exercise today, you will create a subclass of another class and override some methods by using the Source Browser in Java WorkShop to see where your subclass falls in its class hierarchy. You also will get a better feel for how packages work.

When you start programming in Java, the most common use of subclassing is when applets are created. You already relied on subclassing when you wrote `Palindrome` and `JabberwockApplet`. All applets are subclasses of the class `Applet`, which is part of the `java.applet` package. By creating a subclass of `Applet`, you automatically received behavior from windowing and layout classes that enabled your applet to be drawn in the right place and to interact with system operations such as mouse clicks and keypresses.

Jazzing Up `Palindrome`

Today's final project is an applet that is a jazzier version of yesterday's `Palindrome` applet. Use Portfolio Manager to create a new applet with the following fields:

Name: BigPalindrome

Source directory: Enter the full path of your homework directory (`C:/Java-WorkShop/homework` or something similar).

Existing sources: No

Main Class File: You should not be able to change this field because `.class` appears in the field as grayed-out text.

Run page: Leave this field blank.

Create using: Source Editor

To start the example, first construct the class definition for the applet. After deleting the template code that is provided for you, enter the following class definition:

```
public class BigPalindrome extends java.applet.Applet {
// placeholder
}
```

This definition creates a class called `BigPalindrome`. Take a look at `extends java.applet.Applet`—this phrase is what makes `BigPalindrome` a subclass of the `Applet` class. Because the `Applet` class is contained in the `java.applet` package, as opposed to the `java.lang` package, you do not have automatic access to the class. You have to refer to it explicitly by package and class name.

The other part of this class definition is the `public` keyword. The `public` keyword means that your class is available to the Java system at large once it is loaded. Most of the time, you need to make a class `public` only if you want it to be visible to all other classes in your Java program. However, applets must be declared to be `public`. You will learn more about `public` classes in Week 3.

A class definition with nothing in it is pointless—if you don't add anything new, or override the variables or methods of its superclasses, why is the new class needed at all? Add some things to make this class different from its superclass.

First, add an instance variable to contain a `Font` object. Replace the `// placeholder` line with the following:

```
Font f = new Font("TimesRoman", Font.BOLD, 30);
```

The `f` instance variable now contains a new instance of the class `Font`, part of the `java.awt` package. This particular font object is a 30-point Times Roman font in boldface style. In the previous `Palindrome` applet, the font used for the text was the default: 12-point Times Roman. Using a `Font` object, you can change the font of the text displayed in your applet.

By creating an instance variable to hold this `Font` object, you make the object available to all the methods in your class. Now, you will create a method that uses it.

Overriding a Method

When you write applets, there are several standard methods defined in the Applet superclass that you normally will override in the class of your applet. These include methods to initialize the applet, to start it running, to handle operations such as mouse movements, and to clean up when the mouse stops running.

One of these methods in the Applet superclass is the paint() method, which displays your applet on-screen. The default definition of paint() does nothing at all—it's an empty method. By overriding paint(), you tell the applet what should be drawn on-screen. After the Font line, enter the following definition for paint():

```
public void paint(Graphics g) {
    g.setFont(f);
    g.setColor(Color.red);
    g.drawString("Go hang a salami, I'm a lasagna hog.", 5, 25);
}
```

Note that this method is declared public, just as the applet itself was. Unlike the applet, however, the paint() method is public because the method it is overriding also is public. If the method of a superclass is defined as public, the method to override it also has to be public or an error will occur when the class is compiled.

Also note that the paint() method takes a single argument: an instance of the Graphics class. The Graphics class provides platform-independent behavior for rendering fonts, colors, and basic drawing operations. You will learn more about the Graphics class beginning on Day 8, "Applet Basics," when you create more extensive applets.

Inside your paint() method, you have done the following:

- ☐ You told the Graphics object that the default drawing font will be the one contained in the instance variable f.
- ☐ You told the Graphics object that the default color is an instance of the Color class for the color red.
- ☐ You told the Graphics object to draw the palindrome, Go hang a salami, I'm a lasagna hog., on the applet window at the x and y positions of 5 and 25. The string will be rendered in the new font and color.

Importing a Package

For an applet this simple, no more code seems necessary. However, something is missing. If you don't know what it is, save the source file and compile it using the Build Manager. You will get a bunch of errors like the following:

```
BigPalindrome.java:3: Class Font not found in type declaration.
```

These errors will occur because the classes such as Font and Graphics are part of a package. Remember that the only package you automatically have access to is java.lang. You referred to the Applet class in the first line of the class definition by referring to its full package name (java.applet.Applet). Further down in the program, however, you referred to several other classes as if they already were available.

There are two ways to solve this problem. You can refer to all external classes by full package name, or you can import the appropriate class or package at the beginning of your class file. The solution you choose is mostly a matter of personal choice, but if you refer to a class in another package numerous times, you might want to use import to cut down on the typing required.

In the BigPalindrome example, import the needed classes: Graphics, Font, and Color. All three are part of the java.awt package. Before the first line of the program, insert the following three lines:

```
import java.awt.Graphics;
import java.awt.Font;
import java.awt.Color;
```

TIP

You also can import an entire package of public classes by using an asterisk (*) in place of a specific class name. For example, to import all classes in the awt package, you can use the following:

```
import java.awt.*;
```

Listing 2.2 shows the full source code of the applet.

Listing 2.2. BigPalindrome.java.

```
1: import java.awt.Graphics;
2: import java.awt.Font;
3: import java.awt.Color;
4:
5: public class BigPalindrome extends java.applet.Applet {
6:
7:     Font f = new Font("TimesRoman", Font.BOLD, 30);
8:
9:     public void paint(Graphics g) {
10:         g.setFont(f);
11:         g.setColor(Color.red);
12:         g.drawString("Go hang a salami, I'm a lasagna hog.", 5, 25);
13:     }
14: }
```

Now that the proper classes have been imported into your program, it should work successfully. Compile it with the Build Manager, and then run the applet with Project Tester. The output should look like Figure 2.8.

Figure 2.8.

The output of the BigPalindrome *applet.*

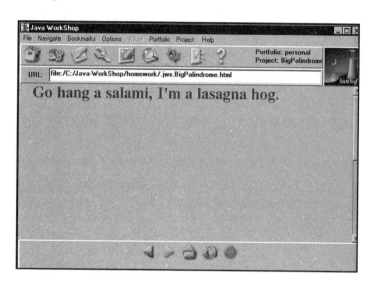

Using the Source Browser

If you need to know the full hierarchy of a class or information related to its methods and other behavior, you can use the Source Browser in Java WorkShop. With BigPalindrome selected as your current project, click the Source Browser icon in the WorkShop command toolbar. It's the magnifying glass icon identified in Figure 2.9.

Figure 2.9.

The Source Browser icon on the WorkShop command toolbar.

Two tabbed dialog boxes are available from the Source Browser page. One enables you to search for a string in the files related to a project or in the files in a specified directory. The other feature, which you will use here, presents information about the classes included in the current project. This feature is the Class Browser.

With the Class Browser dialog box visible, make sure that the Browse option is set to Project instead of Directory. A text field will display all the files associated with the current project— in this example, the full path of BigPalindrome.java will be the only file listed. Click

`BigPalindrome.java`, and a report titled "Class Palindrome" will be generated along the bottom half of the page.

Use the scroll bar to see this report. From top to bottom, the following sections are displayed:

☐ The full class hierarchy of the `BigPalindrome` class. You can travel upwards from superclass to superclass until reaching the top, `java.lang.Object`.

☐ The constructors used in the `BigPalindrome` class. These are special methods that will be discussed on Day 8.

☐ The methods used in the `BigPalindrome` class. In this case, `paint()` is listed along with the method declaration. `paint()` is a hyperlink, and you can click it to go directly to that line in the source code of `BigPalindrome.java`.

In a small program such as the `BigPalindrome` applet, you aren't likely to need the Source Browser. However, for larger, multifile projects that require the creation of numerous subclasses, method overriding, and other behavior, it can be a useful tool.

Summary

If this chapter was your first encounter with object-oriented programming, a lot of the information probably seems both theoretical and overwhelming at this point. You do not have to fully understand the information yet because you will be using object-oriented techniques for the rest of this book. The information will become more familiar to you as you gain more experience.

One of the biggest hurdles of object-oriented programming is not necessarily the concepts, it's their names. There is a lot of jargon. To summarize today's material, here's a glossary of terms and concepts that were covered:

Class: A template for an object that contains variables to describe the object and methods to describe how the object behaves. Classes can inherit variables and methods from other classes.

Object: A concrete instance of a class—in other words, a real instance that has been created using a class as its template. Multiple instances of the same class have access to the same methods, but they often have different values for their instance variables.

Instance: An object made real through the use of a class.

Superclass: A class further up the class hierarchy than another class (the subclass). The subclass inherits variables and methods from all superclasses that are above it in the hierarchy.

Subclass: A class further down the class hierarchy than another class (its superclass). When you create a new class to inherit the behavior of another class, it is called *subclassing.*

Instance method: A method defined in a class that operates on an instance of that class. Instance methods usually are just called *methods.*

Class method: A method defined in a class that operates on the class itself and can be called through the class or any of its instances.

Instance variable: A variable that is owned by an individual instance of a class, and whose value is stored in that instance.

Class variable: A variable that is owned by the class and all of its instances as a whole, and whose value is stored in the class.

Interface: A collection of abstract behavior specifications that can be implemented by individual classes.

Package: A collection of classes and interfaces. Classes from packages other than java.lang must be imported explicitly or referred to by their full package names.

Q&A

Q In effect, methods are functions that are defined inside classes. If they look like functions and act like functions, why aren't they called functions?

A Some object-oriented programming languages do call them functions (C++ calls them *member functions,* for example). Other object-oriented languages differentiate between functions inside and outside a body of a class or object, because in those languages the use of the separate terms is important to understanding how each function works. Because the difference is relevant in other languages, and because the term *method* is now in common use in object-oriented terminology, Java uses the term as well.

Q I understand instance variables and methods, but what are class variables and methods?

A Almost everything you do in a Java program will be done with objects (instances). Some behaviors and attributes, however, make more sense if stored in the class itself rather than in the object. For example, to create a new instance of a class, you need a method that is defined for the class itself, not for an object. Otherwise, you run into a chicken-and-egg dilemma—you can't create a baby object without an existing momma object that has a baby-making method, and no momma object can exist without having been a baby first.

Class variables often are used when you have an attribute with a value that you want to share with all the instances of a class. In most of your programming, you will be dealing with instance variables and methods. You will learn more about class variables and methods later on this week.

FEATURED APPLET Today's Featured Applet

The Java programs you have written in the first two days have used Java to display text, so it is fitting that today's featured applet uses text in a creative way. Clock2, from Per Reedtz Thomsen, displays a configurable digital clock. This applet is based on the Clock applet by Rachel Gollub that is included with the Java Developer's Kit. Figure 2.10 shows the clock centered at the top of a Web page. The current date and time are shown in an applet that continuously updates itself.

Figure 2.10.

The Clock2 applet in action.

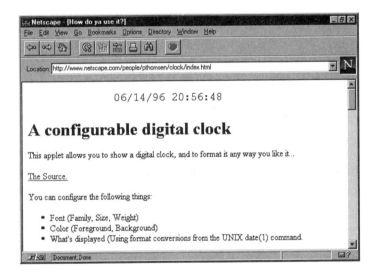

Clock2 files are located on the CD-ROM in the \BOOK\3RDPARTY\DAY2\ directory, including source code in the file Clock2.java. To use Clock2 on a Web page, place the Clock2.class file on your Web site. Place the file in the same directory as the Web page or place it in a subdirectory listed in the CODEBASE parameter of the <APPLET> tag. The CODE tag should be Clock2.class. Listing 2.3 shows the HTML tags used to run Clock2 as it was shown in Figure 2.10.

Listing 2.3. The `<APPLET>` tag for `Clock2`.

```
<APPLET CODE="Clock2.class" WIDTH="275" HEIGHT="30">
<PARAM NAME="FontFamily" VALUE="Courier">
<PARAM NAME="FontSize" VALUE="20">
<PARAM NAME="DateFmt" VALUE="%c">
<PARAM NAME="BGCol" VALUE="f0f0f0">
</APPLET>
```

You can customize `Clock2` parameters within the `<APPLET>` tag as follows:

☐ The `FontFamily` parameter specifies the font to use (`Courier`, `Helvetica`, or the default, `TimesRoman`).

☐ The `FontSize` parameter specifies the point size of the text (`12` is the default).

☐ The `FontWeight` parameter specifies the style of the text (`Bold`, `Italic`, or the default, `Plain`).

☐ The `BGCol` parameter is the background color in hexadecimal RGB format (`c0c0c0`, a shade of gray, is the default).

☐ The `FGCol` parameter is the foreground color in hexadecimal RGB format (`000000`, black, is the default).

☐ The `DateFmt` parameter specifies the format of the date and time string that you want to display, using format conversions from the UNIX `date(1)` command. The string can contain both text and formatting fields. Formatting fields are preceded by the `%` symbol. The following fields are supported:

Field	Description
%a	Abbreviated, 3-character weekday name
%A	Full weekday name
%b	Abbreviated, 3-character month name
%B	Full month name
%c	Appropriate local date and time representation, which is equivalent to using the `toLocaleString()` method of the `java.util.Date` class
%C	Default date and time format
%d	Day of month (shown as 01 to 31)
%D	Date in %m/%d/%y format
%e	Day of month (shown as 1 to 31, with single digits preceded by a blank)

%h	Abbreviated month name (an alias for %b)
%H	Hour (shown as 00 to 23)
%I	Hour (shown as 01 to 12)
%m	Month of year (shown as 01 to 12)
%M	Minute (shown as 00 to 59)
%p	String containing AM or PM indicator
%r	Time in %I:%M:%S %p format
%R	Time in %H:%M format
%S	Seconds (shown as 00 to 61), allowing for leap seconds
%T	Time in %H:%M:%S format
%w	Day of week (Sunday equaling 0)
%y	Year within century (shown as 00 to 99)
%Y	Year as four-digit number
%%	To display the % character in the display

To give you a better idea of how the DateFmt parameter works, consider the following two examples:

☐ The default for the DateFmt parameter, %a, %B %e %T, results in a clock display in the same format as Wed, June 12 21:45:43.

☐ A DateFmt parameter of It is now %R on %d %h %y., results in a clock display in the same format as It is now 21:55 on 12 Jun 96.

More information on Clock2 is available from Per Reedtz Thomsen at the following URL:

http://www.netscape.com/people/pthomsen/clock/index.html

More information on Clock is available from Rachel Gollub at the following URL:

http://java.sun.com/java.sun.com/applets/applets/Clock/index.html

Day 3

Java Language Basics

On Days 1 and 2, you learned about Java programming in broad terms—what a Java program and an executable look like and how to create simple classes. For the remainder of this week, you're going to get down to details and deal with the specifics of what the Java language looks like.

Today, you won't be concerned with how classes and objects are created or how they communicate inside a Java program. Instead, you will be examining simple Java statements—the basic things you can do in Java within a method definition.

The following subjects will be covered:

☐ Java statements and expressions

☐ Variables and data types

☐ Comments

☐ Literals

☐ Arithmetic

☐ Comparisons

☐ Logical operators

NOTE

Java looks a lot like C and C++. Much of the syntax will be familiar if you have worked with those languages. If you are an experienced C or C++ programmer, you might want to pay special attention to Notes (such as this one). They will provide information about the specific differences between Java and other more established languages.

Statements and Expressions

NEW TERM   A *statement* is a single Java operation—the simplest thing you can do in the language. All the following are simple Java statements:

```
int i = 1;
import java.awt.Font;
g.drawString("This is a " + sex + " " + color
        + " jabberwock.", 25, y);
j.hungry = true;
```

The most important thing to remember about Java statements is that each one ends with a semicolon. Forget the semicolon, and your Java program won't compile.

NEW TERM   Statements sometimes return values—for example, when you add two numbers together or test to see whether one value is equal to another. These kind of statements are called *expressions*. They will be discussed later on today.

Java also has compound statements, or block statements, that can be placed wherever a single statement can. Block statements are surrounded by opening braces and closing braces ({ and }). You'll learn more about block statements in Day 5, "Arrays, Conditionals, and Loops."

Variables and Data Types

Variables are locations in memory in which values can be stored. They have a name, a type, and a value. Before you can use a variable, you have to declare it. After it is declared, you then can assign values to it. Java has three kinds of variables: instance variables, class variables, and local variables.

Instance variables, as you learned yesterday, are used to define attributes or the state of a particular object. Class variables are similar to instance variables, except that their values apply to all of that class' instances (and to the class itself) rather than having different values for each object.

Local variables are declared and used inside method definitions—for example, as index counters in loops, as temporary variables, or as a place for values that are needed only inside the method definition itself. You can also use local variables inside block statements. When the method (or block) finishes executing, the variable definition and its value cease to exist, as you will learn about later this week. Use local variables to store information needed by a single method and instance variables to store information needed by multiple methods in the object.

Although all three kinds of variables are declared in much the same way, class and instance variables are accessed and assigned in slightly different ways than local variables. Today, you'll focus on local variables used within method definitions. Tomorrow, you'll learn how to deal with instance and class variables.

 NOTE

> Unlike other languages, Java does not have variables that are global to all parts of a program. You can use instance and class variables to communicate global information among objects. Remember, Java is an object-oriented language, so you should think in terms of objects and how they interact, rather than in terms of programs.

Declaring Variables

To use any variable in a Java program, you first must declare it. Variable declarations consist of a type and a variable name, such as the following:

```
int myAge;
String myName;
boolean isTired;
```

Variable definitions can go anywhere in a method definition (that is, anywhere a regular Java statement can go). They are most commonly declared at the beginning of the definition:

```
public void paint(Graphics g) {
    int count;
    String title;
    boolean isNewCustomer;
    ...
}
```

You can string together variable names with the same type:

```
int x, y, z;
String firstName, LastName;
```

You also can give each variable an initial value when you declare it:

```
int myAge, mySize, numShoes = 28;
String myName = "Beowulf";
boolean isHirsute = true;
int a = 7, b = 6;
```

If multiple variables are on the same line with only one initial value (as in the first of the previous examples), the initial value applies only to the last variable in a declaration. Of the three variables myAge, mySize, and numShoes, only numShoes is set to 28. You also can group individual variables and initial values (also known as *initializers*) on the same line using commas, as with the line that initializes a and b.

You must give values to local variables before you can use the variables. Java programs will not compile if you try to use an unassigned local variable. For this reason, it is always a good idea to give local variables initial values. Instance and class variable definitions do not have this restriction (their initial values depend on the type of the variable, as shown in Table 3.1).

Table 3.1. Initial values for instance and class variables.

Type	Initial value
instances of classes	null
numeric variables	0
characters	\0
booleans	false

Naming Variables

Variable names in Java can start with a letter, an underscore (_), or a dollar sign ($). They cannot start with a number. After the first character, your variable names can include any letter or number. Symbols, such as %, *, and @, often are reserved for operators in Java, so be careful when using symbols in variable names.

NEW TERM The Java language also uses the Unicode character set. *Unicode* is a character set definition that offers the standard ASCII character set along with several thousands of other characters to represent modern and historical languages. You can use accented characters and many non-ASCII characters in variable names, as long as they have a Unicode character number above 00C0.

The Unicode specification includes more than 30,000 characters at present. If you don't understand Unicode or don't think you have a need for it, use plain numbers and letters in your variable names. You will learn more about Unicode later on.

Finally, remember that the Java language is case-sensitive, which means that uppercase letters are different than lowercase letters. The variable X is different from the variable x, and a rose is not a Rose is not a ROSE. Keep this fact in mind as you write your own Java programs and as you read Java code written by others.

By convention, Java variables have meaningful names, often consisting of a combination of several words. The first word is lowercase, but all following words have an initial uppercase letter, as in the following:

```
Button loadFile;
long reallyBigNumber;
boolean playerSetNewHighScore;
```

Variable Types

In addition to the variable name, each variable declaration must have a type, which defines the possible values the variable can hold. The variable type can be one of three things:

☐ One of the eight basic primitive data types

☐ The name of a class or interface

☐ An array

You will learn about how to declare and use array variables on Day 5.

The eight primitive data types handle common types of integers, floating-point numbers, characters, and boolean values (true or false). They're called primitive because they are built into the system and are not actual objects, which makes them easier for programmers to use. Note that these data types are machine-independent, which means that you can rely on their sizes and characteristics to be consistent across your Java programs.

There are four Java integer types, each with a different range of values (as listed in Table 3.2). All are signed, which means they can hold either positive or negative numbers. The type you choose for a variable depends on the range of values you expect the variable to hold. If a value becomes too big for the variable type that has been selected, it automatically is truncated. This can have undesirable results, so make sure that variable values do not outgrow their types.

Table 3.2. Integer types.

Type	Size	Range
byte	8 bits	−128 to 127
short	16 bits	−32,768 to 32,767
int	32 bits	−2,147,483,648 to 2,147,483,647
long	64 bits	−9,223,372,036,854,775,808 to 9,223,372,036,854,775,807

Floating-point numbers are used for numbers with a decimal part. Java floating-point numbers are compliant with IEEE 754, an international standard for defining floating-point numbers and arithmetic. There are two floating-point types: float (32-bit, single-precision numbers) and double (64-bit, double-precision numbers).

The char type is used for individual characters. Because Java uses the Unicode character set, the char type has 16 bits of precision, unsigned. The boolean type can have one of two values, true or false.

NOTE

Note that unlike in other C-like languages, boolean is not a number, nor can it be treated as one. All tests of boolean variables should test for true or false.

In addition to the eight basic data types, variables in Java also can be declared to hold an instance of a particular class:

```
String lastName;
Font basicFont;
OvalShape myOval;
```

Each of these variables then can hold only instances of the given class. As you create new classes, you can declare variables to hold instances of those classes (and their subclasses) as well.

NOTE

Java does not have a typedef statement (as C and C++ do). To declare new types in Java, you declare a new class and then declare variables to be of that class type.

Assigning Values to Variables

Once a variable has been declared, you can assign a value to that variable by using the assignment operator =:

```
score = 200;
tooMuchCaffeine = true;
```

Comments

NEW TERM Comments, which are implemented in most programming languages, are used to make a program more understandable. A *comment* is text that is included in the source code of a program to explain what the program is doing. A statement or operator is used to set off the comments from parts of the program that should be executed. Using comments liberally in your programs probably will benefit you later on, and it definitely will benefit others who have access to your source code.

Java has three kinds of comments: multiline, single line, and Java documentation comments. As in C or C++, /* and */ surround multiline comments. The compiler ignores all the text between the two delimiters, as in the following:

```
/*  This code was written under the influence of off-brand
    supermarket cola. I have no idea why it works, and it
    might be unwise to change anything.
*/
```

The compiler disregards everything after a /* until it sees an */. You cannot use a nested comment (that is, a comment inside a comment) because the first */ that is encountered will cause the compiler to start looking for valid Java code.

A comment confined to a single line can use double slashes (//). When the compiler encounters a //, it ignores everything from that point to the end of a line. Here's an example of a single-line comment:

```
int vices = 7; // are there really only 7 vices?
```

The final type of comment begins with /** and ends with */. These comments are used in an automatic documentation system that has been implemented with Java. You used this system yesterday when looking at the BigPalindrome class with the Java WorkShop Source Browser.

These comments are used to describe classes, methods, and variables that are public, a concept described briefly yesterday. For example, if a /** comment is put in front of a public class declaration, the comment shows up when Class Browser is used on the program.

Automatic documentation is an advanced concept that new Java programmers are unlikely to use, so it is not covered in detail here. On Day 6, "Creating Classes and Applications," you will add some of these comments in a program to see how it works.

WARNING

Some programmers might be in the habit of using long lines of asterisks in certain comment lines, as in the following:

```
/***********************
/** Calculate scores **
/***********************
```

Because these comments begin with /**, they will be interpreted as special Java documentation comments and will show up incorrectly in tools such as the Java WorkShop Source Browser. When programming with Java, you'll have to find other ways to draw attention to comments.

Literals

Literals are used to indicate simple values in Java programs. *Literal*, in programming, means that what you type is what you get. For example, if you type 4 in a Java program, you automatically get an integer with the value 4. If you type an "a", you get a character with the value a. Literals might seem intuitive most of the time, but some special cases of Java literals merit some explanation. Literals are used for different kinds of numbers, boolean values, characters, and strings.

Number Literals

There are several integer literals. For example, 4 is a decimal integer literal of type int (although you can assign it to a variable of type byte or short because it's small enough to fit into those types). A decimal integer literal larger than an int is automatically of type long. You also can force a smaller number to a long by appending an L or l to that number (for example, 4L is a long integer of value 4). Negative integers are preceded by a minus sign, for example, -45.

Integers also can be expressed as octal or hexadecimal numbers. A leading 0 indicates that a number is octal, for example, 0777 or 0004. A leading 0x (or 0X) indicates that a number is hexadecimal (such as 0xFF or 0XAF45).

NOTE

Hexadecimal is a base-16 numbering system, which means that it can express numbers from 0 to 15 as single digits—unlike decimal, a base-10 numbering system that expresses numbers from 0 to 9 as single digits. In hexadecimal, the numbers 0–9 and the letters A–F are used for the 16 digits. Octal is a base-8 numbering system that can express numbers from 0 to 7 as single digits.

Numbering systems such as hexadecimal and octal are used in programming because they are better suited for certain tasks than the decimal system is. Hexadecimal numbers often are used in graphics programming and to represent memory addresses in a machine. In Java, one place you frequently will see hexadecimal being used is with the `java.awt.Color` class. As you can do in HTML with the `BGCOLOR` attribute of the `<BODY>` tag, you can use hexadecimal numbers to select RGB colors. Several of the applets featured at the end of the daily lessons take hexadecimal parameters to set colors.

Floating-point literals usually have two parts: the integer part and the decimal part, as in `5.677777`. Floating-point literals result in a floating-point number of type `double`, regardless of the precision of that number. You can force the number to the type `float` by appending the letter `f` (or `F`) to that number, for example, `2.56F`. You can use exponents in floating-point literals by using the letter `e` or `E` followed by the exponent (which can be a negative number), as in `10e45` or `.36E-2`.

Boolean Literals

Boolean literals are the keywords `true` and `false`. These keywords can be used anywhere you need a test and are the only possible values for boolean variables. Unlike other programming languages, you cannot use `0` and `1` or `T` and `F` to represent boolean values.

Character Literals

Character literals are expressed as a single character surrounded by single quotes: `'a'`, `'#'`, `'3'`, and so on. Characters are stored as 16-bit Unicode characters. Table 3.3 lists the special codes that can represent nonprintable characters, as well as characters from the Unicode character set. The letter *d* in octal, hexadecimal, and Unicode escape codes represents a numeral or a hexadecimal digit (a–f or A–F).

Table 3.3. Character escape codes.

Escape	Meaning
\n	Newline
\t	Tab
\b	Backspace
\r	Carriage return
\f	Formfeed
\\	Backslash
\'	Single quote
\"	Double quote
\ddd	Octal
\xdd	Hexadecimal
\udddd	Unicode character

NOTE | C and C++ programmers should note that Java does not include character codes for \a (a bell) or \v (a vertical tab).

String Literals

A combination of characters is a *string*. Strings in Java are instances of the class String. Strings are not simple arrays of characters, as they are in C or C++, although they do have many array-like characteristics; for example, you can test a string's length, and you can change individual characters. Because string objects are real objects in Java, they have methods that enable you to combine, test, and modify them easily.

String literals consist of a series of characters inside double quotes, as in the following:

```
"Are we not drawn onward to new era?"
"" // an empty string
```

Strings can contain escape codes for characters such as newline, tab, and Unicode characters as well:

```
"Ending balance\t$312.00" // a tab character separating two items
"Nested strings are \"strings inside of\" other strings"
"This string brought to you by Java\u2122"
```

In the last example, the Unicode code sequence for \u2122 produces a trademark symbol (™).

Just because you can represent a character using a Unicode escape code does not mean your computer can display that character—the computer or operating system you are running might not support Unicode, or the font you're using might not have a representation for that character. All that Unicode support in Java provides is a way to encode special characters for systems that support Unicode. These systems include UNIX systems and Microsoft Windows systems to a lesser degree. Windows 95 and NT systems have partial support for Unicode, though the Chinese, Japanese, and Korean characters are among the more notable exceptions.

When you use a string literal in your Java program, Java automatically creates an instance of the class `String` for you with the value you give it. Strings are unusual in this respect. The other literals do not behave in this way (none of the primitive base types are actual objects), and to create a new object, usually you must explicitly create a new instance of a class. You will learn more about strings, the `String` class, and the things you can do with strings later today and tomorrow.

Expressions and Operators

Expressions (statements that return a value) are the simplest statements in Java that actually accomplish something. Arithmetic and tests for equality and magnitude are common examples of expressions. Because they return values, you can assign their results to variables or test those values in other Java statements.

Operators are special symbols that commonly are used in expressions. Operators in Java include arithmetic, various forms of assignment, increment and decrement, and logical operations. This section describes all of these things.

Arithmetic

Java has five operators for basic arithmetic (see Table 3.4).

Table 3.4. Arithmetic operators.

Operator	Meaning	Example
+	Addition	3 + 4
–	Subtraction	5 – 7

continues

Table 3.4. continued

Operator	Meaning	Example
*	Multiplication	5 * 5
/	Division	14 / 7
%	Modulus	20 % 7

Each operator takes two operands, one on either side of the operator. You can also use the subtraction operator (-) to negate a single operand.

Integer division results in an integer. Because integers don't have decimal fractions, any remainder is ignored. The expression 31 / 9, for example, results in 3 (9 goes into 31 only 3 times). Modulus (%) gives the remainder once the operands have been divided evenly. For example, 31 % 9 results in 4 because 9 goes into 31 3 times, with 4 left over. Floating-point division results in a floating-point number, so 31 / 9 in floating-point division would result in 3.44444.

Note that when one operand is an integer, the result type of most operations is an int. If either or both operands is of type long, the result is of type long. If one operand is an integer and another is a floating-point number, the result is a floating-point number.

Creating the Arithmetic Applet

The Arithmetic applet gives you a chance to work with some operators. Use Portfolio Manager to create a new applet with the following fields:

Name: Arithmetic

Source directory: Enter the full path of your homework directory (c:/Java-WorkShop/homework or something similar).

Existing sources: No

Main Class File: You should not be able to change this because .class appears in the field as grayed-out text.

Run page: Leave this field blank.

Create using: Source Editor

After you create the applet, use the Source Editor to input the code from Listing 3.1. As with all examples that you will create in this book, delete the template code that is provided in the Source Editor when a new project is created. Save the program as Arithmetic.java, and compile it with Build Manager.

3

TYPE Listing 3.1. Source code for `Arithmetic.java`.

```
 1: import java.awt.Graphics;
 2:
 3: public class Arithmetic extends java.applet.Applet {
 4:
 5:     public void paint(Graphics g) {
 6:         int x = 6;
 7:         short y = 4;
 8:         float a = .12f;
 9:
10:         g.drawString("You start off with " + x + " pet amoebas.",
11:             5, 50);
12:         g.drawString("Two get married and their spouses move in.",
13:             25, 70);
14:         x = x + 2;
15:         g.drawString("You now have " + x + ".", 5, 90);
16:         g.drawString("Mitosis occurs, doubling the number of amoebas.",
17:             25, 110);
18:         x = x * 2;
19:         g.drawString("You now have " + x + ".", 5, 130);
20:         g.drawString("There's a fight. " + y + " amoebas move out.",
21:             25, 150);
22:         x = x - y;
23:         g.drawString("You now have " + x + ".", 5, 170);
24:         g.drawString("Paramecia attack! You lose one-third of the "
25:             + "colony.", 25, 190);
26:         x = x - (x / 3);
27:         g.drawString("You end up with " + x + " pet amoebas.", 5, 210);
28:
29:         g.drawString("Daily upkeep cost per amoeba: $" + a, 5, 230);
30:         g.drawString("Total daily cost: $" + (a * x), 5, 250);
31:     }
32: }
```

OUTPUT Run the program with Project Tester; the output of the applet should look like the following:

```
You start off with 6 pet amoebas.
    Two get married and their spouses move in.
You now have 8.
    Mitosis occurs, doubling the number of amoebas.
You now have 16.
    There's a fight. 4 amoebas move out.
You now have 12.
    Paramecia attack! You lose one-third of the colony.
You end up with 8 pet amoebas.
Daily upkeep cost per amoeba: $0.12
Total daily cost: $0.96
```

ANALYSIS In this simple Java applet, you initially define three variables in lines 6 through 8: x (a 32-bit integer), y (a 16-bit, short integer), and the floating-point number a. Keep in mind that the default type for floating-point literals (such as .12) is double, so to make sure that this number is of type `float`, you have to use an `f` after it (line 8). The remainder of the program merely does some math with integers and floating-point numbers to track the success of a pet amoeba colony.

One other thing you should note about this program: the method `g.drawString()`. You've seen this method on previous days, but you haven't learned exactly what it does. The `java.awt.Graphics` class has several methods to draw text, images, lines, and shapes. The `drawString()` method takes the following three parameters:

- ☐ a string to display
- ☐ an x coordinate of type `int`
- ☐ a y coordinate of type `int`

The x and y coordinates determine where the string should be drawn. As you will see in more detail on Day 9, "Graphics, Fonts, and Color," the Java coordinate system works differently than other systems you might be familiar with. It begins with (0,0) in the upper left-hand corner. x increases as you go to the right, and y increases as you go downward.

More About Assignment

Variable assignment is a form of expression; in fact, because one assignment expression results in a value, you can string assignments together like this:

```
x = y = z = 0;
```

In this example, all three variables now have the value `0`.

The right side of an assignment expression always is evaluated before the assignment takes place. Expressions such as `x = x + 2` do the right thing: 2 is added to the value of `x`, and then the new value is reassigned to `x`. This sort of operation is so common that Java has several operators borrowed from C and C++ that are shorthand versions of this type of expression. Table 3.5 shows the shorthand assignment operators.

Table 3.5. Assignment operators.

Expression	Is the Same As
x += y	x = x + y
x -= y	x = x - y
x *= y	x = x * y
x /= y	x = x / y

3

Incrementing and Decrementing

As in C and C++, the ++ and -- operators are used to increment or decrement a value by 1. For example, x++ increments the value of x by 1 just as if you had used the expression x = x + 1. Similarly x-- decrements the value of x by 1.

> **NOTE**
>
> Unlike C and C++, Java allows x to be a floating-point number.

The ++ and -- operators can appear before or after the value being incremented or decremented. When the operator appears before the value, as in ++age, it is called a *prefix operator*. When it appears after the value, as in age++, it is called a *postfix operator*. For simple increment or decrement expressions, the operator that you use isn't particularly important. In complex assignments where you are assigning the result of an increment or decrement expression, the one you use makes a difference. Consider the following two expressions:

```
y = x++;
y = ++x;
```

These expressions produce different results because of the difference between prefix and postfix. When you use postfix operators such as x++ or x--, the value is assigned before the increment or decrement takes place. When you use prefix operators such as ++x or --x, the value is assigned after the increment or decrement takes place. For example, if x is equal to 10, the expression y = x++; would cause y to equal 10 and x to equal 11. If instead the expression y = ++x; was used, it would cause y to equal 11 and x to equal 11. Your next project shows these different operators in action.

Creating the PrePost Applet

Use Portfolio Manager to create a new applet with the following fields:

Name: PrePost

Source directory: Enter the full path of your homework directory (`c:/Java-WorkShop/homework` or something similar).

Existing sources: No

Main Class File: You should not be able to change this field because `.class` appears in the field as grayed-out text.

Run page: Leave this field blank.

Create using: Source Editor

After you create the applet, use the Source Editor to input the code from Listing 3.2. Save the program as PrePost.java and compile it with Build Manager.

TYPE | **Listing 3.2. Source code of PrePost.java.**

```
 1: import java.awt.Graphics;
 2:
 3: public class PrePost extends java.applet.Applet {
 4:
 5:     public void paint(Graphics g) {
 6:         int x = 0, y = 0;
 7:         g.drawString("x = " + x + " and y = " + y, 5, 50);
 8:
 9:         x++;
10:         g.drawString("x++ sets x to " + x, 25, 70);
11:
12:         ++x;
13:         g.drawString("++x sets x to " + x, 25, 90);
14:
15:         g.drawString("x = " + x + " and y = " + y, 5, 110);
16:         y = x++;
17:         g.drawString("y = x++ sets x to " + x + " and y to "
18:             + y, 25, 130);
19:
20:         g.drawString("x = " + x + " and y = " + y, 5, 150);
21:         y = ++x;
22:         g.drawString("y = ++x sets x to " + x + " and y to "
23:             + y, 25, 170);
24:     }
25: }
```

OUTPUT Run the program with Project Tester; the output of the applet should look like the following:

```
x = 0 and y = 0
    x++ sets x to 1
    ++x sets x to 2
x = 2 and y = 0
    y = x++ sets x to 3 and y to 2
x = 3 and y = 2
    y = ++x sets x to 4 and y to 4
```

ANALYSIS In the first part of this example, you increment x alone using both prefix and postfix increment operators. In each, x is incremented by 1 each time. In this simple form, using either prefix or postfix works the same way.

In the second part of this example, you use the expression y = x++, in which the postfix increment operator is used. In this result, the value of x is incremented after that value is assigned to y. The result is that y is assigned the original value of x (2), and then x is incremented by 1.

In the third part, you use the `prefix` expression y = ++x. In this part, x is incremented before its value is assigned to y. Because x is 3 from the previous step, its value is incremented (to 4), and then that value is assigned to y. Both x and y end up being 4.

NOTE
> This description is not entirely correct. In reality, Java always evaluates all expressions on the right of an expression before assigning that value to a variable, so the concept of "assigning x to y before x is incremented" isn't precisely right. Instead, Java takes the value of x and stores it temporarily, evaluates (increments) x, and then assigns the original value of x to y. In most simple cases this distinction might not be important, but for more complex expressions with side effects, it might change the overall behavior of the expression.

Comparisons

Java has several expressions for testing equality and magnitude. All these expressions return a boolean value (that is, `true` or `false`). Table 3.6 shows the comparison operators.

Table 3.6. Comparison operators.

Operator	Meaning	Example
==	Equal	x == 3
!=	Not equal	x != 3
<	Less than	x < 3
>	Greater than	x > 3
<=	Less than or equal to	x <= 3
>=	Greater than or equal to	x >= 3

Note the similarity between the comparison operator == and the assignment operator = that you learned about earlier. A common source of programming errors is to confuse these two, especially if you have used a programming language where = is the comparison operator.

Logical Operators

You can combine expressions that result in boolean values (for example, the comparison operators) by using logical operators that represent the logical combinations AND, OR, XOR, and logical NOT.

For AND combinations, you can use the & and && operators. In either case, the expression will evaluate as true only if both expressions also are true. If either expression is false, the entire expression evaluates as false. The difference between the two operators lies in how the expressions are evaluated. With &, both sides of the expression are evaluated regardless of the outcome. With &&, if the left side of the expression is false, the entire expression returns false, and the right side of the expression never is evaluated.

For OR expressions, use ¦ or ¦¦. OR expressions result in true if either or both sides of the expression are true. If both operands are false, the expression evaluates as false. As with & and &&, the single ¦ evaluates both sides of the expression regardless of the outcome. With ¦¦, if the left side of the expression is true, the expression returns true, and the right side never is evaluated.

The XOR operator ^ returns true only if the sides of the expression disagree with each other. In other words, this operator returns true if the left side is true and the right side is false, or the right side is true and the left side is false.

For NOT, use the ! operator with a single-expression argument. The value of the NOT expression is the opposite of the expression: If x is true, !x is false.

In general, only the && and ¦¦ operators are used commonly in logical combinations. &, ¦, and ^ are used primarily for bitwise logical operations, which are summarized in the next section.

Bitwise Operators

The bitwise operators are inherited from C and C++ and are used to perform operations on the individual bits in integers. This advanced topic is beyond the scope of this discussion, and most new Java programmers are not likely to need bitwise operations. Table 3.7 summarizes the bitwise operators.

Table 3.7. Bitwise operators.

Operator	Meaning
&	Bitwise AND
¦	Bitwise OR
^	Bitwise XOR
<<	Left shift
>>	Right shift
>>>	Zero fill right shift
~	Bitwise complement

3

Operator	Meaning
<<=	Left shift assignment (x = x << y)
>>=	Right shift assignment (x = x >> y)
>>>=	Zero fill right shift assignment (x = x >>> y)
x&=y	AND assignment (x = x & y)
x¦=y	OR assignment (x + x ¦ y)
x^=y	XOR assignment (x = x ^ y)

Operator Precedence

Operator precedence determines the order in which expressions are evaluated. This order determines the overall value of the expression. For example, look at the following expression:

```
y = 6 + 4 / 2
```

Depending on whether the 6 + 4 expression or the 4 / 2 expression is evaluated first, the value of y can end up being 5 or 8. Operator precedence determines the order in which expressions are evaluated, so you can determine the outcome of an expression. In general, the following rules of precedence apply:

- Increment and decrement are evaluated before arithmetic.
- Arithmetic expressions are evaluated before comparisons.
- Comparisons are evaluated before logical expressions.
- Assignment expressions are evaluated last.

Table 3.8 shows the specific precedence of operators in Java. Operators higher up the table are evaluated first. For example, given the same expression y = 6 + 4 / 2, you now know according to this table that division is evaluated before addition. The value of y will be 8. Operators on the same line of the table have the same precedence and are evaluated from left to right, based on how they appear in the expression itself.

Table 3.8. Operator precedence.

Operator	Notes
. [] ()	Parentheses () are used to group expressions; a dot (.) is used for access to methods and variables within objects and classes (as discussed tomorrow); and [] is used for arrays (discussed later in the week)

continues

Table 3.8. continued

Operator	Notes
++ -- ! ~ instanceof	Increment, decrement, logical NOT, bitwise complement, and instanceof; the instanceof operator, which will be discussed tomorrow, returns true or false based on whether the object is an instance of the named class or any of that class' superclasses
new (type)expression	The new operator is used to create new instances of classes; () in this case is for casting a value to another type (you'll learn about both of these tomorrow)
* / %	Multiplication, division, modulus
+ -	Addition, subtraction
<< >> >>>	Bitwise left shift, right shift, and zero fill right shift
< > <= >=	Relational comparison tests
== !=	Equality comparison tests
&	AND
^	XOR
¦	OR
&&	Logical AND
¦¦	Logical OR
? :	Shorthand for if...then...else (discussed on Day 5)
= += -= *= /= %= ^=	Various assignments
&= ¦= <<= >>= >>>=	

You always can change the order in which expressions are evaluated by using parentheses around the expressions that should be evaluated first. You can nest parentheses to make sure that expressions evaluate in the order you want them to—the innermost parenthetical expression is evaluated first. Consider the following expression:

```
y = (6 + 4) / 2
```

This expression results in a value of 5 because the 6 + 4 expression is evaluated first, and then the result of that expression (10) is divided by 2.

Parentheses also can be useful in cases where the precedence of an expression isn't immediately clear—in other words, they can make your code easier to comprehend. Adding parentheses doesn't hurt, so if they help you figure out how expressions are evaluated, use them liberally.

String Arithmetic

One special expression in Java is the use of the addition operator (+) to create and concatenate strings. If you have not encountered the term before, *concatenate* means to link two things together. In previous examples, you have seen several lines that look something like this:

```
g.drawString(firstName + " is a " + size + " turkey.", 5, 50);
```

The first parameter of the drawString method is the string that is displayed. The + operator concatenates the firstName and size variables with the text is a and turkey. A single string is formed with the value of the variables inserted in the right places.

When used with strings and other objects, the + operator creates a single string that contains the concatenation of all its operands. If any of the operands in string concatenation is not a string, it automatically is converted to a string, making it easy to create these sorts of output lines.

NOTE

> You can convert an object or type to a string if you implement the method toString(). All objects have a default string representation, but most classes override toString() to provide a more meaningful printable representation.

String concatenation makes lines such as the previous one especially easy to construct. To create a string, just add all of the parts together, the descriptions plus the variables, and output the result anywhere.

The += operator, which you learned about earlier, also works for strings. For example, take the following expression:

```
myFullName += " Jr.";
```

This expression is equivalent to the following:

```
myFullName = myFullName + " Jr.";
```

This operator works the same as it would for numbers. In the preceding, the expression changes the value of myFullName (which might be something like Efrem Zimbalist) to have a Jr. at the end (Efrem Zimbalist Jr.).

Summary

As you learned in the last two lessons, a Java program is made up primarily of classes and objects. Classes and objects, in turn, are made up of methods and variables, and methods are made up of statements and expressions. Variables, statements, and expressions are the basic building blocks that enable you to create classes and methods and build them into a full-fledged Java program.

You learned how to declare and assign values to variables. You also learned how to use literals, which are used to easily create numbers, characters, and strings, and how to use operators, which are used for arithmetic, true/false tests, and other operations. With this basic syntax, you are prepared for tomorrow's lesson. You will be learning how to work with objects to create simple, useful Java programs. As a reference to what you have learned, Table 3.9 lists all the operators you learned about today.

Table 3.9. Java operators.

Operator	Meaning
+	Addition
–	Subtraction
*	Multiplication
/	Division
%	Modulus
<	Less than
>	Greater than
<=	Less than or equal to
>=	Greater than or equal to
==	Equality comparison test
!=	Not equal
&&	Logical AND
||	Logical OR
!	Logical NOT
&	AND
|	OR
^	XOR
<<	Left shift
>>	Right shift

3

Operator	Meaning
>>>	Zero fill right shift
~	Bitwise complement
=	Assignment
++	Increment
--	Decrement
+=	Add and assign
-=	Subtract and assign
*=	Multiply and assign
/=	Divide and assign
%=	Modulus and assign
&=	AND and assign
|=	OR and assign
<<=	Left shift and assign
^=	XOR and assign
>>=	Right shift and assign
>>>=	Zero fill right shift and assign

Q&A

Q Is there any way to define constants?

A You can't create local constants in Java; you only can create constant instance and class variables. You'll learn how to do this tomorrow.

Q What happens if you assign an integer value to a variable that is too large for that variable to hold?

A Logically, you would think that the variable is just converted to the next larger type, but this isn't what happens. What does happen is called *overflow*. If a number becomes too big for its variable, that number overflows, wrapping around to the smallest possible negative number for that type, and the number starts counting upward again. This can result in some confusing and wildly inaccurate results, so make sure that you declare the right integer type for all of your numbers. If there's a chance a number will overflow its type, use the next larger type instead.

Q How can you find out the type of a given variable?

A If you're using the base types (`int`, `float`, `boolean`), and so on, you can't. If you care about the type, you can convert the value to some other type by using casting (you'll learn about this tomorrow). If you're using class types, you can use the instanceof operator, which you'll learn more about tomorrow.

Q Why does Java have all these shorthand operators for arithmetic and assignment? It's really hard to read that way.

A The syntax of Java is based on C++, and therefore on C. One of C's implicit goals is the capability of doing powerful things with a minimum of typing. Because of this, shorthand operators such as the wide array of assignment operators are common. However, there's no rule that requires you to use operators in your own programs. If you find your code to be more readable using the long-form style, no one will come to your house and make you change it.

 # Today's Featured Applet

In today's lesson, you created an applet to do some simple arithmetic. Today's featured applet is a simple calculator. Calc, from Doug Gardner, has buttons for addition, subtraction, multiplication, and division. It also has a square root button that was built with the ImageButton class created by Adam Doppelt. Figure 3.1 shows the applet on a Web page.

Figure 3.1.

The Calc *applet in action.*

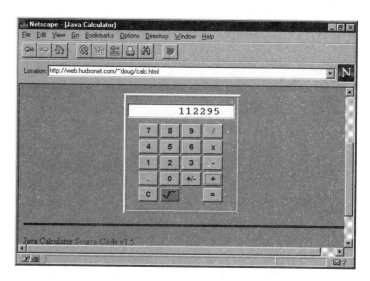

Calc files are located on the CD-ROM in the BOOK\3RDPARTY\DAY3\ directory, including source code in the files Calc.java and ImageButton.java. To use Calc on a Web page, place these eight class files on your Web site: Clock2.class, ImageButton.class, FunctionButton.class, Keypad.class, NumberButton.class, SqrtButton.class, EqualsButton.class, and Display.class. Place these two graphics files on your site as well:

sqrt1.gif and sqrt2.gif. The class files should be placed in the same directory as the Web page or should be placed in a subdirectory listed in the CODEBASE parameter of the <APPLET> tag. The <CODE> tag should be Calc.class.

Listing 3.3 shows the HTML tags used to run Calc as it is shown in Figure 3.1. The TABLE formatting was used by the applet's author as an easy way to create an outer edge for the calculator. Also, the HEIGHT and WIDTH settings must both be set to 200 for the calculator to display correctly.

Listing 3.3. The <APPLET> tag and HTML formatting for Calc.

```
<TABLE BORDER=3><TR><TD>
<APPLET CODE="Calc.class" HEIGHT=200 WIDTH=200>>
</APPLET>
</TD></TR></TABLE>
```

Calc does not use any parameters. More information on the applet is available from Doug Gardner at the following URL:

http://web.hudsonet.com/~doug/calc.html

Also, more information on using ImageButton in a program is available from Adam Doppelt at the following URL:

http://www.cs.brown.edu/people/amd/java/ImageButton/

Day **4**

Working with Objects

Because Java is an object-oriented language, you're going to be dealing with a lot of objects. You will create them, modify them, move them around, change their variables, call their methods, and combine them with other objects. You will develop classes and use your own objects in the mix.

This lesson explores the Java object in its natural habitat. Topics include the following:

- ☐ Creating instances of classes
- ☐ Testing and modifying class and instance variables in your new instances
- ☐ Calling instance methods
- ☐ Converting objects and other data types from one class to another

You also will learn about the Java class libraries and explore some of the features of the Java WorkShop Project Manager.

Creating New Objects

When you write a Java program, you define a set of classes. As you learned on Day 3, "Java Language Basics," classes are templates for objects; for the most part, you merely use the class to create instances and then work with those instances. In this section, therefore, you'll learn how to create a new object from any given class.

Remember strings from yesterday? You learned that using a string literal (a series of characters enclosed in double-quotes) creates a new instance of the class String with the value of that string. The String class is unusual in that respect. Although it's a class, there's an easy way to create instances of that class using a literal. The other classes don't have that shortcut; to create instances of those classes, you have to do so explicitly by using the new operator.

NOTE   What about the literals for numbers and characters—don't they create objects, too? Actually, they don't. The primitive data types for numbers and characters create numbers and characters, but for efficiency, they actually aren't objects. You can put object wrappers around them if you need to treat them like objects (as you'll learn to do later).

Using new

To create a new object, you use new with the name of the class you want to create an instance of, followed by parentheses:

```
String teamName = new String();
Random randInfo = new Random();
Jabberwock j = new Jabberwock();
```

The parentheses are important; don't leave them off. The parentheses can be empty, in which case the most simple, basic object is created, or the parentheses can contain arguments that determine the initial values of instance variables or other initial qualities of that object. The number and type of arguments you can use with new are defined by the class itself by using a special method called a constructor.

WARNING   Some classes might not allow you to create instances without any arguments. Check the documentation for the class you are using to make sure that allows such a constructor.

To illustrate the use of the new command and parenthetical arguments, create the `CreateDate1` applet, which creates `Date` objects. The applet uses three different ways of creating a `Date` object using `new`. Use Portfolio Manager to create a new applet with the following fields:

Name: CreateDate1

Source directory: Enter the full path of your homework directory (`C:/Java-WorkShop/homework` or something similar).

Existing sources: No

Main Class File: You should not be able to change this field because `.class` appears in the field as grayed-out text.

Run page: Leave this field blank.

Create using: Source Editor

After you create the applet, use the Source Editor to input the code from Listing 4.1. When you're done, save the program as `CreateDate1.java` and compile it with Build Manager.

TYPE   **Listing 4.1. The source code for `CreateDate1.java`.**

```
 1: import java.awt.Graphics;
 2: import java.util.Date;
 3:
 4: public class CreateDate1 extends java.applet.Applet {
 5:
 6:     public void paint(Graphics g) {
 7:         Date d1, d2, d3;
 8:
 9:         d1 = new Date();
10:         g.drawString("Date 1: " + d1, 5, 50);
11:
12:         d2 = new Date(71, 7, 1, 7, 30);
13:         g.drawString("Date 2: " + d2, 5, 70);
14:
15:         d3 = new Date("April 3 1993 3:24 PM");
16:         g.drawString("Date 3: " + d3, 5, 90);
17:     }
18: }
```

Run the applet with Project Tester; the output should resemble the following:

OUTPUT
```
Date 1: Mon Sep 16 20:59:45 1996
Date 2: Sun Aug 01 07:30:00 1971
Date 3: Sat Apr 03 15:24:00 1993
```

ANALYSIS   In this example, three different dates are created. The first instance (line 9) uses `new Date` with no arguments, which creates a `Date` object for the current date.

The second Date object you created in this example (line 12) has five integer arguments: year, month, day, hours, and minutes. As the output shows, this creates a Date object for that particular date: Sunday, August 1, 1971, at 7:30 AM. You might have noticed an apparent error in line 12 of the source code: the month parameter is 7 although August is the eighth month. However, the Date class uses a value of 0 for January and counts upward, so the value of the month parameter is one lower than you might expect.

The third version of Date takes one argument: a text string representing the date. When the Date object is created, the text string is parsed, and a Date object with that date and time is created (see the third line of the output).

 NOTE

> The date string can take many different formats, as described in the documentation for the Java Application Programmer Interface (API). The documentation is available in HTML format as part of Java WorkShop. To see the documentation, choose Help | Java API Documentation (1.0). The Date() method is part of the java.util package.

What new Does

When you use the new operator, several things happen: The new instance of the given class is created, memory is allocated for it, and a special method defined in the given class is called. This special method is called a constructor.

NEW TERM   *Constructors* are special methods for creating and initializing new instances of classes. Constructors initialize the new object and its variables, create any other objects that the object needs, and perform any other operations that the object needs to initialize itself.

Multiple constructor definitions in a class each can have a different number or type of arguments. When you use new, you can specify different arguments in the argument list, and the right constructor for those arguments will be called. Multiple constructor definitions are what enabled the Date class in the previous example to accomplish different things with the different versions of new. When you create your own classes, you can define as many constructors as you need to implement the behavior of those classes, as you will learn later.

A Note on Memory Management

If you are familiar with other object-oriented programming languages, you might wonder whether the new command has an opposite command to destroy the object when it's no longer needed.

Memory management in Java is dynamic and automatic. When you create a new object, Java automatically allocates the right amount of memory for that object. You don't have to allocate any memory for objects explicitly. Java does it for you.

When you're finished with an object, you do not need to deallocate the memory that the object uses because Java memory management is automatic. When you are finished with an object, that object no longer has any live references to it (it won't be assigned to any variables you still are using, or stored in any arrays). Java has a garbage collector that looks for unused objects and reclaims the memory the objects are using. You don't have to free the memory—you just have to make sure you're not still holding on to an object you want to get rid of. You'll learn about the Java garbage collector and how it works in great detail on Day 21, "Advanced Concepts."

Introduction to Parameters

As you might have noticed in the featured applets at the end of each day's lessons, applets can be run with parameters. The parameters are specified with an HTML tag and are used to customize applets in a variety of ways. Parameters are a powerful way for the actions of an applet to be changed without requiring changes in the code.

The HTML tag <PARAM> is used to send parameters to an applet, as shown in the following example of <APPLET> usage:

```
<APPLET CODE="NeonSign.class" HEIGHT=200 WIDTH=100>
<PARAM NAME="Text" VALUE="Choosy mothers choose Java">
<PARAM NAME="TextColor" VALUE="Red">
</APPLET>
```

Within the <PARAM> tag, the NAME attribute defines the name of the parameter, and the VALUE attribute defines the value to assign to the parameter. In the preceding example, the Text parameter is set to Choosy mothers choose Java and the TextColor parameter is set to Red.

To read a parameter from within a Java applet, you use the getParameter method. The getParameter method is part of the java.applet.Applet class, so you can use it in all applets because they are a subclass of that class. The method takes a string and returns the parameter that is associated with the string, if any parameter has been specified.

Using Project Manager

At this point, you are becoming an old pro at creating new projects and running them under Java WorkShop. To expand your skills, you now will write the CreateDate2 applet to use an HTML APPLET parameter. This project requires you to use the WorkShop Project Manager.

Creating the `CreateDate2` Applet

Use Portfolio Manager to create a new applet with the following fields:

Name: CreateDate2

Source directory: Enter the full path of your homework directory (`c:/Java-WorkShop/homework` or something similar).

Existing sources: No

Main Class File: You should not be able to change this field because `.class` appears in the field as grayed-out text.

Run page: Leave this blank.

Create using: Source Editor

After creating the applet, use the Source Editor to input the code from Listing 4.2. When you're done, save the program as `CreateDate2.java`. Compile the program, but don't run it yet.

TYPE   **Listing 4.2. The source code for `CreateDate2.java`.**

```
 1: import java.awt.Graphics;
 2: import java.util.Date;
 3:
 4: public class CreateDate2 extends java.applet.Applet {
 5:     String paramDate;
 6:
 7:     public void init() {
 8:         paramDate = getParameter("Date");
 9:     }
10:
11:     public void paint(Graphics g) {
12:         Date d1, d2, d3;
13:
14:         d1 = new Date();
15:         g.drawString("Date 1: " + d1, 5, 50);
16:
17:         d2 = new Date(71, 7, 1, 7, 30);
18:         g.drawString("Date 2: " + d2, 5, 70);
19:
20:         d3 = new Date(paramDate);
21:         g.drawString("Date 3: " + d3, 5, 90);
22:     }
23: }
```

This program is a modification of `CreateDate1`. The following changes were made:

☐ An instance variable called `paramDate` has been added to store the value of the parameter that is received.

☐ An init() method has been added that uses getParameter("Date") to retrieve the Date parameter and stores it in paramDate. The init() method will be discussed on Day 8, "Applet Basics." This method is called automatically when an applet starts running.

☐ The Date object d3 has been changed to use paramDate as the string that determines the value of d3.

Before you can test the modified CreateDate2 applet with Project Tester, you need to set up Java WorkShop so that it sends a Date parameter to the applet. To accomplish this, you need to load Project Manager.

Project Manager Features

Project Manager is used in Java WorkShop to determine how a program is compiled, debugged, and executed. With the CreateDate2 project selected as your current project, click the Project Manager icon on the WorkShop command toolbar. It's the gear icon as identified in Figure 4.1.

Figure 4.1.
The Project Manager icon on the WorkShop command toolbar.

└─PROJECT MANAGER

4

The main page of Project Manager includes the following six tabbed dialog boxes:

☐ In the General dialog box, you can change the nature of the current project (from applet to application, for example) and group projects together.

☐ In the Build dialog box, you can choose the source files to include when the project is being compiled and change advanced configuration options that affect compilation.

☐ The Debug/Browse dialog box enables you to make changes that affect the way the debugger operates.

☐ In the Run dialog box, you can choose how the project will be run, and if it's an applet, you can determine the page to execute from and the elements of the <APPLET> tag to use.

☐ The Publish dialog box enables you to group the project's files together and accomplish other organizational tasks required for the distribution of the project.

☐ In the Portfolio dialog box, you can customize the icon for the project, identify the author, and select other attributes.

Click the Run tab to bring that dialog box to the front. Scroll down to the Name and Value text fields. In the Name field, enter Date. In the Value field, enter Nov 22 1995 1:30 PM. Click the Add button below the Name and Value text fields, and the parameter you have added will appear in the Parameters text area on the dialog box, as shown in Figure 4.2.

Figure 4.2.

Part of the Run dialog box in Project Manager.

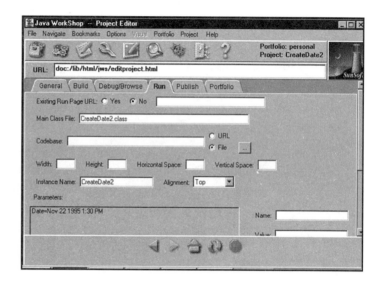

To finish making this change, you must scroll down to the bottom of the Run dialog box and click the Apply button. Otherwise, the change will not take effect. Forgetting to click Apply is an easy mistake to make when working with dialog boxes in Java WorkShop.

Run the applet with Project Tester; the output should reflect the parameter that you sent to the applet, as shown:

```
Date 1: Tue Sep 17 09:09:13 1996
Date 2: Sun Aug 01 07:30:00 1971
Date 3: Wed Nov 22 13:30:00 1995
```

Accessing and Setting Class and Instance Variables

At this point, you could create your own object with class or instance variables defined in it, but how do you work with those variables? Easy! Class and instance variables behave in the same way as the local variables you learned about yesterday. You just refer to them slightly differently than you refer to regular variables in your code.

Getting Values

To get to the value of an instance variable, you use dot notation. With *dot notation*, an instance or class variable name has two parts: the object on the left side of the dot, and the variable on the right side of the dot.

For example, if you have an object assigned to the variable `myCustomer`, and that object has a variable called `orderTotal`, you refer to that variable's value like this:

```
myCustomer.orderTotal;
```

This form of accessing variables is an expression (that is, it returns a value), and both sides of the dot also are expressions. This means that you can nest instance variable access. If that `orderTotal` instance variable itself holds an object, and that object has its own instance variable called `layaway`, you can refer to it like this:

```
myCustomer.orderTotal.layaway;
```

Dot expressions are evaluated from left to right, so you start with `myCustomer`'s variable `orderTotal`, which points to another object with the variable `layaway`. You end up with the value of that `layaway` variable.

Changing Values

4

Assigning a value to that variable is just as easy—just tack an assignment operator on the right side of the expression:

```
myCustomer.orderTotal.layaway = false;
```

This expression sets the value of the `layaway` variable to `false`.

To see how to assign values to instance variables, create the `TestPoint` class, which tests and modifies the instance variables in a `Point` object. `Point` is part of the `java.awt` package and refers to a coordinate point with an x and y value. Use Portfolio Manager to create a new applet with the following fields:

> **Name:** TestPoint
>
> **Source directory:** Enter the full path of your homework directory (`C:/Java-WorkShop/homework` or something similar).
>
> **Existing sources:** No
>
> **Main Class File:** You should not be able to change this field because `.class` appears in the field as grayed-out text.
>
> **Run page:** Leave this blank.
>
> **Create using:** Source Editor

After creating this applet, use the Source Editor to input the code from Listing 4.3. When you're done, save the program as TestPoint.java.

TYPE **Listing 4.3. The source code of TestPoint.java.**

```
 1: import java.awt.Graphics;
 2: import java.awt.Point;
 3:
 4: public class TestPoint extends java.applet.Applet {
 5:
 6:     public void paint(Graphics g) {
 7:         Point thePoint = new Point(10,10);
 8:
 9:         g.drawString("X is " + thePoint.x, 5, 50);
10:         g.drawString("Y is " + thePoint.y, 5, 70);
11:
12:         g.drawString("Setting X to 5.", 25, 90);
13:         thePoint.x = 5;
14:
15:         g.drawString("Setting Y to 15.", 25, 110);
16:         thePoint.y = 15;
17:
18:         g.drawString("X is " + thePoint.x, 5, 130);
19:         g.drawString("Y is " + thePoint.y, 5, 150);
20:     }
21: }
```

OUTPUT Run the applet with Project Tester, and the output should resemble the following:

```
X is 10
Y is 10
    Setting X to 5.
    Setting Y to 15.
X is 5
Y is 15
```

ANALYSIS In this example, you first create an instance of Point where X and Y are both 10 (line 7). Lines 9 and 10 display those values, and you can see dot notation at work there. Lines 13 and 15 change the values of those variables to 5 and 15, respectively. Finally, lines 18 and 19 display the values of X and Y again to show how they've changed.

Class Variables

Class variables, as you learned previously, are variables that are defined and stored in the class itself. Their values, therefore, apply to the class and to all its instances.

With instance variables, each new instance of the class gets a new copy of the instance variables that the class defines. Each instance then can change the values of those instance variables without affecting any other instances. With class variables, only one copy of that variable exists. Every instance of the class has access to that variable, but there is only one value. Changing the value of that variable changes it for all instances of that class.

You define class variables by including the static keyword before the variable itself. For example, take the following partial class definition:

```
class FamilyMember {
    static String surname = "Johnson";
    String name;
    int age;
    ...
}
```

Instances of the class FamilyMember each have their own values for name and age. But the class variable surname has only one value for all family members. Change surname, and all the instances of FamilyMember are affected.

To access class variables, you use the same dot notation used with instance variables. To retrieve or change the value of the class variable, you can use either the instance or the name of the class on the left side of the dot. Both lines of output in this example display the same value:

```
FamilyMember dad = new FamilyMember()
g.drawString("Family's surname is: " + dad.surname, 5, 70);
g.drawString("Family's surname is: " + FamilyMember.surname, 5, 70);
```

Because you can use an instance to change the value of a class variable, it's easy to become confused about class variables and where their values are coming from—remember, the value of a class variable affects all its instances. For this reason, it's a good idea to use the name of the class when you refer to a class variable. It makes your code easier to read and makes strange results easier to debug.

Calling Methods

Calling a method in an object is similar to referring to its instance variables. You use dot notation. The object whose method you're calling is on the left side of the dot, and the name of the method and its arguments are on the right side of the dot, as in the following:

```
myCustomer.addToOrder(itemNumber, price, quantity);
```

Note that all methods must have parentheses after them, even if the method takes no arguments:

```
myCustomer.cancelAllOrders();
```

If the method called results in an object that itself has methods, you can nest methods as you would variables:

```
myCustomer.cancelAllOrders().talkToManager();
```

You can combine nested method calls and instance variable references as well:

```
myCustomer.orderTotal.putOnLayaway(itemNumber, price, quantity);
```

Listing 4.4 shows an example of calling some methods defined in the String class. Strings include methods for string tests and modification, similar to what you would expect in a string library in other languages.

Use Portfolio Manager to create a new applet with the following fields:

> **Name:** TestString
>
> **Source directory:** Enter the full path of your homework directory (C:/Java-WorkShop/homework or something similar).
>
> **Existing sources:** No
>
> **Main Class File:** You should not be able to change this field because .class appears in the field as grayed-out text.
>
> **Run page:** Leave this field blank.
>
> **Create using:** Source Editor

After creating the applet, use the Source Editor to input the code from Listing 4.4. When you're done, save the program as TestString.java.

TYPE   Listing 4.4. Source code of TestString.java.

```
 1: import java.awt.Graphics;
 2:
 3: public class TestString extends java.applet.Applet {
 4:
 5:     public void paint(Graphics g) {
 6:         String str = "Free the bound periodicals";
 7:
 8:         g.drawString("The string is: " + str, 5, 50);
 9:         g.drawString("Length of this string: "
10:             + str.length(), 5, 70);
11:         g.drawString("The character at position 5: "
12:             + str.charAt, 5, 90);
13:         g.drawString("The substring from 17 to 22: "
14:             + str.substring(17, 22), 5, 110);
15:         g.drawString("The index of the character d: "
16:             + str.indexOf('d'), 5, 130);
17:         g.drawString("The index of the beginning of the "
18:             + "substring \"bound\": "
19:             + str.indexOf("bound"), 5, 150);
20:         g.drawString("The string in upper case: "
21:             + str.toUpperCase(), 5, 170);
22:     }
23: }
```

OUTPUT   Run the applet with Project Tester; the output should resemble the following:

```
The string is: Free the bound periodicals
Length of this string: 26
The character at position 5: t
The substring from positions 17 to 22: riodi
The index of the character d: 13
The index of the beginning of the substring "bound": 9
The string in upper case: FREE THE BOUND PERIODICALS
```

ANALYSIS   In line 6, you create a new instance of String by using a string literal (it's easier that way than using new and then putting the characters in individually). The remainder of the program calls different string methods to do different operations on that string:

☐ Line 8 displays the value of the string you created in line 6: Free the bound periodicals.

☐ Lines 9 and 10 call the length() method in the new String object. This string has 26 characters.

☐ Lines 11 and 12 call the charAt() method, which returns the character at the given position in the string. Note that string positions start at 0, so the character at position 5 is t.

☐ Lines 13 and 14 call the substring() method, which takes two integers indicating a range and returns the substring at those starting and ending points. You also can call the substring() method with only one argument, which returns the substring from that position to the end of the string.

☐ Lines 15 and 16 call the indexOf() method, which returns the position of the first instance of the given character (here, 'd').

☐ Lines 17–19 show a different use of the indexOf() method, taking a string argument and returning the position of the beginning of that string.

☐ Lines 20 and 21 use the toUpperCase() method to return a copy of the string in uppercase letters.

Class Methods

Class methods, like class variables, apply to the class as a whole and not to its instances. Class methods commonly are used for general utility methods that might not operate directly on an instance of that class, but fit with that class conceptually. For example, the String class contains a class method called valueOf() that can take many types of arguments (integers, booleans, other objects, and so on). The valueOf() method then returns a new instance of String containing the string value of the argument. This method doesn't operate directly on an existing instance of String, but getting a string from another object or data type is definitely a String-like operation, and it makes sense to define it in the String class.

Class methods also can be useful for gathering general methods together in one place (the class). For example, the Math class, defined in the java.lang package, contains a large set of mathematical operations as class methods; there are no instances of the class Math, but you still can use its methods with numeric or boolean arguments.

To call a class method, use dot notation as you do with instance methods. As with class variables, you can use either an instance of the class or the class itself on the left side of the dot. However, for the same reasons noted in the discussion on class variables, using the name of the class for class methods makes your code easier to read. The last two lines in this example produce the same result:

```
String s, s2;
s = "item";
s2 = s.valueOf;
s2 = String.valueOf;
```

References to Objects

As you work with objects, one important thing going on behind the scenes is the use of references to those objects. When you assign objects to variables, or pass objects as arguments to methods, you are passing references to those objects, not the objects themselves or copies of those objects.

Examine the following snippet of code:

```
Point pt1, pt2;
pt1 = new Point(100, 100);
pt2 = pt1;

pt1.x = 200;
pt1.y = 200;
g.drawString("Point1: " + pt1.x + ", " + pt1.y, 5, 50);
g.drawString("Point2: " + pt2.x + ", " + pt2.y, 5, 70);
```

In this program, you declare two variables of type Point and assign a new Point object to pt1 with x and y each set to 100. You then assign the value of pt1 to pt2. Now, here's the challenge: After changing pt1's x and y instance variables each to 200, what will pt2 look like?

Here's the output of that program:

```
Point1: 200, 200
Point2: 200, 200
```

As you can see, pt2 also was changed. When you assign the value of pt1 to pt2, you create a reference from pt2 to the same object to which pt1 refers. Change the object that pt1 refers to, and you also change the object that pt2 points to because both are references to the same object.

The fact that Java uses references becomes particularly important when you pass arguments to methods. You'll learn more about this later on today, but keep these references in mind.

NOTE

> There are no explicit pointers or pointer arithmetic in Java, just references. However, with these references, and with Java arrays, you have most of the capabilities of pointers without the confusion and lurking bugs that explicit pointers can create.

Converting Objects and Primitive Types

Sometimes in your Java programs, you might have a value stored somewhere that is the wrong type. Maybe it's an instance of the wrong class, or perhaps it's a `float`, and you want it to be an `int`. To convert the value of one type to another, you use a mechanism called casting. *Casting* is a way to convert the value of an object or primitive type into another type. The result of a cast is a new reference or value—casting does not affect the original object or value.

Although the concept of casting is a simple one, the rules for what types in Java can be converted to what other types are complicated by the fact that Java has both primitive types (`int`, `float`, and `boolean`) and object types (`String`, `Point`, `Window`, and so on). Three forms of casts and conversions are described in this section:

☐ Casting between primitive types: `int` to `float`

☐ Casting between object types: from one class instance to another class instance

☐ Converting primitive types to objects and then extracting primitive values back out of those objects

Casting Primitive Types

Casting between primitive types enables you to convert the value of one type to another primitive type—for example, to assign a number of one type to a variable of another type. Casting between primitive types most commonly occurs with the numeric types; boolean values cannot be cast to or from any other primitive type.

Often, if the type you are casting to is larger in terms of storage size than the type of the value you're converting, you might not have to use an explicit cast. You often automatically can treat a `byte` or a `char` as an `int`, for example, or an `int` as a `long`, an `int` as a `float`, or anything as a `double`. In most cases, because the larger type provides more precision than the smaller type, no loss of information occurs when the value is set. As an example, you can store the sum of two bytes in an int without an explicit cast, and the value will be what you would expect it to be.

The exception is casting integers to floating-point values. Casting an int or a long to a float or a long to a double might cause some loss of precision. Consider the following code:

```
int a = 2000000025;
float b = a;
int c = (int)b;
```

The first line sets the integer a to 2000000025 (two billion and twenty-five). The second line sets the floating-point number b by using the integer a—without requiring a cast. The final line sets the integer c with an explicit cast of the floating-point number b. An explicit cast was required in this case.

If you displayed the values of a, b, and c, the following values would be output:

```
a=2000000025
b=2e+009
c=2000000000
```

The second line, which uses exponential notation, shows that the floating-point number has a value of two billion (2e+009), and the third line confirms this. The loss of precision caused by casting from an integer to a floating-point number was 25 in this example.

To convert a large value to a smaller type, you must use an explicit cast because converting that value might result in a loss of precision. Explicit casts look like this:

```
(typename) value
```

In this form, *typename* is the name of the type you're converting to (for example: short, int, float, or boolean), and *value* is an expression that results in the value you want to convert. The following expression divides the value of x by the value of y and casts the result to an int:

```
(int) (x / y);
```

Note that because the precedence of casting is higher than that of arithmetic, you have to use parentheses so that the result of the division is what gets cast to an int.

Casting Objects

You can also cast instances of classes to instances of other classes, with one restriction: The class of the object you're casting and the class of the object you're casting it to must be related by inheritance. You can cast an object only to an instance of its superclass or a subclass, not to any random class.

4

Analogous to converting a primitive value to a larger type, some objects might not need to be cast explicitly. In particular, because subclasses contain all of the information in the superclass, you can use an instance of a subclass anywhere a superclass is expected. Suppose you have a method that takes two arguments: one of type Object, and one of type Number. You don't have to pass instances of those particular classes to that method. For the Object argument, you can pass any subclass of Object (any object, in other words), and for the Number argument you can pass in any instance of any subclass of Number (Integer, Boolean, Float, and so on).

Casting an object to an instance of one of that object's superclasses loses the information the original subclass provided and requires a specific cast. To cast an object to another class, you use the same casting operation that you used for base types:

```
(classname) object
```

In this case, *classname* is the name of the class you want to cast the object to, and *object* is a reference to the object you're casting. Note that casting creates a reference to the old object of the type *classname*; the old object still continues to exist as it did before.

Here's an example of casting an instance of the class GreenApple to an instance of the class Apple, where GreenApple is a subclass of Apple:

```
GreenApple a;
Apple a2;
a = new GreenApple();
a2 = (Apple) a;
```

In addition to casting objects to classes, you also can cast objects to interfaces, but only if that object's class or one of its superclasses implements that interface. Casting an object to an interface then enables you to call one of that interface's methods even if that object's class does not directly implement that interface. You'll learn more about interfaces in Week 3.

Casting Primitive Types to Objects and Vice Versa

Now you know how to cast a primitive type to another primitive type and how to cast between classes. How can you cast one to the other? You can't! Primitive types and objects are very different things in Java, and you can't automatically cast or convert between the two. However, the java.lang package includes several special classes that correspond to each primitive data type: Integer for int, Float for float, Boolean for boolean, and so on.

Using class methods defined in these classes, you can create an object-equivalent for all of the primitive types using new. The following line of code creates an instance of the Integer class with the value 35:

```
Integer intObject = new Integer(35);
```

Once you have actual objects, you can treat those values as objects. Then, when you want the primitive values back again, there are methods for that as well. For example, the intValue() method extracts an int primitive value from an Integer object:

```
int theInt = intObject.intValue();   // returns 35
```

See the Java API documentation, available from the Help pull-down menu in Java WorkShop, for specifics on the methods used to convert between primitive types and objects.

Odds and Ends

This section is a catch-all for other information about working with objects, in particular the following:

- ☐ Comparing objects
- ☐ Finding out the class of any given object
- ☐ Testing to see whether an object is an instance of a given class

Comparing Objects

Yesterday, you learned about operators for comparing values: equals, not equals, less than, and so on. Most of these operators work only on primitive types, not on objects. If you try to use other values as operands, the Java program will not compile successfully. The exception to this rule is the operators for equality: == (equal) and != (not equal). These operators, when used with objects, test whether the two operands refer to exactly the same object.

What should you do if you want to compare instances of your class and have meaningful results? You have to implement special methods in your class, and you have to call those methods using those method names.

NOTE

Java does not have the concept of operator overloading—that is, the capability of defining the behavior of the built-in operators by defining methods in your own classes. The built-in operators remain defined only for numbers.

A good example of this situation is the String class. It is possible to have two strings, two independent objects in memory, with the same values. For example, the variables myName and yourName both could have the value Pudding N. Tane. You might think that the expression myName == yourName would evaluate as true. According to the == operator, however, those two

String objects will not be equal. This is a result of the following logic: Although their contents are the same, they are not the same object. Two people with the same name are not the same person.

The String class, therefore, defines a method called equals() that tests each character in the string and returns true if the two strings have the same values. Examine the following snippet of code:

```
String str1, str2;
str1 = "She sells sea shells by the sea shore.";
str2 = str1;

g.drawString("String1: " + str1, 5, 50);
g.drawString("String2: " + str2, 5, 70);
g.drawString("Same object? " + (str1 == str2), 5, 90);

str2 = new String(str1);

g.drawString("String1: " + str1, 5, 110);
g.drawString("String2: " + str2, 5, 130);
g.drawString("Same object? " + (str1 == str2), 5, 150);
g.drawString("Same value? " + str1.equals(str2), 5, 170);
```

This code produces the following output:

```
String1: She sells sea shells by the sea shore.
String2: She sells sea shells by the sea shore.
Same object? true
String1: She sells sea shells by the sea shore.
String2: She sells sea shells by the sea shore.
Same object? false
Same value? true
```

The first part of this program declares two variables: str1 and str2. It assigns the literal She sells sea shells by the sea shore. to str1, and then assigns that value to str2. As you know from object references, this causes str1 and str2 to point to the same object, and the Same object? test proves that.

In the second part, you create a new String object with the value of str1. Now you have two different string objects with the same value. Testing them to see whether they're the same object by using the == operator returns false, because they are not the same object. Testing them using the equals method to compare their values returns true, because they have the same value.

NOTE

> Why can't you just use another literal when you change str2, rather than using new? String literals are optimized in Java; if you create a string using a literal, and then use another literal with the same characters, Java knows enough to give you the first String object back. Both strings are the same objects—to create two separate objects you have to use new.

Determining the Class of an Object

Want to find out the class of an object? Here's the way to do it for an object assigned to the variable obj:

```
String name = obj.getClass().getName();
```

What does this code do? The getClass() method is defined in the Object class, and as such is available for all objects. The result of that method is a Class object (where Class is itself a class), which has a method called getName(). getName() returns a string representing the name of the class.

For example, recall the Monster class hierarchy that you created on Day 2, "Object-Oriented Programming." What if you have an object assigned to the variable creature and you want to determine its class, to see if it's a Jabberwock, Dragon, or something else? The following would be used:

```
String creatureClass = creature.getClass().getName();
```

Another useful test is the instanceof operator. instanceof has two operands: an object on the left, and the name of a class on the right. The expression returns true or false based on whether the object is an instance of the named class or any of its subclasses. For example, the expression "Millard Fillmore" instanceof String; returns true.

Also, if the variable pt is declared as follows, Point pt = new Point(10,10);, the expression pt instanceof String; will return false because pt is an instance of the class Point.

```
Point pt = new Point(10, 10);
pt instanceof String;
```

The instanceof operator also can be used for interfaces. If an object implements an interface, using the instanceof operator with that interface name on the right side returns true. You'll learn about interfaces in Week 3.

The Java Class Library

To finish up today, you'll be introduced to the Java class library. Actually, you've had some experience with parts of it already, so it shouldn't seem that strange. The Java class library provides the set of classes that are guaranteed to be available in every commercial Java environment (for example, in HotJava or in Netscape Navigator 2.0).

Those classes are in the java package and include all of the classes you've seen so far in this book, plus many more classes you will learn about later in this book. The only class that you won't get much opportunity to learn about during this 21-day course is the java.net package. All others will be featured in sample programs that you create.

In Java WorkShop, the documentation for these classes is available using the Help | Java API Documentation 1.0 command. Descriptions are included for each class' instance variables, methods, constructors, interfaces, and related material. Appendix C, "The Java Class Library," provides a summary of the classes that are available in the library to help you find tools to use in the development of your own Java programs.

The following class packages are part of the Java class library:

□ java.lang: Classes that apply to the language itself, which include the Object class, the String class, and the System class. This package also contains special classes for the primitive types (Integer, Character, Float, and so on).

□ java.util: Utility classes, such as Date, and simple collection classes, such as Vector and Hashtable.

□ java.io: Input and output classes for writing to and reading from streams (such as standard input and output) and for handling files.

□ java.net: Classes for networking support, including Socket and URL (a class to represent references to documents on the World Wide Web).

□ java.awt: The Abstract Windowing Toolkit, a package of classes to implement a graphical user interface, including classes for Window, Menu, Button, Font, CheckBox, and so on. This package also includes classes for processing images (in the java.awt.Image package).

□ java.applet: Classes to implement Java applets, including the Applet class itself, as well as the AudioClip interface.

In addition to the Java classes, development environments might include additional classes that provide other utilities or functionality. Java WorkShop introduces new classes that are used by Visual Java to make the creation and implementation of graphical user interfaces easier. These will be discussed on Day 13, "Visual Java and the Abstract Windowing Toolkit."

4

Although these additional classes can be useful, they are not part of the standard Java library, so you cannot rely on users having the classes when your programs are run. You have to take special steps to provide the additional classes along with the class files you have created. This is particularly important for applets because applets are expected to be executable on any Java-capable browser. Only classes in the `java` package are guaranteed to be available on all browsers and Java environments.

Summary

Today, you learned how to deal with objects: creating them, finding and changing the values of their variables, and calling their methods. You also learned how to copy and compare them, and how to convert them into other objects. You also used the Project Manager in Java WorkShop to send parameters to an applet and used the `getParameter` method to retrieve those parameters. Finally, you learned a bit about the Java class libraries, which give you a large number of classes to play with in your own programs.

You now have the fundamentals of how to deal with most simple things in Java. All you have left are arrays, conditionals, and loops, which you'll learn about tomorrow. After that, you will learn how to define and use classes in Java applications. With just about everything in your Java programs, you always come back to objects.

Q&A

Q I'm confused—what are the differences between objects and the primitive data types such as `int` and `boolean`?

A The primitive types in the language (`byte`, `short`, `int`, `long`, `float`, `double`, `boolean` and `char`) represent the smallest things in the language. They are not objects, although in many ways they can be handled like objects—they can be assigned to variables and passed in and out of methods. Most of the operations that work exclusively on objects, however, will not work on them.

Objects are instances of classes. As such, they usually are more complex data types than simple numbers and characters, often containing numbers and characters as instance or class variables.

Q In the section on calling methods, you had examples of calling a method with a different number of arguments each time, and it gave a different kind of result. How is that possible?

A This is called *method overloading*. Overloading enables the same function name to have different behavior based on the arguments it is called with, and the number and type of arguments can vary. When you define methods in your own classes, you define separate method signatures with different sets of arguments and different definitions. When a method is called, Java figures out which definition to execute based on the number and type of arguments the method was called with.

Q What is the advantage of not having operator overloading in Java (something that is used in C++)?

A Java was designed to be simpler than C++, so some features of C++ have not been adopted by Java. The argument against operator overloading is that because the operator can be defined to mean anything, it makes it difficult to figure out what any given operator is doing at any one time. This can result in confusing code.

FEATURED APPLET Today's Featured Applet

The featured applet for today, `StarField`, is a relatively short Java program with some neat visual effects. Like the Microsoft Windows screen saver, the applet depicts a field of stars moving past the applet window. One added feature is rotation—you can click on the applet surface and set the window spinning. `StarField` was written by Will Schenk. Figure 4.3 shows a screen capture of the applet.

Figure 4.3.

The `StarField` *applet in action.*

`StarField` files are located on the CD-ROM in the `\BOOK\3RDPARTY\DAY4\` directory, including source code in the file `StarField.java`. To use `StarField` on a Web page, place these two class files on your Web site: `StarField.class` and `Star.class`. Place these files in the same directory as the Web page or place them in a subdirectory listed in the `CODEBASE` parameter of the `<APPLET>` tag. The `<CODE>` tag should be `StarField.class`. Listing 4.5 shows the HTML tags used to run `StarField` as it was shown in Figure 4.3.

Listing 4.5. The `<APPLET>` tag for `StarField`.

```
<APPLET CODE=StarField.class WIDTH=600 HEIGHT=225>
<PARAM NAME=STARS VALUE=250>
<PARAM NAME=SPEED VALUE=15>
</APPLET>
```

StarField parameters can be customized within the `<APPLET>` tag as follows:

- [ ] The `stars` parameter defines the number of stars to display (`30` is the default).
- [ ] The `speed` parameter is the speed of the stars (`50` is the default).
- [ ] The `spin` parameter is the normal amount of spin (`0` is the default; `0.01` is recommended).
- [ ] The `maxspin` parameter defines the maximum spin before the spin reverses itself (`0.1` is the default).
- [ ] The `ddx` parameter is an approximation of the second derivative of theta, which can be modified to affect the display (`.005` is the default).

More information on `StarField` is available from the author at the following URL:

```
http://www.personal.psu.edu/users/c/h/chilly/applets/beta/stars.html
```

Day **5**

Arrays, Conditionals, and Loops

Although you could write Java programs using what you've learned so far, those programs would be pretty dull. Much of the good stuff in Java, or in any programming language, comes from using arrays to store values and using loops and conditionals to execute different parts of a program based on tests. Today, you will find out about the following:

- [ ] Arrays, for collecting objects or primitive types into an easy-to-manage list
- [ ] Block statements, for grouping together related statements
- [ ] if and switch statements, for conditional tests
- [ ] for and while loops, for repeating part of a program multiple times

Arrays

NEW TERM   *Arrays* are a way to store a list of items. Each slot of the array holds an individual element, and you can place elements into slots and change the contents of slots as needed. Arrays can contain any type of element value (primitive types or objects), but a single array cannot be used to store different types. You can have an array of integers, an array of strings, or an array of arrays, but you can't have an array that contains both strings and integers, for example.

Java implements arrays differently than some other languages. In Java, arrays are objects that can be treated just like other objects. To create an array in Java, use these steps:

1. Declare a variable to hold the array.
2. Create a new array object and assign it to the array variable.
3. Store things in that array.

Declaring Array Variables

The first step of creating an array is declaring a variable that will hold the array. Array variables indicate the type of object the array will hold and the name of the array, followed by empty brackets ([]). The following lines are all typical array variable declarations:

```
String difficultWords[];
Point hits[];
int donations[];
```

An alternative method of defining an array variable is to put the brackets after the array type instead of after the array name. Putting the brackets after the array name is not as readable as the alternative. To see for yourself, take a look at the preceding three declarations redone with the brackets after the array type:

```
String[] difficultWords;
Point[] hits;
int[] guesses;
```

Creating Array Objects

After you declare the array variable, the next step is to create an array object and assign it to that variable. The two ways to do this step are as follows:

- ☐ Use the new operator
- ☐ Initialize the contents of the array directly

Because arrays are objects in Java, you can use the new operator to create a new instance of an array, as in the following line:

```
String[] playerNames = new String[10];
```

This line creates a new array of strings with 10 slots containing elements. When you create an array object using new, you must indicate how many slots the array will hold.

Array objects can contain primitive types such as integers or booleans, just as they can contain objects:

```
int[] temps = new int[99];
```

When you create an array object using new, all of its slots automatically are initialized (0 for numeric arrays, false for boolean, '\0' for character arrays, and null for objects).

You also can create and initialize an array at the same time. Instead of using new to create the new array object, enclose the elements of the array inside braces, separated by commas:

```
String[] chiles = { "jalapeno", "anaheim", "serrano",
    "habanero", "thai" };
```

Each of the elements inside the braces must be the same type as the variable that holds the array. When you create an array with initial values in this manner, the array will be the same size as the number of elements you have included within the braces. The preceding example creates an array of String objects named chiles that contains five elements.

Accessing Array Elements

Once you have an array with initial values, you can retrieve, change, and test the values in each slot of that array. The value in a slot is accessed with the array name followed by a subscript enclosed within square brackets. This name and subscript can be put into expressions, as in the following:

```
contestantScore[40] = 470;
```

The subscript expression specifies the slot to access within the array. Array subscripts start with 0, as they do in C and C++, so an array with 10 elements has array slots that are accessed by using subscripts 0 through 9.

All array subscripts are checked to make sure that they are inside the boundaries of the array, as specified when the array was created. This check occurs either when the Java program is compiled or when it is run. It is impossible in Java to use an array slot outside the boundaries of the array. Note the following two statements:

```
String[] beatleSpeak = new String[10];
beatleSpeak[10] = "I am the eggman.";
```

5

A program with the preceding two lines of code will produce a compilation error when `beatleSpeak[10]` is used. The error occurs because the `beatleSpeak` array does not have a slot 10—it has 10 slots that begin at `0` and end at 9. The Java compiler will catch this error.

If the array subscript is calculated when the program is running (for example, as part of a loop), and the subscript ends up outside the boundaries of the array, the Java interpreter produces an error. Actually, to be technically correct, it throws an exception. You will learn more about exceptions later on next week and on Day 17, "Exceptions."

How can you keep from overrunning the end of an array accidentally in your programs? Test for the length of the array in your programs using the `length` instance variable—it's available for all array objects, regardless of type, as in the following:

```
int len = beatleSpeak.length
```

This line would return a `10` because the `beatleSpeak` array has 10 elements.

Changing Array Elements

As you saw in the previous examples, you can assign a value to a specific slot of an array by putting an assignment statement after the array name and subscript, as in the following:

```
myGrades[4] = 85;
sentence[0] = "The";
sentence[10] = sentence[0];
```

An important thing to note is that an array of objects in Java is an array of references to those objects (similar in some ways to an array of pointers in C or C++). When you assign a value to a slot in an array, you are creating a reference to that object. When you move values around inside arrays (as in the last of the preceding lines), you are reassigning the reference, not copying a value from one slot to another. Arrays of a primitive type such as `int` or `float` do copy the values from one slot to another.

Arrays of references to objects, as opposed to objects themselves, are particularly useful because you can have multiple references to the same objects both inside and outside of arrays. For example, you can assign an object contained in an array to a variable and refer to that same object by using either the variable or the array position.

Multidimensional Arrays

Java does not support multidimensional arrays. However, you can declare and create an array of arrays (and those arrays can contain arrays, and so on, for as many dimensions as you need). The following lines show how to access these arrays of arrays:

```
int[][] coords = new int[12][12];
coords[0][0] = 1;
coords[0][1] = 2;
```

Block Statements

NEW TERM   A block statement is a group of statements surrounded by braces ({ and }). You can use a block statement anywhere a single statement would go, and the block statement creates a local scope for the statements inside it. This local scope means that you can declare and use local variables inside a block statement, and those variables will cease to exist after the block statement is finished executing. For example, the following block statement is inside a method definition that declares the new variables x and y:

```
void testBlock() {
    int x = 10;
    { // start of block
      int y = 40;
    y = y + x;
    } // end of block
}
```

Because x was declared outside of the block statement, it can be used inside and outside of the block statement. In contrast, y was declared inside the block statement, which limits its local scope to the block statement. It cannot be used outside of it.

Block statements usually are not used in this way (alone in a method definition). To this point, you mostly have seen block statements surrounding class and method definitions. Another common use of block statements is in the control-flow constructs you will be learning about next.

if Conditionals

The if conditional, which enables you to execute different sections of code based on a simple test in Java, is nearly identical to if statements in C. An if conditional contains the keyword if, followed by a boolean test, followed by a statement (often a block statement) to execute if the test is true:

```
if (x < y)
    g.drawString("x is smaller than y", 5, 110);
```

An optional else keyword provides the statement to execute if the test is false, as shown in the following code:

```
if (x < y)
    g.drawString("x is smaller than y", 5, 110);
else g.drawString("y is bigger than x", 5, 110);
```

5

NOTE

> The difference between `if` conditionals in Java and those in C or C++ is that Java requires the test to return a boolean value (`true` or `false`). In C, the test can return an integer.

These `if...else` constructs often will be used with block statements so that more than one statement is executed. To offer a range of possible options, `if` and `else` statements can be nested inside other `if` and `else` statements. Note the following snippet of code, an extension of the `Jabberwock` object you created on Day 2, "Object-Oriented Programming,":

```
if (attitude == "angry" ) {
    g.drawString("The jabberwock is angry.", 5, 110);
    g.drawString("Have you made out a will?", 5, 130);
} else {
    g.drawString("The jabberwock is in a good mood.", 5, 110);
    if (hungry)
        g.drawString("It still is hungry, though.", 5, 130);
    else g.drawString("It wanders off.", 5. 130);
}
```

This example uses the test (`attitude == "angry"`) to determine whether to display that the jabberwock is angry or happy. If the jabberwock is happy, the test (`hungry`) is used to see whether the jabberwock also is hungry—assuming that a hungry jabberwock is a thing to avoid, even if it's a happy jabberwock. The conditional `if (hungry)` is another way of saying `if (hungry == true)`. For boolean tests of this type, leaving off the last part of the expression is a common programming shortcut.

The Conditional Operator

An alternative to using the `if` and `else` keywords in a conditional statement is to use the conditional operator, sometimes called the ternary operator. The *conditional operator* is called a *ternary operator* because it has three terms.

The conditional operator is an expression, meaning that it returns a value (unlike the more general `if`, which only can result in a statement or block being executed). The conditional operator is most useful for short or simple conditionals and looks like the following line:

```
test ? trueresult : falseresult
```

The *test* is an expression that returns `true` or `false`, just like the test in the `if` statement. If the test is true, the conditional operator returns the value of *trueresult*. If the test is false, the conditional operator returns the value of *falseresult*. For example, the following conditional tests the values of `myScore` and `yourScore`, returns the larger of the two as a value, and assigns that value to the variable `ourBestScore`:

```
int ourBestScore = myScore > yourScore ? myScore : yourScore;
```

This use of the conditional operator is equivalent to the following if-else code:

```
if (myScore > yourScore)
        ourBestScore = myScore;
else
        ourBestScore = yourScore;
```

The conditional operator has a very low precedence—it usually is evaluated only after all its subexpressions are evaluated. The only operators lower in precedence are the assignment operators. For a refresher on operator precedence, see the precedence chart from Day 3, "Java Language Basics."

switch Conditionals

A common programming practice in any language is to test a variable against some value, and if it doesn't match that value, to test it again against a different value, and so on. Using only if statements, this process can become unwieldy, depending on how many different values you have to test. For example, you might end up with a set of if statements something like the following:

```
if (oper == '+')
    addargs(arg1, arg2);
else if (oper == '-')
    subargs(arg1, arg2);
else if (oper == '*')
    multargs(arg1, arg2);
else if (oper == '/')
    divargs(arg1, arg2);
```

This use of if statements is called a nested if because each else statement contains another if until all possible tests have been made.

A shorthand mechanism for nested ifs that you can use in some programming languages is to group tests and actions together in a single statement. In Java, you can group actions together with the switch statement, which behaves as it does in C. The following is an example of switch usage:

```
switch (grade) {
    case 'A':
            g.drawString("Great job — an A!", 5, 130);
        break;
    case 'B':
            g.drawString("Good job — a B!", 5, 130);
        break;
    case 'C':
            g.drawString("Your grade was a C.", 5, 130);
        break;
    default: g.drawString("An F — you can do better!", 5, 130);
}
```

5

The `switch` statement is built on a test; in the preceding example, the test is on the value of the `grade` variable. The test variable, which can be any of the primitive types `byte`, `char`, `short`, or `int`, is compared in turn with each of the `case` values. If a match is found, the statement or statements after the test are executed. If no match is found, the `default` statement or statements are executed. The `default` is optional. If it is omitted, and there is no match for any of the `case` statements, the `switch` statement completes without executing anything.

The Java implementation of `switch` is limited—tests and values can be only simple primitive types that are castable to `int`. You cannot use larger primitive types such as `long` or `float`, strings, or other objects within a `switch`, nor can you test for any relationship other than equality. These restrictions limit `switch` to the simplest cases. In contrast, nested `if` statements can work for any kind of test on any type.

The following is a revision of the nested `if` example shown previously. It has been rewritten as a `switch` statement:

```
switch (oper) {
    case '+':
        addargs(arg1, arg2);
        break;
    case '*':
        subargs(arg1, arg2);
        break;
    case '-':
        multargs(arg1, arg2);
        break;
    case '/':
        divargs(arg1, arg2);
        break;
}
```

Note the `break` statements included with each `case` section. Without a `break` statement, once a match is made, the statements for that match and also all the statements further down the `switch` are executed until a `break` or the end of the switch is found. In some cases, this might be exactly what you want to do. However, in most cases, you should include the `break` to ensure that only the right code is executed.

One handy use of falling through without a `break` occurs when multiple values should execute the same statements. To accomplish this task, you can use multiple `case` lines with no result, and the `switch` will execute the first statements that it finds. For example, in the following `switch` statement, the string `x is an even number.` is printed if x has the values of 2, 4, 6, or 8. All other values of x cause the string `x is an odd number.` to be printed.

```
switch {
    case 2:
    case 4:
    case 6:
    case 8:
        g.drawString("x is an even number.", 5, 50);
```

```
        break;
    default: g.drawString("x is an odd number.", 5, 50);
}
```

for **Loops**

The for loop repeats a statement a specified number of times until a condition is met. Although for loops frequently are used for simple iteration in which a statement is repeated a certain number of times, for loops can be used for just about any kind of loop.

The for loop in Java looks roughly like the following:

```
for (initialization; test; increment) {
    statement;
}
```

The start of the for loop has three parts:

- ☐ initialization is an expression that initializes the start of the loop. If you have a loop index, this expression might declare and initialize it, such as int i = 0. Variables that you declare in this part of the for loop are local to the loop itself; they cease to exist after the loop is finished executing. You can initialize more than one variable in this section by separating each expression with a comma. The statement int i = 0, int j = 10 in this section would declare the variables i and j, and both would be local to the loop.

- ☐ test is the test that occurs after each pass of the loop. The test must be a boolean expression or a function that returns a boolean value, such as i < 10. If the test is true, the loop executes. Once the test is false, the loop stops executing.

- ☐ increment is any expression or function call. Commonly, the increment is used to change the value of the loop index to bring the state of the loop closer to returning false and stopping the loop. As you can do in the initialization section, you can put more than one expression in this section by separating each expression with a comma.

The *statement* part of the for loop is the statement that is executed each time the loop iterates. As with if, you can include either a single statement or a block statement; the previous example used a block because that is more common. The following example is a for loop that sets all slots of a String array to the value Mr.:

```
String[] salutation = new String[10];
int i; // the loop index variable

for (i = 0; i < salutation.length; i++)
    salutation[i] = "Mr.";
```

Any part of the for loop can be an empty statement—that is, you can include a semicolon with no expression or statement and that part of the for loop will be ignored. You also can have an empty statement as the body of your for loop if everything you want to do is in the first line of that loop. For example, the following for loop finds the first prime number higher than 4,000:

```
for (i = 4001; notPrime; i += 2)
    ;
```

A common mistake in for loops is to accidentally put a semicolon at the end of the line that includes the for statement:

```
for (i = 0; i < 10; i++);
    x = x * i; // this line is not inside the loop!
```

In this example, the first semicolon ends the loop without executing x = x * i as part of the loop. The x = x * i line will be executed only once because it is outside of the for loop entirely. Be careful not to make this mistake in your Java programs.

while **and** do **Loops**

The remaining types of loop to learn about are the while and do loops. Like for loops, while and do loops enable a block of Java code to be executed repeatedly until a specific condition is met. Whether you use a for, while, or do loop is mostly a matter of your programming style. while and do loops are exactly the same as in C and C++, except that the test condition must be a boolean in Java.

while **Loops**

The while loop is used to repeat a statement as long as a particular condition is true. The following is an example of a while loop:

```
while (i < 10) {
    x = x * i++; // the body of the loop
}
```

The condition that accompanies the while keyword is a boolean expression—i < 10 in the preceding example. If the expression returns true, the while loop executes the body of the loop and then tests the condition again. This process repeats until the condition is false. Although the preceding loop uses opening and closing braces to form a block statement, the braces are not needed because the loop contains only one statement—x = x * i++. Using the braces does not create any problems, though, and the braces will be required if you add another statement inside the loop later on.

while loops and other loops can use more complicated expressions than the ones shown up to this point. The following loop copies the elements of an array of integers (in userData1) to an array of floating-point numbers (in userData2), casting each element to a float as it goes. The one catch is that if any element in userData1 is a 0, the loop immediately exits at that point. To cover both cases—copying all elements and exiting when an element is equal to 0, you can use a compound test with the && operator, as shown in the following code:

```
int count = 0;
while ( count < userData1.length && userData1[count] !=0) {
    userData2[count] = (float) userData1[count++];
}
```

Note that if the condition is false the first time it is tested (for example, if the first element in the first array is 0), the body of the while loop never will be executed. If you need to execute the loop at least once, you can do one of two things:

☐ Duplicate the body of the loop outside of the while loop

☐ Use a do loop (described next)

The do loop is considered the better solution of the two.

do...while **Loops**

The do loop is just like a while loop, except that do executes a given statement until the condition is false (as opposed to doing so while the condition is true). At first, they might sound the same, but the distinction is this: while loops test the condition before looping, so if the condition is false the first time it is tested, the body of the loop never will execute. do loops execute the body of the loop at least once before testing the condition, so if the condition is false the first time it is tested, the body of the loop already will have executed once.

It's the difference between asking dad to borrow the car and telling him later that you borrowed it. If dad nixes the idea in the first case, you don't get to borrow it. If he nixes the idea in the second case, you already have borrowed it once.

do loops look like the following:

```
do {
    x = x * i++; // the body of the loop
} while (i < 10);
```

The body of the loop is executed once before the test condition, i < 10, is evaluated. Then, if the test evaluates as true, the loop runs again. If it is false, the loop exits. Keep in mind that with do loops, the body of the loop executes at least once.

5

The following is a simple example of a do loop that displays a message each time the loop iterates:

```
int x = 1;
do {
    g.drawString("Looping, round " + x, 5, 30+(x*20));
    x++;
} while (x <= 10);
```

The output of these statements is as follows:

```
Looping, round 1
Looping, round 2
Looping, round 3
Looping, round 4
Looping, round 5
Looping, round 6
Looping, round 7
Looping, round 8
Looping, round 9
Looping, round 10
```

Breaking Out of Loops

In all of the loops, the loop ends when a tested condition is met. There might be times when something occurs during execution of a loop and you want to exit the loop early. For that, you can use the break and continue keywords.

You already have seen break as part of the switch statement; break stops execution of the switch statement, and the program continues. The break keyword, when used with a loop, does the same thing—it immediately halts execution of the current loop. If you have nested loops within loops, execution picks up with the next outer loop. Otherwise, the program merely continues executing the next statement after the loop.

For example, recall the while loop that copied elements from an integer array into an array of floating-point numbers until the end of the array or a 0 was reached. You can test for that latter case inside the body of the while loop, and then use break to exit the loop:

```
int count = 0;
while (count < userData1.length) {
    if (userData1[count] == 0) {
        break;
    }
    userData2[count] = (float) userData1[count++];
}
```

The continue keyword starts the loop over at the next iteration. For do and while loops, this means that the execution of the block statement starts over again; for for loops, the increment expression is evaluated and then the block statement is executed. The continue keyword is useful when you want to make a special case out of elements within a loop. With the previous example of copying one array to another, you could test for whether the current element is equal to 0, and use continue to restart the loop after every 0 so that the resulting array never will contain zero. Note that because you're skipping elements in the first array, you now have to keep track of two different array counters:

```
int count = 0;
int count2 = 0;
while (count++ <= userData1.length) {
    if (userData1[count] == 0)
        continue;

    userData2[count2++] = (float)userData1[count];
}
```

Labeled Loops

Both break and continue can have an optional label that tells Java where to resume execution of the program. Without a label, break jumps outside the nearest loop to an enclosing loop or to the next statement outside the loop. The continue keyword restarts the loop it is enclosed within. Using break and continue with a label enables you to use break to go to a point outside a nested loop or to use continue to go to a loop outside the current loop.

To use a labeled loop, add the label before the initial part of the loop, with a colon between the label and the loop. Then, when you use break or continue, add the name of the label after the keyword itself, as in the following:

```
out:
    for (int i = 0; i <10; i++) {
        while (x < 50) {
            if (i * x++ > 400)
                break out;
            // inner loop here
        }
        // outer loop here
    }
```

In this snippet of code, the label out labels the outer loop. Then, inside both the for and while loops, when a particular condition is met, a break causes the execution to break out of both loops. Without the label out, the break statement would exit the inner loop and resume execution with the outer loop.

The following program contains a nested for loop. Inside the innermost loop, if the summed value of the two loop counters is greater than 4, both loops exit at once through the break sumLoops statement:

```
sumLoops:
    for (int i = 1; i <= 5; i++)
        for (int j = 1; j <= 3; j++) {
            System.out.println("i is " + i + ", j is " + j);
            if ((i + j) > 4)
```

5

```
            break sumLoops;
        }
System.out.println("End of loops.");
```

Here's the output of this program:

```
i is 1, j is 1
i is 1, j is 2
i is 1, j is 3
i is 2, j is 1
i is 2, j is 2
i is 2, j is 3
End of loops.
```

As you can see, the loop iterated until the sum of i and j was greater than 4, and then both loops exited back to the outer block and the final message was displayed. This program uses System.out.println, a method used in applications to display text. This topic will be covered tomorrow when you start writing stand-alone Java programs.

Debugging with Java WorkShop

An inevitable part of software design is removing bugs from code. The bigger the project, the more likely that a misplaced bit of punctuation or a logic error will cause unexpected results until the error is corrected. Actually, if there's only one error when you try to compile a program for the first time, you're doing remarkably well!

Java WorkShop includes two powerful tools to find and correct errors: jump-to-error icons and the Debugger. The jump-to-error icons are available in the Build Manager and the Source Editor. The two jump-to-error icons are the Go to Previous Error icon (an up arrow next to a "!" road sign) and the Go to Next Error icon (a down arrow next to a "!" road sign). The icons are shown on the Source Editor command toolbar in Figure 5.1, and they look the same in Build Manager. You will see how to use these icons in the next program that you write.

The Debugger has sophisticated features that make it easier to find bugs in your programs. To get a first look at this feature, click the Debugger icon on the WorkShop command toolbar. It's the bug icon shown in Figure 5.2.

The main page of Debugger includes six tabbed dialog boxes: Threads/Stack, Expressions, Breakpoints, Exceptions, Classes, and Messages. Most of these boxes will make more sense to you later on, when you are introduced to Java concepts such as threads, exceptions, and other advanced features. However, you can make use of the Breakpoints dialog box right away.

A *breakpoint* is a stopping place inserted into a computer program for debugging purposes. When the breakpoint is encountered, the program pauses, offering a chance for you to check the value of variables and other aspects of the program.

Figure 5.1.
The main Source Editor page.

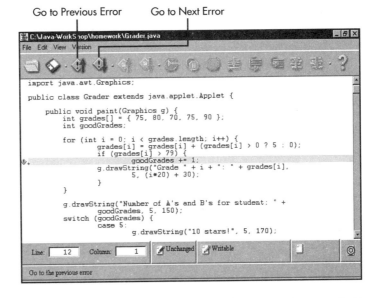

Figure 5.2.
The Debugger icon on the WorkShop command toolbar.

So that you have a need for jump-to-error icons and breakpoints, your next Java program, the `Grader` applet, will start off with some bugs in it. The `Grader` applet also gives you a chance to start working with arrays, conditionals, and loops.

Creating the `Grader` Applet

Use Portfolio Manager to create a new applet with the following fields:

Name: Grader

Source directory: Enter the full path of your homework directory (`C:/Java-WorkShop/homework` or something similar).

Existing sources: No

Run page: Leave this field blank.

Main Class File: You should not be able to change this field because `.class` will appear in the field as grayed-out text.

Create using: Source Editor

Then use the Source Editor to input the code from Listing 5.1. Remember that this code is supposed to have errors so that you can practice using WorkShop's debugging features. Be sure to type it exactly as shown—though for the wrong reasons this time around. You don't want to accidentally correct any of the errors through careless typing! When you're done, save the program as Grader.java.

TYPE   **Listing 5.1. Source code for Grader.java.**

```
 1: import java.awt.Graphics;
 2:
 3: public class Grader extends java.applet.Applet {
 4:
 5:     public void paint(Graphics g) {
 6:         int grades[] = { 75, 80, 70, 75, 90 };
 7:         int goodGrades;
 8:
 9:         for (int i = 0; i < grades.length; i++) {
10:             grades[i] = grades[i] + (grades[i] > 0 ? 5 : 0);
11:             if (grades[i] > 79) {
12:                 goodGrades += 1;
13:                 g.drawString("Grade " + i + ": " + grades[i],
14:                     5, (i*20) + 30);
15:             }
16:         }
17:
18:         g.drawString("Number of A's and B's for student: " +
19:             goodGrades, 5, 150);
20:         switch (goodGrades) {
21:             case 5:
22:                 g.drawString("10 stars!", 5, 170);
23:             case 4:
24:             case 3:
25:                 g.drawString("5 stars!", 5, 170);
26:             case 2:
27:             case 1:
28:                 g.drawString("3 stars!", 5, 170);
29:             default:
30:                 g.drawString("No stars.", 5, 170);
31:         }
32:     }
33: }
```

OUTPUT   After saving the file, use Build Manager to compile the applet. You should see the following two error messages:

```
Grader.java:12: Variable goodGrades may not have been initialized.
                        goodGrades += 1;
Grader.java:19: Variable goodGrades may not have been initialized.
                    goodGrades, 5, 150);
```

When you are debugging a program, the first errors you must correct are compilation errors such as these. Fortunately, the error messages generated by the compiler show the following items:

☐ The program statement, expression, or variable nearest to the error

☐ A description of the specific error

This information often gives you a good idea of what needs to be fixed. In the preceding example, your use of the goodGrades variable is causing two compiler errors because the variable was not given an initial value. As you might recall from Day 3 a local variable must be given an initial value before it is used. The goodGrades variable is declared on line 7, but it is not assigned a value.

Note that in many cases, the part of the program shown in the error message is not the cause of the error. In the preceding example, goodGrades += 1; is a valid statement in Java that should not cause any errors. However, because goodGrades was not initialized earlier, goodGrades += 1; caused the compiler to cry foul.

Jumping to Errors

When the Build Manager reports that an error has occurred during compilation, you can use the jump-to-error icons to go directly to the line in your program where the error occurred. Click the Go to Next Error icon on the Build Manager command toolbar, and Java WorkShop will open the Source Editor with the relevant line highlighted. Using the Go to Previous Error and Go to Next Error icons, you quickly can go through the program and make corrections.

In this case, however, the error occurs before the lines that Build Manager shows. So that the goodGrades local variable has an initial value, change line 7 to the following:

```
int goodGrades = 0;
```

Save the file and use Build Manager to compile the program. You should get the familiar Done. message that indicates a successful compilation.

What the Grader Applet Is Supposed to Do

After successfully compiling the Grader applet, you now can use Project Tester to run the applet. Before doing so, however, you need to understand what the Grader applet should be accomplishing if it runs correctly. The Grader applet was written for a teacher who rewards good students with stars on a classroom poster. The scores on five tests determine how many stars a student will receive, according to the following criteria:

☐ Five A or B test grades: 10 stars

☐ Three or four A or B grades: five stars

☐ One or two A or B grades: three stars

☐ No A or B grades: no stars

The reward system is complicated by one thing: The teacher has decided that the tests were a little too hard. To make up for it, five points are being added to each of the student's five test scores, unless the student missed a test and received zero points. In those cases, no five-point bonus will be awarded on the specific tests.

The Java program should go over the five test scores for a student, add the five-point bonus to each test when appropriate, and tell the teacher how many stars should be awarded to the student. Use Project Tester to run the applet and see whether this is what happens.

Figure 5.3 shows what the output of the applet should be at this point. Four grades are listed instead of five, the number of A's and B's are reported as 4, and a line after that is unreadable because it is several words displayed on top of each other. As you can tell, there still is some debugging work to do.

Figure 5.3.

The output of the
Grader *applet.*

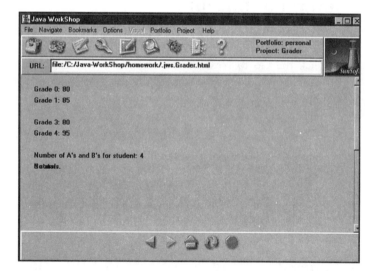

Fixing the Errors

Your Java applet compiles and can execute, but it doesn't do what it is supposed to do. At this point, a line-by-line look at the code might indicate where the problems lie.

ANALYSIS Lines 1 through 5 are standard fare: the `java.awt.Graphics` class is imported, the public class `Grader` is declared as a subclass of `java.applet.Applet`, and the `paint` method is declared.

Line 6 declares and initializes an integer array called `grades` with five slots. The five slots are given the values 75, 80, 70, 75, and 90, respectively. Line 7, which you corrected during the compilation stage, declares the local variable `goodGrades` with an initial value of 0.

Line 9 creates a `for` loop with an index variable called `i` that begins with a value of 0 and increments by 1 (`i++`) during each loop. The loop continues until `i` is equal to or greater than the maximum size of the `grades` array.

The block of statements inside the `for` loop, lines 10 through 15, should be executed five times—the same number of times as the number of test scores stored in the `grades` array.

Line 10 is an expression with the following in parenthesis:

```
(grades[i] > 0 ? 5 : 0);
```

This is a conditional operator, an alternative to the `if` and `else` statements that you learned about earlier today. The conditional operator will return one of two values, depending on whether the expression `grades[i] > 0` is true or false. If it is true, the first value after the `?` is returned (which is 5). If the expression is false, the second value is returned.

Line 10 is equivalent to the following `if` statement:

```
if (grades[i] > 0)
    grades[i] = grades[i] + 5;
```

Lines 11 to 12 use an `if` statement to keep count of how many test grades are A's or B's. Lines 13 and 14 display each of the student's test scores. However, the middle score of 70 is not being displayed for some reason, as Figure 5.3 shows.

Lines 18 and 19 are the first statement executed after the `for` loop ends (the statement has been formatted over two lines for readability—remember that Java ignores indentation and spacing when programs are compiled). The statement in lines 18 and 19 displays the number of A's or B's that the student received on the tests.

Lines 20 to 31 are a `switch` block statement that is supposed to display the number of stars the student should receive based on the number of A's and B's that were received on the five tests. The key phrase here is "supposed to." Lines 20 to 31 are displaying several words on top of each other instead of text such as 5 stars!.

The `switch` Error

Lines 18 to 19 are working correctly, as shown in the output. If you add five points to each of the test scores 75, 80, 70, 75, and 90, the resulting scores are 80, 85, 75, 80, and 90. Four grades are A's or B's, so the student should receive five stars.

This indicates that an error after line 19 is causing the words-on-words problem. If you think back to the section today on switch statements, you might recall that a break statement can be used in each case section.

If a break statement is not used at the end of a case section, all statements after the first matching case will be executed. When your program runs, the first matching case statement is case 4 because the student has four A or B grades. All statements from case 4 downward are executed. The lines 5 stars!, 3 stars!, and No stars. all are displayed.

Add break statements to the switch block so that it appears as follows:

```
switch (goodGrades) {
    case 5:
        g.drawString("10 stars!", 5, 170);
        break;
    case 4:
    case 3:
        g.drawString("5 stars!", 5, 170);
        break;
    case 2:
    case 1:
        g.drawString("3 stars!", 5, 170);
        break;
    default:
        g.drawString("No stars.", 5, 170);
    }
}
```

When you're done, compile and run the applet. You should see the line 5 stars! at the end of the output. That change leaves one error left to fix—the problem preventing the third test score from being displayed.

Using Breakpoints

Lines 13 and 14 in Listing 5.1 display one test score in the grades array, using the loop variable i to determine which array element to display. The parameters 5 and (i*20) + 30 are used to determine the x and y coordinates used by the drawString method when it displays text. It appears that lines 13 and 14 are not being executed five times; if they were, five test scores would be displayed when the program is run.

You can use a breakpoint to see whether a statement in a loop is being executed as many times as you think that it is. Click the Debugger icon on the WorkShop command toolbar, and an active debugging session will start. Return to the Source Editor and place your cursor in front of the statement that displays one test score. To place a breakpoint there, click the Toggle Breakpoint icon on the Source Editor toolbar. It is the stop sign icon with a triangle and rectangle on top of the sign (see Figure 5.4).

5

Figure 5.4.

The Toggle Breakpoint icon on the Source Editor toolbar.

TOGGLE BREAKPOINT

When you run the applet with the breakpoint set, you will discover that lines 13 to 14 are executed four times. As you already might have determined, the error is caused by a misplaced end brace on line 15. This brace ends a block that only will be executed when `grades[i]` > 79. None of the statements in the block will be executed when the test grade is not an A or a B, including the statement that displays the test grade. This means that the third test score will not be displayed (`grades[3]` is 75).

To correct the problem, move the brace so that it is after the line `goodGrades += 1;`. That section of code then should look like the following:

```
if (grades[i] > 79) {
    goodGrades += 1;
}
g.drawString("Grade " + i + ": " + grades[i],
    5, (i*20) + 30);
```

Save the file, use Build Manager to compile it, and use Project Tester to run it. You should see a screen resembling Figure 5.5. Congratulations!

Figure 5.5.

The output of the corrected Grader *applet.*

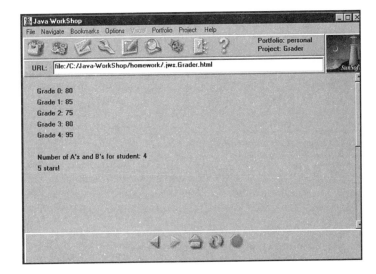

This exercise is just an introduction to the debugging features offered in Java WorkShop. As you learn more about the advanced aspects of Java programming, you also will learn more about the Debugger.

Summary

Today, you encountered three things you will be using often in your Java programs: arrays, conditionals, and loops.

You learned how to declare an array variable, create and assign an array object to that variable, and access and change elements within that array. With the `if` and `switch` conditional statements, you can branch to different parts of your program based on a boolean test. You learned about the `for`, `while`, and `do` loops, each enabling you to execute a portion of your program repeatedly until a given condition is met.

The `Grader` applet, the most complicated Java program that you have created so far, provided an example of arrays, conditionals, and loops in action. As you wrote this applet, you also were introduced to the process of debugging code with Java WorkShop.

Now that you have learned about the smaller parts of a Java program, the next step is to go over bigger issues: declaring classes and creating methods where instances of those classes can communicate with each other. Get to bed early tonight, because tomorrow is going to be a wild ride.

Q&A

Q If arrays are objects (you use `new` to create them, and they have an instance variable `length`), where is the `Array` class? I didn't see it in the Java class libraries.

A Arrays are implemented in an unusual way in Java. The `Array` class is constructed automatically when your Java program runs. This class provides the basic framework for arrays, including the `length` variable. Additionally, each primitive type and object has an implicit subclass of `Array` that represents an array of that class or object. When you create a new array object, it might not have an actual class, but it behaves as if it does.

Q Does Java have `goto` statements?

A The Java language defines the keyword `goto`, but this keyword currently is not used for anything. This means that it cannot be used in your programs as it would be in other languages.

Q I declared a variable inside a block for an `if` statement. When the `if` statement was done, the definition of that variable vanished. Where did it go?

A In technical terms, a block statement forms a new scope. If you declare a variable inside the braces that define the block, the variable only is visible and usable inside that block. Once the block finishes executing, variables declared inside the block disappear.

It's a good idea to declare most of your variables in the outermost block in which they'll be needed—usually at the top of a block. The exception might be simple variables, such as index counters in `for` loops, where declaring them in the first line of the `for` loop is an easy shortcut. You'll learn more about variables and scope tomorrow.

Q Why can't you use `switch` with strings?

A Strings are objects, and `switch` in Java works only for the primitive types `byte`, `char`, `short`, and `int`. To compare strings, you have to use nested `if` statements, which enable more general expression tests, including string comparison.

Q It seems to me that a lot of `for` loops could be written as `while` loops, and vice versa. Is this true?

A Yes. The `for` loop is actually a special case of `while` that enables you to iterate a loop a specific number of times. You could just as easily do the same thing with a `while` loop and a counter that is incremented inside the loop. Either method works equally well, so deciding which one to use mostly is a question of programming style and personal choice.

FEATURED APPLET Today's Featured Applet

The featured applet for today is `SharkLine`, a fun animation applet written by Ken Shirriff of Sun. `SharkLine` puts a horizontal line on a Web page that looks like one produced by an `<HR>` tag, but the applet adds a wrinkle—a surfacing shark. Figure 5.6 shows a screen capture of the applet.

`SharkLine` files are located on the CD-ROM in the `\BOOK\3RDPARTY\DAY5\` directory, including source code in the file `SharkLine.java`. To use `SharkLine` on a Web page, place the `SharkLine.class` file on your Web site. Place the file in the same directory as the Web page or place it in a subdirectory listed in the `CODEBASE` parameter of the `<APPLET>` tag. The `<CODE>` tag should be `SharkLine.class`.

Listing 5.2 shows the HTML tags used to run `SharkLine` as shown in Figure 5.6.

Figure 5.6.

The SharkLine *applet in action.*

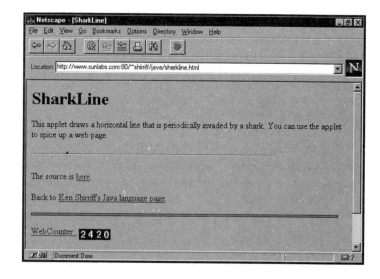

Listing 5.2. The <APPLET> **tag for** SharkLine.

```
<APPLET CODE="SharkLine.class" ALIGN=middle WIDTH=450 HEIGHT=8>
</APPLET>
```

You can customize the following SharkLine parameters within the <APPLET> tag:

Parameter	Description
width	The width of the image that is drawn
height	The height of the image that is drawn
delay	The delay between each surfacing of the shark

More information on SharkLine is available from the author at the following URL:

http://www.sunlabs.com:80/~shirriff/java/sharkline.html

Day 6

Creating Classes and Applications

For most of the first five days, you have focused either on the broad (general object-oriented theory) or the minute (arithmetic and other expressions). You have written classes, created instance variables and methods, and run programs to perform simple tasks. Today, you pull all this information together. You will learn how to create classes, and why you might want to create them, by using the following basics:

- [ ] The parts of a class definition
- [ ] The creation and use of instance variables
- [ ] The creation and use of methods
- [ ] The main() method, used in Java applications
- [ ] The use of arguments passed to a Java program

Defining Classes

You should be familiar with the basics of class definition because you have created classes during each of the previous lessons. A class is defined by using the `class` keyword and the name of the class, as in the following example:

```
class Ticker {
    // body of the class
}
```

If the new class is a subclass of another class, use the `extends` keyword to indicate the superclass of the new class:

```
class SportsTicker extends Ticker {
    // body of the class
}
```

If the new class implements a specific interface, use the `implements` keyword to refer to that interface:

```
class MessageBox implements Runnable {
    // body of the class
}
```

Both `extends` and `implements` are optional. You'll learn about using and defining interfaces on Day 16, "Packages and Interfaces."

Creating Instance and Class Variables

By necessity, when you create a class, you will have something that needs to be added to make the new class different from its superclasses. Inside each class definition, variables and methods are declared and defined—for the class and for each instance. In this section, you learn all about instance and class variables. The next section talks about methods.

Defining Instance Variables

On Day 3, "Java Language Basics," you learned how to declare and initialize local variables, which are variables inside method definitions. Instance variables are declared and defined in almost the same way as local variables. The main difference is their location in the class definition. Variables are considered instance variables if they are declared outside a method definition. Customarily, however, most instance variables are defined right after the first line of the class definition. For example, the following is a simple class definition for the class `Jabberwock`, which inherits from its superclass, `Reptile`:

```
class Jabberwock extends Reptile {

    String color;
    String sex;
    boolean hungry;
    int age;
```

This class definition contains four instance variables:

- [ ] The `color` variable is the color of the jabberwock (for example, orange or burnt sienna).
- [ ] The `sex` variable is a string that indicates the gender of the jabberwock.
- [ ] The `hungry` variable is a boolean variable that is `true` if the jabberwock is hungry and `false` otherwise.
- [ ] The `age` variable is the age of the jabberwock in years.

Constants

Constants are useful to define shared values for all methods of an object—in other words, for giving meaningful names to object-wide values that never will change. In Java, you can create constants only for instance or class variables, not for local variables. A *constant variable* or *constant* is a variable whose value never changes (which might seem strange given the meaning of the word "variable").

To declare a constant, use the `final` keyword before the variable declaration and include an initial value for that variable, as in the following:

```
final float pi = 3.141592;
final boolean debug = false;
final int numberOfJenny = 8675309;
```

NOTE

> The only way to define constants in Java is by using the `final` keyword. Neither #define nor const (C and C++ constructs) are available in Java, though const is reserved to help prevent its accidental use.

6

Constants can be useful for naming various states of an object and then testing for those states. Suppose you have a text label that can be aligned to the left, right, or center. You can define those values as constant integers:

```
final int LEFT = 0;
final int RIGHT = 1;
final int CENTER = 2;
```

As a place to store the current alignment of the text, the variable `alignment` then is declared as an `int`:

```
int alignment;
```

Later on in the body of a method definition, you can set the alignment with the following:

```
this.alignment = CENTER;
```

You also can test for a given alignment:

```
switch (this.alignment) {
    case LEFT:
        // deal with left alignment
        break;
    case RIGHT:
        // deal with right alignment
        break;
    case CENTER:
        // deal with center alignment
        break;
}
```

Using constants often makes a program easier to understand. When a programmer is looking over a section of code, a statement such as `this.alignment = CENTER` is more instructive than `this.alignment = 2` would be. On Day 2, "Object-Oriented Programming," you used constants in the `BigPalindrome` applet to set the color of the text with the following line of code:

```
g.setColor(Color.blue);
```

In the preceding line, `blue` is a constant variable of the `setColor` method. It is initialized with the numeric value that represents the color blue.

Class Variables

As you learned in previous lessons, class variables are global to a class and to all instances of that class. Think of class variables as being even more global than instance variables. Class variables are good for communicating between different objects of the same class or for keeping track of global states among a set of objects.

To declare a class variable, use the `static` keyword in the class declaration, as in the following:

```
static int sum;
static final int maxObjects = 10;
```

Creating Methods

As you learned on Day 4, "Working with Objects," methods define an object's behavior, which consists of what happens when that object is created and the various operations that the object can perform during its lifetime. This section introduces method definition and how methods work. Tomorrow's lesson has more detail about advanced things you can do with methods.

Defining Methods

Method definitions have four basic parts:

- ☐ The name of the method
- ☐ The type of object or primitive type returned by the method
- ☐ A list of parameters
- ☐ The body of the method

The method's *signature* is a combination of the method name, the object or type returned by the method, and a list of parameters.

NOTE

To keep things simpler today, two optional parts of the method definition have been left out: a modifier, such as `public` or `private`, and the `throws` keyword, which indicates the exceptions a method can throw. You'll learn about these parts of a method definition during Week 3.

In other languages, the name of the method (or function, subroutine, or procedure) is enough to distinguish it from other methods in the program. In Java, you can have different methods that have the same name but a different return type or argument list. This situation is called *method overloading*, and you'll learn more about it tomorrow.

Here's what a basic method definition looks like:

```
returntype methodname(type1 arg1, type2 arg2, type3 arg3 ...) {
    // body of the method
}
```

`returntype` is the primitive type or class of the value returned by the method. It can be one of the primitive types, a class name, or `void` if the method does not return a value at all.

6

Note that if this method returns an array object, the array brackets can go either after *returntype* or after the parameter list. Because the former way is easier to read, it is used in the examples today (and throughout this book), as in the following:

```
int[] makeRange(int lower, int upper) {
    // body of this method
}
```

The method's parameter list is a set of variable declarations, separated by commas, inside a pair of parentheses. These parameters become local variables in the body of the method, receiving their values when the method is called.

The makeRange() method just described could be called with the following:

```
makeRange(10,30);
```

Within the makeRange() method, the local variable lower would be initialized with the value 10, and the local variable upper would be initialized as 30.

Inside the method body, you can have statements, expressions, method calls to other objects, conditionals, loops, and so on—everything you've learned about in the previous lessons. If your method has a real return type (that is, it has not been declared to return void), you need to return a value somewhere inside the body of the method. Use the return keyword to do this. The following is an example of a statement that returns a value:

```
return (seconds * 60);
```

Trying Out Methods

To see how makeRange() could be used in a program and to try out other aspects of method programming, you now will write the Range applet. Use Portfolio Manager to create a new applet with the following fields:

> **Name**: Range
>
> **Source directory**: Enter the full path of your homework directory (C:/Java-WorkShop/homework or something similar).
>
> **Existing sources**: No
>
> **Run page**: Leave this blank.
>
> **Main Class File**: You should not be able to change this field because .class appears in the field as grayed-out text.
>
> **Create using**: Source Editor

The Range applet is an example of a class that defines a makeRange() method. The makeRange() method takes two integers, a lower boundary and an upper boundary, and creates an array that contains all integers between those two boundaries, including the boundaries themselves. Use the Source Editor to enter the source code from Listing 6.1. When you're done, save the file.

TYPE **Listing 6.1. Source code of** `Range.java`**.**

```
 1: import java.awt.Graphics;
 2:
 3: public class Range extends java.applet.Applet {
 4:
 5:     public void paint(Graphics g) {
 6:         int theArray[];
 7:         RangeClass theRange = new RangeClass();
 8:         String output = "The array: [ ";
 9:
10:         theArray = theRange.makeRange(1, 10);
11:         for (int i = 0; i < theArray.length; i++) {
12:             output += theArray[i] + " ";
13:         }
14:         output += "]";
15:         g.drawString(output, 5, 50);
16:     }
17: }
18: class RangeClass {
19:     int[] makeRange(int lower, int upper) {
20:         int arr[] = new int[ (upper - lower) + 1 ];
21:
22:         for (int i = 0; i < arr.length; i++) {
23:             arr[i] = lower++;
24:         }
25:         return arr;
26:     }
27: }
```

OUTPUT Compile the project with Build Manager and run it with Project Tester. The output should look like the following:

```
The array: [ 1 2 3 4 5 6 7 8 9 10 ]
```

The `paint()` method in this class tests the `makeRange()` method by creating a range with the lower and upper boundaries of 1 and 10, respectively (see line 10). A `for` loop then is used to display the values of the new array.

The `this` Keyword

In the body of a method definition, you might want to refer to the current object (the object the method was called on) to use that object's instance variables or to pass the current object as an argument to another method. To refer to the current object in these cases, use the `this` keyword.

The `this` keyword refers to the current object, and you can use it any place the object might appear: in dot notation to refer to the object's instance variables, as an argument to a method, as the return value for the current method, and so on. The following are some examples of using `this`:

```
t = this.x;              // the x instance variable for this object
this.resetData(this);    // call the resetData method, defined in
                         // this class, and pass it the current
                         // object
return this;             // return the current object
```

In many cases, however, you might not need the `this` keyword. You can refer to both instance variables and method calls defined in the current class simply by name—the `this` is implicit in those references. Therefore, you could write the first two examples like the following:

```
t = x;              // the x instance variable for this object
resetData(this);    // call the resetData method, defined in this
                    // class
```

> **NOTE**
>
> The viability of omitting the `this` keyword for instance variables, as was done in the preceding code example, depends on whether variables of the same name are declared in the local scope. See the next section for details.

Keep in mind that because `this` is a reference to the current instance of a class, you should use it only inside the body of an instance method definition. Class methods (that is, methods declared with the `static` keyword) cannot use `this`.

Variable Scope and Method Definitions

When you refer to a variable within your method definitions, Java checks for a definition of that variable first in the current scope (which might be a block), and then in the outer scopes up to the current method definition. If the variable is not a local variable, Java then checks for a definition of that variable as an instance or class variable in the current class. If Java still does not find the variable definition, it searches each superclass in turn. Because of the way Java checks for the scope of a given variable, it is possible for you to create a variable in a lower scope that hides the original value of that variable and introduce subtle and confusing bugs into your code.

For example, note the following small Java applet:

```
import java.awt.Graphics;

public class ScopeTest extends java.applet.Applet {
    int test = 10;

    public void paint(Graphics g) {
        int test = 20;
        g.drawString("test = " + test, 5, 50);
    }
}
```

In this class, you have two variables with the same name and definition. The first, an instance variable, has the name test and is initialized with the value 10. The second is a local variable with the same name, but with the value 20. The local variable test within the paint() method hides the instance variable test. The drawString() method inside paint() will display that test is 20. You can get around this problem by using this.test to refer to the instance variable and using just test to refer to the local variable.

A more insidious example occurs when you redefine a variable in a subclass that already occurs in a superclass. This can create subtle bugs in your code; for example, you might call methods that are intended to change the value of an instance variable, but the wrong variable is changed. Another bug might occur when you cast an object from one class to another; the value of your instance variable might mysteriously change because it was getting that value from the superclass instead of your class. The best way to avoid this behavior is to be aware of the variables defined in all superclasses of your class. This awareness will prevent you from duplicating a variable that's in use higher up in the class hierarchy.

Passing Arguments to Methods

When you call a method with object parameters, the objects you pass into the body of the method are passed by reference. Whatever you do to the objects inside the method affects the original objects. Keep in mind that such objects include arrays and all objects that are contained in arrays. When you pass an array into a method and modify its contents, the original array is affected. Primitive types, on the other hand, are passed by value.

To demonstrate how this process works, the following code shows a simple class definition that includes a single method called oneToZero():

```
class PassByReference {
    int oneToZero(int arg[]) {
        int count = 0;

        for (int i = 0; i < arg.length; i++) {
            if (arg[i] == 1) {
                count++;
                arg[i] = 0;
            }
```

```
        }
        return count;
    }
}
```

The oneToZero() method does two things:

1. It counts the number of ones in the array and returns that value.

2. If it finds a 1 in the array, it substitutes a 0 in its place.

The Passer applet uses the oneToZero() method. Use Portfolio Manager to create a new applet with the following fields:

> **Name:** Passer
>
> **Source directory:** Enter the full path of your homework directory (C:/Java-WorkShop/homework or something similar).
>
> **Existing sources:** No
>
> **Run page:** Leave this field blank.
>
> **Main Class File:** You should not be able to change this field because .class will appear in the field as grayed-out text.
>
> **Create using:** Source Editor

Use the Source Editor to enter the source code from Listing 6.2, and then save and compile the file.

TYPE   **Listing 6.2. The source code of Passer.java.**

```
 1: import java.awt.Graphics;
 2:
 3: public class Passer extends java.applet.Applet {
 4:
 5:     public void paint(Graphics g) {
 6:         int arr[] = { 1, 3, 4, 5, 1, 1, 7 };
 7:         PassByReference test = new PassByReference();
 8:         int numOnes;
 9:         String output;
10:
11:         output = "Values of the array: [ ";
12:         for (int i = 0; i < arr.length; i++) {
13:             output += arr[i] + " ";
14:         }
15:         output += "]";
16:         g.drawString(output, 5, 50);
17:
18:         numOnes = test.oneToZero(arr);
19:         g.drawString("Number of Ones = " + numOnes, 5, 70);
20:         output = "New values of the array: [ ";
21:         for (int i = 0; i < arr.length; i++) {
```

```
22:                     output += arr[i] + " ";
23:                 }
24:             output += "]";
25:             g.drawString(output, 5, 90);
26:         }
27: }
28: class PassByReference {
29:     int oneToZero(int arg[]) {
30:         int count = 0;
31:
32:         for (int i = 0; i < arg.length; i++) {
33:             if (arg[i] == 1) {
34:                 count++;
35:                 arg[i] = 0;
36:             }
37:         }
38:         return count;
39:     }
40: }
```

OUTPUT

When you run the project, you should see the following output:

```
Values of the array: [ 1 3 4 5 1 1 7 ]
Number of Ones = 3
New values of the array: [ 0 3 4 5 0 0 7 ]
```

ANALYSIS

A line-by-line look at the paint() method will show how the oneToZero() method is being used. Lines 6 through 9 set up the initial variables for this example:

☐ arr[] is an array of integers with seven elements of the values 1, 3, 4, 5, 1, 1, and 7, respectively.

☐ test is an instance of the class PassByReference.

☐ numOnes is an integer to hold the number of ones in the array.

☐ output is a string used to store the text that will be displayed in the applet.

Line 11 initializes output with the first part of the text that will be displayed: Values of the array: [. Lines 12 through 14 use a for loop to append the values of the array to the output string, in order from slot 1 through slot 7. Line 15 finishes output off with a], and line 16 uses the drawString() method to display output at the x, y coordinates of 5, 50.

Line 18 is where the real work takes place; this line is where you call the oneToZero() method defined in the object test and pass it the array stored in arr as a parameter. The oneToZero() method returns the number of ones in the array, which is assigned to the variable numOnes. Line 19 uses drawString() to display the number of ones, which you just received from the oneToZero() method and stored in the variable numOnes.

The next section of the program displays the array values again. Because a reference to the arr array (an object) was passed to the oneToZero() method, changing the array inside that method changes its values. Displaying the values in lines 20 through 25 proves that the

6

original array has changed because the program's output shows that all the ones in the array are now zeros.

Class and Instance Methods

In addition to class and instance variables, there are class and instance methods that operate in an analogous manner. Class methods are available to any instance of the class itself and can be made available to other classes, regardless of whether an instance of the class exists.

For example, the Java class libraries include a class called Math. The Math class defines a set of math operations that you can use in any program or any of the various number types, as in the following:

```
float root = Math.sqrt(453.0);
g.drawString("The larger of x and y is " + Math.max(x, y), 5, 110);
```

To define class methods, use the static keyword in front of the method definition, just as you would use static in front of a class variable. For example, the class method max() used in the preceding example might have the following signature:

```
static int max(int arg1, int arg2) {
    // body of the method
}
```

Java supplies wrapper classes for each of the base types; for example, Java supplies Integer, Float, and Boolean classes. Using class methods defined in those classes, you can convert objects to primitive types and convert primitive types to objects. For example, the parseInt() class method in the Integer class takes a string and a radix (a *radix* indicates whether the integer is a decimal, hexadecimal, or binary number). The value of the string is returned as an integer:

```
int count = Integer.parseInt("42", 10); // returns 42
```

The lack of a static keyword in front of a method name makes it an instance method. Instance methods operate on a particular object, rather than a class of objects. On Day 2 you created an instance method called feedJabberwock() that fed an individual jabberwock.

Most methods that operate on or affect a particular object should be defined as instance methods. Methods that provide some general capability but do not directly affect an instance of the class should be declared as class methods.

Creating Java Applications

Now that you know how to create classes, objects, class and instance variables, and class and instance methods, you can put it all together into a Java program. Up to this point, you have created Java applets—programs designed to run over the Internet. Java also can be used to design stand-alone programs that do not need a Java-capable World Wide Web browser to run. These programs are called applications.

A Java application consists of one or more classes and can be as large or as small as needed. Java WorkShop is an example of a Java application. The only thing required to make a Java application run is a class that serves as the starting point for the rest of the Java program. Some small programs might need only this starting class.

The starting class for your program must have a main() method. When the application is run, the main() method is the first thing that gets called. The signature for the main() method always looks like the following lines:

```
public static void main(String args[]) {
    // body of method
}
```

The parts of the main() method are explained in the following list:

☐ public means that this method is available to other classes and objects. The main() method must be declared public. You learn more about public and private methods during Week 3.

☐ static means that main() is a class method.

☐ void means that the main() method doesn't return a value.

☐ main() takes one parameter, which is an array of strings. This argument is used for program arguments, which you'll learn about in the next section.

The body of the main() method contains any code you need to start your application, such as the initialization of variables or the creation of class instances.

When Java executes the main() method, keep in mind that main() is a class method. An instance of the class that holds main() is not created automatically when your program runs. If you want to treat that class as an object, you have to create an instance of it in the main() method.

Java Applications and Program Arguments

Because Java applications are stand-alone programs, it's useful to pass arguments or options to an application. You can use the arguments to determine how the application is going to run or enable a generic application to operate on different kinds of input. You can use program arguments for many different purposes, such as to turn on debugging input or to indicate a filename to load.

Passing Arguments to Java Applications

To pass arguments to a Java application from within Java WorkShop, you use Project Manager. As stated, the main() method of an application receives arguments as a string array. The following line is an example of arguments that could be specified within Project Manager:

```
argumentOne 2 three
```

When the main() method receives this information, it will be interpreted as three arguments: argumentOne, 2, and three. A space is used to separate arguments, so the following line would produce three arguments:

```
Java is cool
```

To group arguments, surround them with double quote marks. You could modify the preceding example to make Java is cool a single argument, as follows:

```
"Java is cool"
```

The double quotes are stripped off before the argument gets to your Java application.

Handling Arguments in Your Java Application

When an application is run with arguments, Java stores the arguments as an array of strings and passes the array to the application's main() method. Take another look at the signature for main():

```
public static void main (String args[]) {
    // body of method
}
```

Here, args is the name of the array of strings that contains the list of arguments. You can call this array anything you like. Inside the main() method, you then can handle the arguments your program was given by iterating over the array of arguments and handling them in some manner. The next project, which is the first application that you create with Java, involves an example of this process.

Use Portfolio Manager to create a new project. Instead of filling in the fields of the Applet dialog box, click the Standalone Program tab to bring that dialog box to the front. You should see a screen resembling Figure 6.1.

Figure 6.1.

The top half of the Standalone Program dialog box in Portfolio Manager.

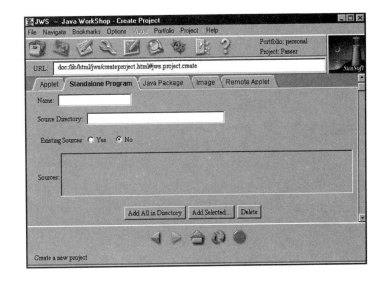

In the Standalone Program dialog box, enter the following information:

Name: EchoArgs

Source directory: Enter the full path of your homework directory (C:/Java-WorkShop/homework or something similar).

Existing sources: No

Main Class File: EchoArgs.class

Create using: Source Editor

Use the Source Editor to enter the code from Listing 6.3. Save the file and compile it with Build Manager, but don't run it yet.

TYPE   **Listing 6.3. Source code for EchoArgs.java.**

```
1: class EchoArgs {
2:     public static void main(String args[]) {
3:         for (int i = 0; i < args.length; i++) {
4:             System.out.println("Argument " + i + ": " + args[i]);
5:         }
6:     }
7: }
```

Setting Program Arguments

Before you can run the application, you need to use the Java WorkShop Project Manager to set the arguments that will be sent to the program. Click the Project Manager icon on the WorkShop command toolbar (the gear icon identified in Figure 6.2).

Figure 6.2.

The Project Manager icon on the WorkShop command toolbar.

PROJECT MANAGER

You will see six tabbed dialog boxes on the main screen of Project Manager. Click the Run tab to bring that dialog box to the front. In the Program Arguments field, enter the following: `Wilhelm Niekro Hough 49`. Click the Apply button when you're done, and then use Project Tester to run the application.

WARNING

As of Dev6 release, Java WorkShop cannot run applications in the same way that applets are run. When you click the Project Tester icon, no output is displayed. Java WorkShop sends the output to a file called `weblog`, which you can find in a `.jws` subdirectory on your system. (On Windows 95 systems, the full pathname of the file on a `c:` drive is `C:\Windows\.jws\weblog`).

The `weblog` file is a text file that can be read with any text editor or viewer. To see it from within Java WorkShop, load the Source Editor, which still should have the `EchoArgs.java` source code loaded in it. Choose View | New Window to open a new text file, and choose `weblog`.

In future releases of Java WorkShop, applications will open a window where output can be displayed and input can be accepted.

The output of the program should resemble the following:

```
Argument 0: Wilhelm
Argument 1: Niekro
Argument 2: Hough
Argument 3: 49
```

NOTE

The array of arguments in Java is not analogous to argv in C and UNIX. In particular, arg[0], the first element in the array of arguments, is the first argument after the name of the class—not the name of the program as it would be in C. Be aware of this fact as you write your Java programs.

An important thing to note: all arguments passed to a Java application will be stored in an array of strings. To treat them as something other than strings, you must convert them.

Converting Arguments

To see how arguments are converted, and to have more opportunity to work with Java applications, create the SumAverage application. This application displays both the sum and the average of the numeric arguments it receives.

Use Portfolio Manager to create a new application, remembering to click the Standalone Program tab. Enter the following fields:

> **Name**: SumAverage
>
> **Source directory**: Enter the full path of your homework directory (C:/Java-WorkShop/homework or something similar).
>
> **Existing sources**: No
>
> **Main Class File**: SumAverage.class
>
> **Create using**: Source Editor

Use the Source Editor to enter the source code from Listing 6.4, and save the file.

TYPE

Listing 6.4. Source code for SumAverage.java.

```
 1: class SumAverage {
 2:     public static void main (String args[]) {
 3:         int sum = 0;
 4:
 5:         for (int i = 0; i < args.length; i++) {
 6:             sum += args[i];
 7:         }
 8:
 9:         System.out.println("Sum is: " + sum);
10:         System.out.println("Average is: " +
11:             (float)sum / args.length);
12:     }
13: }
```

6

This application uses a `for` loop to iterate through the array of arguments, sums them up, and then displays the sum and average. When you use Build Manager to compile the file, you will get the following error:

```
SumAverage.java:6: Incompatible type for +=. Can't convert java.lang.String to
int.
    sum += args[i];
```

This error occurs because the argument array is an array of strings. Even though you are going to pass integers into the application, those integers will be converted to strings before being stored in the array. You have to convert them from strings to integers using a class method for the `Integer` class called `parseInt`. Change line 6 to use that method, as follows:

```
sum += Integer.parseInt(args[i]);
```

 The program will compile successfully. Before running it with Project Tester, use Project Manager and set the Program Arguments field in the Run dialog box to 1 2 3. Run the application, and you should see the following output:

```
Sum is: 6
Average is: 2
```

Running Applications from the Command Line

You can run Java applications from a command prompt by using the Java bytecode interpreter. As you might recall from Day 1, "Introduction to Java and Java WorkShop," a Java program is compiled into bytecodes that are saved as a `.class` file. This file is executed by an interpreter.

Before integrated development environments such as Java WorkShop were released, Java programming required a set of command-line tools called the Java Developer's Kit (JDK). The JDK, which has reached version 1.0.2 as of this writing, is available for Windows 95, Windows NT, MacOS System 7.5, SPARC Solaris (2.3 or later), and Intel x86 Solaris systems. Java WorkShop has its own built-in JDK, which is called behind the scenes by such features as Build Manager, Project Tester, and Source Browser.

You can execute the applications that you create, such as EchoArgs and SumAverage from today's lesson, from the command line with the Java interpreter if your system is configured to run the JDK tools that come with Java WorkShop. The syntax to run a program from the command line is as follows:

```
java classfilename argument
```

classfilename is the name of the file that contains the `main()` method of the application. *argument* is an optional list of arguments that are sent to the application, as described earlier. You could run the `EchoArgs` class from the command line in the following manner:

```
java EchoArgs Wilhelm Niekro Hough 49
```

Applications execute the same whether they are run from a command prompt or Java WorkShop.

Summary

Today you put together everything you've learned about creating Java classes and using them in programs. Subjects included the following:

- ☐ Instance and class variables, which hold the attributes of the class and its instances. You learned how to declare them, how they are different from regular local variables, and how to declare constants.
- ☐ Instance and class methods, which define the behavior of a class. You learned how to define methods, including the parts of a method signature, how to return values from a method, how arguments are passed in and out of methods, and how to use the `this` keyword to refer to the current object.
- ☐ Java applications. You learned all about the `main()` method and how it works and how to pass arguments to a Java application.

Tomorrow, you will finish off Week 1 by learning some advanced aspects of programming with methods.

Q&A

Q I tried to create a constant variable inside a method, and I got a compiler error. What was I doing wrong?

A In Java, only constant class or instance variables can be created. Local variables cannot be constant.

Q `static` and `final` are not exactly the most descriptive words for creating class variables, class methods, and constants. Why not use `class` and `const`?

A The `static` keyword comes from Java's C++ heritage. C++ uses `static` to retain memory for class variables and methods (though they aren't called class methods and variables in that programming language—`static` member functions and variables are more common terms).

6

The `final` keyword, however, is new. This keyword is used in a more general way for classes and methods to indicate that those things cannot be subclassed or overridden. Using the `final` keyword for variables is consistent with that behavior. `final` variables are not quite the same as constant variables in C++, which is why the `const` keyword is not used.

Q In my class, I have an instance variable called `name`. I also have a local variable called `name` in a method, which gets hidden by the local variable because of variable scope. Is there any way to get hold of the instance variable's value?

A The easiest way is not to give your local variables the same names as your instance variables. If you feel you must, you can use `this.name` to refer to the instance variable and `name` to refer to the local variable.

Q I wrote a program to take four arguments, but if I give it too few arguments, it crashes with a run-time error. What's wrong?

A Java won't check the number and type of arguments when it passes them to a `main()` method, so you have to take care of this in your program. If the program requires four arguments to run properly, test to be sure that it has received four arguments.

FEATURED APPLET Today's Featured Applet

The featured applet for today is `NeedleDemo`, an applet that shows how the `Needle` class can be used in a Java program. Both `NeedleDemo` and `Needle` were created by Liam Relihan. `Needle` is a class that can be used by Java programs to implement a needle gauge such as a speedometer. The `NeedleDemo` applet shows three sample gauges that were created with the `Needle` class. Figure 6.3 shows a screen capture of the applet.

`NeedleDemo` files are located on the CD-ROM in the `\BOOK\3RDPARTY\DAY6\` directory, including source code in the files `NeedleDemo.java` and `Needle.java`. To use the `Needle` class with your own Java project, compile the file `Needle.java` along with the other files in the project or make the compiled `Needle.class` file available to your program when it runs. The class files that will be created when `Needle.java` is compiled are `Needle.class`, `MeterZone.class`, and `ScalablePlane.class`. The `NeedleDemo` applet uses the class file `NeedleDemo.class`, which is needed only to run the demonstration applet. Listing 6.5 shows the HTML tags used to run `NeedleDemo` as it was shown in Figure 6.3.

Figure 6.3.

The NeedleDemo *applet in action.*

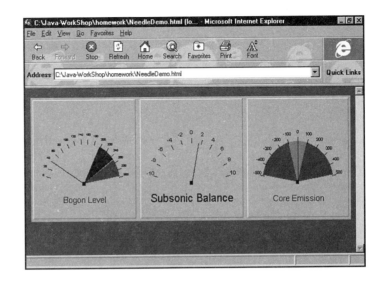

Listing 6.5. The <APPLET> tag for NeedleDemo.

```
<APPLET NAME="NeedleDemo" CODE="NeedleDemo.class" WIDTH="600" HEIGHT="225">
</APPLET>
```

NeedleDemo does not take any parameters. If you would like to use the Needle class in a project that you are writing, add the Needle.java file to the project in Java WorkShop and use the Source Browser to see the documentation for the class. A large number of configurable options have been implemented, including the ability to change the scale of a gauge, define colored zones for "danger" and similar criteria, and other features. The Needle class exemplifies the strength of object-oriented programming—you can plug useful objects into your own programs easily and effectively.

More information on NeedleDemo and the Needle class is available from the author at the following URL:

```
http://itdsrv1.ul.ie/~relihanl/scripts/needle/guagedemo.html
```

Day 7

More About Methods

Methods are arguably the most important part of any object-oriented language. Classes and objects provide a framework. Class and instance variables provide a way of holding the class or object's attributes and state. But methods provide an object's behavior and define how the object interacts with other objects.

Yesterday, you learned some things about defining methods, and you could use this knowledge to create Java programs. However, you would be missing some features that make methods powerful—features that make your objects and classes more efficient and easier to understand. Today, you will learn about the following features:

- ☐ Overloading methods—creating methods with multiple signatures and definitions but with the same name

- ☐ Creating constructor methods—methods that enable you to initialize objects to set up their initial state when created

- ☐ Overriding methods—creating a different definition for a method that has been defined in a superclass

- ☐ Finalizer methods—methods that clean up after an object before it is removed from the system

After you explore each of these features, you will learn how to put documentation in your code that can be seen with the Java WorkShop Source Browser and other class documentation systems. This documentation can make your objects more understandable and more reusable.

Creating Methods with the Same Name but Different Arguments

Yesterday, you learned how to create methods with a single name and a single signature. Methods in Java also can be overloaded. *Overloading* is the capability to create methods that have the same name but different signatures and different definitions. Method overloading enables instances of your class to have a simpler interface to other objects, eliminating the need for entirely different methods that do essentially the same thing. Overloading also makes it possible for methods to behave differently based on the input to the method. When you call a method in an object, Java matches up the method name and arguments in order to choose which method definition to execute.

To create an overloaded method, you create different method definitions in your class, each with the same name but with different argument lists. The difference can be in the number or type of arguments. Java allows method overloading as long as each argument list is unique for the same method name.

Note that Java differentiates overloaded methods based on the number and type of arguments to a method, not on its return type. If you attempt to create two methods with the same name, same argument list, and different return types, you will get a compiler error. The variable names that you choose for each argument to the method are irrelevant—all that matters is the number and the type of arguments.

Creating the MyRect Class

The next example gives you a chance to create an overloaded method and see how it works. The MyRect class defines a rectangular shape with four instance variables to define the upper-left and lower-right corners of the rectangle: x1, y1, x2, and y2.

NOTE

> The name of this class, MyRect, was chosen to avoid a conflict with a class in Java's awt package called Rectangle. MyRect implements much of the same behavior as Rectangle, but creating the new class is worthwhile for instructional purposes.

Examine the following definition of the MyRect class and the four instance variables:

```
class MyRect {
    int x1 = 0;
    int y1 = 0;
    int x2 = 0;
    int y2 = 0;
}
```

When a new instance of the myRect class is created, all of its instance variables are initialized to 0. To set the variables to their correct values as two corners of a rectangle, you can add a buildRect() instance method. buildRect() takes four integer arguments and returns the resulting rectangle object. Because the arguments have the same names as the instance variables, the keyword this is used when referring to the instance variables. The following is the code for buildRect():

```
MyRect buildRect(int x1, int y1, int x2, int y2) {
    this.x1 = x1;
    this.y1 = y1;
    this.x2 = x2;
    this.y2 = y2;
    return this;
}
```

This method can be used to create rectangles, but what if you wanted to define a rectangle's dimensions in a different way? An alternative would be to use Point objects rather than individual coordinates. To implement this alternative, you can overload buildRect() so that its argument list takes two Point objects, as in the following:

```
MyRect buildRect(Point topLeft, Point bottomRight) {
    x1 = topLeft.x;
    y1 = topLeft.y;
    x2 = bottomRight.x;
    y2 = bottomRight.y;
    return this;
}
```

In order for the preceding method to work, the Point class must be imported at the top of the source file so that Java can find it.

Another possible way to define the rectangle would be to use a top corner, height, and width. The following is a definition for an overloaded method to do this:

```
MyRect buildRect(Point topLeft, int w, int h) {
    x1 = topLeft.x;
    y1 = topLeft.y;
    x2 = (x1 + w);
    y2 = (y1 + h);
    return this;
}
```

7

To finish this example, you can add a method to display the rectangle's coordinates. Use Portfolio Manager to create a new applet with the following fields:

Name: RectApplet

Source directory: Enter the full path of your homework directory (C:/Java-WorkShop/homework or something similar).

Existing sources: No

Main Class File: You should not be able to change this field because .class appears in the field as grayed-out text.

Run page: Leave this field blank.

Create using: Source Editor

Use the Source Editor to enter the source code from Listing 7.1. Be sure to include all of the comment lines—these lines are part of the special Java documentation system that was introduced previously and will be described later today. When you finish entering the code, save and compile the file.

TYPE   **Listing 7.1. The source code of** `RectApplet.java.`

```
 1: import java.awt.Graphics;
 2: import java.awt.Point;
 3:
 4: /** This class creates MyRect objects that are similar in function
 5:  * to the class java.awt.Rectangle.
 6:  * @see java.awt.Rectangle
 7:  * @author <a href="mailto:rcade@airmail.net">Rogers Cadenhead</a>
 8:  * @version 1.0
 9:  */
10: public class RectApplet extends java.applet.Applet {
11:     /**
12:      * This method creates a new MyRect object, calls buildRect()
13:      * with three different method signatures, and displays the
14:      * results.
15:      */
16:     public void paint(Graphics g) {
17:         MyRect rect = new MyRect();
18:
19:         g.drawString("Calling buildRect with coordinates "
20:             + "25, 25 and 50,50:", 5, 50);
21:         rect.buildRect(25, 25, 50, 50);
22:         rect.printRect(g, 70);
23:
24:         g.drawString("Calling buildRect with points "
25:             + "(10,10) and (20,20):", 5, 110);
```

```
26:          rect.buildRect(new Point(10,10), new Point(20,20));
27:          rect.printRect(g, 130);
28:
29:          g.drawString("Calling buildRect with 1 point (10,10),"
30:              + " width (50), and height (50):", 5, 170);
31:
32:          rect.buildRect(new Point(10,10), 50, 50);
33:          rect.printRect(g, 190);
34:          }
35: }
36: /** This is the private class that is used to establish
37:   * the initial values for MyRect objects, display MyRect
38:   * object values, and set the coordinates of MyRect
39:   * objects.
40:   */
41: class MyRect {
42:     int x1 = 0;
43:     int y1 = 0;
44:     int x2 = 0;
45:     int y2 = 0;
46:
47:     void printRect(Graphics g, int y) {
48:         g.drawString("MyRect: <" + x1 + ", " + y1
49:             + ", " + x2 + ", " + y2 + ">", 5, y);
50:     }
51:
52:     MyRect buildRect(int x1, int y1, int x2, int y2) {
53:         this.x1 = x1;
54:         this.y1 = y1;
55:         this.x2 = x2;
56:         this.y2 = y2;
57:         return this;
58:     }
59:
60:     MyRect buildRect(Point topLeft, Point bottomRight) {
61:         x1 = topLeft.x;
62:         y1 = topLeft.y;
63:         x2 = bottomRight.x;
64:         y2 = bottomRight.y;
65:         return this;
66:     }
67:
68:     MyRect buildRect(Point topLeft, int w, int h) {
69:         x1 = topLeft.x;
70:         y1 = topLeft.y;
71:         x2 = (x1 + w);
72:         y2 = (y1 + h);
73:         return this;
74:     }
75: }
```

7

OUTPUT Run the applet with Project Tester, and the output should resemble the following:

```
Calling buildRect with coordinates 25,25 and 50,50:
MyRect: <25, 25, 50, 50>

Calling buildRect with points (10,10) and (20,20):
MyRect: <10, 10, 20, 20>

Calling buildRect with 1 point (10,10), width (50), and height (50):
MyRect: <10, 10, 60, 60>
```

As you can see from this example, all of the `buildRect()` methods work based on the arguments they are called with. You can define as many versions of a method as you need to implement the behavior that is needed for that class.

Constructor Methods

NEW TERM In addition to regular methods, you also can define constructor methods in your class definition. A *constructor method* is a special kind of method that determines how an object is initialized when it's created. Unlike regular methods, you can't call a constructor method directly. Instead, Java calls constructor methods automatically.

When you use `new` to create a new instance of a class, Java does three things:

1. Allocates memory for the object
2. Initializes that object's instance variables, either to initial values or to a default (`0` for numbers, `null` for objects, `false` for booleans, or `'\0'` for characters)
3. Calls the constructor method of the class, which might be one of several methods

If a class doesn't have any special constructor methods defined, you still will end up with an object. However, you might have to set its instance variables or call other methods the object needs to initialize itself. All examples you have created up to this point have behaved like this.

By defining constructor methods in your own classes, you can set initial values of instance variables, call methods based on those variables, call methods on other objects, and set the initial properties of an object. You also can overload constructor methods, as you can do with regular methods, to create an object that has specific properties based on the arguments you give to `new`.

Basic Constructor Methods

Constructor methods look a lot like regular methods, with two basic differences:

1. Constructor methods always have the same name as the class.
2. Constructor methods don't have a return type.

The Person class, which you will create next, uses a constructor method to initialize its instance variables based on arguments for new. The class also includes a method for the object to introduce itself.

Use Portfolio Manager to create a new applet with the following fields:

Name: PersonApplet

Source directory: Enter the full path of your homework directory (C:/Java-WorkShop/homework or something similar).

Existing sources: No

Main Class File: You should not be able to change this field because .class appears in the field as grayed-out text.

Run page: Leave this field blank.

Create using: Source Editor

Enter the source code from Listing 7.2 using the Source Editor, and then save and compile the file.

TYPE **Listing 7.2. The source code of** PersonApplet.java.

```
 1: import java.awt.Graphics;
 2:
 3: public class PersonApplet extends java.applet.Applet {
 4:     public void paint(Graphics g) {
 5:         Person p;
 6:
 7:         p = new Person("Harold", 20);
 8:         p.printPerson(g, 50);
 9:         p = new Person("Maude", 80);
10:         p.printPerson(g, 110);
11:     }
12: }
13: class Person {
14:     String name;
15:     int age;
16:
17:     Person(String n, int a) {
18:         name = n;
19:         age = a;
20:     }
21:
22:     void printPerson(Graphics g, int y) {
23:         g.drawString("Hi, my name is " + name + ".", 5, y);
24:         g.drawString("I am " + age + " years old.", 5, y+20);
25:     }
26: }
```

7

Run the applet with Project Tester, and you should see the following output:

```
Hi, my name is Harold.
I am 20 years old.

Hi, my name is Maude.
I am 80 years old.
```

Calling Another Constructor Method

In some cases, you might have a constructor method that needs to duplicate the behavior of an existing constructor method, with some new behavior added. Rather than duplicating identical behavior in multiple constructor methods in your class, you can call the first constructor method from inside the body of the second constructor method. To call a constructor method defined in the current class, use the following:

```
this(arg1, arg2, arg3);
```

The arguments for `this` are the arguments for the constructor method. For example, the `Person` constructor method in Listing 7.2 could be called inside a new constructor method as follows:

```
this(n, a);
```

`n` is the string representing the name of the `Person` object, and `a` is the integer representing the age.

Overloading Constructor Methods

Like regular methods, constructor methods also can take varying numbers and types of parameters. This capability enables you to create an object with exactly the properties you want it to have or to let the object calculate properties from different kinds of input.

For example, the `buildRect()` methods that you defined in the `MyRect` class earlier today would make excellent constructor methods because what they're doing is initializing an object's instance variables to the appropriate values. The next example, the `MyRect2` applet, replaces the `buildRect()` method with overloaded constructor methods.

Use Portfolio Manager to create a new applet with the following fields:

> **Name:** RectApplet2
>
> **Source directory:** Enter the full path of your homework directory (`C:/Java-WorkShop/homework` or something similar).
>
> **Existing sources:** No

Main Class File: You should not be able to change this field because .class appears in the field as grayed-out text.

Run page: Leave this field blank.

Create using: Source Editor

Instead of entering the source code from Listing 7.3, you might want to cut and paste the code from RectApplet.java. To try this procedure, open the Source Editor and choose View | New Window to open RectApplet. Highlight all of the source code and hit Ctrl-C or (Edit | Copy) to copy it to the clipboard. Close the RectApplet Source Editor window and open the RectApplet2 Source Editor window. Highlight all of the template text that was created for you, and replace it by pressing Ctrl-V or (Edit | Paste). This command pastes the contents of the clipboard into the current document.

WARNING

> Some implementations of the DR5 release of Java WorkShop have a bug involving text highlighting. If you cannot highlight the entire text of a document by clicking and dragging your mouse, as you can with other word processing software, you can use a different method. Place your cursor at the spot where you want to begin selecting text. Hold down the Shift key and use the down arrow key to highlight each line.

After entering the code in Listing 7.3, save and compile the file as RectApplet2.java.

TYPE   **Listing 7.3. The source code of** RectApplet2.java.

```
1: import java.awt.Graphics;
2: import java.awt.Point;
3:
4: public class RectApplet2 extends java.applet.Applet {
5:     public void paint(Graphics g) {
6:         MyRect2 rect;
7:
8:         g.drawString("Calling MyRect2 with coordinates "
9:             + "25, 25 and 50,50:", 5, 50);
10:         rect = new MyRect2(25, 25, 50,50);
11:         rect.printRect(g, 70);
12:
13:         g.drawString("Calling MyRect2 with points "
14:             + "(10,10) and (20,20):", 5, 110);
15:         rect= new MyRect2(new Point(10,10), new Point(20,20));
16:         rect.printRect(g, 130);
17:
18:         g.drawString("Calling MyRect2 with 1 point (10,10),"
```

7

continues

Listing 7.3. continued

```
19:                    + " width (50), and height (50):", 5, 170);
20:                 rect = new MyRect2(new Point(10,10), 50, 50);
21:                 rect.printRect(g, 190);
22:                 }
23: }
24:
25: class MyRect2 {
26:     int x1 = 0;
27:     int y1 = 0;
28:     int x2 = 0;
29:     int y2 = 0;
30:
31:     MyRect2(int x1, int y1, int x2, int y2) {
32:         this.x1 = x1;
33:         this.y1 = y1;
34:         this.x2 = x2;
35:         this.y2 = y2;
36:     }
37:
38:     MyRect2(Point topLeft, Point bottomRight) {
39:         x1 = topLeft.x;
40:         y1 = topLeft.y;
41:         x2 = bottomRight.x;
42:         y2 = bottomRight.y;
43:     }
44:
45:     MyRect2(Point topLeft, int w, int h) {
46:         x1 = topLeft.x;
47:         y1 = topLeft.y;
48:         x2 = (x1 + w);
49:         y2 = (y1 + h);
50:     }
51:
52:     void printRect(Graphics g, int y) {
53:         g.drawString("MyRect2: <" + x1 + ", " + y1
54:             + ", " + x2 + ", " + y2 + ">", 5, y);
55:     }
56: }
```

OUTPUT When you run the program with Project Tester, the output should be the same as RectApplet because the overloaded constructor methods perform the same task that the buildRect() methods did. The output is as follows:

```
Calling MyRect2 with coordinates 25,25 and 50,50:
MyRect2: <25, 25, 50, 50>

Calling MyRect2 with points (10,10) and (20,20):
MyRect2: <10, 10, 20, 20>

Calling MyRect2 w/1 point (10,10), width (50), and height (50):
MyRect2: <10, 10, 60, 60>v
```

Overriding Methods

When you call a method of an object, Java looks for that method definition in the object's class. If it doesn't find one, it passes the method call up the class hierarchy until a method definition is found. Method inheritance enables you to define and use methods repeatedly in subclasses without having to duplicate the code.

However, there might be times when you want an object to respond to the same methods but have different behavior when that method is called. In this case, you can override the method. To override a method, you define a method in a subclass with the same signature as a method in a superclass. Then, when the method is called, the subclass method is found and executed instead of the one in the superclass.

Creating Methods that Override Existing Methods

To override a method, all you have to do is create a method in your subclass that has the same signature (name, return type, and argument list) as a method defined by a superclass of your class. Because Java executes the first method definition it finds that matches the signature, the new signature hides the original method definition.

The next code example shows a simple class with a method called printMe(). The printMe() method displays the name of the class and the values of its instance variables. Here's the class:

```
class PrintClass {
    int x = 0;
    int y = 1;

    void printMe() {
        System.out.println("X is " + x + ", Y is " + y);
        System.out.println("I am an instance of the class " +
            this.getClass().getName());
    }
}
```

Next, a PrintSubClass class is created that is a subclass of PrintClass. The only difference between the new class and its superclass is that the new class has a z instance variable:

```
class PrintSubClass extends PrintClass {
    int z = 3;

    public static void main(String args[]) {
        PrintSubClass obj = new PrintSubClass();
        obj.printMe();
    }
}
```

If you ran this application, the output would be as follows:

```
X is 0, Y is 1
I am an instance of the class PrintSubClass
```

7

In the `main()` method of `PrintSubClass`, a `PrintSubClass` object was created and the `printMe()` method was called. Because the `PrintSubClass` does not define this method, Java looks for it in the superclasses of `PrintSubClass`, starting with `PrintClass`. `PrintClass` has a `printMe()` method, so it is executed. Unfortunately, this method does not display the z instance variable, as you can see from the preceding output.

To correct this, a new method is added to `PrintSubClass`. This new method will have the same name and signature as the `printMe()` method in `PrintClass`. Here's the new method:

```
void printMe() {
    System.out.println("x is " + x + ", y is " + y +
        ", z is " + z);
    System.out.println("I am an instance of the class " +
        this.getClass().getName());
}
```

Now, when a `PrintSubClass` object is instantiated and the `printMe()` method is called, the `PrintSubClass` version of `printMe()` is called instead of the one in the superclass `PrintClass`. The following would be the output:

```
x is 0, y is 1, z is 3
I am an instance of the class PrintSubClass
```

Calling the Original Method

Usually, there are two reasons why you want to override a method that a superclass already has implemented:

1. To replace the definition of that original method completely

2. To augment the original method with additional behavior

You already have learned about the first reason—overriding a method and giving the method a new definition hides the original method definition. But there are times when behavior should be added to the original definition instead of replacing it completely, particularly when behavior is duplicated in both the original method and the method that overrides it. By calling the original method in the body of the overriding method, you can add only what you need.

To call the original method from inside a method definition, use the `super` keyword. This keyword passes the method call up the hierarchy, as shown in the following:

```
void myMethod (String a, String b) {
    // do stuff here
    super.myMethod(a, b);
    // maybe do more stuff here
}
```

The super keyword, somewhat like the this keyword, is a placeholder for the superclass of the class. You can use it anywhere you use this, but super refers to the superclass rather than the current class. For example, the following code shows the two printMe() methods:

```
// from PrintClass
    void printMe() {
        System.out.println("X is " + x + ", Y is " + y);
        System.out.println("I am an instance of the class" +
        this.getClass().getName());
    }

//from PrintSubClass
    void printMe() {
        System.out.println("X is " + x + ", Y is " + y
            + ", Z is " + z);
        System.out.println("I am an instance of the class " +
            this.getClass().getName());
    }
```

Rather than duplicating most of the behavior of the superclass' method in the subclass, you can rearrange the superclass' method so that additional behavior can be added easily, as follows:

```
// from PrintClass
    void printMe() {
        System.out.println("I am an instance of the class" +
            this.getClass().getName());
        System.out.println("X is " + x);
        System.out.println("Y is " + y);
}
```

Then, when you override the printMe() method in the subclass, you can call the original method and just add the extra stuff:

```
// From PrintSubClass
    void printMe() {
        super.printMe();
        System.out.println("Z is " + z);
}
```

The following would be the result of calling printMe() on an instance of the subclass:

```
I am an instance of the class PrintSubClass
X is 0
Y is 1
Z is 3
```

Overriding Constructor Methods

Technically, constructor methods cannot be overridden. Because they always have the same name as the current class, new constructor methods are created instead of being inherited.

Much of the time, this system is fine, because when your class' constructor method is called, the constructor method with the same signature for all your superclasses is called also, so initialization can happen for all parts of a class that you inherit.

However, when you are defining constructor methods for your own class, you might want to change how your object is initialized, not only by initializing new variables added by your class, but also by changing the contents of variables that already are there. To do this, you explicitly call the constructor methods of the superclass and subsequently change whatever variables need to be changed.

To call a regular method in a superclass, you use super.*methodname*(*arguments*). Because constructor methods don't have a method name to call, the following form is used:

```
super(arg1, arg2, ...);
```

Similar to using this(...) in a constructor method, super(...) calls the constructor method for the immediate superclass (which might, in turn, call the constructor of its superclass, and so on).

For example, the following shows a class called NamedPoint, which extends the class Point from Java's awt package. The only constructor method of the Point class takes an x and a y argument and returns a Point object. NamedPoint has an additional instance variable (a string for the name), and it defines a constructor method to initialize x, y, and the name:

```
import java.awt.Point;

class NamedPoint extends Point {
    String name;

    NamedPoint(int x, int y, String name) {
    super(x,y);
    this.name = name;
    }
}
```

The constructor method defined here for NamedPoint calls Point's constructor method to initialize the instance variables of Point (x and y). Although you can just as easily initialize x and y yourself, you might not know what other things Point is doing to initialize itself. Therefore, it always is a good idea to pass constructor methods up the hierarchy to make sure everything is set up correctly.

Finalizer Methods

Finalizer methods are almost the opposite of constructor methods. A constructor method is used to initialize an object, and finalizer methods are called just before the object is collected for garbage and has its memory reclaimed.

The finalizer method is finalize(). The Object class defines a default finalizer method that does nothing. To create a finalizer method for your own classes, override the finalize() method using this signature:

```
protected void finalize() {
    ...
}
```

Inside the body of that finalize() method, include any cleaning up that you want to do for that object. You also can call super.finalize() to enable the superclasses of your class to finalize the object, if necessary.

You can call the finalize() method yourself at any time—it's just a method like any other. However, calling finalize() does not trigger an object to be collected in the garbage. Only removing all references to an object causes it to be marked for deletion.

Finalizer methods are used best for optimizing the removal of an object (for example, by removing references to other objects). In most cases, you don't need to use finalize() at all. During Day 21, "Advanced Concepts," you will learn more about garbage collection and finalize().

Java Documentation

The last subject to cover today is the special type of comment that Java uses for class, method, and variable documentation. In the RectApplet project that you created first today, there were several unusual comment sections that began with the /** characters and ended with the */ characters. You can extract the special Java documentation comments that use /** and */ from code by using tools such as the Java WorkShop Source Browser.

Normally, comments in a program are intended for the benefit of programmers who are reading the source code. Comments are used to describe the operation of the program and provide guidance that enables people to understand what the code is doing.

Using Source Browser

Using Portfolio Manager, select RectApplet as your current project, and then click the Source Browser icon in the WorkShop command toolbar (the magnifying glass icon shown in Figure 7.1).

Two tabbed dialog boxes are available from the main Source Browser page. Make sure that the Class Browser dialog box is visible in front, and that the Browse option is set to Project instead of Directory.

7

Figure 7.1.
*The Source Browser icon
on the WorkShop
command toolbar.*

Source Browser

A text field displays all files associated with the current project—in this case, the full path of
`RectApplet.java`. Click `RectApplet.java`, and along the bottom half of the page, you will see
a report titled "Class RectApplet." Use the scroll bar to see this report. From top to bottom,
the following things are displayed:

☐ The class hierarchy of the `RectApplet` class

☐ The constructor methods used in the `RectApplet` class

☐ The methods used in the `RectApplet` class

In three places in the documentation, you will see text that should look familiar to you. The
text is explanatory material that you put into the source code as special Java documentation
comments.

Inserting Comments into Code

The following snippet of code is from the `RectApplet` project. It shows a Java comment that
precedes the declaration of the `RectApplet` class:

```
/** This class creates MyRect objects that are similar in function
  * to the class java.awt.Rectangle.
  * @see java.awt.Rectangle
  * @author <a href="mailto:rcade@airmail.net">Rogers Cadenhead</a>
  * @version 1.0
  */
public class RectApplet extends java.applet.Applet {
```

This is the format to use for all comments of this nature. In addition to text, the comments
can include some HTML tags such as the `MAILTO` hyperlink that is used in the example. You
also can use tags such as `<PRE>` and `<TT>` to display code examples and the like. Do not,
however, use HTML structuring tags such as `<H1>` and `<CENTER>` in these comments because
programs such as the WorkShop Source Browser control how the documentation will be
formatted.

Some special tags are preceded with a `@` character, as you can see in the sample comments.
The tags are as follows:

☐ `@author` *text*. Place an entry beginning with `Author:` that is followed with the
text. You can use this tag only before a class definition.

☐ `@version` *text*. Place an entry beginning with `Version:` followed by the *text*. You
can use this tag only before a class definition.

- ☐ `@exception` *fullclassname description*. Place an entry beginning with `Throws:` that is followed by the class name, in full, and a *description*. You can use this tag only before a method definition.

- ☐ `@param` *parametername description*. Place an entry in a `Parameters:` section of a method definition, with the *parametername* field and *description* used to describe the parameter.

- ☐ `@return` *description*. Place an entry in a `Returns:` section that describes what is returned by a method. You can use this tag only before a method definition.

- ☐ `@see` *classname*. Place a `See Also:` entry that lists the class specified in *classname*. You can use this tag before classes, methods, and variables.

- ☐ `@see` *fullclassname*. Place a different kind of `See Also:` entry that lists the class, in full, that is specified in *fullclassname*. You can use this tag before classes, methods, and variables.

- ☐ `@see` *fullclassname#methodname*. Place a third kind of `See Also:` entry that lists the *fullclassname* class along with the *methodname* specified. You can use this tag before classes, methods, or variables.

Final Word on Commenting

By using these comments in your Java code, you can provide a lot of valuable information for yourself and anyone else who will be working with your source code files. An important thing to keep in mind is that the private aspects of the code cannot use this documentation.

For example, if you had placed some special Java documentation comments in front of the `printRect()` method of the `MyRect` class, it would be ignored by the Java WorkShop Source Browser because that method is available only within a private class and cannot be used by other classes.

You don't have to use this kind of documentation in your Java programs, and on small projects, creating such documentation probably will seem cumbersome. However, one of the biggest advantages of object-oriented programming is the capability to reuse code. Well-documented code is much easier to reuse, so the long-term benefits could make the effort to document worthwhile.

Summary

Today, you learned all kinds of techniques for using, reusing, defining, and redefining methods. You learned how to overload a method name so that the same method can have different behavior based on the arguments it is called with. You learned about constructor methods, which are used to initialize a new object when it is created. You learned about method inheritance and how to override methods that have been defined in a class' superclasses. You learned about finalizer methods, which can be used to clean up after an object right before the object is collected in the garbage and the object's memory has been reclaimed. You finished off with a brief look at special Java documentation comments.

Congratulations on completing your first week of *Teach Yourself SunSoft Java WorkShop in 21 Days*! Starting next week, you will apply everything you have learned this week to writing more sophisticated Java applets. You will be programming with graphics, graphical user interface elements, events, and windowing—making use of the standard Java class libraries and Visual Java, the most powerful feature of Java WorkShop.

Q&A

Q I created two methods with the following signatures:

```
int total(int arg1, int arg2, int arg3) {...}
float total(int arg1, int arg2, int arg3) {...}
```

The Java compiler complains when I try to compile the class with these method definitions, even though their signatures are different. What have I done wrong?

A Method overloading in Java works only if the argument lists are different—either in number or type of arguments. The return type is not relevant for method overloading because Java does not know which method to call.

Q Can I overload overridden methods—in other words, can I create methods that have the same name as an inherited method, but a different parameter list?

A As long as parameter lists vary, you can. It does not matter whether you have defined a new method name or one that has been inherited from a superclass.

FEATURED APPLET Today's Featured Applet

The featured applet for today is Lines by Patrick Martin. This Java animation looks like a familiar screen saver. Lines draws a variable number of lines and moves their endpoints around the screen in random directions, changing the color of the lines as it goes. Figure 7.2 shows a screen capture of the applet.

Figure 7.2.

The Lines *applet in action.*

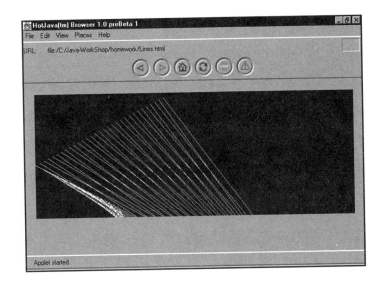

Files for Lines are located on the CD-ROM in the \BOOK\3RDPARTY\DAY7\ directory, including source code in the files Lines.java and Line.java. To use Lines on a Web page, place these two class files on your Web site: Lines.class and Line.class. Place the files in the same directory as the Web page, or place them in a subdirectory listed in the CODEBASE parameter of the <APPLET> tag. The <CODE> tag should be Lines.class.

Listing 7.4 shows the HTML tags used to run Lines as it is shown in Figure 7.2.

Listing 7.4. The <APPLET> tag for Lines.

```
<APPLET CODE="Lines.class" NumLines="50" HEIGHT=400 WIDTH=400>
</APPLET>
```

Lines has one parameter that can be customized within the <APPLET> tag. The lines parameter specifies the number of lines to draw. More information on Lines is available from its author at the following URL:

```
http://www.streetside.com/pat/src/java/Lines/Lines.html
```

7

WEEK 2

at a Glance

- [ ] Applet Basics
  Including an applet on a Web page
  Passing parameters
- [ ] Graphics, Fonts, and Color
  Graphics primitives
  The Color class
- [ ] Simple Animation and Threads
  Painting and repainting
  Reducing animation flicker
  Writing applets with threads

☐ More Animation, Images, and Sound
   Scaling options, executing sound effectively
   Double-buffering

☐ Simple Events and Interactivity
   MouseDown and MouseUp
   Keyboard events
   The Java event handler

☐ Visual Java and the Abstract Windowing Toolkit
   Canvases, text components, and widgets
   Window construction components

☐ Windows, Networking, and Other Tidbits
   Programming menus
   Creating links inside applets

Day **8**

Applet Basics

Much of Java's current popularity has come about because of Java-capable World Wide Web browsers and their support for applets. Applets can be run in any browser that supports Java, including Netscape Navigator and Sun's HotJava browser. Learning how to create applets is most likely the reason you bought this book.

This week, now that you have the basics down, you will explore fully the programming of applets. As you do, you will learn about many of the classes in the standard Java class library. Today, you'll start with the basics:

☐ A review of differences between Java applets and applications

☐ The basics of how an applet works and how to create your own simple applets

☐ How to include an applet on a Web page by using the <APPLET> tag and how you can use features of that tag

☐ How to pass parameters to applets

How Applets and Applications Differ

Although you explored the differences between Java applications and Java applets on an earlier day, it is worthwhile to review them here. Java applications are stand-alone Java programs that can be run by using just the Java interpreter, from a command line, for example. You created your first Java application on Day 6, "Creating Classes and Applications."

Java applets, however, are run from a World Wide Web browser. Java WorkShop functions as a browser, and this functionality was used by Project Tester when you executed applets. A reference to an applet is embedded in a Web page using a special HTML tag. When a user with a Java-enabled browser loads a Web page with an applet in it, the browser downloads that applet from a Web server. The applet then is executed on the user's local system.

Because Java applets run inside a Java browser, they have the advantage of the structure the browser provides: an existing window, an event-handling and graphics context, and the surrounding user interface. Java applications also can create this structure, but they don't require it (you'll learn how to create Java applications that use applet-like graphics and user interface features on Day 14, "Windows, Networking, and Other Tidbits").

The convenience that applets have over applications, in terms of structure and interface capabilities, is hampered by restrictions on what applets can do. Because Java applets can be downloaded from anywhere and run on a client's system, restrictions are necessary to prevent an applet from causing system damage or security breaches. Without these restrictions in place, Java applets could be written to contain viruses or trojan horses (programs that seem friendly but do some sort of damage to the system) or could be used to compromise the security of the system that runs them. The restrictions on what an applet can do include the following:

☐ Applets cannot read or write to the reader's file system, except in specific directories (which are defined by the user through an access control list that is empty by default). Some browsers might not even allow an applet to read or write to the file system at all.

☐ Applets usually cannot communicate with a server other than the one that originally had stored the applet. This feature might be configurable by the browser, but applet programmers cannot depend on having this capability available.

☐ Applets cannot run any programs on the reader's system. For UNIX systems, this restriction includes forking a process.

☐ Applets cannot load programs native to the local platform, including shared libraries such as DLLs.

8

In addition, Java itself includes various forms of security and consistency checking in the Java compiler and interpreter to prevent unorthodox use of the language (you will learn more about this on Day 21, "Advanced Concepts"). This combination of restrictions and security features makes it more difficult for a rogue Java applet to do damage to the user's system.

NOTE

> These restrictions prevent many ways of causing damage, but it's impossible to be absolutely sure that a malicious programmer cannot work around the security measures. Sun investigates reports of security violations and improves Java in response. You will learn about more issues in Java security on Day 21.

Creating Applets

Today and in the days to follow, you will be expanding your knowledge of how applets are developed. You will need a good grasp of how an applet works, what features an applet has, and where to start when you first create your own applets.

To create an applet, you create a subclass of the class `Applet` in the `java.applet` package. The `Applet` class provides behavior to enable your applet to work within the browser and also to take advantage of the capabilities of the Abstract Windowing Toolkit (AWT). The AWT enables you to include user interface elements into a program, handle mouse and keyword events, and draw to the screen.

Although your applet can have as many helper classes as it needs, the `Applet` class is the main class that triggers the execution of the applet. The subclass of `Applet` that you create always has a signature like the following:

```
public class myClass extends java.applet.Applet {
    ...
}
```

Note the `public` keyword. Java requires that your `Applet` subclass be declared `public`. This requirement is true only of your main `Applet` class; any helper classes you create can be `public` or `private`. Public, private, and other forms of access control are described on Day 15, "Modifiers."

When Java encounters your applet in a Web page, it loads your initial applet class and any other helper classes that are used by the first class. In applications, the `main()` method is called directly on your initial class. When an applet is loaded, however, Java creates an instance of that class, and a series of `Applet` methods are called on that instance. Different applets that use the same class use different instances, so each one can behave differently than the other applets running in the same browser.

Major Applet Activities

To create a basic Java application, your class has to have one method, main(), with a specific signature. When the application starts up, main() is executed. Within the main() method, an application programmer can set up the behavior that the application needs.

Applets are similar but more complicated. Applets have many different activities, such as initialization, painting, and mouse events, that correspond to various major events in the life cycle of the applet. Each activity has a corresponding method, so when an event occurs, the browser or other Java-capable tool calls those specific methods.

By default, the implementations of these activity methods do nothing. For example, the paint() method that you have used throughout Week 1 does not inherit any behavior. To provide behavior for an event, you must override the appropriate method in your applet's subclass. For example, you overrode paint() each time last week in order for something to be displayed. You don't have to override all of the methods, of course; different applet behavior requires different methods to be overridden.

You will learn about the important methods to override as the week progresses. For a general overview, the following sections describe five of the more important methods in an applet's execution: initialization, starting, stopping, destruction, and painting.

Initialization

Initialization occurs when the applet first is loaded. Initialization might include creating the objects the applet needs, setting up an initial state, loading images or fonts, or setting parameters. To provide behavior for the initialization of an applet, you override the init() method as follows:

```
public void init() {
    // initialization code goes here
}
```

Starting

After an applet is initialized, it is started. Starting also can occur if the applet was previously stopped. For example, an applet is stopped if the browser user follows a link to a different page, and it is started again when the user returns to the page containing the applet.

Starting can occur several times during an applet's life cycle, but initialization happens only once. To provide startup behavior for your applet, override the start() method as follows:

```
public void start() {
    // starting code goes here
}
```

Functionality that you put in the start() method might include starting up a thread to control the applet, sending the appropriate messages to helper objects, or in some way telling the applet to begin running. You will learn more about starting applets on Day 10, "Simple Animation and Threads."

Stopping

Stopping and starting go hand in hand. Stopping occurs when the user leaves the page that contains a currently running applet, or when an applet stops itself by calling stop() directly. By default, when the user leaves a page, any threads the applet had started will continue running. (You will learn more about threads on Day 10.) By overriding stop(), you can suspend execution of these threads, and then restart them if the applet is viewed again. The following shows the form of a stop() method:

```
public void stop() {
    // stopping code goes here
}
```

Destruction

Destruction sounds more harsh than it is. The destroy() method enables the applet to clean up after itself just before it is freed from memory or the browser exits. You can use this method to kill any running threads or to release any other running objects, for example. Generally, you won't want to override destroy() unless you have specific resources that need to be released, such as threads that the applet has created. To provide cleanup behavior for your applet, override the destroy() method as follows:

```
public void destroy() {
    // destuction code goes here
}
```

NOTE

You might be wondering how destroy() is different from finalize(), which was described on Day 7, "More About Methods." The destroy() method applies only to applets, and finalize() is a more general-purpose way for a single object of any type to clean up after itself.

As you will learn during Day 21, Java has an automatic garbage collector that manages memory for you. The collector reclaims memory from resources after the program is done using them, so you don't normally have to use methods such as destroy().

Painting

Painting is how an applet displays something on-screen, be it text, a line, a colored background, or an image. Painting can occur many hundreds of times during an applet's life cycle: once after the applet is initialized, again if the browser window is brought out from behind another window on-screen, again if the browser window is moved to a different position on-screen, and so on. You must override the paint() method of your Applet subclass in order to display anything. The paint() method looks like the following:

```
public void paint(Graphics g) {
    // painting code goes here
}
```

Note that unlike other methods described in this section, paint() takes an argument: an instance of the class Graphics. This object is created and passed to paint() by the browser, so you don't have to worry about it. However, you always must import the Graphics class (part of the java.awt package) into your applet code, usually through an import statement at the top of your Java source file, as in the following:

```
import java.awt.Graphics;
```

TIP

If you are importing several classes from the same package, such as the Abstract Windowing Toolkit classes, you can use a wildcard character to load all of them at the same time. For example, the statement import java.awt.*; will make every public class in the java.awt package available. The import statement does not include subclasses of the package, however, so the import java.awt.*; statement would not include the classes of the java.awt.image package.

A Simple Applet

On Day 2, "Object-Oriented Programming," you created a simple applet called BigPalindrome—the one with the big blue text Go hang a salami, I'm a lasagna hog. You created and used that applet as an example of creating a subclass. You now will review the code for that applet, this time looking at it differently in light of what you just learned about applets. Listing 8.1 shows the code for that applet.

Listing 8.1. The `BigPalindrome` applet.

```
 1: import java.awt.Graphics;
 2: import java.awt.Font;
 3: import java.awt.Color;
 4:
 5: public class BigPalindrome extends java.applet.Applet {
 6:
 7:     Font f = new Font("TimesRoman", Font.BOLD, 36);
 8:
 9:     public void paint(Graphics g) {
10:         g.setFont(f);
11:         g.setColor(Color.blue);
12:         g.drawString("Go hang a salami, I'm a lasagna hog.", 5, 50);
13:     }
14: }
```

This applet overrides paint(), one of the major methods described in the previous section. Because the applet just displays a few words on the screen, there is nothing to initialize. Therefore, you don't need a start(), stop(), or init() method.

The paint() method is where the real work of this applet occurs. The Graphics object passed into the paint() method holds the graphics state, which is the current features of the drawing surface. Lines 10 and 11 set up the font and color for this graphics state (here, the font object held in the f instance variable and an object representing the color blue that is stored in the Color class variable blue).

Line 12 then draws the string Go hang a salami, I'm a lasagna hog. by using the current font and color at the position 5,50. Note that the 0 point for x,y is at the top left of the applet's drawing surface, with positive y moving downward, so 50 is at the bottom of the applet. Figure 8.1 shows how the applet's bounding box and the string are drawn on the page.

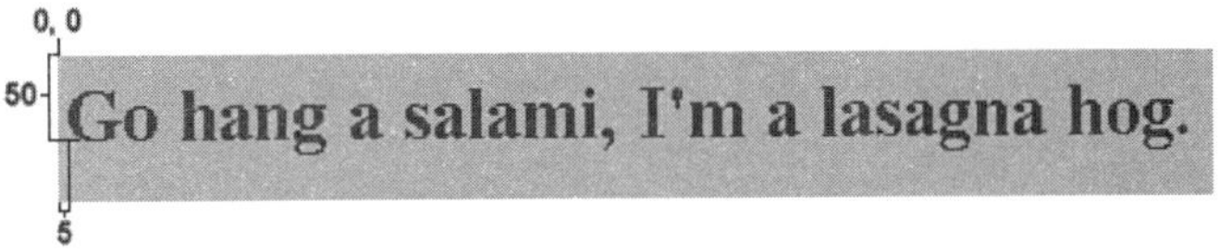

Figure 8.1.

Drawing the BigPalindrome *applet.*

0, 0

50

Go hang a salami, I'm a lasagna hog.

5

Including an Applet on a Web Page

After you create the class or classes that compose your applet and compile them into class files, you must create a Web page that will hold that applet. Java WorkShop does this for you when you test an applet, but this page is just for testing purposes. When you are ready to put an applet on an actual page, you edit HTML files to add the applet yourself. In order to do this, you need to know about the <APPLET> tag.

As you have seen in previous examples, <APPLET> is a special HTML tag for embedding applets in Web pages. Java-capable browsers use the information contained in the tag to find and execute the applet's compiled class files. In this section, you will learn how to put Java applets on a Web page and how to serve the executable Java files to the Web at large.

NOTE

The following section assumes you have at least a passing understanding of HTML. If you need help in this area, you might find the Sams.net book *Teach Yourself Web Publishing with HTML in 14 Days* useful. It was written by Laura Lemay, one of the authors of this book.

The <APPLET> Tag

To include an applet on a Web page, you use the <APPLET> tag. <APPLET> is a special extension to HTML for the inclusion of applets in Web pages. To get a closer look at an <APPPLET> tag, you will create the HTML file for BigPalindrome, one of the applets that you created on Day 2. Use Portfolio Manager to select BigPalindrome as your current project, and click the Source Editor icon to load the source code for BigPalindrome.java.

No changes are needed in this file, but you need the Source Editor open to create a new file. Choose File | New to open a new document for editing. Enter the text from Listing 8.2, and save the result as BigPalindrome.html.

TYPE **Listing 8.2. The HTML code for BigPalindrome.html.**

```
 1: <HTML>
 2: <HEAD>
 3: <TITLE>The Big Palindrome Page</TITLE>
 4: </HEAD>
 5: <BODY>
 6: <P>My favorite meat-related palindrome is:
 7: <BR>
 8: <APPLET CODE="BigPalindrome.class" WIDTH="500" HEIGHT="600">
 9: A secret if your browser does not support Java!
10: </APPLET>
11: </BODY>
12: </HTML>
```

ANALYSIS There are three things to note about the <APPLET> tag in this page:

☐ The CODE attribute indicates the name of the class file that contains this applet, including the .class extension. In this case, the class file must be in the same directory as this HTML file. To indicate applets are in a specific directory, you can use CODEBASE, described later today.

☐ WIDTH and HEIGHT are required and are used to indicate the bounding box of the applet—that is, how big a box to draw for the applet on the Web page. Be sure that WIDTH and HEIGHT are set to an appropriate size for the applet. Depending on the browser, if your applet draws outside the boundaries of the space you've given it, you might not be able to see or get to the parts of the applet outside the bounding box.

☐ The text between the <APPLET> and </APPLET> tags is displayed by browsers that do not understand the <APPLET> tag (which includes most browsers that are not Java-capable). Because your page will be viewed with many different kinds of browsers, it is a good idea to include text here so that readers of your page who don't have Java will see something other than a blank line. In the current example, the text that displays above the applet reads My favorite meat-related palindrome is: Users who have Java browsers will see the rest of this statement as the BigPalindrome applet. Users who don't have Java will see the alternate text that has been provided—namely, A secret if your browser does not support Java!

Note that the APPLET tag, like the IMG tag, is not itself a paragraph. It should be enclosed inside a more general text tag, such as <P> or one of the heading tags (<H1>, <H2>, and the like).

Testing the Result

Now that you have an applet class file and an HTML file that refers to the class, you're ready to test the HTML file with the BigPalindrome applet. Almost ready, actually, you need to set up Java WorkShop to run the applet with the HTML file that you just created.

Using Project Manager, click the Run tab and change Existing Run Page URL from No to Yes. In the text field next to this question, enter BigPalindrome.html. Click the Apply button at the bottom of the dialog box to make the change permanent. Click Project Tester, and the output should resemble Figure 8.2.

In Java WorkShop, you also can load an HTML file the way you would in a Java-capable browser, by typing the URL in the Location field. The BigPalindrome applet can be loaded with a URL such as the following:

```
file:/C:/Java-WorkShop/homework/BigPalindrome.html
```

The preceding would be used if the full path name of the HTML file is C:/Java-WorkShop/homework/BigPalindrome.html. The path of your file might be different.

Figure 8.2.

The output of
`BigPalindrome.html`.

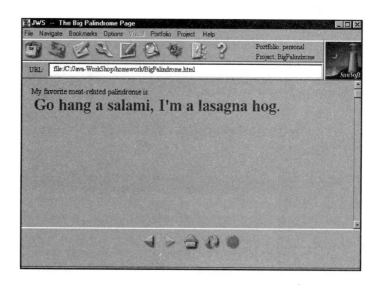

Putting Applets on the Web

After you have an applet and an HTML file, and you have verified that everything is working correctly on your local system, the last step is to make the applet available to the World Wide Web so that anyone with a Java-capable browser can view it.

Java applets are served by a Web server in the same way that HTML files, images, and other media are. You don't need special server software to make Java applets available on the Web; you don't even need to configure your server to handle Java files. If you have a Web server running, or space on a Web server available to you, all you must do is move the applet's HTML and class files to that server, as you would any other file.

More About the <APPLET> Tag

In its simplest form, the <APPLET> tag uses CODE, WIDTH, and HEIGHT to create a space of the appropriate size, and then loads and runs the applet in that space. However, <APPLET> includes several other attributes that can help you better integrate an applet into the overall design of a Web page.

NOTE

The attributes available for the <APPLET> tag are almost identical to those for the HTML <IMG> tag.

8

ALIGN

The ALIGN attribute defines how the applet will be aligned on the page. This attribute can have one of nine values: LEFT, RIGHT, TOP, TEXTTOP, MIDDLE, ABSMIDDLE, BASELINE, BOTTOM, and ABSBOTTOM.

In the case of ALIGN=LEFT and ALIGN=RIGHT, the applet is placed between the text following the applet and the left or right margins of the page, depending on the ALIGN value. The text will continue to flow to the left or right until the lower edge of the applet is reached. You can use a line break tag (BR) with the CLEAR attribute to start the next line of text below the applet. The CLEAR attribute can have one of three values: CLEAR=LEFT starts the text at the next clear left margin, CLEAR=RIGHT does the same for the right margin, and CLEAR=ALL starts the text at the next line where both margins are clear.

For example, this snippet of HTML code aligns an applet against the left margin, has some text flowing alongside the applet, and then breaks the text at the end of the paragraph so that the next bit of text starts below the applet:

```
<P><applet
    code="SmallPalindrome.class"
    width="275"
    height="100"
    align="left">
Madam I'm Adam
</applet>
To the left of this paragraph is an applet. It's a
simple, unassuming applet, in which a small string is
printed in red type, set in 32 point Times bold.
<BR CLEAR=ALL>
<P>In the next part of the page, we demonstrate how
under certain conditions, styrofoam peanuts can be
used as a healthy snack.
```

Figure 8.3 shows how this applet and the text surrounding it might appear in a Java-capable browser.

For smaller applets, you might want to include your applet within a single line of text. There are seven values for ALIGN that determine how the applet is vertically aligned with the text. They are as follows:

- [ ] ALIGN=TEXTTOP aligns the top of the applet with the top of the tallest text in the line.
- [ ] ALIGN=TOP aligns the applet with the topmost item in the line (which can be another applet, or an image, or the top of the text).

☐ `ALIGN=ABSMIDDLE` aligns the middle of the applet with the middle of the largest item in the line.

☐ `ALIGN=MIDDLE` aligns the middle of the applet with the middle of the baseline of the text.

☐ `ALIGN=BASELINE` aligns the bottom of the applet with the baseline of the text. `ALIGN=BASELINE` is the same as `ALIGN=BOTTOM`, but `ALIGN=BASELINE` is a more descriptive name.

☐ `ALIGN=ABSBOTTOM` aligns the bottom of the applet with the lowest item in the line (which can be the baseline of the text or another applet or image).

Figure 8.3.

An example of aligning an applet with text.

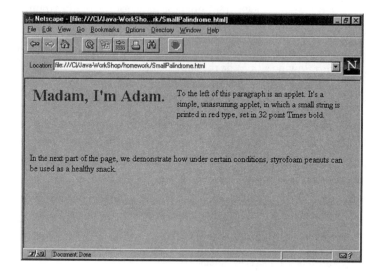

Figure 8.4 shows the various alignment options, in which the line is an image and the arrow is a small applet.

Figure 8.4.

Applet alignment options.

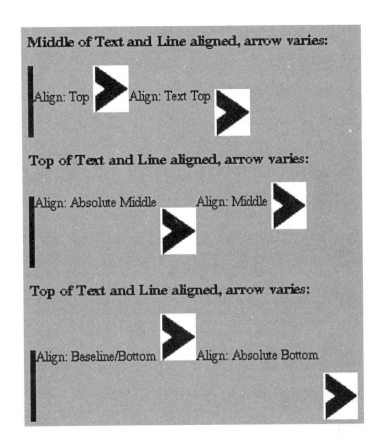

HSPACE **and** VSPACE

The HSPACE and VSPACE attributes are used to set the amount of space, in pixels, between an applet and its surrounding text. HSPACE controls the horizontal space (the space to the left and right of the applet). VSPACE controls the vertical space (the space above and below the applet).

CODE **and** CODEBASE

The CODE attribute is used to indicate the name of the class file that holds the current applet. If CODE is used alone in the <APPLET> tag, the class file is searched for in the same directory as the HTML file that references it.

If you want to store your class files in a different directory than that of your HTML files, you must tell the Java-capable browser where to find the class files. To do this, you use the CODEBASE attribute. CODE contains only the name of the class file; CODEBASE contains an alternate path name where classes are contained. For example, if you store your class files in a subdirectory called classes, which is in the same directory as your HTML files, CODEBASE would be indicated as in the following:

```
<APPLET CODE="MyClass.class" CODEBASE="classes"
    WIDTH=100 HEIGHT=100>
</APPLET>
```

Passing Parameters to Applets

With Java applications, you can pass parameters to the main() method by using arguments on the command line. You then can parse those arguments inside the body of your class, and the application acts accordingly based on the arguments it is given.

Applets, however, don't have a command line. How do you pass different arguments to an applet? Applets can get different input from the HTML file that contains the <APPLET> tag through the use of applet parameters. To set up and handle parameters in an applet, you need two things:

☐ A special parameter tag in the HTML file

☐ Code in your applet to parse those parameters

Applet parameters come in two parts: a name, which is simply a name you pick, and a value, which determines the value of that particular parameter. For example, you can indicate the color of text in an applet by using a parameter with the name color and the value red. You can determine an animation's speed using a parameter with the name speed and the value 5.

In the HTML file that contains the embedded applet, you indicate each parameter using the <PARAM> tag, which has two attributes for the name and the value called (surprisingly enough) NAME and VALUE. The <PARAM> tag goes inside the opening and closing <APPLET> tags, as in the following:

```
<APPLET CODE="QueenMab.class" WIDTH=100 HEIGHT=100>
<PARAM NAME=font VALUE="TimesRoman">
<PARAM NAME=size VALUE="24">
A Java applet appears here.
</APPLET>
```

This particular example defines two parameters to the QueenMab applet: one named font with a value of TimesRoman, and one named size with a value of 24.

Parameters are passed to your applet when it is loaded. In the init() method for your applet, you can retrieve these parameters by using the getParameter() method. The getParameter() method takes one argument, a string representing the name of the parameter you're looking for, and returns a string containing the corresponding value of that parameter. (Like

8

arguments in Java applications, all parameter values are returned as strings.) To get the value of the font parameter from the HTML file, you might have a line such as the following in your init() method:

```
String theFontName = getParameter("font");
```

NOTE

> The names of the parameters as specified in <PARAM> and the names of the parameters in getParameter() must match identically, including the same case. In other words, <PARAM NAME="eecummings"> is different from <PARAM NAME="EECummings">. If your parameters are not being properly passed to your applet, make sure the parameter cases match.

Note that if a parameter you expect has not been specified in the HTML file, getParameter() returns null. Most often, you will want to test for a null parameter and supply a reasonable default, as shown:

```
if (theFontName == null)
    theFontName = "Courier";
```

Keep in mind that getParameter() returns strings; if you want a parameter to be some other object or type, you have to convert it yourself. For example, consider the HTML file for the QueenMab applet. To parse the size parameter and assign it to an integer variable called theSize, you might use the following lines:

```
int theSize;
String s = getParameter("size");
if (s == null)
    theSize = 12;
else theSize = Integer.parseInt(s);
```

Get it? Not yet? In order to get comfortable with parameter passing, you will create an example of an applet that uses this technique.

Passing Parameters to BigPalindrome

You will modify the BigPalindrome applet so that it displays a specific name, for example, Dennis and Edna sinned or No, sir, prefer prison. The name is passed into the applet through an HTML parameter. The project will be called BiggerPalindrome. Before using Java WorkShop on this project, read along as the steps of the project are detailed.

Start by copying the original BigPalindrome class, with a change to reflect the new class name:

```
import java.awt.Graphics;
import java.awt.Font;
import java.awt.Color;
```

```
public class BiggerPalindrome extends java.applet.Applet {

    Font f = new Font("TimesRoman", Font.BOLD, 36);

    public void paint(Graphics g) {
       g.setFont(f);
       g.setColor(Color.blue);
       g.drawString("Go hang a salami, I'm a lasagna hog.", 5, 50);
    }
}
```

The first thing you need to add to this class is a place for the palindrome parameter to be stored in. Because you'll need that name throughout the applet, you add an instance variable for the name right after the variable for the font:

```
String palindrome;
```

To set a value for the name, you have to get the parameter. The best place to handle parameters to an applet is inside an init() method. The init() method is defined similarly to paint() (public, with no arguments, and a return type of void). Make sure when you test for a parameter that you test for a value of null. If a palindrome isn't indicated, the default, in this case, is to display Dennis and Edna sinned, as the following illustrates:

```
public void init() {
    palindrome = getParameter("palindrome");
        if (palindrome == null)
        palindrome = "Dennis and Edna sinned";
    }
```

Once that change is made, all that's left is to modify the paint() method. The original drawString() method looked like this:

```
g.drawString("Go hang a salami, I'm a lasagna hog.", 5, 50);
```

To draw the new string you have stored in the name instance variable, all you need to do is substitute that variable for the literal string:

```
g.drawString(palindrome, 5, 50);
```

Use Portfolio Manager to create a new applet called BiggerPalindrome with the following fields:

Name: BiggerPalindrome

Source directory: Enter the full path of your homework directory
(C:/Java-WorkShop/homework or something similar).

Existing sources: No

Main Class File: You should not be able to change this field because .class
appears in the field as grayed-out text.

Run page: Leave this field blank.

Create using: Source Editor

Use the Source Editor to enter the source code from Listing 8.3, and then save and compile the file.

TYPE **Listing 8.3. The** `BiggerPalindrome` **class.**

```
 1: import java.awt.Graphics;
 2: import java.awt.Font;
 3: import java.awt.Color;
 4:
 5: public class BiggerPalindrome extends java.applet.Applet {
 6:
 7:     Font f = new Font("TimesRoman", Font.BOLD, 37);
 8:     String palindrome;
 9:
10:     public void paint(Graphics g) {
11:         g.setFont(f);
12:         g.setColor(Color.blue);
13:         g.drawString(palindrome, 5, 50);
14:     }
15:
16:     public void init() {
17:         palindrome = getParameter("palindrome");
18:             if (palindrome == null)
19:             palindrome = "Dennis and Edna sinned";
20:     }
21: }
```

Instead of using Java WorkShop's automatically generated HTML page, create the HTML file that contains this applet. From the Source Editor, choose File | New to open a new document for editing. Enter the text from Listing 8.4, and save the result as `BiggerPalindrome.html`.

TYPE **Listing 8.4. The HTML code for** `BiggerPalindrome.html.`

```
 1: <HTML>
 2: <HEAD>
 3: <TITLE>The Bigger Palindrome Page</TITLE>
 4: </HEAD>
 5: <BODY>
 6: <P>
 7: <APPLET CODE="BiggerPalindrome.class" WIDTH=300 HEIGHT=100>
 8: <PARAM NAME=palindrome VALUE="No, sir, prefer prison">
 9: You need to view this with a Java browser!
10: </APPLET>
11: </BODY>
12: </HTML>
```

Note the <APPLET> tag, which designates the class file for the applet and the appropriate width and height (300 and 100, respectively). Just below it (line 8) is the <PARAM> tag, which is used to pass the palindrome to the applet. In this example, the NAME parameter is palindrome, and the VALUE is the string No, sir, prefer prison. After changing the project to run using the BiggerPalindrome.html file (which you can do with Project Manager), run the applet. The output should resemble Figure 8.5.

Figure 8.5.

The output of the BiggerPalindrome *applet.*

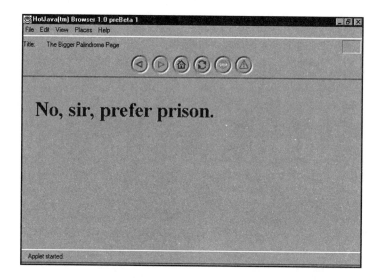

Changing a Parameter

In the code for BiggerPalindrome, if no palindrome is specified, the default is the palindrome Dennis and Edna sinned. Using the Source Browser again, open BiggerPalindrome.html and delete the line containing the <PARAM> tag and the palindrome "No, sir, prefer prison." Listing 8.5 shows the file after the change.

Listing 8.5. Alternative HTML code for BiggerPalindrome.html.

```
 1: <HTML>
 2: <HEAD>
 3: <TITLE>The Bigger Palindrome Page</TITLE>
 4: </HEAD>
 5: <BODY>
 6: <P>
 7: <APPLET CODE="BiggerPalindrome.class" WIDTH=300 HEIGHT=100>
 8: You need to view this with a Java browser!
 9: </APPLET>
10: </BODY>
11: </HTML>
```

8

Save the file, and you can run it immediately with Project Tester. You don't have to compile the project again or do anything to the source code. One advantage of parameter use is that a program can vary its performance without requiring programming changes. Several of the applets featured in the Today's Featured Applet sections of the book have used parameters to increase their flexibility.

When you run the applet again, the applet uses the default palindrome because none was specified as a parameter. The result is shown in Figure 8.6.

Figure 8.6.

The output of the `BiggerPalindrome` *applet.*

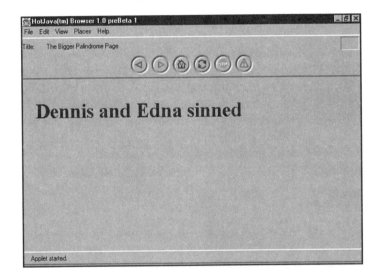

Summary

Applets represent the most common use of the Java language today. Because they are executed and displayed within Web pages, applets can use the graphics, user interface, and event structure provided by the Web browser. This capability provides the applet programmer with a lot of functionality without a lot of extra toil.

Today, you learned the basics of applet creation, including the following things:

☐ All applets you develop using Java inherit from the `Applet` class, part of the `java.applet` package. The `Applet` class provides basic behavior for how the applet will be integrated with the browser and how it will react to input and other changes in state from the browser. By subclassing `Applet`, you have access to all of its behavior.

☐ Applets have five main methods, which are used for the basic activities an applet performs during its life cycle: init(), start(), stop(), destroy(), and paint(). Although you don't need to override all of these methods, they are the most common methods you will see repeated in many of the applets you will create in this book and in other sample programs.

☐ To run a compiled applet class file, you include it in an HTML Web page by using the <APPLET> tag. When a Java-capable browser comes across <APPLET>, it loads and runs the applet described in that tag. Note that to offer Java applets on the World Wide Web alongside HTML files, you do not need special server software—any plain old Web server will do just fine.

☐ Unlike applications, applets do not have a common line on which to pass arguments, so those arguments must be passed to the applet through the HTML file that contains the applet. Parameters in an HTML file are indicated by using the <PARAM> tag inside the opening and closing <APPLET> tags. <PARAM> has two attributes: NAME for the name of the parameter, and VALUE for its value. Inside the body of your applet (usually in init()), you then can gain access to those parameters using the getParameter() method.

Q&A

Q **In the first part of today's lesson, you say that applets are downloaded from Web servers and run on the user's system. What's to stop an applet developer from creating an applet that deletes all the files on the user's system, or in some other way compromises the security of the system?**

A Java applets have several restrictions that make it difficult for the more obvious malicious behavior to take place. For example, because Java applets cannot read or write files on the client system, they cannot delete files or read system files that might contain private information. Because they cannot run programs on the user's system without the user's permission, they cannot, for example, run system programs pretending to be the user. Nor can they run so many programs that a system crashes.

In addition, Java's architecture makes it difficult to circumvent these restrictions. The language, the Java compiler, and the Java interpreter all have checks to make sure that no bogus code is executed and no tricks are being played with the system itself. You'll learn more about these security checks on Day 21, "Advanced Concepts." Of course, no system can claim to be 100-percent secure, and the fact that Java applets are run on your system should make you naturally cautious. See Day 21 for more information about security issues.

8

Q Wait a minute—if I can't read files, write files, or run programs on the system the applet is running on, doesn't that limit me to writing simple animations and flashy graphics? How can I save state in an applet? How can I create, say, a word processor or a spreadsheet as a Java applet?

A For every person who doesn't believe that Java is secure enough, there is someone who believes that Java's security restrictions are too severe. The functionality of Java applets is limited because of the security restrictions, but given the possibility for abuse and the newness of code delivered over the Web, it seems better to err on the side of caution. Hundreds of applets on the Web show what can be done. Visit the Gamelan site at http://www.gamelan.com to get an indication of what's being accomplished on the Web with applets.

Keep in mind, also, that Java applications have none of the restrictions that Java applets do, but because they are also compiled to bytecode, they can be portable across platforms. If applet security is limiting a project that you are planning, you might want to consider implementing it as an application instead.

Q I noticed in my documentation that the <APPLET> tag also has a NAME attribute. What does it do?

A NAME is used when you have multiple applets on a page that need to communicate with each other. You'll learn about this attribute later this week.

Q I have an applet that takes parameters and an HTML file that passes it those parameters. But when my applet runs, all I get are null values. What's going on here?

A Do the names of your parameters (in the NAME attribute) match exactly with the names you're testing for in getParameter()? They must be exact, including case, for the match to be made. Also, make sure that your <PARAM> tags are inside the opening and closing <APPLET> tags and that you haven't misspelled anything.

FEATURED APPLET Today's Featured Applet

The featured applet for today is Graph by Ciarán Treanor, and it is an excellent example of how parameters can be used to create dynamic applets. This applet uses Treanor's PieChartCanvas class to create a pie chart. The graphic is customized based on parameters that specify how the chart will be displayed. Figure 8.7 shows a screen capture of the applet.

Files for Graph are located on the CD-ROM in the \BOOK\3RDPARTY\DAY8\ directory, including source code in the file Graph.java. To use Graph on a Web page, place these two class files on your Web site: Graph.class and PieChartCanvas.class. Place the files in the same directory as the Web page, or place them in a subdirectory listed in the CODEBASE parameter of the <APPLET> tag. The <CODE> tag should be Graph.class.

Figure 8.7.

The Graph *applet in action.*

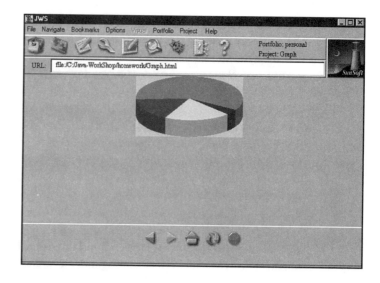

Listing 8.6 shows the HTML tags used to run Graph as it was shown in Figure 8.7.

Listing 8.6. The <APPLET> tag for Graph.

```
<APPLET code="Graph.class" width=200 height=200 align=center>
<param name=depth value="30">
<param name=radius value="200">
<param name=values value="10-red,150-green,40-magenta,50-yellow">
</APPLET>
```

Graph has three parameters that you can customize within the <APPLET> tag, as follows:

☐ The depth parameter specifies how tall the pie chart should be (20 is the default).

☐ The radius parameter specifies the radius of the pie chart (100 is the default).

☐ The values parameter is a string defining the colors and quantity of each pie slice in *value-color* pairs. The values can be floating-point numbers. The colors can be green, red, blue, yellow, magenta, cyan, orange, pink, white, or black. (For example: 10-red,150-green,40-magenta,50-yellow).

More information on Graph is available from its author at the following URL:

```
http://www.broadcom.ie/~ct/java/
```

8

Day **9**

Graphics, Fonts, and Color

Now that you have a basic understanding of how applets work, you will cover the sorts of things you can do with applets for the remainder of this week. Many of these things involve using the built-in Java class libraries and combining them to produce interesting effects.

Today you will learn how to draw to the screen—how to produce lines and shapes with the built-in graphics primitives, how to display text using fonts, and how to use and modify color in your applets. The following specifics will be detailed:

☐ How the graphics system works in Java: the `Graphics` class, the coordinate system used to draw to the screen, and how applets paint and repaint

☐ How to use the Java graphics primitives, including drawing and filling lines, rectangles, ovals, and arcs

☐ How to create and use fonts, including how to draw characters and strings and how to find out the measurements of a given font for better layout

☐ All about color in Java, including the Color class and how to set the foreground and background colors for your applet

NOTE

> Today's lesson discusses many of the basic operations available to you with the Java class library regarding graphics, fonts, and color. However, the lesson is intended to be an introduction and overview of class library features rather than an exhaustive description of everything that is available. Be sure to check out the Java API documentation for more information on the classes that are described.

The Graphics **Class**

With Java's graphics capabilities, you can draw lines, shapes, characters, and images to the screen on your applet. Most of the graphics operations in Java are methods defined in the Graphics class. You don't have to create an instance of Graphics in order to draw something in your applet. In your applet's paint() method (which you learned about yesterday), you are given a Graphics object as a parameter. By drawing on that object, you draw onto your applet, and the results appear on-screen.

The Graphics class is part of the java.awt package, so if your applet does any painting (as it usually will), make sure to import that class at the beginning of your Java file with an import java.awt.Graphics; statement.

The Graphics Coordinate System

To draw an object on the screen, you call one of the drawing methods available in the Graphics class. All the drawing methods take arguments representing endpoints, corners, or starting locations of the object as values in the applet's coordinate system. For example, a line may start at the point 10,10 and end at the point 20,20.

Java's coordinate system has the origin (0,0) in the top left corner. Positive x values increase to the right, and positive y values increase downward. All pixel values are integers; there are no partial or fractional pixels. Figure 9.1 shows how you might draw a simple square by using this coordinate system.

Figure 9.1.
The Java graphics coordinate system.

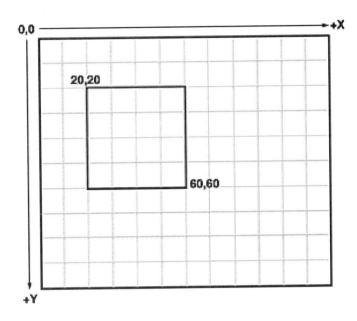

Java's coordinate system is different from many painting and layout programs that have their x and y origin in the bottom left. If you're not used to working with Java's graphics system, it might take some practice to become familiar with it.

Drawing and Filling

The Graphics class provides a set of simple built-in graphics primitives for drawing, including lines, rectangles, polygons, ovals, and arcs.

NOTE

> You can also draw bitmap images, such as GIF files, by using the Graphics class. You'll learn about this tomorrow.

Lines

To draw straight lines, use the drawLine() method. The drawLine() method takes four arguments: the x and y coordinates of the starting point, and the x and y coordinates of the ending point, as in the following:

```
public void paint(Graphics g) {
    g.drawLine(25,25,75,75);
}
```

Figure 9.2 shows the result of this snippet of code.

Figure 9.2.
Drawing lines.

Rectangles

The Java graphics primitives provide three kinds of rectangles:

- [ ] Plain rectangles
- [ ] Rounded rectangles
- [ ] Three-dimensional rectangles, which are drawn with a shaded border

For each of these rectangles, you have two methods to choose from: one that draws the rectangle in outline form, and one that draws the rectangle filled in with a color.

To draw a plain rectangle, use either the `drawRect()` or `fillRect()` method. Both take four arguments: the x and y coordinates of the top left corner of the rectangle, and the width and height of the rectangle to draw. For example, the following `paint()` method draws two squares:

```
public void paint(Graphics g) {
    g.drawRect(20,20,60,60);
    g.fillRect(120,20,60,60);
}
```

The first square drawn is an outline, and the second is filled, as shown in Figure 9.3.

Figure 9.3.
Rectangles.

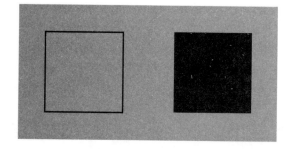

Rounded rectangles are, as you might expect, rectangles with rounded edges. The `drawRoundRect()` and `fillRoundRect()` methods draw rounded rectangles, and they are similar to the methods for regular rectangles, except that rounded rectangles have two extra arguments. The last two arguments determine how far along the edges of the rectangle the corner arc begins. The first argument is for the horizontal plane, and the second argument is for the vertical plane. Larger values make the overall rectangle more rounded, and values equal to the width and height of the entire rectangle produce a circle. Figure 9.4 shows some examples of rounded corners and the corner arguments used to create them.

Figure 9.4.

Rounded corners.

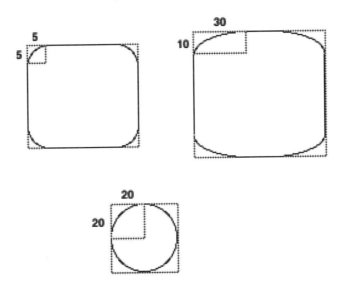

The following `paint()` method draws two rounded rectangles—one as an outline with a rounded corner 10 pixels square, and the other as a filled rectangle with a rounded corner 20 pixels square:

```
public void paint(Graphics g) {
    g.drawRoundRect(20,20,60,60,10,10);
    g.fillRoundRect(120,20,60,60,20,20);
}
```

Figure 9.5 shows the resulting rectangles.

Three-dimensional rectangles are the last type of rectangles you can use. These rectangles aren't really 3-D, of course; they have a shadow effect that makes them appear either raised or indented from the surface of the applet.

Three-dimensional rectangles have five arguments. The first four are the x and y of the start position, and the width and height of the rectangle. The fifth argument is a boolean value indicating whether the 3-D effect raises the rectangle (`true`) or indents it (`false`).

Figure 9.5.

Rounded rectangles.

As with the other rectangles, there are also different methods for drawing and filling the 3-D rectangles: draw3DRect() and fill3DRect(), respectively. The following paint() method draws two 3-D rectangles:

```
public void paint(Graphics g) {
    g.draw3DRect(20,20,60,60,true);
    g.draw3DRect(120,20,60,60,false);
}
```

The first rectangle drawn is raised, as indicated by the true value in the fifth argument, and the second rectangle is indented (see Figure 9.6).

Figure 9.6.

Three-dimensional rectangles.

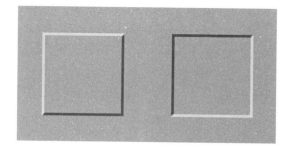

 NOTE

In the current version of the Java class library, it is difficult to see the 3-D effect of these rectangles because of the small line width (in fact, Figure 9.6 was enhanced to better show the effect). If you are having trouble with 3-D rectangles, this line width might be why. Also, drawing 3-D rectangles in any color other than black makes them easier to see.

Polygons

Polygons are shapes with an unlimited number of sides. To draw a polygon, you need a set of x and y coordinates. The drawing method starts at one coordinate, draws a line to the second, then draws a line to the third, and so on.

As with rectangles, you can draw an outline of a polygon or a filled polygon (by using the drawPolygon() and fillPolygon() methods, respectively). You also have a choice of how you want to indicate the list of coordinates—either as arrays of x and y coordinates or as an instance of the Polygon class.

When you are drawing a polygon by using arrays, the drawPolygon() and fillPolygon() methods take three arguments:

- ☐ An array of integers representing x coordinates
- ☐ An array of integers representing y coordinates
- ☐ An integer for the total number of points

The x and y arrays should have the same number of elements, of course.

The following is an example of using arrays to draw a polygon's outline (Figure 9.7 shows the result):

```
public void paint(Graphics g) {
    int xvalues[] = { 39,94,97,142,53,58,26 };
    int yvalues[] = { 33,74,36,70,108,80,106 };
    int pts = xvalues.length;

    g.drawPolygon(xvalues, yvalues, pts);
}
```

Figure 9.7.

A polygon.

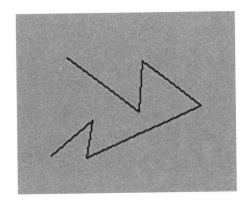

Note that Java does not automatically close the polygon when the `drawPolygon()` method is used. If you want to complete the shape, you have to include the starting point of the polygon at the end of the array. Drawing a filled polygon takes care of this automatically by connecting the starting and ending points.

The second way to draw a polygon is to use a `Polygon` object. The `Polygon` class is useful if you intend to add points to the polygon or if you're building the polygon on the fly. The `Polygon` class enables you to treat the polygon as an object rather than having to deal with individual arrays.

You can create a `Polygon` object by instantiating an empty polygon, as follows:

```
Polygon poly = new Polygon();
```

You can also create a polygon from a set of points using integer arrays, as in the previous `xvalues` and `yvalues` example. Once you have a `Polygon` object, you can append points to the polygon with a statement such as the following:

```
poly.addPoint(20,35);
```

To draw the polygon, use the `Polygon` object as an argument to `drawPolygon()` or `fillPolygon()`. Here's the previous example, rewritten this time with a `Polygon` object. Also, the polygon is filled instead of being an outline (Figure 9.8 shows the output):

```
public void paint(Graphics g) {
    int xvalues[] = { 39,94,97,142,53,58,26 };
    int yvalues[] = { 33,74,36,70,108,80,106 };
    int pts = xvalues.length;
    Polygon poly = new Polygon(xvalues, yvalues, pts);
    g.fillPolygon(poly);
}
```

Figure 9.8.

Another polygon.

Ovals

Ovals, which can be ellipses or circles, are handled just like rectangles with overly rounded corners. They are drawn using four arguments: the x and y of the top corner, and the width and height of the oval itself. Note that because an oval is being drawn, the starting point is some distance to the left and above the actual outline of the oval itself. Again, if you think of it as a rectangle, the starting place is easier to understand.

The drawOval() method draws an outline of an oval, and the fillOval() method draws a filled oval. The following is an example of two ovals—a circle and an ellipse:

```
public void paint(Graphics g) {
    g.drawOval(20,20,60,60);
    g.fillOval(120,20,100,60);
}
```

Figure 9.9 shows how these two ovals appear on-screen.

Figure 9.9.

Ovals.

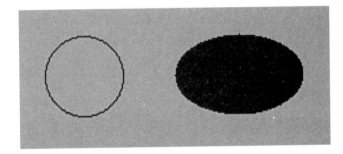

Arcs

Of all the drawing operations, arcs are the most complex to construct, which is why they were saved for last. An arc is a part of a oval; in fact, the easiest way to think of an arc is as a section of a complete oval. Figure 9.10 shows some arcs.

The drawArc() method takes six arguments: the coordinates of the starting corner, the width and height, the angle at which to start the arc, and the degrees of the arc to draw before stopping.

The drawArc() method draws the arc's outline, and the fillArc() method draws a filled arc. Filled arcs are drawn as though they were sections of a pie—instead of joining the two endpoints, both endpoints are joined to the center of the circle.

The important thing to understand about arcs is that you actually are drawing the arc as an oval with only part of the oval being drawn. The starting corner, width, and height are not the starting point, width, and height of the actual arc as drawn on-screen. Instead, they are the starting corner, width, and height of the full ellipse that the arc is part of. Those first points determine the size and shape of the arc. The last two arguments (for the degrees) determine the starting and ending points of the arc.

Figure 9.10.

Arcs.

Consider a simple arc—a C shape on a circle as shown in Figure 9.11.

Figure 9.11.

A C arc.

To construct the method to draw this arc, the first thing to do is think of it as a complete circle. Then, you find the x and y coordinates and the width and height of that circle. Those four values are the first four arguments to the drawArc() or fillArc() methods. Figure 9.12 shows how to get those values from the arc.

To get the last two arguments, think in terms of degrees around the circle. The starting position, 0 degrees, is at 3 o'clock; 90 degrees is at 12 o'clock; 180 degrees is at 9 o'clock; and 270 degrees is at 6 o'clock. The starting point of the arc is the degree value of the start of the arc. In this example, the starting point is the top of the C at 90 degrees, so 90 is the fifth argument to the drawArc() or fillArc() methods.

Figure 9.12.

Constructing a circular arc.

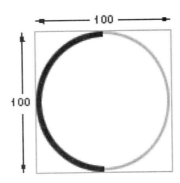

9

The sixth and last argument is another degree value indicating how far around the circle to sweep and the direction to go (it's not the ending degree angle, as you might think). In this case, because you're going halfway around the circle, you're sweeping 180 degrees. You are sweeping in a counter-clockwise direction, which is considered the positive direction in Java, so 180 is the last argument in the arc. If you were sweeping 180 degrees in a clockwise direction, the last argument would be -180. See Figure 9.13 for an illustration of the degree positions for the fifth argument and the counter-clockwise sweep of 180 degrees.

Figure 9.13.

Arcs on circles.

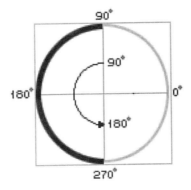

NOTE

It doesn't matter which side of the arc you start with, because the shape of the arc already has been determined by the complete oval it is a section of. The end result is the same.

The following is the code to draw the arc that just has been described. For this example, an outline of the C is drawn to the left, and a filled version is drawn to the right (see Figure 9.14):

```
public void paint(Graphics g) {
    g.drawArc(20,20,60,60,90,180);
    g.fillArc(120,20,60,60,90,180);
}
```

Figure 9.14.

Two circular arcs.

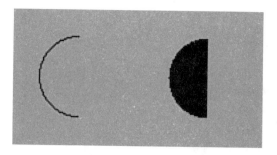

Circles are an easy way to visualize arcs on circles; arcs on ellipses are slightly more difficult. Figure 9.15 shows an example of an elliptical arc.

Figure 9.15.

An elliptical arc.

Like the arc on the circle, this arc is a piece of a complete oval—in this case, an elliptical oval. By completing the oval that this arc is a part of, you can get the starting points, width, and height arguments for the drawArc() or fillArc() method you want to use (see Figure 9.16).

Figure 9.16.

Arcs on ellipses.

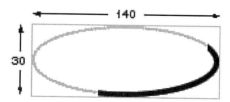

Then all you need to do is figure out the starting angle and the angle to sweep. This arc doesn't start on a nice boundary such as 90 or 180 degrees, so you'll need some trial-and-error attempts in order to get it right. This arc starts somewhere around 25 degrees, and then sweeps clockwise about 130 degrees (see Figure 9.17).

Figure 9.17.

Starting and ending points.

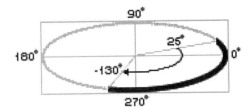

With all portions of the arc in place, you can write the code. Here's the Java code for this arc, both drawn and filled:

```
public void paint(Graphics g) {
    g.drawArc(10,20,150,50,25,-130);
    g.fillArc(10,80,150,50,25,-130);
}
```

Figure 9.18 shows the two elliptical arcs. Note in the filled case how filled arcs are drawn as if they were pie sections.

Figure 9.18.

Two elliptical arcs.

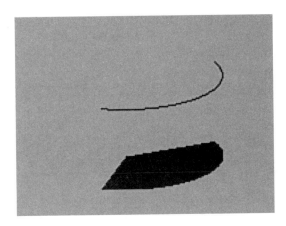

To summarize, here are the steps required to construct arcs in Java:

1. Think of the arc as a slice of a complete oval.
2. Construct the full oval with the starting point, width, and height (it often helps to draw the full oval on the screen first to get an idea of the right positioning).
3. Determine the starting angle for the beginning of the arc.
4. Determine how far to sweep the arc, and in which direction (counter-clockwise indicates positive values, and clockwise indicates negative).

A Simple Graphics Example

The next applet you will create, Lamp, uses many of the built-in graphics primitives to draw a rudimentary shape. It's a lamp with a spotted shade (or a sort of cubist mushroom, depending on your point of view).

Use Portfolio Manager to create a new applet with the following fields:

Name: Lamp

Source directory: Enter the full path of your homework directory
(C:/Java-WorkShop/homework or something similar).

Existing sources: No

Main Class File: You should not be able to change this field because .class appears in the field as grayed-out text.

Run page: Leave this field blank.

Create using: Source Editor

Use the Source Editor to enter the source code from Listing 9.1, and then save and compile the file.

TYPE   **Listing 9.1. Source code of Lamp.java.**

```
 1: import java.awt.*;
 2:
 3: public class Lamp extends java.applet.Applet {
 4:
 5:     public void paint(Graphics g) {
 6:         // the lamp platform
 7:         g.fillRect(0,250,290,290);
 8:
 9:         // the base of the lamp
10:         g.drawLine(125,250,125,160);
11:         g.drawLine(175,250,175,160);
12:
13:         // the lamp shade, top and bottom edges
14:         g.drawArc(85,157,130,50,-65,312);
15:         g.drawArc(85,87,130,50,62,58);
16:
17:         // lamp shade, sides
18:         g.drawLine(85,177,119,89);
19:         g.drawLine(215,177,181,89);
20:
21:         // dots on the shade
22:         g.fillArc(78,120,40,40,63,-174);
23:         g.fillOval(120,96,40,40);
24:         g.fillArc(173,100,40,40,110,180);
25:     }
26: }
```

When you run the file, you will see a drawing composed of lines, circles, and other polygons, as shown in Figure 9.19.

Figure 9.19.

The output of the Lamp *applet.*

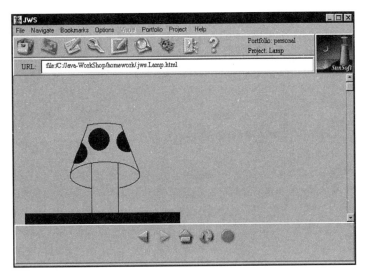

Copying and Clearing

Once you have drawn a few things on the screen, you might want to move them around or clear the entire applet. The Graphics class provides methods for doing both of these things.

The copyArea() method copies a rectangular area of the screen to another area of the screen. This method takes six arguments: the x and y of the top corner of the rectangle to copy, the width and the height of that rectangle, and the distance in the x and y directions to copy it to. For example, the following statement copies a square area 100 pixels on a side 100 pixels directly to its right:

```
g.copyArea(0,0,100,100,100,0);
```

To clear a rectangular area, use the clearRect() method. This method, which takes the same four arguments as the drawRect() and fillRect() methods, fills the given rectangle with the current background color of the applet (you'll learn how to set the current background color later today).

To clear the entire applet, you can use the size() method, which returns a Dimension object representing the width and height of the applet. You then can get to the actual values for width and height by using the width and height instance variables, as in the following statement:

```
g.clearRect(0,0,size().width,size().height);
```

Text and Fonts

The Graphics class, in conjunction with the Font class (and sometimes the FontMetrics class), also enables you to display text on the screen. The Font class represents a given font—its name, style, and point size—and FontMetrics gives you information about that font (for example, the actual height or width of a given character) so that you can lay out text precisely in your applet. Note that the text here is drawn to the screen once and is intended to stay there. You will learn about entering text from the keyboard later this week.

Creating Font Objects

To draw text on-screen, first you need to create an instance of the Font class. Font objects represent an individual font—its name, style (bold, italic, and so on), and its point size. Font names are strings representing the family of the font (for example, "TimesRoman", "Courier", or "Helvetica"). Font styles are constants defined by the Font class; you can get to them by using class variables—for example, Font.PLAIN, Font.BOLD, or Font.ITALIC. You can add these constants to create combined styles. For example, Font.BOLD + Font.ITALIC produces a font that is both bold and italic. Finally, the point size is the size of the font, as defined by the font itself. The point size might or might not be the height of the characters.

To create an individual Font object, use these three arguments to the Font class' new constructor:

```
Font f = new Font("TimesRoman", Font.BOLD, 24);
```

This example creates a Font object for the TimesRoman BOLD font in 24 points. Note that, like most Java classes, you have to import this class before you can use it.

The fonts you have available to you in your applets depend on which fonts are installed on the system where the applet is running. If you pick a font for your applet and that font isn't available on the current system, Java will substitute a default font (usually Courier). For best results, it's a good idea to stick with standard fonts such as "TimesRoman", "Helvetica", and "Courier".

You also can use the getFontList() method, defined in the java.awt.Tookit class, to get a listing of the current fonts available on the system. You can use this list to make choices about which fonts to use on the fly. If you are interested in trying out this method, see the method's description in the API documentation, which is available from the Help pull-down menu in Java WorkShop.

Drawing Characters and Strings

With a Font object in hand, you can draw text on-screen using the methods `drawChars()` and `drawString()`. First, though, you need to set the current font to your Font object using the `setFont()` method.

The current font is part of the graphics state that is maintained by the Graphics object you're drawing on. Each time you draw a character or a string to the screen, that text is drawn using the current font. To change the font of the text, first change the current font. The following `paint()` method creates a new font, sets the current font to that font, and draws the string `"I'm very font of you."` at the point 10,100.

```
public void paint(Graphics g) {
    Font f = new Font("TimesRoman", Font.PLAIN, 72);
    g.setFont(f);
    g.drawString("I'm very font of you.", 10, 100);
}
```

This code should look familiar to you—it was used frequently in the applets created during Week 1. The latter two arguments to `drawString()` determine the point where the string will start. The x value is the start of the leftmost edge of the text, and y is the baseline for the entire string.

Similar to `drawString()` is the `drawChars()` method, which takes an array of characters as an argument instead of taking a string. The `drawChars()` method has five arguments: the array of characters, an integer representing the first character in the array to draw, another integer for the last character in the array to draw, and the x and y coordinates for the starting point. Note that all characters are drawn between the first and last character specified. Most of the time, `drawString()` is more useful than `drawChars()`.

To try out some of the variations of font usage, you now will create an applet that draws several lines of text in different fonts. Use Portfolio Manager to create a new applet called ManyFonts with the following fields:

Name: ManyFonts

Source directory: Enter the full path of your homework directory (`C:/Java-WorkShop/homework` or something similar).

Existing sources: No

Main Class File: You should not be able to change this field because `.class` appears in the field as grayed-out text.

Run page: Leave this field blank.

Create using: Source Editor

Enter the source code from Listing 9.2, and then save and compile the file.

TYPE **Listing 9.2. Source code of** `ManyFonts.java.`

```
 1: import java.awt.Font;
 2: import java.awt.Graphics;
 3:
 4: public class ManyFonts extends java.applet.Applet {
 5:
 6: public void paint(Graphics g) {
 7:     Font f = new Font("TimesRoman", Font.PLAIN, 18);
 8:     Font fb = new Font("TimesRoman", Font.BOLD, 18);
 9:     Font fi = new Font("TimesRoman", Font.ITALIC, 18);
10:     Font fbi = new Font("TimesRoman", Font.BOLD + Font.ITALIC, 18);
11:
12:     g.setFont(f);
13:     g.drawString("This is a plain font", 10, 25);
14:     g.setFont(fb);
15:     g.drawString("This is a bold font", 10, 50);
16:     g.setFont(fi);
17:     g.drawString("This is an italic font", 10, 75);
18:     g.setFont(fbi);
19:     g.drawString("This is a bold italic font", 10, 100);
20:     }
21: }
```

Run the applet with Project Tester; the output should resemble Figure 9.20.

Figure 9.20.

The output of the ManyFonts *applet.*

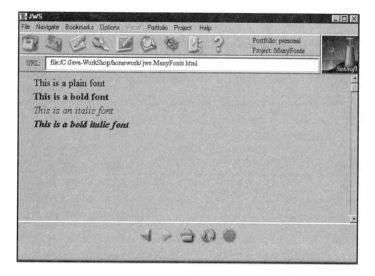

Finding Out Font Information

Sometimes, you might want to make decisions in your Java program based on the attributes of the current font, such as its point size, or the total height of its characters. You can find out basic information about fonts and font objects by using simple methods on the Graphics object and on the Font object. Table 9.1 shows some of these methods.

Table 9.1. Font methods.

Method Name	In Object	Action
getFont()	Graphics	Returns the current font object as previously set by setFont()
getName()	Font	Returns the name of the font as a string
getSize()	Font	Returns the current font size (an integer)
getStyle()	Font	Returns the current style of the font (styles are integer constants: 0 is plain, 1 is bold, 2 is italic, and 3 is bold italic)
isPlain()	Font	Returns true if the font's style is plain, false otherwise
isBold()	Font	Returns true if the font's style is bold, false otherwise
isItalic()	Font	Returns true if the font's style is italic, false otherwise

For more detailed information about the qualities of the current font (for example, the length or height of given characters), you need to work with font measurements (or *metrics*). The FontMetrics class describes information specific to a given font: the leading between lines, the height and width of each character, and so on. To work with these sorts of values, you create a FontMetrics object based on the current font by using the applet method getFontMetrics(), as in the following:

```
Font f = new Font("TimesRoman", Font.BOLD, 36);
FontMetrics fmetrics = getFontMetrics(f);
g.setFont(f);
```

Table 9.2 shows some of the things you can find out using font metrics. All the methods in the table should be called on a FontMetrics object.

Table 9.2. Font metrics methods.

Method Name	Action
stringWidth(*string*)	Given a string, returns the full width of that string, in pixels
charWidth(*char*)	Given a character, returns the width of that character
getAscent()	Returns the ascent of the font—that is, the distance between the font's baseline and the top of the characters
getDescent()	Returns the descent of the font—that is, the distance between the font's baseline and the bottom of the characters (for characters such as p and q that drop below the baseline)
getLeading()	Returns the leading for the font—that is, the spacing between the descent of one line and the ascent of another line
getHeight()	Returns the total height of the font, which is the sum of the ascent, descent, and leading values

Using Font Metrics

As an example of how font metrics can be used, the Centered applet automatically centers a string horizontally and vertically inside an applet. The centering position is different depending on the font and font size; by using font metrics to find out the actual size of a string, you can draw the string in the appropriate place.

Note the applet.size() method that is used in this applet. This method returns the width and height of the overall applet area as a Dimension object. You can retrieve the applet's width and height by using the width and height instance variables of the Dimension object.

Use Portfolio Manager to create a new applet called Centered with the following fields:

Name: Centered

Source directory: Enter the full path of your homework directory (C:/Java-WorkShop/homework or something similar).

Existing sources: No

Main Class File: You should not be able to change this field because .class will appear in the field as grayed-out text.

Run page: Leave this field blank.

Create using: Source Editor

Enter the source code from Listing 9.3, and then save and compile the file. Before you can run the applet, you will need to set the applet's size through Project Manager.

| TYPE | **Listing 9.3. Source code of** Centered.java. |

```
 1: import java.awt.Font;
 2: import java.awt.Graphics;
 3: import java.awt.FontMetrics;
 4:
 5: public class Centered extends java.applet.Applet {
 6:
 7:     public void paint(Graphics g) {
 8:         Font f = new Font("TimesRoman", Font.PLAIN, 24);
 9:         FontMetrics fm = getFontMetrics(f);
10:         g.setFont(f);
11:
12:         String s = "So long, and thanks for all the fish.";
13:         int xstart = (size().width - fm.stringWidth(s)) / 2;
14:         int ystart = (size().height) / 2;
15:
16:         g.drawRect(0, 0, size().width - 1, size().height - 1);
17:         g.drawString(s, xstart, ystart);
18:     }
19: }
```

Before using Project Tester to run the applet, use Project Manager to change the applet's width to 400 and its height to 200 (remembering to click Apply when the changes have been made). When you run the applet, the output should resemble Figure 9.21. You also might want to change the string indicated in line 12, and the font size indicated in line 8, so that you can see how the applet continues to center the text correctly despite the changes.

Figure 9.21.

The output of the Centered *applet.*

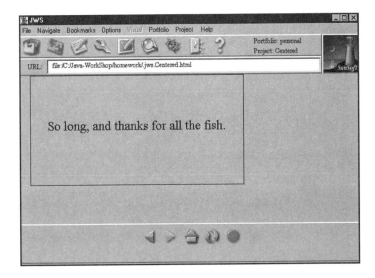

Color

Drawing black on a gray background is nice, but being able to use different colors is much nicer. Java provides methods and behavior for dealing with color through the Color class and also provides methods for setting the current foreground and background colors so that you can draw with the colors you created.

Java's abstract color model uses 24-bit color, which represents a color as a combination of red, green, and blue values. Each component of the color can have a number between 0 and 255. 0,0,0 is black, 255,255,255 is white, and Java can represent millions of colors between the two extremes.

Java's abstract color model maps to the color model of the platform that Java is running on, which often has 256 colors or fewer from which to choose. If a requested color in a Color object is not available for display, the resulting color might be mapped to another color or dithered, depending on how the browser viewing the color implemented it and the platform that the applet is running on. In other words, although Java provides the capability to create and use millions of colors, few might actually be available to you in real use.

Using Color Objects

To draw an object in a particular color, you must create an instance of the Color class to represent that color. The Color class defines a set of standard color objects, stored in class variables, that enable you quickly to get a Color object for some of the more popular colors. For example, Color.red gives you a Color object representing red (RGB values of 255, 0, and 0), Color.white gives you a white color (RGB values of 255, 255, and 255), and so on. Table 9.3 shows the standard colors defined by variables in the Color class.

Table 9.3. Standard colors.

Color Name	RGB Value
Color.white	255,255,255
Color.black	0,0,0
Color.lightGray	192,192,192
Color.gray	128,128,128
Color.darkGray	64,64,64
Color.red	255,0,0
Color.green	0,255,0
Color.blue	0,0,255

Color Name	RGB Value
Color.yellow	255,255,0
Color.magenta	255,0,255
Color.cyan	0,255,255
Color.pink	255,175,175
Color.orange	255,200,0

9

If the color you want to draw in is not one of the standard color objects, fear not. You can create a `Color` object for any combination of red, green, and blue, as long as you have the values of the color you want. Just create a new `Color` object, as in the following statement:

```
Color c = new Color(140,140,140);
```

This line of Java code creates a `Color` object representing a dark gray. You can use any combination of red, green, and blue values to construct a color object. Alternatively, you also can create a `Color` object using three floating-point numbers from 0.0 to 1.0:

```
Color c = new Color(0.55,0.55,0.55)
```

Testing and Setting the Current Colors

To draw an object or text using a `Color` object, you have to set the current color to be that `Color` object. Use the `setColor()` method (a method for `Graphics` objects) to do this, as in the following statement:

```
g.setColor(Color.green);
```

After you set the current color, all drawing operations will occur in that color.

In addition to setting the current color for the graphics context, you also can set the background and foreground colors for the applet itself by using the `setBackground()` and `setForeground()` methods. Both of these methods are defined in the `java.awt.Component` class, which `Applet` (and therefore your classes) automatically inherits.

The `setBackground()` method sets the background color of the applet, which is usually a gray color. It takes a single argument, a `Color` object:

```
setBackground(Color.white);
```

The `setForeground()` method also takes a single color as an argument and affects everything that has been drawn on the applet, regardless of the color in which it has been drawn. You can use setForeground() to change the color of everything in the applet at once, rather than having to redraw everything. The following statement sets everything drawn on the applet to black:

```
setForeground(Color.black);
```

In addition to the setColor(), setForeground(), and setBackground() methods, there are corresponding get methods that enable you to retrieve the current graphics color, background, or foreground. Those methods are getColor() (defined in Graphics objects), getForeground() (defined in Applet), and getBackground() (also in Applet). You can use these methods to choose colors based on existing colors in the applet, as in the following:

```
setForeground(g.getColor());
```

A Color Example

The final applet that you create today, ColorBoxes, fills the drawing area with square boxes that have randomly chosen colors. The applet is written to handle any size of applet, and it automatically fills the area with the right number of boxes.

Use Portfolio Manager to create the ColorBoxes applet with the following fields:

> **Name**: ColorBoxes
>
> **Source directory**: Enter the full path of your homework directory
> (C:/Java-WorkShop/homework or something similar).
>
> **Existing sources**: No
>
> **Main Class File**: You should not be able to change this field because .class appears in the field as grayed-out text.
>
> **Run page**: Leave this field blank.
>
> **Create using**: Source Editor

Enter the source code from Listing 9.4, and then save and compile the file.

TYPE   **Listing 9.4. Source code for the ColorBoxes applet.**

```
 1: import java.awt.Graphics;
 2: import java.awt.Color;
 3:
 4: public class ColorBoxes extends java.applet.Applet {
 5:
 6:     public void paint(Graphics g) {
 7:         int rval, gval, bval;
 8:
 9:         for (int j = 30; j < (size().height -25); j += 30)
10:             for (int i = 5; i < (size().width -25); i += 30) {
```

```
11:                    rval = (int)Math.floor(Math.random() * 256);
12:                    gval = (int)Math.floor(Math.random() * 256);
13:                    bval = (int)Math.floor(Math.random() * 256);
14:
15:                    g.setColor(new Color(rval,gval,bval));
16:                    g.fillRect(i, j, 25, 25);
17:                    g.setColor(Color.black);
18:                    g.drawRect(i-1, j-1, 25, 25);
19:                }
20:            }
21:        }
```

ANALYSIS The two for loops are the heart of this example. The first one draws the rows, and the second draws the individual boxes within the row. When a box is drawn, the random color is calculated first, and then the box is drawn. A black outline is drawn around each box because some colors tend to blend into the background of the applet.

This paint() method generates new colors each time the applet is painted and will generate new ones whenever you move the window around or cover the applet's window with another window. Figure 9.22 shows a sample of the applet's output at a width of 400 and a height of 200, which you can designate using Project Tester if desired. However, the black-and-white figure definitely pales before the actual appearance of this colorful applet.

Figure 9.22.

The output of the ColorBoxes *applet.*

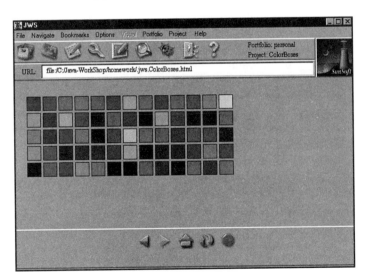

Summary

For the first week, the only thing that you displayed on an applet was text. Today, you learned how to draw lines, rectangles, and ovals by drawing onto a `Graphics` object. You learned the basics of using the `paint()` method—how to draw rudimentary shapes, how to use fonts and font metrics to draw text, and how to use `Color` objects to change the color of what you're drawing.

This foundation is what enables you to do animation inside an applet, because animation basically involves repeated painting to the screen. It also gives you the background to work with images. These are topics you will learn about tomorrow.

Q&A

Q In all the examples you show, and in all the tests I've made, the graphics primitives such as `drawLine()` and `drawRect()` produce lines that are one pixel wide. How can I draw thicker lines?

A At present, you can't draw thicker lines with the `Graphics` class—no methods exist for changing the default line width. If you need a thicker line, you have to draw multiple lines one pixel apart to produce that effect. Some classes have been created by Java programmers in an attempt to rectify the situation. Visit the Gamelan site at `http://www.gamelan.com` and search its public directory of Java applets for classes of this kind.

Q I wrote an applet to use the Helvetica font. It worked fine on my system, but when I run it on my friend's system, everything is in Courier. Why?

A Your friend most likely doesn't have the Helvetica font installed on his or her system. When Java can't find a font, it substitutes a default font instead—in your case, Courier. The best way to deal with this situation is to query the user's font list using the `getFontList()` method in the `java.awt.Toolkit` class to see what fonts are available.

Q I tried out the applet that draws boxes with random colors, but each time it draws, a lot of the boxes are the same color. If the colors truly are random, why is it doing this?

A Two reasons. The first is that the random number generator used in that code (from the `Math` class) isn't a very good random number generator; the documentation for that method says as much. For a better random number generator, use the `Random` class from the `java.util` package.

The second and more likely reason is that there aren't enough colors available in your browser or on your system to draw all the colors that the applet is generating. If your system can't produce the wide range of colors available using the `Color` class, or if the browser has allocated too many colors for other things, you might end up with duplicate colors in the boxes, depending on how the browser and the system have been designed to handle color usage. Usually your applets won't use quite as many colors as `ColorBoxes`, so you won't run into this problem often.

FEATURED APPLET **Today's Featured Applet**

Today's featured applet is an example of combining a background graphic with drawn animation. `Eowyn4` by Alexandre Fenyo draws a shrinking red circle over an image of a square, in the manner of a radar circle shrinking on a monitor. Figure 9.23 shows three side-by-side screen captures of the applet.

Figure 9.23.

The `Eowyn4` *applet in action.*

Files for `Eowyn4` are located on the CD-ROM in the `\BOOK\3RDPARTY\DAY9\` directory, including source code in the file `Eowyn4.java`. To use `Eowyn4` on a Web page, place these two class files on your Web site: `Eowyn4.class` and `Zone.class`. Place the files in the same directory as the Web page, or place them in a subdirectory listed in the `CODEBASE` parameter of the `<APPLET>` tag. The `<CODE>` tag should be `Eowyn4.class`.

Listing 9.5 shows the HTML tags used to run `Eowyn4` as it is shown in Figure 9.23. The line containing the `<IMG>` tag is sent only to users without a Java-capable browser.

Listing 9.5. The `<APPLET>` tag for `Eowyn4`.

```
<APPLET CODE=Eowyn4.class WIDTH=112 HEIGHT=105>
<IMG SRC=masi.gif ALT="" WIDTH=113 HEIGHT=115>
</APPLET>
```

Eowyn4 has no parameters to customize, but the applet loads the background image from two files called javaimg.gif and javaimgA.gif, which both should be located in the same directory as the applet. The HEIGHT and WIDTH attributes should be around the same size as the background image that you store in the two image files. The two images should be identical, or close to it, to produce the effect shown in Figure 9.23.

More information on Eowyn4 is available from its author at the following URL:

http://humanus.ibp.fr

Day 10

Simple Animation and Threads

The first exposure to Java for many people was the sight of animated text or moving images on a Web page. These kinds of animation are simple, requiring only a few methods to implement in Java, but those methods are the basis for any applet that requires dynamic updates to the screen. Starting with simple animation is a good way to build up to more complicated applets.

Today, you'll learn how the various parts of Java work together so that you can create moving figures and dynamically updated applets. You will learn about the following fundamentals:

☐ How Java animations work—the paint() and repaint() methods, starting and stopping dynamic applets, and how to use and override these methods in your own applets

☐ Threads—what they are and how they can make your applets more well-behaved with other applets and with the system in general

☐ How to reduce animation flicker, a common problem with animation in Java

Throughout today, you also will work with lots of examples of real applets that create animations or perform some kind of dynamic movement.

Creating Animation in Java

Animation in Java involves two steps: constructing a frame of animation, and asking Java to paint that frame. These two steps are repeated as necessary to create the illusion of movement. The basic, static applets that you created yesterday taught you how to construct a frame. What's left is to tell Java to paint a frame.

Painting and Repainting

The paint() method, as you learned yesterday, is called by Java whenever the applet needs to be painted. Java calls this method when the applet initially is drawn, when the window containing the applet is moved, or when another window is moved off the top of the applet. You also can ask Java to repaint the applet whenever you want.

To change the appearance of what is on-screen, you construct the image (frame) that you want to paint, and then ask Java to paint the frame. If you do this repeatedly, and do it fast enough, you produce animation inside your Java applet. That's all there is to it.

All these actions don't take place in the paint() method, however. All paint() does is put dots on the screen—in other words, the method is responsible only for the current frame of the animation. The real work of modifying the frame for an animation occurs elsewhere in the definition of an applet. The frame is constructed. Variables are set that paint() will use. Color, Font, and other objects are created. Then, the repaint() method is called. The repaint() method is the trigger that causes Java to call paint(), which causes the frame to be drawn.

NOTE

A Java applet can contain many different components that all need to be painted (as you'll learn later this week). In fact, applets are embedded inside a larger Java application that also paints to the screen in similar ways. When you call repaint(), and therefore paint(), you actually are not immediately drawing to the screen as you would be in other windowing or graphical toolkits. Instead, repaint() in Java is a request to repaint the applet as soon as the larger Java application can repaint it. Also, if too many repaint() requests are made in a short amount of time, the system might only call repaint() once for all of them. Much of the time, the delay between the call to the repaint() method and the actual screen repainting is negligible.

Starting and Stopping an Applet's Execution

As you will recall from Day 8, "Applet Basics," start() and stop() are the methods that trigger an applet to start and stop running. These methods are empty when your applet inherits them from java.applet.Applet, so you have to override them in order to do anything at the start or the conclusion of your program. You didn't use start() and stop() yesterday because the applets on that day only needed to use paint() once. With animation and other Java applets that are processing and running over time, you need to use start() and stop() to trigger the start of your applet's execution and to stop it from running when you leave the page that contains your applet. For many applets, you will want to override start() and stop() for just these reasons.

The start() method triggers the execution of the applet. You can either do all of the applet's work inside that method, or you can call other objects' methods to do the work. Usually, start() is used to create and begin execution of a thread so the applet can run in its own time.

The stop() method, on the other hand, suspends an applet's execution. If you don't use this method, the applet keeps running and using system resources even after a user leaves the page in which the applet is displaying. Most of the time when you create a start() method, you also should create a corresponding stop() .

Putting It Together

Listing 10.1 shows a sample applet that, at first glance, uses basic applet animation to display the date and time and updates it every second, creating a simple animated digital clock. Figure 10.1 shows what a frame of the clock's animation should look like.

Figure 10.1.

Frame of an animated clock applet.

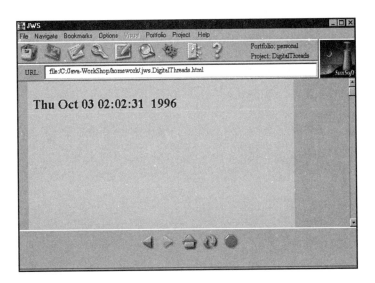

The words "at first glance" in the previous paragraph are important, because the applet shown in Listing 10.1 doesn't work! In spite of this, you can learn a lot about basic animation from the program, so working through the code will be valuable. Afterward, you will learn just what's wrong with it. See whether you can figure out what's going on with this code before moving on to the analysis. You don't need to create the applet at this time.

Listing 10.1. The source code of `DigitalClock.java`.

```
 1: import java.awt.Graphics;
 2: import java.awt.Font;
 3: import java.util.Date;
 4:
 5: public class DigitalClock extends java.applet.Applet {
 6:
 7:     Font theFont = new Font("TimesRoman", Font.BOLD, 24);
 8:     Date theDate;
 9:
10:     public void start() {
11:         while (true) {
12:             theDate = new Date();
13:             repaint();
14:             try { Thread.sleep(1000); }
15:             catch (InterruptedException e) { }
16:         }
17:     }
18:
19:     public void paint(Graphics g) {
20:         g.setFont(theFont);
21:         g.drawString(theDate.toString(), 10, 50);
22:     }
23: }
```

ANALYSIS Lines 7 and 8 define two instance variables, `theFont` and `theDate`, which hold objects representing the current font and the current date, respectively. You will learn about these variables later. The `start()` method triggers the execution of the applet. Note the `while` loop inside this method—`while (true)` always returns `true`, so the loop never exits. A single animation frame is constructed inside the `while` loop by using the following steps:

☐ The `Date` class represents a date and time (`Date` is part of the `java.util` package, which specifically was imported in line 3). Line 12 creates a new instance of the `Date` class, which holds the current date and time and assigns it to the instance variable `theDate`.

☐ Line 13 calls the `repaint()` method.

☐ Lines 14 and 15, as complicated as they look, do nothing except pause for 1000 milliseconds (one second) before the loop repeats. The `sleep()` method, part of the `Thread` class, is what causes the applet to pause. Without a specific `sleep()` method, the applet would run as fast as it possibly could—which, for most computer systems, is much faster than needed. Using sleep() enables you to control exactly how fast the animation takes place. The try and catch statements around the method enable Java to manage errors if they occur. The try and catch keywords handle exceptions, and they are described on Day 17, "Exceptions."

In the paint() method that begins on line 19, two things occur: the current font is set, and the date is displayed on-screen (note that the toString() method is required to convert the date to a string). Because paint() is called repeatedly, the string is updated every second to reflect the current date stored in the theDate object.

There are a few things to note from this example. First, you might think it would be easier to create the new Date object inside the paint() method. That way, to pass the Date object around, a local variable could be used instead of an instance variable. Although this technique creates cleaner code, it also results in a less efficient program. The paint() method is called every time a frame needs to be changed. In this case, this fact is not that important, but in an animation that changes frames quickly, the paint() method has to slow down to create the new object every time. By calculating new objects beforehand and letting paint() just paint the screen, you can make painting as efficient as possible. For this same reason, the Font object also is in an instance variable.

Introduction to Threads

Depending on your experience with operating systems and environments within those systems, you might have encountered the concept of threads. When a program runs, it starts executing, runs its initialization code, calls methods or procedures, and continues running until it is complete or until the program is exited. The program uses a single thread; the *thread* is a single point of control for the program.

Multithreading, implemented in Java, enables several different execution threads to run at the same time inside the same program. These threads run in parallel, without interfering with each other. Suppose you have a long computation near the start of a program's execution. This long computation might not be needed until later in the program's execution. In a single-threaded program, you have to wait for that computation to finish before the rest of the program can continue running. In a multithreaded system, you can put that computation in its own thread, enabling the rest of the program to continue running independently.

Using threads in Java, you can create an applet that runs in its own thread, and it will run all by itself without interfering with any other part of the system. With threads, you can have lots of applets running at once on the same page. Depending on how many are running, you eventually might tax the system and cause all applets to run more slowly, but they still will run independently.

Even if you don't want to run numerous applets at once, using threads in your applets is good Java programming practice. The general rule of thumb for well-behaved applets is this: Whenever you have something processing that is likely to continue for a long time (such as an animation loop, or a bit of code that takes a long time to execute), you should use a thread.

The Problem with `DigitalClock`

The `DigitalClock` applet in the last section does not use threads. Instead, the `while` loop that cycles through the animation is in the `start()` method. As a result, when the applet starts running, it keeps going until the user quits the software that is running the applet.

Although this approach might seem like a good solution to the problem, the clock won't work because the `while` loop in the `start()` method is monopolizing all system resources, including painting. If you compile and run the `DigitalClock` applet, all you get is a blank screen. You also won't be able to stop the applet normally because there's no way to call a `stop()` method.

The solution to this problem is to rewrite the applet so that it uses threads. Threads enable the applet to do the following:

☐ Animate on its own without interfering with other system operations
☐ Start and stop
☐ Run in parallel with other applets

Writing Applets with Threads

How do you create an applet that uses threads? You need to do several things, but none of them is difficult. A lot of the basics of using threads in applets is just boilerplate code that can be copied and pasted from one applet to another. Because it's so easy, there's almost no reason not to use threads in your applets, given the benefits.

There are five modifications you need to make to create an applet that uses threads:

☐ Change the signature of your applet class to include the words `implements Runnable`
☐ Include an instance variable to hold your applet's thread
☐ Modify your `start()` method to do nothing but spawn a thread and start it running
☐ Create a `run()` method that contains the code that starts your applet running
☐ Create a `stop()` method to suspend execution of the thread when a user leaves the page containing the applet

The first change is to the first line of your class definition. The applets that you have created up to this point have a definition like the following:

```
public class EatSandwich extends java.applet.Applet {
    // class code goes here
}
```

To use threads, you change the class definition to the following:

```
public class EatSandwich extends java.applet.Applet  implements Runnable {
    // class code goes here
}
```

This change includes support for the Runnable interface in an applet. If you think way back to Day 2, you'll remember that interfaces are a way to collect method names common to different classes so that the methods can be mixed in and implemented inside different classes that must implement the behavior. The Runnable interface defines the behavior that an applet needs in order to run a thread. In particular, it provides a default definition for the run() method. Runnable makes it possible to call the run() method on instances.

The second step is to add an instance variable to hold an applet's thread. Call it anything you like—it's a variable of the type Thread. Because Thread is a class in java.lang, it does not have to be imported. The following creates a Thread instance variable called runner:

```
Thread runner;
```

Next, add a start() method or modify the existing one so that it does nothing but create a new thread and start it running. Here's a typical example:

```
public void start() {
    if (runner == null) {
        runner = new Thread(this);
        runner.start();
    }
}
```

If you modify start() to do nothing but spawn a thread, where does the body of your applet go? It goes into a new method, run(), which looks like the following:

```
public void run() {
    // what your applet actually does
}
```

The run() method can contain anything that you want to run in the separate thread: initialization code, the loop for the applet, or anything else that needs to run in its own thread. You also can create new objects and call methods from inside run(), and they also will run inside that thread. The run() method is the heart of your applet.

Now that threads have a place to run and a start() method to start them, you should add a stop() method to suspend execution of the thread when a user leaves the page containing the applet. Stopping the thread stops whatever the applet is doing at the time. A stop() method usually is something along these lines:

```
public void stop() {
  if (runner != null) {
     runner.stop();
     runner = null;
  }
}
```

The stop() method here does two things: it stops the thread from executing and also sets the thread's variable runner to null. Setting the variable to null makes the Thread object it previously contained available for garbage collection, which allows the applet to be removed from memory after a certain amount of time. If the user comes back to the page containing a stopped applet, the start() method creates a new thread and starts up the applet once again.

Fixing DigitalClock

Now that you can create threads, you can use one to fix the DigitalClock applet and get some hands-on experience writing threads. First, modify the class definition to include the Runnable interface, and change the name of the class to DigitalThreads:

```
public class DigitalThreads extends java.applet.Applet implements Runnable {
```

Second, add an instance variable for Thread, as follows:

```
Thread runner;
```

For the third step, put the code that was in a method called start() in a method called run(). If you entered the source code for DigitalClock.java, you could make the change simply by replacing start() with run().

Finally, add the boilerplate start() and stop() methods:

```
public void start() {
      if (runner == null); {
          runner = new Thread(this);
          runner.start();
      }
  }

  public void stop() {
      if (runner != null) {
          runner.stop();
          runner = null;
      }
  }
```

To try the new, improved DigitalClock out, use Portfolio Manager to create a new applet with the following fields:

Name: DigitalThreads

Source directory: Enter the full path of your homework directory
(`C:/Java-WorkShop/homework` or something similar).

Existing sources: No

Main Class File: You should not be able to change this field because `.class`
appears in the field as grayed-out text.

Run page: Leave this field blank.

Create using: Source Editor

Use the Source Editor to enter the source code from Listing 10.2, and then save and run the
file. If you enter everything correctly, the applet will look like Figure 10.1.

TYPE   Listing 10.2. The source code for `DigitalThreads.java.`

```
 1: import java.awt.Graphics;
 2: import java.awt.Font;
 3: import java.util.Date;
 4:
 5: public class DigitalThreads extends java.applet.Applet
 6:     implements Runnable {
 7:
 8:     Font theFont = new Font("TimesRoman", Font.BOLD, 24);
 9:     Date theDate;
10:     Thread runner;
11:
12:     public void start() {
13:         if (runner == null); {
14:             runner = new Thread(this);
15:             runner.start();
16:         }
17:     }
18:
19:     public void stop() {
20:         if (runner != null) {
21:             runner.stop();
22:             runner = null;
23:         }
24:     }
25:
26:     public void run() {
27:         while (true) {
28:             theDate = new Date();
29:             repaint();
30:             try { Thread.sleep(1000); }
31:             catch (InterruptedException e) { }
32:         }
33:     }
34:
35:     public void paint(Graphics g) {
```

continues

Listing 10.2. continued

```
36:          g.setFont(theFont);
37:          g.drawString(theDate.toString(),10,50);
38:      }
39: }
```

Reducing Animation Flicker

If you've been following along with this book and trying the examples as you go, rather than reading on an airplane or in the bathtub, you might have noticed that when the DigitalThreads applet runs, there is an occasional annoying flicker in the animation. This flicker isn't a mistake or an error in the program; unfortunately, that flicker is a side effect of creating animation in Java. Because it is annoying, however, this part of today's lesson explains how to reduce flicker, making animation run more cleanly and look better on-screen.

Avoiding Flicker

Flicker is caused by the way Java paints and repaints each frame of an applet. At the beginning of today's lesson, you learned that when you call the repaint() method, repaint() calls paint(). That's not precisely true. A call to paint() does indeed occur in response to a repaint(), but what actually happens are the following steps:

1. The call to repaint() results in a call to the method update().
2. The update() method clears the screen of any existing content (in essence, filling it with the current background color), and then calls paint().
3. The paint() method draws the contents of the current frame.

Step 2, the call to update(), is the cause of animation flicker. Because the screen is cleared between frames, the parts of the screen that do not change between frames alternate rapidly between being painted and being cleared—in other words, they flicker.

There are two major ways to avoid flicker in your Java applets:

☐ Override the update() method so that it either does not clear the screen or only clears the parts of the screen that you've changed.

☐ Override both the update() and paint() methods and use double-buffering.

If the second way sounds complicated, that's because it is. Double-buffering involves drawing to an off-screen graphics surface and then copying that entire surface to the screen. Because it's more complicated, you'll explore that one tomorrow. Today, let's cover the easier solution: overriding update().

How to Override update()

The cause of flicker lies in the update() method. This method is found in the Component class, which you'll learn more about on Day 13, "Visual Java and the Abstract Windowing Toolkit." Here's the default version of update():

```java
public void update(Graphics g) {
    g.setColor(getBackground());
    g.fillRect(0, 0, width, height);
    g.setColor(getForeground());
    paint(g);
}
```

The update() method clears the screen by filling the applet's bounding rectangle with the background color, sets the color back to normal, and then calls paint(). When you override update() with your own version of the method, you have to keep these two things in mind and make sure that your version of update() does something similar. In the next two sections, you'll work through some examples of overriding update() to reduce flicker.

Solution 1: Don't Clear the Screen

The first solution to reducing flicker is not to clear the screen at all. This solution works only for some applets, of course. For example, the ColorSwirl applet displays a single string (Look to the cookie!), but the string is presented in different colors that fade into each other dynamically.

Use Portfolio Manager to create a new applet with the following fields:

Name: ColorSwirl

Source directory: Enter the full path of your homework directory (C:/Java-WorkShop/homework or something similar).

Existing sources: No

Main Class File: You should not be able to change this field because .class appears in the field as grayed-out text.

Run page: Leave this field blank.

Create using: Source Editor

Enter Listing 10.3 into the Source Editor, and then save and run the applet.

TYPE   **Listing 10.3. The source code of** `ColorSwirl.java.`

```
 1: import java.awt.Graphics;
 2: import java.awt.Color;
 3: import java.awt.Font;
 4:
 5: public class ColorSwirl extends java.applet.Applet
 6:     implements Runnable {
 7:
 8:     Font f = new Font("TimesRoman",Font.BOLD,48);
 9:     Color colors[] = new Color[50];
10:     Thread runThread;
11:
12:     public void start() {
13:         if (runThread == null) {
14:             runThread = new Thread(this);
15:             runThread.start();
16:         }
17:     }
18:
19:     public void stop() {
20:         if (runThread != null) {
21:             runThread.stop();
22:             runThread = null;
23:         }
24:     }
25:
26:     public void run() {
27:
28:         // initialize the color array
29:         float c = 0;
30:         for (int i = 0; i < colors.length; i++) {
31:             colors[i] =
32:                 Color.getHSBColor(c, (float)1.0,(float)1.0);
33:             c += .02;
34:         }
35:
36:         // cycle through the colors
37:         int i = 0;
38:         while (true) {
39:             setForeground(colors[i]);
40:             repaint();
41:             i++;
42:             try { Thread.sleep(50); }
43:             catch (InterruptedException e) { }
44:             if (i == colors.length ) i = 0;
45:         }
46:     }
47:
48:     public void paint(Graphics g) {
49:         g.setFont(f);
50:         g.drawString("Look to the cookie!", 15, 50);
51:     }
52: }
```

10

Figure 10.2 shows a screen capture from the ColorSwirl applet. As you will see when you run it, the applet flickers terribly as it cycles through the different colors.

Figure 10.2.

The output of the ColorSwirl applet.

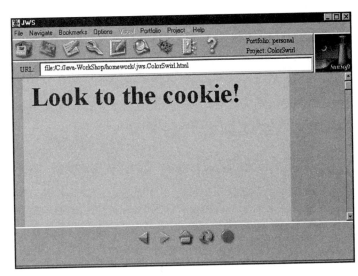

ANALYSIS Three new things about this applet might look strange to you:

☐ When the applet starts, the first thing you do (in lines 28 through 34) is to create an array of Color objects that contains all the colors the text will display. By creating the colors beforehand, you then can draw text in one color at a time; it's easier to precompute all the colors at once.

☐ To create the different colors, a method in the Color class called getHSBColor() creates a Color object based on values for hue, saturation, and brightness, rather than the standard red, green, and blue. By incrementing the hue value and keeping saturation and brightness constant, you can create a range of colors without having to know the RGB value for each color. If you don't understand this code, don't worry about it—it's just an easy way to create the color array.

☐ The applet then cycles through the array of colors, setting the foreground to each one in turn and calling repaint(). When the applet gets to the end of the array, it starts over again (line 44), so the process repeats continuously.

Now that you understand what the applet does, it's time to fix the flicker. The flicker is occurring because each time the applet is painted, there's a moment where the screen is cleared. Instead of the text cycling neatly from red to a nice pink to purple, the text is going from red to gray, to pink to gray, to purple to gray, and so on—not nice-looking at all.

Because the screen clearing is all that's causing the problem, the solution is easy: override `update()` and remove the part where the screen is cleared. It doesn't need to get cleared anyhow because nothing is changing except for the color of the text. With the screen clearing behavior removed from `update()`, all `update()` needs to do is call `paint()`. Here's what the `update()` method should look like in the revised `ColorSwirl` applet:

```
public void update(Graphics g) {
    paint(g);
}
```

Adding these three lines stops the flicker. Change the applet in the Source Editor, compile the applet, and test out this change.

Solution 2: Redraw Only What You Have To

For some applets, the solution to flicker won't be as easy as it was for `ColorSwirl`. In the next example, which is called `Checkers1`, a red checker piece moves from a black square to a white square, as if on a checkerboard. Use Portfolio Manager to create a new applet with the following fields:

> **Name**: Checkers1
>
> **Source directory**: Enter the full path of your homework directory (`C:/Java-WorkShop/homework` or something similar).
>
> **Existing sources**: No
>
> **Main Class File**: You should not be able to change this field because `.class` appears in the field as grayed-out text.
>
> **Run page**: Leave this field blank.
>
> **Create using**: Source Editor

Enter Listing 10.4 into the Source Editor, and then save and compile the applet.

TYPE **Listing 10.4. The source code of** `Checkers1.java.`

```
 1: import java.awt.Graphics;
 2: import java.awt.Color;
 3:
 4:  public class Checkers1 extends java.applet.Applet
 5:      implements Runnable {
 6:
 7:      Thread runner;
 8:      int xpos;
 9:
10:      public void start() {
11:          if (runner == null); {
```

```
12:                runner = new Thread(this);
13:                runner.start();
14:            }
15:        }
16:
17:        public void stop() {
18:            if (runner != null) {
19:                runner.stop();
20:                runner = null;
21:            }
22:        }
23:
24:        public void run() {
25:            setBackground(Color.blue);
26:            while (true) {
27:                for (xpos = 5; xpos <= 105; xpos+=4) {
28:                    repaint();
29:                    try { Thread.sleep(100); }
30:                    catch (InterruptedException e) { }
31:                }
32:                for (xpos = 105; xpos > 5; xpos -=4) {
33:                    repaint();
34:                    try { Thread.sleep(100); }
35:                    catch (InterruptedException e) { }
36:                }
37:            }
38:        }
39:
40:        public void paint(Graphics g) {
41:            // Draw background
42:            g.setColor(Color.black);
43:            g.fillRect(0, 0, 100, 100);
44:            g.setColor(Color.white);
45:            g.fillRect(101, 0, 100, 100);
46:
47:            // Draw checker
48:            g.setColor(Color.red);
49:            g.fillOval(xpos, 5, 90, 90);
50:        }
51: }
```

When you run the Checkers1 applet, the output should resemble Figure 10.3.

ANALYSIS In this applet, an instance variable, xpos, keeps track of the current starting position of the checker (because it moves horizontally, the y stays constant and the x changes). In the run() method, you change the value of x and repaint, waiting 100 milliseconds between each move. The checker moves from one side of the screen to the other and then moves back (hence the two for loops in that method). In the paint() method, the background squares are painted (one black and one white), and then the checker is drawn at its current position.

Figure 10.3.

The Checkers1 *applet.*

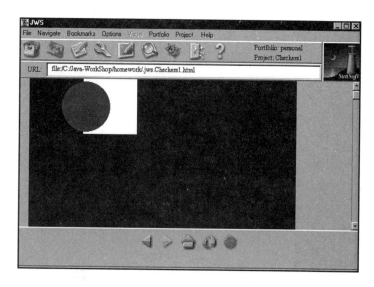

This applet, like the ColorSwirl applet, also has a terrible flicker. (In line 25, the background is set to blue to emphasize it, so if you run this applet, you definitely will see the flicker.) However, the solution to solving the flicker problem for this applet is more difficult than for the last one because you want to clear the screen before the next frame is drawn. Otherwise, the red checker won't have the appearance of leaving one position and moving to another; it just will leave a red smear from one side of the checkerboard to the other.

How do you get around this? You still clear the screen in order to get the animation effect, but you clear only the part that you changed. By limiting the redraw to a small area, you can eliminate much of the flicker that results from redrawing the entire screen. To limit what gets redrawn, you need a few things.

First, you need a way to restrict the drawing area so that each time paint() is called, only the part that needs to get redrawn gets redrawn. Fortunately, this task is easy when you use a mechanism called *clipping*. Clipping, part of the Graphics class, enables you to restrict the drawing area to a small portion of the full screen. Although the entire screen might get instructions to redraw, only the portions inside the clipping area are drawn.

The second thing you need is a way to keep track of the area to redraw. Both the left and right edges of the drawing area change for each frame of the animation (one side to draw the new oval, the other to erase the part of the oval left over from the previous frame). To keep track of those two x values, you need instance variables for both the left side and the right.

With those two concepts in mind, you can start modifying the Checkers1 applet to redraw only what needs to be redrawn. First, add instance variables for the left and right edges of the drawing area. Call those instance variables ux1 and ux2 (u for update), where ux1 is the left side of the area to draw and ux2 the right, as shown in the following code:

```
int ux1,ux2;
```

Now modify the run() method so that it keeps track of the area to be drawn. You would think that step would be easy—just update each side for each iteration of the animation. However, things can get complicated because of the way Java uses paint() and repaint(). The problem with updating the edges of the drawing area with each frame of the animation is that for every call to repaint() there might not be an individual corresponding paint(). If system resources get tight (because of other programs running on the system or for any other reason), paint() might not get executed immediately, and several calls to paint() might queue up waiting for their turn to change the pixels on the screen. In this case, rather than trying to make all those calls to paint() in order (and be potentially behind all the time), Java catches up by executing only the most recent call to paint() and skips all the others.

If you update the edges of the drawing area with each repaint(), and a couple of calls to paint() are skipped, you end up with bits of the drawing surface not being updated and bits of the oval left behind. A simple way around this problem is to update the leading edge of the oval each time the frame updates, but only update the trailing edge if the most recent paint() has occurred. This way, if a couple of calls to paint() get skipped, the drawing area will get larger for each frame, and when paint() finally gets caught up, everything will be repainted correctly. Admittedly, this solution is complex, but without this mechanism, the applet will not get repainted correctly. Go through the following process slowly so that you can get a better grasp of what's going on at each step.

In the run() method, each frame of the animation takes place. In this method, you calculate each side of the drawing area based on the old position of the oval and the new position of the oval. When the oval is moving toward the left side of the screen, this calculation is easy. The value of ux1 (the left side of the drawing area) is the previous oval's x position (xpos), and the value of ux2 is the x position of the current oval plus the width of that oval (90 pixels in this example).

Here's what the old run() method looked like, to refresh your memory:

```
public void run() {
    setBackground(Color.blue);
    while (true) {
        for (xpos = 5; xpos <= 105; xpos+=4) {
            repaint();
            try { Thread.sleep(100); }
            catch (InterruptedException e) { }
        }
        for (xpos = 105; xpos > 5; xpos -=4) {
            repaint();
```

10

```
            try { Thread.sleep(100); }
            catch (InterruptedException e) { }
        }
    }
}
```

In the first `for` loop in the `run()` method, where the oval is moving to the right, you first update ux2 (the right edge of the drawing area):

```
ux2 = xpos + 90;
```

Then after the `repaint()` has occurred, you update ux1 to reflect the old x position of the oval. However, you want to update this value only if the `paint()` method happened. How can you determine this? You can reset ux1 in `paint()` to a given value (0), and then test to see whether you can update that value or whether you have to wait for the `paint()` to occur:

```
if (ux1 == 0) ux1 = xpos;
```

Here's the new, completed `for` loop for when the oval is moving to the right:

```
for (xpos = 5; xpos <= 105; xpos += 4) {
    ux2 = xpos + 90;
    repaint();
    try { Thread.sleep(100); }
    catch (InterruptedException e) { }
    if (ux1 == 0) ux1 = xpos;
}
```

When the oval is moving to the left, everything flips. The left side, ux1, is the leading edge of the oval that gets updated every time, and ux2, the right side, has to wait to make sure it gets updated. So in the second `for` loop, you first update ux1 to be the x position of the current oval:

```
ux1 = xpos;
```

Then after the `repaint()` is called, you test to make sure the `paint()` method happened and update ux2:

```
if (ux2 == 0) ux2 = xpos + 90;
```

Here's the new version of the second `for` loop inside `run()`:

```
for (xpos = 105; xpos > 5; xpos -= 4) {
    ux1 = xpos;
    repaint();
    try { Thread.sleep(100); }
    catch (InterruptedException e) { }
    if (ux2 == 0) ux2 = xpos + 90;
}
```

Those are the only modifications that run() needs. The next task is to override update() to limit the region being painted to the left and right edges of the drawing area that were set inside run(). To clip the drawing area to a specific rectangle, use the clipRect() method. The clipRect() method, like drawRect(), fillRect(), and clearRect(), is defined for Graphics objects, and it takes four arguments: x and y starting positions and the width and height of the region. ux1 is the x point of the top corner of the region, and ux2 - ux1 produces the width of the region. Finally, to finish update(), you call paint(), as follows:

```
public void update(Graphics g) {
        g.clipRect(ux1, 5, ux2 - ux1, 95);
        paint(g);
    }
```

Note that with the clipping region in place, you don't have to do anything to the paint() method. The paint() method goes ahead and draws to the entire screen each time, but only the areas inside the clipping region get changed.

Finally, you need to update the trailing edge of each drawing area inside paint() in case several calls to paint() were skipped. Because you are testing for a value of 0 inside run(), you merely reset ux1 and ux2 to 0 after drawing everything:

```
ux1 = ux2 = 0;
```

Once you make these changes, this applet will draw only the parts of the applet that have changed and will manage the case where some frames don't get updated immediately. Although this solution does not eliminate all flicker in the animation, it reduces it a great deal. Make the changes to the Checkers1 applet so that it matches Listing 10.5.

TYPE   **Listing 10.5. The revised source code of** Checkers1.java.

```
 1: import java.awt.Graphics;
 2: import java.awt.Color;
 3:
 4: public class Checkers1 extends java.applet.Applet implements Runnable {
 5:
 6:     Thread runner;
 7:      int xpos;
 8:      int ux1,ux2;
 9:
10:     public void start() {
11:         if (runner == null); {
12:             runner = new Thread(this);
13:             runner.start();
14:         }
15:     }
16:
17:     public void stop() {
```

continues

Listing 10.5. continued

```
18:            if (runner != null) {
19:                runner.stop();
20:                runner = null;
21:            }
22:        }
23:
24:        public void run() {
25:            setBackground(Color.blue);
26:            while (true) {
27:                for (xpos = 5; xpos <= 105; xpos += 4) {
28:                    ux2 = xpos + 90;
29:                    repaint();
30:                    try { Thread.sleep(100); }
31:                    catch (InterruptedException e) { }
32:                    if (ux1 == 0) ux1 = xpos;
33:                }
34:                for (xpos = 105; xpos >= 5; xpos -= 4) {
35:                    ux1 = xpos;
36:                    repaint();
37:                    try { Thread.sleep(100); }
38:                    catch (InterruptedException e) { }
39:                    if (ux2 == 0) ux2 = xpos + 90;
40:                }
41:            }
42:        }
43:
44:        public void update(Graphics g) {
45:            g.clipRect(ux1, 5, ux2 - ux1, 95);
46:            paint(g);
47:        }
48:
49:        public void paint(Graphics g) {
50:            // Draw background
51:            g.setColor(Color.black);
52:            g.fillRect(0, 0, 100, 100);
53:            g.setColor(Color.white);
54:            g.fillRect(101, 0, 100, 100);
55:
56:            // Draw checker
57:            g.setColor(Color.red);
58:            g.fillOval(xpos, 5, 90, 90);
59:
60:            // reset the drawing area
61:            ux1 = ux2 = 0;
62:        }
63: }
```

Summary

Congratulations on getting through Day 10! This day was a bit rough; you've learned a lot, and it all might seem overwhelming. You learned about a plethora of methods to use and override: `start()`, `stop()`, `paint()`, `repaint()`, `run()`, and `update()`. You also received a solid foundation in the creation and use of threads.

After today, you're over the worst hurdles in terms of understanding animation. Other than handling bitmap images, which you'll learn about tomorrow, you now have the background to create just about any animation you want in Java.

Q&A

Q **Why all the indirection with `paint()` and `repaint()` and `update()` and all that? Why not have a simple `paint()` method that just puts stuff on the screen when you want it there?**

A The windowing implementations available through Java WorkShop, the Abstract Windowing Toolkit, and Visual Java enable you to nest drawable surfaces within other drawable surfaces. When a `paint()` takes place, all parts of the system are redrawn, starting from the outermost surface and moving downward into the most nested one. Because the drawing of your applet takes place at the same time everything else is drawn, your applet doesn't get any special treatment. Your applet will be painted when everything else is painted. Although with this system you sacrifice some of the immediacy of instant painting, it enables your applet to coexist with the rest of the system more cleanly.

Q **Are Java threads like threads on other systems?**

A The implementation of threads in Java was influenced by other multithreading systems, and if you're used to working with threads, many of the concepts in Java threading will be familiar to you. You'll learn more next week on Day 18, "Multithreading."

Q **When an applet uses threads, I just have to tell the thread to start and it starts, and tell it to stop and it stops? That's it? I don't have to test anything in my loops or keep track of its state? It just stops?**

A It just stops. When you put your applet into a thread, Java can control the execution of your applet much more readily. By causing the thread to stop, your applet just stops running, and then resumes when the thread starts up again. It's all automatic.

10

Q The `ColorSwirl` applet seems to display only five or six colors. What's going on here?

A This is the same problem that you might have encountered yesterday where there might not be enough colors on your system to display all of the ones used by `ColorSwirl`. If you're running into this problem, you could upgrade your hardware, or you might try quitting other applications running on your system. Other browsers, or image editing tools, might be hogging colors that Java wants to use.

Q Even with the changes that were made, the `Checkers1` applet still flickers. Why?

A Reducing the size of the drawing area by using clipping significantly reduces the flicker, but it doesn't stop it entirely. For many applets, using either of the methods described today might be enough to reduce animation flicker to the point where your applet looks good. To get totally flicker-free animation, you'll need to use a technique called double-buffering, which you'll learn about tomorrow.

 Today's Featured Applet

Today's featured applet is `Fan` from Leon Cho, a class that causes text to start at the center and fan out to the left and right. Figure 10.4 shows three successive screen captures of the applet.

Figure 10.4.
The Fan *applet in action.*

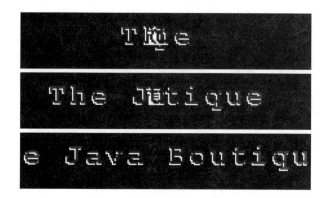

Files for `Fan` are located on the CD-ROM in the `\BOOK\3RDPARTY\DAY10\` directory, including source code in the file `Fan.java`. To use `Fan` on a Web page, place the `Fan.class` class file on your Web site. Place the file in the same directory as the Web page or place it in a subdirectory listed in the `CODEBASE` parameter of the `<APPLET>` tag. The `<CODE>` tag should be `Fan.class`.

Listing 10.7 shows the HTML tags used to run `Fan` as it was shown in Figure 10.4.

Listing 10.7. The `<APPLET>` tag for Fan.

```
<applet code=Fan.class width=350 height=30>
<param name=TEXT VALUE="The Java Boutique">
<param name=SPEED VALUE="4">
<param name=SPACING VALUE="4">
<param name=VSPACING VALUE="20">
<param name=FONT VALUE="Courier">
<param name=FONTSIZE VALUE="22">
</applet>
```

Fan has six parameters that can be customized within the `<APPLET>` tag, as follows:

☐ The text parameter is the text string to display.

☐ The speed parameter specifies the distance to move the text, in pixels (4 is the default).

☐ The spacing parameter is a factor that determines the amount of space to allocate for each character in the text (4 is the default).

☐ The vspacing parameter specifies the amount of space, in pixels, to put between the top of the applet and the text (20 is the default). The spacing parameter is multiplied with the speed parameter to determine the space allocated for each character.

☐ The font parameter is the font to use for the text, which is recommended to be a fixed-width font for best effect (Courier is the default).

☐ The fontsize parameter specifies the size of the text (22 is the default).

More information on Fan is available from its author at the following URL:

http://homepage.interramp.com/cd004397/textfan.html

10

Day 11

More Animation,
Images, and Sound

Animations are fun and easy to do in Java, but there's only so much you can do with the built-in Java methods for drawing lines, fonts, and colors. For really interesting animations, you have to provide your own images for each frame of the animation; having sounds is nice, as well. Today, you'll do more with animations, incorporating images and sounds into Java applets.

Specifically, you'll explore the following topics:

- [ ] Using images—getting them from the server, loading them into Java, and displaying them in your applet
- [ ] Creating animations by using images, including an extensive example
- [ ] Using sounds—getting them and playing them at the appropriate times
- [ ] Sun's Animator applet—an easy way to organize animations and sounds in Java
- [ ] Double-buffering—hard-core flicker avoidance

Retrieving and Using Images

Basic image handling in Java is easy. The Image class in java.awt provides abstract methods to represent common image behavior, and special methods defined in Applet and Graphics give you everything you need to load and display images in your applet. In this section, you'll learn how to get and draw images in your Java applets.

Getting Images

To display an image in your applet, you first must load that image into your Java program. Images are stored as separate files from your Java class files, so you have to tell Java where to find the images.

The Applet class method getImage() loads an image and automatically creates an instance of the Image class for you. To use this method, all you have to do is import the java.awt.Image class, and then give getImage() the URL of the image you want to load. There are two ways of doing the latter step:

☐ Use the getImage() method with a single argument (an object of type URL) to retrieve the image at that URL

☐ Use the getImage() method with two arguments: the base URL (also a URL object) and a string representing the path or file name of the actual image (relative to the base)

Although the first way might seem easier (just plug in the URL as a URL object), the second is more flexible. Remember, because you're compiling Java files, if you include a hard-coded URL of an image and then move your files around to a different location, you have to recompile all your Java files.

The second way, therefore, is usually the one to use. The Applet class also provides two methods that will help with the base URL argument to getImage():

☐ The getDocumentBase() method returns a URL object representing the directory of the HTML file that contains this applet. For example, if the HTML file is located at http://www.sylvester.com/htmlfiles/javahtml/, the getDocumentBase() method returns a URL pointing to that path.

☐ The getCodeBase() method returns a string representing the directory in which this applet is contained—which might or might not be the same directory as the HTML file, depending on whether the CODEBASE attribute in APPLET is set.

Whether you use getDocumentBase() or getCodeBase() depends on whether your images are relative to your HTML files or relative to your Java class files. Use whichever one applies better to your situation. Note that either of these methods is more flexible than hard-coding

11

a URL or path name into the `getImage()` method; using either `getDocumentBase()` or `getCodeBase()` enables you to move your HTML files and applets around and have Java still be able to find your images.

The following examples of `getImage()` should give you an idea of how to use it. This first call to `getImage()` retrieves the file at that specific URL (`"http://www.sylvester.com/files/tweety.gif"`). If any part of that URL changes, you have to recompile your Java applet to take the new path into account:

```
Image img = getImage(
    new URL("http://www.sylvester.com/files/tweety.gif"));
```

In the following form of `getImage()`, the `tweety.gif` file is in the same directory as the HTML files that refer to this applet:

```
Image img = getImage(getDocumentBase(), "tweety.gif")
```

In this similar form, the file `tweety.gif` is in the same directory as the applet itself:

```
Image img = getImage(getCodeBase(), "tweety.gif")
```

If you have lots of image files, it's common to put them into their own subdirectory. This form of `getImage()` looks for the file `tweety.gif` in the subdirectory `images`, which, in turn, is in the same directory as the Java applet:

```
Image img = getImage(getCodeBase(), "images/tweety.gif")
```

If `getImage()` can't find the file indicated, it returns `null`. A `drawImage()` method on a `null` image will draw nothing. Using a `null` image in other ways will probably cause an error.

NOTE

> Currently, Java supports images in the GIF and JPEG formats. Other image formats might be available later, but for now, your images should be in either GIF or JPEG format.

Drawing Images

All that stuff with `getImage()` does nothing except go off and retrieve an image and stuff it into an instance of the `Image` class. Now that you have an image, you have to do something with it. The most likely thing you're going to want to do is display it as you would a rectangle or a text string. The `Graphics` class provides two methods to do just this, and both are calls to `drawImage()`.

The first version of drawImage() takes four arguments: the image to display, the x and y positions of the top left corner, and this, as shown in the following:

```
public void paint() {
    g.drawImage(img, 10, 10, this);
}
```

This first form draws the image in its original dimensions with the top left corner at the given x and y positions.

Your first exercise today is a program that uses drawImage() to display a GIF file. Use Portfolio Manager to create a new applet with the following fields:

Name: DrawDrink

Source directory: Enter the full path of your homework directory (C:/Java-WorkShop/homework or something similar).

Existing sources: No

Main Class File: You should not be able to change this field because .class appears in the field as grayed-out text.

Run page: Leave this field blank.

Create using: Source Editor

Enter Listing 11.1 into the Source Editor, and then save and compile the applet. This simple applet loads in an image called HotDrink.gif and displays it.

TYPE **Listing 11.1. The source code of DrawDrink.java.**

```
 1: import java.awt.Graphics;
 2: import java.awt.Image;
 3:
 4: public class DrawDrink extends java.applet.Applet {
 5:
 6:     Image img;
 7:
 8:     public void init() {
 9:     img = getImage(getCodeBase(),
10:         "images/HotDrink.gif");
11:     }
12:
13:     public void paint(Graphics g) {
14:         g.drawImage(img, 10, 10, this);
15:     }
16: }
```

Before you can run the program, you need to put the HotDrink.gif file in a subdirectory called images. The subdirectory should be located in the same directory as the DrawDrink applet (in many cases, this directory will be something like C:\Java-WorkShop\homework\images).

The image file `HotDrink.gif` and the other image and sound files used in today's lesson are on the CD-ROM along with the Day 11 source code files. If for some reason you can't use this image, you can substitute any GIF file that's no larger than 5 by 5 inches. The size limitation is only required so that the image can be seen fully within the boundaries of the applet.

When you run the applet, the output should resemble Figure 11.1.

Figure 11.1.

The output of the `DrawDrink` *applet.*

In this example, the instance variable `img` holds the `HotDrink.gif` image, which is loaded in the `init()` method. The `paint()` method then draws that image on the screen.

The second form of `drawImage()` takes six arguments: the image to draw, the x and y coordinates, a width and height of the image bounding box, and `this`. If the width and height arguments for the bounding box are smaller or larger than the image, the image automatically is scaled to fit. Using those extra arguments enables you to squeeze and expand images into whatever space you need them to fit in (keep in mind, however, that there might be some image degradation from scaling an image smaller or larger than its intended size).

One helpful hint for scaling images is to find out the size of the image that you've loaded, so you then can scale it to a specific percentage and avoid distortion in either direction. Two methods defined for the `Image` class enable you do this: `getWidth()` and `getHeight()`. Both take a single argument, an instance of `ImageObserver`, which is used to track the loading of the image (more about this argument later). Most of the time, you can use `this` as an argument to either `getWidth()` or `getHeight()`.

If you stored the `HotDrink.gif` image in a variable called `img`, for example, this line returns the width of that image, in pixels:

```
theWidth = img.getWidth(this);
```

To practice scaling images, use Portfolio Manager to create a new applet with the following fields:

Name: DrawDrink2

Source directory: Enter the full path of your homework directory (C:/Java-WorkShop/homework or something similar).

Existing sources: No

Main Class File: You should not be able to change this field because .class appears in the field as grayed-out text.

Run page: Leave this field blank.

Create using: Source Editor

Enter Listing 11.2 into the Source Editor, and then save and compile the applet. This program draws the HotDrink.gif image at several different sizes.

TYPE **Listing 11.2. The source code of DrawDrink2.java.**

```
1: import java.awt.Graphics;
2: import java.awt.Image;
3:
4: public class DrawDrink2 extends java.applet.Applet {
5:
6:     Image img;
7:
8:     public void init() {
9:         img = getImage(getCodeBase(),
10:         "images/HotDrink.gif");
11:     }
12:
13:     public void paint(Graphics g) {
14:         int iwidth = img.getWidth(this);
15:         int iheight = img.getHeight(this);
16:         int xpos = 10;
17:
18:         // 25 percent
19:         g.drawImage(img, xpos, 10,
20:         iwidth / 4, iheight / 4, this);
21:
22:         // 50 percent
23:         xpos += (iwidth / 4) + 10;
24:         g.drawImage(img, xpos , 10,
25:         iwidth / 2, iheight / 2, this);
26:
27:         // 100 percent
28:         xpos += (iwidth / 2) + 10;
29:         g.drawImage(img, xpos, 10, this);
30:
```

11

```
31:            // 150 percent x, 25 percent y
32:            g.drawImage(img, 10, iheight + 30,
33:              (int)(iwidth * 1.5), iheight / 4, this);
34:     }
35: }
```

When you run the program, the output should resemble Figure 11.2.

Figure 11.2.

The output of the
DrawDrink2 *applet.*

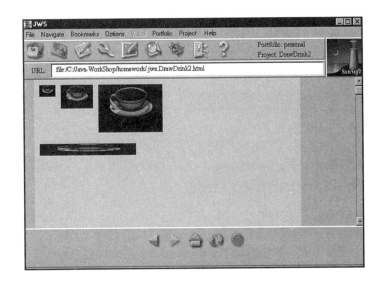

At this point, you probably are wondering about that last argument to drawImage(): the mysterious this, which also appears as an argument to getWidth() and getHeight(). Why is this argument used? Its official use is to pass in an object that functions as an ImageObserver (that is, an object that implements the ImageObserver interface). Image observers enable you to watch the progress of how far along an image is in the loading process and to make decisions when the image is either fully or partially loaded. The Applet class, which your applet inherits from, contains default behavior for watching for images that should work in the majority of cases—hence, the this argument to drawImage(), getWidth(), and getHeight(). The only reason you'll want to use a different argument is if you are tracking lots of images loading asynchronously. See the Java API Documentation on the java.awt.image.ImageObserver class for more details.

Modifying Images

In addition to the image-handling basics described in this section, the java.awt.image package provides more classes and interfaces that enable you to modify images and their internal colors or to create bitmap images by hand. Most of these classes require background knowledge in image processing, including a good grasp of color models and bitwise operations. All these things are outside the scope of an introductory book on Java, but if you have this background (or you're interested in trying out these features), the classes in java.awt.image will be helpful to you. For examples of image creation and manipulation, you can use the source code of the applets on the JavaSoft Web site at http://java.sun.com. Also, several of the programs chosen as Today's Featured Applet use graphics in inventive ways.

Creating Animation Using Images

Creating animations by using images is much the same as creating images by using fonts, colors, or shapes; you use the same methods and the same procedures for painting, repainting, and reducing flicker that you learned about yesterday. The only difference is that you have a stack of images to flip through rather than a set of painting methods. Probably the best way to show you how to use images for animation is to walk through an example. The following sections develop an extensive example of an animation of a small penguin called Pixel Pete.

An Example: Pete

Pixel Pete is the starring character in the Iceblox videogame applet created by Karl Hörnell. Iceblox is the featured applet on Day 15, "Modifiers," but you get a chance to meet Pete today. In addition to being an extremely inventive programmer, Hörnell is a talented cartoonist, and he created a variety of images for Pixel Pete's movement in the game. The penguin can walk, raise his wings up and down, face the user, and blink.

For this example, you'll implement a small animation based on the original Pixel Pete graphics. This applet causes Pete to run in from the left side of the screen, stop in the middle, blink several times, wave his wings, and then run off to the right. The movements are repeated until you quit running the program.

NOTE

This is the largest applet discussed in this book, so only the new material is discussed in detail. The basics regarding threads, the run() method, and the like were covered yesterday. All the code is printed later today so that you can put it all together.

Before you begin writing Java code to construct an animation, you should have all the images that form the animation itself. The Pete applet has six images, as shown in Figure 11.3.

Figure 11.3.

The images for the `Pete` *applet.*

You should store these images in a subdirectory of your homework directory called images. You can store them elsewhere if desired, as long as you take note of where you've put them, because you'll need that information.

The basic idea of creating animation by using images is that you rapidly display a set of images one at a time so they give the appearance of movement. The easiest way to manage this process in Java is to store the images in an array of class Image, and then to have a special variable that stores a reference to the current image.

For the Pete applet, you include instance variables to implement both these things: an array to hold the images called petepics and a variable of type Image to hold the current image:

```
Image petepics[] = new Image[9];
Image currentimg;
```

Because you'll need to pass the position of the current image around between the methods in this applet, you also need to keep track of the current x and y positions. The y stays constant for this particular applet, but the x might vary. Two instance variables are added for those two positions:

```
int xpos;
int ypos = 50;
```

During the applet's initialization, you read in all the images and store them in the petepics array. This sort of operation works especially well in an init() method.

Given that you have six images with six different file names, you could do a separate call to getImage() for each one. You can save some typing, however, by creating an array of the file names (petesrc, an array of strings) and then just using a for loop to iterate over each one. This init() method for the Pete applet loads all the images into the petepics array:

```
public void init() {

    String petesrc[] = { "right1.gif", "right2.gif",
            "right3.gif", "stop.gif", "blink.gif",
            "wave.gif" };

    for (int i=0; i < petepics.length; i++) {
        petepics[i] = getImage(getCodeBase(),
            "images/" + petesrc[i]);
    }
}
```

Note here in the call to getImage() that the directory these images are stored in is included as part of the path. If your directory is not images, you need to make a change at this point in the code when you enter the program into the Source Editor later.

With the images loaded, the next step is to start animating the bits of the applet. You do this inside the applet's thread's run() method. In this applet, Pete does four things:

☐ Runs in from the left side of the screen

☐ Stops in the middle and blinks three times

☐ Waves his wings four times

☐ Runs off the right side of the screen

Because you could animate this applet by merely painting the right image to the screen at the right time, it makes sense to write this applet so that many of Pete's activities are contained in individual methods. This way, you can reuse some of the activities (the animation of Pete running, in particular) if you want Pete to do things in a different order.

The first step is to create a method to make Pete run. Because you're going to be using this method twice, making it generic is a good plan. You create the peterun() method, which takes two arguments: the x position to start, and the x position to end. Pete then runs between those two positions (the y remains constant).

Three images represent Pete running, so to create the running effect, you need to alternate between those three images (stored in positions 0, 1, and 2 of the image array) and move them across the screen. The moving part is a simple for loop between the start and end arguments, setting the x position to the current loop value. To swap the images, you use the showpic method variable. This variable is initialized with the value 0 and is incremented by 1 during each iteration of the for loop. When showpic is greater than 2, it is set to 0 again.

After each new frame is drawn, you'll call repaint() and sleep() for a bit. Because this applet does a lot of sleeping for various intervals, it makes sense to create a method that does the sleeping for the appropriate time interval. Call this method pause, and define it as follows:

```
void pause(int time) {
    try { Thread.sleep(time); }
    catch (InterruptedException e) { }
}
```

The peterun() method iterates from the start position to the end position. For each turn of the loop, it sets the current x position, sets currentimg to the right animation frame, calls repaint(), and pauses. The following is the definition of peterun():

```
void peterun(int start, int end) {
    int showpic = 0;
    for (int i = start; i < end; i+=10) {
        xpos = i;
        // swap images
        currentimg = petepics[showpic];
        repaint();
        pause(150);
        showpic++;
        if (showpic > 2)
```

```
                showpic = 0;
        }
}
```

Note that in that for line you increment the loop by 10 pixels. Why 10 pixels, and not, say, five or eight? The answer is determined mostly through trial and error to see what looks right. Ten seems to work best for the animation. When you write your own animations, you have to play with both the distances and the sleep times until you get an animation you like.

The paint() method, which paints each frame, is just responsible for painting the current image at the current x and y positions. All that information is stored in instance variables, so the paint() method has only a single line in it:

```
public void paint(Graphics g) {
    g.drawImage(currentimg, xpos, ypos, this);
}
```

Now back up to the run() method, where the main processing of this animation is happening. You've created the peterun() method, and in run(), you'll call that method with the appropriate values to make Pete run from the left edge of the screen to the center:

```
// run from one side of the screen to the middle
peterun(0, size().width / 2);
```

The second major thing Pete does in this animation is stop and pause. You have a single frame for this action, so you don't need a separate method for it. All you need to do is set the appropriate image, call repaint(), and pause for the right amount of time. This example pauses for a second after Pete stops walking, an interval chosen through trial and error:

```
// stop and pause
currentimg = petepics[3];
repaint();
pause(1000);
```

The third part of the animation is the blinking. There's no horizontal movement for this part of the animation. You alternate between the eyes-open and eyes-closed images (stored in positions 3 and 4 of the image array). Because blinking is a distinct action, you create a separate method for it.

The peteblink() method takes a single argument: the number of times to blink. With that argument, you can iterate and then, inside the loop, alternate between the two blinking images and repaint each time:

```
void peteblink(int numtimes) {
    for (int i = numtimes; i > 0; i--) {
        currentimg = petepics[4];
        repaint();
        pause(50);
        currentimg = petepics[3];
        repaint();
        pause(250);
    }
}
```

Inside the run method, you can then call peteblink() with an argument of (3):

```
// blink three times
peteblink(3);
```

After blinking, Pete waves. Again, you have two images for waving, one the standing-still, eyes-open pose from position 3 in the array and the other in position 5. These two images are alternated a certain number of times. The following is the petewave() method, which takes a single number argument and animates for that many turns:

```
void petewave(int numtimes) {
    for (int i = numtimes; i > 0; i--) {
        currentimg = petepics[3];
        repaint();
        pause(150);
        currentimg = petepics[5];
        repaint();
        pause(150);
    }
}
```

Call petewave() in the run() method like this:

```
// wave four times
petewave(4);
```

Finally, to finish off the applet, Pete runs off to the right side of the screen. You can reuse the peterun() method to do this action:

```
// wake up and run off
pause(500);
peterun(xpos, size().width + 10);
pause(1500);
```

There's one more thing left to do to finish the applet. The images for the animation all have black backgrounds. Drawing those images on the default applet background (a medium gray) means an unsightly black box around each image. To get around the problem, set the applet's background to black at the start of the run() method:

```
setBackground(Color.black);
```

Got all that? There's a lot of code in this applet and a lot of individual methods to accomplish a rather simple animation, but it's not all that complicated. The heart of it, as in the heart of all Java animations, is to set up the frame and then call repaint() to enable the screen to be drawn.

Note that you don't do anything to reduce the amount of flicker in this applet. It turns out that the images are small enough, and the drawing area also small enough, that flicker is not a problem for this applet. It's always a good idea to write your animations to do the simplest thing first, and then add behavior to make them run cleaner.

You now can enter the entire code for the Pete applet and see it in action. Using Portfolio Manager, create a new applet with the following fields:

Name: Pete

Source directory: Enter the full path of your homework directory
(C:/Java-WorkShop/homework or something similar).

Existing sources: No

Main Class File: You should not be able to change this field because .class
appears in the field as grayed-out text.

Run page: Leave this field blank.

Create using: Source Editor

Enter Listing 11.3 into the Source Editor, and then save and compile the applet.

TYPE | **Listing 11.3. The final** Pete **applet.**

```
 1: import java.awt.Graphics;
 2: import java.awt.Image;
 3: import java.awt.Color;
 4:
 5: public class Pete extends java.applet.Applet
 6:     implements Runnable {
 7:
 8:     Image petepics[] = new Image[6];
 9:     Image currentimg;
10:     Thread runner;
11:     int xpos;
12:     int ypos = 50;
13:
14:     public void init() {
15:         String petesrc[] = { "right1.gif", "right2.gif",
16:             "right3", "stop.gif", "blink.gif",
17:             "wave.gif" };
18:
19:         for (int i=0; i < petepics.length; i++) {
20:             petepics[i] = getImage(getCodeBase(),
21:             "images/" + petesrc[i]);
22:         }
23:     }
24:     public void start() {
25:         if (runner == null) {
26:             runner = new Thread(this);
27:             runner.start();
28:         }
29:     }
30:
31:     public void stop() {
32:         if (runner != null) {
33:             runner.stop();
34:             runner = null;
35:         }
```

continues

Listing 11.3. continued

```
36:      }
37:
38:      public void run() {
39:
40:          while (true) {
41:              setBackground(Color.black);
42:
43:              // run from one side of the screen to the middle
44:              peterun(0, size().width / 2);
45:
46:              // stop and pause
47:              currentimg = petepics[3];
48:              repaint();
49:              pause(1000);
50:
51:              // blink three times
52:              peteblink(3);
53:
54:              // wave four times
55:              petewave(4);
56:
57:              // pause and then run off
58:              pause(500);
59:              peterun(xpos, size().width + 10);
60:              pause(1500);
61:          }
62:      }
63:
64:      void peterun(int start, int end) {
65:          int showpic = 0;
66:          for (int i = start; i < end; i += 10) {
67:              xpos = i;
68:              // swap images
69:              currentimg = petepics[showpic];
70:              repaint();
71:              pause(150);
72:              showpic++;
73:              if (showpic > 2)
74:                  showpic = 0;
75:          }
76:      }
77:      void peteblink(int numtimes) {
78:          for (int i = numtimes; i > 0; i--) {
79:              currentimg = petepics[4];
80:              repaint();
81:              pause(50);
82:              currentimg = petepics[3];
83:              repaint();
84:              pause(250);
85:          }
86:      }
87:
88:      void petewave(int numtimes) {
89:          for (int i = numtimes; i > 0; i--) {
```

```
 90:                 currentimg = petepics[3];
 91:                 repaint();
 92:                 pause(150);
 93:                 currentimg = petepics[5];
 94:                 repaint();
 95:                 pause(150);
 96:             }
 97:     }
 98:
 99:     void pause(int time) {
100:         try { Thread.sleep(time); }
101:         catch (InterruptedException e) { }
102:     }
103:
104:     public void paint(Graphics g) {
105:         g.drawImage(currentimg, xpos, ypos, this);
106:     }
107: }
```

Run the applet, and you'll see output resembling Figure 11.4.

Figure 11.4.

The output of the Pete *applet.*

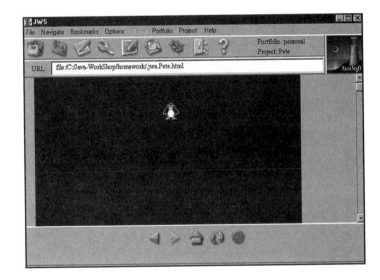

NOTE

A version of Iceblox is included on the CD-ROM, as described during Day 15's Featured Applet section. To see other applets written by Karl Hörnell, visit his Web site at the following URL:

http://www.tdb.uu.se/~karl

Hörnell makes a lot of source code available for the benefit of other Java programmers, so it's a site well-worth checking out.

Retrieving and Using Sounds

Java has built-in support for playing sounds in conjunction with running animations or for playing sounds on their own. Support for sound, like support for images, is built into the Applet and awt classes, so using sound in your Java applets is as easy as loading and using images.

Currently, the only sound format that Java supports is Sun's AU format, sometimes called mu-law format. AU files tend to be smaller than sound files in other formats, but the sound quality is not very good. If you're especially concerned with sound quality, you might want your sound clips to be references in the traditional HTML way (as links to external files) rather than being included in a Java applet.

The simplest way to retrieve and play a sound is through the play() method, which is part of the Applet class and therefore available to you in your applets. The play() method is similar to the getImage() method in that it takes one of two forms:

☐ play() with one argument, a URL object, loads and plays the given audio clip at that URL.

☐ play() with two arguments, one a base URL and one a path name, loads and plays that audio file. The first argument can be a call to getDocumentBase() or getCodeBase().

For example, the following line of code retrieves and plays the sound sound.au, which is contained in the audio subdirectory. The audio subdirectory, in turn, is located in the same directory as this applet:

```
play(getCodeBase(), "audio/sound.au");
```

The play() method retrieves and plays the given sound as soon as possible after it is called. If it can't find the sound, you won't get an error; you just won't get any audio when you expect it.

If you want to play a sound repeatedly by starting and stopping the sound clip or running the clip as a loop (playing it over and over), things are slightly more complicated—but not much more so. In this case, you use the applet method getAudioClip() to load the sound clip into an instance of the class AudioClip (part of java.applet—don't forget to import it) and then operate directly on that AudioClip object.

Suppose that you have a sound loop that you want to play in the background of your applet. In your initialization code, you can use this line to get the audio clip:

```
AudioClip clip = getAudioClip(getCodeBase(),
    "audio/worldmusic.au");
```

11

Then, to play the clip once, use the play() method:

```
clip.play();
```

To stop a currently playing sound clip, use the stop() method:

```
clip.stop();
```

To loop the clip (play it repeatedly), use the loop() method:

```
clip.loop();
```

If the getAudioClip() method can't find the sound you indicate, or can't load it for any reason, it returns null. It's a good idea to test for this case in your code before trying to play the audio clip, because trying to call the play(), stop(), and loop() methods on a null object will result in an error (actually, an exception).

In your applet, you can play as many audio clips as you need; all the sounds you use will mix together properly as they are played by your applet. Note that if you use a background sound, which is a sound clip that loops repeatedly, that sound clip will not stop playing automatically when you suspend the applet's thread. Even if your reader moves to another page, the first applet's sounds will continue to play. You can fix this problem by stopping the applet's background sound in the stop() method:

```
public void stop() {
    if (runner != null) {
        if (bgsound != null)
            bgsound.stop();
        runner.stop();
        runner = null;
    }
}
```

The next applet you create illustrates how sounds are played in Java. Create a new applet with the following fields:

Name: AudioLoop

Source directory: Enter the full path of your homework directory (C:/Java-WorkShop/homework or something similar).

Existing sources: No

Main Class File: You should not be able to change this field because .class appears in the field as grayed-out text.

Run page: Leave this field blank.

Create using: Source Editor

Enter Listing 11.4, and then save and compile the applet. The program is a simple one that plays two sound files located in a audio subdirectory: worldmusic.au and sound.au. The first is a background sound that plays repeatedly. The second is played every five seconds, and it sounds like one of the Mario Brothers landing on a springboard or Cupid firing an arrow.

TYPE **Listing 11.4. The source code of** AudioLoop.java.

```
 1: import java.awt.Graphics;
 2: import java.applet.AudioClip;
 3:
 4: public class AudioLoop extends java.applet.Applet
 5:     implements Runnable {
 6:
 7:     AudioClip bgsound;
 8:             AudioClip sound;
 9:     Thread runner;
10:
11:     public void start() {
12:         if (runner == null) {
13:             runner = new Thread(this);
14:             runner.start();
15:         }
16:     }
17:
18:     public void stop() {
19:         if (runner != null) {
20:             if (bgsound != null)
21:                 bgsound.stop();
22:             runner.stop();
23:             runner = null;
24:         }
25:     }
26:
27:     public void init() {
28:         bgsound = getAudioClip(getCodeBase(),"audio/worldmusic.au");
29:             sound = getAudioClip(getCodeBase(), "audio/sound.au");
30:     }
31:
32:     public void run() {
33:             if (bgsound != null) bgsound.loop();
34:         while (runner != null) {
35:             try { Thread.sleep(5000); }
36:             catch (InterruptedException e) { }
37:                 if (sound != null) sound.play();
38:
39:         }
40:     }
41:
42:     public void paint(Graphics g) {
43:         g.drawString("Playing sounds ...", 5, 50);
44:     }
45: }
46:
```

11

When you run the applet with Project Tester, you should hear both sounds playing indefinitely.

NOTE

> The sound file `worldmusic.au` comes from `infinite.am`, a Web site that offers music for use by the multimedia and music industries. It is located at the following URL:
>
> `http://indigo.ie/~infinite/home.htm`

Sun's Animator Applet

Because most Java animations have a lot of code in common, being able to reuse that code as much as possible makes creating animations with images and sounds much easier, particularly for Java developers who aren't as good at the programming side of Java. For just this reason, Sun provides an `Animator` applet as part of the standard Java release.

The `Animator` applet provides a simple, general-purpose animation interface. You compile the code and create an HTML file with the appropriate parameters for the animation. Using `Animator`, you can do the following:

- ☐ Create an animation loop—that is, an animation that plays repeatedly
- ☐ Add a soundtrack to the applet
- ☐ Add sounds to be played at individual frames
- ☐ Indicate the speed at which the animation is to occur
- ☐ Specify the order of the frames in the animation, which means that you can reuse frames that repeat during the course of the animation

Even if you don't intend to use Sun's `Animator` code, it's a great example of how animations work in Java and the sorts of clever tricks you can use in a Java applet. The most current version of the `Animator` applet is available from the JavaSoft Web site at the following URL:

`http://java.sun.com/java.sun.com/applets/applets/Animator/index.html`

Double-Buffering

Yesterday, you learned two simple ways to reduce flicker in animations. Although you learned specifically about animations using drawing, flicker also can result from animations using images. In addition to the two flicker-reducing methods described yesterday, there is one other way to reduce flicker in an application: double-buffering.

New Term With *double-buffering,* you create a second surface that is off-screen and paint to that surface each of the elements you want to display at one time. When that has been done, you draw the whole off-screen surface at once onto the actual applet. Because all the work goes on behind the scenes, there's no opportunity for interim parts of the drawing process to appear accidentally and disrupt the smoothness of the animation.

Double-buffering isn't always the best solution. If your applet is suffering from flicker, first try overriding update() and drawing only portions of the screen to solve your problem. Double-buffering is less efficient than regular buffering, and it also takes up more memory and space, so if you can avoid it, make an effort to do so. In terms of nearly eliminating animation flicker, however, double-buffering works exceptionally well.

Creating Applets with Double-Buffering

To create an applet that uses double-buffering, you need two things: an off-screen image to draw on and a graphics context for that image. Those two elements together mimic the effect of the applet's drawing surface: the graphics context (an instance of Graphics) to provide the drawing methods, such as drawImage() and drawString(), and the Image to hold the dots that get drawn.

There are four major steps to adding double-buffering to your applet. First, your off-screen image and graphics context need to be stored in instance variables so that you can pass them to the paint() method. Declare the following instance variables in your class definition:

```
Image offscreenImage;
Graphics offscreenGraphics;
```

Second, during the initialization of the applet, you'll create an Image and a Graphics object and assign them to these variables (you have to wait until initialization so you know how big they're going to be). The createImage() method gives you an instance of Image, which you can then send the getGraphics() method in order to get a new graphics context for that image:

```
offscreenImage = createImage(size().width,
    size().height);
offscreenGraphics = offscreenImage.getGraphics();
```

Now, whenever you have to draw to the screen (usually in your paint() method), rather than drawing to the Graphics object used by paint(), draw to the off-screen Graphics object. For example, to draw an image called img at position 10,10, use this line:

```
offscreenGraphics.drawImage(img, 10, 10, this);
```

Finally, at the end of your paint() method, after the drawing to the off-screen image is done, add the following line to place the off-screen buffer on-screen:

```
g.drawImage(offscreenImage, 0, 0, this);
```

Of course, you most likely will want to override `update()` so that it doesn't clear the screen between paintings:

```
public void update(Graphics g) {
    paint(g);
}
```

Review those four steps:

1. Add instance variables to hold the image and graphics contexts for the off-screen buffer.

2. Create an image and a `Graphics` context object when your applet is initialized.

3. Do all your applet painting to the off-screen buffer, not the applet's drawing surface.

4. At the end of your `paint` method, draw the off-screen buffer to the real screen.

An Example: Checkers2 **Revisited**

Yesterday's example featured the animated moving red oval to demonstrate animation flicker and how to reduce it. Even with the operations you did yesterday, however, the `Checkers2` applet still flashed occasionally. As your last project today, you will revise that applet to include double-buffering. Use Portfolio Manager to switch back to the `Checkers2` project and make the following changes.

First, add the instance variables for the off-screen image and its graphics context:

```
Image offscreenImg;
Graphics offscreenG;
```

Second, add an `init()` method to initialize the off-screen buffer:

```
public void init() {
    offscreenImg = createImage(size().width,
    size().height);
    offscreenG = offscreenImg.getGraphics();
}
```

Third, modify the `paint()` method to draw to the off-screen buffer instead of to the main `Graphics` buffer:

```
public void paint(Graphics g) {
    // Draw background
    offscreenG.setColor(Color.black);
    offscreenG.fillRect(0, 0, 100, 100);
    offscreenG.setColor(Color.white);
    offscreenG.fillRect(100, 0, 100, 100);
```

11

```
                // Draw checker
                offscreenG.setColor(Color.red);
                offscreenG.fillOval(xpos, 5, 90, 90);

                g.drawImage(offscreenImg, 0, 0, this);
        }
```

Note that you still are clipping the main graphics rectangle in the update() method, as you did yesterday; you don't have to change that part. The only part that is relevant is that final paint() method wherein everything is drawn off-screen before finally being displayed.

After these changes have been made to use double-buffering, you can remove the code that pertained to the clipRect() method that was used as a flicker-reduction technique. When you're done, the source code should match Listing 11.5. Save, compile, and run the applet.

Listing 11.5. The revised source code of Checkers2.java.

```
 1: import java.awt.Graphics;
 2: import java.awt.Color;
 3: import java.awt.Image;
 4:
 5: public class Checkers2 extends java.applet.Applet implements Runnable {
 6:
 7:         Thread runner;
 8:         int xpos;
 9:         Image offscreenImg;
10:         Graphics offscreenG;
11:
12:         public void init() {
13:             offscreenImg = createImage(size().width, size().height);
14:             offscreenG = offscreenImg.getGraphics();
15:         }
16:
17:         public void start() {
18:             if (runner == null); {
19:                 runner = new Thread(this);
20:                 runner.start();
21:             }
22:         }
23:
24:         public void stop() {
25:             if (runner != null) {
26:                 runner.stop();
27:                 runner = null;
28:             }
29:         }
30:
31:         public void run() {
32:             setBackground(Color.blue);
33:             while (true) {
34:                 for (xpos = 5; xpos <= 105; xpos += 2) {
35:                     repaint();
36:                     try { Thread.sleep(50); }
```

```
37:                    catch (InterruptedException e) { }
38:                }
39:                for (xpos = 105; xpos > 5; xpos -= 2) {
40:                    repaint();
41:                    try { Thread.sleep(50); }
42:                    catch (InterruptedException e) { }
43:                }
44:            }
45:        }
46:
47:        public void update(Graphics g) {
48:            paint(g);
49:        }
50:
51:        public void paint(Graphics g) {
52:            // Draw background
53:            offscreenG.setColor(Color.gray);
54:            offscreenG.fillRect(0, 0, size().width, size().height);
55:            offscreenG.setColor(Color.black);
56:            offscreenG.fillRect(0, 0, 100, 100);
57:            offscreenG.setColor(Color.white);
58:            offscreenG.fillRect(101, 0, 100, 100);
59:
60:            // Draw checker
61:            offscreenG.setColor(Color.red);
62:            offscreenG.fillOval(xpos, 5, 90, 90);
63:
64:            g.drawImage(offscreenImg, 0, 0, this);
65:        }
66: }
```

11

Summary

Three major topics were the focus of today's lesson:

☐ Using images in your applets—locating them, loading them, using the drawImage() method to display them, and creating animations with them.

☐ Using sounds, which can be included in your applets any time you need them—at specific moments, or as background sounds that can be repeated while the applet executes. You learned how to locate, load, and play sounds both using the play() and the getAudioClip() methods.

☐ Using double-buffering, a technique that enables you to virtually eliminate flicker in animations, at some expense of animation efficiency and speed. Using images and graphics contexts, you can create an off-screen buffer to draw to, the result of which is then displayed to the screen at the last possible moment.

Q&A

Q In the `Pete` program, you put the image loading into the `init()` method. It seems to me that it might take Java a long time to load all those images, and because `init()` isn't in the main thread of the applet, there's going to be a distinct pause there. Why not put the image loading at the beginning of the `run()` method instead?

A There are sneaky things going on behind the scenes of the `Pete` applet. The `getImage()` method doesn't actually load the image; in fact, it returns an `Image` object almost instantaneously, so it isn't taking up a large amount of processing time during initialization. The image data that `getImage()` points to isn't loaded until the image is needed. This way, Java doesn't have to keep enormous images around in memory if the program is going to use only a small piece. Instead, it can just keep a reference to that data and retrieve what it needs later.

Q I wrote an applet to do a background sound using the `getAudioClip()` and `loop()` methods. The sound works great, but it won't stop. I've tried suspending the current thread and killing, but the sound goes on. What can I do?

A Background sounds don't run in the main thread of the applet, so if you stop the thread, the sound keeps going. The solution is easy; in the same method where you stop the thread, also stop the sound, like this:

```
runner.stop();   //stop the thread
bgsound.stop();  //also stop the sound
```

FEATURED APPLET **Today's Featured Applet**

Today's featured applet is Michael Thelen's `LimeSweeper`, a variation on the MineSweeper game. Instead of dodging exploding mines, players try to avoid opening boxes that contain limes. Figure 11.5 shows an example of `LimeSweeper` in action.

Files for `LimeSweeper` are located on the CD-ROM in the `\BOOK\3RDPARTY\DAY11\` directory, including source code in the file `Sweeper.java`. To use `LimeSweeper` on a Web page, place these six files on your Web site: `Sweeper.java`, `StatusBar.java`, `Timer.java`, `Minefield.java`, `MessageBar.java`, and `Box.java`. Place these class files in the same directory as the Web page or place them in a subdirectory listed in the `CODEBASE` parameter of the `<APPLET>` tag. The `<CODE>` tag should be `Sweeper.class`. Listing 11.6 shows the HTML tags used to run `LimeSweeper` as it is shown in Figure 11.5.

11

Figure 11.5.

The LimeSweeper *applet in action.*

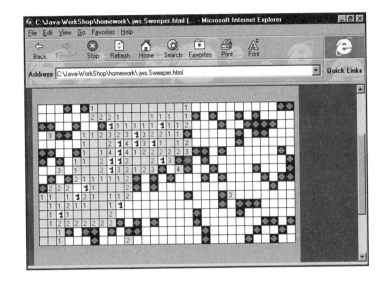

Listing 11.6. The `<APPLET>` tag for LimeSweeper.

```
<APPLET code="Sweeper.class" width=500 height=400>
</APPLET>
```

LimeSweeper takes no parameters. More information on the applet is available from its author at the following URL:

```
http://www.cs.hope.edu/~thelenm/java/applets/Sweeper/
```

Day **12**

Simple Events and Interactivity

In Java, events are part of the Abstract Windowing Toolkit (AWT), a package that is used to create windows, buttons, and other graphical interface features. The AWT uses events in its communication by sending messages to other AWT components or parts of a program when something has happened. The occurrence that triggers an event can be input from the user (mouse movements, mouse clicks, or keypresses), changes in the system environment (a window opening or closing, the window being scrolled up or down), or a variety of other things that might affect the operation of the program.

NOTE

> Java's Abstract Windowing Toolkit is a package of classes that implements most common UI components. In Java WorkShop, the AWT is used in conjunction with Visual Java to manage the user interface.

In other words, whenever something happens to a Java AWT component (including an applet), an event is generated. Some events are handled automatically by the AWT or browser. paint() methods, for example, are generated and handled by the browser; all you have to do is tell the AWT what you want painted when it gets to your part of the window. Some events, however, you need to know about—such as a mouse click inside the boundaries of your applet. Writing your Java programs to handle these kinds of events enables you to get input from the user and have your applet change its behavior based on that input.

Today, you'll learn about managing simple events, including the following basics:

☐ Mouse clicks

☐ Mouse movements, including mouse dragging

☐ Keyboard actions

You also will learn about the handleEvent() method, which is the basis for collecting, handling, and passing events of all kinds from your applet to other user interface components in the window, or in your applet itself. Tomorrow, you'll learn how to combine events with the AWT and Visual Java to create a complete interface for your applet.

Mouse Clicks

The most common event you might be interested in are mouse clicks. Mouse-click events occur when a user clicks the mouse somewhere in the body of your applet. You can intercept mouse clicks to do simple things such as toggling the sound on and off in your applet, moving to the next slide in a presentation, or clearing the screen and starting over, or you can use mouse clicks in conjunction with mouse movements to perform more complex motions in your applet.

mouseDown **and** mouseUp

When you click the mouse once, the AWT generates two events: a mouseDown event when the mouse button is pressed, and a mouseUp event when the button is released. Why two individual events for a single mouse action? Because you might want to do different things for the "down" and the "up." For example, look at a pull-down menu. The mouseDown event extends the menu, and the mouseUp event selects an item (with mouseDrags in between, as you will learn later). If you have only one event for both actions (mouseUp and mouseDown), you cannot implement that sort of user interaction.

Handling mouse events in your applet is easy; all you have to do is override the right method definition in your applet. That method will be called when that particular event occurs. Here's an example of the method signature for a mouseDown event:

```
public boolean mouseDown(Event evt, int x, int y) {
    // method code here
}
```

The mouseDown() and mouseUp() methods take three parameters: the event itself and the x and y coordinates where the mouseDown or mouseUp event occurred. The event argument is an instance of the class Event. All system events generate an instance of the Event class, which contains information about where and when the event took place, the kind of event it is, and other information that you might want to know about the event. Sometimes having this kind of information about an event object is useful, as you'll discover later in this section. The x and the y coordinates of the event, as passed in through the x and y arguments, are used to determine precisely where the mouse click took place.

For example, this simple method displays information about a mouseDown event when it occurs:

```
public boolean mouseDown(Event evt, int x, int y) {
    System.out.println("Mouse down at " + x + "," + y);
    return true;
}
```

If you include this method in your applet, this message will be displayed every time a user clicks the mouse inside your applet. Note that this method, unlike the other system methods you've studied this far, returns a boolean value instead of not returning anything (void). This fact becomes important tomorrow when you create user interfaces and then manage input to these interfaces; having an event handler return true or false determines whether a given user interface component can intercept an event or whether it needs to pass it on to the enclosing component. The general rule is that if your method deals with the event, it should return true. For today's lesson, this is almost always the case.

The second half of the mouse click is the mouseUp() method, which is called when the mouse button is released. To handle a mouseUp event, add the mouseUp() method to your applet. mouseUp() looks just like mouseDown():

```
public boolean mouseUp(Event evt, int x, int y) {
    // method code here
}
```

An Example: Spots

In this section, you'll create an example of an applet that uses mouse events, mouseDown in particular. The Spots applet starts with a blank screen and then waits. When you click the mouse on that screen, a blue dot is drawn. You can place up to 10 dots on the screen. Figure 12.1 shows the Spots applet.

12

Figure 12.1.

Sample output of the Spots *applet.*

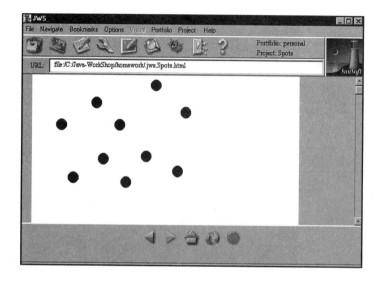

Follow along as the parts of this applet are described. The applet is listed in full later, and you can enter the code into the Java WorkShop Source Editor at that point. The first part of the program is the initial class definition:

```
import java.awt.Graphics;
import java.awt.Color;
import java.awt.Event;

public class Spots extends java.applet.Applet {

    final int MAXSPOTS = 10;
    int xspots[] = new int[MAXSPOTS];
    int yspots[] = new int[MAXSPOTS];
    int currspots = 0;

}
```

This class uses three other AWT classes: Graphics, Color, and Event. That last class, Event, needs to be imported in any applets that use events. The Spots class has four instance variables: a constant to determine the maximum number of spots that can be drawn, two arrays to store the x and y coordinates of the spots that already have been drawn, and an integer to keep track of the number of the current spot.

NOTE | The Spots class doesn't include the implements Runnable modifier in its definition. As you will see later as you build this applet, it also doesn't have a run() method. Why not? The reason is that it doesn't do anything on its own; all it does is wait for input and then do stuff when input happens. There's no need for threads if your applet isn't actively doing something all the time.

The init() method of the applet has one line, which sets the background color to white:

```
public void init() {
        setBackground(Color.white);
}
```

Set the background in the init() method instead of in paint(), because paint() is called repeatedly each time a new spot is added. Because you need to set the background only once, putting it in the paint() method unnecessarily slows down that method. Putting it in the init() method is a much better idea.

The main action of this applet occurs in the mouseDown() method:

```
public boolean mouseDown(Event evt, int x, int y) {
    if (currspots < MAXSPOTS)
            addspot(x,y);
        else System.out.println("Too many spots.");
        return true;
}
```

When the mouse click occurs, the mouseDown() method tests to see whether there are less than 10 spots. If so, it calls the addspot() method (which you'll write soon). If not, it just displays an error message. Finally, it returns true, because all the event methods have to return a boolean value (usually true).

What does addspot() do? It adds the coordinates of the spot to the arrays that store the coordinates, increments the currspots variable, and then calls repaint():

```
void addspot(int x, int y) {
        xspots[currspots] = x;
        yspots[currspots] = y;
        currspots++;
        repaint();
    }
```

You might be wondering why you have to keep track of all the past spots in addition to the current spot. The reason is because of repaint(). Each time you paint the screen, you have to paint all the old spots in addition to the newest spot. Otherwise, each time you painted a new spot, the older spots would be erased.

The next bit is the paint()method:

```
public void paint(Graphics g) {
    g.setColor(Color.blue);
    for (int i = 0; i < currspots; i++) {
```

12

```
            g.fillOval(xspots[i] -10, yspots[i] - 10, 20, 20);
        }
}
```

Inside the paint() method, you just loop through the spots you've stored in the xspots and yspots arrays, painting each one. (The paint() method paints the spots a little to the right and upward from the x and y coordinates stored in the arrays. This is done so that the spot is painted around the point where the mouse pointer clicked rather than below and to the right of it.)

That's all you need to do to create an applet that handles mouse clicks. Everything else is handled for you. You have to add the appropriate behavior to mouseDown() or mouseUp() to intercept and handle that event. Listing 12.1 shows the full text for the Spots applet.

Use Portfolio Manager to create a new project called Spots, and make sure that the Source Editor option is chosen. When you compile and run the project, it should resemble Figure 12.1.

TYPE   **Listing 12.1. The source code of** Spots.java.

```
 1: import java.awt.Graphics;
 2: import java.awt.Color;
 3: import java.awt.Event;
 4:
 5: public class Spots extends java.applet.Applet {
 6:
 7:     final int MAXSPOTS = 10;
 8:     int xspots[] = new int[MAXSPOTS];
 9:     int yspots[] = new int[MAXSPOTS];
10:     int currspots = 0;
11:
12:     public void init() {
13:         setBackground(Color.white);
14:     }
15:
16:     public boolean mouseDown(Event evt, int x, int y) {
17:         if (currspots < MAXSPOTS)
18:             addspot(x,y);
19:         else System.out.println("Too many spots.");
20:         return true;
21:     }
22:
23:     void addspot(int x,int y) {
24:         xspots[currspots] = x;
25:         yspots[currspots] = y;
26:         currspots++;
27:         repaint();
28:     }
29:
```

12

```
30:     public void paint(Graphics g) {
31:         g.setColor(Color.blue);
32:         for (int i = 0; i < currspots; i++) {
33:             g.fillOval(xspots[i] - 10, yspots[i] - 10, 20, 20);
34:         }
35:     }
36: }
```

Mouse Movements

Every time the mouse is moved a single pixel in any direction, a mouse movement event is generated. There are two mouse movement events: mouse drags, where the movement occurs with the mouse button pressed down, and plain mouse movements, where the mouse button isn't pressed. To manage mouse movement events, use the mouseDrag() and mouseMove() methods.

mouseDrag and mouseMove

The mouseDrag() and mouseMove() methods, when included in your applet code, intercept and handle mouse movement events. The mouseMove() method, for plain mouse pointer movements without the mouse button pressed, looks much like the mouse click methods:

```
public boolean mouseMove(Event evt, int x, int y) {
    // method code here
}
```

The mouseDrag() method handles mouse movements made with the mouse button pressed down (a complete dragging movement consists of a mouseDown event, a series of mouseDrag events for each pixel the mouse is moved, and a mouseUp event when the button is released). The mouseDrag() method looks like this:

```
public boolean mouseDrag(Event evt, int x, int y) {
    // method code here
}
```

mouseEnter and mouseExit

The mouseEnter() and mouseExit() methods are called when the mouse pointer enters the applet or when it exits the applet. (These methods are useful on components of user interfaces that you might put inside an applet. You'll learn more about these tomorrow.) Both mouseEnter() and mouseExit() have three arguments: the Event object and the x and y coordinates of the point where the mouse entered or exited the applet:

```
public boolean mouseEnter(Event evt, int x, int y) {
    // method code here
```

12

```
        }

    public boolean mouseExit(Event evt, int x, int y) {
        // method code here
    }
```

An Example: Lines

Examples always help to make concepts more concrete. In this section, you create an applet that enables you to draw straight lines on the screen by dragging from the starting point to the endpoint. Figure 12.2 shows the applet at work.

Figure 12.2.

Sample output of the Lines *applet.*

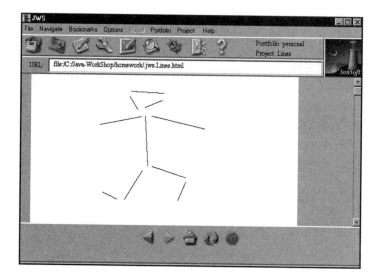

As with the Spots applet (on which this applet is based), follow along as the parts of the program are described. The first thing to do is to create the basic definition. Listing 12.2 shows the first part of the Lines applet.

Listing 12.2. The first part of the Lines applet.

```
1: import java.awt.Graphics;
2: import java.awt.Color;
3: import java.awt.Event;
4: import java.awt.Point;
5:
6: public class Lines extends java.applet.Applet {
7:
8:     final int MAXLINES = 10;
9:     Point starts[] = new Point[MAXLINES]; // starting points
```

```
10:     Point ends[] = new Point[MAXLINES];    // endingpoints
11:     Point anchor;    // start of current line
12:     Point currentpoint; // current end of line
13:     int currline = 0; // number of lines
14:
15:     public void init() {
16:         setBackground(Color.white);
17:     }
```

ANALYSIS   Compared to Spots, this applet added a few extra things. Unlike Spots, which keeps track of individual integer coordinates, this applet keeps track of Point objects. These objects are an x and a y coordinate encapsulated in a single object. To deal with points, you import the Point class (line 4) and set up a bunch of instance variables that hold points:

- The starts array holds points representing the starting points of lines already drawn.
- The ends array holds the endpoints of those same lines.
- anchor holds the starting point of the line currently being drawn.
- currentpoint holds the current endpoint of the line currently being drawn.
- currline holds the current number of lines (to make sure you don't go over MAXLINES).

Finally, the init() method sets the background of the applet to white.

The three main events this applet deals with are mouseDown(), to set the anchor point for the current line; mouseDrag(), to animate the current line as it's being drawn; and mouseUp(), to set the ending point for the new line. Given that you have instance variables to hold each of these values, finishing the applet is merely a matter of plugging the right variables into the right methods. Here's mouseDown(), which sets the anchor point:

```
public boolean mouseDown(Event evt, int x, int y) {
    anchor = new Point(x, y);
    return true;
}
```

While the mouse is being dragged to draw the line, the applet animates the line being drawn. As you drag the mouse around, the new line moves with it from the anchor point to the tip of the mouse. The mouseDrag event contains the current point each time the mouse moves, so use that method to keep track of the current point (and to repaint for each movement so the line animates):

```
public boolean mouseDrag(Event evt, int x, int y) {
    currentpoint = new Point(x, y);
    repaint();
    return true;
}
```

12

The new line doesn't get added to the arrays of old lines until the mouse button is released. The following is the mouseUp() method, which tests to make sure you haven't exceeded the maximum number of lines before calling the addline() method (described next):

```
public boolean mouseUp(Event evt, int x, int y) {
    if (currline < MAXLINES)
        addline(x, y);
    else System.out.println("Too many lines.");
    return true;
}
```

The addline() method is where the arrays of lines are updated and where the applet is repainted to take the new line into effect:

```
void addline(int x, int y) {
    starts[currline] = anchor;
    ends[currline] = new Point(x, y);
    currline++;
    currentpoint = null;
    repaint();
}
```

Note that in this code you also set currentpoint to null. Why? Because the current line you were drawing is finished. By setting currentpoint to null, you can test for that value in the paint() method.

Painting the applet means drawing all the old lines stored in the starts and ends arrays, as well as drawing the current line in process (whose endpoints are in anchor and currentpoint, respectively). To show the animation of the current line, draw it in blue. Here's the paint() method for the Lines applet:

```
public void paint(Graphics g) {

    // Draw existing lines
    for (int i = 0; i < currline; i++) {
        g.drawLine(starts[i].x, starts[i].y,
            ends[i].x, ends[i].y);
    }

    // Draw current line
    g.setColor(Color.blue);
    if (currentpoint != null)
        g.drawLine(anchor.x, anchor.y,
            currentpoint.x, currentpoint.y);
}
```

When you're drawing the current line in paint(), you test first to see whether currentpoint is null. If it is, the applet isn't in the middle of drawing a line, so there's no reason to try drawing a line that doesn't exist. By testing for currentpoint (and by setting currentpoint to null in the addline() method), you can paint only what you need.

12

With just 58 lines of code and a few basic methods, you have a basic drawing application in your Web browser. Listing 12.3 shows the full text of the Lines applet so that you can put the pieces together. When you create the applet with Java WorkShop, the output should resemble Figure 12.2.

TYPE | **Listing 12.3. The source code of Lines.java.**

```
1: import java.awt.Graphics;
2: import java.awt.Color;
3: import java.awt.Event;
4: import java.awt.Point;
5:
6: public class Lines extends java.applet.Applet {
7:
8:     final int MAXLINES = 10;
9:     Point starts[] = new Point[MAXLINES]; // starting points
10:     Point ends[] = new Point[MAXLINES];    // endingpoints
11:     Point anchor;     // start of current line
12:     Point currentpoint; // current end of line
13:     int currline = 0; // number of lines
14:
15:     public void init() {
16:         setBackground(Color.white);
17:     }
18:
19:     public boolean mouseDown(Event evt, int x, int y) {
20:         anchor = new Point(x,y);
21:         return true;
22:     }
23:
24:     public boolean mouseUp(Event evt, int x, int y) {
25:         if (currline < MAXLINES)
26:             addline(x,y);
27:         else System.out.println("Too many lines.");
28:         return true;
29:     }
30:
31:     public boolean mouseDrag(Event evt, int x, int y) {
32:         currentpoint = new Point(x,y);
33:         repaint();
34:         return true;
35:     }
36:
37:     void addline(int x,int y) {
38:         starts[currline] = anchor;
39:         ends[currline] = new Point(x,y);
40:         currline++;
41:         currentpoint = null;
42:         repaint();
43:     }
44:
```

continues

Listing 12.3. continued

```
45:     public void paint(Graphics g) {
46:         // Draw existing lines
47:         for (int i = 0; i < currline; i++) {
48:             g.drawLine(starts[i].x, starts[i].y,
49:                 ends[i].x, ends[i].y);
50:         }
51:
52:         // Draw current line
53:         g.setColor(Color.blue);
54:         if (currentpoint != null)
55:             g.drawLine(anchor.x,anchor.y,
56:                 currentpoint.x,currentpoint.y);
57:     }
58: }
```

Keyboard Events

Keyboard events are generated whenever users press a key on the keyboard. By using key events, you can retrieve the values of keys pressed to perform an action or get character input from users.

keyDown and keyUp Methods

To capture a keyboard event, use the keyDown() method:

```
public boolean keyDown(Event evt, int key) {
    // method code here
}
```

The keys generated by keyDown events (and passed into keyDown() as the key argument) are integers representing ASCII character values, which include alphanumeric characters, function keys, tabs, returns, and so on. To use them as characters (for example, to display them), you need to cast them to characters:

```
currentchar = (char)key;
```

The following simple example of a keyDown() method does nothing but display the key you just typed in both its ASCII and character representations:

```
public boolean keyDown(Event evt, int key) {
    System.out.println("ASCII value: " + key);
    System.out.println("Character: " + (char)key);
    return true;
}
```

As with mouse clicks, each keyDown event also has a corresponding keyUp event. To intercept keyUp events, use the keyUp() method:

```
public boolean keyUp(Event evt, int key)  {
    // method code here
}
```

Default Keys

The Event class provides a set of class variables that refer to several standard non-alphanumeric keys, such as the arrow keys. If your interface uses these keys, you can provide more readable code by testing for these names in your keyDown() method rather than testing for their numeric values. For example, to test whether the up arrow was pressed, you might use the following snippet of code:

```
if (key == Event.UP) {
    // code here
}
```

Because the values these class variables hold are integers, you also can use the switch statement to test for them.

Table 12.1 shows the standard Event class variables for various keys and the keys that they represent.

Table 12.1. Standard keys defined by the Event class.

Class Variable	Represented Key
Event.HOME	The Home key
Event.END	The End key
Event.PGUP	The Page Up key
Event.PGDN	The Page Down key
Event.UP	The up arrow
Event.DOWN	The down arrow
Event.LEFT	The left arrow
Event.RIGHT	The right arrow

12

An Example: Keys

In this section, you create an applet that demonstrates keyboard events. This applet takes the first character that is pressed by the user and displays it in the center of the applet window.

Then, when the arrow keys are pressed, the character moves in the direction indicated by the key. Typing another character at any time changes the character displayed. Figure 12.3 shows an example.

Figure 12.3.

Sample output of the Keys *applet.*

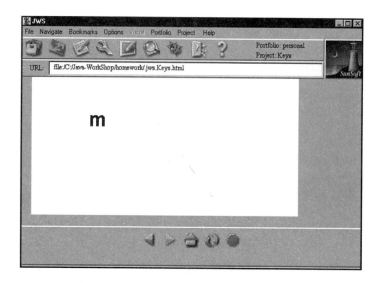

This applet is less complicated than the previous applets you've created today. It has only three methods: init(), keyDown(), and paint(). The instance variables also are simpler because the only things you need to keep track of are the x and y positions of the current character and the value of that character. Here's the top of this class definition:

```
import java.awt.Graphics;
import java.awt.Event;
import java.awt.Font;
import java.awt.Color;

public class Keys extends java.applet.Applet {

    char currkey;
    int currx;
    int curry;
```

The init() method is responsible for three things: setting the background color, setting the applet's font (here, 36 point Helvetica bold), and setting the beginning position for the character (the middle of the screen, minus a few points to nudge it up and to the right):

```
public void init() {
    currx = (size().width / 2) - 8;  // default
    curry = (size().height / 2) - 16;
```

```
    setBackground(Color.white);
    setFont(new Font("Helvetica", Font.BOLD, 36));
}
```

Because this applet's behavior is based on keyboard input, the keyDown() method is where most of the work of the applet takes place:

```
public boolean keyDown(Event evt, int key) {
    switch (key) {
        case Event.DOWN:
            curry += 5;
            break;
        case Event.UP:
            curry -= 5;
            break;
        case Event.LEFT:
            currx -= 5;
            break;
        case Event.RIGHT:
            currx += 5;
            break;
        default:
            currkey = (char)key;
    }

    repaint();
    return true;
}
```

In the center of the keyDown() method, a switch statement tests for different key events. If the event is an arrow key, the appropriate change is made to the character's position. If the event is any other key, the character itself is changed. The method finishes up with a repaint() method and returns true.

The paint() method in this applet is almost trivial; it just displays the current character at the current position. However, note that when the applet starts up, there's no initial character and nothing to draw, so you have to take that fact into account. The currkey variable is initialized to 0, so you paint the applet only if currkey has an actual value:

```
public void paint(Graphics g) {
    if (currkey != 0) {
        g.drawString(String.valueOf(currkey), currx,curry);
    }
}
```

Listing 12.4 shows the complete source code for the Keys applet. When you create the Keys project and run it, you will not be prompted to press a character. Once you do, however, the output should resemble Figure 12.3.

12

TYPE   **Listing 12.4. The source code of** Keys.java.

```
 1: import java.awt.Graphics;
 2: import java.awt.Event;
 3: import java.awt.Font;
 4: import java.awt.Color;
 5:
 6: public class Keys extends java.applet.Applet {
 7:
 8:     char currkey;
 9:     int currx;
10:     int curry;
11:
12:     public void init() {
13:         currx = (size().width / 2) -8;   // default
14:         curry = (size().height / 2) -16;
15:
16:         setBackground(Color.white);
17:         setFont(new Font("Helvetica",Font.BOLD,36));
18:     }
19:
20:     public boolean keyDown(Event evt, int key) {
21:         switch (key) {
22:         case Event.DOWN:
23:             curry += 5;
24:             break;
25:         case Event.UP:
26:             curry -= 5;
27:             break;
28:         case Event.LEFT:
29:             currx -= 5;
30:             break;
31:         case Event.RIGHT:
32:             currx += 5;
33:             break;
34:         default:
35:             currkey = (char)key;
36:         }
37:
38:         repaint();
39:         return true;
40:     }
41:
42:     public void paint(Graphics g) {
43:         if (currkey != 0) {
44:             g.drawString(String.valueOf(currkey), currx,curry);
45:         }
46:     }
47: }
```

Testing for Modifier Keys

The Shift, Control, and Meta keys are modifier keys. They don't generate key events themselves, but when you get an ordinary mouse or keyboard event, you can test to see whether those keys were held down when the event occurred. Sometimes it might be obvious, shifted alphanumeric keys produce different key events than unshifted ones, for example. For other events, however, (mouse events in particular) you might want to handle an event with a modifier key held down differently than a regular version of that event.

The Event class provides three methods for testing whether a modifier key is held down: shiftDown(), metaDown(), and controlDown(). All these methods return boolean values based on whether that modifier key is pressed. You can use these three methods in any of the event handling methods (mouse or keyboard) by calling them on the event object passed into that method:

```
public boolean mouseDown(Event evt, int x, int y ) {
    if (evt.shiftDown())
        // handle shift-click
    else // handle regular click
}
```

The AWT Event Handler

The default methods you've learned about today for handling basic events in applets are called by a generic event handler method called handleEvent(). The handleEvent() method is how the AWT generically deals with events that occur between application components and events based on user input.

In the default handleEvent() method, basic events are processed and the methods you learned about today are called. To handle events other than those mentioned here, to change the default event-handling behavior, or to create and pass around your own events, you need to override handleEvent() in your own Java programs. The handleEvent() method looks like this:

```
public boolean handleEvent(Event evt) {
    // method code here
}
```

To test for specific events, examine the ID instance variable of the Event object that gets passed in. The event ID is an integer, but fortunately, the Event class defines a set of event IDs as class variables that you can test for in the body of the handleEvent() method. Because these class variables are integer constants, a switch statement works particularly well. For example, the following is a simple handleEvent() method to display debugging information about mouse events:

```
public boolean handleEvent(Event evt) {
    switch (evt.id) {
    case Event.MOUSE_DOWN:
        System.out.println("MouseDown: " +
                evt.x + "," + evt.y);
        return true;
    case Event.MOUSE_UP:
        System.out.println("MouseUp: " +
                evt.x + "," + evt.y);
        return true;
    case Event.MOUSE_MOVE:
        System.out.println("MouseMove: " +
                evt.x + "," + evt.y);
        return true;
    case Event.MOUSE_DRAG:
        System.out.println("MouseDown: " +
                evt.x + "," + evt.y);
        return true;
    default:
        return false;
    }
}
```

You can test for the following keyboard events:

☐ Event.KEY_PRESS is generated when a key is pressed (the same as the keyDown() method).

☐ Event.KEY_RELEASE is generated when a key is released.

☐ Event.KEY_ACTION and Event.KEY_ACTION_RELEASE are generated when a key is pressed and released.

You can test for these mouse events:

☐ Event.MOUSE_DOWN is generated when the mouse button is pressed (the same as the mouseDown() method).

☐ Event.MOUSE_UP is generated when the mouse button is released (the same as the mouseUp() method).

☐ Event.MOUSE_MOVE is generated when the mouse is moved (the same as the mouseMove() method).

☐ Event.MOUSE_DRAG is generated when the mouse is moved with the button pressed (the same as the mouseDrag() method).

☐ Event.MOUSE_ENTER is generated when the mouse enters the applet (or a component of that applet). You also can use the mouseEnter() method.

☐ Event.MOUSE_EXIT is generated when the mouse exits the applet. You can also use the mouseExit() method.

12

In addition to these events, the Event class has a whole suite of methods for handling user interface components. You learn more about these events tomorrow.

Note that if you override handleEvent() in your class, none of the default event handling methods you learned about today will get called unless you explicitly call them in the body of handleEvent(), so be careful if you decide to do this. One way to get around this problem is to test for the event you're interested in, and if that event isn't it, call super.handleEvent() so that the superclass that defines handleEvent() can process things. Here's an example of how to do this:

```
public boolean handleEvent(Event evt) {
    if (evt.id == Event.MOUSE_DOWN) {
        // process the mouse down
        return true;
    } else {
        return super.handleEvent(evt);
    }
}
```

Summary

Handling events in Java's Abstract Windowing Toolkit (AWT) is easy. Most of the time, all you need to do is stick the right method in your applet code, and your applet intercepts and handles that method. Here are some of the basic events you can manage in this way:

- ☐ Use mouseUp() and mouseDown() methods for each part of mouse clicks.
- ☐ Use mouseMove() and mouseDrag() for mouse movement with the mouse button released and pressed, respectively; use mouseEnter() and mouseExit() for when the mouse enters and exits the applet area.
- ☐ Use keyDown() and keyUp() for when a key on the keyboard is pressed.

All events in the AWT generate an Event object. Inside that object, you can find out information about the event, when it occurred, and its x and y coordinates (if applicable). You also can test that event to see whether a modifier key was pressed when the event occurred by using the shiftDown(), controlDown(), and metaDown() methods.

Finally, the handleEvent() method is the parent of the individual event methods. The handleEvent() method is what the Java system calls to manage events; the default implementation calls the individual method events where necessary. To override how methods are managed in your applet, override handleEvent().

12

Q&A

Q In the `Spots` applet, the spot coordinates are stored in arrays, which have a limited size. How can I modify this applet so that it will draw an unlimited number of spots?

A You can do one of a couple things:

The first thing to do is test in your `addspot()` method whether the number of spots has exceeded `MAXSPOTS`. Then create a bigger array, copy the elements of the old array into that bigger array (use the `System.arraycopy()` method to do that), and reassign the x and y arrays to that new, bigger array.

The second thing to do is to use the `Vector` class. `Vector`, part of the `java.util` package, implements an array that automatically is expandable—sort of like a linked list is in other languages. The disadvantage of `Vector` is that to put something into `Vector`, it has to be an actual object. This means you'll have to cast integers to `Integer` objects, and then extract their values from `Integer` objects to treat them as integers again. The `Vector` class enables you to access and change elements in `Vector` just as you can in an array (by using method calls, rather than array syntax). Check it out.

Q The `mouseDown()` and `mouseUp()` methods seem to apply to only a single mouse button. How can I determine which button on the mouse has been pressed?

A At the moment, you can't. AWT assumes that you're using only one mouse button or, if you have a mouse with multiple buttons, that you're using only the left one. Although this assumption provides some limitations on the kinds of actions you can perform in your applet, it does provide a cross-platform solution. Different systems have different mice, so writing your applet to do something specific with the right mouse button isn't a good idea if the people running your applet are using Macintoshes and have only one mouse button. If you really want to have different mouse actions perform different things, test for modifier keys in your `mouseDown()` and `mouseUp()` methods.

Q What's a Meta key?

A A Meta key is popular in UNIX systems and is often mapped to Alt on most keyboards. Because Shift and Control are much more popular and widespread, it's probably a good idea to base your interfaces on those modifier keys if you can.

Q How do I test to see whether the Return key has been pressed?

A Return (linefeed) is character 10; Enter (carriage return) is character 13. Note that different platforms might send different keys for the actual key marked Return. In particular, UNIX systems send linefeeds, Macintoshes send carriage returns, and DOS systems send both. So to provide a cross-platform behavior, you might want to test for both linefeed and carriage return.

FEATURED APPLET Today's Featured Applet

Today's featured applet is scroll, an image-scrolling applet that displays parallax, which is distant objects moving at a different vertical rate than close objects. The applet was written by Mark Van Buren, and it shows a train moving in the foreground in front of mountains and a wide body of water. Figure 12.4 shows an example of scroll in action.

Figure 12.4.

The scroll *applet in action.*

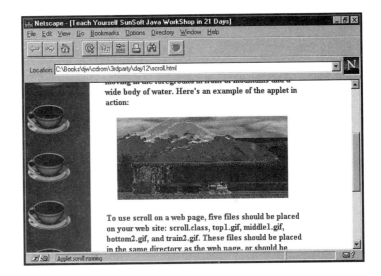

Files for scroll are located on the CD-ROM in the \BOOK\3RDPARTY\DAY12\ directory, including source code in the file scroll.java. To use scroll on a Web page, place these five files on your Web site: scroll.class, top1.gif, middle1.gif, bottom2.gif, and train2.gif. Place these files in the same directory as the Web page or place them in a subdirectory listed in the CODEBASE parameter of the <APPLET> tag. The <CODE> tag should be scroll.class. Listing 12.5 shows the HTML tags used to run scroll as it was shown in Figure 12.4.

Listing 12.5. The <APPLET> tag for scroll.

```
<applet code=scroll.class width=320 height=149>
</applet>
```

The scroll applet takes no parameters, but if you examine the GIF files that are used to create the parallax image, it is possible to create different images for use with the applet. More information on the applet is available from its author at the following URL:

http://www.portraits.com/web/3d/scroll.htm

12

Day 13

Visual Java and the Abstract Windowing Toolkit

For the past five days you've concentrated on creating applets that do simple things: display text, play an animation or a sound, or enable basic interactions with the user. Once you get past that point, however, you might want to create more complex applets that behave like applications that are embedded in a Web page—applets that use graphical user interface features such as buttons, menus, text fields, and other elements of a real application.

Visual Java and the Abstract Windowing Toolkit were designed for this sort of real work in Java applets and applications. You have been using the AWT throughout this book, as you might have guessed from the classes you've been importing. The Applet class and most of the classes used this week are integral parts of the AWT. The AWT provides the following:

- A full set of user interface widgets and other components, including windows, menus, buttons, check boxes, text fields, scrollbars, and scrolling lists
- Support for user interface containers, which can contain other embedded containers or widgets
- An event system for managing system and user events between and among parts of the AWT
- Mechanisms for laying out components in a way that enables platform-independent user interface design

Today, you'll learn how to use these things in your Java applets. Tomorrow, you'll learn about creating windows, menus, and dialog boxes, which enable you to create windows that pop up separately from the browser window. If you find the framework of the Web browser too limiting, you can take your AWT background and start writing full-fledged Java applications. Today's lesson focuses on applets, however.

This background in the AWT will be the basis for your use of Visual Java, the development tool that is part of Java WorkShop. Visual Java enables a programmer to develop a graphical user interface in a visual way—dragging and dropping user interface components, modifying the look of a program, and the like. It's an exciting part of Java WorkShop, and as SunSoft extends Visual Java's capabilities, it will speed up the design process considerably.

NOTE

This lesson is the most complex one. There's a lot to cover and a lot of code to go through today, so if it becomes overwhelming, you may want to take two days or more for this one.

An AWT Overview

The basic idea behind the Abstract Windowing Toolkit is that a Java window is a set of nested components, starting from the outermost window all the way down to the smallest user interface component. Components can include things you see on the screen, such as windows, menu bars, buttons, and text fields, and they also can include containers, which in turn can contain other components. Figure 13.1 shows how a sample page in a Java browser might include several different components, all of which are managed through the AWT.

Figure 13.1.

AWT components.

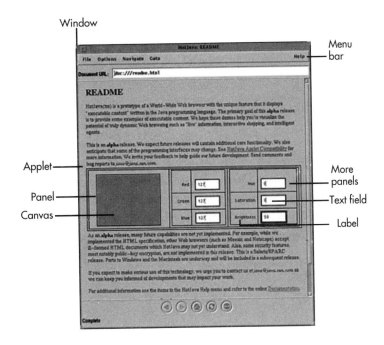

This nesting of components within containers within other components creates a hierarchy of components, from the smallest check box inside an applet to the overall window on the screen. The hierarchy of components determines the arrangement of items on the screen and inside other items, the order in which they are painted, and how events are passed from one component to another.

These are the major components you can work with in the AWT:

☐ *Containers.* Containers are generic AWT components that can contain other components, including other containers. The most common form of container is the panel, which represents a container that can be displayed on-screen. Applets are a form of panel—the Applet class is a subclass of the Panel class.

☐ *Canvases.* A canvas is a simple drawing surface. Although you can draw on panels (as you've been doing all along), canvases are good for painting images or other graphics operations.

☐ *User Interface components.* These components can include buttons, lists, simple pop-up menus, check boxes, text fields, and other typical elements of a user interface.

☐ *Window construction components.* These components include windows, frames, menu bars, and dialog boxes. These components are listed separately from the other user interface components because you'll use these less often—particularly in

13

applets. In applets, the browser provides the main window and menu bar, so you don't have to use these. Your applet might create a new window, however, or you might want to write a Java application that uses these components.

The classes inside the java.awt package are written and organized to mirror the abstract structure of containers, components, and individual user interface components. Figure 13.2 shows some of the class hierarchy that makes up the main classes in the AWT. The root of most AWT components is the class Component, which provides basic display and event-handling features. The classes Container, Canvas, TextComponent, and many of the other user interface components inherit from Component. Inheriting from the Container class are objects that can contain other AWT components, such as the Panel and Window classes. Note that the java.applet.Applet class, even though it lives in its own package, inherits from Panel, so your applets are an integral part of the hierarchy of components in the AWT system.

Figure 13.2.

A partial AWT class hierarchy.

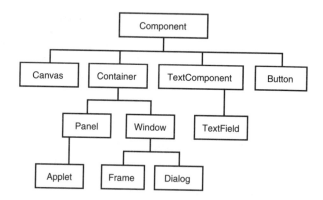

A graphical user interface-based application that you write by using the AWT can be as complex as you like, with dozens of nested containers and components inside each other. AWT was designed so that each component can play its part in the overall AWT system without needing to duplicate or keep track of the behavior of other parts in the system.

The Basic User Interface Components

The simplest kind of AWT component is the basic user interface component. You can create and add these to your applet without needing to know anything about creating containers or panels. Your applet, even before you start handling events, painting, and drawing, is already an AWT container. Because an applet is a container, you can put other AWT components, such as user interface components or other containers, into it.

In this section, you'll learn about the basic user interface components: labels, buttons, check boxes, choice menus, and text fields. In each case, the procedure for creating the component

13

is the same; you first create the component, and then add it to the panel that holds it, at which point it is displayed on-screen.

To add a component to a panel (such as your applet, for example), use the add() method:

```
public void init() {
    Button b = new Button("OK");
    add(b);
}
```

Note that where the component appears in the panel depends on the layout that panel is defined to have. The default layout for panels such as applets is FlowLayout with a centered alignment, which means that components are added from left to right in rows, and then row by row as they fit, with each row centered. You'll learn more about panels and layouts in the next section.

Note also that each of these components has an action associated with it—that is, something that component does when it's activated. Actions generally trigger events or other activities in your applet (often called callbacks in other window toolkits). In this section, you will focus on creating the components themselves. You will learn about adding actions to them later in today's lesson.

Labels

NEW TERM   The simplest form of user interface component is the label. *Labels* are, effectively, text strings that you can use to label other user interface components. The advantages that a label has over an ordinary text string is that it follows the layout of the given panel, and you don't have to worry about repainting it every time the panel is redrawn. Labels also can be aligned easily within a panel, enabling you to attach labels to other user interface components without knowing exact pixel positions.

To create a label, use one of the following constructors:

- [ ] Label() creates an empty label, with its text aligned left.
- [ ] Label(*String*) creates a label with the given text string, also aligned left.
- [ ] Label(*String*, *int*) creates a label with the given text string and the given alignment. The available alignments are stored in class variables in Label: Label.RIGHT, Label.LEFT, and Label.CENTER.

The label's font is determined by the overall font for the component (as set by the setFont() method).

Here's some simple code to create a few labels:

```
add(new Label("aligned left "));
add(new Label("aligned center", Label.CENTER));
add(new Label(" aligned right", Label.RIGHT));
```

13

Figure 13.3 shows how this looks on-screen.

Figure 13.3.
Labels.

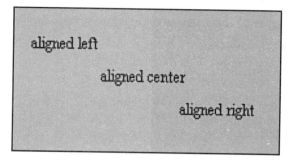

Once you have a label object, you can use methods defined in the Label class to get and set the values of the text, as explained in Table 13.1.

Table 13.1. Label methods.

Method	Action
getText()	Returns a string containing this label's text
setText(String)	Changes the text of this label
getAlignment()	Returns an integer representing the alignment of this label: 0 is Label.LEFT, 1 is Label.CENTER, 2 is Label.RIGHT
setAlignment(int)	Changes the alignment of this label to the given integer (use the class variables indicated above)

Buttons

NEW TERM *Buttons* are simple user interface components that trigger some action in your interface when they are pressed. For example, a calculator applet might have buttons for each number and operator, or a dialog box might have buttons for OK and Cancel.

To create a button, use one of the following constructors:

☐ Button() creates an empty button with no label.

☐ Button(*String*) creates a button with the given string object as a label.

Once you have a button object, you can get the value of the button's label by using the `getLabel()` method, and set the label using the `setLabel(String)` methods. Figure 13.4 shows some simple buttons that were created using the following code:

```
add(new Button("Rewind"));
add(new Button("Play"));
add(new Button("Fast Forward"));
add(new Button("Stop"));
```

Figure 13.4.

Buttons.

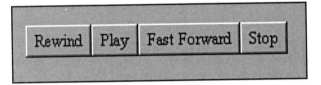

Check Boxes

NEW TERM *Check boxes* are user interface components that have two states: on and off (or checked and not checked, selected and not selected, true and false, and so on). Unlike buttons, check boxes usually don't trigger direct actions in a user interface but instead are used to indicate optional features of some other action.

Check boxes can be used in two ways:

☐ Nonexclusive, meaning that given a series of check boxes, any of them can be selected.

☐ Exclusive, meaning that within one series, only one check box can be selected at a time.

Exclusive check boxes are called radio buttons or check box groups and are described in the next section.

You can create nonexclusive check boxes by using the `Checkbox` class. You can create a check box by using one of the following constructors:

☐ `Checkbox()` creates an empty check box that's not selected.

☐ `Checkbox(String)` creates a check box with the given string as a label.

☐ `Checkbox(String, null, boolean)` creates a check box that is either selected or not selected based on whether the boolean argument is `true` or `false`, respectively. (The `null` is used as a placeholder for a group argument. Only radio buttons have groups, as you'll learn in the next section.)

13

Table 13.2 lists the check box methods. Figure 13.5 shows a few simple check boxes (Socks and Shirt are selected), generated using the following code:

```
add(new Checkbox("Shoes"));
add(new Checkbox("Socks", null, true));
add(new Checkbox("Pants"));
add(new Checkbox("Underwear"));
add(new Checkbox("Shirt", null, true));
```

Table 13.2. Check box methods.

Method	Action
getLabel()	Returns a string containing this check box's label
setLabel(String)	Changes the text of the check box's label
getState()	Returns true or false, based on whether the check box is selected
setState(boolean)	Changes the check box's state to selected (true) or not selected (false)

Figure 13.5.

Check boxes.

Radio Buttons

NEW TERM   *Radio buttons* have the same appearance as check boxes, but only one in a series can be selected at a time. To create a series of radio buttons, first create an instance of CheckboxGroup:

```
CheckboxGroup cbg = new CheckboxGroup();
```

13

Then create and add the individual check boxes, using the group as the second argument and whether that check box is selected (only one in the series can be selected) as the third argument:

```
add(new Checkbox("Yes", cbg, true);
add(new Checkbox("no", cbg, false);
```

Here's a simple example (the results of which are shown in Figure 13.6):

```
CheckboxGroup cbg = new CheckboxGroup();

add(new Checkbox("Red", cbg, false));
add(new Checkbox("Orange", cbg, true));
add(new Checkbox("Yellow", cbg, false));
add(new Checkbox("Green", cbg, false));
add(new Checkbox("Blue", cbg, false));
add(new Checkbox("Indigo", cbg, false));
add(new Checkbox("Violet", cbg, false));
```

Figure 13.6.
Radio buttons.

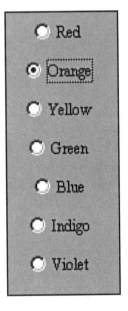

13

If you add more than one check box with its third argument set to `true`, only the last one added will appear with the check box selected.

You can use all the check box methods defined in the previous section with the check boxes in the group. In addition, you can use the `getCheckboxGroup()` and `setCheckboxGroup()` methods to access and change the group of any given check box. You can also use the `getCurrent()` and `setCurrent(Checkbox)` methods, defined in the check box group, to get or set the currently selected check box.

Choice Menus

NEW TERM The choice menu is a more complex user interface component than labels, buttons, or check boxes. *Choice menus* are pop-up (or pull-down) menus that enable you to select an item from that menu. The menu then displays that choice on-screen.

To create a choice menu, create an instance of the `Choice` class, and then use the `addItem()` method to add individual items to it in the order in which they should appear:

```
Choice c = new Choice();

c.addItem("Apples");
c.addItem("Oranges");
c.addItem("Strawberries");
c.addItem("Blueberries");
c.addItem("Bananas");
```

Finally, add the entire choice menu to the panel in the usual way:

```
add(c);
```

Figure 13.7 shows a simple choice menu generated from code in the previous example.

Figure 13.7.

Choice menus.

 TIP

Choice menus allow only one selection per menu. If you want to select multiple items, use a scrolling list instead.

Once your choice menu is created, regardless of whether it's added to a panel, you can continue to add items to that menu by using the `addItem()` method. Table 13.3 shows some other methods that might be useful in working with choice menus.

Table 13.3. Choice menu methods.

Method	Action
`getItem(int)`	Returns the string item at the given position (items inside a choice menu begin at 0, same as arrays)
`countItems()`	Returns the number of items in the menu
`getSelectedIndex()`	Returns the index position of the item that's selected
`getSelectedItem()`	Returns the currently selected item as a string
`select(int)`	Selects the item at the given position
`select(String)`	Selects the item with the given string

Text Fields

 Unlike the user interface components up to this point, which enable you to select only among several options to perform an action, text fields allow you to enter any values. *Text fields* enable your reader to enter text.

To create a text field, use one of the following constructors:

☐ `TextField()` creates an empty textfield that is 0 characters wide.

☐ `TextField(int)` creates an empty text field with the given width in characters.

☐ `TextField(String)` creates a text field 0 characters wide, initialized with the given string.

☐ `TextField(String, int)` creates a text field with the given width in characters and containing the given string. If the string is longer than the width, you can select and drag portions of the text within the field and the box will scroll left or right.

For example, the following line creates a text field 30 characters wide with the string `"Enter Your Name"` as its initial contents.

```
TextField tf = new TextField("Enter Your Name", 30);
add(tf);
```

13

 TIP   Text fields include only the editable field itself. You usually need to include a label with a text field to indicate what belongs in that text field.

NOTE

> Text fields are different from text areas. Text fields are limited in size and are best used for one-line items. Text areas have scrollbars and are better for larger text windows. Both can be edited and enable selections with the mouse. You'll learn about text areas later today.

You also can create a text field that obscures the characters typed into it—for example, for password fields. To do this, first create the text field itself, and then use the setEchoCharacter() method to set the character that is echoed on-screen. Here is an example:

```
TextField tf = new TextField(30);
tf.setEchoCharacter('*');
```

Figure 13.8 shows three text boxes (and labels) that were created by using the following code:

```
add(new Label("Enter your Name"));
add(new TextField("your name here", 45));
add(new Label("Enter your phone number"));
add(new TextField(12));
add(new Label("Enter your password"));
TextField t = new TextField(20);
t.setEchoCharacter('*');
add(t);
```

Figure 13.8.

Text fields.

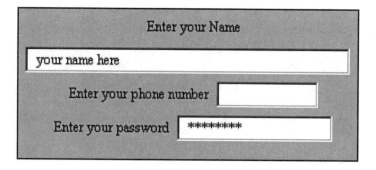

Text fields inherit from the class TextComponent and have a whole suite of methods, both inherited from that class and defined in its own class, that might be useful in your Java programs. Table 13.4 shows a selection of those methods.

Table 13.4. Text field methods.

Method	Action
getText()	Returns the text this text field contains (as a string)
setText(String)	Puts the given text string into the field

13

Method	Action
getColumns()	Returns the width of this text field
select(int, int)	Selects the text between the two integer positions (positions start from 0)
selectAll()	Selects all the text in the field
isEditable()	Returns true or false based on whether the text is editable
setEditable(boolean)	true (the default) enables text to be edited; false freezes the text
getEchoChar()	Returns the character used for masking input
echoCharIsSet()	Returns true or false based on whether the field has a masking character

Panels and Layout

You know at this point that an AWT panel can contain user interface components or other panels. The question now is how those components are arranged and displayed on-screen. In other windowing systems, user interface components often are arranged using hard-coded pixel measurements, (put text field tf at 10,30, for example) the same way you used the graphics operations to paint squares and ovals on-screen. In the AWT, the window can be displayed on many different windowing systems on many different screens and with many different kinds of fonts with different font metrics. Therefore, you need a more flexible method of arranging components on the screen so that a layout that looks nice on one platform isn't a jumbled unusable mess on another. For just this purpose, Java has layout managers, insets, and hints that each component can provide for helping lay out the screen.

Note that the nice thing about AWT components and user interface items is that you don't have to paint them—the AWT system manages all that for you. If you have graphical components or images, or you want to create animations inside panels, you still have to do that by hand, but for most of the basic components, all you have to do is put them on-screen, and Java will handle the rest.

13

Layout Managers

The actual appearance of the AWT components on-screen is determined by the order in which they are added to the panel that holds them and the layout manager that panel currently is using to lay out the screen. The layout manager determines how portions of the screen are sectioned and how components within that panel are placed.

Note that each panel on the screen can have its own layout manager. By nesting panels within panels, and using the appropriate layout manager for each one, you often can arrange your user interface to group and arrange components in a way that is both functionally useful and also looks good on a variety of platforms and windowing systems. You'll learn about nesting panels in a later section.

The AWT provides five basic layout managers: FlowLayout, GridLayout, GridBagLayout, BorderLayout, and CardLayout. To create a layout manager for a given panel, use the setLayout() method for that panel:

```
public void init() {
    setLayout(new FlowLayout());
}
```

Setting the default layout manager, like creating the user interface components, is best done during the applet's initialization, which is why it's included here.

Once the layout manager is set, you can start adding components to the panel. The order in which components are added is often significant, depending on which layout manager is currently active. Read on for information about the specific layout managers and how they present components within the panel to which they apply. The following sections describe the five basic Java AWT layout managers.

The FlowLayout Class

The FlowLayout class is the most basic of layouts. Using the flow layout, components are added to the panel one at a time, row by row. If a component doesn't fit onto a row, it's wrapped onto the next row. The flow layout also has an alignment, which determines the alignment of each row. By default, each row is centered. Figure 13.9 shows a flow layout at its best—a simple row of buttons, centered on a line.

The default panel layout is a basic flow layout with a centered alignment, so if you want to use this layout, you don't have to add any code. In case you're wondering, however, you can specify this layout by entering the following line of code in your panel's initialization:

```
setLayout(new FlowLayout());
```

To create a flow layout with an alignment other than centered, add the FlowLayout.RIGHT or FlowLayout.LEFT class variable as an argument:

```
setLayout(new FlowLayout(FlowLayout.LEFT));
```

You also can set horizontal and vertical gap values by using flow layouts. The gap is the number of pixels between components in a panel; by default, the horizontal and vertical gap values are three pixels, which can be close indeed. Horizontal gap spreads out components to the left and to the right of the panel; vertical gap separates components to the top and bottom of the panel. Add integer arguments to the flow layout constructor to increase the gap:

```
setLayout(new FlowLayout(FlowLayout.LEFT, 10, 10));
```

Figure 13.9.

Flow layout.

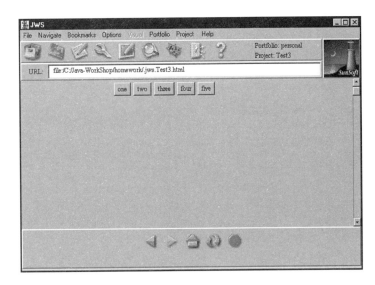

The first argument after `FlowLayout.LEFT` represents the horizontal gap, and the last argument represents the vertical gap. Figure 13.10 shows a layout gap of 10 points in both the horizontal and vertical directions.

Figure 13.10.

Flow layout with a gap of 10 points.

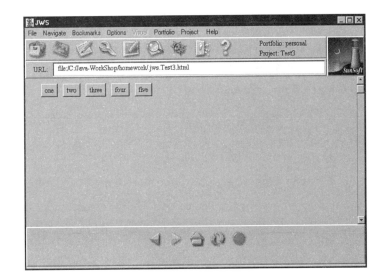

Grid and Grid Bag Layouts

Grid layouts use a layout that offers more control over the placement of components inside a panel. Using a grid layout, you portion off the area of the panel into rows and columns. Each component you then add to the panel is placed in a cell of the grid, starting from the top row and progressing through each row from left to right (here's where the order of calls to the add() method are relevant to how the screen is laid out). By using grid layouts and nested grids, you often can approximate the use of hard-coded pixel values to place your user interface components precisely where you want them. Figure 13.11 shows a grid layout with two rows and three columns.

Figure 13.11.

Grid layout.

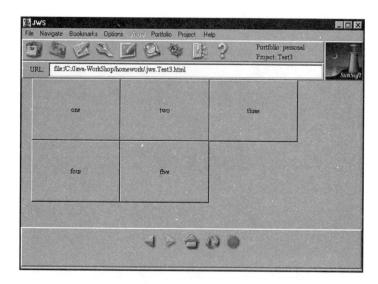

To create a grid layout, indicate the number of rows and columns you want the grid to have when you create a new instance of the GridLayout class:

```
setLayout(new GridLayout(2, 3));
```

Grid layouts also can have a horizontal and vertical gap between components; to create gaps, add those pixel values:

```
setLayout(new GridLayout(2, 3, 10, 15));
```

Figure 13.12 shows a grid layout with a 10-pixel horizontal gap and a 15-pixel vertical gap.

Grid bag layouts, as implemented by the GridBagLayout class, are variations on grid layouts. Grid bag layouts also enable you to lay out your user interface elements in a rectangular grid, but you have much more control over the presentation of each element in the grid. Grid bag layouts use a helper class, GridBagConstraints, to indicate how each cell in the grid is to be formatted.

13

Figure 13.12.
Grid layouts with horizontal and vertical gap.

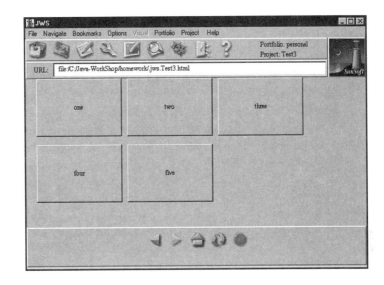

Border Layouts

Border layouts behave differently than flow and grid layouts. When you add a component to a panel that uses a border layout, you indicate its placement as a geographic direction: north, south, east, west, and center (see Figure 13.13). The components around all the edges are laid out with as much size as they need; the component in the center, if any, gets any space left over.

Figure 13.13.
Border layout.

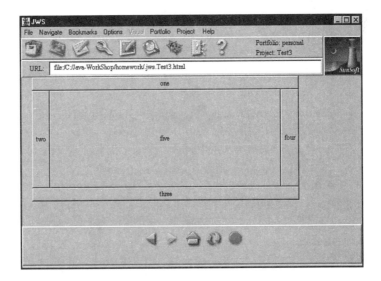

To use a border layout, you create it as you do the other layouts:

```
setLayout(new BorderLayout());
```

Then you add the individual components by using a special add() method. The first argument to add() is a string indicating the position of the component within the layout:

```
add("North", new TextField("Title", 50));
add("South", new TextField("Status", 50));
```

You also can use this form of add() for the other layout managers; the string argument will just be ignored if it's not needed.

Border layouts also can have horizontal and vertical gaps. Note that the north and south components extend all the way to the edge of the panel, so the gap will result in less space for the east, west, and center components. To add gaps to a border layout, include those pixel values as before:

```
setLayout(new BorderLayout(10, 10));
```

Card Layouts

Unlike the other layouts, when you add components to a card layout, they are not all displayed on the screen at once. Card layouts are used to produce slide shows of components that display components one at a time. If you've ever used the HyperCard program on the Macintosh, you've worked with the same basic idea.

Generally when you create a card layout, the components you add to it will be other container components—usually panels. You then can use different layouts for those individual cards so that each screen has its own look. When you add each card to the panel, you can give it a name. Then you can use methods defined in the CardLayout class to move back and forth between different cards in the layout.

For example, here's how to create a card layout containing three cards:

```
setLayout(new CardLayout());
Panel one = new Panel()
add("first", one);
Panel two = new Panel()
add("second", two);
Panel three = new Panel()
add("third", three);
show(this, "second");
```

Insets

As you have seen today, horizontal gap and vertical gap are used to determine the amount of space between components in a panel. Insets are used to determine the amount of space

13

around the panel itself. The Insets class provides values for the top, bottom, left, and right insets, which then are used when the panel is drawn. Figure 13.14 shows the previous BorderLayout example with an inset of 10 pixels around each edge.

Figure 13.14.

Insets.

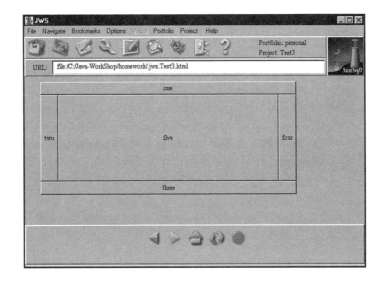

To include an inset, override the insets() method in your class (your Applet class or other class that serves as a panel). The arguments to the insets constructor provide pixel insets for the top, bottom, left, and right edges of the panel. This particular example provides an inset of 10 pixels on all four sides of the panel:

```
public Insets insets() {
    return new Insets(10, 10, 10, 10);
}
```

Handling User Interface Actions and Events

If you stopped reading today's lesson right now, you could go out and create an applet that had lots of user interface components nicely laid out on-screen with the proper layout manager, gap, and insets. However, your applet would be really dull, because none of your user interface components would do anything when pressed, typed into, or selected. For your user interface components to do something when they are activated, you need to hook up the user interface's action with an operation.

Testing for an action by a user interface component is a form of event management; the things you learned yesterday about events will come in handy here. In particular, user interface components produce the special kind of event called an *action*. To intercept an action by any user interface component, you define an action() method in your applet or class:

```
public boolean action(Event evt, Object arg) {
    // method code here
}
```

The action() method should look similar to the basic mouse and keyboard event methods. Like those methods, it gets passed the event object that represents this event. It also gets an extra object, which can be of any type.

The second argument to the action() method depends on the user interface component that's generating the event. The basic definition is that it's any arbitrary argument; when a component generates an event, it can pass along any extra information that might later be needed. Because that extra information might be useful for you, it's passed on through the action() method.

All the basic user interface components (except for labels, which have no action) have different actions and arguments:

☐ Buttons create actions when they are selected, and a button's argument is the label of the button.

☐ Check boxes, both exclusive and nonexclusive, generate actions when a box is checked. The argument is always true.

☐ Choice menus generate an action when a menu item is selected, and the argument is that item.

☐ Text fields create actions when the user presses Enter inside that text field. Note that if the user tabs to a different text field or uses the mouse to change the input focus, an action is not generated. Pressing Enter is the only thing that triggers the action.

Note that with actions, unlike with ordinary events, you can have many different kinds of objects generating the event, as opposed to a single event such as a mouseDown. To deal with those different user interface components and the actions they generate, you have to test for the type of object that created the event in the first place inside the body of your action() method. That object is stored in the event's target instance variable, and you can use the instanceof operator to find out what kind of user interface component sent it:

```
public boolean action(Event evt, Object arg) {
    if (evt.target instanceof TextField)
        handleText(evt.target);
    else if (evt.target instanceof Choice)
        handleChoice(arg);
    // and so on
}
```

13

Although you can handle user interface actions in the body of the `action()` method, it's much more common to define a handler method and call that method from `action()` instead. In this example, there are two handler methods: one to handle the action on the text field (`handleText()`) and one to handle the action on the choice menu (`handleChoice()`). Depending on the action you want to handle, you also might want to pass on the argument from the action, the user interface component that sent it, or any other information that the event might contain.

Listing 13.1 contains the source code for a simple applet that has five buttons labeled with letters and a text field. The `action()` method tests for a button action and then passes the letter of the button pressed to a method called `fillField()`. This method fills the text field with the letter, as shown in Figure 13.15.

Listing 13.1. The source code of `FillText.java`.

```
 1:
 2: import java.awt.*;
 3:
 4: public class FillText extends java.applet.Applet {
 5:     TextField tf = new TextField(70);
 6:
 7:     public void init() {
 8:         setBackground(Color.white);
 9:
10:         add(new Button("H"));
11:         add(new Button("A"));
12:         add(new Button("R"));
13:         add(new Button("P"));
14:         add(new Button("O"));
15:         add(tf);
16:     }
17:
18:     public boolean action(Event evt, Object arg) {
19:         if (evt.target instanceof Button)
20:             fillField((String)arg);
21:         return true;
22:     }
23:
24:     void fillField(String bname) {
25:         String s = "";
26:         for (int i = 0; i < 101; i += 1)
27:             s += bname;
28:         tf.setText(s);
29:     }
30: }
```

13

Figure 13.15.

The FillText *applet.*

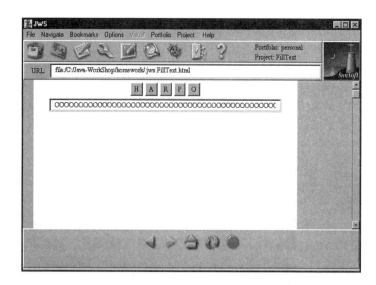

Nesting Panels and Components

Adding user interface components to individual applets is fun, but applets begin to turn into lots of fun when you begin working with nested panels. By nesting different panels inside your applet, and nesting panels inside those panels, you can create different layouts for different parts of the overall applet area, isolate background and foreground colors and fonts to individual parts of an applet, and manage the design of your user interface components much more cleanly and simply. The more complex the layout of your applet, the more likely you're going to want to use nested panels.

Nested Panels

Panels, as you already have learned, are components that can be displayed on-screen; Panel's superclass, Container, provides the generic behavior for holding other components inside it. The Applet class, which your applets all inherit from, is a subclass of Panel. To nest other panels inside an applet, you merely create a new panel and add it to the applet, just as you would add any other user interface component:

```
setLayout(new GridLayout(1, 2, 10, 10));
Panel panel1 = new Panel();
Panel panel2 = new Panel();
add(panel1);
add(panel2);
```

You then can set up an independent layout for those subpanels and add AWT components to them (including still more subpanels) by calling the add() method in the appropriate panel:

```
panel1.setLayout(new FlowLayout());
panel1.add(new Button("Up"));
panel1.add(new Button("Down"));
```

Although you can do all this in a single class, it's common in applets that make heavy use of the panels to factor out the layout and behavior of the subpanels into separate classes, and to communicate between the panels by using method calls. You'll look at an extensive example of this later on in today's lesson.

Events and Nested Panels

When you create applets with nested panels, those panels form a hierarchy from the outermost panel (the applet, usually) to the innermost user interface component. This hierarchy is important to how each component in an applet interacts with the other components in the applet or with the browser that contains that applet; in particular, the component hierarchy determines the order in which components are painted to the screen.

More importantly, the hierarchy also affects event handling, particularly for user input events such as mouse and keyboard events. Events are received by the innermost component in the component hierarchy and passed up the chain to the root component. Suppose that you have an applet with a subpanel that can handle mouse events (using the mouseDown() and mouseUp() methods) and that panel contains a button. Clicking the button means that the button receives the event before the panel does; if the button isn't interested in that mouseDown() method, the event gets passed to the panel, which can then process it or pass it further up the hierarchy.

Remember the discussion about the basic event methods yesterday? You learned that the basic event methods all return boolean values. Those boolean values become important when you're talking about handling events or passing them on. An event handling method, whether it is the set of basic event methods or the more generic handleEvent(), can do one of three things, given any random event:

13

- [ ] Not be interested in the event (this is usually true only for handleEvent(), which receives all the events generated by the system). If this is the case, the event is passed on up the hierarchy until a component processes it (or it is ignored altogether). In this case, the event handling method should return false.

- [ ] Intercept the event, process it, and return true. In this case, the event stops with that event method. Recall that this is the case with the basic mouseDown() and keyDown() methods that you learned about yesterday.

☐ Intercept the method, process it, and pass it on to the next event handler. This case is somewhat unusual, but you may create a user interface by using nested components that will want to do this. In this case, the event method should return `false` to pass the event on to the next handler in the chain.

More User Interface Components

Once you master the basic user interface components and how to add them to panels and manage their events, you can add more user interface components. In this section, you'll learn about text areas, scrolling lists, scrollbars, and canvases.

Note that the user interface components in this section do not produce actions, so you can't use the `action()` method to handle their behavior. Instead, you have to use a generic `handleEvent()` method to test for specific events that these user interface components generate. You'll learn more about this in the next section.

Text Areas

Text areas are like text fields, except they have more functionality for handling large amounts of text. Because text fields are limited in size and don't scroll, they are better for one-line responses and text entry; text areas can be any given width and height and have scrollbars by default, so you can deal with larger amounts of text more easily.

To create a text area, use one of the following constructors:

☐ `TextArea()` creates an empty text area 0 rows long and 0 characters wide. Given that a text area with no dimensions can't be displayed, you should make sure you change the dimensions of this new text area before adding it to a panel (or just use the next constructor instead).

☐ `TextArea(int, int)` creates an empty text area with the given number of rows and columns (characters).

☐ `TextArea(String)` creates a text area displaying the given string, 0 rows by 0 columns.

☐ `TextArea(String, int, int)` creates a text area displaying the given string and with the given dimensions.

Figure 13.16 shows a simple text area generated from the following code:

```
String str = "\"After all, Watson,\" said Holmes, reaching up his hand for
his\n" + "clay pipe, \"I am not retained by the police to supply their
deficiencies.\n" + "If Horner were in danger it would be another thing, but this
fellow will\n" + "not appear against him, and the case must collapse. I suppose
that I am\n" + "committing a felony, but it is just possible I am saving a
soul.\""; add(new TextArea(str,10,60));
```

13

Figure 13.16.

A text area.

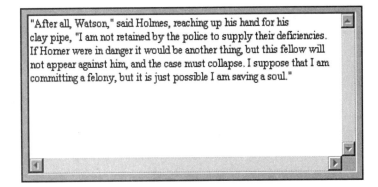

"After all, Watson," said Holmes, reaching up his hand for his clay pipe, "I am not retained by the police to supply their deficiencies. If Horner were in danger it would be another thing, but this fellow will not appear against him, and the case must collapse. I suppose that I am committing a felony, but it is just possible I am saving a soul."

Both text areas and text fields inherit from the `TextComponent` class, so a lot of the behavior for text fields (particularly getting and setting text and selections) is usable on text areas as well (refer to Table 13.4). Text areas also have a number of their own methods that you might find useful. Table 13.5 shows a sampling of those methods.

Table 13.5. Text area methods.

Method	Action
`getColumns()`	Returns the width of the text area, in characters or columns.
`getRows()`	Returns the number of rows in the text area (not the number of rows of text that the text area contains).
`insertText(String, int)`	Inserts the string at the given position in the text (text positions start at `0`).
`replaceText(String, int, int)`	Replaces the text between the given integer positions with the new string.
`setLineIncrement(int inc)`	Changes the increment for how far to scroll when the endpoints of the scrollbar are selected. The default is `1`.
`getLineIncrement()`	Returns the increment for how far to scroll when the endpoints of the scrollbar are selected.
`setPageIncrement(int inc)`	Change the increment for how far to scroll when the inside range of the scrollbar is selected. The default is `10`.
`getPageIncrement()`	Returns the increment for how far to scroll when the inside range of the scrollbar is selected.

13

Scrolling Lists

Remember the choice menu, which enables you to choose one of several different options? A scrolling list is functionally similar to a choice menu in that it lets you pick several options from a list. Scrolling lists differ in two significant ways:

☐ Scrolling lists are not pop-up menus. They're lists from which you can choose one or more items. If the number of items is larger than the list box, a scrollbar automatically is provided so that you can see the other items.

☐ A scrolling list can be defined to accept only one item at a time (exclusive) or multiple items (nonexclusive).

To create a scrolling list, create an instance of the List class, and then add individual items to that list. The List class has two constructors:

☐ List() creates an empty scrolling list that enables only one selection at a time.

☐ List(int, boolean) creates a scrolling list with the given number of visible lines on the screen (you're unlimited as to the number of items you can add to the list). The boolean argument indicates whether this list enables multiple selections (true) or not (false).

After creating a List object, add items to it using the addItem() method and then add the list itself to the panel that contains it. Here's an example, the result of which is shown in Figure 13.17:

```
List lst = new List(5, true);

lst.addItem("Hamlet");
lst.addItem("Claudius");
lst.addItem("Gertrude");
lst.addItem("Polonius");
lst.addItem("Horatio");
lst.addItem("Laertes");
lst.addItem("Ophelia");

add(lst);
```

Figure 13.17.

A scrolling list.

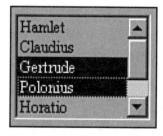

Table 13.6 shows some of the methods available to scrolling lists. See the API documentation for a complete set.

Table 13.6. Scrolling list methods.

Method	Action
getItem(int)	Returns the string item at the given position
countItems()	Returns the number of items in the menu
getSelectedIndex()	Returns the index position of the item that's selected (used for lists that enable only single selections)
getSelectedIndexes()	Returns an array of index positions (used for lists that enable multiple selections)
getSelectedItem()	Returns the currently selected item as a string
getSelectedItems()	Returns an array of strings containing all the selected items
select(int)	Selects the item at the given position
select(String)	Selects the item with that string

Scrollbars and Sliders

Text areas and scrolling lists come with their own scrollbars, which are built into those user interface components and enable you to manage both the body of the area or the list and its scrollbar as a single unit. You also can create individual scrollbars, or sliders, to manipulate a range of values.

Scrollbars are used to select a value between a maximum and a minimum value. To change the current value of that scrollbar, you can use three different parts of the scrollbar (see Figure 13.18):

- ☐ Arrows on either end, which increment or decrement the values by some small unit (1 by default).
- ☐ A range in the middle, which increments or decrements the value by a larger amount (10 by default).
- ☐ A box in the middle, often called an *elevator* or *thumb*, whose position shows where in the range of values the current value is located. Moving this box with the mouse causes an absolute change in the value, based on the position of the box within the scrollbar.

13

Figure 13.18.

Scrollbar parts.

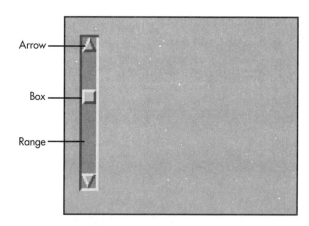

Choosing any of these visual elements causes a change in the scrollbar's value; you don't have to update anything or handle any events. All you have to do is give the scrollbar a maximum and minimum, and Java will handle the rest.

To create a scrollbar, you can use one of three constructors:

☐ `Scrollbar()` creates a scrollbar with `0`, `0` as its initial maximum and initial minimum values, in a vertical orientation.

☐ `Scrollbar(int)` creates a scrollbar with `0`, `0` as its initial maximum and initial minimum values. The argument represents an orientation, for which you can use the class variables `Scrollbar.HORIZONTAL` and `Scrollbar.VERTICAL`.

☐ `Scrollbar(int, int, int, int, int)` creates a scrollbar with the following arguments (each one is an integer, and the arguments must be presented in this order):

The first argument is the orientation of the scrollbar: `Scrollbar.HORIZONTAL` and `Scrollbar.VERTICAL`.

The second argument is the initial value of the scrollbar, which should be a value between the scrollbar's maximum and minimum values.

The third argument is the overall width (or height, depending on the orientation) of the scrollbar's box. In user interface design, a larger box implies that a larger amount of the total range is currently showing (this applies best to things such as windows and text areas).

The fourth and fifth arguments are the minimum and maximum values for the scrollbar.

13

Here's a simple example of a scrollbar that increments a single value (see Figure 13.19). The label to the left of the scrollbar is updated each time the scrollbar's value changes:

```java
import java.awt.*;

public class SliderTest extends java.applet.Applet {
    Label l;

    public void init() {
        l = new Label("0");
        add(l);
        add(new Scrollbar(Scrollbar.HORIZONTAL, 1, 0, 1, 100));
    }

    public boolean handleEvent(Event evt) {
        if (evt.target instanceof Scrollbar) {
            int v = ((Scrollbar)evt.target).getValue();
            l.setText(String.valueOf(v));
        }
        return true;
    }
}
```

Figure 13.19.

A scrollbar.

The Scrollbar class provides several methods for managing the values within scrollbars (see Table 13.7).

Table 13.7. Scrollbar methods.

Method	Action
getMaximum()	Returns the maximum value
getMinimum()	Returns the minimum value
getOrientation()	Returns the orientation of this scrollbar: 0 is Scrollbar.HORIZONTAL, 1 is Scrollbar.VERTICAL
getValue()	Returns the scrollbar's current value
setValue(int)	Sets the current value of the scrollbar

Canvases

NEW TERM A *canvas* is a component that you can draw on. Although you can draw on most AWT components, such as panels, canvases do little except let you draw on them. They can't contain other components, but they can accept events, and you can create animations and display images on them. Canvases, in other words, could have been used for much of the stuff you learned about earlier this week.

To create a canvas, use the Canvas class and add it to a panel as you would any other component:

```
Canvas can = new Canvas();
add(can);
```

More User Interface Events

Yesterday, you learned about some basic event types that are generated from user input to the mouse or the keyboard. These event types are stored in the Event object as the event ID and can be tested for in the body of a handleEvent() method by using class variables defined in Event. For many basic events, such as mouseDown() and keyDown(), you can define methods for those events to handle the event directly. You learned a similar mechanism today for user interface actions where creating an action() method handled a specific action generated by a user interface component.

The most general way of managing events, however, continues to be the handleEvent() method. For events relating to scrollbars and scrolling lists, the only way to intercept these events is to override handleEvent(). To intercept a specific event, test for that event's ID. The available IDs are defined as class variables in the Event class, so you can test them by name. You learned about some of the basic events yesterday. Table 13.8 shows additional events that may be useful to you for the components you've learned about today (or that you might find useful in general).

Table 13.8. Additional events.

Event ID	What It Represents
ACTION_EVENT	Generated when a user interface component action occurs
KEY_ACTION	Generated when text field action occurs
LIST_DESELECT	Generated when an item in a scrolling list is deselected
LIST_SELECT	Generated when an item in a scrolling list is selected
SCROLL_ABSOLUTE	Generated when a scrollbar's box has been moved
SCROLL_LINE_DOWN	Generated when a scrollbar's bottom or right arrow is selected

13

Event ID	What It Represents
SCROLL_LINE_UP	Generated when a scrollbar's top or left arrow (button) is selected
SCROLL_PAGE_DOWN	Generated when the scrollbar's range below (or to the right of) the box is selected
SCROLL_PAGE_UP	Generated when the scrollbar's range above (or to the left of) the box is selected

A Complete Example: RGB to HSB Converter

The next program that you create is a larger applet that puts together much of what you've learned so far. The ColorTest applet demonstrates layouts, nesting panels, creating user interface components, and catching and handling actions, as well as using multiple classes to put together a single applet. In short, it's the most complex applet you will have created up to this point.

Figure 13.20 shows the applet you will be creating in this example. The ColorTest applet enables you to pick colors based on RGB (red, green, and blue) and HSB (hue, saturation, and brightness) values and immediately see the results of your selection.

Figure 13.20.

The ColorTest *applet.*

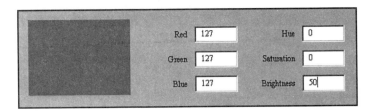

ColorTest has three main parts: a colored box on the left side and two groups of text fields on the right. The group on the left indicates RGB values, and the group on the right indicates HSB values. By changing any of the values in any of the text boxes, the colored box is updated to the new color, as are the values in the other group of text boxes.

This applet uses two classes:

☐ ColorTest, which inherits from Applet. This is the controlling class for the applet itself.

☐ ColorControls, which inherits from Panel. You create this class to represent a group of three text fields and to handle actions from those text fields. Two instances of this class, one for the RGB values and one for the HSB ones, are created and added to the applet.

Before entering any code, work through this example step by step, because it's very complicated and can get confusing. All the code for this applet is shown at the end of this section.

Create the Applet Layout

The best way to start creating an applet that uses AWT components is to worry about the layout first and then worry about the functionality. When dealing with the layout, you also should start with the outermost panel first and work inward.

Making a sketch of your user interface design can help you figure out how to organize the panels inside your applet or window to best take advantage of layout and space. Figure 13.21 shows the ColorTest applet with a grid drawn over it so that you can get an idea of how the panels and embedded panels work.

Figure 13.21.

The ColorTest applet panels and components.

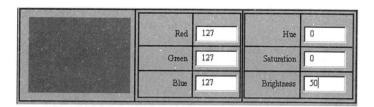

Create the Panel Layout

Start with the outermost panel—the applet itself. The ColorTest class is the applet class and inherits from Applet. You also import the AWT classes at this point (note that because you use so many of them in this program, it's easiest to import the entire package):

```
import java.awt.*;

public class ColorTest extends java.applet.Applet {
    // class code here
}
```

The applet panel has three parts: the color box on the left, the RGB text fields in the middle, and the HSB fields on the right. Set up instance variables to hold the three major components of this applet. You need to keep hold of these objects so you can update things when a value changes.

There are two subpanels, and although they have different labels and values, they essentially are the same panel. You could just create code for each one here, but you'd end up duplicating a lot of the same code. This is a perfect opportunity, therefore, to create another class to represent the subpanels with the text fields on them. Call it ColorControls (you'll get around to creating the class later) and define two variables, rgbControls and hsbControls, to hold the subpanels:

```
ColorControls rgbControls, hsbControls;
```

The color box is easy; it's just a canvas. Call it swatch:

```
Canvas swatch;
```

Next, you move on to the init() method, where all the basic initialization and layout takes place. There are four major steps:

1. Set the layout for the big parts of the panel. Although a flow layout would work, a grid layout with one row and three columns is a much better idea. Use a gap of ten points to separate each of the components:

   ```
   setLayout(new GridLayout(1, 3, 10, 10));
   ```

2. Create the three components of this applet: a canvas for the color box and two subpanels for the text fields. You have an instance variable to hold the canvas:

   ```
   swatch = new Canvas();
   ```

   You need to create two instances of your as-of-yet nonexistent ColorControls panels here as well, but you don't know exactly what you need to create them yet, so put in some basic constructors and fill in the details later:

   ```
   rgbControls = new ColorControls()
   hsbControls = new ColorControls();
   ```

3. Add those components to the applet:

   ```
   add(swatch);
   add(rgbControls);
   add(hsbControls);
   ```

4. Initialize the default color and update all the panels to reflect that default color.

While you're working on layout, add an inset just for fun—10 points along all the edges:

```
public Insets insets() {
    return new Insets(10, 10, 10, 10);
}
```

Got it so far? Now you have a skeleton init() method and an insets() method in your ColorTest class. The next step is to create the subpanel layout, which means creating that ColorControls class.

13

Define the Subpanels

The ColorControls class has behavior for laying out and handling the subpanels that represent the RGB and HSB values for the color. ColorControls doesn't need to be a subclass of Applet because it isn't an applet, it's just a panel. Define it to inherit from Panel:

```
class ColorControls extends Panel {
    // class code here
}
```

NOTE

> You can put the ColorControls class in the same file as the ColorTest class. You haven't been doing this often because most of the applets and applications you've been creating had only one class. If you remember way back to Day 1, "Introduction to Java and Java WorkShop," however, you learned that you can have multiple class definitions in a single file as long as only one of those definitions is declared public. In this case, the ColorTest class is public (it's an applet, so it has to be), but the ColorControls class doesn't need to be, so everything works out fine. Normally, you'd put ColorControls in a separate file, anyway.

You need a couple of instance variables in this class. The first thing you need is a hook back up to the applet class that contains this panel. Why? The applet class is the class that oversees how the subcomponents work, so it's going to be the class that updates everything. Eventually, you're going to have to call a method in that class to indicate that something in this panel has changed. Without a reference to that outer class, there's no way to do this. Instance variable number one is a reference to the class ColorTest:

```
ColorTest outerparent;
```

If you figure that the applet class is the one that's going to be updating everything, that class is going to need a way to get hold of the pieces inside this class. In particular, it's going to be interested in the individual text fields, so you're going to need instance variables to hold those. This code creates three such variables:

```
TextField f1, f2, f3;
```

Now for the constructor for this class. Again, this class isn't an applet, so you don't use init(); all you need is a constructor method. What do you need inside that constructor? You need to set the layout for the subpanel, create the text fields, and add them to the panel. The goal here is to make the ColorControls class generic enough so that you can use it for both the RGB fields and the HSB fields.

13

The two different panels differ in two respects: the labels for the text fields and the initial values for the text fields. That's six values to get before you can create the object. You can pass those six values in through the constructors in ColorTest. Because you need that hook back to the applet class, you also should pass in a reference to that object as part of the constructor.

You now have seven arguments to the basic constructor for the ColorControls class. Here's the signature for that constructor:

```
ColorControls(ColorTest target,
        String l1, String l2, String l3,
        int v1, int v2, int v3) {
}
```

Given those arguments, you can assign the right values to your instance variables:

```
outerparent = target;

f1 = new TextField(String.valueOf(v1),10);
f2 = new TextField(String.valueOf(v2),10);
f3 = new TextField(String.valueOf(v3),10);
```

Note that because the first argument to the TextField constructor is a string, and the values that you passed in were integers, you have to use the valueOf() class method (defined in String) to convert the integer to a string before creating each text field.

Next, you create the layout for this panel. You also use a grid layout for these subpanels, as you did for the applet panel, but this time the grid will have three rows (one for each of the text field and label pairs) and two columns (one for the labels and one for the fields).

Given the 3-by-2 grid, you now can add the text fields and labels to that panel. Note that by separating the labels and the text fields into separate cells in the grid, you can align the labels, creating a nice aligned layout.

```
add(new Label(l1, Label.RIGHT));
add(f1);
add(new Label(l2, Label.RIGHT));
add(f2);
add(new Label(l3, Label.RIGHT));
add(f3);
```

Finally, you will inset the contents of the subpanel a bit (only on the top and bottom edges) by including an insets() method:

```
public Insets insets() {
        return new Insets(10, 10, 0, 0);
  }
```

You're almost there. You have 98 percent of the layout in place and ready to go, but you're missing two things: creating the ColorControls objects in ColorTest and initializing everything so that all the components have the right values. For both, you need to go back to the ColorTest class and the init() method you defined there. Start with the initialization part, because that's easy. The default color is black. Set up a local variable to hold that color object:

```
Color theColor = new Color(0, 0, 0);
```

To set the initial color of the color box, all you need to do is set its background:

```
swatch.setBackground(theColor);
```

Now, you are ready to initialize those subpanels. The constructor for ColorControls has seven arguments: the ColorTest object, three labels (strings), and three initial values for the text fields (integers). Do the RGB controls first, because you easily can extract the initial red, green, and blue values out of the Color object:

```
rgbControls = new ColorControls(this, "Red", "Green", "Blue",
        theColor.getRed(), theColor.getGreen(),
        theColor.getBlue());
```

Things get complicated on the HSB side of the panel. The Color class provides you with a method to get the HSB values out of a Color object, but there are two problems:

☐ The RGBtoHSB() method is a single class method that insists on returning an array of the three values.

☐ The HSB values are measured in floating-point values. It is preferable to think of HSB as integers, wherein the hue is a degree value around a color wheel (0 through 360), and saturation and brightness are percentages from 0 to 100. Having HSB as integer values also enables you to have a generic subpanel, as was the intent.

Initializing the HSB subpanel is going to be a little difficult. First, extract those HSB values. Given that the method takes three RGB arguments—an array of three floats—and returns an array of three floats, you have to go through this process to get those values:

```
float[] HSB = Color.RGBtoHSB(theColor.getRed(),
    theColor.getGreen(), theColor.getBlue(),(new float[3]));
```

Now you have an array of floats, where hsb[0] is the hue, hsb[1] is the saturation, and hsb[2] is the brightness. You can now initialize the HSB side of the applet, making sure that when you pass those HSB values into the subpanel, you multiply them by the right values (360 for the hues, 100 for the saturation and the brightness) and convert them to integers:

```
hsbcontrols = new ColorControls(this,
        "Hue", "Saturation", "Brightness",
        (int)(hsb[0] * 360), (int)(hsb[1] * 100),
        (int)(hsb[2] * 100));
```

Ready to give up? Fear not—you've done the hard part. When you have your layout working, you can compile your Java program and see how it looks. None of your user interface components do anything yet, but perfecting the layout is half the battle.

13

Handle the Actions

After creating the layout, you set up actions with the user interface components so that when the user interacts with the applet, the applet can respond. The action of this applet occurs when the user changes a value in any of the text fields. By causing an action in a text field, the color changes, the color box updates to the new color, and the values of the fields in the opposite subpanel change to reflect the new color.

The ColorTest class is responsible for doing the updating, because it keeps track of all the subpanels. You should be tracking and intercepting events in the subpanel in which they occur, however. Because the action of the applet is a text action, you can use an action() method to intercept it:

```
public boolean action(Event evt, Object arg) {
        if (evt.target instanceof TextField) {
            outerparent.update(this);
            return true;
        }
        else return false;
    }
```

In the action() method, you test to make sure the action was indeed generated by a text field (because there are only text fields available, that's the only action you'll get, but it's a good idea to test for it anyhow). If so, call the update() method, defined in ColorTest, to update the applet to reflect all the new values. Because the outer applet is responsible for doing all the updating, you need that hook back to the applet, so you can call the right method at the right time.

Update the Result

The only part left now is to update all the values and the color swatch if one of the values changes. For this part, you define the update() method in the ColorTest class. This update() method takes a single argument—the ColorControls instance that contains the changed value (you get that argument from the action() method in the subpanel).

13

NOTE Won't this update() method interfere with the system's update() method? Nope. Remember, methods can have the same names, but different signatures and definitions. Because this update() has a single argument of type ColorControls, it doesn't interfere with the other version of update(). Normally, all methods called update() should mean basically the same thing; it's not true here, but it's only an example.

The update() method is responsible for updating all the panels in the applet. To know which panel to update, you need to know which panel changed. You can find out by testing to see whether the argument you got passed is the same as the subpanels you have stored in the RGBcontrols and HSBcontrols instance variables:

```
void update(ColorControls in) {

    if (in == rgbControls) { // the change was in rgb
    // code here
    }
    else { // change was in hsb
}
```

This test is the heart of the update() method. Start with that first case—a number has been changed in the RGB text fields. Based on those new RGB values, you have to generate a new color object and update the values on the HSB panel. To reduce some typing, you create a few local variables to hold some basic values. In particular, the values of the text fields are strings, and you get into them by accessing the text field instance variables for the ColorControls panel (f1, f2, f3) and then using the getText() method to extract the values. Extract those values and store them in string variables so that you don't have to keep typing:

```
String v1 = in.f1.getText();
String v2 = in.f2.getText();
String v3 = in.f3.getText();
```

Given those string values for RGB, you now create a color object by converting those strings to integers:

```
Color c;
c = new Color(Integer.parseInt(v1),Integer.parseInt(v2), Integer.parseInt(v3));
```

NOTE

This part of the example isn't very robust; it assumes that the user has entered real numbers into the text fields. A better version of this would test to make sure that no parsing errors had occurred, but this step was omitted here to keep this example small.

When you have a Color object, you can update the color swatch:

```
swatch.setBackground(c);
```

The next step is to update the HSB panel to the new HSB values. Doing this in the init() method is no fun at all, and it's even less fun here. To do this, you call RGBtoHSB to get the floating-point values, convert them to integers with the right values, convert them to strings, and then put them back into the text fields for the HSB subpanel. Got all that? Here's the code:

```
float[] HSB = Color.RGBtoHSB(c.getRed(),c.getGreen(),
          c.getBlue(), (new float[3]));
hsb[0] *= 360;
hsb[1] *= 100;
hsb[2] *= 100;
hsbControls.f1.setText(String.valueOf((int)hsb[0]));
hsbControls.f2.setText(String.valueOf((int)hsb[1]));
hsbControls.f3.setText(String.valueOf((int)hsb[2]));
```

The second part of the update() method is called when a value on the HSB side of the panel is changed. This is the "else" in the if-else statement that determines what to update, given a change.

Believe it or not, it's easier to update RGB values given HSB than it is to do it the other way around. First, convert the string values from the HSB text fields to integers by using these lines:

```
int f1 = Integer.parseInt(v1);
int f2 = Integer.parseInt(v2);
int f3 = Integer.parseInt(v3);
```

There's a class method in the Color class that creates a new color object when given three HSB values. The catch is that those values are floats, and they're not the values you currently have. To call getHSBColor() (that's the name of the method), convert the integers to floats and divide by the right amounts:

```
c = Color.getHSBColor((float)f1 / 360, (float)f2 / 100, (float)f3/100);
```

Now that you have a Color object, the rest is easy. Set the color swatch:

```
swatch.setBackground(c);
```

Then update the RGB text fields with the new RGB values from the color object:

```
rgbControls.f1.setText(String.valueOf(c.getRed()));
rgbControls.f2.setText(String.valueOf(c.getGreen()));
rgbControls.f3.setText(String.valueOf(c.getBlue()));
```

At the end of the update() method, the following statement makes sure that the color of the swatch is updated to reflect changes to the RGB and HSB values:

```
swatch.repaint();
```

The Complete Source Code

Listing 13.2 shows the complete source code for the ColorTest applet. Often it's easier to figure out what's going on when the code's in one place and you can follow the method calls and how values are passed back and forth.

13

Listing 13.2. The source code of `ColorTest.java`.

```
 1: import java.awt.*;
 2:
 3: public class ColorTest extends java.applet.Applet {
 4:     ColorControls rgbControls, hsbControls;
 5:     Canvas swatch;
 6:
 7:     public void init() {
 8:         Color theColor = new Color(0, 0, 0);
 9:         float[] hsb = Color.RGBtoHSB(theColor.getRed(),
10:             theColor.getGreen(), theColor.getBlue(),
11:             (new float[3]));
12:
13:         setLayout(new GridLayout(1, 3, 10, 10));
14:
15:         // The color swatch
16:         swatch = new Canvas();
17:         swatch.setBackground(theColor);
18:
19:         // the control panels
20:         rgbControls = new ColorControls(this,
21:             "Red", "Green", "Blue",
22:             theColor.getRed(), theColor.getGreen(),
23:             theColor.getBlue());
24:
25:         hsbControls = new ColorControls(this,
26:             "Hue", "Saturation", "Brightness",
27:             (int)(hsb[0] * 360), (int)(hsb[1] * 100),
28:             (int)(hsb[2] * 100));
29:
30:         add(swatch);
31:         add(rgbControls);
32:         add(hsbControls);
33:     }
34:
35:     public Insets insets() {
36:         return new Insets(10, 10, 10, 10);
37:     }
38:
39:     void update(ColorControls in) {
40:         Color c;
41:         String v1 = in.f1.getText();
42:         String v2 = in.f2.getText();
43:         String v3 = in.f3.getText();
44:
45:         if (in == rgbControls) {     // change to RGB
46:             c = new Color(Integer.parseInt(v1),
47:                     Integer.parseInt(v2),
48:                     Integer.parseInt(v3));
49:             swatch.setBackground(c);
50:
51:             float[] hsb = Color.RGBtoHSB(c.getRed(),c.getGreen(),
52:                     c.getBlue(), (new float[3]));
53:             hsb[0] *= 360;
54:             hsb[1] *= 100;
```

13

```
55:                    hsb[2] *= 100;
56:                    hsbControls.f1.setText(String.valueOf((int)hsb[0]));
57:                    hsbControls.f2.setText(String.valueOf((int)hsb[1]));
58:                    hsbControls.f3.setText(String.valueOf((int)hsb[2]));
59:                }
60:            else {     // change to HSB
61:                int f1 = Integer.parseInt(v1);
62:                int f2 = Integer.parseInt(v2);
63:                int f3 = Integer.parseInt(v3);
64:                c = Color.getHSBColor((float)f1 / 360,
65:                        (float)f2 / 100, (float)f3/100);
66:                swatch.setBackground(c);
67:                rgbControls.f1.setText(String.valueOf(c.getRed()));
68:                rgbControls.f2.setText(String.valueOf(
69:                    c.getGreen()));
70:                rgbControls.f3.setText(String.valueOf(c.getBlue()));
71:            }
72:            swatch.repaint();
73:        }
74: }
75:
76:
77: class ColorControls extends Panel {
78:        TextField f1, f2, f3;
79:        ColorTest outerparent;
80:
81:        ColorControls(ColorTest target,
82:                String l1, String l2, String l3,
83:                int v1, int v2, int v3) {
84:
85:            this.outerparent = target;
86:            setLayout(new GridLayout(3,4,10,10));
87:
88:            f1 = new TextField(String.valueOf(v1),10);
89:            f2 = new TextField(String.valueOf(v2),10);
90:            f3 = new TextField(String.valueOf(v3),10);
91:
92:            add(new Label(l1, Label.RIGHT));
93:            add(f1);
94:            add(new Label(l2, Label.RIGHT));
95:            add(f2);
96:            add(new Label(l3, Label.RIGHT));
97:            add(f3);
98:        }
99:
100:        public Insets insets() {
101:            return new Insets(10,10,0,0);
102:        }
103:
104:        public boolean action(Event evt, Object arg) {
105:            if (evt.target instanceof TextField) {
106:                outerparent.update(this);
107:                return true;
108:            }
109:            else return false;
110:        }
111: }
```

13

Introduction to Visual Java

With the Abstract Windowing Toolkit, you have the ability to make your Java programs as "GUI" as possible. Your graphical user interface can include buttons, text fields, scrollbars, and all the other features associated with a windowing environment. You even can add your own custom widgets, which then can be added to your own programs or made available to other programmers. However, using the AWT takes a lot of work, and results are only evident when the program is compiled and run.

With Visual Java, the work of creating a graphical user interface becomes a lot easier. This Java WorkShop development tool enables you to design your interface visually and see exactly how the program will look right away so you can make changes immediately. The tool was developed as a complement to the AWT. AWT components such as buttons and text fields are available from within Visual Java in the same way that paintbrushes are available in a graphics program. The components are shown on a palette toolbar, and you click the one that you want to put on the screen. The best way to show how it works is to dive right into a Visual Java project.

Designing an Interface

The program that you are developing is a number-guessing applet. The computer generates a random number from 1 to 32,767, and responds to guesses with one of three responses: "Too high!", "Too low!", or "That's right!". Three other bits of information are tracked: the last low guess, the last high guess, and the number of guesses. Figure 13.22 shows what the applet looks like when you're done.

Figure 13.22.

The Guesser *applet.*

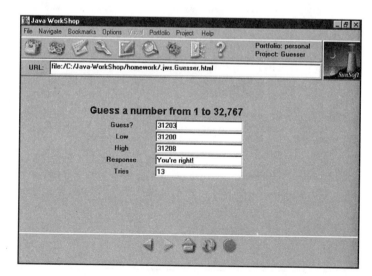

As you did with the ColorTest applet and the AWT, the first thing to work on is the program's interface. You will be laying out 11 components with Visual Java: five text fields with five labels next to them, and a label at the top.

To get started, create a new applet project with Portfolio Manager. Give it the name Guesser, and make sure that Visual Java is selected this time instead of Source Editor. When you click the Apply button, Visual Java should load automatically. If not, you can load it by clicking the Visual Java button on the WorkShop command toolbar. This button is the pencil-and-monitor icon identified in Figure 13.23.

Figure 13.23.

The Visual Java icon on the WorkShop command toolbar.

VISUAL JAVA

When Visual Java loads, two different windows will open. One will be a Panel work area with one or more gray boxes arranged at the center of the window. This is the place where you lay out the elements of your program. It is a grid, and each of the gray boxes can hold a component such as a button, scroll bar, or custom widget. The gray boxes also can hold grids, giving you even more control over the look of the interface. Figure 13.24 shows a grid that is three rows tall and four columns wide.

Figure 13.24.

The Panel work area.

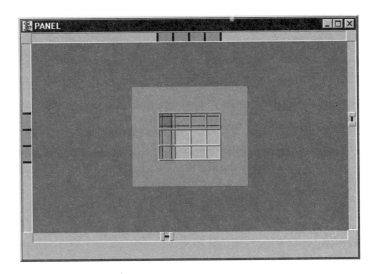

As you can see, the grid cell in the upper left corner has several lines intersecting inside it. This is the active cell in the grid. In order to make changes to a cell, you have to make it active by clicking the mouse within its boundaries.

Modifying a Panel Grid

A good place to start when you're developing an interface with Visual Java is to establish the number of cells you will need. In this case, you will need a grid that is two cells wide and six cells tall.

Make one of the grid cells active and press one of the arrow keys, making note of which one you pressed. This is how you can expand the grid; the up and down arrows add a row in the direction of the key, and the left and right arrows do likewise for the columns. Try it out several times until you have far more grid cells than you need for this project.

To delete cells, make a cell active and press the Delete key. This will delete a row and column, depending on which cell currently is active. Experiment with this feature until you have a grid that is the needed size: two columns wide, and six columns tall. When you have that accomplished, you can place your first component.

Using the Palette Toolbar

To put a component on a grid cell, you first must choose that component from the Palette toolbar. This toolbar is located on a different window than the Panel work area. Figure 13.25 shows what the Palette toolbar window looks like—the Palette is the vertical row of icons at far left.

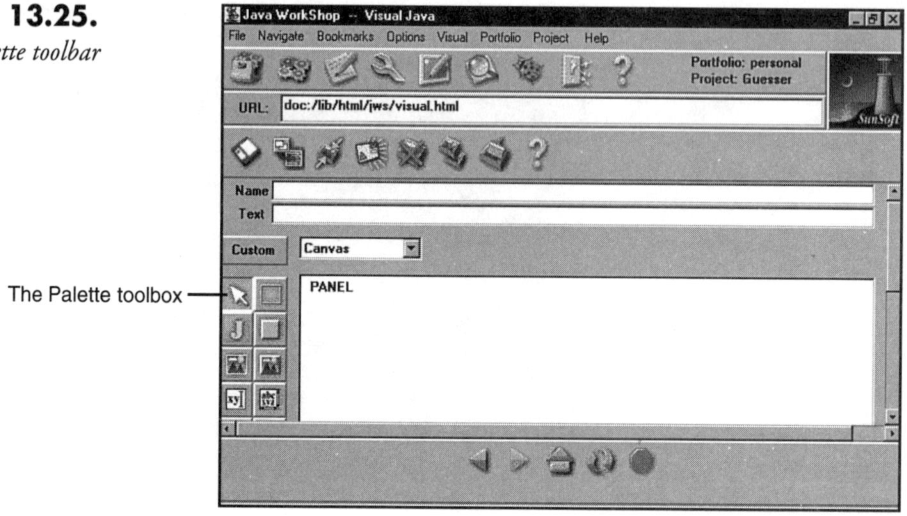

Figure 13.25.

The Palette toolbar window.

The Palette toolbox

The first type of component that you will place is a label. A label is represented by the "J" icon on the Palette toolbar. Click the icon to select it, and switch back to the Panel work area. Then click in the upper-left hand grid cell to put a label at that spot in the grid. You will see the word label appear in that cell, surrounded by a thick purple border inside the cell.

You have put this component in your applet, but it is set to the default attributes, including the text label. You need to change the text to read, Guess a number from 1 to 32,767. To do this, click the right mouse button anywhere on the purple border of the cell. (You also can choose Visual | Edit | Attribute from the menu bar.)

An Attributes window will pop up, enabling you to change several things about this component. The configurable options include the alignment of the label's text, its foreground and background colors, its name, and its text. Change the text to read Guess a number from 1 to 32,767. You can change the font by clicking the ellipsis button (...) next to the Font text field. Set it to 18-point, bold Helvetica. Click the OK button to make the change official.

Stretching a Component

When you return to the Panel work area, you will see the new label in place. However, as you might recall from Figure 13.22, this label is supposed to stretch over the whole applet, not just the left-hand column. To stretch a component over more than one cell in the grid, you have to grab the edge you want to stretch and pull it over a neighboring cell.

In this example, position your cursor over the purple border just to the right of the text 32,767. Move the mouse in that border until your cursor changes to a pair of arrows pointing left and right. When it does, click and hold down the left mouse button. Drag the whole thing over the cell to the right of it, and release the button. The Guess a number label now should be over both columns, with 10 empty cells beneath it. The next step is to lay out the other five labels.

Placing Multiple Labels

Because you're putting down five of the same kind of component, it is handy to use a shortcut method here. Go back to the Palette toolbar and select the Label icon again (the "J"). You will be putting a label component in each of the empty cells in the left-hand column. In the Panel work area, hold down the Ctrl key and click once in each of these empty cells. Five more label components will be placed, each with the default text of label. Change these components in the same way that you changed the Guess a number label. In order from top to bottom, the text of the labels should be Guess?, Low, High, Response, and Tries.

13

In the remaining five empty cells, each in the right-hand column, you need to put a text field component. Return to the Palette toolbar and click the text field icon—it's the letters "xy" next to a cursor. In the Panel area, hold down the Ctrl key and click once in each of the empty cells. An empty text field appears.

You do not have any default text to change this time, but each of these text fields needs to be given a descriptive name. This name is used later in your program when you're trying to use the text field by retrieving or changing its contents. The name is an attribute just like the text is, so you can change it from the Attributes window. From top to bottom, the names of the text fields should be as follows: guess, low, high, response, and numGuesses. Make sure to capitalize these names exactly as they are shown. This step completes the design of the interface, and you can use it to create a working, executable copy of the applet.

TIP

At this point, it probably would be wise to save your work. The layout of your graphical interface and all other elements of Visual Java are not saved in the same place as your Java programs. Visual Java information is saved in a file with the extension .gui and the same name as the project. To save your work, choose the Visual | Save command from the menu bar, or click the disk icon on the Visual Java toolbar.

Generating the Interface Code

In order to make this Visual Java interface work as a Java program, you have to generate source code. Choose the Visual | Generate command from the menu bar. This command causes Java source code files to be generated that transparently control the Visual Java interface you have created. The first time you generate source code, three source code files are created. Two, GuesserRoot.java and GuesserMain.java, are support files needed to run Visual Java programs and should never be modified. The third file, Guesser.java, is the place where you add source code to handle events and other tasks the program needs to accomplish.

Writing the Program

Before making any changes to source code, you can compile the files that were created by Visual Java and try out the interface. Use Build Manager to compile all files associated with the project, and then use Project Manager to change the width to 500 pixels and the height to 225 pixels. When you run the applet, you are able to enter text in each of the fields, but nothing happens in response. To give the applet a brain to go with its fetching new appearance, use Source Editor to edit the file Guesser.java.

There are two things you need to do to make this applet functional. First, you need to create some instance variables to store the following things:

- ☐ The number to guess
- ☐ The number of attempts to guess it
- ☐ The most recent guess that was lower than the number
- ☐ The most recent guess that was higher than the number

These variables are declared and initialized right below the line in Guesser.java that reads private GuesserRoot gui;. Add the following statements:

```
int numGuesses = 0;
int low = -1;
int high = 32768;
int num = (int)Math.floor(Math.random()*32767);
```

These statements should be straightforward, except for the last one. It uses two methods in the java.lang.Math class to create a random number (actually pseudo-random, because the sequence of random numbers eventually is repeated, but it's more than adequate for this applet).

The second thing that must be done to make the applet functional is to add an Action() method.

Handling Events

As you have learned today and in previous lessons, interface components generate events to communicate changes in their state and other information to the rest of the program. Programs created using Visual Java are aware of AWT events that are generated and know how to pass them and to handle them. In the Guesser applet, something needs to happen when a user chooses a number in the guess text field.

To make this something happen, you need to add an Action() method to the Guesser.java program. Enter the method as it is shown in lines 82 to 109 of Listing 13.3. This listing shows the source code of Guesser.java up to line 125, with the Action() method already added. The rest of the source code was created automatically when you generated source code in Visual Java, and you will not be changing it. The only thing you need to add is the code for the Action() method. Insert the Action() method between the initRoot() method and initGroup() method.

13

Listing 13.3. The final source code of Guesser.java.

```
 1: /**
 2:  * This is a template.  You may modify this file.
 3:  *
 4:  * Runtime vendor: SunSoft, Inc.
 5:  * Runtime version: 0.6
 6:  *
 7:  * Visual vendor: SunSoft, Inc.
 8:  * Visual version: 0.6
 9:  */
10:
11:
12: import sunsoft.jws.visual.rt.base.*;
13: import sunsoft.jws.visual.rt.shadow.java.awt.*;
14: import java.awt.*;
15:
16:
17: public class Guesser extends Group {
18:    private GuesserRoot gui;
19:    int numGuesses = 0;
20:    int low = -1;
21:    int high = 32768;
22:    int num = (int)Math.floor(Math.random()*32767);
23:
24:    /**
25:     * Sample method call ordering during a group's lifetime:
26:     *
27:     * Constructor
28:     * initRoot
29:     * initGroup
30:     * (setOnGroup and getOnGroup may be called at any time in any
31:     *  order after initGroup has been called)
32:     * createGroup
33:     * showGroup/hideGroup + startGroup/stopGroup
34:     * destroyGroup
35:     */
36:
37:    /**
38:     * All the attributes used by the group must be defined in the
39:     * constructor.  setOnGroup is called at initialization for all
40:     * the attributes.  If the attribute has not been set prior to
41:     * initialization, setOnGroup is called with the default value.
42:     */
43:    public Guesser() {
44:       /**
45:        * Define the group's custom attributes here.
46:        *
47:        * For example:
48:        *
49:        * attributes.add("customString", "java.lang.String",
50:        *     "Default String", 0);
51:        */
52:
53:       /**
54:        * This method defines the attributes that will be forwarded to
```

13

```
55:        * the main child (either a window or a panel).  All attributes
56:        * defined by this method are marked with the FORWARD flag.
57:        */
58:       addPanelAttributes();
59:    }
60:
61:    /**
62:     * initRoot must be overridden in group subclasses to initialize
63:     * the shadow tree.  The return value must be the root of the
64:     * newly initialized shadow tree.
65:     */
66:    protected Root initRoot() {
67:       /**
68:        * Initialize the gui components
69:        */
70:       gui = new GuesserRoot(this);
71:
72:       /**
73:        * This method registers an attribute manager with the group, such
74:        * that attributes marked with the FORWARD flag will be sent to
75:        * this attribute manager.
76:        */
77:       addAttributeForward(gui.getMainChild());
78:
79:       return gui;
80:    }
81:
82:    public boolean action(Message msg, Event evt, Object what) {
83:       boolean handled = false;
84:
85:       if (msg.target == gui.guess) {
86:          String guess = (String)gui.guess.get("text");
87:          // increment number of guesses
88:          numGuesses += 1;
89:          gui.numGuesses.set("text", ""+numGuesses);
90:
91:          // check current guess
92:          int g = Integer.parseInt(guess);
93:          if (g > num) {
94:             high = g;
95:             gui.high.set("text", ""+high);
96:             gui.response.set("text", "Too high!");
97:          }
98:          if (g < num) {
99:             low = g;
100:            gui.low.set("text", ""+low);
101:            gui.response.set("text", "Too low!");
102:         }
103:         if (g == num) {
104:            gui.response.set("text", "You're right!");
105:         }
106:         handled = true;
107:      }
108:      return handled;
109:   }
```

continues

Listing 13.3. continued

```
110:
111:
112:    /**
113:     * initGroup is called during initialization.  It is called just after
114:     * initRoot is called, but before the sub-groups are initialized and
115:     * before the attributes are sent to the setOnGroup method.
116:     *
117:     * initGroup is only called once in the lifetime of the Group.
118:     * This is because groups cannot be uninitialized.  Anything that
119:     * needs to be cleaned up should be created in createGroup instead
120:     * of initGroup, and then can be cleaned up in destroyGroup.
121:     * createGroup and destroyGroup may be called multiple times during
122:     * the lifetime of a group.
123:     */
124:    protected void initGroup() { }
125:
```

When you're done, save Guesser.java and build all files in the project with Build Manager. Run the project with Project Tester, and the applet should look like the applet shown in Figure 13.22.

Because Visual Java is still incomplete at this point, a full description of how it handles events and works in conjunction with the AWT is not yet possible. However, an explanation of a few of the features in the preceding Action() method should whet your appetite.

The following two lines are used to access text fields that you named from within Visual Java:

```
String guess = (String)gui.guess.get("text");
gui.numGuesses.set("text", ""+numGuesses);
```

The first retrieves the value of the guess text field. The second changes the value of the numGuesses text field. As shown in line 18, gui is an instance of the class GuesserRoot, one of the support classes that was created when you generated source code from your interface.

The get method returns a value from the interface, and the set method changes a value in the interface. If you're eager to try more with Visual Java, choose the Help icon on the Visual Java toolbar to read the online documentation and a Visual Jave tutorial.

Visual Java puts a new layer between the programmer and the complexities of the AWT and windowing programming, and it should be a powerful complement to the windowing capabilities that were introduced originally with the Java Developer's Kit.

Summary

A lot of ground has been covered in a single day. You've learned about two tools for the creation of windowing software: the Abstract Windowing Toolkit and Visual Java. Both are packages of Java classes and interfaces for creating full-fledged access to a window-based graphical user interface system, with mechanisms for graphics display, event management, text and graphics primitives, user interface components, and cross-platform layout. Applets are an integral part of each.

The lesson has brought together everything you've learned up to this point about simple applet management and added a lot more about creating applets, panels, and user interface components and managing the interactions between all of them. With the information you got today and the few bits that you'll learn tomorrow, you can create cross-platform Java applications that do just about anything you would want to do.

Q&A

Q You've mentioned a lot about the `Component` and `Container` classes, but it looks like the only `Container` objects that ever get created are `Panels`. What do the `Component` and `Container` classes give me?

A Those classes factor out the behavior for components (generic AWT components) and containers (components that can contain other components). Although you don't necessarily create direct instances of these classes, you can create subclasses of them if you want to add behavior to the AWT that the default classes do not provide. As with most of the Java classes, any time you need a superclass' behavior, don't hesitate to extend that class by using your own subclass.

Q Can I put a user interface component at a specific x and y position on the screen?

A By using the existing layout managers supplied with the AWT toolkit, no. This limitation is actually a good thing because you don't know what kind of display environment your applet will be run under, what kind of fonts are installed, or what kind of fonts are being currently used. By using the layout managers provided with the AWT, you can be reasonably sure that every portion of your window will be viewable and readable and usable (fonts may cause you trouble). You can't guarantee anything like that with hard-coded layouts.

Q I was exploring the AWT package, and I saw this subpackage called `peer`. There's also references to the `peer` classes sprinkled throughout the API documentation. What do peers do?

A `peers` are responsible for the platform-specific parts of the AWT. For example, when you create a Java AWT window, you have an instance of the `Window` class that provides generic window behavior, and then you have an instance of a class implementing `WindowPeer` that creates the very specific window for that platform— a motif window under X Window, a Macintosh-style window under the

Macintosh, or a Windows 95 window under Windows 95. These peer classes also handle communication between the window system and the Java window itself. By separating the generic component behavior (the AWT classes) from the system implementation and appearance (the peer classes), Java enables you to focus on providing behavior in your Java application and let the Java implementation deal with the platform-specific details.

FEATURED APPLET Today's Featured Applet

Today's featured applet is Abacus, a version of the ancient calculating device implemented with Java by Luis Fernandes. The applet uses bitmapped images to draw the parts of the abacus and has added a numerical digit at the top of each row of beads. Figure 13.26 shows an example of Abacus in action.

Figure 13.26.

The Abacus *applet in action.*

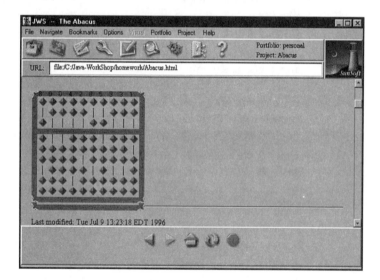

Files for Abacus are located on the CD-ROM in the \BOOK\3RDPARTY\DAY13\ directory, including source code in the file Abacus.java. To use Abacus on a Web page, place one class file and three image files on your Web site: Abacus.class, frame.gif, diamond.gif, and nodiamond.gif. Place the class file in the same directory as the Web page, or place it in a subdirectory listed in the CODEBASE parameter of the <APPLET> tag. Place the image files in a subdirectory called images. The <CODE> tag should be Abacus.class. Listing 13.4 shows the HTML tags used to run Abacus as it was shown in Figure 13.26.

13

Listing 13.4. The `<APPLET>` tag for Abacus.

```
<applet code=scroll.class width=320 height=149>
</applet>
```

Abacus has four parameters that can be customized within the `<APPLET>` tag, as follows:

- [ ] The `value` parameter is the initial value of the abacus.
- [ ] The `frameImg` parameter specifies the image to use as the frame of the abacus (`frame.gif` is the default).
- [ ] The `beadImg` parameter specifies the image to use as the abacus bead (`diamond.gif` is the default).
- [ ] The `nobeadImg` parameter is the image to use as an empty part of the abacus (`nodiamond.gif` is the default).

More information on the applet is available from its author at the following URL:

```
http://www.ee.ryerson.ca:8080/~elf/abacus/
```

13

Day **14**

Windows, Networking, and Other Tidbits

Here you are on the last day of the second week, and you're just almost finished with applets and the AWT. With the information you'll learn today, you can create a wide variety of applets and applications using Java. Next week's lessons provide more of the advanced stuff that you'll need if you start doing really serious work in Java.

Today, to finish up this week, there are three very different topics:

☐ Windows, menus, and dialog boxes—the last of the AWT classes that enable you to pop up real windows from applets and to create stand-alone Java applications that have their own windows

☐ Networking—how to load new HTML files from an Java-enabled browser, how to retrieve files from Web sites, and some basics on how to work with generic sockets in Java

☐ Extra tidbits—the smaller stuff that didn't fit in anywhere else, but that might be useful to you as you write your Java applets and applications

Windows, Menus, and Dialog Boxes

Today, you'll finish up the last bits of the AWT that didn't fit into yesterday's lesson. In addition to all the graphics, events, user interface components, and layout mechanisms that the AWT provides, it provides windows, menus, and dialog boxes, enabling to you create fully featured applications either as part of your applet or independently for stand-alone Java applications.

Frames

The AWT Window class enables you to create windows that are independent of the browser window containing the applet—that is, separate pop-up windows with their own titles, resize handles, and menu bars. The Window class provides basic behavior for windows. Most commonly, instead of using the Window class, you'll use Window's subclasses, Frame and Dialog. The Frame class enables you to create a fully functioning window with a menu bar. Dialog is a more limited window for dialog boxes. You'll learn more about dialog boxes later on in this section.

To create a frame, use one of the following constructors:

- ☐ new Frame() creates a basic frame without a title.
- ☐ new Frame(*String*) creates a basic frame with the given title.

Frames are containers, just like panels are, so you can add other components to them just as you would regular panels, using the add() method. The default layout for frames is BorderLayout:

```
win = new Frame("My Cool Window");
win.setLayout(new BorderLayout(10, 20));
win.add("North", new Button("Start"));
win.add("Center", new Button("Move"));
```

To set a size for the new window, use the resize() method. To set a location for where the window appears, use the move() method. Note that the location() method can tell you where the applet window is on the screen so that you can pop up the extra window in a relative position to that window (all these methods are defined for all containers, so you can use them for applets, windows, and the components inside them, subject to the current layout):

```
win.resize(100, 200);
Dimension d = location();
win.move(d.width + 50, d.height + 50);
```

When you initially create a window, it's invisible. You need to use the show() method to make the window appear on-screen (you can use hide() to hide it again):

```
win.show();
```

14

Listing 14.1 shows an example of a simple applet with a pop-up window (both the applet and the window are shown in Figure 14.1). The applet has two buttons: one to show the window, and one to hide the window. The window itself, created from a subclass called MyFrame, contains a single label: "This is a Window". You use this basic window and applet all through this section, so the more you understand what's going on here the easier it will be later.

Listing 14.1. A pop-up window example.

```
 1: import java.awt.*;
 2:
 3: public class GUI extends java.applet.Applet {
 4:     Frame window;
 5:
 6:     public void init() {
 7:         add(new Button("Open Window"));
 8:         add(new Button("Close Window"));
 9:
10:         window = new MyFrame("A Popup Window");
11:         window.resize(150, 150);
12:         window.show();
13:     }
14:
15:     public boolean action(Event evt, Object arg) {
16:         if (evt.target instanceof Button) {
17:             String label = (String)arg;
18:             if (label.equals("Open Window")) {
19:                 if (!window.isShowing())
20:                     window.show();
21:             }
22:             else if (label == "Close Window") {
23:                 if (window.isShowing())
24:                     window.hide();
25:             }
26:             return true;
27:         }
28:         else return false;
29:     }
30: }
31:
32: class MyFrame extends Frame {
33:     Label l;
34:     MyFrame(String title) {
35:       super(title);
36:       setLayout(new GridLayout(1, 1));
37:       l = new Label("This is a Window", Label.CENTER);
38:       add(l);
39:     }
40: }
```

14

Figure 14.1.

Windows.

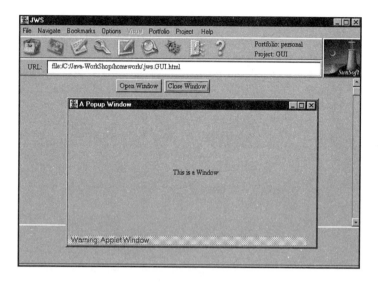

Menus

Each new window you create can have its own menu bar along the top of the screen. Each menu bar can have a number of menus, and each menu, in turn, can have menu items. The AWT provides classes for all these things called, respectively, `MenuBar`, `Menu`, and `MenuItem`.

Menus and Menu Bars

To create a menu bar for a given window, create a new instance of the class `MenuBar`:

```
MenuBar mb = new MenuBar();
```

To set this menu bar as the default menu for the window, use the `setMenuBar()` method on the window:

```
window.setMenuBar(mb);
```

Add individual menus (File, Edit, and so on) to the menu bar by creating them and then adding them to the menu bar:

```
Menu m = new Menu("File");
mb.add(m);
```

Some systems enable you to indicate a special help menu, which might be drawn on the right side of the menu bar. You can indicate that a specific menu is the help menu by using the `setHelpMenu()` method. The given menu should already be added to the menu bar itself:

```
Menu hm = new Menu("Help");
mb.add(hm);
mb.setHelpMenu(hm);
```

14

If for any reason you want to prevent a user from selecting a menu, you can use the `disable()`
command on that menu (and the `enable()` command to make it available again):

```
m.disable();
```

Menu Items

There are four kinds of items you can add to individual menus:

- ☐ Instances of the class `MenuItem`, for regular menu items
- ☐ Instances of the class `CheckBoxMenuItem`, for toggled menu items
- ☐ Other menus, with their own menu items
- ☐ Separators, for lines that separate groups of items on menus

You add regular menu items by using the `MenuItem` class. Add the items to a menu using the
`add()` method:

```
Menu m = new Menu("Tools");
m.add(new MenuItem("Info"));
m.add(new MenuItem("Colors"));
```

You can add submenus by creating a new instance of `Menu` and adding it to the first menu.
You then can add items to that menu:

```
Menu sb = new Menu("Sizes");
m.add(sb);
sb.add(new MenuItem("Small"));
sb.add(new MenuItem("Medium"));
sb.add(new MenuItem("Large"));
```

The `CheckBoxMenuItem` class creates a menu item with a check box on it, enabling the menu
state to be toggled on and off (selecting it once makes the check box appear selected; selecting
it again deselects the check box). You can create and add a check box menu item the same
way you create and add regular menu items:

```
CheckboxMenuItem coords =
    new CheckboxMenuItem("Show Coordinates");
m.add(coords);
```

Finally, to add a separator to a menu (a line used to separate groups of items in a menu), create
and add a menu item with a single dash (-) as the label, as follows:

```
MenuItem msep = new MenuItem("-");
m.add(msep);
```

You can disable any menu item by using the `disable()` method and enable it again using
`enable()`. Disabled menu items cannot be selected:

```
MenuItem mi = new MenuItem("Fill");
m.addItem(mi);
mi.disable();
```

14

Menu Actions

The act of selecting a menu item causes an action event to be generated. You can handle that action the same way you handle other `action()` methods—by overriding `action()`. Both regular menu items and check box menu items have actions that generate an extra argument representing the label for that menu. You can use that label to determine which action to take. Also note that because `CheckBoxMenuItem` is a subclass of `MenuItem`, you don't have to treat that menu item as a special case:

```
public boolean action(Event evt, Object arg) {
    if (evt.target instanceof MenuItem) {
        String label = (String)arg;
        if (label.equals("Show Coordinates")) toggleCoords();
        else if (label.equals("Fill")) fillcurrentArea();
        return true;
    }
    else return false;
}
```

An Example

Suppose you wanted to add a menu to the window you created in the previous section. To add it to the constructor method in the `MyFrame` class, you would use the following code (Figure 14.2 shows the resulting menu):

```
MyFrame(String title) {
    super(title);
    MenuBar mb = new MenuBar();
    Menu m = new Menu("Colors");
    m.add(new MenuItem("Red"));
    m.add(new MenuItem("Blue"));
    m.add(new MenuItem("Green"));
    m.add(new MenuItem("-"));
    m.add(new CheckboxMenuItem("Reverse Text"));
    mb.add(m);
    mb.setHelpMenu(m);
    setMenuBar(mb);
    ...
}
```

This menu has four items: one each for the colors red, blue, and green (which, when selected, change the background of the window) and one check box menu item for reversing the color of the text (to white). To handle these menu items, you need an `action()` method:

```
public boolean action(Event evt, Object arg) {
    String label = (String)arg;
    if (evt.target instanceof MenuItem) {
      if (label.equals ("Red")) setBackground(Color.red);
      else of (label.equals("Blue")) setBackground(Color.blue);
      else if (label.equals("Green")) setBackground(Color.green);
      return true;
    }
```

```
if (evt.target instanceof CheckboxMenuItem) {
  if (getForeground() == Color.black)
    setForeground(Color.white);
  else setForeground(Color.black);
  return true;
}
return false;
}
```

Figure 14.2.

A menu.

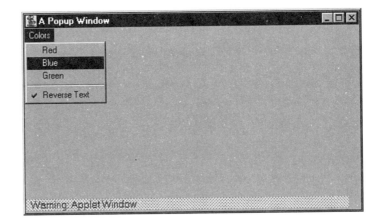

Dialog Boxes

Dialog boxes are similar functionally to frames in that they pop up new windows on the screen. However, dialog boxes are intended to be used for transient windows, windows that let you know about warnings, windows that ask you for specific information, and so on. Dialog boxes don't usually have title bars or many of the more general features that windows have (although you can create one with a title bar), and they can be made nonresizable or modal.

NEW TERM A *modal dialog* prevents input to any of the other windows on the screen until that dialog is dismissed.

The AWT provides two kinds of dialog boxes: the Dialog class, which provides a generic dialog, and FileDialog, which produces a platform-specific dialog to choose files to save or open. To create a generic dialog, use one of these constructors:

☐ Dialog(Frame, boolean) creates an initially invisible dialog, attached to the current frame, which is either modal (true) or not (false).

☐ Dialog(Frame, String, boolean) is the same as the previous constructor with the addition of a title bar and a title indicated by the string argument.

14

Note that because you have to give a dialog a `Frame` argument, you can attach dialogs only to windows that already exist independently of the applet itself. The dialog window, like the frame window, is a panel on which you can lay out and draw user interface components and perform graphics operations, just as you would any other panel. Like other windows, the dialog is invisible initially, but you can show it with `show()` and hide it with `hide()`.

To practice working with dialog boxes, you can add a dialog to the example with the pop-up window. Add a menu item for changing the text of the window, which brings up the Enter Text dialog box (see Figure 14.3).

Figure 14.3.

The Enter Text dialog box.

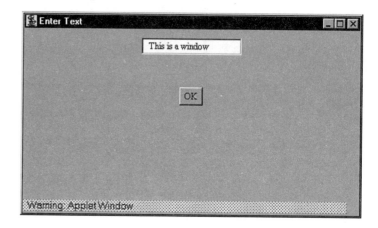

To add this dialog box, first add a menu item to that window (the constructor method for the `MyFrame` class) to change the text that the pop-up window displays:

```
m.add(new MenuItem("Set Text..."));
```

In that same method, you can create the dialog box and lay out the parts of it (it's invisible by default, so you can do whatever you want to it and it won't appear on-screen until you show it):

```
dl = new Dialog(this, "Enter Text", true);
dl.setLayout(new GridLayout(2, 1, 30, 30));
tf = new TextField(l.getText(), 20);
dl.add(tf);
dl.add(new Button("OK"));
dl.resize(150, 75);
```

The action of choosing the menu item you just added displays the dialog box; choosing the OK button dismisses it. You need to add behavior to this class' `action()` method so that the dialog box works correctly. Add a line for the new menu item to the menu item tests:

```
if (evt.target instanceof MenuItem) {
    if (label.equals("Red")) setBackground(Color.red);
    if (label.equals("Blue")) setBackground(Color.blue);
    if (label.equals("Green")) setBackground(Color.green);
    if (label.equals("Set Text...")) dl.show();
}
```

Then, because OK is a button, you have to add a special case for that button separate from the menu items. In this special case, set the text of the window to the text that was typed into the text field, and then hide the dialog box again:

```
if (evt.target instanceof Button) {
    if (label.equals("OK")) {
        l.setText(tf.getText());
        dl.hide();
    }
}
```

File Dialog Boxes

FileDialog provides a basic file open/save dialog box that enables you to access the file system. The FileDialog class is system-independent, but depending on the platform, the standard Open File dialog is displayed.

NOTE

For applets, you can display the file dialog, but due to security restrictions, you can't do anything with it (or, if you can, access to any files on the local system is severely restricted). FileDialog is much more useful in stand-alone applications.

To create a file dialog, use the following constructors:

☐ FileDialog(Frame, String) creates an Open File dialog, attached to the given frame, with the given title. This form creates a dialog box to load a file.

☐ FileDialog(Frame, String, int) also creates a file dialog, but that integer argument is used to determine whether the dialog is for loading a file or saving a file (the only difference is the labels on the buttons; the file dialog does not open or save anything). The possible options for this argument are FileDialog.LOAD and FileDialog.SAVE.

After you create a FileDialog instance, use show() to display it:

```
FileDialog fd = new FileDialog(this, "FileDialog");
fd.show();
```

14

When readers choose a file in the file dialog and dismiss it, you then can access the filename they chose by using the getDirectory() and getFile() methods; both return strings indicating the values the readers chose. You can open that file by using the stream and file handling methods (which you'll learn about next week) and then read from or write to that file.

Window Events

Yesterday, you learned about writing your own event handler methods, and you noted that the Event class defines many standard events for which you can test. Window events are part of that list, so if you use windows, these events may be of interest to you. Table 14.1 shows those events.

Table 14.1. Window events from the Event class.

Event	Description
WINDOW_DESTROY	Generated when a window is destroyed (for example, when the browser or applet viewer has quit)
WINDOW_EXPOSE	Generated when the window is brought forward from behind other windows
WINDOW_ICONIFY	Generated when the window is iconified
WINDOW_DEICONIFY	Generated when the window is restored from an icon
WINDOW_MOVED	Generated when the window is moved

Using AWT Windows in Applications

Because frames are general-purpose mechanisms for creating AWT windows with panels, you can use them in your stand-alone Java applications and easily take advantage of all the applet capabilities you learned about this week. To do this, write your application as if it were an applet (inheriting from the Applet class and using threads, graphics, and user interface components as necessary), and then add a main() method. Here's one for a class called MyAWTClass:

```
public static void main(String args[]) {
    Frame f = new Frame("My Window");
    MyAWTClass mc = new MyAWTClass();
    mc.init();
    mc.start();
```

14

```
    f.add("Center", mc);
    f.resize(300, 300);
    f.show();
}
```

This `main()` method does five things:

- ☐ It creates a new frame to hold the applet.
- ☐ It creates an instance of the class that defines that method.
- ☐ It duplicates the applet environment calls to `init()` and `start()`.
- ☐ It adds the applet to the frame and resizes the frame to be 300 pixels square.
- ☐ It shows the frame on-screen.

By using this mechanism, you can create a Java program that can function equally well as an applet or an application—just include `init()` for applets and `main()` for applications.

If you do create an application that uses this mechanism, be careful of your `init()` methods that get parameters from an HTML file. When you run an applet as an application, you don't have the HTML parameters passed into the `init()` method. Pass them in as command-line arguments, instead, and handle them in your `main()` method. Then set a flag so that the `init()` method doesn't try to read parameters that don't exist.

Networking in Java

Networking is the capability of making connections from your applet or application to a system over the network. Networking in Java involves classes in the `java.net` package, which provide cross-platform abstractions for simple networking operations, including connecting and retrieving files by using common Web protocols and creating basic UNIX-like sockets. Used in conjunction with input and output streams (which you'll learn much more about next week), reading and writing files over the network becomes as easy as reading or writing to files on the local disk.

There are restrictions, of course. Java applets cannot read from or write to the disk on the machine that's running them without permission. Some browser software does not support this feature at all. Depending on the browser, Java applets might not be able to connect to systems other than the one upon which they were originally stored. Even given these restrictions, you still can accomplish a great deal and take advantage of the Web to read and process information over the Net. Also, all types of file and network access are possible with Java applications, which do not need the same security restrictions as applets.

14

This section describes three ways you can communicate with systems on the Net:

- [ ] showDocument(), which enables an applet to tell the browser to load and link to another page on the Web
- [ ] openStream(), a method that opens a connection to a URL and enables you to extract data from that connection
- [ ] The socket classes, Socket and ServerSocket, which enable you to open standard socket connections to hosts and read to and write from those connections

Creating Links Inside Applets

Probably the easiest way to use networking inside an applet is to tell the browser running that applet to load a new page. You can use this, for example, to create animated image maps that load a new page when clicked. To link to a new page, you create a new instance of the class URL. You saw some of this when you worked with images.

The URL class represents a uniform resource locator. To create a new URL, you can use one of four different forms:

- [ ] URL(String, String, int, String) creates a new URL object, given a protocol (http, ftp, gopher, file), a host name (www.yahoo.com, ftp.netcom.com), a port number (80 for http), and a file name or path name.
- [ ] URL(String, String, String) does the same thing as the previous form, minus the port number.
- [ ] URL(URL, String) creates a URL, given a base path and a relative path. For the base, you can use getDocumentBase() for the URL of the current HTML file, or getCodeBase() for the URL of the Java applet class file. The relative path is tacked onto the last directory in those base URLs (just like with images and sounds).
- [ ] URL(String) creates a URL object from a URL string (which should include the protocol, host name, optional port name, and file name).

For that last one (creating a URL from a string), you have to catch a malformed URL exception, so surround the URL constructor with a try...catch:

```
String url = "http://www.yahoo.com/";
try { theURL = new URL(url); }
catch ( MalformedURLException e) {
    System.out.println("Bad URL: " + theURL);
}
```

Getting a URL object is the hard part. Once you have one, all you have to do is pass it to the browser. Do this by using this single line of code, where theURL is the URL object to link to:

```
getAppletContext().showDocument(theURL);
```

The browser that contains your URL loads and displays the document at that URL.

Listing 14.2 shows a simple applet that displays three buttons representing different Web locations (the buttons are shown in Figure 14.4). Clicking the buttons causes the document to be loaded from the locations to which those buttons refer.

Listing 14.2. The source code of `ButtonLink.java`.

```
 1: import java.awt.*;
 2: import java.net.URL;
 3: import java.net.MalformedURLException;
 4:
 5: public class ButtonLink extends java.applet.Applet {
 6:
 7:     Bookmark bmlist[] = new Bookmark[3];
 8:
 9:     public void init() {
10:         bmlist[0] = new Bookmark("Teach Yourself SunSoft Java WorkShop Home
          ➥Page",
11:             "http://www.spiderbyte.com/java/");
12:         bmlist[1] = new Bookmark("Sams.Net Publishing",
13:             "http://www.mcp.com/sams/");
14:         bmlist[2]= new Bookmark("JavaSoft Home Page",
15:             "http://java.sun.com");
16:
17:         setLayout(new GridLayout(bmlist.length,1, 10, 10));
18:         for (int i = 0; i < bmlist.length; i++) {
19:             add(new Button(bmlist[i].name));
20:         }
21:     }
22:
23:     public boolean action(Event evt, Object arg) {
24:         if (evt.target instanceof Button) {
25:             LinkTo((String)arg);
26:             return true;
27:         }
28:         else return false;
29:     }
30:
31:     void LinkTo(String name) {
32:         URL theURL = null;
33:         for (int i = 0; i < bmlist.length; i++) {
34:             if (name.equals(bmlist[i].name))
35:                 theURL = bmlist[i].url;
36:         }
37:         if (theURL != null)
38:             getAppletContext().showDocument(theURL);
39:     }
40: }
41:
```

continues

14

Listing 14.2. continued

```
42: class Bookmark {
43:     String name;
44:     URL url;
45:
46:     Bookmark(String name, String theURL) {
47:         this.name = name;
48:         try { this.url = new URL(theURL); }
49:         catch ( MalformedURLException e) {
50:             System.out.println("Bad URL: " + theURL);
51:         }
52:     }
53: }
```

Figure 14.4.

Bookmark buttons.

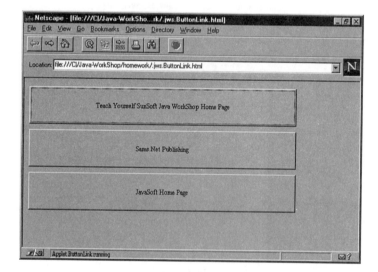

Two classes make up this applet: the first implements the applet, and the second is a class representing a bookmark. Bookmarks have two parts: a name and an URL. This particular applet creates three bookmark instances and stores them in an array of bookmarks (this applet could be modified easily to accept bookmarks as parameters from an HTML file). For each bookmark, a button is created whose label is the value of the bookmark's name. When the buttons are pressed, the linkTo() method is called, which tells the browser to load the URL referenced by that bookmark.

14

Opening Web Connections

Rather than asking the browser to just load the contents of a file, sometimes you might want to get hold of that file's contents so that your applet can use them. If the file you want to grab is stored on the Web, and can be accessed using the more common URL forms (http, ftp, and so on), your applet can use the URL class to get it.

Note that for security reasons, applets can by default connect back only to the same host from which they originally loaded. This means that if you have your applets stored on a system called www.myhost.com, the only machine your applet can open a connection to will be that same host (and that same host *name*, so be careful with host aliases). If the file the applet wants to retrieve is on that same system, using URL connections is the easiest way to get it.

openStream()

URL defines a method called openStream(), which opens a network connection using the given URL and returns an instance of the class InputStream (part of the java.io package). If you convert that stream to a DataInputStream (with a BufferedInputStream in the middle for better performance), you then can read characters and lines from that stream (you'll learn all about streams on Day 19, "Streams"). For example, these lines open a connection to the URL stored in the variable theURL, and then read and echo each line of the file to the standard output:

```
try {
    InputStream in = theURL.openStream();
    DataInputStream data = new DataInputStream(new BufferedInputStream(in);

    String line;
    while ((line = data.readLine()) != null) {
        System.out.println(line);
    }
}
catch (IOException e) {
    System.out.println("IO Error: " + e.getMessage());
}
```

NOTE You need to wrap all those lines in a try...catch statement to catch any IOExceptions that are generated.

14

The following is an example of an applet that uses the openStream() method to open a connection to a Web site, reads a file from that connection (Edgar Allan Poe's poem, "The Raven"), and displays the result in a text area. Listing 14.3 shows the code; Figure 14.5 shows the result after the file has been read.

Listing 14.3. The GetRaven class.

```
 1: import java.awt.*;
 2: import java.io.DataInputStream;
 3: import java.io.BufferedInputStream;
 4: import java.io.InputStream;
 5: import java.io.IOException;
 6: import java.net.URL;
 7: import java.net.URLConnection;
 8: import java.net.MalformedURLException;
 9:
10: public class GetRaven extends java.applet.Applet
11:     implements Runnable {
12:
13:     URL theURL;
14:     Thread runner;
15:     TextArea ta = new TextArea("Getting text...", 30, 70);
16:
17:     public void init() {
18:         String url = "http://www.spiderbyte.com/java/raven.txt";
19:         try { this.theURL = new URL(url); }
20:         catch ( MalformedURLException e) {
21:             System.out.println("Bad URL: " + theURL);
22:         }
23:         add(ta);
24:     }
25:
26:     public Insets insets() {
27:         return new Insets(10,10,10,10);
28:     }
29:
30:     public void start() {
31:         if (runner == null) {
32:             runner = new Thread(this);
33:             runner.start();
34:         }
35:     }
36:
37:     public void stop() {
38:         if (runner != null) {
39:             runner.stop();
40:             runner = null;
41:         }
42:     }
43:
44:     public void run() {
45:         InputStream conn;
46:         DataInputStream data;
```

```
47:            String line;
48:            StringBuffer buf = new StringBuffer();
49:
50:            try {
51:                conn = theURL.openStream();
52:                data = new DataInputStream(new BufferedInputStream(
53:                    conn));
54:
55:                while ((line = data.readLine()) != null) {
56:                    buf.append(line + "\n");
57:                }
58:
59:                ta.setText(buf.toString());
60:            }
61:            catch (IOException e) {
62:                System.out.println("IO Error:" + e.getMessage());
63:            }
64:        }
65: }
```

Figure 14.5.

The GetRaven *applet.*

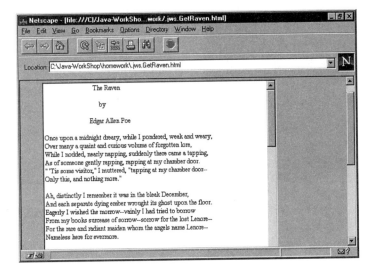

ANALYSIS   The init() method (lines 17 to 24) sets up the URL and the text area in which that file will be displayed. The URL could be easily passed into the applet via an HTML parameter; in this example, it's hard-coded for simplicity. Because it might take some time to load the file over the network, you put that routine into its own thread and use the familiar start(), stop(), and run() methods to control that thread.

Inside run() (lines 44 to 64), the work takes place. Here, you initialize a bunch of variables and then open the connection to the URL (using the openStream() method in line 51). Once the connection is open, you set up an input stream in lines 52 to 57 and read from it, line

14

by line, putting the result into an instance of `StringBuffer` (a string buffer is a modifiable string). Once all the data has been read, line 59 converts the `StringBuffer` object into a real string and then puts that result in the text area.

One other thing to note about this example is that the part of the code that opened a network connection, read from the file, and created a string is surrounded by a `try` and `catch` statement. If any errors occur while you're trying to read or process the file, these statements enable you to recover from them without the entire program crashing (in this case, the program exits with an error, because there's little else to be done if the applet can't read the file). The `try` and `catch` statement gives you the capability of handling and recovering from errors. You'll learn more about this statement on Day 17, "Exceptions."

The `URLconnection` Class

`URL`'s `openStream()` method is a simplified use of the `URLconnection` class. `URLconnection` provides a way to retrieve files by using URLs on Web or FTP sites, for example. `URLconnection` also enables you to create output streams if the protocol allows it.

To use a URL connection, you first create a new instance of the class `URLconnection`, set its parameters (whether it enables writing, for example), and then use the `connect()` method to open the connection. Keep in mind that, with a URL connection, the class handles the protocol for you based on the first part of the URL, so you don't have to make specific requests to retrieve a file. All you have to do is read it.

Sockets

For networking applications beyond what the `URL` and `URLconnection` classes offer (for example, for other protocols or for more general networking applications), Java provides the `Socket` and `ServerSocket` classes as an abstraction of standard socket programming techniques.

NOTE

There isn't enough space to devote to a full explanation of how socket programming works. If you haven't worked with sockets before, see whether `openStream()` will meet your needs. If you need to do more, any book that discusses socket programming will give you the background you need to work with Java's sockets.

The Socket class provides a client-side socket interface similar to standard UNIX sockets. To open a connection, create a new instance of Socket (where *hostname* is the host to connect to, and *portnum* is the port number):

```
Socket connection = new Socket(hostname, portnum);
```

NOTE

If you use sockets in an applet, you are still subject to the security restrictions about where you can connect.

Once the socket is open, you can use input and output streams to read and write from that socket (you'll learn all about input and output streams on Day 19):

```
DataInputStream in = new DataInputStream(
    new BufferedInputStream(connection.getInputStream()));
DataOutputStream out= new DataOutputStream(
    new BufferedOutputStream(connection.getOutputStream()));
```

When you're done with the socket, don't forget to close it (this action also closes all the input and output streams you might have set up for that socket):

```
connection.close();
```

Server-side sockets work similarly, with the exception of the accept() method. A server socket listens on a TCP port for a connection from a client; when a client connects to that port, the accept() method accepts a connection from that client. By using both client and server sockets, you can create applications that communicate with each other over the network.

To create a server socket and bind it to a port, create a new instance of ServerSocket with the port number:

```
ServerSocket sconnection = new ServerSocket(8888);
```

To listen on that port (and to accept a connection from any clients if one is made), use the accept() method:

```
sconnection.accept();
```

Once the socket connection is made, you can use input and output streams to read from and write to the client. See the java.net package for more information about Java sockets.

14

Other Applet Hints

On this, the last section of the last day of the second week, you will finish with things that didn't fit in anywhere else: using showStatus() to print messages in the browser's status window, providing applet information, and communicating between multiple applets on the same page.

The showStatus() Method

The showStatus() method, available in the applet class, enables you to display a string in the status bar of the browser, which contains the applet. You can use this method for printing error, link, help, or other status messages:

```
getAppletContext().showStatus("Change the color");
```

The getAppletContext() method enables your applet to access features of the browser that contains it. You already saw a use of this method with links, wherein you could use the showDocument() method to tell the browser to load a page. The showStatus() method uses that same mechanism to print status messages.

 NOTE

> The showStatus() method might not be supported in all browsers, so do not depend on it for your applet's functionality or interface. It is a useful way of communicating optional information to your user; if you need a more reliable method of communication, set up a label in your applet and update it to reflect changes in its message.

Applet Information

The AWT gives you a mechanism for associating information with your applet. Usually, there is a mechanism to view display information in the browser running the applet. You can use this mechanism to display your name or your organization name to your applet or to provide contact information so that users can get hold of you if they want. To provide information about your applet, override the getAppletInfo() method:

```
public String getAppletInfo() {
    return "GetRaven copyright 1996 Laura Lemay";
}
```

14

Communicating Between Applets

Sometimes you want to have an HTML page that has several different applets on it. To do this, all you have to do is include several different iterations of the <APPLET> tag; the browser will create different instances of your applet for each one that appears on the HTML page.

But what if you want to communicate between those applets? What if you want a change in one applet to affect the other applets in some way? The best way to do this is to use the applet context to get to different applets on the same page. You already have seen the getAppletContext() method used for several other purposes. You also can use it to get hold of the other applets on the page. For example, to call a method called sendMessage() on all the applets on a page (including the current applet), use the getApplets() method and a for loop that looks something like this:

```
for (Enumeration e = getAppletContext().getApplets();
        e.hasMoreElements();) {
    Applet current = (Applet)(e.nextElement());
    current.sendMessage();
}
```

The getApplets() method returns an Enumeration object with a list of the applets on the page. Iterating over the Enumeration object in this way enables you to access each element in the Enumeration in turn.

If you want to call a method in a specific applet, it's slightly more complicated. To do this, you give your applets a name and then refer to them by name inside the body of code for that applet. To give an applet a name, use the NAME parameter in your HTML file:

```
<P>This applet sends information:
<APPLET CODE="MyApplet.class" WIDTH=100 HEIGHT=150
    NAME="sender"> </APPLET>
<P>This applet receives information from the sender:
<APPLET CODE="MyApplet.class" WIDTH=100 HEIGHT=150
    NAME="receiver"> </APPLET>
```

To get a reference to another applet on the same page, use the getApplet() method from the applet context with the name of that applet. This gives you a reference to the applet of that name. You then can refer to that applet as if it were just another object by calling methods, setting its instance variables, and so on:

```
// get ahold of the receiver applet
Applet receiver = getAppletContext().getApplet("receiver");
// tell it to update itself.
reciever.update(text, value);
```

In this example, you use the getApplet() method to get a reference to the applet with the name receiver. Given that reference, you then can call methods in that applet as if it were

14

just another object in your own environment. In this example, if both applets have an update() method, you can tell receiver to update itself by using the information the current applet has.

Naming your applets and then referring to them by using the methods described in this section enables your applets to communicate and stay in sync with each other, providing uniform behavior for all the applets on your page.

Summary

Congratulations! Take a deep breath; you're finished with Week 2. This week has been full of useful information about creating applets and using the Java AWT classes along with Visual Java to display, draw, animate, process input, and create fully fledged interfaces in your applets.

Today, you finished exploring applets and the AWT by learning about three concepts. First, you learned about windows, frames, menus, and dialog boxes, which enable you to create a framework for your applets or enable your Java applications to take advantage of applet features.

Second, you had a brief introduction to Java networking through some of the classes in the java.net package. Applet networking includes things as simple as pointing the browser to another page from inside your applet, but it also can include retrieving files from the Web by using standard Web protocols (http, ftp, and so on). For more advanced networking capabilities, Java provides basic socket interfaces that can be used to implement many basic network-oriented applets, such as client-server interactions and chat sessions.

Finally, you finished up with the tidbits—small Java AWT and applet features that didn't fit anywhere else. These tidbits included showStatus(), providing information about your applet, and communicating between multiple applets on a single page.

Q&A

Q When I create pop-up windows, they all show up with this big yellow bar that says Warning: Applet Window. What does this mean?

A The warning is to tell users of an applet that the window being displayed was generated by an applet, and not by the browser itself. This is a security feature to keep an applet programmer from popping up a window that masquerades as a browser window and, for example, asks users for their passwords. There's nothing you can do to hide or obscure the warning.

Q **What good is having a file dialog box if you can't read or write files from the local file system?**

A Applets often can't read or write from the local file system depending on the browser, but you can use AWT components in Java applications as well as applets, and the file dialog box also is useful for them.

Q **How can I mimic an HTML form submission in a Java applet?**

A Currently, applets make it difficult to do this. The best (and easiest way) is to use GET notation to get the browser to submit the form contents for you. HTML forms can be submitted in two ways: by using the GET request or by using POST. If you use GET, your form information is encoded in the URL itself, something like this:

```
http://www.blah.com/cgi-bin/myscript?mail=1&yes=2&name=Fozzie
```

Because the form input is encoded in the URL, you can write a Java applet to mimic a form, get input from the user, and then construct a new URL object with the form data included on the end. Then just pass that URL to the browser by using getAppletContext().showDocument(), and the browser will submit the form results itself. For simple forms, this is all you need.

Q **How can I do POST form submissions?**

A You'll have to mimic what a browser does to send forms using POST: open a socket to the server and send the data, which looks something like this (the exact format is determined by the HTTP protocol; this is only a subset of it):

```
POST /cgi-bin/mailto.cgi HTTP/1.0
Content-type: application/x-www-form-urlencoded
Content-length: 36

{your encoded form data here}
```

If you've done it right, you get the CGI form output back from the server. It's then up to your applet to handle that output properly. Note that if the output is in HTML, there really isn't a way to pass that output to the browser that is running your applet yet. This capability might end up in future Java releases. If you get back an URL, however, you can redirect the browser to that URL.

Q **showStatus() doesn't work in my browser. How can I give my readers status information?**

A As you learned in the section on showStatus(), whether a browser supports showStatus() is dependent on to that browser. If you must have status-like behavior in your applet, consider creating a status label in the applet itself that is updated with the information you need to present.

14

Q It looks like the `openStream()` method and the `Socket` classes implement TCP sockets. Does Java support UDP (datagram) sockets?

A The JDK 1.0 provides two classes, `DatagramSocket` and `DatagramPacket`, which implement UDP sockets. The `DatagramSocket` class operates similarly to the `Socket` class. Use instances of `DatagramPacket` for each packet you send or receive over the socket. See the API documentation for the `java.net` package for more information.

Today's Featured Applet

Today's featured applet is `NowShowing`, a configurable marquee applet created by Rogers Cadenhead, one of the co-authors of this book. The applet draws a sign around text and creates a lighting effect around the sign that resembles a movie marquee. Figure 14.6 shows an example of `NowShowing` in action.

Figure 14.6.

The `NowShowing` *applet in action.*

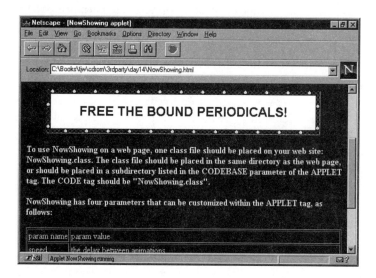

Files for `NowShowing` are located on the CD-ROM in the `\BOOK\3RDPARTY\DAY14\` directory, including source code in the file `NowShowing.java`. To use `NowShowing` on a Web page, place the `NowShowing.class` class file on your Web site. Place the class file in the same directory as the Web page, or place it in a subdirectory listed in the `CODEBASE` parameter of the `<APPLET>` tag. The `<CODE>` tag should be `NowShowing.class`.

Listing 14.4 shows the HTML tags used to run `NowShowing` as it was shown in Figure 14.6.

Listing 14.4. The `<APPLET>` tag for `NowShowing`.

```
<applet code="NowShowing.class" width="512" height="80" align="Top">
<param name="speed" value="100">
<param name="blink" value="5">
<param name="text" value="FREE THE BOUND PERIODICALS!">
<param name="fontsize" value="24">
</applet>
```

`NowShowing` has seven parameters that can be customized within the `<APPLET>` tag, as follows:

- ☐ The `speed` parameter is the delay between animations (`100` is the default).
- ☐ The `blink` parameter is the distance, in bulbs, between two lighted bulbs on the marquee (`4` is the default).
- ☐ The `text` parameter specifies the text to center on the marquee (`Free the bound periodicals!` is the default).
- ☐ The `fontSize` parameter is the size of the font to display (`24` is the default).
- ☐ The `font` parameter specifies the name of the font to use (`Arial` is the default).
- ☐ The `circle` parameter is the radius of each bulb (`6` is the default).
- ☐ The `randomColor` parameter sets the colors to random display if it exists; the colors are yellow otherwise.

More information on the applet is available from the author at the following URL:

```
http://www.spiderbyte.com/java
```

14

WEEK 3

15

16

17

18

19

20

21

At A Glance

- ☐ Modifiers
  Method and variable access control
- ☐ Packages and Interfaces
  Hiding classes
  Design versus implementation inheritance
- ☐ Exceptions
  Proper throw statements
  Using the finally clause
- ☐ Multithreading
  Synchronization problems
  More about Point

- ☐ Streams

   Input and output, `flush()` and `close()`

- ☐ Native Methods and Libraries

   Built-in optimizations

   Generating header and stub files

- ☐ Advanced Concepts

   Java bytecodes

   Security and consistency checking

   Garbage collection

Day **15**

Modifiers

After you have programmed in Java for a while, you will discover that making all your classes, methods, and variables public can become troublesome. The larger your program becomes, and the more you reuse your classes for new projects, the more you will want some control over their visibility. One of the large-scale solutions to this problem, packages, will be described tomorrow. Today, you'll explore what you can do within a class itself.

You will learn how to create and use the following:

☐ Methods and variables that control access by other classes

☐ Class variables and methods

☐ Constant variables, classes that cannot be subclassed, and methods that cannot be overridden

☐ Abstract classes and methods

NEW TERM *Modifiers* are prefixes that can be applied in various combinations to the methods and variables within a class and, in some cases, to the class itself. All the modifiers are optional, and do not have to appear in a declaration. Good style suggests the use of as many modifiers as needed to describe the intended use of, and restrictions on, what is being declared. In some special situations, certain modifiers are defined implicitly for you, and you do not need to use them in a declaration. One example of implicit modifiers is inside an interface, which will be described tomorrow.

You can use modifiers in any order in a Java statement. The order of modifiers is a matter of taste, but you should pick a style and be consistent with it throughout your classes. The following is the recommended order of modifiers:

```
access static abstract synchronized unusual final native
```

This list will make more sense to you as you learn about each of the modifiers today. However, some modifiers will be described later because of how they are used. How access modifiers apply to classes is covered tomorrow. The synchronized modifier has to do with multithreaded methods, so it will be described on Day 18, "Multithreading." The native modifier, covered on Day 20, "Native Methods and Libraries," specifies that a method is implemented in a native language of your computer (usually C) rather than in Java.

NOTE

An *unusual* modifier can be volatile or transient. The volatile modifier has to do with multithreading, and it will be discussed on Day 18. The transient modifier is used to declare a variable to be outside the persistent part of an object. This modifier makes persistent object storage systems easier to implement in Java, and though the compiler supports it, it is not used by the current implementation of the Java system.

Method and Variable Access Control

Access control is about controlling visibility. When a method or variable is visible to another class, its methods can be called by the other class, and its variables can be modified by the other class. This kind of access is called *referencing*. To prevent a method or variable from being referenced, you can use one of the four levels of visibility, depending on how much access should be restricted. You set these levels through the access modifier. The levels of visibility are the four P's of protection: public, package, protected, and private. To understand their use, you must understand the relationships that a method or variable within a class can have with other classes.

public

Each class is an island unto itself, so the first relationship to consider involves the distinction between the inside and the outside of the class. A method or variable is visible to the class in which it is defined. In order to make it visible to all classes, the method or variable should be declared to have `public` access.

For simplicity's sake, almost every method and variable defined this week will be declared `public`. If you use any of the book's examples in your own code, you probably will want to restrict access further. Because you're just learning now, it's a good idea to begin with the widest possible access. You can narrow this access as you gain design experience. The following are some examples of `public` declarations:

```
public class  Sandwich {
    public float        weightOfSandwich;
    public String     typeOfMeat;

    public boolean     takeABite() {
        // code for sandwich-biting method
    }
}
```

NOTE The use of two or more spaces after the modifiers and type in these declarations is intentional. It makes finding the variable or method name on each line a little easier. Later, you'll see that the type and the name sometimes are separately lined up in a column to make the code even more readable. When you see several modifiers on the same line, you'll begin to appreciate these small touches.

A variable or method with `public` access has the widest possible visibility. Any other class can see it. Any other class can use it. This might not always be what you want, of course, so more restrictive access is possible.

Package

In C, a name can be hidden so that only the functions within a given source file can see it. In Java, source files are replaced by the more explicit notion of packages, which can group classes. You will learn about packages tomorrow. For now, all you need to know is that the relationship to consider is between a class and other classes that are part of the same system, library, or program (or any other grouping of related classes). This defines the next level of increased protection and narrowed visibility.

Due to an idiosyncrasy of the Java language, this level of access has no precise name. This level is indicated by the lack of any access modifier in a declaration. Historically, this level has been called various suggestive names such as *friendly* and *package*. The latter seems most appropriate and is the one used here. Perhaps in a later release of Java, it will be possible to say package explicitly, but for now it is simply the default protection when no modifier has been specified.

Most of the declarations you've seen in the past two weeks have used this default level of protection. Here's a reminder of what they look like:

```
public class  Gambler {
    int  moneyInPocket = 70;
    int  chanceToBluff = 25;

    boolean  anteUp() {
        // method code here
    }
}
```

In the Gambler class, the anteUp() method has no access modifier, which means it is accessible only from within the same package. Now take a look at Hand, another class in the same package:

```
public class  Hand {
    public void  dealCards() {
        Gambler  bret = new Gambler();

        bret.anteUp();
        g.drawString("$" + bret.moneyInPocket, 5, 50);
    }
}
```

If a class from any other package tried to access bret the way that Hand does in this example, it would generate compile-time errors.

Why was package made a default? When you're designing a large system and you divide your classes into groups to implement smaller pieces of that system, the classes often need to share more with one another than with the outside world. The need for this level of sharing is common enough that it was made the default level of protection. But what if you have some details of your implementation that you don't want to share even within a package? The answer is the next level of protection.

protected

The third relationship to consider is between a class and its present and future subclasses. These subclasses are much closer to a parent class than to any outside classes, for the following reasons:

☐ Subclasses usually are more intimately aware of the internals of a parent class.

- ☐ Subclasses often are written by you or by someone who has been given your source code.
- ☐ Subclasses frequently need to modify or enhance the representation of data within a parent class.

No other class is allowed this level of access and must use the public interface that the class offers. To support the level of access reserved for subclasses, modern programming languages have invented an intermediate level of access between the previous two levels (public, package) and full privacy (private). This intermediate level provides more protection and narrows visibility further than a package does, but it still allows subclasses to have full access. In Java, this level of protection is provided by the protected modifier, as in the following code:

```
public class  Knob {
    private protected int     notches = 10;
    private protected String  knobLabel = "Volume";

    private protected boolean  crankItUp() {
        notches = 11;
        return true;
    }
}

public class  GlowingKnob extends Knob {
    public void  tryItOut() {
        GlowingKnob  k = new GlowingKnob();

        System.out.println(k.knobLabel);
        k.crankItUp();
        System.out.println("Notches: " + k.notches);
    }
}
```

In the preceding example, the Knob class has two private protected instance variables, notches and knobLabel. It also has a private protected method, crankItUp(). These can be used freely by the GlowingKnob class because it is a subclass of Knob. However, consider the following class, Doohickey, which is not a subclass of Knob:

```
public class  Doohickey {
    public void  tryItOut() {
        GlowingKnob  k = new GlowingKnob();

        System.out.println(k.knobLabel);
        k.crankItUp();
    }
}
```

Even though Doohickey is in the same package as GlowingKnob, it is not a subclass of it (it's a subclass of Object, because no superclass is indicated in the declaration). Only subclasses are allowed to see, or to use, private protected variables and methods. The declarations in

Knob are prefixed by private protected because in the current version of Java, adding private is required to get the behavior described here. Using protected alone allows both subclasses and classes in the same package to have access (which offers a fifth level of protection that can be used).

One of the most striking examples of the need for this special level of access is when you are supporting a public abstraction with your class. As far as the outside world is concerned, you have a simple, public interface (through methods) to whatever abstraction you've built for your users. A more complex representation, and the implementation that depends on it, is hidden inside. When subclasses extend and modify this representation, or even just your implementation of it, they need to get to the underlying, concrete representation and not simply to the abstraction, as shown in the following:

```
public class  SortedList {
    private protected BinaryTree  theBinaryTree;

    // code here
    public Object[]  theList() {
        return theBinaryTree.asArray();
    }

    public void       add(Object o) {
        theBinaryTree.addObject(o);
    }
}

public class  InsertSortedList extends SortedList {
    public void        insert(Object o, int position) {
        theBinaryTree.insertObject(o,     position);
    }
}
```

Without being able to access theBinaryTree directly, the insert() method would have had to get the list as an array of Objects, through the public method theList(), allocate a new, bigger array, and insert the new object by hand. By seeing that its parent is using a BinaryTree to implement the sorted list, it can call upon BinaryTree's built-in method insertObject() to get the job done.

Some languages have experimented with more explicit ways of raising and lowering your level of abstraction to solve this same problem in a more general way. In Java, protected solves only a part of the problem by allowing you to separate the concrete from the abstract. The rest is up to you.

private

The final relationship comes back to the distinction between the inside and outside of the class. private is the most narrowly visible, highest level of protection that you can get—the opposite of `public`. `private` methods and variables cannot be seen by any class other than the one in which they are defined, as in the following:

```
public class  Gambler {
    private int      CardUpSleeve;

    private int   UseSleeveCard() {
        // method code here
    }
}
```

This level might seem extremely restrictive, but it is a commonly used level of protection. Any private data, internal state, or representations unique to your implementation—anything that shouldn't be directly shared with subclasses—is `private`. Remember that an object's primary job is to encapsulate its data, to hide it from sight and limit its manipulation. The best way to do that is to make as much data as private as possible.

Your methods always can be less restrictive, but keeping a tight rein on your internal representation is important. It minimizes the amount of information one class needs to know about another to get its job done and reduces the extent of the code changes you need when your representation changes.

Conventions for Instance Variable Access

A good rule of thumb is that unless an instance variable is constant (you'll soon see how to specify this), it should almost certainly be `private`. If you don't do this, you have the following problem:

```
public class  Love {
    public String  termOfEndearment;
    termOfEndearment = "snookie-lump";
}
```

This class might have set up `termOfEndearment` for the use of other classes, expecting them to read it only. Consider the case of two objects, a `Romeo` object and a `Juliet` object. Even though these objects come from completely different class hierarchies, they have fallen in love with each other. At some point in the Java program, the `Romeo` object might want to use a term of endearment to express its affection for the `Juliet` object. It could use the `termOfEndearment` instance variable from the `Love` class to do so.

However, `termOfEndearment` is not `private`. Because it isn't, another class could change it at will. A `Tybalt` object, say, could do the following:

```
Love  l = new Love();

l.termOfEndearment = "hen-pecked shrew";
```

As you can see, `Romeo` can't count on the `public` variable `termOfEndearment` because it can be changed like this. An instance variable that can be publicly read also can be written to. Because there is no way to specify separately the level of protection for reading and writing to instance variables, they almost always should be declared `private`.

NOTE

> The careful reader might recall that this rule has been violated in many examples in this book. Most of the time, this was done for clarity's sake and to make the examples shorter. (You will see soon that it takes more space to do the right thing.) One use cannot be avoided: the `System.out.println()` calls scattered throughout the book must use the `public` variable `out` directly. You cannot change this `final` system class (which you might have written differently). You can imagine the disastrous results if anyone accidentally modifies the contents of this global `public` variable!

Accessor Methods

If instance variables are `private`, how do you provide access to them for the outside world? The answer is to write accessor methods, as in the following:

```
public class  Love {
    private String   termOfEndearment;

    public String   termOfEndearment() { // get the string
        return termOfEndearment;
    }

    private protected void  termOfEndearment(String s) { // set the string
        termOfEndearment = s;
    }
}
```

Using methods to access an instance variable is a common technique in object-oriented programs. Applying it liberally through your classes repays you numerous times over with more robust and reusable programs. Notice how separating the reading and writing of the instance variable allows you to specify a `public` method to return its value and a `protected` method to set it. This pattern of protection is often useful because it is common for everyone to need the ability to see the value of a variable, but only an object and its subclasses should be able to change it. This pattern of protection also enables you to control the values that the variable can be set to by adding code to the set method.

If the variable is a particularly private piece of data, you could make its set method `private` and its get method `protected` or any other combination that suits the data's sensitivity.

15

NOTE

> The compiler and Java 1.0 language specification will permit an instance variable and method to have the same name, as in the preceding example where there is a `termOfEndearment` instance variable and a `termOfEndearment()` method. However, some people might find this convention confusing and will find it more understandable to add prefixes to the get and set methods. For example, in the preceding example, the methods could be named `getTermOfEndearment` and `setTermOfEndearment`.
>
> Giving the variable and methods the same name can make sense if used consistently, and it saves typing. As long as a convention of some kind is followed, there should be no problem.

Whenever you want to append to your own instance variable, you should use your own accessor, as in the following:

```
aTitle(aTitle() + ", lord of the jungle");
```

Just like a method outside the class would do, you're using accessor methods to change the string `aTitle`. Why are you doing this? You protected the variable in the first place to control how your class would be used by others, but the protection doesn't guard against your use of the class. Your code should be protected from knowing too much about its own representation, except in those few places that need to know about it. Then, if you must change something about `aTitle`, the change will not affect every use of that variable in your class (as it would without accessor methods). Instead, a change to `aTitle` would affect only the implementations of its accessor methods.

One of the powerful side effects of maintaining this level of indirection regarding your own instance variables is that if special code needs to be performed each time `aTitle` is accessed, that code can be put in one place where the methods in your class and in all others will call that special code. Here's an example:

```
private protected void  aTitle(String s) { // the set method
    aTitle = s;
    performSomeImportantBookkeepingOn(s);
}
```

Although it might seem cumbersome to replace a statement such as

```
x = 12 + 5 * x;
```

with

```
x(12 + 5 * x());
```

the result will be greater reusability and easier maintenance.

Class Variables and Methods

What if you want to create a shared variable that all your instances can see and use? If you use an instance variable, each instance has its own copy of the variable, defeating its whole purpose. If you place it in the class itself, however, there is only one copy, and all instances of the class share it. This kind of variable is called a class variable. The following example uses the class variable `pi`, which is identified as a class variable because of its use of the modifier `static`:

```
public class  Circle {
    public static float  pi = 3.14159265F;

    public float  area(float r) {
        return  pi * r * r;
    }
}
```

 TIP

Java uses the word `static` to declare class variables and methods. Whenever you see the word `static`, remember to mentally substitute the word *class*.

Instances can refer to their own class variables as though they were instance variables, as in the last example. Because the `pi` variable is `public`, methods in other classes also can refer to `pi`:

```
float  circumference = 2 * Circle.pi * r;
```

 NOTE

Instances of `Circle` also can use this form of access. For clarity, this form of access is preferred in most cases, even for instances. It clarifies that a class variable is being used and helps the reader to know instantly that the variable is global to all instances.

If you might change your mind later about how a class variable is accessed, created, and so forth, create instance (or even class) accessor methods to hide any uses of it from these changes.

Class methods are defined in much the same way. They can be accessed in the same two ways just described by instances of their class, but only through the full class name by instances of other classes. The following class defines class methods to help it count its own instances:

```
public class  InstanceCounter {
    private static int  instanceCount = 0; // a class variable

    private protected static int  instanceCount() { // a class method
        return instanceCount;
    }

    private static void  incrementCount() {
        ++instanceCount;
    }

    InstanceCounter() {
        InstanceCounter.incrementCount();
    }
}
```

In this example, an explicit use of the class name calls the method `incrementCount()`. Though this might seem verbose, it immediately tells someone reading the code which object is expected to handle the method (the class, in this case, rather than the instance). This is especially useful if the reader needs to find where that method is declared in a large class that places all its class methods at the beginning (the recommended practice, by the way).

Note the initialization of `instanceCount` to `0`. Just as an instance variable is initialized when its instance is created, a class variable is initialized when its class is created. This class initialization happens essentially before anything else can happen to that class or its instances, so the class in the example will work as planned.

Finally, the conventions you learned for accessing an instance variable are applied in this example to access a class variable. The accessor methods are therefore class methods. (There is no set method here, just an increment method, because no one is allowed to set `instanceCount` directly.) Note that only subclasses are allowed to ask what the `instanceCount` is because that is a relatively intimate detail. Here's a test of `InstanceCounter` in action:

```
public class  InstanceCounterTester extends InstanceCounter {
    public static void  main(String arg[]) {
        for (int  i = 0;  i < 10;  ++i)
            new InstanceCounter();
        System.out.println("made " + InstanceCounter.instanceCount());
    }
}
```

Not shockingly, this example displays the following:

```
made 10
```

The `final` Modifier

Using the `final` modifier, you can accomplish the following:

- [ ] When the `final` modifier is applied to a class, it means that the class cannot be subclassed.
- [ ] When it is applied to a variable, it means that the variable is constant.
- [ ] When it is applied to a method, it means that the method cannot be overridden by subclasses.

`final` Classes

Here's a `final` class declaration:

```
public final class  LastClass {
    // class code here
}
```

You declare a class `final` for only two reasons. The first is security. You expect to use its instances as unchangeable capabilities, and you don't want anyone else to be able to subclass and create new and different instances of them. The second is efficiency. You want to count on instances of only that one class (and no subclasses) being around in the system so that you can optimize for them.

NOTE

> The Java class library uses `final` classes extensively. You can flip through the class hierarchy diagrams in Appendix B, "Class Hierarchy Diagrams," to see them (`final` classes are lightly shaded). Examples of the security advantage of `final` are the classes `java.lang.System`, `java.net.InetAddress`, and `java.net.Socket`. A good example of the efficiency advantage is `java.lang.String`. Strings are so common in Java, and so central to it, that the run-time system handles them specially (for security reasons as well).

You will rarely create a `final` class, although you will have plenty of opportunity to be upset because certain system classes are `final`. Such is the price of security and efficiency.

15

15

final **Variables**

To declare constants in Java, use final variables, as in the following:

```
public class  Football {
    public static final int     touchdown   = 7;
    public          final String  cheer = "Go, team!";
}
```

NOTE The unusual spacing in the last line of the example is an attempt to make it clearer that the top variable is a class variable and the bottom one isn't, but that both are public and final.

You can use final class and instance variables in expressions just like normal class and instance variables, but you cannot modify them. As a result, final variables must be given their value at the time of declaration. These variables function like a better, typed version of the #define constants of C. Classes can provide useful constants to other classes through final class variables such as touchdown in the last example and BOLD, ITALIC, and PLAIN in java.awt.Font. Other classes reference the variables as before, such as in the statement BengalsScore += Football.touchdown;.

Local variables (those inside blocks of code surrounded by braces, such as variables in while or for loops) can't be declared final. In fact, local variables can't have modifiers in front of them at all.

final **Methods**

Here's an example of using final methods:

```
public class  MorphImage {
    public static final void  combineFaces() {
        // a unique and really useful method
    }

    public          final void  checkRegistration() {
        // no one gets to override this
    }
}
```

Subclasses cannot override final methods. It is a rare thing that a method truly wants to declare itself the final word on its own implementation, so why does this modifier apply to methods? The answer is efficiency. If you declare a method final, the compiler then can place it in-line where methods are calling it because the compiler knows that no other class ever can subclass and override the method to change its meaning. Although you might not use final right away when writing a class, as you fine-tune the system later, you might discover that a few methods have to be final to make your class fast enough. Almost all your methods will be fine as they are, however.

The Java class library declares a lot of commonly used methods final so that you will benefit from the increased execution speed. In the case of classes that already are final, this makes perfect sense and is a wise choice. The few final methods declared in non-final classes will annoy you because your subclasses can no longer override them. When efficiency becomes less of an issue for the Java environment, many of these final methods might be unfrozen again, restoring this lost flexibility to the system.

NOTE

Effectively, private methods are final, as are all methods declared in a final class. Marking these latter methods final (as the Java library sometimes does) is legal but redundant; the compiler already treats them as final.

It's possible to use final methods for some of the same security reasons that you use final classes, but it's a much rarer event.

If you use accessor methods a lot (as recommended), and you are worried about efficiency, here's a rewrite of Love that's much faster:

```
public class  Love {
    private String  termOfEndearment;

    public final String  termOfEndearment() { // get the string
        return termOfEndearment;
    }

    private protected final void  termOfEndearment(String s) { // set the string
        termOfEndearment = s;
    }
}
```

NOTE

Future Java compilers almost will certainly be smart enough to place simple methods in-line automatically, so you won't need to use final in such cases.

abstract **Methods and Classes**

15

Whenever you arrange classes into an inheritance hierarchy, the presumption is that higher classes are more abstract and general, and lower subclasses are more concrete and specific. Often, as you design a set of classes, you factor out common design and implementation into a shared superclass. If the primary reason that a superclass exists is to act as this common repository, and if only its subclasses expect to be used, that superclass is called an abstract class.

abstract classes can create no instances, but they can contain anything a normal class can contain. In addition, abstract classes are allowed to prefix any of their methods with the modifier abstract. Non-abstract classes are not allowed to use this modifier; using it on even one method requires that the whole class be declared abstract. The following example includes a method called loadPalindromeFile() that must be implemented by any subclass that extends PalindromeClass:

```
public abstract class  PalindromeClass {
    int  wordcount; // an instance variable

    public abstract int  loadPalindromeFile();

    public boolean  isAPalindrome() {
        // code of a normal method
    }
}
public class  PalindromeSubclass extends PalindromeClass {
    public int  loadPalindromeFile() {
        // code for method that must be implemented
    }
}
```

The following are two attempted uses of these classes:

```
Object  a = new PalindromeClass();
Object  c = new PalindromeSubClass();
```

The first attempt is illegal because an abstract class cannot be instantiated. The second is permitted because PalindromeSubclass is a concrete subclass of the abstract class. Notice that abstract methods need no implementation; non-abstract subclasses, however, must provide an implementation. The abstract class simply provides the template for the methods, which are implemented later by subclasses. In the Java class library, several abstract classes have no documented subclasses in the system, but simply provide a base for subclassing to occur in programs. If you look at the diagrams in Appendix B, abstract classes are shaded darker than final classes and are quite common in the library.

Using an abstract class to embody a pure design—that is, nothing but abstract methods—is better accomplished in Java by using an interface, a topic that will be discussed tomorrow. Whenever a design calls for an abstraction that includes instance state or a partial implementation, however, an abstract class is your only choice. In earlier object-oriented languages, abstract classes were simply a convention. They proved to be so valuable that Java supports them not only in the form described here, but in the richer form of interfaces.

Summary

Today, you learned how variables and methods can control their visibility and access by other classes through the four P's of protection: public, package, protected, and private. You also learned that although instance variables are most often declared private, declaring accessor methods enables you to control the reading and writing of them separately. Protection levels allow you to separate your public abstractions from their concrete representations.

You also learned how to create class variables and methods, which are associated with the class itself, and how to declare final variables, methods, and classes to represent constants and fast or secure methods and classes.

Finally, you discovered how to declare and use abstract classes, which cannot be instantiated, and abstract methods, which have no implementation and must be overridden in subclasses. Together, abstract classes and methods provide a template for subclasses to fill in and act as a variant of the powerful interfaces of Java.

Q&A

Q Why are there so many different levels of protection in Java?

A Each level of protection, or visibility, provides a different view of your class to the outside world. Each is a logically well-defined and useful separation that Java supports directly in the language (as opposed to accessor methods, for example, which are a convention you must follow).

Q Won't using accessor methods everywhere slow down my Java code?

A Not always. Soon, Java compilers will be smart enough to make these methods fast automatically, but if you're concerned about speed, you always can declare accessor methods to be final, and they'll be just as fast as direct instance variable accesses.

Q Are class methods (static **methods) inherited just like instance methods?**

A No. Class methods are now final by default. How, then, can you ever declare a non-final class method? The answer is that you can't. Inheritance of class methods is not allowed, breaking the symmetry with instance methods. Because this rule goes against a part of Java's philosophy (making everything as simple as possible), perhaps it will be reversed in a later release.

Q Based on what I've learned, it seems like private **abstract methods and** final **abstract methods or classes don't make sense. Are they legal?**

A Nope—they cause compile-time errors, as you have guessed. To be useful, abstract methods must be overridden, and abstract classes must be subclassed. Neither of those operations would be legal if the classes and methods were also private or final.

FEATURED APPLET Today's Featured Applet

Today's featured applet is Iceblox, an animated videogame from Karl Hörnell. Players control a penguin who is dodging fire monsters while trying to collect gold coins encased in ice. The applet is an excellent example of how buffering is used to eliminate flickering. Figure 15.1 shows a screen capture from Iceblox.

Figure 15.1.

The Iceblox *applet in action.*

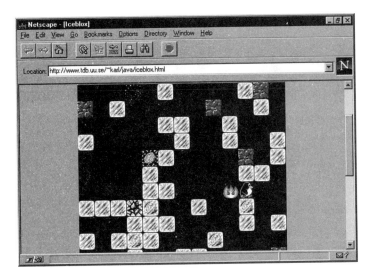

Files for Iceblox are located on the CD-ROM in the \BOOK\3RDPARTY\DAY15\ directory, including source code in the file Iceblox.java. To use Iceblox on a Web page, place these two files on your Web site: the class file Iceblox.class and the image file Iceblox.gif. Place the files in the same directory as the Web page, or place them in a subdirectory listed in the CODEBASE parameter of the <APPLET> tag. The <CODE> tag should be Iceblox.class.

Listing 15.1 shows the HTML tags used to run Iceblox as it was shown in Figure 15.1.

Listing 15.1. The <APPLET> tag for Iceblox.

```
<applet code="Iceblox.class" width=390 height=350>
</applet>
```

Iceblox takes no parameters. More information on the applet and other animation and games written by the same author are available from the following URL:

```
http://www.tdb.uu.se/~karl/java/iceblox.html
```

15

Day **16**

Packages and Interfaces

When you examine a new feature of Java, ask yourself two questions:

1. How can this feature be used to better organize the parts of my Java program?
2. How can it be used in the code of my methods?

The first question is a reference to what often is called programming in the large, and the second is a reference to what is called programming in the small. Bill Joy, a founder of Sun Microsystems, likes to say that Java feels like C (familiar and powerful) when programming in the small and like Smalltalk (extendable and expressively powerful) when programming in the large.

The separation of designing from coding is one of the most fundamental advances of programming in the past quarter-century, and object-oriented languages such as Java implement a strong form of this separation. The first part of this separation already has been described on previous days. When you develop a Java program, first you design the classes and decide on the relationships between these classes. When that has been done, you implement the Java code needed for each of the methods in your design. If you are careful enough with both these processes, you can change your mind about aspects of the design without affecting anything but small, local pieces of your Java code, and you can change the implementation of any method without affecting the rest of the design.

As you begin to explore more advanced Java programming, however, you'll find that this simple model becomes too limiting. As you explore these limitations, both for programming in the large and in the small, you will learn why the following two features are needed:

☐ Packages, which are used to organize classes

☐ Interfaces, which are used to implement behavior for use by several classes that can be in different class hierarchies

Packages

Packages, Java's way of doing large-scale design and organization, are used to categorize and group classes. The following sections explore why you might need to use packages.

Programming in the Large

When you begin to develop Java programs that use a large number of classes, you quickly will discover some limitations in the model presented thus far for designing and building them. For one thing, as the number of classes that you build grows, the likelihood of wanting to reuse a short, simple class name increases. When you reuse your own classes, or use classes designed by others such as the Java library, you might not remember or even know all class names that are being used. To avoid conflicts, you need to know how to hide a class inside a package.

You first declare the name of the package by using the `package` statement. Then you define a class, as you would normally. That class, and any other classes also declared with the same package name, are grouped together. (These other classes usually are located in separate source files.) Here's a simple example of the creation of a package in a Java source file:

```
package  wordProcessor;

public class  CheckSpelling {
    // class code here
}
```

NOTE

If a package statement appears in a Java source file, it must be the first statement in that file other than comments or blank lines.

Packages can be organized further into a hierarchy that is somewhat analogous to the inheritance hierarchy, where each level usually represents a smaller, more specific grouping of classes. The Java class library itself is organized along these lines (as shown in Appendix B, "Class Hierarchy Diagrams"). The top level is called java; the next level includes io, net, util, and awt and others. The last of these, awt, has an even lower level that includes the package image. The ColorModel class, which is located in the image package, can be uniquely referred to anywhere in Java code as java.awt.image.ColorModel.

NOTE

By convention, the first level of the hierarchy specifies the globally unique name of the company that developed the Java package. For example, Sun Microsystems classes, which are not part of the standard Java environment, all begin with the prefix sun. The standard package, java, is an exception to this rule because it is so fundamental, and because it might be implemented by multiple companies in the future.

Sun has specified a more formal procedure for package naming to be followed in the future. The top-level domains of the Internet (EDU, COM, GOV, FR, US, and so on) will form the first part of package names, in uppercase letters. This part will be followed by the domain name of the company that created the package, and it can go further down the hierarchy of the company as needed.

By this procedure, the sun packages would be called COM.sun, for example. A package further down an organization's domain tree could be called something like GOV.whitehouse.president.reelect.to.committee.WiretapOpponent. Because domain names already are guaranteed to be unique globally, this naming scheme solves the thorny naming problem nicely. As a bonus, the applets and packages from the potentially thousands of Java programmers automatically will be stored into a growing hierarchy below your classes directory, giving you a way to find and categorize them all in a comprehensible manner.

Because each Java class usually is located in a separate source file, the grouping of classes provided by a hierarchy of packages is analogous to the grouping of files into a hierarchy of directories on your file system. The Java compiler reinforces this analogy by requiring the creation of a directory hierarchy that exactly matches the hierarchy of packages you have created and the placement of the class in the directory with the same name and level as the package in which it's defined. Java WorkShop handles this task for you when a package statement is used in one of your programs or when you use Project Manager to create a package.

The directory hierarchy for the Java class library exactly mirrors its package hierarchy. For example, the class referenced as `java.awt.image.ColorModel` is stored in a file named `ColorModel.class` in a subdirectory with the partial path `java/awt/image`.

Consider the case of a package called `esperanto` that has been declared within the `wordProcessor` package, as follows:

```
package  wordProcessor.esperanto;

public class  CheckSpelling {
    // class code here
}
```

In this example, the Java source file `CheckSpelling.java` must be located in a directory called `wordProcessor/esperanto` for the compiler to find it. When the compiler generates the file `CheckSpelling.class`, it places the file into this same directory. The compiler enforces the hierarchy.

NOTE

For today's first example, the source file `CheckSpelling.java` would be stored in a subdirectory called `wordProcessor`. When classes are defined without a `package` statement, the compiler places the classes in a default, unnamed package, and their `.java` and `.class` files can be located in the current directory, a `classes` subdirectory, or a directory indicated by the `CLASSPATH` environment variable. The compiler and interpreter both search this list of paths to find any classes you reference. On some implementations, the Java class library's `.class` files are located in an archive file named `classes.zip` in the `lib` subdirectory to conserve space.

In Java WorkShop, you can use Project Manager to view the current setting of `CLASSPATH`. You also can add directories to the path. These features are available through the Build tabbed dialog box in Project Manager, but you should not need them in most circumstances.

Programming in the Small

When you refer to a class by name in your Java code, you are using a package. Most of the time you aren't aware of it because commonly used classes in the system are in java.lang, a package that the Java compiler automatically imports for you. For example, consider the following statement:

```
String  favoriteSongTitle;
```

If the String class were not part of java.lang, you would have to refer to it by its full package name, java.lang.String, or use an import statement in the program.

If you tried to use the CheckSpelling class in the package wordProcessor in a program, you might try the following statement:

```
CheckSpelling  cs;
```

This statement would result in a compiler error stating that the class CheckSpelling is not defined in the package java.lang. To solve this problem, prefix a class name with the name of the package that defines the class:

```
wordProcessor.CheckSpelling  cs;
```

As this example demonstrates, the package and class names together form a globally unique name because the wordProcessor package can have only one class called CheckSpelling. Other packages can use the class name CheckSpelling without conflicting with this particular class.

NOTE

> By convention, package names begin with a lowercase letter to distinguish them from class names, which begin with an uppercase letter. In something such as java.awt.image.PixelGrabber, this convention helps to make the class name, PixelGrabber in this case, easier to spot.

Suppose you want to use a lot of classes from a package, a package with a long name, or both. Referring to something like EDU.unt.athletics.spirit.handsign.EagleClaw would be unwieldy. Instead, you can use the import statement to import the names of classes into a program. You can refer to the classes in an imported package without a prefix, just like java.lang classes. For example, to import the EagleClaw class, you would use the following statement:

```
import EDU.unt.athletics.spirit.handsign.EagleClaw;
```

After the package has been imported, the class can be referred to throughout a Java program without using the package name, as in the following:

```
EagleClaw  e = new EagleClaw();
```

NOTE | All `import` statements must appear after any `package` statement, but before any class definitions. Thus, they must be at the top of a source file.

If you are using several classes from the same package, you can use the wildcard character * in an `import` statement. Using this character causes all public classes at the spot of the wildcard to be imported.

The following is a series of statements that do not use a wildcard:

```
GOV.whitehouse.president.reelect.to.committee.KissBabies          k;
GOV.whitehouse.president.reelect.to.committee.WooContributors      w;
GOV.whitehouse.president.reelect.to.committee.FundProjectsInIowa   f;
```

You can accomplish the same task with a single `import` statement, as shown:

```
import GOV.whitehouse.president.reelect.to.committee.*;
```

This `import` statement makes the following statements usable in Java:

```
KissBabies          k;
WooContributors      w;
FundProjectsInIowa   f;
```

NOTE | The asterisk wildcard is not exactly like the one you might use at a command prompt to specify the contents of a directory. For example, if you listed the contents of the directory `classes/java/awt/*`, the directory listing would include all `.class` files and subdirectories such as `image` and `peer`. However, using `import java.awt.*` does not import subpackages such as `image` and `peer`. To import all classes in a complex package hierarchy, you must explicitly import each level of the hierarchy by hand.

If you plan to use a class or a package only a few times in your source file, it probably is not worth importing the class. The question to ask yourself is whether the loss in clarity introduced by using `import` is worth the convenience of typing fewer characters in the code.

16

A full package name shows anyone reading the code where to find more information about the class, right at the spot where the class is being used, rather than in an `import` statement at the top of the source file.

Although package use allows classes to have the same name, this still can cause a conflict if two packages are imported that use the same class name. Consider the following package and class declarations:

```
package  fernando.pitch;

public class  Curveball {
    // class code here
}

package  fernando.pitch;

public class  Slider {
    // class code here
}
```

In a second package, you have the following declarations:

```
package  nolan.pitch;

public class  Curveball {
    // class code here
}

package  nolan.pitch;

public class  Fastball {
    // class code here
}
```

You then write the following, in a new program:

```
import fernando.pitch;
import nolan.pitch;

Curveball  c;
```

There are two possible locations for the class referred to in `Curveball c;`: the `fernando.pitch` package, and the `nolan.pitch` package. Because this is ambiguous, it causes a compiler error. It must be fixed by using a more explicit reference to the intended class, as shown:

```
import fernando.pitch;
import nolan.pitch;

fernando.pitch.Curveball    c1;
nolan.pitch.Curveball       c2;
```

The two statements referring to `Curveball` classes will now work because of the explicit reference indicating which class is being referred to.

Although most examples in this section have used declarations, any use of a class name follows the same rules.

Hiding Classes

The astute reader might have noticed that the discussion of importing with an asterisk stated that it imported a whole package of `public` classes. Why would you want to have classes of any other kind? Take a look at the following:

```
package  collections;

public class  LinkedList {
    private Node  root;

    public  void  add(Object o) {
        root = new Node(o, root);
    }
    // code here
}

class  Node { // not public
    private Object   contents;
    private Node     next;

    Node(Object o, Node n) {
        contents = o;
        next     = n;
    }
    // code here
}
```

NOTE

If this all were in one file, you might think it violates the compiler's rule regarding one class per Java source file. Actually, the compiler cares only about each `public` class being in a separate file (although it still is good style to use separate files for each class).

The goal of the `LinkedList` class is to provide a set of useful public methods (such as `add()`) to any other classes that might want to use them. These other classes don't need to know about any support classes `LinkedList` needs to get its job done. In addition, because `LinkedList` is designed, the `Node` class probably should be local to its implementation.

16

For methods and variables, this would be addressed by the four P's of protection discussed yesterday: `private`, `protected`, `package`, and `public`, listed in order of increasing visibility. You already have explored many `public` classes, and because both the `private` and `protected` modifiers make sense only inside a class definition, you cannot put the modifiers outside of one. `Node` has no protection modifier in its declaration. This limits the class to use only in the same package that it was defined in. In this case, this is the `collections` package. You might use `LinkedList` as follows:

```
import collections.*;

LinkedList    aLinkedList;
Node          n;

aLinkedList.add(new Integer(1138));
aLinkedList.add("THX-");
```

This code would cause a compile-time error. The `Node` class is not imported by the statement `import collections.*;` because the statement only can import `public` classes, so a `Node` variable cannot be declared.

NOTE

> You also could import or declare a `LinkedList` using `collections.LinkedList`. Because `LinkedList` refers to `Node`, that class automatically is loaded and used, and the compiler verifies that `LinkedList` has the right to create and use the `Node` class as part of package `collections`. However, this class still cannot be used by other classes that aren't in the same package.

One of the advantages of hidden classes is that they can introduce complexity into a class without making it complex to the classes that import it. Creating a good package consists of defining a small, clean set of `public` classes and methods for other classes to use, and then implementing them by using as many hidden `package` support classes as needed. You will see another use for hidden classes later today.

Interfaces

Interfaces, like the abstract classes and methods you saw yesterday, provide templates of behavior that other classes are expected to implement. However, they are much more powerful.

Programming in the Large

When you first begin to design object-oriented programs, the class hierarchy seems to provide all the functionality you will ever need. Within that single tree, you can express a hierarchy of numeric types (number, complex, floating-point, rational, integer), relationships between objects and processes outside of the object, and any number of necessary features.

After some deeper thought, or more complex design experience, this wonderful tree begins to feel restrictive. The power and discipline you have achieved by carefully placing only one copy of each idea somewhere in the tree can come back to haunt you whenever you need to use the same idea on other, distant parts of the tree.

Some languages address these problems by introducing more flexible run-time power, such as the code block and the perform: method of Smalltalk. Others choose to provide more complex inheritance hierarchies, such as multiple inheritance. With the latter complexity comes a host of confusing and error-prone ambiguities and misunderstandings, and with the former, a harder time implementing safety and security. The language also becomes harder to learn. Java has chosen to take neither of these paths, but in the spirit of Objective-C's protocols, the language has adopted a separate hierarchy altogether to gain the expressive power needed to loosen the restrictiveness.

This new hierarchy is a hierarchy of interfaces. Interfaces are not limited to a single superinterface, so they allow a form of multiple inheritance. But they pass on only method descriptions to their children, not method implementations nor instance variables. This difference helps to eliminate many of the complexities of full multiple inheritance.

Interfaces, like classes, are declared in source files, one interface to a file. Like classes, they also are compiled into `.class` files. In fact, almost everywhere that this book has a class name in any of its examples or discussions, you can substitute an interface name. Java programmers often say "class" when they mean "class or interface." Interfaces complement and extend the power of classes, and the two can be treated almost exactly the same. One of the few differences between them is that an interface cannot be instantiated: new can create only an instance of a class. The following is an example of a declaration of an interface:

```
package  wordProcessor;

public interface  CheckSpelling extends WordInterface, DocInterface, ... {
    // interface code here
}
```

All methods in the interface are public and abstract. All variables are public and final. This example is a rewritten version of the first example in today's lesson. It now adds a new public interface to the package wordProcessor instead of a new public class. Note that multiple parents can be listed in an interface's extends clause.

NOTE
> If no extends clause is given, interfaces do not default to inheriting
> from Object because Object is a class. Interfaces don't have a topmost
> interface from which they all are guaranteed to descend.

Any methods defined in a public interface implicitly are prefixed by the public and abstract modifiers, and variables are prefixed by the public, static, and final modifiers. Only those modifiers can appear. Consider the following:

```
public interface  Worldview {
    public static final int  theAnswer = 42;
    public abstract      int  lifeTheUniverseAndEverything();

    long  bigBangCounter = 0;   // OK, becomes public, static, final
    long  ageOfTheUniverse();   // OK, becomes public and abstract

    private protected int  aConstant;
          private   int  getAnInt();
}
```

In this example, the declarations for theAnswer and lifeTheUniverseAndEverything() are correct. The declarations of bigBangCounter and ageOfTheUniverse() are acceptable as well because they will default to the correct modifiers. The last two declarations will generate errors, however.

NOTE
> If an interface is declared non-public (that is, package), no public
> modifiers are implicitly prefixed. If you say public inside such an
> interface, you're making a real statement that the method or variable is
> public. It's not often, though, that an interface is shared only by the
> classes inside a package. Most will need to be shared by the classes using
> that package as well.

Design Versus Implementation Revisited

One of the most powerful things interfaces add to Java is the capability of separating design inheritance from implementation inheritance. In the single-class inheritance tree, these two are bound inextricably. Sometimes, you want to be able to describe an interface to a class of objects abstractly, without having to create a particular implementation of it yourself. You could create an abstract class, such as those described yesterday. In order for a new class to use this type of interface, however, it has to become a subclass of the abstract class and accept its position in the tree. If this new class also needs to be a subclass of some other class in the tree, for implementation reasons, what could it do? What if it wants to use two such "interfaces" at once? Take a look:

```
class  CrunchNumbers extends NewMath implements AbacusInterface {
    // code here
}

class  CountStuff implements AbacusInterface, FingerAndToeInterface {
    // code here
}
```

The first class is stuck in the single inheritance tree just below the class NewMath, but it is free to implement an interface as well. The second class is stuck just below Object but has implemented two interfaces (it could have implemented any number of them). Implementing an interface means promising to implement all methods specified in the interface.

NOTE

> An abstract class is allowed to ignore this strict promise and can implement any subset of the methods (or even none of them), but all its non-abstract subclasses must fulfill the promise.

Because interfaces are in a separate hierarchy, they can be mixed in with classes in the single inheritance tree at any place where they are needed. Thus, the single inheritance class tree can be viewed as containing only the implementation hierarchy. The design hierarchy (full of abstract methods, mostly) is contained in the multiple inheritance interface tree. This powerful way of thinking about the organization of your program is highly recommended, although it takes a little getting used to.

Examine a simple example of this separation—the creation of the new class Orange. Suppose you already have a good implementation of the class Fruit and an interface, Fruitlike, that represents what a Fruit can do. You want an orange to be a fruit, but you also want it to be a spherical object that can be tossed, rotated, and so on. Here's how to express it all:

```
interface  Fruitlike extends Foodlike {
    void  decay();
    void  squish();
    // and so on
}

class  Fruit extends Food implements Fruitlike {
    private Color  myColor;
    private int    daysTilIRot;
    // and so on
}
```

16

```
interface  Spherelike {
    void  toss();
    void  rotate();
    // and so on
}

class  Orange extends Fruit implements Spherelike {
    // toss()ing may squish() me (a behavior unique to me)
}
```

You use this example again later today. For now, notice that class Orange doesn't have to say implements Fruitlike. By extending Fruit, it already has! The reverse is not true, however. Implementing an interface implies nothing about the implementation hierarchy of a class.

One of the nice things about this structure is that you can change your mind about what class Orange extends (if a great Sphere class is implemented, for example), yet class Orange still will understand the same two interfaces:

```
class  Sphere implements Spherelike { // extends Object
    private float  radius;
    // class code here
}

class  Orange extends Sphere implements Fruitlike {
    // users of Orange never need know about the change!
}
```

The capability to mix in interfaces enables several classes, scattered across the single-inheritance tree, to implement the same set of methods. Although these classes share a common superclass, it is likely that below this common parent are many subclasses that are not interested in this set of methods. Adding the methods to the parent class, or even creating a new abstract class to hold them and inserting it into the hierarchy above the parent, is not an ideal solution.

Instead, use an interface to specify the method or methods. It can be implemented by every class that shares the need and by none of the other classes that would have been forced to implement it in the single-inheritance tree. Users of the interface now can specify variables and arguments to be of a new interface type that can refer to any of the classes that implement the interface—a powerful abstraction, as you'll see later. Some examples of mix-in facilities are object persistence (through read() and write() methods), producing or consuming something (the Java library does this for images), and providing useful constants. The last of these might look like the following:

```
public interface  NeededConstants {
    public static final int     num1    = 4133;
    public static final float   num2    = 7.234F;
    public static final String  name    = "Earth";
}

public class  AnyClass implements NeededConstants {
```

```
    public static void  main(String argv[]) {
    double  calculation = num1 * num2;

    System.out.println("Wonders of the " + name + ": " + calculation);
    }
}
```

This code demonstrates that the class AnyClass can refer directly to variables defined in the interface NeededConstants. Normally, you refer to such variables and constants through the class, as you would refer to the constant BOLD, which is provided by the Font class. If a set of constants is used widely, or their class name is long, the shortcut of being able to refer to them directly (as num1 rather than as NeededConstants.num1, for example) makes it worth placing them into an interface and implementing it widely.

Programming in the Small

How do you use these interfaces? Remember, almost everywhere that you can use a class, you can use an interface instead. For example, use the interface Worldview defined previously:

```
Worldview  o = getTheRightObjectSomehow();

long  age = o.ageOfTheUniverse();
```

Once you declare o to be of type Worldview, you can use o as the receiver of any message that the interface defines or inherits.

What does the previous declaration mean? When a variable is declared to be of an interface type, it simply means that any object the variable refers to is expected to have implemented that interface—that is, it is expected to understand all methods that the interface specifies. It assumes that a promise made between the designer of the interface and its eventual implementors has been kept. Although this is a rather abstract notion, it allows, for example, the previous code to be written long before any classes that qualify are implemented or even created. In traditional object-oriented programming, you are forced to create a class with stub implementations to get the same effect.

Here's a more complicated example:

```
Orange      anOrange    = getAnOrange();
Fruit       aFruit      = (Fruit) getAnOrange();
Fruitlike   aFruitlike  = (Fruitlike) getAnOrange();
Spherelike  aSpherelike = (Spherelike) getAnOrange();

aFruit.decay();          // fruits decay
aFruitlike.squish();     //  and squish

aFruitlike.toss();       // not OK
aSpherelike.toss();      // OK

anOrange.decay();        // oranges can do it all
```

16

```
anOrange.squish();
anOrange.toss();
anOrange.rotate();
```

Declarations and casts are used in this example to restrict an orange to act more like a mere fruit or sphere, simply to demonstrate the flexibility of the structure built previously. If the second structure built (the one with the new `Sphere` class) were being used instead, most of this code still would work. (In the lines containing `Fruit`, all instances of `Fruit` need to be replaced by `Sphere`. The `aFruit.decay()` method could be replaced, for example, by `aSphere.rotate()`. Everything else is the same.)

16

NOTE   The direct use of implementation class names is for demonstration purposes only. Normally, you would use only interface names in those declarations and casts so that none of the code in the example would have to change to support the new structure.

Interfaces are implemented and used throughout the Java class library, whenever a behavior is expected to be implemented by a number of disparate classes. In Appendix B, you'll find the interfaces `java.lang.Runnable`, `java.util.Enumeration`, `java.util.Observable`, `java.awt.image.ImageConsumer`, and `java.awt.image.ImageProducer`. Using one of these interfaces, `Enumeration`, to revisit the `LinkedList` example described previously ties together today's lesson by demonstrating a good use of packages and interfaces together:

```
package  collections;

public class  LinkedList {
    private Node  root;

    //
    public Enumeration  enumerate() {
    return new LinkedListEnumerator(root);
    }
}

class  Node {
    private Object  contents;
    private Node    next;

    //
    public  Object  contents() {
        return contents;
    }

    public  Node    next() {
        return next;
    }
}
```

```
class  LinkedListEnumerator implements Enumeration {
    private Node   currentNode;

    LinkedListEnumerator(Node   root) {
        currentNode = root;
    }

    public boolean  hasMoreElements() {
        return currentNode != null;
    }

    public Object    nextElement() {
        Object  anObject = currentNode.contents();

        currentNode = currentNode.next();
        return  anObject;
    }
}
```

Here is a typical use of Enumeration:

```
collections.LinkedList  aLinkedList = createLinkedList();
java.util.Enumeration    e = aLinkedList.enumerate();

while (e.hasMoreElements()) {
    Object  anObject = e.nextElement();
    // do something useful with anObject
}
```

Note that Enumeration is being used as if you know what it is, but you do not. It is an instance of a hidden class (LinkedListEnumerator) that you cannot see or use directly. By a combination of packages and interfaces, the LinkedList class has managed to provide a transparent public interface to some of its most important behavior (through the already defined interface java.util.Enumeration), and it still hides its two implementation classes.

Handing out an object like this sometimes is called *vending*. Often, the vendor gives out an object that a receiver can't create itself, but that it knows how to use. By giving it back to the vendor, the receiver can prove it has a certain capability, authenticate itself, or do any number of useful tasks—all without knowing much about the object given out. This powerful capability can be applied in a broad range of situations.

Summary

Today, you learned how packages collect and categorize classes into meaningful groups. Packages are arranged in a hierarchy, which not only better organizes your programs, but enables you and the thousands of Java programmers on the Internet to name and share projects. You also learned how to use packages, both your own creations and the packages that make up the Java class library.

You then discovered how to declare and use interfaces, a powerful mechanism for extending the traditional single inheritance of Java's classes and for separating design inheritance from implementation inheritance in programs. Interfaces often are used to call common shared methods when the exact class involved is not known. You will see further uses of interfaces tomorrow and the day after.

Finally, packages and interfaces can be combined to provide useful abstractions, such as LinkedList, that appear simple yet actually are hiding almost all of their implementation from their users. This technique is powerful.

16

Q&A

Q What will happen to package/directory hierarchies when some sort of archiving is added to Java?

A Java systems might soon be able to download an entire archive of packages, classes, and resources over the Internet. When this happens, the simple mapping between directory hierarchy and package hierarchy will break down, and you will not be able to tell as easily where each class is stored (that is, in which archive). Presumably these new, advanced Java systems will provide tools that make this task and the task of compiling and linking your programs much easier.

Q Can you say import some.package.B* to import all the classes in that package that begin with B?

A No—the import asterisk (*) does not act like a command-line asterisk. The import statement imports all public classes that are directly inside the package named, and not inside one of its subpackages. You only can import exactly this set of classes, or exactly one explicitly named class, from a given package. By the way, Java loads the information for a class only when you refer to that class in your code, so the * form of import is no less efficient than naming each class individually.

Q Is there any way that a hidden class (a package class) somehow can be forced out of hiding?

A A case in which a hidden class can be forced into visibility occurs if the class has a public superclass and someone casts an instance of the class to the superclass. Any public variables or methods of that superclass now can be accessed or called through your hidden class instance, even if those variables or methods were not thought of by you as public in the hidden class. Usually, these public methods and variables are ones you don't mind having your instances use, or you wouldn't have declared them to have the public superclass. This isn't always the case. Many of the system's built-in classes are public—you might have no choice. Luckily, this event is rare.

Q Why is full multiple inheritance so complex that Java abandoned it?

A It's not that it is too complex, but that it makes the language much more complicated, and as you'll learn on the final day, this complexity can cause larger systems to be less trustworthy and thus less secure. For example, if you were to inherit from two different parents, each having an instance variable with the same name, you would be forced to allow the conflict and explain how the exact same references to that variable name in each of your superclasses are different. Instead of being able to call superclass methods to get more abstract behavior accomplished, you always would need to worry about which of the possibly many identical methods you wanted to call in which parent. Java's run-time method dispatching would have to be more complex as well.

Finally, because so many people are providing classes for reuse on the Internet, the normally manageable conflicts that would arise in your own program would be confounded by thousands of users mixing and matching multi-inherited classes at will. In the future, if these issues are resolved, more powerful inheritance might be added to Java, but its current capabilities should be sufficient for most of your programs.

Q abstract classes don't have to implement all methods in an interface themselves, but do all their subclasses have to?

A Actually, no. Because of inheritance, the precise rule is that an implementation must be provided by some class for each method, but it doesn't have to be a specific class. If a class implements all methods of an interface, the subclasses of that class do not also have to implement the methods. Whatever the abstract class doesn't implement, the first non-abstract class below it must implement. Then, any further subclasses need do nothing further.

Q You didn't mention callbacks. Aren't they an important use of interfaces?

A Callbacks often are used in user interfaces (such as windowing systems) to specify what set of methods are going to be sent whenever the user does a certain set of things (such as clicking the mouse somewhere, typing, and so forth). Because the user interface classes should not know anything about the classes using them, an interface's ability to specify a set of methods separate from the class tree is crucial in this case.

However, callbacks using interfaces are not as general as using, for example, the perform: method of Smalltalk. This is because a given object only can request that a user interface object call it back using a single method name. Suppose that the object wanted two user interfaces objects of the same class to call it back, using different names to tell them apart? This cannot be done in Java, and the object must use a special state and tests to tell them apart. Although interfaces are quite valuable in this case, they are not the ideal callback facility, and the compexity of their use made them too unwieldy to discuss here.

FEATURED APPLET Today's Featured Applet

Today's featured applet is SmartMap, an image map and text display applet created by Rogers Cadenhead, one of the co-authors of this book. The applet superimposes text over an image depending on where the mouse is located. It uses the same COORDS and HREF attributes of the HTML extensions for client-side image maps and adds a TEXT attribute for a cutline that is displayed atop the image until the mouse is moved out of the cutline's mapping.

In order to display the text, SmartMap uses a new class called Cutline that also was created by Cadenhead. The Cutline class takes a line of text and can display it in a box, with the text separated over up to five different lines. The font, font size, and font style all are configurable.

For the demonstration included on the CD-ROM that accompanies this book, SmartMap uses a map from The Dargon Project, the longest running fantasy fiction anthology on the Internet. The project is located at the following URL:

```
http://www.shore.net/~dargon
```

Figure 16.1 shows a screen capture of the SmartMap applet.

Figure 16.1.

The SmartMap *applet in action.*

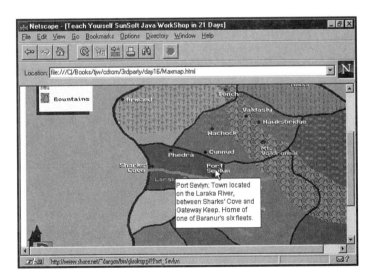

Files for SmartMap are located on the CD-ROM in the \BOOK\3RDPARTY\DAY16\ directory, including source code in the files SmartMap.java and Cutline.java. To use SmartMap on a Web page, place these three files on your Web site: the class files SmartMap.class and Cutline.class and the image file to display. Place the files in the same directory as the Web page, or place them in a subdirectory listed in the CODEBASE parameter of the <APPLET> tag. The <CODE> tag should be SmartMap.class.

Listing 16.1 shows the HTML tags used to run SmartMap as it was shown in Figure 16.1. The MAP tag is included near the end, and all of this material will be displayed to Web users who do not have a Java-capable browser. It is shown here to illustrate how the SmartMap applet is compatible with the HTML extensions for client-side image maps.

Listing 16.1. The <APPLET> tag for SmartMap.

```
<applet code="SmartMap.class" height=480 width=640>
<param name="image" value="maxmap.gif">

<param name="text1" value="Dargon: Coastal town in northern Baranur. Seat of the
duchy of Dargon, area of heavy trade and adventure.">
<param name="coords1" value="302,26,357,61">
<param name="href1" value="http://www.shore.net/~dargon/bin/glookup.pl?Dargon">

<param name="text2" value="Coldwell: River running through Dargon.">
<param name="coords2" value="383,44,467,61">
<param name="href2" value="http://www.shore.net/~dargon/bin/
glookup.pl?Coldwell">

<param name="text3" value="Shireton: A small agrarian community near the forest
south of Dargon. Home of Trissa, Corambis' daughter.">
<param name="coords3" value="302,77,380,93">
<param name="href3" value="http://www.shore.net/~dargon/bin/
glookup.pl?Shireton">

<param name="text4" value="Armand: Capital of Narragan and home of one of the 6
Baranurian Fleets.">
<param name="coords4" value="174,161,293,174">
<param name="href4" value="http://www.shore.net/~dargon/bin/glookup.pl?Armand">

<param name="text5" value="Tench: One cow town at crossroads near Dargon;
located near Morion's fighting school Pentamorlo. Anything can be bought here
for a price.">
<param name="coords5" value="356,147,401,164">
<param name="href5" value="http://www.shore.net/~dargon/bin/glookup.pl?Tench">

<param name="text6" value="Valdasly: Barony in Arvalia.">
<param name="coords6" value="401,181,467,201">
<param name="href6" value="http://www.shore.net/~dargon/bin/
glookup.pl?Valdasly">

<param name="text7" value="Hawksbridge: The ducal seat of Arvalia.">
<param name="coords7" value="431,200,529,218">
```

```
<param name="href7" value="http://www.shore.net/~dargon/bin/
glookup.pl?Hawksbridge">

<param name="text8" value="Mount Voldronnai: Volcano in the Windbourne mountain
range. Currently inactive. Only volcano in Baranur.">
<param name="coords8" value="435,244,516,277">
<param name="href8" value="http://www.shore.net/~dargon/bin/
glookup.pl?Mount_Voldronnai">

<param name="text9" value="Cynnd: A town in Baranur.">
<param name="coords9" value="329,255,392,273">
<param name="href9" value="http://www.shore.net/~dargon/bin/glookup.pl?Cynnyd">

<param name="text10" value="Phedra: Small farming community in Quinnat.">
<param name="coords10" value="262,256,318,275">
<param name="href10" value="http://www.shore.net/~dargon/bin/glookup.pl?Phedra">

<param name="text11" value="Shark's Cove: Port town on the river delta at the
mouth of the Laraka River. This town has a reputation for being rather rough and
seedy.">
<param name="coords11" value="171,284,242,302">
<param name="href11" value="http://www.shore.net/~dargon/bin/
glookup.pl?Sharks'_Cove">

<param name="text12" value="Laraka: The mighty river of Baranur.">
<param name="coords12" value="234,306,312,321">
<param name="href12" value="http://www.shore.net/~dargon/bin/glookup.pl?Laraka">

<param name="text13" value="Port Sevlyn: Town located on the Laraka River,
between Sharks' Cove and Gateway Keep. Home of one of Baranur's six fleets. ">
<param name="coords13" value="332,284,385,314">
<param name="href13" value="http://www.shore.net/~dargon/bin/
glookup.pl?Port_Sevlyn">

<param name="text14" value="Gateway Keep: Castle/Keep constructed to protect the
river trade route from Magnus to the rest of the world.">
<param name="coords14" value="373,320,448,345">
<param name="href14" value="http://www.shore.net/~dargon/bin/
glookup.pl?Gateway_Keep">

<param name="text15" value="Magnus: Capital of the Kingdom of Baranur; a large
town on the Laraka River. Population of about 50,000+ people.">
<param name="coords15" value="385,362,451,378">
<param name="href15" value="http://www.shore.net/~dargon/bin/glookup.pl?Magnus">

<param name="text16" value="The Dargon Project: Click now to visit the web
site.">
<param name="coords16" value="3,394,53,472">
<param name="href16" value="http://www.shore.net/~dargon">

<img src="maxmap.gif" alt="Dargon map" height=480 width=640 ismap
usemap="#Dargon">
<map name="Dargon">
```

continues

Listing 16.1. continued

```
<area shape="rect" coords="302,26,357,61" href="http://www.shore.net/~dargon/
bin/glookup.pl?Dargon">
<area shape="rect" coords="383,44,467,61" href="http://www.shore.net/~dargon/
bin/glookup.pl?Coldwell">
<area shape="rect" coords="302,77,380,93" href="http://www.shore.net/~dargon/
bin/glookup.pl?Shireton">
<area shape="rect" coords="174,161,293,174" href="http://www.shore.net/~dargon/
bin/glookup.pl?Armand">
<area shape="rect" coords="356,147,401,164" href="http://www.shore.net/~dargon/
bin/glookup.pl?Tench">
<area shape="rect" coords="401,181,467,201" href="http://www.shore.net/~dargon/
bin/glookup.pl?Valdasly">
<area shape="rect" coords="431,200,529,218" href="http://www.shore.net/~dargon/
bin/glookup.pl?Hawksbridge">
<area shape="rect" coords="435,244,516,277" href="http://www.shore.net/~dargon/
bin/glookup.pl?Mount_Voldronnai">
<area shape="rect" coords="329,255,392,273" href="http://www.shore.net/~dargon/
bin/glookup.pl?Cynnyd">
<area shape="rect" coords="262,256,318,275" href="http://www.shore.net/~dargon/
bin/glookup.pl?Phedra">
<area shape="rect" coords="171,284,242,302" href="http://www.shore.net/~dargon/
bin/glookup.pl?Sharks'_Cove">
<area shape="rect" coords="234,306,312,321" href="http://www.shore.net/~dargon/
bin/glookup.pl?Laraka">
<area shape="rect" coords="332,284,385,314" href="http://www.shore.net/~dargon/
bin/glookup.pl?Port_Sevlyn">
<area shape="rect" coords="373,320,448,345" href="http://www.shore.net/~dargon/
bin/glookup.pl?Gateway_Keep">
<area shape="rect" coords="385,362,451,378" href="http://www.shore.net/~dargon/
bin/glookup.pl?Magnus">
<area shape="rect" coords="3,394,53,472" href="http://www.shore.net/~dargon">
</map>
</applet>
```

SmartMap has seven or more parameters that can be customized within the <APPLET> tag, as follows:

☐ The image parameter is the file name of the image to display.

☐ The coords1 parameter specifies the x1,y1 and x2,y2 coordinates of image map item 1 (for example, "50,50,200,200" will create a rectangular image map with (50,50) as the upper left corner and (200,200) as the lower right corner).

☐ The coords# parameter specifies the x1,y1 and x2,y2 coordinates of image map item # (where # is a number from 1 to 30).

☐ The text1 parameter specifies the text to display when the image is over map item 1.

☐ The text# parameter specifies the text to display when the image is over map item # (where # is a number from 1 to 30).

16

☐ The `href1` parameter is the URL, if any, to load when the mouse is clicked while over map item 1.

☐ The `href#` parameter is the URL, if any, to load when the mouse is clicked over map item # (where # is a number from 1 to 30).

☐ The `font` parameter specifies the name of the font to use for text (`Arial` is the default).

☐ The `fontSize` specifies the size of the font to use (12 is the default).

☐ The `fontStyle` specifies the style of the font to use (`BOLD`, `ITALIC`, or normal if left off).

More information on the applet is available from the author at the following URL:

```
http://www.spiderbyte.com/java
```

Day **17**

Exceptions

Today, you'll learn about exception conditions in Java. The following topics will be covered:

- ☐ How to declare when you are expecting one
- ☐ How to handle them in your code
- ☐ How to create them
- ☐ How your code is limited by them, but also made more robust

Programming languages have labored long to find the right way to deal with unusual events in normally reliable code. Consider the following example:

```
int  status = callSomethingThatAlmostAlwaysWorks();

if (status == FUNNY_RETURN_VALUE) {
    . . .              // something unusual happened, handle it
    switch(someGlobalErrorIndicator) {
        . . . // handle more specific problems
    }
} else {
    . . .              // all is well
}
```

This seems like a lot of work just to handle a rare case. What's worse, if the function that is called returns an int as part of its normal answer, you must distinguish one special integer (FUNNY_RETURN_VALUE) to indicate an error. What if that function needs all the integers? In that case, you must do something even more ugly.

Even if you manage to find a distinguished value (such as NULL in C for pointers, -1 for integers, and so forth), what if there are multiple errors that must be produced by the same function? Often, some global variable is used as an error indicator. The function stores a value in it, but what happens if another error occurs before the caller gets to handle the error? Multiple errors propagate badly, if at all. There are also numerous problems with generalizing such a variable for use in large programs, with complex errors, and so forth.

NEW TERM   Luckily, there is an alternative. You can use exceptions to help you handle abnormal conditions in your programs. An *exception* is any object that is an instance of the class Throwable (or any of its subclasses). Exceptions make the normal, nonexceptional code cleaner and easier to read.

Programming in the Large

When you begin to build complex programs in Java, you will discover something after designing the classes, interfaces, and their method descriptions. Even when this is done, you have not defined all the behavior of your objects. After all, an interface describes the normal way to use an object and doesn't include any strange, exceptional cases. In many systems, the documentation takes care of this problem by explicitly listing the distinguished values used in hacks like the previous example. Because the system knows nothing about these hacks, it cannot check them for consistency. In fact, the compiler can do nothing at all to help you with these exceptional conditions, in contrast to the helpful warnings and errors it produces if a method is used incorrectly.

More importantly, you have not captured this important aspect of your program in your design. Instead, you are forced to make up a way to describe it in the documentation and hope you have not made any mistakes when you implement it later. What's worse, others will devise different ways of describing the same thing. Clearly, you need some uniform way of declaring the intentions of classes and methods with respect to these exceptional conditions. Java provides just such a way:

```
public class  SampleClass {
    public void  readData() throws DataReadException {
        // code of this method
    }
}
```

In this example, you warn the reader (and the compiler) that the code might throw an exception called DataReadException.

You can think of a method's description as a contract between the designer of that method or class and the caller of the method. Usually, this description tells the types of a method's arguments, what it returns, and the general semantics of what it normally does. You are being told, as well, what abnormal things it can do. This information makes explicit all places where exception conditions should be handled in a program, and that makes large-scale design easier.

Because exceptions are instances of classes, they can be put into a hierarchy that naturally can describe the relationships among the different types of exceptions. If you take a moment to glance in Appendix B at the diagrams for java.lang errors and java.lang exceptions, you will see that the class Throwable has two large hierarchies of classes beneath it. The roots of these two hierarchies are subclasses of Throwable called Exception and Error. These hierarchies embody the rich set of relationships that exist between exceptions and errors in the Java run-time environment.

When you know that a particular kind of error or exception can occur in your method, you are supposed to either handle it yourself or explicitly warn potential method callers about the possibility through the throws clause. Not all errors and exceptions must be listed; instances of either class Error or RuntimeException (or any of their subclasses) do not have to be listed in the throws clause. They get special treatment because they can occur anywhere within a Java program and are usually conditions that the program did not directly cause. One good example is the OutOfMemoryError, which can happen anywhere, at any time, and for any number of reasons. You can, of course, choose to list these errors and run-time exceptions in your throws clause if you like, but the callers of your methods will not be forced to handle them. Only non-run-time exceptions must be handled.

NOTE

> Whenever you see the word *exception* by itself, it almost always means *exception or error* (that is, an instance of Throwable). The previous discussion makes it clear that Exceptions and Errors form two separate hierarchies, but they act exactly the same, except for the throws clause rule.

If you examine the diagrams in Appendix B more carefully, you'll notice that there are only six types of exceptions (in java.lang) that must be listed in a throws clause (remember that all Errors and RuntimeExceptions are exempt). They are as follows:

- ☐ ClassNotFoundException
- ☐ CloneNotSupportedException
- ☐ IllegalAccessException

☐ `InstantiationException`

☐ `InterrupedException`

☐ `NoSuchMethodException`

Each of these names suggests something that explicitly is caused by the programmer, not some behind-the-scenes event such as `OutOfMemoryError`.

If you look further in Appendix B, near the bottom of the diagrams for `java.util` and `java.io`, you'll see that each package adds some new exceptions. The `java.util` package adds two exceptions, `EmptyStackException` and `NoSuchElementException`, and they are placed under `RuntimeException`. The `java.io` package adds a whole new tree under `IOException`. These exceptions are caused more explicitly by the programmer, and so they are rooted under `Exception`. Thus, `IOExceptions` must be described in `throws` clauses. Finally, package `java.awt` (in diagram `java.awt-components`) defines one of each style, an exception (`AWTException`) and an error (`AWTError`).

The Java class library uses exceptions everywhere, and to good effect. If you examine the detailed API documentation, you will see that many of the methods in the library have `throws` clauses, and some of them document when they might throw one of the implicit errors or exceptions. This documentation is just a nicety, because you are not required to catch conditions like that. If it weren't obvious that such a condition could happen at that point, and if for some reason you cared about catching it, this documentation would be useful information.

Programming in the Small

Now that you have a feeling for how exceptions can help you design a program and a class library better, how do you use exceptions? In the next example, you will try to call the `readData()` method defined earlier, which throws `DataReadException`:

```
public void  loadAllData() throws DataReadException {
    SampleClass  sc = new SampleClass();

    sc.readData();
}
```

Looking more closely at the code, if you assume that `DataReadException` is a subclass of `Exception`, it means that if you don't handle it in the code of `loadAllData()`, you must warn your callers about it. Because your code calls `readData()` without doing anything about the fact that it might throw `DataReadException`, you must add that exception to your `throws` clause. This action is perfectly legal, but it does defer to your caller something that perhaps you should be responsible for doing yourself. (It depends on the circumstances, of course.)

Suppose that that you feel responsible today and decide to handle the exception. Because you're now declaring a method without a `throws` clause, you must catch the expected exception and do something useful with it:

```
public void  loadAllData() {
    SampleClass  sc = new SampleClass();

    try {
        sc.readData();
    } catch (DataReadException d) {
        . . . // do something terribly significant
    }
}
```

The `try` statement says basically, "Try running the code inside these braces, and if there are exceptions thrown, I will attach handlers to take care of them." (You first saw a `try` statement on Day 10, "Simple Animation and Threads.") You can have as many `catch` clauses at the end of a `try` statement as needed. Each `catch` clause allows you to handle all exceptions that are instances of the class listed in parentheses, of any of its subclasses, or of a class that implements the interface listed in parentheses. In the `catch` clause in the preceding example, exceptions of the class `DataReadException` (or any of its subclasses) are being handled.

What if you want to combine both of the approaches shown so far? You want to handle the exception yourself but also point it out to your caller. You can do this by explicitly rethrowing the exception:

```
public void  loadAllData() throws DataReadException {
    SampleClass  sc = new SampleClass();

    try {
        sc.readData();
    } catch (DataReadException d) {
        . . .            // do something responsible
        throw d;         // rethrow the exception
    }
}
```

This code works because exception handlers can be nested. You handle the exception by doing something responsible with it, but decide that it is too important to not give an exception handler that might be in your caller a chance to handle it as well. Exceptions float all the way up the chain of method callers this way (usually not being handled by most of them), until at last the system itself handles any uncaught ones by aborting your program and displaying an error message. In a stand-alone program, this system is not such a bad idea, but in an applet, it can cause the browser to crash. Most browsers protect themselves from this disaster by catching all exceptions themselves whenever they run an applet, but you never can tell. If it's possible for you to catch an exception and do something intelligent with it, you should.

To see what throwing a new exception looks like, today's first example is fleshed out as follows:

```
public class  SampleClass {
    public void  readData() throws DataReadException {
        . . .
        if (someThingUnusualHasHappened()) {
            throw new DataReadException();
            // execution never reaches here
        }
    }
}
```

NOTE

> throw is a little like a break statement—nothing beyond it in the block is executed.

The fundamental way that all exceptions are generated is that something creates an exception object and throws it. The whole hierarchy under the class Throwable would be worth much less if throw statements were not scattered throughout the code in the Java library at just the right places. Because exceptions propagate up from any depth down inside methods, any method call you make might generate a plethora of possible errors and exceptions. Luckily, only the ones listed in the throws clause of that method need to be thought about; the rest travel silently past on their way to becoming an error message (or being caught and handled higher up in the system).

The following is an unusual demonstration of this process, where the throw and the handler that catches it are very close together:

```
System.out.print("Karl Malden ");
try {
    System.out.print("is ");
    throw new ArticleException();
    System.out.print("like");
} catch (ArticleException m) {
    System.out.print("so ");
}
System.out.print("rad!\n");
```

It displays the following: `Karl Malden is so rad!`

In addition to handling the exceptions that you must deal with because a method throws them, you can create your own exceptions. These must be subclasses of Exception or one of its subclasses. The reason to create your own exceptions is to handle exceptional circumstances in the most organized way possible. Exceptions enable you to put error handling in a program without making the rest of the program harder to understand. The throw statement is used to throw your created exception, and the exception is treated like any other exception in your programs.

Exceptions are a quite powerful way of partitioning the space of all possible error conditions into manageable pieces. Because the first matching `catch` clause is executed, you can build chains such as the following:

```
try {
    someReallyExceptionalMethod();
} catch (NullPointerException n) {  // a subclass of RuntimeException
    . . .
} catch (RuntimeException r) {      // a subclass of Exception
    . . .
} catch (IOException i) {           // a subclass of Exception
    . . .
} catch (MyFirstException m) {      // our subclass of Exception
    . . .
} catch (Exception e) {             // a subclass of Throwable
    . . .
} catch (Throwable t) {
    . . . // Errors & anything else not caught are caught here
}
```

By listing subclasses before their parent classes, the parent catches anything it normally would catch that also is not one of the subclasses that precede it. By juggling chains like these, you can express almost any combination of tests. If there's some obscure case you can't handle, perhaps you can use an interface to catch it instead. That would allow you to design your exceptions hierarchy using multiple inheritance. Catching with an interface rather than a class also can be used to test for a property that many exceptions share but that cannot be expressed in the single-inheritance tree alone.

Suppose that a scattered set of your exception classes requires a reboot after being thrown. You create an interface called `NeedsReboot`, and all these classes implement the interface. (None of them needs to have a common parent exception class.) Then the highest level of exception handler simply catches classes that implement `NeedsReboot` and performs a reboot:

```
public interface  NeedsReboot { }    // needs no contents at all

try {
    someMethodThatGeneratesExceptionsThatImplementNeedsReboot();
} catch (NeedsReboot n) {     // catch an interface
    . . .                     // clean up
    SystemClass.reboot();     // reboot using a made-up system class
}
```

By the way, if you need really unusual behavior during an exception, you can place the behavior into the exception class itself! Remember that an exception is also a normal class, so it can contain instance variables and methods. Although using them is a little unusual, it might be valuable on a few occasions. Here's what such an exception might look like:

```
try {
    someExceptionallyStrangeMethod();
} catch (ComplexException e) {
    switch (e.internalState()) { // probably returns an instance variable value
        case e.COMPLEX_CASE: // a class variable of the exception's class
```

17

```
            e.performComplexBehavior(myState, theContext, etc);
            break;
        . . .
    }
}
```

Limitations Placed on the Programmer

As powerful as all of this exception handling sounds, it also is limiting. Suppose you want to override one of the standard methods of the Object class, toString(), to be smarter about how displays are handled:

```
public class  MyIllegalClass {
    public String  toString() {
    someReallyExceptionalMethod();
        . . . // returns some String
    }
}
```

Because the superclass (Object) defined the method declaration for toString() without a throws clause, any implementation of the method in any subclass must obey this restriction. In particular, you cannot just call someReallyExceptionalMethod(), as you did previously, because it will generate a host of errors and exceptions, some of which are not exempt from being listed in a throws clause (such as IOException and MyFirstException). If all of the exceptions thrown were exempt, you would have no problem, but because some are not, you have to catch at least those few exceptions for this code to be legal in Java:

```
public class  MyLegalClass {
    public String  toString() {
        try {
            someReallyExceptionalMethod();
        } catch (IOException e) {
        } catch (MyFirstException m) {
        }
        . . . // returns some String
    }
}
```

In both cases, you elect to catch the exceptions and do absolutely nothing with them. Although this is legal, it is not always the right thing to do. You might need to think for a while to come up with the best nontrivial behavior for any particular catch clause. This extra thought and care makes your program more robust, better able to handle unusual input, and more likely to work correctly when used by multiple threads (you'll see this tomorrow).

The toString() method of MyIllegalClass produces a compiler error to remind you to reflect on these issues. This extra care will reward you richly as you reuse your classes in later projects and in larger and larger programs. Of course, the Java class library has been written with exactly this degree of care, and that's one of the reasons it's robust enough to be used in constructing your Java projects.

The `finally` **Clause**

The final aspect of exceptions to discuss is the `finally` clause. Suppose you absolutely must do an action, no matter what happens. Usually, this action is to free some external resource after acquiring it, to close a file after opening it, or something similar. To be sure that the action is taken, even in the case of exceptions, you use a `finally` clause in the `try` statement:

```
SomeFileClass  f = new SomeFileClass();

if (f.open("/a/file/name/path")) {
    try {
        someReallyExceptionalMethod();
    } finally {
        f.close();
    }
}
```

This use of `finally` behaves much like the following code:

```
SomeFileClass  f = new SomeFileClass();

if (f.open("/a/file/name/path")) {
    try {
        someReallyExceptionalMethod();
    } catch (Throwable t) {
        f.close();
        throw t;
    }
}
```

The difference is that `finally` can be used to clean up after things other than exceptions, such as `return`, `break`, and `continue` statements. The code in the `finally` block is executed regardless of whether an exception is thrown in the `try` block and regardless of whether an exception is caught in a `catch` block. Because the `finally` block always is executed, you can use it for cleanup tasks that must be handled no matter what occurs in the code.

Here's a complex demonstration of exception handling code that uses a `finally` clause:

```
public class  MyFinalExceptionalClass extends ContextClass {
    public static void  main(String argv[]) {
        int  mysteriousState = getContext();

        while (true) {
            System.out.print("Who ");
            try {
                System.out.print("is ");
                if (mysteriousState == 1)
                    return;
                System.out.print("that ");
                if (mysteriousState == 2)
                    break;
                System.out.print("strange ");
                if (mysteriousState == 3)
                    continue;
```

```
                System.out.print("but kindly ");
                if (mysteriousState == 4)
                    throw new UncaughtException();
                System.out.print("not at all ");
            } finally {
                System.out.print("amusing man?\n");
            }
            System.out.print("I'd like to meet the man");
        }
        System.out.print("Please tell me.\n");
    }
}
```

Here is the output produced, depending on the value of `mysteriousState`:

☐ 1   Who is amusing man?

☐ 2   Who is that amusing man? Please tell me

☐ 3   Who is that strange amusing man? ...

☐ 4   Who is that strange but kindly amusing man?

☐ 5   Who is that strange but kindly not at all amusing man? I'd like to meet the man Who is that strange...

NOTE

In cases 3 and 5, the output never ends. In 4, an error message generated by the `UncaughtException` also is printed.

Summary

Today, you learned about how exceptions improve your program's design, robustness, and multithreading capability. You also learned about the vast array of exceptions defined and thrown in the Java class library and how to try methods while catching any of a hierarchically ordered set of possible exceptions and errors. Java's reliance on strict exception handling places some restrictions on the programmer, but you learned that these restrictions are light compared to the rewards. The `finally` clause, which provides a foolproof way to be certain that something is accomplished, no matter what, was discussed also.

Q&A

Q **I'm still not sure I understand the differences between `Exceptions`, `Errors`, and `RuntimeExceptions`. Is there another way of looking at them?**

A `Errors` are caused by dynamic linking or virtual machine problems and are thus too low-level for most programs to care about (although sophisticated development libraries and environments probably care a great deal about them). `RuntimeExceptions` are generated by the normal execution of Java code, and though they occasionally reflect a condition you will want to handle explicitly, more often they reflect a coding mistake by the programmer and thus simply need to print an error to help flag that mistake. Exceptions that are not `RuntimeExceptions` (`IOExceptions`, for example) are conditions that, because of their nature, should be explicitly handled by any robust and well-thought-out code. The Java class library has been written using only a few of these, but those few are extremely important to using the system safely and correctly. The compiler helps you handle these exceptions properly through its `throws` clause checks and restrictions.

Q **Is there any way to get around the strict restrictions placed on methods by the `throws` clause?**

A Yes. Suppose you thought long and hard and have decided that you need to circumvent this restriction. This almost is never the case, because the right solution is to go back and redesign your methods to reflect the exceptions that you need to `throw`. Imagine, however, that for some reason a system class has you in a strait-jacket. Your first solution is to subclass `RuntimeException` to make up a new, exempt exception of your own. Now you can throw it to your heart's content because the `throws` clause that was annoying you does not need to include this new exception. If you need a lot of such exceptions, an elegant approach is to mix in some novel exception interfaces to your new `Runtime` classes. You're free to choose whatever subset of these new interfaces you want to `catch` (none of the normal `Runtime` exceptions needs to be caught), and any leftover new `Runtime` exceptions are allowed to go through that otherwise annoying standard method in the library.

Q **I'm still a little confused by long chains of `catch` clauses. Can you label the previous example, identifying which exceptions are handled by each line of code?**

A Certainly. Here it is:

```
try {
    someReallyExceptionalMethod();
} catch (NullPointerException n) {
 . . .// handles NullPointerExceptions
} catch (RuntimeException r) {
 . . .// handles RuntimeExceptions that are not
     // NullPointerExceptions
} catch (IOException i) {
 . . .// handles IOExceptions
} catch (MyFirstException m) {
 . . .// handles MyFirstExceptions
} catch (Exception e) {
 . . .// handles Exceptions that are not
```

```
        // RuntimeExceptions nor IOExceptions
 . . .// nor MyFirstExceptions
} catch (Throwable t) {
 . . .// handles Throwables that are not Exceptions
    // (that is, errors)
}
```

Q **Given how annoying it sometimes can be to handle exception conditions properly, what's stopping me from surrounding any method as follows:**

```
try { thatAnnoyingMethod(); } catch (Throwable t) { }
```

and simply ignoring all exceptions?

A Nothing, other than your own conscience. In some cases, you should do nothing, because it is the correct thing to do for your method's implementation. Otherwise, you should struggle through the annoyance and gain experience. Good style is a struggle even for the best of programmers, but the rewards are rich indeed.

FEATURED APPLET **Today's Featured Applet**

Today's featured applet is `Eliza`, Charles Hayden's adaptation of the famous artificial intelligence program described by Joseph Weizenbaum in *Communications of the ACM* in January 1966. This applet uses a script of recognized words and verbal patterns, and uses it to converse with someone in the manner of a psychiatrist. Hayden's Java applet is described as a faithful adaptation of Weizenbaum's original. Figure 17.1 shows an example of `Eliza` in action.

Figure 17.1.

The `Eliza` *applet in action.*

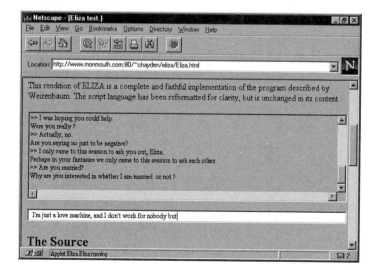

17

Files for Eliza are located on the CD-ROM in the \BOOK\3RDPARTY\DAY17\ directory, including source code in the following files:

- ☐ Decomp.java: Decomposition rule
- ☐ DecompList.java: List of decomposition rules
- ☐ Eliza.java: The main applet program
- ☐ ElizaApp.java: The main application program, use either this or Eliza.java, not both
- ☐ ElizaMain.java: The main driver
- ☐ EString.java: String matching and transformation helper functions
- ☐ Key.java: String key that will be the first thing the program looks for in the input
- ☐ KeyList.java: The list of all keys
- ☐ KeyStack.java: The arrangement of all keys found in the input into a rank-ordered stack
- ☐ Mem.java: Response storage for later use
- ☐ PrePost.java: Word pairs for pre- or post-rewriting
- ☐ PrePostList.java: List of all the pre or post rules
- ☐ ReasembList.java: List of reassembly rules (goes with a decomposition rule)
- ☐ SynList.java: List of EWordList synonym lists
- ☐ WordList.java: List of words used for synonyms

To use Eliza on a Web page, place all of the preceding files on your Web site, with the exception of ElizaApp.java, which should not be included. The site also must have the script file that tells Eliza how to respond to comments and questions. This file should have a full URL to work properly, as shown in Listing 17.1. Place the Eliza files in the same directory as the Web page, in a directory indicated in the CODE attribute, or in a subdirectory listed in the CODEBASE parameter of the <APPLET> tag. The <CODE> tag should be Eliza.class. Listing 17.1 shows the HTML tags used to run Eliza as it was shown in Figure 17.1.

Listing 17.1. The <APPLET> tag for Eliza.

```
<APPLET code="Eliza/Eliza.class" width=600 height=200>
<PARAM name="script"
        value="file:///C¦/Java-WorkShop/homework/Eliza/script">
</APPLET>
```

Eliza has one parameter that you can customize within the <APPLET> tag: script. This parameter specifies the full URL of the file that contains Eliza's script. More information on Eliza is available from Charles Hayden at the following URL:

```
http://www.monmouth.com:80/~chayden/eliza/Eliza.html
```

Day **18**

Multithreading

Today, you'll learn more about the threads mentioned briefly during Week 2 and expand your knowledge of the following topics:

- ☐ How to "think multithreaded"
- ☐ How to protect your methods and variables from unintended thread conflicts
- ☐ How to create, start, and stop threads and threaded classes
- ☐ How the scheduler works in Java

Threads are a relatively recent invention in the computer science world. Although processes, their larger parent, have been around for decades, threads only recently have been accepted into the mainstream. What's odd about this fact is that threads are extremely valuable, and programs written with them are noticeably better in performance. Some of the best individual, Herculean efforts over the years have involved implementing a threads-like facility by hand to give a program a more friendly feel to its users.

Imagine that you're using your favorite text editor on a large file. When it starts up, does it need to examine the entire file before it lets you edit? Does it need to make a copy of the file? If the file is huge, you may have a long wait before you can start typing. Wouldn't it be nicer for the text editor to show the first page, enabling you to begin editing, and somehow complete the slower tasks necessary for initialization in the background? Threads allow exactly this kind of within-the-program parallelism.

Perhaps the best example of threading (or lack of it) is a Web browser. Can your browser download several files and Web pages at once while still enabling you to continue browsing? While these pages are downloading, can your browser download all the pictures, sounds, and so forth in parallel, interleaving the fast and slow download times of multiple Internet servers? Sun's HotJava browser, which was written in Java, can do all of these things and more by using the built-in threading capabilities of the language.

The Problem with Parallelism

As you might be asking at this point, if threading is so wonderful, why doesn't every system have it? Many modern operating systems have the basic primitives needed to create and run threads, but they are missing a key ingredient. The rest of their environment is not thread-safe. Imagine that you are in a thread, one of many, and each thread is sharing some important data managed by the system. If you were managing that data, you could take steps to protect it (as you'll see later today), but the system is managing it. Now visualize a piece of code in the system that reads a crucial value, thinks about it for a while, and then adds 1 to the value:

```
if (blackjackHand == loser) {
    . . . // think about how much to pay
    casinoAccount += amountOfBet;
}
```

Remember that any number of threads might be calling upon this part of the system at once. The disaster occurs when two threads have both executed the `if` test before either has incremented the `casinoAccount`. In that case, the value is clobbered by them both with the `casinoAccount += amountOfBet` statement, and one of the amounts is lost. This problem might not seem so bad to you, although it certainly would be bad for the casino owner, but imagine instead that the crucial value affects the state of the screen as it is being displayed. In that case, unfortunate ordering of the threads can cause the screen to be updated incorrectly. In the same way, mouse or keyboard events can be lost, databases can be inaccurately updated, and so forth.

This disaster is inescapable if any significant part of the system has not been written with threads in mind. The barrier to a mainstream threaded environment is the large effort required to rewrite existing libraries for thread safety. Java was written from scratch with this is mind, and every Java class in its library is thread-safe. Thus, you have to worry only about your own synchronization and thread-ordering because you can assume that the Java system will handle threading correctly.

NOTE

Some readers might wonder what the fundamental problem with the `blackjackHand` example is. Can't you just make the code in the `think about how much to pay` area in the example small enough to reduce or eliminate the problem? Without atomic operations, the answer is no. Even if the code took zero time, the program must access the value of some variable to make any decision and then change something to reflect that decision. These two steps can never be made to happen at the same time without an atomic operation. Unless you're given one by the system, it is impossible to create your own.

Even the line `casinoAccount += amountOfBet;` involves multiple steps: get the current values, add one to the other, and store it. Each of these steps requires several machine instructions, so a single line of Java code such as `casinoAccount += amountOfBet;` will require several dozen individual machine instructions when the bytecode interpreter executes the line. Because of this, you can never consider a Java statement to be a single line of code that will be executed all at once. So that all of the steps happen at once (atomically), threads are used. Special Java primitives, at the lowest levels of the language, provide the basic atomic operations needed to build safe, threaded programs.

18

NEW TERM

Atomic operations are operations that appear to other threads to happen exactly at the same time.

Thinking Multithreaded

Getting used to threads takes a new way of thinking. Rather than imagining that you always know exactly what's happening when you look at a method you've written, you have to ask yourself some additional questions. What will happen if more than one thread calls into this method at the same time? Do you need to protect it in some way? What about your class as a whole? Are you assuming that only one of its methods is running at the same time? Often you make such assumptions, and a local instance variable is messed up as a result. For example, look at the following case:

```
public class ThreadCounter {
    int crucialValue;

    public void countMe() {
        crucialValue += 1;
    }
}
```

```
    public int    howMany() {
        return crucialValue;
    }
}
```

This code suffers from the most pure form of the synchronization problem: the += takes more than one step, and you might miscount the number of threads as a result. (Don't worry about how threads are created yet, just imagine that a whole bunch of them are able to call countMe() at once, at slightly different times.) Java enables you to fix this problem:

```
public class  SafeThreadCounter {
    int  crucialValue;

    public synchronized void  countMe() {
        crucialValue += 1;
    }

    public              int  howMany() {
        return crucialValue;
    }
}
```

The synchronized keyword tells Java to make the block of code in the method thread-safe. Only one thread will be allowed inside this method at once, and others have to wait until the currently running thread is finished with it before they can begin running it. Although this keyword works in many situations, synchronizing a large, long-running method is almost always a bad idea. All your threads would end up stuck at this bottleneck, waiting single file to get their turn at this one slow method.

Because the compiler can keep unsynchronized variables around in registers during computations, and a thread's registers can't be seen by other threads (especially if they're on another processor in a true multiprocessor computer), a variable can be updated in such a way that no possible order of thread updates could have produced the result. To avoid this bizarre case, you can label a variable volatile, meaning that you know it will be updated asynchronously by multiprocessor-like threads. Java then loads and stores the variable each time it's needed and does not use registers.

NOTE

In early releases of Java, variables that were safe from these bizarre effects were labeled threadsafe. Because most variables are safe to use, however, they are now assumed to be thread-safe unless you mark them volatile. Using volatile is an extremely rare event. In the 1.0 release, the Java library does not use volatile anywhere.

18

Synchronization

The method howMany() in the last example doesn't need to be synchronized, because it simply returns the current value of an instance variable. Something higher in the call chain, such as something that uses the value returned from the method, might need to be synchronized, though. Here's an example:

```
public class  Point {              // redefines class Point from package java.awt
    private float  x, y;           // OK because we're in a different package here

    public  float  x() {           // needs no synchronization
        return x;
    }

    public  float  y() {           // ditto
        return y;
    }
    . . .                                  // methods to set and change x and y
}

public class  UnsafePointPrinter {
    public void  print(Point p) {
        System.out.println("The point's x is " + p.x()
                           + " and y is " + p.y() + ".");
    }
}
```

The analogous methods to howMany() are x() and y(). They need no synchronization, because they just return the values of instance variables. The caller of x() and y() has to decide whether it needs to synchronize itself, and in this case, it does. Although the method print() simply reads values and displays them, it reads two values. There is a chance that some other thread, running between the call to p.x() and the call to p.y(), could have changed the value of x and y stored inside the Point p. Remember, you don't know how many other threads have a way to reach and call methods in this Point object! Thinking multithreaded comes down to being careful any time you make an assumption that something has not happened between two parts of your program (even two parts of the same line, or the same expression, such as the string + expression in this example).

Making the Method Safe

You could try to make a safe version of print() by adding the synchronized keyword modifier to it, or you could take a slightly different approach, as follows:

```
public class  TryAgainPointPrinter {
    public void  print(Point p) {
        float  safeX, safeY;
```

```
        synchronized(this) {
            safeX = p.x();       // these two lines now
            safeY = p.y();       // happen atomically
        }
        System.out.print("The point's x is " + safeX
                                    + " y is " + safeY);
    }
}
```

The synchronized statement takes an argument that says what object you would like to lock to prevent more than one thread from executing the enclosed block of code at the same time. In this example, you use this (the instance itself), which is exactly the object that would have been locked by the synchronized method as a whole if you had changed print() to be like your safe countMe() method. You have an added bonus with this new form of synchronization; you can specify exactly what part of a method needs to be safe, and the rest can be left unsafe.

Notice how you took advantage of this freedom to make the protected part of the method as small as possible, while leaving the String creations, concatenations, and printing (which together take a small but nonzero amount of time) outside the protected area. This is both good style (as a guide to the reader of your code) and more efficient, because fewer threads get stuck waiting to get into protected areas.

Making the Method Safer

The last example still has a problem. You made sure that no one executes your calls to x() and y() out of order, but have you prevented the Point p from changing? The answer is no—you still have not solved the problem. You really do need the full power of the synchronized statement:

```
public class  SafePointPrinter {
    public void  print(Point p) {
        float  safeX, safeY;

        synchronized(p) {        // no one can change p
            safeX = p.x();       // while these two lines
            safeY = p.y();       // are happening atomically
        }
        System.out.print("The point's x is " + safeX
                                    + " y is " + safeY);
    }
}
```

Now you've got it. You need to protect the Point p from changes, so you lock it by giving it as the argument to your synchronized statement. Now when x() and y() happen together, they can be sure to get the current x and y of the Point p without any other thread being able to call a modifying method between. You're still assuming, however, that the Point p has properly protected itself. (You always can assume this about system classes, but you wrote this Point class.) You can make sure by writing the only method that can change x and y inside p yourself:

18

```
public class  Point {
    private float  x, y;

    . . . // the x() and y() methods

    public synchronized void  setXAndY(float  newX,  float  newY) {
        x = newX;
        y = newY;
    }
}
```

By synchronizing the only set method in Point, you guarantee that any other thread trying to grab the Point p and change it out from under you has to wait. You've locked the Point p with your synchronized(p) statement, and any other thread has to try to lock the same Point p through the implicit synchronized(this) statement p now executes when entering setXAndY(). Thus, at last, you are thread-safe.

NOTE

By the way, if Java had some way of returning more than one value at once, you could write a synchronized getXAndY() method for Point that returns both values safely. In the current Java language, such a method could return a new, unique Point to guarantee to its callers that no one else has a copy that might be changed. You can use this sort of trick to minimize the parts of the system that need to worry about synchronization.

Making the Method Safest

An added benefit of using the synchronized modifier on methods (or of using synchronized(this) {. . .}) is that only one of these methods or blocks of code can run at once.

NOTE

Programmers who have tackled multithreading with languages such as C and Fortran will be familiar with the concept of critical sections— blocks of code that must be executed without interruption. The synchronized statement is Java's approach to the concept of protecting critical sections from other threads that might interrupt them.

You can use that knowledge to guarantee that only one of several crucial methods in a class will run at once, as in the following code:

```
public class  ReallySafePoint {
    private float  x, y;
```

```
public synchronized Point  getUniquePoint() {
    return new Point(x, y);                 // can be a less safe Point
}                                           // because only the caller has it

public synchronized void   setXAndY(float  newX,  float  newY) {
    x = newX;
    y = newY;
}

public synchronized void   scale(float  scaleX,  float  scaleY) {
    x *= scaleX;
    y *= scaleY;
}

public synchronized void   add(ReallySafePoint  aRSP) {
    Point  p = aRSP.getUniquePoint();

    x += p.x();
    y += p.y();
}   // Point p is soon thrown away by GC; no one else ever saw it
}
```

This example combines several of the ideas mentioned previously. To prevent callers from needing to synchronize(p) whenever getting your x and y, you give them a synchronized way to get a unique Point (like returning multiple values). Each method that modifies the object's instance variables also is synchronized to prevent it from running between the x and y references in getUniquePoint() and from stepping on another method as it modifies the local x and y. Note that add() itself uses getUniquePoint() to avoid having to say synchronized(aRSP).

Classes that are this safe are a little unusual; it is more often your responsibility to protect yourself from other threads using commonly held objects (such as a Point). Only when you know for certain that you're the only one that knows about an object can you fully relax. Of course, if you created the object yourself and gave it to no one else, you can be that certain.

Protecting a Class Variable

Suppose that you want a class variable to collect some information across all of a class' instances:

```
public class  StaticCounter {
    private static int  crucialValue;

    public synchronized void  countMe() {
        crucialValue += 1;
    }
}
```

Is this safe? If crucialValue were an instance variable, it would be. Because it's a class variable, however, and there is only one copy of it for all instances, you still can have multiple threads modifying it by using different instances of the class. (Remember, the synchronized modifier locks the object this, an instance.) Luckily, you already know the tools you need to solve this problem:

```
public class  StaticCounter {
    private static int  crucialValue;

    public void  countMe() {
        synchronized(getClass()) { // can't directly name StaticCounter
            crucialValue += 1;              // the (shared) class is now locked
        }
    }
}
```

The trick is to lock on a different object—not on an instance of the class, but on the class itself. Because a class variable is inside a class, just as an instance variable is inside an instance, this shouldn't be all that unexpected. In a similar way, classes can provide global resources that any instance (or other class) can access directly by using the class name and lock by using that same class name. In the last example, crucialValue was used from within an instance of StaticCounter, but if crucialValue were declared public instead, from anywhere in the program, it would be safe to say the following:

```
synchronized(Class.forName("StaticCounter")) {
    StaticCounter.crucialValue += 1;
}
```

NOTE

> The direct use of another object's variable is bad style; it's used here to demonstrate a point quickly. StaticCounter normally would provide a countMe()-like class method of its own to do this sort of dirty work.

You now can begin to appreciate how much work the Java team has done by considering these issues for every class and method in the Java class library.

Creating and Using Threads

Now that you understand the power (and the dangers) of having many threads running at once, you probably want to know how those threads are created.

WARNING

The system itself always has a few so-called daemon threads running, one of which is constantly doing the tedious task of garbage collection for you in the background. A main user thread listens for events from your mouse and keyboard. If you're not careful, you can sometimes lock up this main thread. If you do, no events are sent to your program, and it appears to be dead. A good rule of thumb is that whenever you're doing something that can be done in a separate thread, it probably should be. Threads in Java are relatively cheap to create, run, and destroy, so don't use them too sparingly.

If you have noticed the java.lang.Thread class, you might have guessed (correctly) that you can create a thread by subclassing this class:

```
public class  MyFirstThread extends Thread { // a.k.a., java.lang.Thread
    public void  run() {
        . . .                    // do something useful
    }
}
```

You now have a new type of Thread called MyFirstThread, which does something when its run() method is called. Of course, no one has created this thread or called its run() method, so it does absolutely nothing at the moment. To create and run an instance of your new thread class, you write the following:

```
MyFirstThread  aMFT = new MyFirstThread();

aMFT.start();    // calls your run() method
```

What could be simpler? You create a new instance of your thread class, and then ask it to start running. Whenever you want to stop the thread, you use this line:

```
aMFT.stop();
```

Besides responding to start() and stop(), a thread also can be temporarily suspended and later resumed:

```
Thread  t = new Thread();

t.suspend();
. . .            // do something special while t isn't running
t.resume();
```

A thread automatically will suspend() and then resume() when it's first blocked at a synchronized point and then later unblocked (when it's that thread's turn to run).

The Runnable **Interface**

Creating a thread is simple if every time you want to create one you have the luxury of being able to place it under the Thread class in the single-inheritance class tree. What if it more naturally belongs under some other class, from which it needs to get most of its implementation? The interfaces of Day 16, "Packages and Interfaces," come to the rescue:

```
public class  MySecondThread extends ImportantClass implements Runnable {
    public void  run() {
        . . .                    // do something useful
    }
}
```

By implementing the interface Runnable, you declare your intention to run a separate thread. The class Thread itself implements this interface, as you might expect from the design discussions on Day 16. As you also might guess from the example, the interface Runnable specifies only one method: run(). As in MyFirstThread, you expect something to create an instance of a thread and call your run() method. Here's how this task is accomplished:

```
MySecondThread  aMST = new MySecondThread();
Thread          aThread = new Thread(aMST);

aThread.start();   // calls your run() method, indirectly
```

First, you create an instance of MySecondThread. Then, by passing this instance to the constructor making the new Thread, you make it the target of that Thread. Whenever that new Thread starts up, its run() method calls the run() method of the target it was given (assumed by the Thread to be an object that implements the Runnable interface). When start() is called, aThread indirectly calls your run() method. You can stop aThread with stop(). If you don't need to talk to the Thread explicitly or to the instance of MySecondThread, here's a one line shortcut:

```
new Thread(new MySecondThread()).start();
```

NOTE

> As you can see, the class name MySecondThread is a bit of a misnomer; this class does not descend from Thread, nor is it the thread that you start() and stop(). This class probably should have been called MySecondThreadedClass or ImportantRunnableClass.

Testing Runnable

The following is a longer example of implementing the Runnable interface:

```
public class  SimpleRunnable implements Runnable {
    public void  run() {
```

```
            System.out.println("in thread named '"
                              + Thread.currentThread().getName() + "'");
    }  // any other methods run() calls are in current thread as well
}

public class  ThreadTester {
    public static void  main(String argv[]) {
        SimpleRunnable  aSR = new SimpleRunnable();

        while (true) {
            Thread  t = new Thread(aSR);

            System.out.println("new Thread() " + (t == null ?
                                              "fail" : "succeed") + "ed.");
            t.start();
            try { t.join(); } catch (InterruptedException ignored) { }
                        // waits for thread to finish its run() method
        }
    }
}
```

NOTE

> You might be worried that only one instance of the class SimpleRunnable is created, but many new Threads are using it. Don't they get confused? Remember to separate in your mind the aSR instance (and the methods it understands) from the various threads of execution that can pass through it. aSR's methods provide a template for execution, and the multiple threads created are sharing that template. Each remembers where it is executing and whatever else it needs to make it distinct from the other running threads. They all share the same instance and the same methods. That's why you need to be so careful to imagine numerous threads running rampant over each of your methods when adding synchronization.

The class method currentThread() can be called to get the thread in which a method currently is executing. If the SimpleRunnable class were a subclass of Thread, its methods would know the answer already (it is the thread running). Because SimpleRunnable just implements the Runnable interface, however, and counts on something else to create the thread (ThreadTester's main()), its run() method needs another way to get its hands on that thread. Often, you'll be deep inside methods called by your run() method when suddenly you need to get the current thread. The class method shown in this example works no matter where you are.

You can do some reasonably disastrous things with your knowledge of threads. For example, if you're running in the main thread of the system and you think you are in a different thread, you might use the following statement:

```
Thread.currentThread().stop();
```

This statement has unfortunate consequences for your soon-to-be-dead program! When in doubt, you can make sure you're stopping the right thread by testing for the name of currentThread() first. Then, if it's what you expected, you can use currentThread() in a method call such as the preceding call to stop(). Thread naming is described in the next section.

The example calls getName() on the current thread to get the thread's name (usually something helpful, such as Thread-23) so it can tell the world in which thread run() is running. The final thing to note is the use of the join() method, which, when sent to a thread, means that the program or thread that called join() will wait forever until the joined thread finishes its run() method. You don't want to use this method lightly; if you have anything else important to get done in your thread any time soon, you can't count on how long the joined thread might take to finish. In the example, its run() method is short and finishes quickly, so each loop can wait safely for the previous thread to die before creating the next one. (Of course, in this example, you didn't have anything else you wanted to do while waiting for join() anyway.)

Here's the output produced:

```
new Thread() succeeded.
in thread named 'Thread-1'
new Thread() succeeded.
in thread named 'Thread-2'
new Thread() succeeded.
in thread named 'Thread-3'
```

This is just the beginning of the output, because it would continue until interrupted.

Named Threads

If you want your threads to have particular names, you can assign them yourself by using a two-argument form of Thread's constructor:

```
public class NamedThreadTester {
    public static void  main(String argv[]) {
        SimpleRunnable  aSR = new SimpleRunnable();
```

```
        for (int i = 1; true; ++i) {
            Thread t = new Thread(aSR, "" + (100 - i)
                                      + " threads on the wall...");

            System.out.println("new Thread() " + (t == null ?
                                      "fail" : "succeed") + "ed.");
            t.start();
            try { t.join(); } catch (InterruptedException ignored) { }
        }
    }
}
```

OUTPUT   The constructor takes a target object, as before, and a `String` that names the new thread. Here's the output:

```
new Thread() succeeded.
in thread named '99 threads on the wall...'
new Thread() succeeded.
in thread named '98 threads on the wall...'
new Thread() succeeded.
in thread named '97 threads on the wall...'
```

Naming a thread is an easy way to pass it some information. This information flows from the parent thread to its new child. Giving threads meaningful names (such as `network input`) also is useful for debugging purposes so that when the names appear during an error, in a stack trace, for example, you easily can identify which thread caused the problem. You might also think of using names to help group or organize your threads, but Java provides you with a `ThreadGroup` class to perform this function. A `ThreadGroup` allows you to group threads, to control them all as a unit, and to keep them from being able to affect other threads (useful for security).

Putting several threads into a `ThreadGroup` enables you to take action on all of the grouped threads at the same time. Anyone who uses a Web browser has seen something like this in action when a Web page stops loading several graphics on a page after something is clicked with the mouse. Each graphic could be loading in its own thread, and if these threads were grouped in `ThreadGroup page`, a call to `page.stop()` would stop all of the threads with the single method call. The `ThreadGroup` class also has `resume()` and `suspend()` methods.

Knowing When a Thread Has Stopped

Imagine a different version of the last example, one that creates a thread and then hands the thread off to other parts of the program. Suppose the program then would like to know when that thread dies so that it can perform some cleanup operation. If `SimpleRunnable` were a subclass of `Thread`, you might try to catch `stop()` whenever it is sent, but look at `Thread`'s declaration of the `stop()` method:

```
public final void stop() { . . . }
```

The final here means that you can't override this method in a subclass. In any case, SimpleRunnable is not a subclass of Thread, so how can this imagined example possibly catch the death of its thread? The answer is to use the following:

```
public class  SingleThreadTester {
    public static void  main(String argv[]) {
        Thread  t = new Thread(new SimpleRunnable());

        try {
            t.start();
            someMethodThatMightStopTheThread(t);
        } catch (ThreadDeath  aTD) {
            . . .             // do some required cleanup
            throw aTD;        // re-throw the error
        }
    }
}
```

You should understand most of this code from yesterday's lesson. All you need to know is that if the thread created in the example dies, it throws an error of class ThreadDeath. The code catches that error and performs the required cleanup. It then rethrows the error, allowing the thread to die. The cleanup code is not called if the thread exits normally (its run() method completes), but that's fine because you assume the cleanup is needed only when stop() is used on the thread.

NOTE

> Threads can die in other ways; for example, they can throw exceptions that no one catches. In these cases, stop() never is called, and the previous code is not sufficient. (If the cleanup always has to occur, even at the normal end of a thread's life, you can put it in a finally clause.) Because unexpected exceptions can come out of nowhere to kill a thread, multithreaded programs that carefully catch and handle all their exceptions are more predictable, robust, and easier to debug.

Thread Scheduling

You might wonder exactly what order your threads will run in and how you can control that order. Unfortunately, the current implementation of the Java system cannot tell you precisely the order your threads will run in; with a lot of work, however, you always can control the order. The part of the system that decides the real-time ordering of threads is called the *scheduler.*

Preemptive Versus Non-preemptive

Normally, any scheduler has two fundamentally different ways of looking at its job: non-preemptive scheduling and preemptive time-slicing.

NEW TERM With *non-preemptive scheduling*, the scheduler runs the current thread forever, requiring that thread explicitly to tell it when it is safe to start a different thread. With *preemptive time-slicing*, the scheduler runs the current thread until it has used up a certain tiny fraction of a second, and then preempts it, suspends it, and resumes another thread for the next tiny fraction of a second.

Non-preemptive scheduling is courtly, always asking for permission to schedule, and is valuable in extremely time-critical, real-time applications where being interrupted at the wrong moment, or for too long, could be disastrous. However, most modern schedulers use preemptive time-slicing, because, except for a few time-critical cases, it makes writing multithreaded programs much easier. For one thing, it does not force each thread to decide exactly when it should yield control to another thread. Instead, every thread can just run blindly on, knowing that the scheduler will be fair about giving all other threads their chance to run.

Preemptive time-slicing is still not the ideal way to schedule threads, however. This approach gives a little too much control to the scheduler. The final touch many modern schedulers add is to allow you to assign each thread a priority. This priority creates a total ordering of all threads, making some threads more important than others. Being higher priority often means that a thread gets run more often (or gets more total running time), but it always means that it can interrupt other, lower-priority threads, even before their timeslice has expired.

The current Java release does not specify precisely the behavior of its scheduler. Threads can be assigned priorities, and when a choice is made between several threads that all want to run, the highest-priority thread wins. However, among threads that are all the same priority, the behavior is not well-defined. In fact, the different platforms on which Java currently runs have different behaviors—some behaving more like a preemptive scheduler, and some more like a non-preemptive scheduler.

NOTE

> This incomplete specification of the scheduler presumably will be corrected in later releases. Not knowing the fine details of how scheduling occurs is all right, but not knowing whether equal-priority threads must explicitly yield or face running forever is not all right. For example, all the threads you have created so far are equal-priority threads, so you don't know their basic scheduling behavior!

Testing Your Scheduler

To find out what kind of scheduler you have on your system, try the following:

```java
public class RunnablePotato implements Runnable {
    public void run() {
        while (true)
            System.out.println(Thread.currentThread().getName());
    }
}

public class PotatoThreadTester {
    public static void main(String argv[]) {
        RunnablePotato aRP = new RunnablePotato();

        new Thread(aRP, "one potato").start();
        new Thread(aRP, "two potato").start();
    }
}
```

OUTPUT For a non-preemptive scheduler, this code displays the following:

```
one potato
one potato
one potato
. . .
```

The output will continue until the program is interrupted.

OUTPUT A preemptive scheduler that time-slices repeats the line one potato a few times, followed by the same number of two potato lines, over and over:

```
one potato
one potato
...
one potato
two potato
two potato
...
two potato
. . .
```

This output will continue until the program is interrupted. What if you want to be sure the two threads will take turns, no matter what the system scheduler wants to do? You rewrite RunnablePotato as follows:

```java
public class RunnablePotato implements Runnable {
    public void run() {
        while (true) {
            System.out.println(Thread.currentThread().getName());
            Thread.yield();  // let another thread run for a while
        }
    }
}
```

18

TIP

> Normally you would have to say `Thread.currentThread().yield()` to get your hands on the current thread, and then call `yield()`. Because this pattern is so common, however, the `Thread` class provides a shortcut.

OUTPUT

The `yield()` method explicitly gives any other threads that want to run a chance to begin running. (If there are no threads waiting to run, the thread that made the `yield()` continues.) In this example, there's another thread that's just dying to run, so when you now execute the class `ThreadTester`, it should output the following:

```
one potato
two potato
one potato
two potato
one potato
two potato
. . .
```

This output should occur even if your system scheduler is non-preemptive and never would normally run the second thread.

Testing Priority Threads

To see whether priorities are working on your system, try this code:

```
public class  PriorityThreadTester {
    public static void  main(String argv[]) {
        RunnablePotato  aRP = new RunnablePotato();
        Thread          t1  = new Thread(aRP, "one potato");
        Thread          t2  = new Thread(aRP, "two potato");

        t2.setPriority(t1.getPriority() + 1);
        t1.start();
        t2.start();    // at priority Thread.NORM_PRIORITY + 1
    }
}
```

TIP

> The values representing the lowest, normal, and highest priorities that threads can be assigned are stored in class variables of the `Thread` class: `Thread.MIN_PRIORITY`, `Thread.NORM_PRIORITY`, and `Thread.MAX_PRIORITY`. The system assigns new threads, the priority `Thread.NORM_PRIORITY` by default. Priorities in Java currently are defined in a range from 1 to 10, with 5 being normal, but you shouldn't depend on these values; use the class variables or tricks like the one shown in this example.

18

If one potato is the first line of output, your system does not preempt using priorities. Why? Imagine that the first thread (t1) has just begun to run. Even before it has a chance to display anything, along comes a higher-priority thread (t2) that wants to run right away. That higher-priority thread should preempt the first and get a chance to display two potato before t1 finishes printing anything. If you use the RunnablePotato class that never yields, t2 stays in control forever, displaying two potato lines, because it's a higher priority than t1 and it never yields control. If you use the latest RunnablePotato class (with yield()), the output is alternating lines of one potato and two potato as before, but the output starts with two potato.

The following example demonstrates how complex threads behave:

```
public class  ComplexThread extends Thread {
    private int   delay;

    ComplexThread(String   name,   float   seconds) {
        super(name);
        delay = (int) seconds * 1000;    // delays are in milliseconds
        start();                          // start up!
    }

    public void  run() {
        while (true) {
            System.out.println(Thread.currentThread().getName());
            try {
                Thread.sleep(delay);
            } catch (InterruptedException e) {
                return;
            }
        }
    }

    public static void  main(String argv[]) {
        new ComplexThread("one potato",    1.1F);
        new ComplexThread("two potato",    1.3F);
        new ComplexThread("three potato", 0.5F);
        new ComplexThread("four",          0.7F);
    }
}
```

ANALYSIS This example combines the thread and its tester into a single class. Its constructor takes care of naming itself and of starting itself, because it is now a Thread. The main() method creates new instances of its own class, because that class is a subclass of Thread. The run() method is also more complicated because it now uses, for the first time, a method that can throw an unexpected exception.

The Thread.sleep() method forces the current thread to yield() and then waits for at least the specified amount of time to elapse before allowing the thread to run again. However, the thread might be interrupted by another thread while sleeping. In such a case, it throws an InterruptedException. Now, because run() is not defined as throwing this exception, you must hide the fact by catching and handling it yourself. Because interruptions usually are requests to stop, you should exit the thread, which you can do by returning from the run() method.

OUTPUT This program should output a repeating but complex pattern of four different lines, where every once in a great while you see the following:

```
. . .
one potato
two potato
three potato
four
. . .
```

Study the output pattern to prove to yourself that true parallelism is going on inside Java programs. You might also begin to appreciate that, if even this simple set of four threads can produce such complex behavior, many more threads must be capable of producing near chaos if not carefully controlled. Luckily, Java provides the synchronization and thread-safe libraries you need to control that chaos.

Summary

Today, you learned that parallelism is desirable and powerful, but introduces many new problems (methods and variables now need to be protected from thread conflicts, for instance) that can lead to chaos if not carefully controlled.

By "thinking multithreaded," you can detect the places in your programs that require synchronized statements or modifiers to make them thread-safe. A series of Point examples demonstrated the various levels of safety you can achieve, and ThreadTesters showed how subclasses of Thread, or classes that implement the Runnable interface, are created and run() to generate multithreaded programs.

You also learned how to yield(), how to start(), stop(), suspend(), and resume() your threads, and how to catch ThreadDeath whenever it happens. Finally, you learned about preemptive and non-preemptive scheduling, both with and without priorities, and how to test your Java system to see which of them your scheduler is using.

This wraps up the description of threads. You now know enough to write the most complex of programs: multithreaded ones. As you get more comfortable with threads, you might begin to use the ThreadGroup class or the enumeration methods of Thread to get your hands on all threads in the system. Don't be afraid to experiment.

Q&A

Q How exactly do these threads get created and run? What about applets?

A When a simple, stand-alone Java program starts up, the system creates a main thread, and its run() method calls the simple program's main() method to start it

18

automatically. Likewise, when a simple applet loads in a Java-capable browser, a `Thread` already has been created by the browser, and its `run()` method calls the applet's `init()` and `start()` methods to start the applet. In either case, a new `Thread()` of some kind was created by the Java environment itself.

Q The `ThreadTester` class has an infinite loop that creates threads and then uses `join()` on them. Is the loop really infinite?

A In theory, yes. In actuality, how far the loop runs determines the resource limits and tests the stability of the threads package and garbage collector in Java. Over time, all Java releases will converge on making the loop truly infinite.

Q I know Java releases are still a little fuzzy about the scheduler's behavior, but what's the current story?

A Here are the gruesome details, relayed by Arthur van Hoff at Sun: the way Java schedules threads "depends on the platform. It is usually preemptive, but not always time-sliced. Priorities are not always observed, depending on the underlying implementation." This final clause gives you a hint that all this confusion is an implementation problem, and that in some future release, the design and implementation will both be clear about scheduling behavior.

Q Does Java support more complex multithreaded concepts, such as semaphores?

A The class `Object` in Java provides methods that can be used to build up condition variables, semaphores, and any higher-level parallel construct you might need. The method `wait()` (and its two variants with a timeout) causes the current thread to wait until some condition has been satisfied. The `notify()` method (or `notifyAll()`), which must be called from within a `synchronized` method or block, tells the thread (or all threads) to wake up and check that condition again, because something has changed. By careful combinations of these two primitive methods, any data structure can be manipulated safely by a set of threads, and all the classical parallel primitives needed to implement published parallel algorithms can be built.

Q My parallel friends tell me I should worry about something called "deadlock." Should I?

A Not for simple multithreaded programs. However, in more complicated programs, one of the biggest worries does become one of avoiding a situation in which one thread has locked an object and is waiting for another thread to finish, while that other thread is waiting for the first thread to release that same object before it can finish. That's a deadlock—both threads will be stuck forever. Mutual dependencies like this involving more than two threads can be quite intricate, convoluted, and difficult to locate, much less rectify. They are one of the main challenges in writing complex multithreaded programs.

18

Today's Featured Applet

Today's featured applet is BallDrop from David Krider, an educational applet that uses Java to demonstrate probability. The applet tracks the movement of balls through a pachinko-like grid and shows how the seemingly random fall of the balls conforms to a predictable distribution. The Java applet demonstrates the use of graphics and of math to drive the movement of graphics. Figure 18.1 shows an example of BallDrop in action.

Figure 18.1.

The BallDrop *applet in action.*

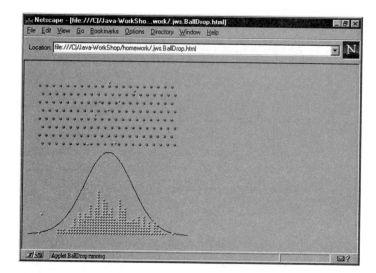

Files for BallDrop are located on the CD-ROM in the \BOOK\3RDPARTY\DAY18\ directory, including source code in the file BallDrop.java. To use BallDrop on a Web page, four files should be placed on your Web site: the class files BallDrop.class and Ball.class, and the image files for the pin and ball images (smallpin.gif and smallball.gif are provided with the applet, and are the defaults). These files should be placed in the same directory as the Web page, or should be placed in a subdirectory listed in the CODEBASE parameter of the <APPLET> tag. The <CODE> tag should be BallDrop.class. Listing 18.1 shows the HTML tags used to run BallDrop as it was shown in Figure 18.1.

Listing 18.1. The <APPLET> tag for BallDrop.

```
<applet
  name="BallDrop"
  code="BallDrop.class"
  width="300"
  height="300"
  align="Top">
</applet>
```

`BallDrop` has eight parameters that can be customized within the `<APPLET>` tag as follows:

- ☐ The `BallImage` parameter is the name of the file containing the ball graphic (smallball.gif is the default).

- ☐ The `PinImage` parameter is the name of the file containing the pin graphic (smallpin.gif is the default).

- ☐ The `NumRows` parameter is the number of rows of the grid (8 is the default).

- ☐ The `NumColumns` parameter is the number of columns of the grid (20 is the default).

- ☐ The `NumBalls` parameter is the number of balls to have dropping at the same time (10 is the default).

- ☐ The `Delay` parameter is the delay between screen updates (10 is the default).

- ☐ The `TopSpace` parameter is the amount of space to leave at the top (30 is the default).

- ☐ The `SideSpace` parameter is the amount of space to leave at the side (20 is the default).

More information on the applet is available from its author at the following URL:

`http://www.cco.caltech.edu/~ekrider/Finance/BallDrop/BallDrop.html`

18

Day 19

Streams

NEW TERM One of the innovations of the UNIX operating system was the pipe. A *pipe* is an uninterpreted stream of bytes that can be used for communicating between programs, between forked copies of your own program, or for reading and writing to arbitrary peripheral devices and files. By unifying many disparate ways of communicating into a single metaphor, UNIX paved the way for a whole series of related inventions, culminating in the abstraction known as streams.

NEW TERM A *stream* is a path of communication between the source of some information and its destination. This information, an uninterpreted byte stream, can come from any pipe source, the computer's memory, or even from the Internet. The source and destination of a stream are completely arbitrary producers and consumers of bytes, respectively. Therein lies the power of the abstraction. You don't need to know about the source of the information when reading from a stream, and you don't need to know about the final destination when writing to one.

General-purpose methods that can read from any source accept a stream argument to specify that source; general methods for writing accept a stream to specify the destination. Arbitrary processors of data (or *filters*) have two stream arguments. They read from the first, process the data, and write the results to the second. These processors have no idea of either the source or the destination of the data they are processing. Sources and destinations can vary widely. For instance, they could be two memory buffers on the same local computer, the extremely low frequency transmissions to and from a submarine at sea, or the real-time data streams of a NASA probe in deep space.

By separating the consuming, processing, or producing of data from the sources and destinations of that data, you can mix and match any combination of them as you write your program. In the future, when new forms of sources or destinations appear (or new forms of consumers, processors, or producers), they can be used within the same framework with no changes to your classes. In addition, new stream abstractions, supporting higher levels of interpretation on top of the bytes, can be written completely independent of the underlying transport mechanisms for the bytes themselves.

The foundations of this stream framework are the two abstract classes, InputStream and OutputStream. If you turn briefly to the diagram for java.io in Appendix B, "Class Hierarchy Diagrams," you'll see that below these classes is a virtual cornucopia of categorized classes, demonstrating the wide range of streams in the system, but also demonstrating an extremely well-designed hierarchy of relationships between these streams—one well worth learning from. The place to start is with the parents.

Today, you'll explore the use of input and output streams in Java, including the following topics:

- ☐ Creating input/output streams
- ☐ Using input/output streams
- ☐ Detecting the end of an input stream
- ☐ Filtered input streams, which can be nested to great effect
- ☐ Stream interfaces that make reading and writing typed streams much easier
- ☐ Utility classes that are used to access the file system

Input Streams

All of the methods you will explore today are declared to throw IOExceptions. This new subclass of Exception conceptually embodies all of the possible input/output errors that might occur while using streams. Several subclasses of it define a few more specific exceptions that can be thrown as well. For now, it is enough to know that in order to be a well-behaved user of streams, you must either catch an IOException or be in a method that can pass it along.

WARNING

Many of the examples in today's lesson assume that they appear inside a method that has `IOException` in its `throws` clause, so they don't have to worry about catching those exceptions and handling them more reasonably. Your code should be a little less cavalier.

The abstract **Class** `InputStream`

`InputStream` is an abstract class that defines the fundamental ways in which a destination (consumer) reads a stream of bytes from some source. The identity of the source and the manner of the creation and transport of the bytes are irrelevant. When using an input stream, you are the destination of those bytes, and that's all you need to know.

read()

The most important method to the consumer of an input stream is the one that reads bytes from the source. This method, `read()`, comes in many flavors, and each is demonstrated in an example in today's lesson.

Each of these `read()` methods is defined to wait (that is, *to block*) until all of the input requested becomes available. Don't worry about this limitation; because of multithreading, you can do as many other things as you like while this one thread is waiting for input. In fact, it is common to assign a thread to each stream of input (and for each stream of output) that is responsible solely for reading from the stream (or writing to it). These input threads might then hand off the information to other threads for processing. This multithreading naturally overlaps the input/output time of your program with its compute time.

The first form of `read()` is as follows:

```
InputStream   s      = getAnInputStreamFromSomewhere();
byte[]        buffer = new byte[1024]; // any size will do

if (s.read(buffer) != buffer.length)
    System.out.println("I got less than I expected.");
```

NOTE

In this code, and throughout the rest of today's lesson, it is assumed that an `import java.io.*;` statement was used at the beginning of the source code. If it was omitted, the Java compiler would generate an error because of classes that could not be found.

This form of `read()` attempts to fill the entire buffer given. If it cannot (usually due to reaching the end of the input stream), it returns the number of bytes that were read into the buffer. After that, any further calls to `read()` return -1, indicating that you are at the end of the stream. Note that the `if` statement still works even in this case, because -1 != 1024 (this number corresponds to an input stream with no bytes in it all).

 NOTE

> Don't forget that, unlike in C, the -1 case in Java is not used to indicate an error. Any input/output errors `throw` instances of `IOException` (which you're not using `catch` to handle yet). You learned yesterday that all uses of distinguished values can be replaced by the use of exceptions, and so they should. The -1 in the last example is a bit of an anachronism. You soon will see a better approach to indicating the end of the stream using the class `DataInputStream`.

You also can read into a slice of your buffer by specifying the offset into the buffer, and the length desired, as arguments to `read()`:

```
s.read(buffer, 100, 300);
```

This example tries to fill in bytes 100 through 399 and otherwise behaves exactly the same as the previous `read()` method:

```
public int  read(byte[]  buffer) throws IOException {
    return  read(buffer, 0, buffer.length);
}
```

Finally, you can read in bytes one at a time:

```
InputStream  s = getAnInputStreamFromSomewhere();
byte         b;
int          byteOrMinus1;

while ((byteOrMinus1 = s.read()) != -1) {
    b = (byte) byteOrMinus1;
    . . .      // process the byte b
}
. . .      // reached end of stream
```

 NOTE

> Because of the nature of integer promotion in Java in general, and because in this case the `read()` method returns an `int`, using the `byte` type in your code might be a little frustrating. You'll find yourself constantly having to explicitly cast the result of arithmetic expressions,

or of `int` return values, back to your size. Because `read()` should be returning a `byte` in this case, declaring and using it this way makes clearer the size of the data being read. In cases where you feel the range of a variable naturally is limited to a `byte` (or a `short`) rather than an `int`, please take the time to declare it that way and pay the small price necessary to gain the added clarity. By the way, a lot of the Java class library code stores the result of `read()` in an `int`—which shows that everyone makes style mistakes.

skip()

What if you want to skip over some of the bytes in a stream, or start reading a stream from some point other than its beginning? A method similar to `read()` does the trick:

```
if (s.skip(1024) != 1024)
    System.out.println("I skipped less than I expected.");
```

This example skips over the next 1024 bytes in the input stream. The `skip()` method takes and returns a long integer, because streams are not required to be limited to any particular size. The default implementation of `skip()` in this Java release uses `read()`:

```
public long  skip(long n) throws IOException {
    byte[]  buffer = new byte[(int) n];

    return  read(buffer);
}
```

NOTE This default implementation does not support large skips correctly, because its `long` argument is cast to an `int`. Subclasses must override this default implementation if they want to handle this situation more properly. Overriding this implementation won't be as easy as you might think, because the current release of the Java system does not allow integer types larger than `int` to act as array subscripts. One possible solution would be to implement a series of skips with values stored as `int` that add up to the `long` argument you needed to use.

available()

If for some reason you would like to know how many bytes are in the stream right now, you can ask:

```
if (s.available() < 1024)
    System.out.println("Too little is available right now.");
```

This method tells you the number of bytes that you can read() without blocking. Because of the abstract nature of the source of these bytes, streams might or might not be able to provide a reasonable answer to this question. For example, some streams always return 0. Unless you use specific subclasses of InputStream that you know provide a reasonable answer to this question, you shouldn't rely upon this method. Remember, multithreading eliminates many of the problems associated with blocking while waiting for a stream to fill again. Thus, one of the strongest rationales for the use of available() is no longer an issue.

mark() **and** reset()

Some streams support the notion of marking a position in the stream and then later resetting the stream to that position to reread the bytes there. Clearly, the stream would have to remember all of those bytes, so there is a limitation on how far apart in a stream the mark and its subsequent reset can occur. There also is a method that asks whether the stream supports the notion of marking at all. Here's an example:

```
InputStream  s = getAnInputStreamFromSomewhere();

if (s.markSupported()) {      // does s support the notion?
    . . .             // read the stream for a while
    s.mark(1024);
    . . .             // read less than 1024 more bytes
    s.reset();
    . . .             // we can now reread those bytes
} else {
    . . .                     // no, perform some alternative
}
```

When marking a stream, you specify the maximum number of bytes you intend to allow to pass before resetting it. This number allows the stream to limit the size of its byte memory. If this number of bytes goes by and you have not yet reset(), the mark becomes invalid, and attempting to reset() will throw an exception.

Marking and resetting a stream is most valuable when you are attempting to identify the type of the stream (or the next part of the stream), but to do so, you must consume a significant piece of it in the process. Often, this is because you have several parsers that you can hand the stream to, but they will consume an unknown number of bytes before determining whether the stream is of their type. Set a large size for the read limit, and let each parser run until it either throws an error or completes a successful parse. If an error is thrown, reset() and try the next parser.

close()

Because you don't know what resources an open stream represents, or how to deal with them properly when you're finished reading the stream, you usually should close down a stream explicitly so that it can release these resources. Of course, garbage collection and a finalization method can do this for you, but what if you need to reopen that stream or those resources before they have been freed by this asynchronous process? At best, this is annoying or confusing; at worst, it introduces an unexpected, obscure, and difficult-to-track-down bug. Because you're interacting with the world of external resources, it's safer to be explicit about closing streams when you're finished using them:

```
InputStream  s = alwaysMakesANewInputStream();

try {
    . . .        // use s to your heart's content
} finally {
    s.close();
}
```

Get used to using finally; it's a useful way to make sure that something (such as closing the stream) always gets done. Of course, you're assuming that the stream always is successfully created. If this is not always the case, and null is sometimes returned instead, here's the correct way to be safe:

```
InputStream  s = tryToMakeANewInputStream();

if (s != null) {
    try {
        . . .
    } finally {
        s.close();
    }
}
```

All input streams descend from the abstract class InputStream. All share in common the few methods described so far. Thus, stream s in the previous examples could have been any of the more complex input streams described in the next few sections.

ByteArrayInputStream

ByteArrayInputStream creates an input stream from an array of bytes:

```
byte[]  buffer = new byte[1024];

fillWithUsefulData(buffer);

InputStream  s = new ByteArrayInputStream(buffer);
```

19

Readers of the new stream s see a stream 1024 bytes long, containing the bytes in the array buffer. Just as read() has a form that takes an offset and a length, so does this class' constructor:

```
InputStream  s = new ByteArrayInputStream(buffer, 100, 300);
```

In this example, the stream is 300 bytes long and consists of bytes 100–399 from the array buffer.

NOTE

Finally, you've seen your first examples of the creation of a stream. These new streams are attached to the simplest of all possible sources of data, an array of bytes in the memory of the local computer.

ByteArrayInputStream simply implements the standard set of methods that all input streams do. In this stream, however, the available() method has a particularly simple job; it returns 1024 and 300, respectively, for the two instances of ByteArrayInputStream you created previously, because it knows exactly how many bytes are available. Finally, calling reset() on a ByteArrayInputStream resets it to the beginning of the stream (buffer) no matter where the mark is set.

FileInputStream

One of the most common uses of streams, and historically the earliest, is to attach them to files in the file system. The following is the creation of such an input stream on a UNIX system:

```
InputStream  s = new FileInputStream("/some/path/and/fileName");
```

WARNING

Applets attempting to open, read, or write streams based on files in the file system can cause security violations (depending on the security level set by the user of the browser). Try to create applets that do not depend on files at all by using servers to hold shared information. (Stand-alone Java applications have none of these problems, of course.)

You also can create the stream from a previously opened file descriptor:

```
int          fd = openInputFileInTraditionalUNIXWays();
InputStream  s  = new FileInputStream(fd);
```

In either case, because the created input stream is based on an actual (finite length) file, the stream can implement available() precisely and can skip() like a champ (just as ByteArrayInputStream can, by the way). In addition, FileInputStream knows a few more tricks:

```
FileInputStream  aFIS = new FileInputStream("aFileName");

int  myFD = aFIS.getFD();

/* aFIS.finalize(); */  // will call close() when automatically called by GC
```

 TIP

To call the new methods, you must declare the stream variable aFIS to be of type FileInputStream, because plain InputStreams don't know about them.

The first line is obvious: getFD() returns the file descriptor of the file on which the stream is based. The second, though, is an interesting shortcut that allows you to create FileInputStreams without worrying about closing them later. FileInputStream's implementation of finalize(), a protected method, closes the stream. Unlike in the contrived call shown as a comment, you almost never can call a finalize() method directly (nor should you). The garbage collector calls it after noticing that the stream is no longer in use, but before actually destroying the stream. Thus, you can go merrily along using the stream, never closing it, and all will be well. The system eventually takes care of closing it.

You can get away with this because streams based on files tie up very few resources, and these resources cannot be accidentally reused before garbage collection (these were the things worried about in the previous discussion of finalization and close()). Of course, if you also were writing to the file, you would have to be more careful. Reopening the file too soon after writing might make it appear in an inconsistent state because the finalize() method, and thus the close(), might not have happened yet. Just because you don't *have* to close the stream doesn't mean you might not want to do so anyway. For clarity, or if you don't know precisely what type of an InputStream you were handed, you might choose to call close() yourself.

FilterInputStream

The FilterInputStream abstract class provides a pass-through for all of the standard methods of InputStream. It holds inside itself another stream, by definition one further down the chain of filters, to which it forwards all method calls. It implements nothing new but allows itself to be nested:

```
InputStream        s  = getAnInputStreamFromSomewhere();
FilterInputStream  s1 = new FilterInputStream(s);
FilterInputStream  s2 = new FilterInputStream(s1);
FilterInputStream  s3 = new FilterInputStream(s2);

... s3.read() ...
```

Whenever a read is performed on the filtered stream s3, it passes along the request to s2; then s2 does the same to s1, and finally s is asked to provide the bytes. Subclasses of FilterInputStream do some nontrivial processing of the bytes as they flow past. The rather verbose form of "chaining" in the previous example can be made more elegant:

```
s3 = new FilterInputStream(new FilterInputStream(new FilterInputStream(s)));
```

You should use this kind of statement in your code whenever you can. It clearly expresses the nesting of chained filters and easily can be parsed and "read aloud" by starting at the innermost stream s and reading outward, each filter stream applying to the one within, until you reach the outermost stream s3.

NOTE

> FilterInputStream is called abstract rather than abstract because it is not actually declared to be abstract. As a result, you can create instances of FilterInputStream directly. The same is true for its corresponding output stream class, described later today.

The following sections examine each of the subclasses of FilterInputStream.

BufferedInputStream

BufferedInputStream is one of the most valuable of all streams. It implements the full complement of InputStream's methods, but it does so by using a buffered array of bytes that acts as a cache for future reading. This array separates the rate and the size of the chunks you're reading from the more regular, larger block sizes in which streams are most efficiently read (from, for example, peripheral devices, files in the file system, or the network). It also allows smart streams to read ahead when they expect that you will want more data soon.

Because the buffering of BufferedInputStream is so valuable, and it's also the only class able to handle mark() and reset() properly, you might wish that every input stream could somehow share its valuable capabilities. Normally, because those stream classes do not implement them, you would be out of luck. Fortunately, you already saw a way that filter streams can wrap themselves around other streams. Suppose that you would like a buffered FileInputStream that can handle marking and resetting correctly. The following code creates a buffered input stream based on the file arcdata that can mark() and reset():

```
InputStream  s = new BufferedInputStream(new FileInputStream("arcdata"));
```

Now you can begin to see the power of nesting streams. Any capability provided by a filter input stream (or output stream, as you'll see soon) can be used by any other basic stream through nesting.

DataInputStream

All of the methods that instances of the DataInputStream class understand are defined in a separate interface, which is implemented by both DataInputStream and RandomAccessFile (another class in java.io). This interface, called DataInput, is general-purpose enough that you might want to use it yourself in the classes you create.

The DataInput Interface

When you begin using streams to any degree, you quickly will discover that byte streams are not a helpful format into which to force all data. In particular, the primitive types of the Java language embody a nice way of looking at data, but with the streams you've been defining thus far in this book, you could not read data of these types. The DataInput interface specifies a higher-level set of methods that, when used for both reading and writing, can support a more complex, typed stream of data. Here are the set of methods this interface defines:

```
void   readFully(byte[]  buffer) throws IOException;
void   readFully(byte[]  buffer, int  offset, int  length) throws IOException;
int    skipBytes(int n) throws IOException;

boolean  readBoolean()          throws IOException;
byte     readByte()             throws IOException;
int      readUnsignedByte()     throws IOException;
short    readShort()            throws IOException;
int      readUnsignedShort()    throws IOException;
char     readChar()             throws IOException;
int      readInt()              throws IOException;
long     readLong()             throws IOException;
float    readFloat()            throws IOException;
double   readDouble()           throws IOException;

String   readLine()             throws IOException;
String   readUTF()              throws IOException;
```

The first three methods are new names for the two forms of read() and skip() you've seen previously. Each of the next 10 methods reads in a primitive type or its unsigned counterpart (useful for using every bit efficiently in a binary stream). These latter methods must return an integer of a wider size than you might think; because integers are signed in Java, the unsigned value does not fit in anything smaller. The final two methods read a newline-terminated string of characters ('\r', '\n', or "\r\n") from the stream—the first in ASCII, and the second in Unicode.

Now that you know what the interface that `DataInputStream` implements looks like, look at it in action:

```
DataInputStream  s = new DataInputStream(getNumericInputStream());

long  size = s.readLong();     // the number of items in the stream

while (size— > 0) {
    if (s.readBoolean()) {     // should I process this item?
        int    anInteger    = s.readInt();
        int    magicBitFlags = s.readUnsignedShort();
        double aDouble       = s.readDouble();

        if ((magicBitFlags & 0100000) != 0) {
            . . .     // high bit set, do something special
        }
            . . .        // process anInteger and aDouble
    }
}
```

Because the class implements an interface for all of its methods, you also can use the following interface:

```
DataInput  d = new DataInputStream(new FileInputStream("anything"));
String     line;

while ((line = d.readLine()) != null) {
    . . .        // process the line
}
```

The `EOFException`

When the end of a stream is reached, most of `DataInputStream`'s methods throw an `EOFException`. This exception is tremendously useful, and it allows you to rewrite all of the kludgy uses of -1 you saw earlier today in a much nicer fashion:

```
DataInputStream  s = new DataInputStream(getAnInputStream());

try {
    while (true) {
        byte  b = (byte) s.readByte();
        . . .     // process the byte b
    }
} catch (EOFException e) {
    . . .      // reached end of stream
}
```

This code works just as well for all but the last two of the read methods of `DataInputStream`.

WARNING

> The `skipBytes()` method does nothing at all on end of stream, `readLine()` returns `null`, and `readUTF()` might throw a `UTFDataFormatException`, if it notices the problem at all.

LineNumberInputStream

In an editor or a debugger, line numbering is crucial. To add this valuable capability to your programs, use the filter stream `LineNumberInputStream`, which keeps track of line numbers as its stream flows through the stream. It's even smart enough to remember a line number and later restore it during a `mark()` and `reset()`. You might use this class as follows:

```
LineNumberInputStream  al;
al = new LineNumberInputStream(new FileInputStream("source"));

DataInputStream  s = new DataInputStream(al);
String          line;

while ((line = s.readLine()) != null) {
    . . .     // process the line
    System.out.println("Did line #: " + al.getLineNumber());
}
```

In this example, two filter streams are nested around the `FileInputStream` that provides the data. The first filter stream reads lines one at a time, and the second keeps track of the line numbers of these lines as they go by. You must explicitly name the intermediate filter stream, `al`, because if you did not, you couldn't call `getLineNumber()` later. Note that if you invert the order of the nested streams, reading from the `DataInputStream` does not cause the `LineNumberInputStream` to see the lines.

You must put any filter streams acting as monitors in the middle of the chain and pull the data from the outermost filter stream so that the data will pass through each of the monitors in turn. In the same way, buffering should occur as far inside the chain as possible, because it won't be able to do its job properly unless most of the streams that need buffering come after it in the flow. For example, here's a silly order:

```
new BufferedInputStream(new LineNumberInputStream(
        _new DataInputStream(new FileInputStream("scores")));
```

This order is much better:

```
new DataInputStream(new LineNumberInputStream(
        _new BufferedInputStream(new FileInputStream("scores")));
```

You can also tell `LineNumberInputStream`s to `setLineNumber()`, for those few times when you know more than they do.

PushbackInputStream

The filter stream class `PushbackInputStream` commonly is used in parsers to push back a single character in the input (after reading it) while trying to determine what to do next—a simplified version of the `mark()` and `reset()` utility you learned about earlier. Its only addition to the standard set of `InputStream` methods is `unread()`, which, as you might guess, pretends that it never read the byte passed in as its argument, and then gives that byte back as the return value of the next `read()`.

The following is a simple implementation of readLine() using the PushbackInputStream class:

```
public class  SimpleLineReader {
    private FilterInputStream  s;

    public  SimpleLineReader(InputStream  an) {
        s = new DataInputStream(an);
    }

    . . .    // other read() methods using stream s

    public String  readLine() throws IOException {
        char[]  buffer = new char[100];
        int     offset = 0;
        byte    thisByte;

        try {
loop:       while (offset < buffer.length) {
                switch (thisByte = (byte) s.read()) {
                    case '\n':
                        break loop;
                    case '\r':
                        byte  nextByte = (byte) s.read();

                        if (nextByte != '\n') {
                            if (!(s instanceof PushbackInputStream)) {
                                s = new PushbackInputStream(s);
                            }
                            ((PushbackInputStream) s).unread(nextByte);
                        }
                        break loop;
                    default:
                        buffer[offset++] = (char) thisByte;
                        break;
                }
            }
        } catch (EOFException e) {
            if (offset == 0)
                return null;
        }
        return String.copyValueOf(buffer, 0, offset);
    }
}
```

ANALYSIS This implementation demonstrates numerous things. For the purpose of this example, readLine() is restricted to reading the first 100 characters of the line. In this respect, it demonstrates how not to write a general-purpose line processor (you should be able to read any size line). It also reminds you how to break out of an outer loop and how to produce a String from an array of characters (in this case, from a slice of the array of characters). This example also includes standard uses of InputStream's read() method for reading bytes one at a time and for determining the end of the stream by enclosing it in a DataInputStream and catching an EOFException.

One of the more unusual aspects of the example is the way `PushbackInputStream` is used. To be sure that `'\n'` is ignored following `'\r'`, you have to look ahead one character; but if it is not a `'\n'`, you must push back that character. Look at the two lines after `if (nextByte != '\n') {` as if you didn't know much about the s stream. The general technique used is instructive. First, you see whether s is already an `instanceof` some kind of `PushbackInputStream`. If so, you can use it. If not, you enclose the current stream (whatever it is) inside a new `PushbackInputStream` and use this new stream.

The subsequent line wants to call the method `unread()`. The problem is that s has a compile-time type of `FilterInputStream`, and thus doesn't understand that method. The previous two lines have guaranteed, however, that the run-time type of the stream in s is `PushbackInputStream`, so you safely can cast the stream to that type and then call `unread()`.

NOTE

> This example was done in an unusual way for demonstration purposes. You could have declared a `PushbackInputStream` variable and always enclosed the `DataInputStream` in it. (Conversely, `SimpleLineReader`'s constructor could have checked whether its argument was already of the right class, the way `PushbackInputStream` did, before creating a new `DataInputStream`.) The interesting thing about this approach of wrapping a class only when needed is that it works for any `InputStream` that you hand it, and it does additional work only if it needs to. Both of these are good general design principles.

All the subclasses of `FilterInputStream` now have been described. It's time to return to the direct subclasses of `InputStream`.

PipedInputStream

The `PipedInputStream` class, along with its corresponding class `PipedOutputStream`, are covered later today (they need to be demonstrated together). For now, all you need to know is that together they create a simple, two-way communication conduit between threads. Interthread communication can be used as a means to synchronize threads and keep up with what the individual threads of a program are accomplishing.

SequenceInputStream

Suppose that you have two separate streams, and you would like to make a composite stream that consists of one stream followed by the other (like appending two strings together). This task is exactly what `SequenceInputStream` was created for:

```
InputStream  s1 = new FileInputStream("theFirstPart");
InputStream  s2 = new FileInputStream("theRest");

InputStream  s  = new SequenceInputStream(s1, s2);

... s.read() ...   // reads from each stream in turn
```

You could have faked this example by reading each file in turn, but what if you had to hand the composite stream s to some other method that was expecting only a single InputStream? Here's an example (using s) that numbers the lines of the two previous files with a common numbering scheme:

```
LineNumberInputStream  al = new LineNumberInputStream(s);

... al.getLineNumber() ...
```

NOTE
Stringing together streams this way is especially useful when the streams are of unknown length and origin and were just handed to you by someone else.

What if you want to string together more than two streams? You can try the following:

```
Vector  v = new Vector();
. . .   // set up all the streams and add each to the Vector
InputStream  s1 = new SequenceInputStream(v.elementAt(0),
                                          v.elementAt(1));
InputStream  s2 = new SequenceInputStream(s1, v.elementAt(2));
InputStream  s3 = new SequenceInputStream(s2, v.elementAt(3));
. . .
```

NOTE
A Vector is an expandable array of objects that can be filled, referenced (with elementAt()), and enumerated.

However, it's much easier to use a different constructor that SequenceInputStream provides:

```
InputStream  s  = new SequenceInputStream(v.elements());
```

This constructor takes an enumeration of all the streams you want to combine and returns a single stream that reads through the data of each in turn.

StringBufferInputStream

StringBufferInputStream is exactly like ByteArrayInputStream, but instead of being based on a byte array, it's based on an array of characters (a String):

```
String      buffer = "Everybody polka!";
InputStream  s      = new StringBufferInputStream(buffer);
```

All comments that were made about ByteArrayInputStream apply here as well. (See the earlier section on that class.)

NOTE StringBufferInputStream is a bit of a misnomer, because this input stream is based on a String. It should be called StringInputStream.

Output Streams

Output streams are in almost every case paired with an InputStream that you already have learned about. If an InputStream performs a certain operation, its corresponding OutputStream performs the inverse operation.

The abstract Class OutputStream

OutputStream is the abstract class that defines the fundamental ways in which a source (producer) writes a stream of bytes to some destination. The identity of the destination and the manner of the transport and storage of the bytes are irrelevant. When using an output stream, you are the source of those bytes, and that's all you need to know. Because all output streams descend from the abstract class OutputStream, all output streams share the following few methods in common.

19

write()

The most important method to the producer of an output stream is the one that writes bytes to the destination. This method, write(), comes in many flavors, each demonstrated in an example that follows.

NOTE Every one of these write() methods is defined to block (wait) until all of the output requested has been written. You don't need to worry about this limitation—see the note under InputStream's read() method if you don't remember why.

The following code writes the contents of a 1,024-byte array to an output stream:

```
OutputStream   s      = getAnOutputStreamFromSomewhere();
byte[]         buffer = new byte[1024];    // any size will do

fillInData(buffer);    // the data we want to output
s.write(buffer);
```

You also can write a "slice" of your buffer by specifying the offset into the buffer, and the length desired, as arguments to write():

```
s.write(buffer, 100, 300);
```

This example writes out bytes 100 through 399 and otherwise behaves exactly the same as the previous write() method:

```
public void  write(byte[]  buffer) throws IOException {
    write(buffer, 0, buffer.length);
}
```

Finally, you can write out bytes one at a time:

```
while (thereAreMoreBytesToOutput()) {
    byte  b = getNextByteForOutput();

    s.write(b);
}
```

flush()

Because you don't know what an output stream is connected to, you might be required to flush your output through some buffered cache to get it to be written (in a timely manner, or at all). OutputStream's version of this method does nothing, but it is expected that subclasses that require flushing (for example, BufferedOutputStream and PrintStream) will override this version to do something nontrivial.

close()

Just like for an InputStream, you usually should close down an OutputStream explicitly so that it can release any resources it might have reserved on your behalf. (All the same notes and examples from InputStream's close() method apply here, with the prefix In replaced everywhere by Out.)

ByteArrayOutputStream

The inverse of ByteArrayInputStream, which creates an input stream from an array of bytes, is ByteArrayOutputStream, which directs an output stream into an array of bytes:

```
OutputStream  s = new ByteArrayOutputStream();

s.write(123);
. . .
```

The size of the internal byte array grows as needed to store a stream of any length. You can provide an initial capacity as an aid to the class, if you like:

```
OutputStream  s = new ByteArrayOutputStream(1024 * 1024);   // 1M
```

NOTE
> You just have seen your first examples of the creation of an output stream. These new streams were attached to the simplest of all possible destinations of data: an array of bytes in the memory of the local computer.

Once the ByteArrayOutputStream s has been filled, it can be output to another output stream:

```
OutputStream            anotherOutputStream = getTheOtherOutputStream();
ByteArrayOutputStream  s = new ByteArrayOutputStream();

fillWithUsefulData(s);
s.writeTo(anotherOutputStream);
```

It also can be extracted as a byte array or converted to a String:

```
byte[]  buffer             = s.toByteArray();
String  bufferString       = s.toString();
String  bufferUnicodeString = s.toString(upperByteValue);
```

NOTE
> The last method allows you to fake Unicode (16-bit) characters by filling in their lower bytes with ASCII and then specifying a common upper byte (usually 0) to create a Unicode String result.

ByteArrayOutputStreams have two utility methods: one returns the current number of bytes stored in the internal byte array, and the other resets the array so that the stream can be rewritten from the beginning:

```
int  sizeOfMyByteArray = s.size();

s.reset();      // s.size() now would return 0
s.write(123);
. . .
```

19

FileOutputStream

One of the most common uses of streams is to attach them to files in the file system. The following example is the creation of such an output stream on a UNIX system:

```
OutputStream  s = new FileOutputStream("/some/path/and/fileName");
```

WARNING

Applets attempting to open, read, or write streams based on files in the file system can cause security violations. See the note under `FileInputStream` for more details.

You also can create the stream from a previously opened file descriptor:

```
int             fd = openOutputFileInTraditionalUNIXWays();
OutputStream  s = new FileOutputStream(fd);
```

`FileOutputStream` is the inverse of `FileInputStream`, and it knows the same tricks:

```
FileOutputStream  aFOS = new FileOutputStream("aFileName");

int  myFD = aFOS.getFD();

/* aFOS.finalize(); */  // will call close() when automatically called by GC
```

NOTE

To call the new methods, you must declare the stream variable `aFOS` to be of type `FileOutputStream`, because plain `OutputStreams` don't know about them.

The first trick is obvious: `getFD()` returns the file descriptor for the file on which the stream is based. The second, commented, contrived call to `finalize()` is there to remind you that you might not have to worry about closing this type of stream; closing is done for you automatically. (See the discussion under `FileInputStream` for more.)

FilterOutputStream

The `FilterOutputStream` abstract class provides a pass-through for all the standard methods of `OutputStream`. It holds inside itself another stream, by definition one further down the chain of filters, to which it forwards all method calls. It implements nothing new but allows itself to be nested:

```
OutputStream          s  = getAnOutputStreamFromSomewhere();
FilterOutputStream  s1 = new FilterOutputStream(s);
```

19

```
FilterOutputStream  s2 = new FilterOutputStream(s1);
FilterOutputStream  s3 = new FilterOutputStream(s2);

... s3.write(123) ...
```

Whenever a write is performed on the filtered stream s3, it passes along the request to s2. Then s2 does the same to s1, and finally s is asked to output the bytes. Subclasses of FilterOutputStream, of course, do some nontrivial processing of the bytes as they flow past. This chain can be tightly nested—see the section on FilterInputStream for more information. The following sections examine each of the subclasses of FilterOutputStream.

BufferedOutputStream

BufferedOutputStream is one of the most valuable of all streams. All it does is implement the full complement of OutputStream's methods, but it does so by using a buffered array of bytes that acts as a cache for writing. This array separates the rate and the size of the chunks you're writing from the more regular, larger block sizes in which streams are most efficiently written (to peripheral devices, files in the file system, or the network, for example).

BufferedOutputStream is one of two classes in the Java library to implement flush(), which pushes the bytes you've written through the buffer and out of the other side. Because buffering is so valuable, you might wish that every output stream could somehow be buffered. Fortunately, you can surround any output stream in such a way as to achieve that goal:

```
OutputStream  s = new BufferedOutputStream(new FileOutputStream("ed"));
```

You now have a buffered output stream based on the file "ed" that can use flush(). As with filter input streams, any capability provided by a filter output stream can be used by any other basic stream through nesting.

19

DataOutputStream

All the methods that instances of the DataOutputStream class understand are defined in a separate interface, which both DataOutputStream and RandomAccessFile implement. This interface, called DataOutput, is general-purpose enough that you might want use it yourself in the classes you create.

The DataOutput Interface

In cooperation with its inverse interface, DataInput, DataOutput provides a higher-level, typed-stream approach to the reading and writing of data. Rather than dealing with bytes, this interface deals with writing the primitive types of the Java language directly:

```
void  write(int i) throws IOException;
void  write(byte[]  buffer) throws IOException;
void  write(byte[]  buffer, int  offset, int  length) throws IOException;
```

```
void  writeBoolean(boolean b)  throws IOException;
void  writeByte(int i)         throws IOException;
void  writeShort(int i)        throws IOException;
void  writeChar(int i)         throws IOException;
void  writeInt(int i)          throws IOException;
void  writeLong(long l)        throws IOException;
void  writeFloat(float f)      throws IOException;
void  writeDouble(double d)    throws IOException;

void  writeBytes(String s)  throws IOException;
void  writeChars(String s)  throws IOException;
void  writeUTF(String s)    throws IOException;
```

Most of these methods have counterparts in the interface DataInput. The first three methods mirror the three forms of write() you saw previously. Each of the next eight methods writes out a primitive type. The final three methods write out a string of bytes or characters to the stream—the first one as 8-bit bytes; the second as 16-bit Unicode characters; and the last, as a special Unicode stream (readable by DataInput's readUTF()).

NOTE

> The unsigned read methods in DataInput have no counterparts here. You can write out the data they need through DataOutput's signed methods because they accept int arguments and also because they write out the correct number of bits for the unsigned integer of a given size as a side effect of writing out the signed integer of that same size. The method that reads this integer must interpret the sign bit correctly; the writer's job is easy.

Now that you know what the interface that DataOutputStream implements looks like, look at it in action:

```
DataOutputStream  s    = new DataOutputStream(getNumericOutputStream());
long              size = getNumberOfItemsInNumericStream();

s.writeLong(size);

for (int  i = 0;  i < size;  ++i) {
    if (shouldProcessNumber(i)) {
        s.writeBoolean(true);     // should process this item
        s.writeInt(theIntegerForItemNumber(i));
        s.writeShort(theMagicBitFlagsForItemNumber(i));
        s.writeDouble(theDoubleForItemNumber(i));
    } else
        s.writeBoolean(false);
}
```

This example is the exact inverse of the example that was given for DataInput. Together, they form a pair that can communicate a particular array of structured primitive types across any stream (or transport layer). Use this pair as a jumping-off point whenever you need to do something similar.

In addition to the interface, the DataOutputStream class implements one self-explanatory utility method:

```
int   theNumberOfBytesWrittenSoFar = s.size();
```

Processing a File

One of the most common tasks in file input/output is to open a file, read and process it line-by-line, and output it again to another file. Here's a prototypical example of how that would be done in Java:

```
DataInput    aDI = new DataInputStream(new FileInputStream("source"));
DataOutput   aDO = new DataOutputStream(new FileOutputStream("dest"));
String       line;

while ((line = aDI.readLine()) != null) {
    StringBuffer  modifiedLine = new StringBuffer(line);

    . . .        // process modifiedLine in place
    aDO.writeBytes(modifiedLine.toString());
}
aDI.close();
aDO.close();
```

If you want to process the file byte-by-byte, use this code:

```
try {
    while (true) {
        byte  b = (byte) aDI.readByte();

        . . .           // process b in place
        aDO.writeByte(b);
    }
} finally {
    aDI.close();
    aDO.close();
}
```

The following two lines just copy the file:

```
try { while (true) aDO.writeByte(aDI.readByte()); }
finally { aDI.close(); aDO.close(); }
```

PrintStream

You might not realize it, but you already are intimately familiar with the use of two methods of the PrintStream class. That's because whenever you use these method calls

```
System.out.print(. . .)
System.out.println(. . .)
```

you are using a PrintStream instance located in System's class variable out to perform the output. System.err is also a PrintStream, and System.in is an InputStream.

NOTE On UNIX systems, these three streams will be attached to standard output (STDOUT), standard error (STDERR), and standard input (STDIN), respectively.

PrintStream is uniquely an output stream class (it has no corresponding input class). Because it usually is attached to a screen output device of some kind, it provides an implementation of flush(). It also provides the familiar close() and write() methods, as well as a plethora of choices for outputting the primitive types and Strings of Java:

```
public void   write(int b);
public void   write(byte[]  buffer, int  offset, int  length);
public void   flush();
public void   close();

public void   print(Object o);
public void   print(String s);
public void   print(char[]  buffer);
public void   print(char c);
public void   print(int i);
public void   print(long l);
public void   print(float f);
public void   print(double d);
public void   print(boolean b);

public void   println(Object o);
public void   println(String s);
public void   println(char[]  buffer);
public void   println(char c);
public void   println(int i);
public void   println(long l);
public void   println(float f);
public void   println(double d);
public void   println(boolean b);

public void   println(); // output a blank line
```

You also can wrap PrintStream around any output stream, just like a filter class:

```
PrintStream  s = new PrintStream(new FileOutputStream("Disco"));

s.println("Here's the first line of text in the file Disco.");
```

If you provide a second argument to the constructor for PrintStream, the argument is a boolean that specifies whether the stream should auto-flush. If true, a flush() is sent after each character is written (or for the three-argument form of write(), after a whole group of characters has been written).

The following sample program operates like the UNIX command `cat`, taking the standard input line-by-line and outputting it to the standard output:

```
import java.io.*;

public class  Cat {
    public static void  main(String argv[]) {
        DataInput  d = new DataInputStream(System.in);
        String     line;

      try {  while ((line = d.readLine()) != null)
            System.out.println(line);
        } catch (IOException  ignored) { }
    }
}
```

PipedOutputStream

Together, `PipedInputStream` and `PipedOutputStream` support a UNIX-pipe-like connection between two threads, implementing all of the careful synchronization that allows this sort of shared queue to operate safely. To set up the connection, use the following:

```
PipedInputStream    sIn  = PipedInputStream();
PipedOutputStream   sOut = PipedOutputStream(sIn);
```

One thread writes to `sOut`, and the other reads from `sIn`. By setting up two such pairs, the threads can communicate safely in both directions.

Related Classes

19

The other classes and interfaces in `java.io` supplement the streams to provide a complete I/O system:

- [ ] The `File` class abstracts "file" in a platform-independent way. Given a filename, it can respond to queries about the type, status, and properties of a file or directory in the file system.

- [ ] A `RandomAccessFile` class is created with a file, a filename, or a file descriptor. It combines in one class implementations of the `DataInput` and `DataOutput` interfaces, both tuned for random access to a file in the file system. In addition to these interfaces, `RandomAccessFile` provides certain traditional UNIX-like facilities, such as using `seek()` to go to a random point in the file.

- [ ] The `StreamTokenizer` class takes an input stream and produces a sequence of tokens. By overriding its various methods in your own subclasses, you can create powerful lexical parsers.

You can learn more about all of these other classes from the full API documentation that is included in the Java WorkShop Help pull-down menu.

Summary

Today, you learned about the general idea of streams and input streams based on byte arrays, files, pipes, sequences of other streams, and string buffers, as well as input filters for buffering, typed data, line numbering, and pushing-back characters. You also learned about the corresponding output streams for byte arrays, files, and pipes, and output filters for buffering and typed data, and the unique output filter used for printing.

Along the way, you became familiar with the fundamental methods all streams understand (such as read() and write()), as well as the unique methods many streams add to this repertoire. You learned about catching IOExceptions—especially the most useful of them, EOFException. Finally, you learned that the twice-useful DataInput and DataOutput interfaces form the heart of RandomAccessFile, one of the several utility classes that round out Java's input/output facilities.

Java streams provide a powerful base on which you can build multithreaded, streaming interfaces of the most complex kinds and the programs to interpret them. The higher-level Internet protocols and future services that your applets can build upon this base are limitless.

Q&A

Q In an early read() example, you did something with the variable byteOrMinus1 that seemed a little clumsy. Isn't there a better way? If not, why recommend the cast later?

A Yes, there is something a little odd about those statements. You might be tempted to try something like this instead:

```
while ((b = (byte) s.read()) != -1) {
    . . .     // process the byte b
}
```

The problem with this shortcut occurs when read() returns the value 0xFF (0377). Because this value is signed-extended before the test gets executed, it will appear to be identical to the integer value -1 that indicates end of stream. Only saving that value in a separate integer variable, and then casting it later, will accomplish the desired result. The cast to byte is recommended in the note for orthogonal reasons; storing integer values in correctly sized variables is always good style (and besides, read() should be returning something of byte size here and throwing an exception for the end of the stream).

19

Q What input streams in `java.io` actually implement `mark()`, `reset()`, and `markSupported()`?

A `InputStream` itself does. In their default implementations, `markSupported()` returns `false`, `mark()` does nothing, and `reset()` throws an exception. The only input stream in the current release that correctly supports marking is `BufferedInputStream`, which overrides these defaults. `LineNumberInputStream` implements `mark()` and `reset()`, but in the current release, it doesn't answer `markSupported()` correctly, so it looks as if it does not implement this method.

Q Why is `available()` useful, if it sometimes gives the wrong answer?

A First, for many streams, it gives the right answer. Second, for some network streams, its implementation might be sending a special query to discover some information you couldn't get any other way (for example, the size of a file being transferred by FTP). If you were displaying a progress bar for network or file transfers, for example, `available()` will often give you the total size of the transfer, and when it does not (usually by returning `0`), it will be obvious to you (and your users).

Q What's a good use for the `DataInput`/`DataOutput` pair of interfaces?

A One common use of such a pair is to convert objects into a form that can be stored for movement over a network. Each object implements read and write methods using these interfaces, effectively converting itself to a stream that later can be reconstituted on the other end into a copy of the original object.

FEATURED APPLET Today's Featured Applet

19

Today's featured applet is `Countdown` from Michael Hartman, an applet that counts down to a date and time that can be customized. The Java program uses image files for the elements of the countdown clock, and it uses mouse events to present a text message and make the applet into a hyperlink. The applet is based partially on the CTC5 countdown applet by Tom Carlson. Figure 19.1 shows an example of `Countdown` in action.

Files for `Countdown` are located on the CD-ROM in the `\BOOK\3RDPARTY\DAY19\` directory, including source code in the file `countdown.java`. To use `Countdown` on a Web page, place the class file `countdown.class` on your Web site. The site also must have the graphics files for each digit of the clock, the "T-" and "T+" images, and a blank digit. These range from `01cdb0.gif` to `91cdb0.gif` for the digits, and the remaining three files are `tplus.gif`, `tminus.gif`, and `blank.gif`. Place these files in the same directory as the Web page, or place them in a subdirectory listed in the `CODEBASE` parameter of the `<APPLET>` tag. The `<CODE>` tag should be `countdown.class`. Listing 19.1 shows the HTML tags used to run `Countdown` as it is shown in Figure 19.1.

Figure 19.1.

The Countdown *applet in action.*

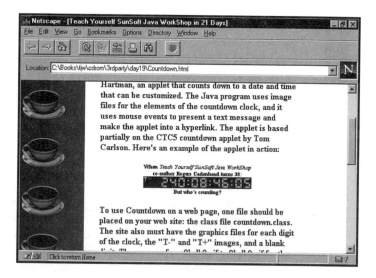

Listing 19.1. The `<APPLET>` tag and surrounding HTML tags for Countdown.

```
<center>
<font size=1>When <i>Teach Yourself SunSoft Java WorkShop</i><br>co-author
Rogers Cadenhead turns 30:</font><br>
<applet code="countdown.class" width=203 height=21>
<param name=text value="Click to return Home">
<param name=dest value="../index.html">
<param name=year value=1997>
<param name=month value=4>
<param name=day value=13>
<param name=hour value=8>
<param name=minute value=30>
</applet><br>
<font size=1>But who's counting?</font><br>
</center>
```

Countdown has eight parameters that can be customized within the `<APPLET>` tag, as follows:

☐ The text parameter is the text string to display when a mouse is dragged over the applet window.

☐ The dest parameter is the URL to load if the mouse is clicked on the applet.

☐ The year parameter is the full year to count down to.

☐ The month parameter is the month, as an integer, to count down to.

☐ The day parameter is the day to count down to.

☐ The hour parameter is the hour to count down to (optional).

☐ The minute parameter is the minute to count down to (optional).

☐ The second parameter is the second to count down to (optional).

More information on Countdown is available from Michael Hartman at the following URL:

`http://www.eng.auburn.edu/~hartmms/countdown.html`

More information on the CTC5 countdown applet is available from Tom Carlson at the following URL:

`http://www.ncsc.dni.us/ncsc/ctc5/java/Countdown.html`

19

Day **20**

Native Methods and Libraries

There are only two reasons that you might need to declare some of your methods to be native—that is, implemented by a language other than Java. The first and best reason to do so is to utilize a special capability of your computer or operating system that the Java class library does not already provide. Such capabilities include interfacing to new peripheral devices or plug-in cards or accessing a different type of networking. Two more concrete examples are acquiring real-time audio input from a microphone or using 3-D accelerator hardware in a library. Neither of these capabilities is provided to you by the current Java environment, so you must implement them outside Java in another language (currently C, or any language that can link with C).

The second reason to implement native methods is speed. This is often unnecessary, because you rarely need the raw speeds gained by this approach. It's even more rare to be unable to gain that speed in other ways (as you'll see later today). Using native methods in this case takes advantage of the fact that the current Java release does not perform as well on many tasks as an optimized

C program. For those tasks, you can write the part that needs to be faster in C and still use a larger Java shell of classes to hide this part from your users. The Java class library uses this approach for certain critical system classes to raise the overall level of efficiency in the system. As a user of the Java environment, you don't see any side effects of this approach (except, perhaps, a few classes or methods that are `final` that might not be otherwise).

Today, you'll learn about the following topics:

☐ `native` methods in Java—how to create them, make headers and stubs for them, and link them into a dynamically loadable library

☐ the language's built-in optimizations

☐ tricks you can use to make programs faster

The place to start, however, is with the reasons not to use `native` methods.

Disadvantages of `native` Methods

Once you decide to use `native` methods in your program, the advantages are gained at the expense of the portability of your Java code. Before, you had a program that could travel to any Java environment. Any new architectures or new operating systems written were irrelevant to your code. All it required was that the Java Virtual Machine be available, and it could run anywhere, anytime—now and in the future.

Now, however, you've created a library of native code that must be linked with your program to make it work properly. The first thing you lose is the program's ability to travel as an applet. No Java-capable browser currently in existence allows native code to be loaded with an applet for security reasons. The Java team has struggled to place as much functionality as possible into the `java` packages because they are the only environment you can count on when developing applets. (The `sun` packages, shipped primarily for use with stand-alone Java programs, are not always available to applets.)

NOTE

> Any classes that are written without native code should be able to be loaded with an applet, as long as they depend only on the `java` packages. Unfortunately, many of the `sun` packages contain classes that must use native code to provide crucial functionality that is missing from the `java` packages. Netscape and Microsoft also have introduced proprietary classes, and these use native code to extend Java at the price of lost platform independence.

20

Because the use of `native` methods prevents a program from being an applet, the program is limited to machines that have a Java Virtual Machine ported to their operating system. Also, because `native` methods often utilize aspects of the operating system, different source code might be needed for each operating system the program should run on. If changing the source is necessary, you can see that a considerable investment of resources is required to make the program available on multiple platforms.

The Illusion of Required Efficiency

Many times, programmers focus on speed of execution, but that energy and creativity often is better spent developing a concise, minimal set of classes and methods that are general, abstract, and reusable. If you spend most of your programming time on thinking and rethinking these fundamental goals and how to achieve them, you are developing code that will hold its usefulness in the future. If you spend your energy worrying about the speed that software will run right now on some computer, your work will be irrelevant after the 18 to 36 months it takes hardware to be fast enough to hide the minor inefficiencies in your program.

Efficiency should not be ignored altogether, however. Some of the great algorithms of computer science deal with solving hard or impossible problems in reasonable amounts of time, and writing your programs carelessly can lead to remarkably slow results. Carelessness, however, can as easily lead to incorrect, fragile, or nonreusable results.

NOTE

> There always are cases where you must be fanatical about efficiency in many parts of a set of classes. The Java class library itself is such a case, as is anything that must run in real-time for some critical real-world application. Such applications are rare, however.
>
> When speaking of a new kind of programming that must emerge, the language's developers like to invoke the four S's of Java: small, simple, safe, and secure. The feel of the Java language itself encourages the pursuit of clarity and the reduction of complexity. The intense pursuit of efficiency, which increases complexity and reduces clarity, is antithetical to these goals.

20

After you build a solid foundation, debug your classes, and your program works as you'd like it to, you can begin optimizing it.

Built-In Optimizations

Your next job is to see whether your release supports turning on the just-in-time compiler or using a Java-to-C translator, two things that can greatly increase performance if they have been implemented. Both are explained on Day 21, "Advanced Concepts."

Simple Optimization Tricks

If the just-in-time compiler and a Java-to-C translator aren't available, or they don't optimize your program enough for your taste, you can profile your applet or program as it runs to determine in which methods it spends the most time. Once you know this, you can begin to make targeted changes to your classes.

The Java interpreter has a command-line option that creates profile information, and it can be set from within Java WorkShop. You can use this option for any applications that you create; the field is located on the Project Manager's Run tabbed dialog box. When you use Project Tester to run the program, a file called java.prof is created that contains the output of the profile feature.

TIP

Before you begin making optimizations, you also might want to save a copy of your clean classes. As soon as computer speeds allow (or a major rewrite necessitates it), you can revert to these classes, which embody the best implementation of your program.

To begin optimizing the program, use the output of the profiler to identify the methods that consume most of the time. There are almost always just a few methods that take up the majority of the program's time, and often it is just a single method. If the time-consuming methods contain loops, examine the inner loops to see whether they do any of the following:

- ☐ Call methods that can be made final
- ☐ Call a group of methods that can be collapsed into a single method
- ☐ Create objects that can be reused rather than created anew each loop

Creating objects and calling methods are two areas that can be optimized as needed. For example, if a chain of four or more method calls is needed to reach a destination method's code, you can call directly to that destination method from the topmost method. This change might require adding a new instance variable to reference the object for that method call directly. A change of this kind often violates layering or encapsulation constraints and makes the code more complex. These are the prices you pay for added speed. If this kind of optimization and others you might have learned do not work, and the Java code still is too slow for your needs, you need to use native methods.

Writing native Methods

Suppose you have decided to add native methods to your program, and you already know which methods in which classes need to be native. To add these methods, on the Java side, all you need to do is the following:

1. Delete the method bodies of each method you picked (the body is all the code between the brackets { and } and the brackets themselves).
2. Replace the deleted code with a single semicolon (;).
3. Add the modifier native to the method's existing modifiers.
4. Add a static initializer to each class that now contains native methods to load the native code library you're about to build. (You can pick any name you like for this library—details follow.)

That's all you need to do in Java to specify a native method. Subclasses of any class containing your new native methods still can override them, and these new Java methods are called for instances of the new subclasses, just as you would expect. Unfortunately, what needs to be done in your native language environment is not so simple, as explained in the following sections.

NOTE

The following discussion assumes that C and UNIX are your language and environment. Some of the steps might differ slightly on your system, but such differences will be outlined in the notes surrounding the Java Developer's Kit documentation on native methods, available on the World Wide Web from the following URL:

http://java.sun.com/books/Series/Tutorial/native/index.html

This discussion parallels the documentation.

20

The Sample Class

Imagine a version of the Java environment that does not provide file input/output. Any Java program needing to use the file system first would have to write native methods to get access to the operating system primitives needed to do file input/output. This example combines simplified versions of two Java library classes, java.io.File and java.io.RandomAccessFile:

```
public class  SimpleFile {
    public static final  char    separatorChar = '>';
    private protected    String  path;
    private protected    int     fd;

    public  SimpleFile(String s) {
        path = s;
    }

    public String  getFileName() {
        int  index = path.lastIndexOf(separatorChar);

        return (index < 0) ? path : path.substring(index + 1);
    }

    public String  getPath() {
        return path;
    }

    public native boolean  open();
    public native void      close();
    public native int       read(byte[]  buffer, int  length);
    public native int       write(byte[]  buffer, int  length);

    static {
        System.loadLibrary("simple");  // runs when class first loaded
    }
}
```

NOTE

> The unusual separatorChar (>) is used to demonstrate what an imple-
> mentation might look like for a file system that didn't use any of the
> more common path separator conventions. Early Xerox computers used
> > as a separator, and several existing computer systems use strange
> separators today, so this is not that farfetched.

SimpleFile objects can be created and used in the usual way:

```
SimpleFile  f = new SimpleFile(">some>path>and>fileName");

f.open();
f.read(...);
f.write(...);
f.close();
```

The first thing to notice about the implementation of SimpleFile is how unremarkable the
first two-thirds of its Java code is. It looks just like any other class, with a class and an instance
variable, a constructor, and two normal method implementations. After this code, there are
four native method declarations. From previous discussions, you'll recognize these as normal

method declarations with the code block replaced by a semicolon and the modifier `native` added. You will be implementing these methods in C code later.

The last part of `SimpleFile` is a mysterious code fragment at the very end of the class. You might recognize the general construct here as a `static` initializer. Any code between the brackets is executed exactly once, when the class is first loaded into the system. You take advantage of that fact to run something you want to run only once—the loading of the native code library you will create later today. This ties together the loading of the class itself with the loading of its native code. If either fails for some reason, the other fails as well, guaranteeing that no partially set-up version of the class ever can be created.

Generating Header and Stub Files

In order to manipulate Java objects and data types in your C code, you need to include some special `.h` files. Most of these files are located in a subdirectory of your Java WorkShop directory called `include`. If you're a glutton for detail punishment, look at `native.h` in that directory in particular and all the headers it points to. Some of the special forms you need must be tailored to fit your class' methods precisely. That's where the `javah` tool comes in.

Using `javah`

To generate the headers you need for your `native` methods, first compile `SimpleFile` in Java WorkShop as you normally would, producing the file `SimpleFile.class`.

There is not a header-generation feature inside Java WorkShop's current release, so you have to use a command-line utility that comes with WorkShop's version of the Java Developer's Kit. This utility, `javah`, generates a header file for a specified class file. To generate a header file for `SimpleFile.class`, use the following command:

```
javah SimpleFile
```

TIP

If the class passed to `javah` is inside a package, the package name is attached to the beginning of the header file name (and to the structure names it generates inside that file), after replacing all dots (.) with underscores (_) in the package's full name. If `SimpleFile` had been contained in a hypothetical package called `acme.widgets.files`, `javah` would have generated a header file named `acme_widgets_files_ SimpleFile.h`, and the various names within the file would have been renamed in a similar manner. When running `javah`, you should pass it only the class name itself, and not the full filename, which has `.class` on the end.

20

The Header File

 Here's the output of `javah SimpleFile`:

```
/* DO NOT EDIT THIS FILE - it is machine generated */
#include <native.h>
/* Header for class SimpleFile */

#ifndef _Included_SimpleFile
#define _Included_SimpleFile
struct Hjava_lang_String;

typedef struct ClassSimpleFile {
#define SimpleFile_separatorChar 62L
struct Hjava_lang_String *path;
long fd;
} ClassSimpleFile;
HandleTo(SimpleFile);

extern /*boolean*/ long SimpleFile_open(struct HSimpleFile *);
extern void SimpleFile_close(struct HSimpleFile *);
extern long SimpleFile_read(struct HSimpleFile *,HArrayOfByte *,long);
extern long SimpleFile_write(struct HSimpleFile *,HArrayOfByte *,long);
#endif
```

> **NOTE** `HandleTo()` is a magic macro that uses the structures created at run time by the stubs you'll generate later today.

The members of the `struct` generated previously are in a one-to-one correspondence with the variables of your class. In order to bring an instance of your class gently into the land of C, use the macro `unhand()` (as in "unhand that object!"). For example, the `this` pseudo-variable in Java appears as a `struct HSimpleFile *` in the land of C, and to use any variables inside this instance (you), you must `unhand()` yourself first. You'll see some examples of this macro in a later section today.

Using `javah -stubs`

 To run interference between the Java world of objects, arrays, and other high-level constructs and the lower-level world of C, you need stubs. *Stubs* are pieces of glue code that automatically translate arguments and return values back and forth between the worlds of Java and C.

Stubs can be automatically generated by `javah`, just like the headers. There isn't much you need to know about the stubs file, just that it has to be compiled and linked with the C code you write to allow it to interface with Java properly. A stubs file (`SimpleFile.c`) is created by running `javah` on your class with the `-stubs` option.

20

NOTE

> One interesting side-effect of stub generation is the creation of *method signatures*, informally called method descriptions elsewhere. These signatures are quite useful; they can be passed to special C functions that allow you to call back into the Java world from C. You can use stub generation to learn what these signatures look like for different method arguments and return values, and then use that knowledge to call arbitrary Java methods from within your C code. Brief descriptions of these special C functions, along with further details, appear later today in the section, "Some Useful Functions."

The Stubs File

OUTPUT

The result of running `javah -stubs SimpleFile` is the following:

```c
/* DO NOT EDIT THIS FILE - it is machine generated */
#include <StubPreamble.h>

/* Stubs for class SimpleFile */
/* SYMBOL: "SimpleFile/open()Z", Java_SimpleFile_open_stub */
stack_item *Java_SimpleFile_open_stub(stack_item *_P_,struct execenv
➥*_EE_) {
    extern long SimpleFile_open(void *);
    _P_[0].i = SimpleFile_open(_P_[0].p);
    return _P_ + 1;
}
/* SYMBOL: "SimpleFile/close()V", Java_SimpleFile_close_stub */
stack_item *Java_SimpleFile_close_stub(stack_item *_P_,struct execenv
➥*_EE_) {
    extern void SimpleFile_close(void *);
    (void) SimpleFile_close(_P_[0].p);
    return _P_;
}
/* SYMBOL: "SimpleFile/read([BI)I", Java_SimpleFile_read_stub */
stack_item *Java_SimpleFile_read_stub(stack_item *_P_,struct execenv
➥*_EE_) {
    extern long SimpleFile_read(void *,void *,long);
    _P_[0].i = SimpleFile_read(_P_[0].p,((_P_[1].p)),((_P_[2].i)));
    return _P_ + 1;
}
/* SYMBOL: "SimpleFile/write([BI)I", Java_SimpleFile_write_stub */
stack_item *Java_SimpleFile_write_stub(stack_item *_P_,struct execenv
➥*_EE_) {
    extern long SimpleFile_write(void *,void *,long);
    _P_[0].i = SimpleFile_write(_P_[0].p,((_P_[1].p)),((_P_[2].i)));
    return _P_ + 1;
}
```

20

ANALYSIS Each comment line contains the method signature for one of the four `native` methods you're implementing. You can use one of these signatures to call into Java and run, for example, a subclass' overriding implementation of one of your `native` methods. More often, you'd learn and use a different signature to call some useful Java method from within C to get something done in the Java world.

You do this by calling a special C function in the Java run-time environment called `execute_java_dynamic_method()`. Its arguments include the target object of the method call and the method's signature. The general form of a fully qualified method signature is any/`package/name/ClassName/methodName(...)X`. (You can see several in the stub's output comments, where `SimpleFile` is the class name and there is no package name.) The `X` is a letter or string that represents the return type, and the "(...)" contains a string that represents each of the argument's types in turn. (Here are the letters and strings used, and the types they represent, in the example: `[T` is array of type `T`, `B` is byte, `I` is int, `V` is void, and `Z` is boolean.)

The method `close()`, which takes no arguments and returns `void`, is represented by the string `"SimpleFile/close()V"`. Its inverse, `open()`, returns a boolean instead and is represented by `"SimpleFile/open()Z."` Finally, `read()`, which takes a byte array and an int as its two arguments and returns an int, is `"SimpleFile/read([BI)I."`

Creating `SimpleFileNative.c`

Now you can, at last, write the C code for your Java `native` methods. The header file generated by `javah`, `SimpleFile.h`, gives you the prototypes of the four C functions you need to implement to make your native code complete. You then write some C code that provides the native facilities that your Java class needs (in this case, some low-level file input/output routines). Finally, you assemble all the C code into a new file, include a bunch of required (or useful) `.h` files, and name it `SimpleFileNative.c`. Here's the result:

```
#include "SimpleFile.h"       /* for unhand(), among other things */

#include <sys/param.h>        /* for MAXPATHLEN */
#include <fcntl.h>            /* for O_RDWR and O_CREAT */

#define LOCAL_PATH_SEPARATOR   '/'    /* UNIX */

static void  fixSeparators(char *p) {
    for (; *p != '\0';  ++p)
        if (*p == SimpleFile_separatorChar)
            *p = LOCAL_PATH_SEPARATOR;
}

long  SimpleFile_open(struct HSimpleFile  *this) {
    int    fd;
    char   buffer[MAXPATHLEN];
```

```
        javaString2CString(unhand(this)->path, buffer, sizeof(buffer));
        fixSeparators(buffer);
        if ((fd = open(buffer, O_RDWR | O_CREAT, 0664)) < 0)    /* UNIX open */
            return(FALSE);    /* or, SignalError() could "throw" an exception */
        unhand(this)->fd = fd;              /* save fd in the Java world */
        return(TRUE);
    }

    void SimpleFile_close(struct HSimpleFile *this) {
        close(unhand(this)->fd);
        unhand(this)->fd = -1;
    }

    long SimpleFile_read(struct HSimpleFile *this, HArrayOfByte *buffer,
    _ long count) {
        char *data    = unhand(buffer)->body;  /* get array data   */
        int  len      = obj_length(buffer);    /* get array length */
        int  numBytes = (len < count ? len : count);

        if ((numBytes = read(unhand(this)->fd, data, numBytes)) == 0)
            return(-1);
        return(numBytes);          /* the number of bytes actually read */
    }

    long SimpleFile_write(struct HSimpleFile *this, HArrayOfByte *buffer,
    _ long count) {
        char *data = unhand(buffer)->body;
        int  len   = obj_length(buffer);

        return(write(unhand(this)->fd, data, (len < count ? len : count)));
    }
```

After you finish writing your .c file, compile it by using your local C compiler. On some systems, you might need to specify special compilation flags that mean "make it relocatable and dynamically linkable."

 NOTE

If you don't have a C compiler, you might want to get a copy of the GNU C compiler (gcc), one of the best C compilers in the world, which runs on almost every machine and operating system on the planet. The best way to get gcc is to buy the "GNU release" on CD-ROM, the profits of which support the Free Software Foundation. You can find both the GNU CD-ROM and the Linux CD-ROM (which includes GNU) in places that sell software or technical books, or you can contact the FSF directly. If you can't afford either of the CD-ROMs, or you already own a CD-ROM but want the latest version of the GNU C compiler, you can download the gzip archive file from the following FTP site:

```
ftp://prep.ai.mit.edu/pub/gnu/gcc-2.7.2.tar.gz
```

20

> This archive contains all 7M of the latest gcc release. If you'd like to
> make a donation to the FSF, or buy gcc and its manual directly, you
> can e-mail them at gnu@prep.ai.mit.edu or call (617) 542-5942.

Some Useful Functions

When writing the C code for native implementations, a whole set of useful internal macros
and functions are available for accessing Java run-time structures. Several of them were used
in SimpleFileNative.c. The following brief digression will help you understand some of
them a little better.

WARNING

> Don't rely on the exact form given for any of the following macros and
> functions. Because they're all internal to Java run time, they're subject
> to change. Check to see what the latest versions of them look like in
> your Java release before using them.

NOTE

> The following brief descriptions are taken from an early release of Java
> and are listed to give you a taste of the capabilities. The main docu-
> mentation page of the JavaSoft Web site is at the following URL:
>
> http://java.sun.com/java.sun.com/doc/

The following returns a pointer to the data portion of an object and returns the length of an
array:

```
Object  *unhand(Handle *)
int      obj_length(HArray *)
```

The actual pointer type returned is not always Object *, but it varies, depending on the type
of Handle (or HArray).

The following finds a class (given its name), makes an array of characters of length length, and
allocates an array of the given length and type:

```
ClassClass    *FindClass(struct execenv *e, char  *name, bool_t  resolve)
HArrayOfChar  *MakeString(char  *string, long  length)
Handle        *ArrayAlloc(int  type, int  length)
```

Use this function to call a Java method from C:

```
long  execute_java_dynamic_method(ExecEnv *e, HObject *obj, char *method_name,
                                       ➥_char *signature, ...);
```

e is NULL to use the current environment. The target of the method call is obj. The method method_name has the given method signature. It can have any number of arguments and returns a 32-bit value (int, Handle *, or any 32-bit C type).

Use the following to call a Java constructor and a class method:

```
HObject  *execute_java_constructor(ExecEnv *e, char *classname, ClassClass *c,
                                       ➥_char *signature, ...);

long  execute_java_static_method(ExecEnv *e, ClassClass *c, char *method_name,
                                       ➥_char *signature, ...);
```

The target class is c; the rest of the arguments are the same as the arguments of the execute_java_dynamic method.

Calling the following posts a Java exception that is thrown when your native method is returned:

```
SignalError(0, JAVAPKG "ExceptionClassName", "message");
```

It is somewhat like the Java code:

```
throw new ExceptionClassName("message");
```

Finally, these are some useful string functions:

```
void  javaStringPrint(Hjava_lang_String *s)
int   javaStringLength(Hjava_lang_String *s)

Hjava_lang_String  *makeJavaString(char  *string, int  length)

char  *makeCString(Hjava_lang_String *s)
char  *allocCString(Hjava_lang_String *s)

unicode  *javaString2unicode(Hjava_lang_String *s, unicode  *buf, int  len)
char     *javaString2CString(Hjava_lang_String *s, char     *buf, int  len)
```

The first two methods print a Java String (like System.out.print()) and get its length, respectively. The third makes a Java String out of a C string. The fourth and fifth do the reverse, turning a Java String into a C string (allocated from temporary or heap storage, respectively). The final two methods copy a Java String into preexisting Unicode or ASCII C buffers.

20

Compiling the Stubs File

The final step you need to take in the C world is to compile the stubs file `SimpleFile.c` by using the same compilation flags you used for `SimpleFileNative.c`.

NOTE
> If you have several classes with `native` methods, you can include all their stubs in the same `.c` file, if you like. Of course, you might want to name it something else, such as `Stubs.c`, in that case.

You now are finished with all the C code that must be written and compiled to make your loadable native library.

A Native Library

Now you finally will be able to tie everything together and create the native library, `simple`, that was assumed to exist at the beginning of today's lesson.

Linking It All

It's time to link everything you've done into a single library file. This code looks a little different on each system that Java runs on, but here's the basic idea, in UNIX syntax:

```
cc -G SimpleFile.o SimpleFileNative.o -o simple
```

The `-G` flag tells the linker that you're creating a dynamically linkable library; the details differ from system to system.

NOTE
> By naming the library `simple`, you're disobeying a UNIX convention that dynamic library names should have the prefix `lib` and the suffix `.so` (on your system, these prefixes and suffixes might differ). You can call your library `libsimple.so` to obey the convention, if you like, but just for the clarity of this example, the simpler name was used.

Using Your Library

Now, when the Java class `SimpleFile` first is loaded into your program, the `System` class attempts to load the library named `simple`, which you just created. Look back at the Java code for `SimpleFile` to remind yourself.

How does it locate it? It calls the dynamic linker, which consults an environment variable named `LD_LIBRARY_PATH` that tells it which sequence of directories to search when loading new libraries of native code. Because the current directory is in Java's load path by default, you can leave `simple` in the current directory, and it will work just fine.

Summary

Today, you learned about the numerous disadvantages of using `native` methods, the many ways you can make your programs run faster, and also about the often illusory need for efficiency. There are times, however, when `native` methods are needed. You learned the procedure for creating `native` methods from both the Java and the C sides by generating header files and stubs, and by compiling and linking a full example.

After working your way through today's difficult material, you've mastered one of the most complex parts of the Java language. You now know how the Java run-time environment itself was created, and how to extend that powerful environment yourself at its lowest levels. As a reward, tomorrow we'll look under the hood at some of the hidden power of Java, and you can just sit back and enjoy the ride.

Q&A

Q Does the Java class library need to call `System.loadLibrary()` to load the built-in classes?

A No, you won't see any `loadLibrary()` calls in the implementation of any classes in the Java class library. That's because the Java team had the luxury of being able to statically link most of their code into the Java environment, something that makes sense only when you're in the unique position of providing an entire system, as they are. Your classes must dynamically link their libraries into an already-running copy of the Java system. This is, by the way, more flexible than static linking; it allows you to unlink old and relink new versions of your classes at any time, making updating them trivial.

Q Can I statically link my own classes into Java like the Java team did?

A You can, if you like, ask Sun Microsystems for the source code to the Java run-time environment itself, and as long as you obey the relatively straightforward legal restrictions on using that code, you can relink the entire Java system plus your classes. Your classes then are statically linked into the system, but you have to give everyone who wants to use your program this special version of the Java environment. Sometimes, if you have strong enough requirements, this is the only way to go, but most of the time, dynamic linking is not only good enough, but preferable.

20

Today's Featured Applet

Today's featured applet is MktView from the Softbear Company. The applet, which tracks stock values provided from an external source, is an example of how Java can be used to dynamically produce graphical information, and it shows an example of using a Common Gateway Interface to provide data for a Java program. Figure 20.1 shows an example of MktView in action.

Figure 20.1.

The MktView *applet in action.*

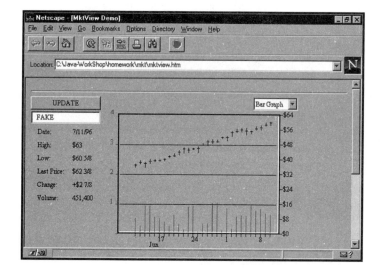

Files for MktView are located on the CD-ROM in the \BOOK\3RDPARTY\DAY20\ directory, including source code in the files MktView.java, MktModel.java, Pretty.java, Quote.java, QuoteView.java, and StackLayout.java. To use MktView on a Web page, place the six class files that correspond in name with the source code files on your Web site. Place these class files in the same directory as the Web page, or place them in a subdirectory listed in the CODEBASE parameter of the <APPLET> tag. The <CODE> tag should be MktView.class. Listing 20.1 shows the HTML tags used to run MktView as it was shown in Figure 20.1.

Listing 20.1. The <APPLET> tag for MktView.

```
<APPLET CODE=MktView.class WIDTH=500 HEIGHT=280>
<param name="stockName" value="FAKE">
<param name="nrDays" value="30">
</APPLET>
```

20

MktView takes the following two parameters:

☐ The stockName parameter is the name of the stock being tracked.

☐ The nrDays parameter specifies the number of days being tracked.

More information on the applet is available from Softbear at the following URL:

http://www.softbear.com/java/mktview/

20

Day 21

Advanced Concepts

As the last lesson of *Teach Yourself SunSoft Java WorkShop in 21 Days*, you will learn about the inner workings of the Java system. You'll find out about the following topics:

- ☐ Java's vision
- ☐ The Java Virtual Machine
- ☐ Bytecodes
- ☐ The garbage collector
- ☐ Security

The place to begin is with a look at the big picture of Java.

The Big Picture

When Java was released, the most ambitious of the design goals was to revolutionize the way software is written and distributed. The starting place for this revolution is the Internet, where the language's developers believe much of the interesting software of the future will live. To achieve such an ambitious goal, a large part of the Internet programming community must be marshaled behind the idea, and they must be given tools to help achieve it. The Java language offers its four S's— small, simple, safe, secure—and its flexible, Net-oriented environment. Its developers believe it can be the focal point for a new legion of programming activity.

Toward this end, Sun Microsystems has done something gutsy: they opened up their language to the public. What was originally a secret, multi-million-dollar research and development project has become a free, open, and relatively unencumbered technology standard. The company is literally giving it away and reserving only the rights it needs to maintain and develop the standard.

Any truly open standard must be supported by at least one excellent, freely available demonstration implementation, and Sun achieved this with its own Java Developer's Kit, along with support for Java applets in Netscape Navigator. The release of Java WorkShop is the next step in the company's plans to further popularize Java. Another important step in Java's growth is support for the language in Microsoft Internet Explorer 3.0, and the planned integration of Java into the next release of the Windows 95 operating system.

Efforts are also being made to duplicate the Java environment, provide support for Java programs in operating systems, and develop new operating systems built specifically for Java. Each of these developments can help it become a more robust and widespread standard.

A Powerful Vision

The computer science world is balkanized, with hundreds of languages, dozens of them widely used, that divide and separate programmers. Because Java is so simple, Internet-capable, and powerful, it has been thrust onto center stage as a way to bring all of this development together. Java deserves the attention. It is the natural outgrowth of ideas that have lain relatively dormant in the mainstream since the early 1970s, when they were hatched inside the Smalltalk group at Xerox PARC. The Smalltalk language invented the first object-oriented bytecode interpreter, and it pioneered many of the ideas that Java builds on today. Those efforts were not embraced over the intervening decades as a solution to the general problems of software development, however.

Today, largely because of the need for safe, executable content delivered over the World Wide Web, Java has generated interest in these ideas. This new vision of software is one in which the Internet becomes a vast collection of objects, classes, and the open APIs between them. These will be mixed and matched, as needed, to build larger software in ways it has never been designed before. The power of networks, and the Internet in particular, will be harnessed by the language.

The goals are ambitious, and the hype that surrounds Java at this time is immense (as shown by the number of books like this one written about Java in the last year). It has attracted a large number of programmers, developers, and managers who believe that Java deserves all the good press it has received.

The Java Virtual Machine

To achieve Java's goals, it must be ubiquitous. It must run on any computer and any operating system. To achieve this level of portability, Java must be precise not only about the language itself, but about the environment in which the language lives. You can see, from earlier in the book and in Appendix B, "Class Hierarchy Diagrams," that the Java environment includes a useful set of class packages and a freely available implementation of them. This structure takes care of a portion of what is needed, but it also is crucial to specify exactly how the run-time environment of Java behaves.

This final requirement is what has stymied many attempts at ubiquity in the past. If you base your system on any assumptions about what is beneath the run-time system, you lose. If you depend in any way on the computer or operating system, you lose. Java solves this problem by inventing an abstract computer of its own and running on that. This abstract computer is the *Java Virtual Machine.*

NEW TERM The Java Virtual Machine runs a special set of instructions called *bytecodes* that are a stream of formatted bytes, each with a precise specification that defines exactly what each bytecode does to the Java Virtual Machine. The Java Virtual Machine also is responsible for certain fundamental capabilities of Java, such as object creation and garbage collection.

Finally, in order to move bytecodes safely across the Internet, you need a bulletproof model of security and how to maintain it and a precise format for how this stream of bytecodes can be sent from one virtual machine to another. Each of these requirements is addressed in today's lesson.

 NOTE This discussion blurs the distinction between the run-time environment and the Java Virtual Machine. This blurring is intentional, but a little unconventional. Think of the Java Virtual Machine as providing all of the capabilities, even those that conventionally are assigned to the run-time environment. This book uses the words "run-time environment" and "Java Virtual Machine" interchangeably. Equating the two highlights the single environment that must be created to support Java. Much of the following description is based closely on the latest "Virtual Machine Specifications" documents.

21

An Overview

The following quote from the introduction to the Java Virtual Machine documentation is relevant to the vision outlined earlier:

> "The Java Virtual Machine specification has a purpose that is both like and unlike equivalent documents for other languages and abstract machines. It is intended to present an abstract, logical machine design free from the distraction of inconsequential details of any implementation. It does not anticipate an implementation technology or an implementation host. At the same time, it gives a reader sufficient information to allow implementation of the abstract design in a range of technologies.
>
> However, the intent of the…Java project is to create a language…that will allow the interchange over the Internet of "executable content," which will be embodied by compiled Java code. The project specifically does not want Java to be a proprietary language and does not want to be the sole purveyor of Java language implementations. Rather, we hope to make documents like this one and source code for our implementation freely available for people to use as they choose.
>
> This vision…can be achieved only if the executable content can be reliably shared between different Java implementations. These intentions prohibit the definition of the Java Virtual Machine from being fully abstract. Rather, relevant logical elements of the design have to be made sufficiently concrete to allow the interchange of compiled Java code. This does not collapse the Java Virtual Machine specification to a description of a Java implementation; elements of the design that do not play a part in the interchange of executable content remain abstract. But it does force us to specify, in addition to the abstract machine design, a concrete interchange format for compiled Java code."

The Java Virtual Machine specification consists of the following:

- ☐ The bytecode syntax, including opcode and operand sizes, values, and types, and their alignment and endian-ness
- ☐ The values of any identifiers (for example, type identifiers) in bytecodes or in supporting structures
- ☐ The layout of the supporting structures that appear in compiled Java code (for example, the constant pool)
- ☐ The Java .class file format

Each of these items is covered today.

Despite this degree of specificity, several elements of the design remain purposely abstract, including the following:

- [ ] The layout and management of the run-time data areas
- [ ] The particular garbage-collection algorithms, strategies, and constraints
- [ ] The compiler, development environment, and run-time extensions (apart from the need to generate and read valid Java bytecodes)
- [ ] Any optimizations performed, once valid bytecodes are received

These places are where the creativity of a virtual machine implementor has full rein.

The Fundamental Parts

The Java Virtual Machine can be divided into five fundamental pieces:

- [ ] A bytecode instruction set
- [ ] A set of registers
- [ ] A stack
- [ ] A garbage-collected heap
- [ ] An area for storing methods

Some of these pieces might be implemented by using an interpreter, a native binary code compiler, or even a hardware chip, but all these logical, abstract components of the Java Virtual Machine must be supplied in some form in every Java system.

NOTE

> The memory areas used by the Java Virtual Machine are not required to be at any particular place in memory, to be in any particular order, or even to use contiguous memory. However, all but the method area must be able to represent aligned 32-bit values (for example, the Java stack is 32 bits wide).

The Java Virtual Machine and its supporting code often are referred to as the run-time environment. When this book refers to something being done at run time, the Java Virtual Machine is what's doing it.

21

Java Bytecodes

The Java Virtual Machine instruction set is optimized to be small and compact. It is designed to travel across the Net and so has traded off speed-of-interpretation for space. (Given that both Net bandwidth and mass storage speeds increase less rapidly than CPU speed, this trade-off seems appropriate.)

As mentioned, Java source code is compiled into bytecodes and stored in a `.class` file. In Java WorkShop, compilation is handled by the Build Manager feature. It is not a traditional compiler because the source code is translated into bytecodes, a lower-level format that cannot be run directly, but must be further interpreted by each computer. Of course, it is exactly this level of indirection that buys you the power, flexibility, and extreme portability of Java code.

NOTE

> Later today you also will learn about the "just-in-time" compiler, which acts more like the back end of a traditional compiler. The use of the same word "compiler" for these two different pieces of Java technology is unfortunate, but somewhat reasonable, because each is really one-half of a more traditional compiler (either the front end or the back end).

A bytecode instruction consists of a one-byte opcode that serves to identify the instruction involved and zero or more operands, each of which may be more than one byte long, that encode the parameters the opcode requires.

NOTE

> When operands are more than one byte long, they are stored in big-endian order, high-order byte first. These operands must be assembled from the byte stream at run time. For example, a 16-bit parameter appears in the stream as two bytes so that its value is `first_byte * 256 + second_byte`. The bytecode instruction stream is only byte-aligned, and alignment of any larger quantities is not guaranteed (except for within the special bytecodes `lookupswitch` and `tableswitch`, which have special alignment rules of their own).

Bytecodes interpret data in the run-time memory areas as belonging to a fixed set of types. These types are the primitive types you've seen several times before: several signed integer types (8-bit `byte`, 16-bit `short`, 32-bit `int`, 64-bit `long`), one unsigned integer type (16-bit `char`), and two signed floating-point types (32-bit `float`, 64-bit `double`), plus the type "reference to an object" (a 32-bit pointer-like type). Some special bytecodes (for example, the

21

dup instructions), treat run-time memory areas as raw data, without regard to type. This is the exception, however.

These primitive types are distinguished and managed by the compiler, not by the Java run-time environment. These types are not "tagged" in memory, and thus cannot be distinguished at run time. Different bytecodes are designed to handle each of the various primitive types uniquely, and the compiler carefully chooses from this palette based on its knowledge of the types stored in the various memory areas. For example, when adding two integers, the compiler generates an `iadd` bytecode; for adding two floats, `fadd` is generated.

Registers

 The registers of the Java Virtual Machine are just like the registers inside a "real" computer. *Registers* hold the machine's state, affect its operation, and are updated after each bytecode is executed.

The following are the Java registers:

☐ `pc`, the program counter, which indicates what bytecode is being executed

☐ `optop`, a pointer to the top of the operand stack, which is used to evaluate all arithmetic expressions

☐ `frame`, a pointer to the execution environment of the current method, which includes an activation record for this method call and any associated debugging information

☐ `vars`, a pointer to the first local variable of the currently executing method

The Java Virtual Machine defines these registers to be 32 bits wide.

NOTE

> Because the Java Virtual Machine is primarily stack-based, it does not use any registers for passing or receiving arguments. This is a conscious choice skewed toward bytecode simplicity and compactness. It also aids efficient implementation on register-poor architectures, which most of today's computers are, unfortunately. Perhaps when the majority of CPUs out there are a little more sophisticated, this choice will be re-examined, though simplicity and compactness might still be reason enough!
>
> By the way, the `pc` register also is used when the run time handles exceptions; `catch` clauses ultimately are associated with ranges of the `pc` within a method's bytecodes.

21

The Stack

NEW TERM The Java Virtual Machine is stack-based. The *stack* is used to supply parameters to bytecodes and methods and to receive results back from them. A Java stack frame is similar to the stack frame of a conventional programming language; it holds the state for a single method call. Frames for nested method calls are stacked on top of this frame.

Each stack frame contains three possibly empty sets of data: the local variables for the method call, its execution environment, and its operand stack. The sizes of these first two sets are fixed at the start of a method call, but the operand stack varies in size as bytecodes are executed in the method. Local variables are stored in an array of 32-bit slots, indexed by the register `vars`. Most types take up one slot in the array, but the `long` and `double` types each take up two slots.

NOTE

Long and double values, stored or referenced through an index N, take up the 32-bit slots[ ]and[ ]+ 1. These 64-bit values thus are not guaranteed to be 64-bit-aligned. Implementors are free to decide the appropriate way to divide these values among the two slots.

The execution environment in a stack frame helps to maintain the stack itself. It contains a pointer to the previous stack frame, a pointer to the local variables of the method call, and pointers to the stack's current "base" and "top." Additional debugging information also can be placed into the execution environment.

The operand stack, a 32-bit first-in-first-out (FIFO) stack, is used to store the parameters and return values of most bytecode instructions. For example, the `iadd` bytecode expects two integers to be stored on the top of the stack. It pops them, adds them together, and pushes the resulting sum back onto the stack.

Each primitive data type has unique instructions that know how to extract, operate, and push back operands of that type. For example, `long` and `double` operands take two slots on the stack, and the special bytecodes that handle these operands take this into account. It is illegal for the types on the stack and the instruction operating on them to be incompatible (the compiler outputs bytecodes that always obey this rule).

NOTE

The top of the operand stack and the top of the overall Java stack are almost always the same. Thus, "the stack" refers to both stacks collectively.

21

The Heap

 The *heap* is that part of memory from which newly created instances (objects) are allocated. The heap often is assigned a large, fixed size when the Java run-time system is started, but on systems that support virtual memory, it can grow as needed, in a nearly boundless fashion.

Because objects automatically are garbage-collected in Java, programmers do not have to (and, in fact, cannot) manually free the memory allocated to an object when they are finished using it. Java objects are referenced indirectly in the run-time environment, through handles, which are a kind of pointer into the heap. Because objects are never referenced directly, parallel garbage collectors can be written that operate independently of your program, moving around objects in the heap at will. You'll learn more about garbage collection later.

The Method Area

Like the compiled code areas of conventional programming language environments or the TEXT segment in a UNIX process, the method area stores the Java bytecodes that implement almost every method in the Java system. (Remember that some methods might be native, and thus implemented, for example, in C.) The method area also stores the symbol tables needed for dynamic linking and any other information that debuggers or development environments might want to associate with each method's implementation.

> **NOTE**
>
> A native method is just like anything else that is called native in Java. It means that code outside of the Java language is involved, usually C.

Because bytecodes are stored as byte streams, the method area is aligned on byte boundaries. (The other areas all are aligned on 32-bit word boundaries.)

The Constant Pool

In the heap, each class has a constant pool attached to it. Usually created by the compiler, these constants encode all names used by any method in a class, such as variables and methods. The class contains a count of how many constants there are and an offset that specifies how far into the class description itself the array of constants begins. These constants are typed through specially coded bytes and have a precisely defined format when they appear in the .class file for a class. Later today, a little of this file format is covered, but everything is specified fully by the Java Virtual Machine specifications.

21

Limitations

The Java Virtual Machine, as currently defined, places some restrictions on legal Java programs by virtue of the choices it has made (some were previously described, and more will be detailed later today). These limitations and their implications are as follows:

- ☐ 32-bit pointers, which imply that the Java Virtual Machine can address only 4G of memory

- ☐ Unsigned 16-bit indices into the exception, line number, and local variable tables, which limit the size of a method's bytecode implementation to 64K

- ☐ Unsigned 16-bit indices into the constant pool, which limits the number of constants in a class to 64K (a limit on the complexity of a class)

In addition, Sun's implementation of the Java Virtual Machine uses so-called _quick bytecodes, which further limit the system. Unsigned 8-bit offsets into objects might limit the number of methods in a class to 256, and unsigned 8-bit argument counts limit the size of the argument list to 255 32-bit words. (Although this means that you can have up to 255 arguments of most types, you can have only 127 of them if they're all long or double.)

Bytecodes in More Detail

One of the main tasks of the Java Virtual Machine is the fast, efficient execution of the Java bytecodes in methods. Unlike in the discussion yesterday about generality versus efficiency, this is a case where speed is of the upmost importance. Every Java program suffers from a slow implementation here, so the run-time environment must use as many tricks as possible to make bytecodes run fast. The key is that Java programmers must not be able to see these tricks in the behavior of their programs. A Java run-time implementor must be extremely clever to accomplish this goal.

The Bytecode Interpreter

A bytecode interpreter examines each opcode byte (bytecode) in a method's bytecode stream in turn and executes a unique action for that bytecode. This process might consume further bytes for the operands of the bytecode and might affect which bytecode will be examined next. The interpreter operates like the hardware CPU in a computer, which examines memory for instructions to carry out in exactly the same manner. It is the software CPU of the Java Virtual Machine.

Your first, naive attempt to write such a bytecode interpreter almost would certainly be disastrously slow. The inner loop, which dispatches one bytecode each time through the loop, is notoriously difficult to optimize. Smart people have been thinking about this problem, in

21

one form or another, for more than 20 years. Luckily, they've gotten results, all of which can be applied to Java.

The final result is that the interpreter shipped in the current release of Java has an extremely fast inner loop. On even a relatively slow computer, this interpreter can perform more than 590,000 bytecodes per second! This is really quite good, because the CPU in that computer does only about 30 times better using hardware. This interpreter is fast enough for most Java programs (those requiring more speed always can use `native` methods), but what if a smart implementor wants to do better?

The Just-in-Time Compiler

About a decade ago, a clever trick was discovered by Peter Deutsch while trying to make Smalltalk run faster. He called it "dynamic translation" during interpretation. Sun calls it "just-in-time" compiling.

The trick is to notice that the really fast interpreter you've just written (in C, for example) already has a useful sequence of native binary code for each bytecode that it interprets: *the binary code that the interpreter itself is executing.* Because the interpreter already has been compiled from C into native binary code, for each bytecode that it interprets, it passes through a sequence of native code instructions for the hardware CPU on which it is running. By saving a copy of each binary instruction as it "goes by," the interpreter can keep a running log of the binary code it *itself* has run to interpret a bytecode. It can just as easily keep a log of the set of bytecodes that it ran to interpret an entire method.

You take that log of instructions and optimize it, just as a smart compiler does. This eliminates redundant or unnecessary instructions from the log and makes it look just like the optimized binary code that a good compiler might have produced.

NOTE
> The compiled look of the code is where the name compiler comes from in the just-in-time compiler, but the just-in-time compiler is really only the back end of a traditional compiler—the part that does code generation. By the way, the front end here is the Java compiler.

The next time that method is run (in exactly the same way), the interpreter simply can execute directly the stored log of binary native code. Because this process optimizes out the inner-loop overhead of each bytecode, as well as any other redundancies between the bytecodes in a method, it can gain a factor of 10 or more in speed. An experimental version of this technology at Sun has shown that Java programs using it can run as fast as compiled C programs. Borland and Microsoft have written "just-in-time" compilers that are running Java programs at much faster speeds than interpreted Java is capable of.

21

NOTE

> The parenthetical in the last paragraph, "(in exactly the same way)," is needed for this reason: If anything is different about the input to the method, it takes a different path through the interpreter and must be relogged. (There are sophisticated versions of this technology that solve this difficulty and others.) The cache of native code for a method must be invalidated whenever the method has changed, and the interpreter must pay a small up-front cost each time a method is run for the first time. However, these small bookkeeping costs are far outweighed by the amazing gains in speed that are possible.

The current release of Java WorkShop does not have a just-in-time compiler feature, although one is being developed at Sun. The latest details on new development tools are available in the Developer's Corner section of the JavaSoft Web site at the following URL:

```
http://java.sun.com
```

Java-to-C Translation

Another, simpler trick, which works well whenever you have a good, portable C compiler on each system that runs your program, is to translate the bytecodes into C and then compile the C into binary native code. If you wait until the first use of a method or class, and then perform this translation as an invisible optimization, it gains you an additional speedup over the approach outlined previously, without the Java programmer needing to know about it.

Of course, this approach limits you to systems with a C compiler, but there are extremely good, freely available C compilers. In theory, your Java code might be able to travel with its own C compiler or know where to pull one from the Net as needed, for each new computer and operating system it faced.

As an example, if you're using Java to write a server that lives only on your computer, it might be appropriate to use Java for its flexibility in writing and maintaining the server (and for its capability of dynamically linking new Java code on the fly), and then to run a java2c utility by hand to translate the basic server itself entirely into native code. You could link the Java run-time environment into that code so that your server remains a fully capable Java program, but it's now an extremely fast one. An experimental version of the java2c translator inside Sun shows that it can reach the speed of compiled and optimized C code. This is the best that you can hope to do!

21

The Garbage Collector

Decades ago, programmers in both the Lisp and the Smalltalk communities realized how valuable it is to be able to ignore memory deallocation. They realized that although allocation is fundamental, deallocation is forced on the programmer by the laziness of the system, which should be able to figure out what is no longer useful and get rid of it. In relative obscurity, these pioneering programmers developed a whole series of garbage collectors to perform this job, each version getting more sophisticated and efficient. Finally, now that the mainstream programming community has begun to recognize the value of this automated technique, Java can become the first widespread application of the technology those pioneers developed.

The Problem

Imagine that you're a programmer in a C-like language. Each time you create something dynamically in such a language, you are completely responsible for tracking the life of this object throughout your program and mentally deciding when it will be safe to deallocate it. This task can be quite difficult, and sometimes impossible, because any of the other libraries or methods you've called might have squirreled away a pointer to the object without your knowledge. When it becomes impossible to know, you simply choose never to deallocate the object, or at least to wait until every library and method call involved has completed, which could be nearly as long.

The uneasy feeling you get when writing such code is a natural, healthy response to what is inherently an unsafe and unreliable style of programming. If you, and everyone who writes every library and method you call, have tremendous discipline, you can, in principle, survive this responsibility without too many mishaps. But aren't you human? Aren't they? There must be some small slips in this perfect discipline due to error. What's worse, such errors are virtually undetectable, as anyone who's tried to hunt down a stray pointer problem in C will tell you. What about the thousands of programmers who don't have that sort of discipline?

Another way to ask this question is: Why should any programmers be forced to have this discipline, when it is entirely possible for the system to remove this heavy burden from their shoulders? Software engineering estimates have shown recently that for every 55 lines of production C-like code in the world, there is one bug. This means that your electric razor has about 80 bugs, and your TV, 400. Soon they will have even more, because the size of this kind of embedded computer software is growing exponentially. When you begin to think of how much C-like code is in your car's engine, it should make you a little nervous.

Many of these errors are due to the misuse of pointers, by misunderstanding or by accident, and to the early, incorrect freeing of allocated objects in memory. Java addresses both of these issues by eliminating explicit pointers from the Java language altogether and by implementing an automatic garbage collector.

21

The Solution

Imagine a run-time system that tracks each object you create, notices when the last reference to it has vanished, and frees the object for you. How could such a thing work?

One brute-force approach, tried early in the days of garbage collecting, is to attach a reference counter to every object. When the object is created, the counter is set to 1. Each time a new reference to the object is made, the counter is incremented, and each time such a reference disappears, the counter is decremented. Because all such references are controlled by the language, as variables and assignments, for example, the compiler can tell whenever an object reference might be created or destroyed, just as it does in handling the scoping of local variables. Thus, it can assist with this task. The system itself holds onto a set of root objects that are considered too important to be freed. The class Object is one example of such an object. Finally, all that's needed is to test after each decrement whether the counter has hit 0. If it has, the object is freed.

If you think carefully about this approach, you soon will convince yourself that it definitely is correct when it decides to free anything. It is so simple that you can immediately tell that it will work. The low-level hacker in you also might feel that if it's that simple, it's probably not fast enough to run at the lowest level of the system—and you'd be right.

Think about all of the stack frames, method arguments, return values, and local variables created in the course of even a few hundred milliseconds of a program's life. For each of these tiny, nano-steps in the program, an extra increment (at best) or decrement, test, and deallocation (at worst) will be added to the running time of the program. The first garbage collectors were slow enough that many predicted they never could be used at all!

Luckily, a whole generation of smart programmers has invented a big bag of tricks to solve these overhead problems. One trick is to introduce special "transient object" areas that don't need to be reference counted. The best of these generational scavenging garbage collectors today can take less than three percent of the total time of your program—a remarkable feat if you realize that many other language features, such as loop overheads, can be as large or larger!

Other problems exist with garbage collection. If you are constantly freeing and reclaiming space in a program, won't the heap of objects soon become fragmented, with small holes everywhere and no room to create new, large objects? Because the programmer is now free from the chains of manual deallocation, won't they create even more objects than usual?

What's worse, there is another way that this simple reference counting scheme is inefficient, in space rather than time. If a long chain of object references eventually comes full circle, back to the starting object, each object's reference count remains at least 1 forever. None of these objects ever will be freed!

NEW TERM Together, these problems imply that a good garbage collector must, every once in a while, step back to compact or to clean up wasted memory. *Compaction* occurs when a garbage collector steps back and reorganizes memory, eliminating the holes created by fragmentation. Compacting memory is simply a matter of repositioning objects one-by-one into a new, compact grouping that places them all in a row, leaving all of the free memory in the heap in one big piece.

NEW TERM Cleaning up the circular garbage still lying around after reference counting is called *marking and sweeping*. A mark-and-sweep of memory involves first marking every root object in the system and then following all of the object references inside those objects to new objects to mark, and so on, recursively. Then, when you have no more references to follow, you sweep away all of the unmarked objects, and compact memory as before.

The good news is that this compaction solves the space problems you were having. The bad news is that when the garbage collector does these operations, a nontrivial amount of time passes during which your program is unable to run—all its objects are being marked, swept, rearranged, and so forth, in what seems like an uninterruptible procedure. Your first hint to a solution is the word "seems."

Garbage collecting can be done a little at a time, between or in parallel with normal program execution, thus dividing up the large amount of time needed into numerous so-small-you-don't-notice-them chunks of time that happen between the cracks. (Of course, years of smart thinking went into the abstruse algorithms that make all of this possible!)

One final problem that might worry you a little has to do with these object references. Aren't these pointers scattered throughout your program and not just buried in objects? Even if they're only in objects, don't they have to be changed whenever the object they point to is moved by these procedures? The answer to both of these questions is a resounding yes, and overcoming this problem is the final hurdle to making an efficient garbage collector.

There are really only two choices. The first, brute force, assumes that all of the memory containing object references needs to be searched on a regular basis, and whenever the object references found by this search match objects that have moved, the old reference is changed. This assumes that there are hard pointers in the heap's memory—ones that point directly to other objects. By introducing various kinds of soft pointers, including pointers that are like forwarding addresses, the algorithm improves greatly. Although these brute-force approaches sound slow, modern computers can do them fast enough to be useful.

21

NOTE

> You might wonder how the brute-force techniques identify object references. In early systems, references were tagged specially with a pointer bit, so they could be unambiguously located. Now, so-called conservative garbage collectors assume that if it looks like an object reference, it is—at least for the purposes of the mark and sweep. Later, when trying to update the reference, they can find out whether it is an object reference.

The final approach to handling object references, and the one Java currently uses, is also one of the first ones tried. It involves using 100-percent soft pointers. An object reference is actually a handle, sometimes called an OOP, to the real pointer, and a large object table exists to map these handles into the actual object reference. Although this approach does introduce extra overhead on almost every object reference (some of which can be eliminated by clever tricks, as you might guess), it's not too high a price to pay for this incredibly valuable level of indirection.

This indirection allows the garbage collector, for example, to mark, sweep, move, or examine one object at a time. Each object can be independently moved out from under a running Java program by changing only the object table entries. This approach not only allows the step back phase to happen in the tiniest steps, but it makes a garbage collector that runs literally in parallel with your program much easier to write. The Java garbage collector is an example of a garbage collector that can run in parallel with other programs.

WARNING

> You need to be careful about garbage collection when you're doing critical, real-time programs, although that probably will be a rare case for most Java applet and application programmers.

Java's Parallel Garbage Collector

Java applies almost all of these advanced techniques to give you a fast, efficient, parallel garbage collector. Running in a separate thread, it silently cleans up the Java environment of almost all trash (it is conservative) in the background, is efficient in both space and time, and never steps back for more than a small amount of time. You should never need to know it's there.

By the way, if you want to force a full mark-and-sweep garbage collection to happen soon, you can do so by calling the System.gc() method. You might want to do this if you just freed up a majority of the heap's memory in circular garbage and want it all taken away quickly. You might also call this method whenever you're idle as a hint to the system about when it would be best to come and collect the garbage. This meta knowledge is rarely needed by the system, however. Ideally, you never will notice the garbage collector.

The Security Story

The security of Java programs, especially applets, is a legitimate concern. It is one of the major technical stumbling blocks to ubiquity and code sharing, two of the goals mentioned earlier in today's lesson. Sun Microsystems, the developers of Java, have made networks the central theme of its software for more than a decade. Providing security is central to its future, because global networks are useless without good security. Because of the obvious risk inherent in Java applets, security has been an integral part of the language's design and implementation.

Java's Security Model

Java protects against potentially damaging or malicious Java code through a series of interlocking defenses that together form an imposing barrier to all such attacks.

WARNING

No security system will protect a user from ignorance or carelessness. The kind of person who blindly downloads binary executables from the Internet browser and runs them is already in more danger than Java ever will pose. Internet users must educate themselves about the possible threats that exist—viruses, trojan horses, and other damaging material. Downloading "auto-running macros" or reading e-mail with "executable attachments" is an especially foolhardy activity.

Java does not introduce any new dangers, but by being the first mainstream use of executable and mobile code on the Net, it has made people aware of the dangers that always have been there. Java is already, as you will soon see, much less dangerous than any of these common activities on the Net, and Java can be made safer still over time.

A good rule of thumb on the Net is not to download an executable program from anyone other than trusted individuals and companies. If you don't care about losing all the data on your hard drive, or about your privacy, you can do anything you like. Fortunately, Java allows you to relax that law. You can run Java applets from anyone, anywhere, in relative safety.

21

Java's powerful security mechanisms act at four different levels of the system architecture. First, the Java language itself was designed to be safe, and the Java compiler ensures that source code doesn't violate these safety rules. Second, all bytecodes executed by the run-time environment are screened to be sure that they also obey these rules. This layer guards against having an altered compiler produce code that violates the safety rules. Third, the class loader ensures that classes don't violate name space or access restrictions when they are loaded into the system. Finally, API-specific security prevents applets from doing destructive things. This final layer depends on the security and integrity guarantees from the other three layers.

The Language and the Compiler

The Java language and its compiler are the first line of defense. Java was designed to be a safe language. Most other C-like languages have facilities to control access to objects, but they also have ways to forge access to objects (or to parts of objects), usually by using pointers and misusing them. This capability introduces two fatal security flaws to any system built on these languages. One is that no object can protect itself from outside modification, duplication, or spoofing (others pretending to be that object). Another is that a language with powerful pointers is more likely to have serious bugs that compromise security. These pointer bugs, where a "runaway pointer" starts modifying some other object's memory, were responsible for most of the public and not-so-public security problems on the Internet this past decade.

Java eliminates these threats by eliminating pointers from the language altogether. Object references are like pointers, but they are carefully controlled to be safe. They are unforgeable, and all casts are checked for legality before being allowed. In addition, powerful new array facilities in Java not only help to offset the loss of pointers, but add safety by strictly enforcing array bounds, catching more bugs for the programmer—bugs that, in other languages, might lead to unexpected and exploitable problems.

The language definition, and the compilers that enforce it, create a powerful barrier to any malicious Java program. Because an overwhelming majority of the "Net-savvy" software on the Internet might soon be Java, its safe language definition and compilers help to guarantee that most of this software has a solid, secure base. With fewer bugs, Net software will be more predictable—a property that thwarts attacks.

Verifying the Bytecodes

What if that malicious programmer gets a little more determined and rewrites the Java compiler to suit his nefarious purposes? The Java run-time environment, getting the lion's share of its bytecodes from the Net, never can tell whether those bytecodes were generated by a "trustworthy" compiler. Therefore, it must verify that they meet all of the safety requirements.

Before running any bytecodes, the run-time environment subjects them to a rigorous series of tests that vary in complexity from simple format checks all the way to running a theorem prover to make certain that they are playing by the rules. These tests verify that the bytecodes do not forge pointers, violate access restrictions, access objects as other than what they are (InputStreams always are used as InputStreams, and never as anything else), call methods with inappropriate argument values or types, nor overflow the stack.

Consider the following Java code sample:

```
public class VectorTest {
    public int  array[];

    public int  sum() {
        int[]  localArray = array;
        int    sum        = 0;

        for (int  i = localArray.length;  —i >= 0;  )
            sum += localArray[i];
        return sum;
    }
}
```

The bytecodes generated when this code is compiled look something like the following:

aload_0	Load this
getfield #10	Load this.array
astore_1	Store in localArray
iconst_0	Load 0
istore_2	Store in sum
aload_1	Load localArray
arraylength	Get its length
istore_3	Store in i
A: iinc 3 -1	Subtract 1 from i
iload_3	Load i
iflt B	Exit loop if < 0
iload_2	Load sum
aload_1	Load localArray
iload_3	Load i
iaload	Load localArray[i]
iadd	Add sum
istore_2	Store in sum
goto A	Do it again
B: iload_2	Load sum
ireturn	Return it

21

NOTE

> The examples and descriptions in this section of the book are paraphrased from the tremendously informative security paper in the alpha Java release. You are encouraged to read the latest version of this document in newer releases if you want to follow the ongoing Java security story.

Extra Type Information and Requirements

Java bytecodes encode more type information than strictly is necessary for the interpreter. Even though, for example, the aload and iload opcodes do exactly the same thing, aload always is used to load an object reference and iload is used to load an integer. Some bytecodes (such as getfield) include a symbol table reference, and that symbol table has even more type information. This extra type information allows the run-time system to guarantee that Java objects and data aren't manipulated illegally.

Conceptually, before and after each bytecode is executed, every slot in the stack and every local variable has some type. This collection of type information, all of the slots and local variables, is called the *type state* of the execution environment. An important requirement of the Java type state is that it must be determinable statically by induction—that is, before any program code is executed. As a result, as the run-time systems read bytecodes, each is required to have the following inductive property: Given only the type state before the execution of the bytecode, the type state afterward must be fully determined.

Given straight-line bytecodes (no branches), and starting with a known stack state, the state of each slot in the stack therefore is always known. For example, starting with an empty stack:

iload_1	Load integer variable. Stack type state is I.
iconst 5	Load integer constant. Stack type state is II.
iadd	Add two integers, producing an integer. Stack type state is I.

NOTE

> Smalltalk and PostScript bytecodes do not have this restriction. Their more dynamic type behavior does create additional flexibility in those systems, but Java needs to provide a secure execution environment. It therefore must know all types at all times, in order to guarantee a certain level of security.

21

Another requirement made by the Java run-time environment is that when a set of bytecodes can take more than one path to arrive at the same point, all such paths must arrive there with exactly the same type state. This strict requirement implies, for example, that compilers cannot generate bytecodes that load all the elements of an array onto the stack. (Because each time through such a loop the stack's type state changes, the start of the loop—the same point in multiple paths—would have more than one type state, which is not allowed.)

The Verifier

Bytecodes are checked for compliance with all of these requirements by a part of the run-time environment called the *verifier*. Using the extra type information in a .class file, the verifier examines each bytecode in turn, constructing the full type state as it goes, and verifies that all of the types of parameters, arguments, and results are correct. Thus, the verifier acts as a gatekeeper to your run-time environment, letting in only those bytecodes that pass muster.

WARNING

> The verifier is the crucial piece of Java's security, and it depends on your having a correctly implemented run-time system. As of this writing, only Sun is producing Java run-time systems, and theirs are secure. In the future, however, you should be careful when downloading or buying another company or individual's version of the Java run-time environment. Eventually, Sun will implement validation suites for run-time environments, compilers, and so forth to be sure that they are safe and correct. In the meantime, caveat emptor! Your run-time environment is the base on which all of the rest of Java's security is built, so make sure it is a good, solid, secure base.

When bytecodes have passed the verifier, they are guaranteed not to do the following: cause any operand stack under- or overflows; use parameter, argument, or return types incorrectly; illegally convert data from one type to another (from an integer to a pointer, for example); nor access any object's fields illegally (that is, the verifier checks that the rules for public, private, package, and protected are obeyed).

As an added bonus, because the interpreter now can count on all of these facts being true, it can run much faster than before. All the required checks for safety have been done up front, so it can run at full throttle. In addition, object references now can be treated as capabilities, because they are unforgeable; capabilities allow, for example, advanced security models for file input/output and authentication to be safely built on top of Java.

21

NOTE

> Because you now can trust that a `private` variable really is private, and that no bytecode can perform some magic with casts to extract information from it (such as your credit card number), many of the security problems that might arise in other, less safe environments vanish! These guarantees also make erecting barriers against destructive applets possible and easier. Because the Java system doesn't have to worry about nasty bytecodes, it can get on with creating the other levels of security it wants to provide to you.

The Class Loader

The class loader is another kind of gatekeeper, albeit a higher-level one. The verifier was the security of last resort. The class loader is the security of first resort. When a new class is loaded into the system, it is placed into (lives in) one of several different realms. In the current release, three realms are possible: your local computer, the firewall-guarded local network on which your computer is located, and the Internet. The class loader treats each of these realms differently.

NOTE

> Actually, there can be as many realms as your desired level of security requires, because the class loader is under your control. As a programmer, you can make your own class loader that implements your own peculiar brand of security. (This is a radical step: you might have to give the users of your program a whole bunch of classes, and the users might have to give you a whole lot of trust, to accomplish this.)
>
> As a user, you can tell your Java-capable browser, or Java system, what realm of security (of the three) you'd like it to implement for you right now or from now on.
>
> As a system administrator, Java has global security policies that you can set up to help guide your users to not give away the store (that is, set all their preferences to be unrestricted, which leaves them susceptible to attack).

In particular, the class loader never allows a class from a less protected realm to replace a class from a more protected realm. The file system's input/output primitives, about which you should be very worried (and rightly so), all are defined in a local Java class, which means that

21

they all live in the local computer realm. Thus, no class from outside your computer (from either the supposedly trustworthy local network or from the Internet) can take the place of these classes and spoof Java code into using nasty versions of these primitives. In addition, classes in one realm cannot call upon the methods of classes in other realms, unless those classes explicitly have declared those methods `public`. This restriction implies that classes from machines other than your local computer cannot even see the file system I/O methods, much less call them, unless you or the system wants them to.

In addition, every new applet loaded from the network is placed into a separate package-like namespace. This means that applets are protected even from each other! No applet can access another's methods (or variables) without its cooperation. Applets from inside the firewall even can be treated differently from those outside the firewall, if you like.

NOTE

> In the current release, an applet is in a package namespace along with any other applets from that source. This source, or origin, is most often a host (domain name) on the Internet. This special subrealm is used extensively in the next section. Depending on where the source is located, either outside the firewall or inside, further restrictions might apply (or be removed entirely). This model is likely to be extended in future releases of Java, providing an even finer degree of control over which classes get to do what.

The class loader essentially partitions the world of Java classes into small, protected little groups, about which you can safely make assumptions that always will be true. This type of predictability is the key to well-behaved and secure programs.

You now have seen the full lifetime of a method. It starts as source code on some computer, is compiled into bytecodes on some possibly different computer, and then can travel (as a `.class` file) into any file system or network anywhere in the world. When you run an applet in a Java-capable browser (or download a class and run it by other means), the method's bytecodes are extracted from its `.class` file and carefully looked over by the verifier. Once they are declared safe, the interpreter can execute them for you (or a code generator can generate native binary code for them using either the "just-in-time" compiler or `java2c`, when they are available. That native code then can be run directly).

At each stage, more security is added. The final level of that security is the Java class library itself, which has several carefully designed classes and APIs that add the final touches to the security of the system.

21

The Security Manager

SecurityManager is an abstract class that recently was added to the Java system to collect, in one place, all of the security policy decisions that the system has to make as bytecodes run. You learned before that you can create your own class loader. You might not have to, because you can subclass SecurityManager to perform most of the same customizations.

An instance of some subclass of SecurityManager always is installed as the current security manager. It has complete control over which of a well-defined set of dangerous methods are allowed to be called by any given class. It takes into account the realms from the last section, the source (origin) of the class, and the type of the class (stand-alone or loaded by an applet). Each of these items can be separately configured to have the effect that you (the programmer) like on your Java system. For non-programmers, the system provides several levels of default security policies from which you can choose.

What is this well-defined set of methods that are protected? File input/output is a part of the set, for obvious reasons. Applets, by default, can open, read, or write files only with the permission of the user, and even then, only in certain restricted directories. (Of course, users always can be foolhardy about this and remove the restrictions.) Also in this protected set are the methods that create and use network connections, both incoming and outgoing.

The final members of the set are those methods that allow one thread to access, control, and manipulate other threads. (Of course, additional methods can be protected as well by creating a new subclass of SecurityManager that handles them.)

For both file and network access, the user of a Java-capable browser can choose between three realms (and one subrealm) of protection:

- *unrestricted* (allows applets to do anything)
- *firewall* (allows applets within the firewall to do anything)
- *source* (allows applets to do things only with their origin Internet host or with other applets from there)
- *local* (disallows all file and network access)

For file access, the *source* subrealm is not meaningful, so a Java-capable browser really has only three realms of protection in this case. (As a programmer, of course, you have full access to the security manager and can set up your own peculiar criteria for granting and revoking privileges to your heart's content.)

For network access, you can imagine wanting many more realms. For example, you might specify different groups of trusted domains (companies), each of which is allowed added privileges when applets from that group are loaded. Some groups can be more trusted than others, and you might even allow groups to grow automatically by allowing existing members to recommend new members for admission. (The Java seal of approval?) In any case, the possibilities are endless, as long as there is a secure way of recognizing the original creator of an applet.

You might think this problem already has been solved, because classes are tagged with their origins. The Java run-time environment goes far out of its way to be sure that that origin information is never lost—any executing method can be dynamically restricted by this information anywhere in the call chain. So why isn't this enough? Because what you'd really like to be able to do is permanently tag an applet with its original creator (its true origin), and no matter where it has traveled, a browser could verify the integrity and authenticate the creator of that applet. Just because you don't know the company or individual that operates a particular server machine doesn't mean that you want to mistrust every applet stored on that machine. It's just that, currently, to be really safe, you should mistrust those applets.

If somehow those applets were tagged irrevocably with the digital signature of their creator, and that signature also could guarantee that the applet had not been tampered with, you'd be golden. Luckily, Sun is planning to do exactly that for Java, as soon as export restrictions can be resolved. Here's a helpful hint of where the team would like to go, from the security documentation: "a mechanism exists whereby public keys and cryptographic message digests securely can be attached to code fragments that not only identify who originated the code, but guarantee its integrity as well. This latter mechanism will be implemented in future releases." Look for these sorts of features in every release of Java; they will be a key part of the future of the Internet!

One final note about security: Despite the best efforts of the Java team, there is always a trade-off between useful functionality and absolute security. For example, Java applets can create windows, an extremely useful capability, but in early versions of the JDK, a malicious applet could use this to spoof the user into typing private password information by showing a familiar program (or operating system) window and then asking an expected, legitimate-looking question in it. This problem has been resolved by adding a Java logo and warning text such as "Untrusted Java Applet Window" to windows of this kind.

Flexibility and security can't both be maximized. Thus far on the Net, people have chosen maximum flexibility and have lived with the minimal security the Net now provides. Let's hope that Java can help tip the scales a bit, enabling much better security while sacrificing only a minimal amount of the flexibility that has drawn so many to the Internet.

Summary

Today, you learned about the grand vision of Java, and about the exciting potential that it has. You learned about the inner workings of the virtual machine, the bytecode interpreter, the garbage collector, the class loader, the verifier, the security manager, and the powerful security features of Java.

21

This is the last day of your 21-day course, but don't put the book down yet! Read the Graduation section that follows to find out more about advancing your knowledge of Java and making use of Java resources that are available online.

Q&A

Q I know you said that garbage collection is something I don't have to worry about, but what if I want or need to?

A For such cases, there is a way to ask the Java run-time environment during startup not to run garbage collection unless forced to, either by an explicit call, System.gc() or by running out of memory. The command-line argument to specify with Project Manager is -noasyncgc. This feature can be useful if you have multiple threads that are messing each other up and want to get the gc thread out of the way while testing them. Don't forget that turning off garbage collection means that any object you create will live a long, long time. If you're real-time, you never want to step back for a full gc, so be sure to reuse objects often, and don't create too many of them!

Q I like the control above; is there anything else I can do to the garbage collector?

A You also can force the finalize() methods of any recently freed objects to be called immediately through System.runFinalization(). You might want to do this if you're about to ask for some resources that you suspect might still be tied up by objects that are gone but not forgotten (waiting for finalize()). This action is even rarer than starting a gc by hand, but it's mentioned here for completeness.

FEATURED APPLET **Today's Featured Applet**

Today's featured applet is CrazyText, a text-manipulation applet created by Patrick Taylor. The applet displays highly configurable, dancing, multicolored text. Because it puts the functionality into a public class called CrazyLabel, it can be used easily in containers and other Java programs. It was based on Daniel Wyszynski's NervousText applet, included with the Java Developer's Kit. Figure 21.1 shows an example of CrazyText in action.

Files for CrazyText are located on the CD-ROM in the \BOOK\3RDPARTY\DAY21\ directory, including source code in the files CrazyText.java, CrazyLabel.java, and CrazyLabelExample.java. To use CrazyText on a Web page, place the class files CrazyText.class and CrazyLabel.class on your Web site. Place the files in the same directory as the Web page, or place them in a subdirectory listed in the CODEBASE parameter of the <APPLET> tag. The <CODE> tag should be CrazyText.class. Listing 21.1 shows the HTML tags used to run CrazyText as it is shown in Figure 21.1.

Figure 21.1.

The CrazyText *applet in action.*

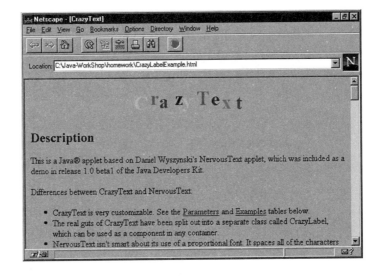

Listing 21.1. The <APPLET> tag for CrazyText.

```
<applet code="CrazyText.class" width=220 height=55>
<param name=text value="CrazyText">
<param name=delay value="100">
<param name=delta value="5">
<param name=hgap value="5">
<param name=clear value="true">
<param name=cycle value="char">
<param name=fontName value="Helvetica">
<param name=fontSize value="24">
<param name=fontBold value="false">
<param name=fontItalic value="false">
</applet>
```

CrazyText has 29 parameters that can be customized within the <APPLET> tag, as follows:

- [ ] The text parameter is the text string to display (CrazyText is the default).

- [ ] The delay parameter specifies the delay between updates, in milliseconds (100 is the default).

- [ ] The delta parameter specifies the craziness factor, which determines how far the individual letters will move, in pixels (5 is the default).

- [ ] The hgap parameter specifies the horizontal gap between characters, in pixels (0 is the default).

- [ ] The vgap parameter specifies the vertical gap between lines, in pixels (0 is the default).

21

☐ The hspace parameter specifies the extra spacing to put on the left and right (0 is the default).

☐ The vspace parameter specifies the extra spacing to put on the top and bottom (0 is the default).

☐ The clear parameter is true if the background should be cleared on update, false otherwise (false is the default).

☐ The cycle parameter specifies the mode for color changes; whole indicates that all letters should have the same color when changes occur, char indicates that each character can change independently, and none indicates that no color changes should take place (whole is the default).

☐ The fgcolor parameter specifies the foreground color in *#rrggbb* format (the color black is the default).

☐ The bgcolor parameter specifies the background color in *#rrggbb* format (the color light gray is the default).

☐ The bgcolor2 parameter specifies a second color to use for a background gradient fill that cycles from bgcolor to bgcolor2 (optional).

☐ The bgGradient parameter specifies the direction, either vertical or horizontal, of the background gradient fill (vertical is the default).

☐ The bgImage parameter specifies the image to use as a background tile (optional).

☐ The borderSize parameter specifies the thickness of the border, excluding depth lines (0 is the default).

☐ The borderOuter parameter specifies the outer depth of the border (0 is the default).

☐ The borderInner parameter specifies the inner depth of the border (0 is the default).

☐ The borderRaised parameter specifies true if the border should appear raised, false otherwise (true is the default).

☐ The borderColor parameter specifies the color of the border, in *#rrggbb* format (the color light gray is the default).

☐ The shadowDepth parameter specifies the depth of the text shadow (0 is the default).

☐ The shadowColor parameter specifies the color of the text shadow, in *#rrggbb* format (the color gray is the default).

☐ The fontName parameter specifies the name of the font to use (TimesRoman is the default).

☐ The fontSize parameter specifies the size of the font (36 is the default).

☐ The fontBold parameter is true if the font should be bold, false otherwise (true is the default).

21

- ☐ The `fontItalic` parameter is `true` if the font should be italicized, `false` otherwise (`false` is the default).
- ☐ The `url` parameter specifies the page to load if the applet is clicked; `none` means that no page should be loaded (the CrazyText home page is the default).
- ☐ The `message` parameter specifies the message to show in the status area when the mouse is over the applet; `$url` shows the URL (CrazyText info is the default).
- ☐ The `resizeMin` parameter is `true` if the applet should be resized to the minimum size (`false` is the default).
- ☐ The `debug` parameter is `true` if debugging information should be sent to the console (`false` is the default).

More information on `CrazyText` is available from Patrick Taylor at the following URL:

`http://www.nicom.com/~taylor/classes/CrazyText/`

More information on `NervousText` is available from Daniel Wyszynski at the following URL:

`http://widelux.poly.edu:8000/classes/Nervous.html`

21

Graduation

Congratulations! You have completed the 21-day course on Java programming and SunSoft Java WorkShop. By now, you probably have a good idea where to go next with this knowledge. However, before you are unleashed on the world, there's a few things you ought to know about.

There are a number of ways you can continue learning about Java, expanding your skills, and following the developments related to the language. You might be interested in other Java books from Sams.net, Java Web sites, and the Java Usenet newsgroups.

Other Java Books

Now that you have developed a broad knowledge of Java, you might want to build on that foundation with some other books from Sams.net Publishing. The following offerings from Sams.net could be of interest to you:

- [ ] *Tricks of the Java Programming Gurus*
- [ ] *Java Unleashed*
- [ ] *Java Developer's Reference*
- [ ] *Peter Norton's Guide to Programming Java*

- *Teach Yourself Database Programming with Java in 21 Days*
- *Creating Web Applets with Java*
- *Teach Yourself Internet Game Programming with Java in 21 Days*
- *Teach Yourself Café in 21 Days*
- *Developing Intranet Applications with Java*
- *Developing Professional Java Applets*

The Sams.net Web site at `http://www.mcp.com/sams` has the most current details on the company's books, and it's well worth visiting because of books that you can sample for free over the Web. One book that now is offered for free over the Web is *Presenting Java* from John December.

Web Sites

Because of its appeal to developers and users on the World Wide Web, Java information is offered at thousands of sites. If you want to learn more about Java on the Web, the following sites will get you started:

- `http://java.sun.com` is the official JavaSoft site. It offers online documentation, news on the latest developments, Java software to download or purchase, and links to other pertinent sites.

- `http://www.gamelan.com` is the largest directory of Java applets and Java-related Web sites. It also offers a chat applet that uses Java to offer America Online–style chat, as shown on Day 1.

- `http://rampages.onramp.net/~ranger/java_workshop.html` is an unofficial Java WorkShop troubleshooting home page that was created by a user who has been helping people use the software since its introduction as a beta release in Spring 1996.

- `http://www.jars.com` is the Java Applet Rating Service, a group that reviews Java applets. The JARS logo, an apple, can be seen with numerous applets on the Web.

- `http://weber.u.washington.edu/~jgurney/java/` is another directory of Java applets, with a smaller number of listings than Gamelan, but with nice collection of useful Java programs that can be added to Web pages.

- `http://www.seas.upenn.edu/~mcrae/projects/macjava/index.html` is Apple-Flavored Java, a site devoted to Macintosh implementations of Java development software and Java programs.

- `http://sunsite.unc.edu/javafaq/javafaq.html` is a list of frequently asked questions about Java answered by participants in the Usenet newsgroup `comp.lang.java`.

- ☐ `http://k2.scl.cwru.edu/~gaunt/java/java-faq.html` is another list of questions about Java called the "Unofficial Obscure Java FAQ," which was established for some answers to infrequently asked questions about the language.

- ☐ `http://www.javaworld.com/` is the home page of JavaWorld Magazine, which puts a lot of articles, sample source code, and news stories online.

- ☐ `http://www.yahoo.com/Computers_and_Internet/Programming_Languages/Java/` is a section of the Yahoo! Directory devoted to Java, with more than 300 links to Web sites.

Usenet Newsgroups

Hundreds of messages are posted on Usenet newsgroups each day by people who are interested in Java. Some are from developers with experience in the language, who are seeking advice and can comment on advanced aspects of the language. Many are from newcomers who need help in their effort to learn Java, and Usenet is a great place to get technical assistance.

The following newsgroups currently are available on Usenet, which can be accessed with an Internet account, a subscription to online services such as CompuServe and America Online, and other means:

- ☐ `comp.lang.java` is the main Java newsgroup, which was split off recently into more specific subgroups. It still is the most heavily used Usenet discussion group devoted to the programming language.

- ☐ `comp.lang.java.advocacy` is a newsgroup for debate and diatribes about Java and other languages that can be compared to it.

- ☐ `comp.lang.java.announce` is a moderated newsgroup with announcements related to Java—often used for company press releases, Web site launches, and similar information.

- ☐ `comp.lang.java.api` is a newsgroup for discussion of the Java Application Programming Interface, the full class library that comes with Java WorkShop, and other development environments for the language.

- ☐ `comp.lang.java.misc` is a newsgroup for discussions that don't seem to belong in any of the other newsgroups, just like `comp.lang.java`.

- ☐ `comp.lang.java.programmer` is a newsgroup for questions, answers, and other talk related to Java programming.

- ☐ `comp.lang.java.security` is a newsgroup where the security issues related to Java are discussed, with an emphasis on the security of executing Java applets over the World Wide Web.

- ☐ `comp.lang.java.setup` is a newsgroup for the discussion of installation problems regarding Java development tools and similar issues.
- ☐ `comp.lang.java.tech` is an advanced newsgroup where technical issues of the Java language are discussed.

The Last Word

Because this is a Graduation section, there is a temptation to tell you that this point is both an ending and a beginning. The best of times, and the worst of times. The first day of the rest of your life; yadda, yadda; blah, blah; murmur!

But this isn't school, and neither you nor the authors are wearing uncomfortable black gowns and funny-looking hats. (Not that there's anything wrong with that.) As a Java programmer, you're part of an exciting new development at the most exciting time to be involved with it. It is hoped that this book helped you develop confidence in your skills with the language and with the use of Java WorkShop as you write programs.

If you have any questions, comments, or large piles of money that you're tired of counting, please contact the authors through the book's Web site at `http://www.spiderbyte.com/java`.

"Don't let it end like this. Tell them I said something."

—The last words of Pancho Villa (1877-1923)

APPENDIX

A

Language Summary

This appendix contains a quick reference for the Java language, as described in this book.

 NOTE

> This appendix is not a grammar overview, nor is it a technical overview of the language itself. It's a quick reference to be used after you already know the basics of how the language works. If you need a technical description of the language, your best bet is to visit the Java Web site (http://java.sun.com) and download the actual specification, which includes a full BNF grammar.

Language keywords and symbols are shown in a monospace font. Arguments and other parts to be substituted are in *italic monospace*. Optional parts are indicated by brackets (except in the array syntax section). If several options are mutually exclusive, they are shown separated by pipe symbols ([¦]) like this:

```
[ public ¦ private ¦ protected ] type varname
```

Reserved Words

The following words are reserved for use by the Java language itself (some of them are reserved but currently not in use). You cannot use these words to refer to classes, methods, or variable names:

abstract	else	interface	super
boolean	extends	long	switch
break	final	native	synchronized
byte	finally	new	this
case	float	null	throw
catch	for	package	throws
char	goto	private	transient
class	if	protected	try
const	implements	public	void
continue	import	return	volatile
do	instanceof	short	while
double	int	static	

A

Comments

```
// this is a single-line comment
/* this is a
multiline comment */
/** Javadoc comment */
```

Literals

Literal	Description
number	Type int
number[l | L]	Type long
0x*hex*	Hex integer
0X*hex*	Hex integer
0*octal*	Octal integer
[*number*].*number*	Type double
number[f | f]	Type float
number[d | D]	Type double
[+ | -] *number*	Signed
*number*e*number*	Exponent
*number*E*number*	Exponent
'*character*'	Single character
"*characters*"	String
""	Empty string
\b	Backspace
\t	Tab
\n	Line feed
\f	Form feed
\r	Carriage return
\"	Double quote
\'	Single quote
\\	Backslash
\u*NNNN*	Unicode escape (*NNNN* is hex)
true	Boolean
false	Boolean

Variable Declaration

Declaration	Description
[byte	short	int	long] varname	Integers (pick one type)
[float	double] varname	Floats (pick one type)
char varname	Characters
boolean varname	Boolean
classname varname	Class types
interfacename varname	Interface types
type varname, varname, varname	Multiple variables

The following options are available only for class and instance variables. You can use any of these options with a variable declaration:

Declaration	Description
[static] variableDeclaration	Class variable
[final] variableDeclaration	Constants
[public	private	protected] variableDeclaration	Access control
[volatile] varname	Modified asynchronously
[transient] varname	Not persistent
	(not yet implemented)

Variable Assignment

Assignment	Description
variable = value	Assignment
variable++	Postfix increment
++variable	Prefix increment
variable--	Postfix decrement
--variable	Prefix decrement
variable += value	Add and assign
variable -= value	Subtract and assign
variable /= value	Multiply and assign
variable ÷= value	Divide and assign

A

Assignment	Description
`variable %= value`	Modulus and assign
`variable &= value`	AND and assign
`variable ¦= value`	OR and assign
`variable ^= value`	XOR and assign
`variable <<= value`	Left-shift and assign
`variable >>= value`	Right-shift and assign
`variable >>>= value`	Zero-fill right-shift and assign

Operators

Operation	Description
`arg + arg`	Addition
`arg - arg`	Subtraction
`arg * arg`	Multiplication
`arg / arg`	Division
`arg % arg`	Modulus
`arg < arg`	Less than
`arg > arg`	Greater than
`arg <= arg`	Less than or equal to
`arg >= arg`	Greater than or equal to
`arg == arg`	Equal
`arg != arg`	Not equal
`arg && arg`	Logical AND
`arg ¦¦ arg`	Logical OR
`! arg`	Logical NOT
`arg & arg`	AND
`arg ¦ arg`	OR
`arg ^ arg`	XOR
`arg << arg`	Left-shift
`arg >> arg`	Right-shift

continues

Operation	Description
arg >>> arg	Zero-fill right-shift
~ arg	Complement
(type)thing	Casting
arg instanceof class	Instance of
test ? trueOp : falseOp	Ternary (if) operator

Objects

Statement or Object	Description
new class()	Create new instance
new class(arg, arg, arg...)	New instance with parameters
object.variable	Instance variable
object.classvar	Class variable
class.classvar	Class variable
object.method()	Instance method (no arguments)
object.method(arg,arg,arg...)	Instance method
object.classmethod()	Class method (no arguments)
object.classmethod(arg,arg,arg...)	Class method
class.classmethod()	Class method (no arguments)
class.classmethod(arg,arg,arg...)	Class method

Arrays

NOTE

The brackets in this section are parts of the array creation or access statements. They do not denote optional parts as they do in other parts of this appendix.

Declaration	Description
`type varname[]`	Array variable
`type[] varname`	Array variable
`new type[numElements]`	New array object
`array[index]`	Element access
`array.length`	Length of array

Loops and Conditionals

Statement	Description
`if ( test ) block`	Conditional
`if ( test ) block` `else block`	Conditional with `else`

`switch (test) {`
    `case value : statements`
    `case value : statements`
    `...`
    `default : statement`
`}`
	`switch` (only with `int` or `char` types)

`for (initializer; test; change ) block`	`for` loop
`while ( test ) block`	`while` loop
`do block` `while (test)`	`do` loop
`break [ label ]`	break from loop or switch
`continue [ label ]`	continue loops
`label:`	Labeled loops

Class Definitions

The syntax for a simple class definition is as follows:

```
class classname block
```

You can add any of the following optional modifiers to the class definition:

Declaration	Description
[final] `class classname block`	Cannot be subclassed
[abstract] `class classname block`	Cannot be instantiated
[public] `class classname block`	Accessible outside package
`class classname` [extends `superclass`] `block`	Define superclass
`class classname` [implements `interfaces`] `block`	Implement one or more interfaces

Method and Constructor Definitions

The basic method looks like this, where *returnType* is a type name, a class name, or void:

```
returnType methodName() block
```

A method with parameters looks like this:

```
returnType methodName(parameter, parameter, ...)block
```

Method parameters look like this:

```
type parameterName
```

Method variations can include any of the following optional keywords:

Declaration	Description
[abstract] `returnType methodName() block`	Abstract method
[static] `returnType methodName() block`	Class method
[native] `returnType methodName() block`	Native method
[final] `returnType methodName() block`	final method
[synchronized] `returnType methodName() block`	Thread lock before executing
[public ¦ private ¦ protected] `returnType methodName()`	Access control

Constructors look like the following:

Statement	Description
`classname() block`	Basic constructor
`classname(parameter, parameter, parameter...) block`	Constructor with parameters
`[public	private	protected] classname() block`	Access control

In the method/constructor body, you can use these references and methods:

Statement	Description
`this`	Refers to current object
`super`	Refers to superclass
`super.methodName()`	Calls a superclass' method
`this(...)`	Calls class' constructor
`super(...)`	Calls superclass' constructor
`return [ value ]`	Returns a value

Packages, Interfaces, and Importing

Statement	Description
`import package.className`	Imports specific class name
`import package.*`	Imports all public classes in package
`package packagename`	Classes in this file belong to this package
`interface interfaceName [ extends anotherInterface ] block`	This class is an interface
`[ public ] interface interfaceName block`	This interface is `public`
`[ abstract ] interface interfaceName block`	This interface is `abstract`

Exceptions and Guarding

Statement	Description
`synchronized ( object ) block`	Waits for lock on *object*
`try block`	Guarded statements
`catch ( exception ) block`	Executed if *exception* is thrown
`[ finally block ]`	Clean-up code
`try block[ catch ( exception ) block ]` `finally block`	Same as previous example (can use optional `catch` or `finally`, but not both)

APPENDIX

B

Class Hierarchy Diagrams

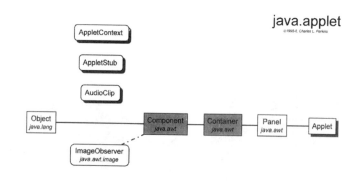

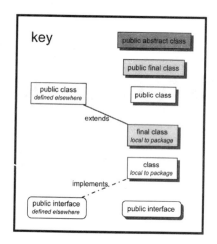

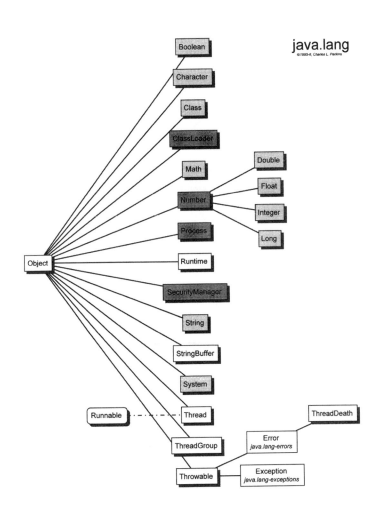

java.lang
©1995-6, Charles L. Perkins

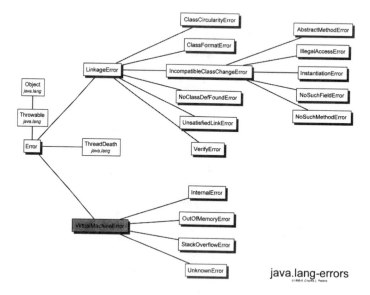

java.lang-errors

java.lang-exceptions

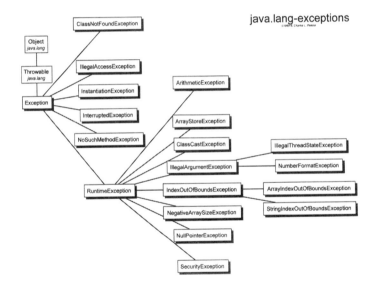

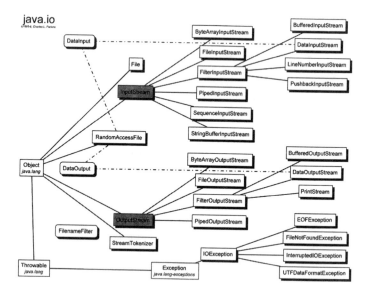

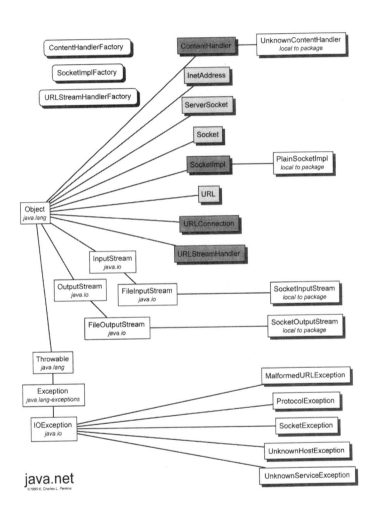

ContentHandlerFactory

SocketImplFactory

URLStreamHandlerFactory

ContentHandler

UnknownContentHandler
local to package

InetAddress

ServerSocket

Socket

SocketImpl

PlainSocketImpl
local to package

URL

URLConnection

URLStreamHandler

Object
java.lang

InputStream
java.io

OutputStream
java.io

FileInputStream
java.io

SocketInputStream
local to package

FileOutputStream
java.io

SocketOutputStream
local to package

Throwable
java.lang

Exception
java.lang-exceptions

IOException
java.io

MalformedURLException

ProtocolException

SocketException

UnknownHostException

UnknownServiceException

java.net
©1995-6, Charles L. Perkins

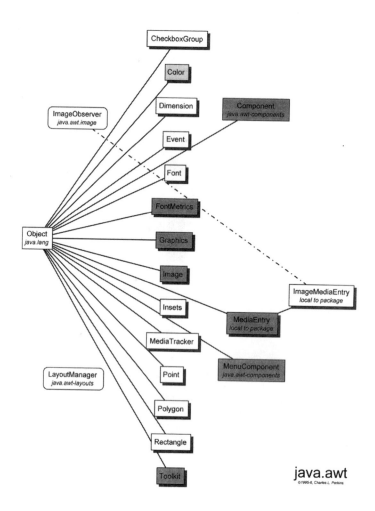

java.awt

©1995-6, Charles L. Perkins

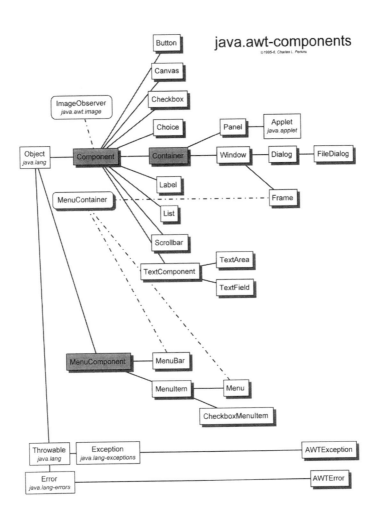

java.awt-components

© 1995-6, Charles L. Perkins

java.awt-layouts

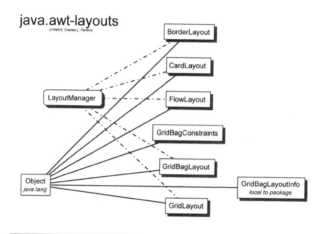

java.awt.image

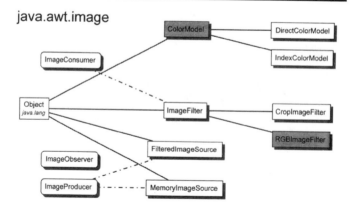

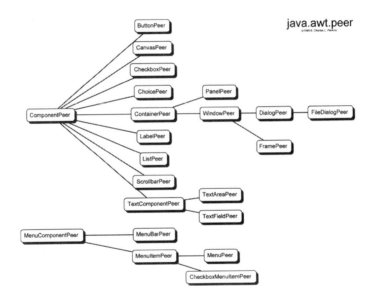

java.awt.peer

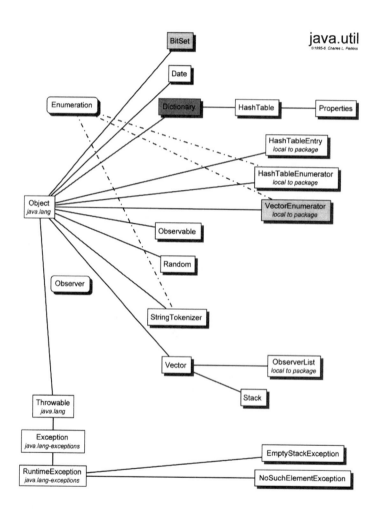

java.util
©1995-6 Charles L. Perkins

About These Diagrams

The diagrams in this appendix are class hierarchy diagrams for the package java and for all the subpackages recursively below it in the Java 1.0 binary release. Each page contains the class hierarchy for one package (or a subtree of a particularly large package) with all its interfaces included, and each class in this tree is shown attached to its superclasses, even if they are on another page. A detailed key is located on the first page of this appendix.

For these diagrams, the API documentation was supplemented through a search of all source files (below src/java) to find all the missing package classes and their relationships. There are various programs that will lay out hierarchies, but these were assembled by hand. One nice side effect of the effort is that the diagrams should be more readable than a computer would produce.

A stylistic note: Lines are attached through the center of each class node, which on occasion can be a little confusing. Follow lines through the center of the classes, not at any corners, and not along lines that do not pass through the center.

APPENDIX C

The Java Class Library

This appendix provides a general overview of the classes available in the standard Java packages (that is, the classes that are guaranteed to be available in any Java implementation). This appendix is intended for general reference; for more information about class inheritance and the exceptions defined for each package, see Appendix B, "Class Hierarchy Diagrams." For more specific information about each class and the methods within each class, see the API documentation from JavaSoft at http://java.sun.com. A copy of the 1.0 API documentation is on the CD-ROM included with this book.

`java.lang`

The `java.lang` package contains the classes and interfaces that make up the core Java language.

Interfaces

Cloneable	Interface indicating that an object may be copied or cloned
Runnable	Methods for classes that want to run as threads

Classes

Boolean	Object wrapper for `boolean` values
Character	Object wrapper for `char` values
Class	Run-time representations of classes
ClassLoader	Abstract behavior for handling loading of classes
Compiler	System class that gives access to the Java compiler
Double	Object wrapper for `double` values
Float	Object wrapper for `float` values
Integer	Object wrapper for `int` values
Long	Object wrapper for `long` values
Math	Utility class for math operations
Number	Abstract superclass of all number classes (`Integer`, `Float`, and so on)
Object	Generic `Object` class, at top of inheritance hierarchy
Process	Abstract behavior for processes such as those spawned using methods in the `System` class

Runtime	Access to the Java run-time environment
SecurityManager	Abstract behavior for implementing security policies
String	Character strings
StringBuffer	Mutable strings
System	Access to Java's system-level behavior, provided in a platform-independent way
Thread	Methods for managing threads and classes that run in threads
ThreadDeath	Class of object thrown when a thread is asynchronously terminated
ThreadGroup	A group of threads
Throwable	Generic exception class; all objects thrown must be a Throwable

java.util

The java.util package contains various utility classes and interfaces, including random numbers, system properties, and other useful classes.

Interfaces

Enumeration	Methods for enumerating sets of values
Observer	Methods for allowing classes to observe Observable objects

Classes

BitSet	A set of bits
Date	The current system date, as well as methods for generating and parsing dates
Dictionary	An abstract class that maps between keys and values (superclass of HashTable)
Hashtable	A hash table
Observable	An abstract class for observable objects
Properties	A hash table that contains behavior for setting and retrieving persistent properties of the system or of a class

Random	Utilities for generating random numbers
Stack	A stack (a last-in-first-out queue)
StringTokenizer	Utilities for splitting strings into a sequence of individual tokens
Vector	A growable array of Objects

java.io

The java.io package provides input and output classes and interfaces for streams and files.

Interfaces

DataInput	Methods for reading machine-independent typed input streams
DataOutput	Methods for writing machine-independent typed output streams
FilenameFilter	Methods for filtering file names

Classes

BufferedInputStream	A buffered input stream
BufferedOutputStream	A buffered output stream
ByteArrayInputStream	An input stream from a byte array
ByteArrayOutputStream	An output stream to a byte array
DataInputStream	Enables you to read primitive Java types (int, char, boolean, and so on) from a stream in a machine-independent way
DataOutputStream	Enables you to write primitive Java data types (int, char, boolean, and so on) to a stream in a machine-independent way
File	Represents a file on the host's file system
FileDescriptor	Holds on to the UNIX-like file descriptor of a file or socket

FileInputStream	An input stream from a file, constructed using a file name or descriptor
FileOutputStream	An output stream to a file, constructed using a file name or descriptor
FilterInputStream	Abstract class that provides a filter for input streams (and for adding stream functionality such as buffering)
FilterOutputStream	Abstract class that provides a filter for output streams (and for adding stream functionality such as buffering)
InputStream	An abstract class representing an input stream of bytes; the parent of all input streams in this package
LineNumberInputStream	An input stream that keeps track of line numbers
OutputStream	An abstract class representing an output stream of bytes; the parent of all output streams in this package
PipedInputStream	A piped input stream, which should be connected to a PipedOutputStream to be useful
PipedOutputStream	A piped output stream, which should be connected to a PipedInputStream to be useful (together they provide safe communication between threads)
PrintStream	An output stream for printing (used by System.out.println(...))
PushbackInputStream	An input stream with a 1-byte, push-back buffer
RandomAccessFile	Provides random-access to a file, constructed from file names, descriptors, or objects
SequenceInputStream	Converts a sequence of input streams into a single input steam
StreamTokenizer	Converts an input stream into a sequence of individual tokens
StringBufferInputStream	An input stream from a String object

java.net

The java.net package contains classes and interfaces for performing network operations, such as sockets and URLs.

Interfaces

ContentHandlerFactory	Methods for creating ContentHandler objects
SocketImplFactory	Methods for creating socket implementations (instance of the SocketImpl class)
URLStreamHandlerFactory	Methods for creating URLStreamHandler objects

Classes

ContentHandler	Abstract behavior for reading data from a URL connection and constructing the appropriate local object, based on MIME types
DatagramPacket	A datagram packet (UDP)
DatagramSocket	A datagram socket
InetAddress	An object representation of an Internet host (host name, IP address)
ServerSocket	A server-side socket
Socket	A socket
SocketImpl	An abstract class for specific socket implementations
URL	An object representation of a URL
URLConnection	Abstract behavior for a socket that can handle various Web-based protocols (http, ftp, and so on)
URLEncoder	Turns strings into x-www-form-urlencoded format
URLStreamHandler	Abstract class for managing streams to objects that are referenced by URLs

java.awt

The java.awt package contains the classes and interfaces that make up the Abstract Windowing Toolkit.

Interfaces

LayoutManager	Methods for laying out containers
MenuContainer	Methods for menu-related containers

Classes

BorderLayout	A layout manager for arranging items in border formation
Button	A push button
Canvas	A canvas for drawing and performing other graphics operations
CardLayout	A layout manager for HyperCard-like metaphors
Checkbox	A check box
CheckboxGroup	A group of exclusive check boxes (radio buttons)
CheckboxMenuItem	A toggle menu item
Choice	A pop-up menu of choices
Color	An abstract representation of a color
Component	The abstract generic class for all user interface components
Container	Abstract behavior for a component that can hold other components or containers
Dialog	A window for brief interactions with users
Dimension	An object representing width and height
Event	An object representing events caused by the system or based on user input
FileDialog	A dialog for getting file names from the local file system
FlowLayout	A layout manager that lays out objects from left to right in rows
Font	An abstract representation of a font
FontMetrics	Abstract class for holding information about a specific font's character shapes and height and width information
Frame	A top-level window with a title
Graphics	Abstract behavior for representing a graphics context, and for drawing and painting shapes and objects
GridBagConstraints	Constraints for components laid out using GridBagLayout
GridBagLayout	A layout manager that aligns components horizontally and vertically based on their values from GridBagConstraints
GridLayout	A layout manager with rows and columns; elements are added to each cell in the grid
Image	An abstract representation of a bitmap image

Insets	Distances from the outer border of the window; used to lay out components
Label	A text label for user interface components
List	A scrolling list
MediaTracker	A way to keep track of the status of media objects being loaded over the Net
Menu	A menu, which can contain menu items and is a container on a menu bar
MenuBar	A menu bar (container for menus)
MenuComponent	The abstract superclass of all menu elements
MenuItem	An individual menu item
Panel	A container that is displayed
Point	An object representing a point (x and y coordinates)
Polygon	An object representing a set of points
Rectangle	An object representing a rectangle (x and y coordinates for the top corner, plus width and height)
Scrollbar	A user interface scrollbar object
TextArea	A multiline, scrollable, editable text field
TextComponent	The superclass of all editable text components
TextField	A fixed-size editable text field
Toolkit	Abstract behavior for binding the abstract AWT classes to a platform-specific toolkit implementation
Window	A top-level window, and the superclass of the Frame and Dialog classes

java.awt.image

The java.awt.image package is a subpackage of the AWT that provides classes for managing bitmap images.

Interfaces

ImageConsumer	Methods for receiving image data created by an ImageProducer

ImageObserver	Methods to track the loading and construction of an image
ImageProducer	Methods for producing image data received by an ImageConsumer

Classes

ColorModel	An abstract class for managing color information for images
CropImageFilter	A filter for cropping images to a particular size
DirectColorModel	A specific color model for managing and translating pixel color values
FilteredImageSource	An ImageProducer that takes an image and an ImageFilter object and produces an image for an ImageConsumer
ImageFilter	A filter that takes image data from an ImageProducer, modifies it in some way, and hands it off to an ImageConsumer
IndexColorModel	A specific color model for managing and translating color values in a fixed-color map
MemoryImageSource	An image producer that gets its image from memory; used after constructing an image by hand
PixelGrabber	An ImageConsumer that retrieves a subset of the pixels in an image
RGBImageFilter	Abstract behavior for a filter that modifies the RGB values of pixels in RGB images

java.awt.peer

The java.awt.peer package is a subpackage of AWT that provides the hidden platform-specific AWT classes (for example, for Motif, Macintosh, or Windows 95) with platform-independent interfaces to implement. Thus, callers using these interfaces need not know which platform's window system these hidden AWT classes currently are implementing.

Each class in the AWT that inherits from either Component or MenuComponent has a corresponding peer class. Each of those classes is the name of the Component with -Peer added (for example, ButtonPeer, DialogPeer, and WindowPeer). Because these classes provide similar behavior, they are not enumerated here.

`java.applet`

The `java.applet` package provides applet-specific behavior.

Interfaces

`AppletContext`	Methods to refer to the applet's context
`AppletStub`	Methods for implementing applet viewers
`AudioClip`	Methods for playing audio files

Class

`Applet`	The base applet class

APPENDIX

D

How Java Differs from C and C++

This appendix contains a description of most of the major differences between C, C++, and Java. If you are a programmer familiar with either C or C++, you might want to review this appendix to avoid some of the common mistakes and assumptions that programmers make when using Java.

Pointers

Java does not have an explicit pointer type. Instead of pointers, all references to objects, including variable assignments, arguments passed into methods, and array elements, are accomplished by using implicit references. References and pointers are essentially the same thing except that you can't do pointer arithmetic on references (nor do you need to).

References also allow structures such as linked lists to be created easily in Java without explicit pointers; simply create a linked list node with variables that point to the next and the previous node. Then, to insert items in the list, assign those variables to other node objects.

Arrays

Arrays in Java are first-class objects, and references to arrays and their contents are accomplished through implicit references rather than through point arithmetic. Array boundaries are enforced strictly; attempting to read past the end of an array causes a compile or run-time error. As with other objects, passing an array to a method passes a reference to the original array, so changing the contents of that array reference changes the original array object.

Arrays of objects are arrays of references that are not initialized automatically to contain actual objects. Using the following Java code produces an array of type MyObject with 10 elements, but the array initially contains only null values:

```
MyObject arrayOfObjs[] = new MyObject[10];
```

You now must add actual MyObject objects to that array:

```
for (int i=0; i < arrayOfObjs.length; i++) {
    arrayofobjs[i] = new MyObject();
```

Java does not support multidimensional arrays as C and C++ do. In Java, you must create arrays that contain other arrays.

Strings

Strings in C and C++ are arrays of characters, terminated by a null character (`'\0'`). To operate on and manage strings, you treat them as you would any other array, with the inherent difficulties of keeping track of pointer arithmetic and being careful not to stray past the end of the array.

Strings in Java are objects, and all methods that operate on strings can treat the string as a complete entity. Strings are not terminated by a null character, nor can you accidentally overstep the end of a string (like arrays, string boundaries are enforced strictly).

Memory Management

All memory management in Java is automatic; memory is allocated automatically when an object is created, and a run-time garbage collector (the gc) frees that memory when the object is no longer in use. C's `malloc()` and `free()` functions do not exist in Java. To force an object to be freed, remove all references to that object (in other words, assign all variables and array elements holding it to `null`). The next time the Java gc runs, that object is reclaimed.

Data Types

As mentioned in the early part of this book, all Java primitive data types (`char`, `int`, `long`, and so on) have consistent sizes and behavior across platforms and operating systems. There are no unsigned data types as in C and C++ (except for `char`, which is a 16-bit unsigned integer).

The `boolean` primitive data type can have two values: `true` or `false`. Boolean is not an integer, nor can it be treated as one, although you can cast `0` or `1` (integers) to boolean types in Java.

Composite data types are accomplished in Java exclusively through the use of class definitions. The `struct`, `union`, and `typedef` keywords all have been removed in favor of classes.

Casting between data types is much more controlled in Java than in C and C++; automatic casting occurs only when there will be no loss of information. All other casts must be explicit. The primitive data types (`int`, `float`, `long`, `char`, `boolean`, and so on) cannot be cast to objects or vice versa; there are methods and special wrapper classes to convert values between objects and primitive types.

D

Operators

Operator precedence and association behaves as it does in C. Note, however, that the new keyword (for creating a new object) binds tighter than dot notation (.), which is different behavior from C++. In particular, note the following expression:

```
new foo().bar;
```

This expression operates as if it were written like this:

```
(new foo()).bar;
```

Operator overloading, as in C++, cannot be accomplished in Java. The , operator of C has been deleted. The >>> operator produces an unsigned logical right shift (remember, there are no unsigned integer data types). Finally, you can use the + operator to concatenate strings.

Control Flow

Although the if, while, for, and do statements in Java are syntactically the same as they are in C and C++, one significant difference exists: The test expression for each control flow construct must return an actual boolean value (true or false). In C and C++, the expression can return an integer.

Arguments

Java does not support mechanisms for varied-length argument lists to functions as in C and C++. All method definitions must have a specific number of arguments.

Command-line arguments in Java behave differently from those in C and C++. The first element in the argument vector (argv[0]) in C and C++ is the name of the program itself; in Java, that first argument is the first of the additional arguments. In other words, Java's argv[0] is argv[1] in C and C++; there is no way to get hold of the actual name of the Java program.

Other Differences

The following are Java's other minor differences from C and C++:

☐ Java does not have a preprocessor, and as such, does not have #define or macros. Constants can be created by using the final modifier when declaring class and instance variables.

☐ Java does not have template classes as C++ does.

☐ Java does not include C's const keyword or the capability to pass arguments by const reference explicitly.

☐ Java classes are singly inherited, with some multiple-inheritance features provided through interfaces.

☐ All functions must be methods. There are no functions that are not tied to classes.

☐ The goto keyword does not exist in Java (it's a reserved word, but currently unimplemented). You can, however, use labeled break and continue statements to break out of and continue executing complex switch or loop constructs.

APPENDIX

E

JDK Command-Line Utilities

Before Java WorkShop was released, Sun's only development environment for Java programming was the Java Developer's Kit. The Kit is a set of command-line utilities that includes an interpreter to run programs, a compiler, an applet viewer, and other tools.

Java WorkShop comes with a modified version of the JDK, and it uses these tools internally. The Project Manager feature includes several dialog boxes where command-line arguments can be specified. You also can use the JDK command-line tools from the command line.

WARNING

> Java WorkShop will not work correctly if a full version of the JDK also is on your system. Deinstall the JDK and remove it from configuration files, such as AUTOEXEC.BAT on Microsoft Windows systems, before installing WorkShop.

The following sections detail how you can use tools in WorkShop's modified JDK, including descriptions of the most common arguments that modify how they operate. They also describe places in WorkShop where you can use these command-line parameters.

For more information, check out the JavaSoft JDK home page on the World Wide Web at the following URL:

```
http://java.sun.com/java.sun.com/products/JDK/index.html
```

javac

The Java compiler, javac, takes one or more .java source code files as input and compiles the code into .class files of executable bytecode. You can create source code files with any text editor that can save files as plain text without any formatting characters. The following command would be used to compile the source code file BurnsAndAllen.java:

```
javac BurnsAndAllen.java
```

If there are no compilation errors, the class file BurnsAndAllen.class is created, along with other .class files for each class included in the source code.

You can insert arguments between javac and the filenames, as in this example:

```
javac -verbose Gildersleeve.java
```

You can use the following arguments to modify how the compiler operates:

- ☐ The -classpath *pathtext* argument overrides the default CLASSPATH environment variable, which determines where javac will look to find classes that are used in the source code. The *pathtext* argument is a list of directories and .zip files.

□ The -d *directoryname* argument changes the directory where the .class file should be stored, unless it is in a package. In that case, *directoryname* is the root directory of the package hierarchy, and the .class file is stored in the proper place in its package.

You can specify these arguments within Java WorkShop in Project Manager's Build tabbed dialog box.

java

The Java interpreter, java, executes Java .class files. The following command would be used to run the bytecode file JohnnyDollar.class:

```
java JohnnyDollar
```

Note that the .class extension is not used. The interpreter runs any Java program that has a main() method with the following signature:

```
public static void main(String args[])
```

You can replace args[] with any valid name for the array. This array is used to receive program arguments, which can be specified after the file name when the program is run. The following is an example of passing two arguments, B and 13, to a Java program:

```
java Cabin B 13
```

You can insert interpreter arguments between java and the bytecode file name, as in this example:

```
java -verify GreenHornet
```

You can use the following arguments to modify how the interpreter operates:

□ The -classpath *pathtext* argument overrides the default CLASSPATH environment variable, which determines where java will look to find classes that are used in the bytecode. The *pathtext* argument is a list of directories and .zip files.

□ The -checksource (or -cs) argument checks the .class file and source file of the file being executed and compiles the .class file again if it is not current.

□ The -noverify argument turns off the bytecode verifier, which stops the interpreter from taking some security measures to prevent the execution of malicious code on your system. Use this argument with caution.

□ The -verify argument runs the bytecode verifier on all .class files, instead of just the classes that are loaded from systems other than your own.

You can specify these arguments for applications within Java WorkShop in the Project Manager's Run tabbed dialog box.

appletviewer

The Java applet browser, `appletviewer`, loads HTML files and executes Java applets that are embedded in those documents. If more than one applet is included in a document, it executes each one in its own window. The following command would be used to view applets in the HTML file `LightsOut.html`:

```
appletviewer LightsOut.html
```

Because Java WorkShop functions as a Web browser, you have the same capability as `appletviewer` if you enter the HTML file name in the URL field of any WorkShop page.

javadoc

The Java documentation creator, `javadoc`, takes a `.java` source code file or package name as input and generates documentation in HTML format on how the file or package is used. In order for `javadoc` to be able to create full documentation, a special type of comment statement must have been used in the source code. See Day 7, "More About Methods," for a description of these comments.

The following command would be used to create HTML documentation from the source code file `OneMansFamily.java`:

```
javadoc OneMansFamily.java
```

The HTML file `OneMansFamily.class` is created. If a package name were specified instead of a file name, HTML files would be created for each `.java` file in the package, and an HTML file indexing the package also would be created.

You can insert arguments between `javadoc` and the file names, as in this example:

```
javadoc -d otr/classic TheShadow.java
```

You can use the following arguments to modify how the documentation creator operates:

- ☐ The `-classpath` *pathtext* argument overrides the default CLASSPATH environment variable, which determines where `javadoc` will look to find the file or package name. The *pathtext* argument is a list of directories and `.zip` files.
- ☐ The `-d` *directoryname* argument changes the directory where the `.HTML` output should be stored.

You can use the Java WorkShop Source Browser to see this kind of documentation for any Java class or package.

javah

The Java native method C generator, javah, takes Java source files as input and generates the C code necessary to use native methods in those Java programs. The process is described on Day 20, "Native Methods and Libraries."

javap

The Java class disassembler, javap, provides a list of virtual machine instructions used by a class and can detail class and method declarations, constructors, static initializers, and other information about what the bytecode is doing.

APPENDIX

F

Java WorkShop
Troubleshooting

If you're experiencing problems in the operation of Java WorkShop or the use of its features, the following questions and answers might help. If you want to reach the developers of WorkShop, use the Send Comments command on the Help menu to contact them by e-mail.

Also, a Java WorkShop user has established an "unofficial troubleshooting guide" on the World Wide Web at the following URL:

```
http://rampages.onramp.net/~ranger/java_workshop.html
```

The page is available in Dutch, French, and Spanish versions in addition to English. There is also a *Teach Yourself SunSoft Java WorkShop in 21 Days* Web page at the following URL:

```
http://www.spiderbyte.com/java
```

You are encouraged to visit it if you want to contact the authors of the book or ask a question about any of the material that has been covered here. Co-author Rogers Cadenhead maintains the site, and his current e-mail address will be given there.

Questions and Answers

Q I get an error message when I try to run `setupws.exe`, the file I downloaded to run a beta copy of Java WorkShop. Do I have to download that huge file again?

A Unfortunately, you do. If the installation archive that you downloaded was working correctly, you would've been guided through the setup process. Delete the existing copy of `setupws.exe` and download a new copy if SunSoft still is making beta versions available over the World Wide Web.

Q I installed Java WorkShop successfully, but it won't run. What is causing this?

A The primary culprit of problems of this kind is a prior version of the Java Developer's Kit on your system. Java WorkShop includes its own modified version of the JDK, and if there is another one on your system, they will conflict with each other. Deinstall the other JDK and remove all references to it from configuration files such as `AUTOEXEC.BAT` and `CONFIG.SYS`. Then reinstall Java WorkShop, and it should run correctly.

Q When I run a Java application, I get an error that says, `Unable to initialize threads: Cannot find java/lang/Thread`. What do I need to do to fix this?

A This error sounds like something was not configured correctly during the installation of Java WorkShop. Make sure that your `CLASSPATH` environment variable includes the `JDK/classes` subdirectory (which will have a full path that begins with the directory where you installed Java WorkShop). You also ought to consider reinstalling the software.

Q: **When I have been using Java WorkShop for a while, windows sometimes begin to open and close more slowly and the system goes into a funk. What can I do to prevent this from happening?**

A: Because Java WorkShop is one of the largest programs developed with Java, and it's still in early beta release at the time of this writing, it has a number of performance glitches. The best thing to do when you believe that the performance is worsening is to close down the software and load it again. Also, try not to run other programs when running WorkShop.

Q: **Occasionally when I run Java WorkShop, I get a warning dialog box about how the weblog file could not be copied. What is this file?**

A: Java WorkShop sends some program output and error messages to a file called weblog. This file is backed up to a file called weblog.bak when WorkShop is first run, but if another copy of WorkShop is running, this will result in the warning that you saw. The warning also can happen if you load more than one copy of WorkShop at the same time, by double-clicking once too often on the program's icon in Windows 95, for example. There's no harm in running Java WorkShop after you see this message, but if more than one copy of the software is loaded on your system, you should close the extra copies.

Q: **I have a copy of Symantec Café on my system. Can I use WorkShop at the same time?**

A: Because both development environments use environment variables, you need to make sure that none of the Café configuration statements are being executed if you want to run WorkShop. If you have SET CLASSPATH, SET HOMEDRIVE, SET HOMEPATH, SET JAVA_HOME, or SET PATH statements in your configuration file AUTOEXEC.BAT, you need to put a REM statement in front of those statements. This statement causes the line in your configuration to be ignored, but keeps it around if you want to use Café later on. This same conflict might occur with other Java development tools.

Q: **I just downloaded the Dev6 release, but when I try to use Build Manager to compile a program, I get the following error: javac: invalid argument: null. What's wrong?**

A: Java WorkShop is having trouble running javac, the JDK tool it uses behind the scenes to compile the file. Make sure that your CLASSPATH environment variable is set to refer to Java WorkShop directories instead of directories for the JDK, Café, or another product that uses the JDK. If that does not work, remove or use REM statements to disregard all lines in your configuration files referring to Java tools, and then reinstall Java WorkShop. Reportedly, future versions of Java WorkShop will not rely on these configuration files, which should alleviate many of these problems.

F

Q **I wrote a stand-alone program that compiles with no errors, but when I click the Project Tester icon, nothing happens. What's wrong?**

A The Dev5 release of Java WorkShop, only applets can be viewed as they are run from the Project Tester feature. Applications do run when you click the Project Tester icon, but you don't get to see them. The output is directed to a file on your system, and you cannot interact with the program. The file is called `weblog`, with no file extension, and the file can be found in a `.jws` subdirectory on your system. On Microsoft Windows systems, the `.jws` subdirectory will be located off of your main Windows system directory (such as `C:\Windows\.jws`).

Q **I created an applet with Java WorkShop's Visual Java, and it would not run when I put the class files on my Web site. The error messages were referring to classes that could not be found. What can I do to use this applet?**

A With Visual Java programs created from the Dev6 release of Java WorkShop, you have to include extra class files in the directory specified with the `CODEBASE` attribute. All classes in the `jws/visual/rt` directory and its subdirectories should be copied into this directory. SunSoft permits this use of the classes. Developers are investigating ways to remove this requirement for future releases.

Q **My problem isn't answered in this appendix, and I couldn't find an answer anywhere in this book. Where can I go for help?**

A Visit the Web site given at the beginning of this appendix, and let us know what problem you're having—especially if it relates to the examples and lessons in this book. If there's a need for it, we'll answer the commonly asked questions there. You also can find many helpful people by asking questions on the Java Usenet newsgroups such as `comp.lang.java` and `comp.lang.java.misc`. They're described in full in the Graduation section after Day 21.

APPENDIX

G

What's on the CD-ROM

On the *Teach Yourself SunSoft Java Workshop in 21 Days* CD-ROM you will find all the sample files that have been presented in this book along with a wealth of other applications and utilities. The following sections list some of the CD-ROM's highlights.

 NOTE

> Please refer to the readme file on the CD-ROM for the latest listing of software.

Explorer

- ☐ Microsoft Internet Explorer 3.0

HTML Tools

- ☐ Microsoft Internet Assistants for Access, Excel, PowerPoint, Schedule+, and Word
- ☐ CSE 3310 HTML Validator for Windows 95/NT v1.00
- ☐ W3e HTML Editor version 4.2.1, which includes HTML, VRML, and a Java editor/browser
- ☐ HotDog 32 HTML editor
- ☐ HTMLed 32 HTML editor

Graphics and Sound Applications

- ☐ Goldwave sound editor, player, and recorder
- ☐ Paint Shop Pro 3.12 graphics editor and graphic file format converter for Windows
- ☐ ThumbsPlus image viewer and browser
- ☐ MapThis ImageMap utility

Java

- ☐ Sun's Java Developer's Kit for Windows 95/NT, version 1.02
- ☐ 21 sample applets

Utilities

- ☐ Microsoft Viewers for Excel, PowerPoint, and Word
- ☐ Adobe Acrobat viewer
- ☐ Microsoft PowerPoint Animation Player & Publisher
- ☐ WinZip for Windows NT/95
- ☐ WinZip Self-Extractor, which is a utility program that creates native Windows self-extracting ZIP files

About Shareware

Shareware is not free. Please read all documentation associated with a third-party product (usually contained with files named `readme.txt` or `license.txt`) and follow all guidelines.

G

INDEX

Symbols

" (double quotes) string literals, 62

' (single quotes) character literals, 61

— (decrement assignment operator), 67

! (exclamation point) not logical operator, 70

!= (not equal comparison operator), 69

% (percent sign) modulus operator, 64

& (ampersand)
    and logical operator, 70
    bitwise AND operator, 70

&= (AND assignment operator), 71

* (asterisks)
    comments, 60
    importing classes, 409
    importing packages, 45
    import statements, 398
    multiplication operator, 64
    wildcard character, importing classes, 176

+ (plus sign)
    addition operator, 63
    string concatenation, 73

++ (increment assignment operator), 67

- (minus sign) subtraction operator, 63

< (less than comparison operator), 69

<= (less than or equal to comparison operator), 69

> (greater than comparison operator), 69

>= (greater than or equal to comparison operator), 69

/ (forward slash) division operator, 64

; (semicolons)
    for loops, 112
    statements, 54

<< (left shift operator), 70

<<= (left shift assignment operator), 71

== (equal comparison operator), 69

>> (right shift operator), 70

>>= (right shift assignment operator), 71

>>> (zero fill right shift operator), 70

>>>= (zero fill right shift assignment operator), 71

[ ] (brackets) declaring array variables, 104

^ (caret)
bitwise XOR operator, 70
xor logical operator, 70

{ } (braces) block statements, 107

| (vertical bar)
bitwise OR operator, 70
|or logical operator, 70

|= (OR assignment operator), 71

|= (XOR assignment operator), 71

~ (tilde) bitwise complement operator, 70

A

Abacus applet, 344
Web site, 345
ABSBOTTOM value (<APPLET> HTML tag ALIGN attribute), 182
ABSMIDDLE value (<APPLET> HTML tag ALIGN attribute), 182
abstract classes, 389-390
InputStream, 457-461
methods, 410
OutputStream, 471-472
abstract methods, 389-390, 404
Abstract Windowing Toolkit, see AWT
accept( ) method, sockets, 365
access modifiers, 376, 390
classes, 401
instance variables, 381-382
interfaces, 403

package, 377-378
private, 380-381
protected, 378-380
public, 377
accessor methods, 382-383
speed considerations, 390
ACTION EVENT, user interface components, 322
action( ) method
adding, 339
defining, 312
menus, 352
actions
handling, 329
methods, 313
objects, testing, 312
user interface components, handling, 311-313
add( ) method
adding components to panels, 297
border layouts, 310
frames, 348
menu items, 351
addItem( ) method, choice menus, 302
addition operator, 63
ALIGN attribute (<APPLET> HTML tag), 181-182
aligning
applets, 181-182
panel components, 306-307
text lables, 129-130
alternative HTML code for BiggerPalindrome.html (listing), 188
ampersand (&)
and logical operator, 70
bitwise AND operator, 70
AND assignment operator (&=), 71
and logical operator, 70
animation
creating, 222-225
Animator applet, 263
images, 252-259
Pixel Pete, 252-259

flicker, 230
avoiding, 230-240
clipping, 236
double-buffering, 242, 263-267
for loops, 254
frames, 223-225
images, arrays, 253
instance variables, 253
loops, 226
methods, 254-256
painting, 222
creating objects, 225
SharkLine applet, 125-126
threads, 254
Animator applet, 263
Web site, 263
applications, main( ) method, 139
Applet class, 570
applications, creating, 356-357
subclassing, 173
Applet dialog box, 30
projects, creating, 15
<APPLET> HTML tag, 5, 177-179
attributes, 180-184
<APPLET> tag and HTML formatting for Calc (listing), 77
<APPLET> tag and surrounding HTML tags for Countdown (listing), 482
<APPLET> tag for Abacus (listing), 345
<APPLET> tag for BallDrop (listing), 452
<APPLET> tag for Eliza (listing), 429
<APPLET> tag for Eowyn4 (listing), 219
<APPLET> tag for Fan (listing), 243
<APPLET> tag for Graph (listing), 192

<APPLET> tag for Iceblox
(listing), 392
<APPLET> tag for Lines
(listing), 167
<APPLET> tag for MktView
(listing), 500
<APPLET> tag for
NeedleDemo (listing), 147
<APPLET> tag for
NowShowing (listing), 371
<APPLET> tag for scroll
(listing), 291
<APPLET> tag for SharkLine
(listing), 126
<APPLET> tag for SmartMap
(listing), 412-414
<APPLET> tag for SparkleText
on a simple HTML page
(listing), 22
<APPLET> tag for StarField
(listing), 102
AppletContext interface, 570
applets, 3
    Abacus, 344-345
    actions, handling, 329
    aligning, 181-182
    animation, 223-225
        painting, 222
        SharkLine, 125-126
    Animator, 263
    Arithmetic, creating, 64-66
    AudioLoop, creating,
      261-263
    BallDrop, 452-453
    BiggerPalindrome, 185-189
        creating, 186
    BigPalindrome, creating,
      42-43
    browsers, 172
    Calc
        creating, 76
        Web site, 77
    Centered, creating, 212-213
    Checkers1, animation,
      234-240
    Checkers2, adding double-
      buffering, 265-266
    classes, 99

clearing, 207
Clock2, 49-50
    Web site, 51
color, creating arrays, 233
ColorBoxes, creating,
  216-217
ColorSwirl, animation,
  231-234
ColorTest, creating, 323-333
communicating between
  applets, 367-368
compared to applications,
  172-173
compiling, 17-18
    Build Manager, 34
Countdown, 481-483
CrazyText, 528-531
CreateDate1, creating, 81-82
CreateDate2, creating, 83-85
creating, 4, 14-19, 30-34,
  42-43, 64-69, 81-91,
  150-154, 173-177, 338
    double-buffering, 264-265
    Source Editor, 31
debugging, 119-124
destroying, 175-176
DigitalClock, 223-225
    adding threads, 228-230
    troubleshooting, 226
DigitalThreads, creating,
  228-230
DrawDrink, creating, 248
DrawDrink2, creating,
  250-251
EarthWeb Chat, 4
Eliza, 428-430
embedding HTML tags, 172
Eowyn4, 219-220
events, 174
Fan, 242-243
File dialog boxes, 355
files, retrieving, 361
FillText, creating, 313
forms, 369
GetRaven, creating, 362-364
Grader, 119-120
    creating, 117-118
Graph, 191-192

Guesser, creating, 334-342
Iceblox, 391-392
icons, 30
images, loading, 246-247
information, displaying, 366
initializing, 174
    creating layout managers,
      306
input streams, file system,
  462
JabberwockApplet, creating,
  30-34
    running, 35
Keys, creating, 283-286
Lamp, creating, 206-207
layouts, creating, 324
LimeSweeper, 268-269
limitations, 191
Lines, 166-167
    creating, 278-282
    Web site, 167
loading, 173
ManyFonts, creating,
  209-210
methods, 174
MKTView, 500-501
MyRect, creating, 150-154
naming, calling methods, 367
native methods, 486
NeedleDemo, 146-147
networking
    browsers, 357
    creating links, 358
NowShowing, 370-371
painting, 176, 241
    importing Graphics class,
      194
panels
    creating layouts, 324-325
    creating subpanels,
      326-328
parameters
    changing, 188-189
    passing, 184-189
Passer, creating, 136-138
PersonApplet, creating,
  155-156

Pete
creating, 256-259
images, 253
PrePost, creating, 67-69
programming, Source
Browser, 46-47
projects, 14
publishing, 180
Range, creating, 132-133
RectApplet, creating,
152-154
RectApplet2, creating,
156-158
reports, displaying, 163
running, 5, 35, 85, 174
as applications, 357
methods, 223
parameters, 83
Project Tester, 30, 35
threads, 225
Visual Java, 586
scroll, 291
security, 172, 190-191, 525
signatures, 173
SmartMap, 411-415
sockets, 365
SparkleText, 21
Web site, 22
Spots
creating, 273-277
modifying, 290
StarField, 101
Web site, 102
starting, 174
stopping, 175
threads, 241
streams, 474
testing, 5, 179
Project Tester, 18-19
TestPoint, creating, 87-88
TestString, creating, 90-91
text alternatives, 179
threads, creating, 226-228,
450
updating, 329-331
user interface components,
adding, 296-297

Web pages, adding, 177-180
windows, warnings, 368
AppletStub interface, 570
appletviewer, 580
applications, 3
arguments, 139
handling, 140-141
passing, 140
compared to applets, 172-173
creating, 139-144, 174
Applet class, 356-357
networking, sockets, 364-365
parameters, passing, 184
running, 142
command-line, 144-145
Project Tester, 586
SumAverage, creating,
143-144
threads
creating, 450
weblog file, 142
windows, 356-357
archiving packages/directories,
409
arcs, drawing, 201-205
arguments, 574
action( ) method, 312
applications, 139
handling, 140-141
passing, 140
converting, 143
dialog boxes, 354
drawChars( ) method, 209
drawImage( ) method,
248-249
drawLine( ) method, 195
fonts, creating, 208
methods, passing, 135-138
mouse click events, 273
objects, creating, 80
play( ) method, 260
read( ) method, 458
registers, 509
Scrollbar( ) method, 320
setting, Project Manager,
142-143
skip( ) method, 459

storage, 143
write( ) method, 472
Arithmetic applet, creating,
64-66
arithmetic operators, 63-66
arrays, 104, 542, 572
accessing elements, 105
assignment statements, 106
color applets, 233
images, animations, 253
initializing, 105
length, testing, 106
methods, 132
multidimentional, 106
objects
creating, 104-105
references, 106
polygons, drawing, 199
primitive data types, 105
streams, 461-462
strings, 62
subscripts, 105
variables, declaring, 104
vectors, 470
assigning variables, 540
assignment operators, 66
incrementing/decrementing,
67
variables, assigning values,
87-88
assignment statements, arrays,
106
asterisk (*)
comments, 60
import statements, 398
importing classes, 409
importing packages, 45
multiplication operator, 64
wildcard character, importing
classes, 176
atomic operations, 433
threads, 433
attributes
<APPLET> HTML tag,
178-184
instance variables, 54
NAME (<PARAM> HTML
tag), 83

objects, 27-28
  <PARAM> HTML tag, 184
  VALUE (<PARAM> HTML
    tag), 83
variables, 27
**Attributes window, user
  interface components (Visual
  Java), 337**
AU format (audio files), 260
audio
  AU format, 260
  background, 261
  loops, 261
  playing
    repeating, 260
    stopping, 261
  sounds, 260-263
  stopping, 268
  URLs, loading files, 260
AudioClip interface, 570
**AudioLoop applet, creating,
  261-263**
author documentation tag, 164
available( ) method, 481
  input streams, 459-462
**AWT (Abstract Windowing
  Toolkit), 99, 294**
  applets, creating, 173
  class hierarchy, 296
  components, 294-296
  events, 271-272
  frames, 348-349
  panels, 305-311
  user interface components,
    296-305
awt portfolio, 30

B

backgrounds
  color, 215
    setting with init( )
      method, 275
  sounds, 261
BallDrop applet, 452
  Web site, 453

**BASELINE value (<APPLET>
  HTML tag ALIGN attribute),
  182**
behavior
  defining, methods, 28
  objects, 28
**BiggerPalindrome applet,
  185-189**
  creating, 186
**BiggerPalindrome class
  (listing), 187**
BigPalindrome applet
  creating, 42-43
  listing, 177
**BigPalindrome.java (listing),
  45**
bitmap images, drawing, 195
BitSet class, 563
bitwise AND operator, 70
**bitwise complement operator
  (~), 70**
bitwise operators, 71
bitwise OR operator, 70
bitwise XOR operator, 70
block statements, 54, 107
  if-else conditionals, 108
bookmarks, URLs, 360
boolean
  data types, 31
  literals, 61
  values, event methods, 315
  variable types, 58
Boolean class, 562
**BorderLayout class, 309-310,
  567**
**braces ({ }) block statements,
  107**
**brackets ([ ]) declaring array
  variables, 104**
break keyword, 114-115
  labels, 115-116
**break statements, switch
  conditionals, 110**
breakpoints, 116
  debugging, 122-124
browsers
  applets, 172
    networking, 357
    text alternatives, 179

HotJava, 6
  threads, 432
Internet Explorer, 4
Java compatibility, 4
Netscape Navigator 2.0, 4
showStatus( ) method,
  support, 366
status bar, creating messages,
  366
threads, 432
URLs, passing, 358
**BufferedInputStream class,
  464-465, 564**
**BufferedOutputStream class,
  475, 564**
buffers
  output streams, 475
  streams, 457-458
**Build All Files command, Build
  Manager, 34**
**Build All Files icon (Build
  Manager), 17**
**Build dialog box, Project
  Manager, 85**
Build Manager, 11
  applets, compiling, 34
  commands, Build All Files,
    34
  debugging, 116
  icon, 17
  projects, compiling, 17
  source code, compiling, 338
**buildRect( ) method, creating,
  151**
Button class, 567
**Button( ) constructor method,
  298**
**buttons (user interface
  components), 298-299**
  actions, 312
  bookmarks, creating, 360
  command toolbar, Visual
    Java, 335
  labels, 299
  mouse, events, 290
  see also radio buttons
**ByteArrayInputStream class,
  461-462, 564**

**ByteArrayOutputStream class,
472-473, 564**
bytecode, 505, 508-509
  alignment, 508
  compiling, just-in-time,
    513-514
  converting to C code, 514
  data types, 508
    security considerations,
      522-523
  interpreter, 512-513
  opcode, 508
  speed considerations,
    512-514
  verifying, 523
    security considerations,
      520-522
bytecodes
  interpreters, 8
  speed considerations, 10

C

C
  code, native methods,
    494-496
  compared to Java, 54
  compilers, converting
    bytecode, 514
  composite data types,
    compared to classes, 26
  functions, 496-497
C++
  compared to Java, 54,
    572-575
  OOP, relationship to Java, 10
caching, streams, 464
Calc applet
  creating, 76
  Web site, 77
callbacks, interfaces, 410
calling
  constructor methods, 156
    superclasses, 162
  event handlers, overriding
    handleEvent( ) method, 289

  methods, 89-92, 160-161
  objects, 28
Canvas class, 322, 567
**canvases (user interface
  components), 295, 322**
CardLayout class, 310, 567
caret (^)
  bitwise XOR operator, 70
  XOR logical operator, 70
case-sensitivity, 33, 57
  applet parameters, 185
casting
  data types, 93
  explicit, 94
  integers, read( ) method, 458
  keyDown events, converting
    to characters, 282
  objects, 94-95
    to interfaces, 95
    to primitive data types,
      95-96
  primitive data types, 93
    to objects, 95-96
**catch clause, exception
  handling, 421**
**Centered applet, creating,
  212-213**
char data types, 58
Character class, 562
character literals
  objects, creating, 80
characters
  drawing, 209-210
  escape codes, 62
  literals, 61
  Unicode, 56
    creating strings, 473
charWidth( ) method, 212
**check boxes (user interface
  components), 299-300**
  actions, 312
  exclusive, 299
  nonexclusive, 299
Checkbox class, 567
  methods, 299
**Checkbox( ) constructor
  method, 299**

CheckboxGroup class, 567
  radio buttons, creating, 300
CheckBoxMenuItem class, 351
CheckboxMenuItem class, 567
**Checkers1 applet, animation,
  234-240**
**Checkers2 applet, double-
  buffering, 265-266**
Choice class, 567
  choice menus, creating, 302
**choice menus (user interface
  components), 302-303**
  actions, 312
  compared to scrolling lists,
    318
**Choose command, Portfolio
  Manager, 30**
Class Browser, 46
Class class, 562
class instances, variables, 58
class keyword, 128
class libraries, 8
class loader, 524-525
**class methods, 48, 91-92, 138,
  385**
  defining, 138
  inheritance, 391
  naming, 92
**class variables, 48, 54, 86-88,
  384**
  accessing, dot notation, 89
  creating, 128
  declaring, 130
  defining, 89
  initial values, 56
  naming, 89
  protecting, 438-439
classes, 25-27, 47
  abstract, 389-390
    InputStream, 457-461
    methods, 404-410
    OutputStream, 471-472
    protected access modifiers,
      380
  access modifiers, 401
  Applet, 570
    creating applications,
      356-357
    subclassing, 173

applets, 99
applications, 139
attributes, 27-28
behavior, 28
BitSet, 563
Boolean, 562
BorderLayout, 309-310, 567
BufferedInputStream,
    464-465, 564
BufferedOutputStream, 475,
    564
Button, 567
ByteArrayInputStream,
    461-462, 564
ByteArrayOutputStream,
    472-473, 564
Canvas, 567
Canvases, 322
CardLayout, 310, 567
casting, 94-95
Character, 562
Checkbox, 567
    methods, 299
CheckboxGroup, 567
    creating radio buttons,
        300
CheckBoxMenuItem, 351
CheckboxMenuItem, 567
Choice, 567
    creating choice menus,
        302
Class, 562
ClassLoader, 562
Color, 214, 567
ColorControls, 324
ColorModel, 569
ColorTest, 323
compared to composite data
    types (C programming
    language), 26
compared to interfaces, 402
comparing, methods, 96
Compiler, 562
Component, 343, 567
components, 27-28
constant pool, 511
Container, 343, 567
ContentHandler, 566

creating, 26-35
    constructor methods, 82
    defining, 31
    inheritance, 36
    Portfolio Manager, 29-30
    subclassing, 37-39
CropImageFilter, 569
DatagramPacket, 566
DatagramSocket, 566
DataInputStream, 465-466,
    564
DataOutputStream, 475-477,
    564
Date, 224, 563
declaring
    final, 386
    protected, 379
    public, 377
defining, 43, 128, 274, 543
    default packages, 396
    threads, 227
Dialog, 348, 567
Dictionary, 563
Dimension, 567
DirectColorModel, 569
directories, hierarchies, 396
Double, 562
Error, 419
Event, 567
exceptions, 419-420
File, 479, 564
FileDescriptor, 564
FileDialog, 355-367
FileInputStream, 462-463,
    564
FileOutputStream, 474, 565
FilteredImageSource, 569
FilteredOutputStream,
    474-475
FilterInputStream, 463-464,
    565
FilterOutputStream, 565
final modifier, 386-388
Float, 562
FlowLayout, 306-307, 567
Font, 208, 567
    creating instances, 43
FontMetrics, 208, 211, 567

Frame, 348, 567
Graphics, 194-195, 567
    primitives, 195
GridBagConstraints, 308,
    567
GridBagLayout, 308, 567
GridLayout, 308, 567
Hashtable, 563
hiding, 394, 400-401
    forcing visibility, 409
hierarchies, diagrams, 547,
    559
hierarchy, 36-37
    creating, 37-39
Image, 246, 567
ImageFilter, 569
importing, 397-400
    * (asterisks), 409
    multiple, 176
IndexColorModel, 569
InetAddress, 566
inheritance, 36-40
    multiple, 40
    single, 40
InputStream, 457-461, 565
    methods, 481
Inset, 310-311
Insets, 568
instance variables, 27
    creating, 326
instances, 26
Integer, 562
    converting argument
        arrays, 144
interfaces, 99
    inheritance, 404
Jabberwock, creating, 29
Java language, 99
java.io, 479
Label, 568
    methods, 298
libraries, 27, 562-570
    java package, 99-100
    packages, 42
LineNumberInputStream,
    467, 565
linking, 499

List, 568
    creating scrolling lists, 318
loading, 499
    security considerations,
        524-525
Long, 562
Math, 138, 562
MediaTracker, 568
MemoryImageSource, 569
Menu, 568
MenuBar, 568
MenuComponent, 568
MenuItem, 351, 568
methods, calling, 28
    modifiers, 375-376
    naming conventions, 397
native methods, 489-491
Needle, Web site, 147
networks, 99
Number, 562
Object, 37, 562
objects, determining, 98
Observable, 563
organization, 296
organizing, 36
OutputStream, 471-472, 565
packages, 42, 394-401
    accessing, 42
    hiding, 394
    importing, 44-46
Panel, 568
PipedInputStream, 469, 565
PipedOutputStream, 479,
    565
PixelGrabber, 569
Point, 568
Polygon, 200, 568
PrintClass, 159
PrintStream, 477-479, 565
PrintSubClass, 159
Process, 562
Properties, 563
PushBackInputStream,
    467-469, 565
Random, 564
RandomAccessFile, 479, 565
Rectangle, 568
RGBImageFilter, 569

Runnable interface, adding,
    228
Runtime, 563
RuntimeException, 419
Scrollbar, 321, 568
SecurityManager, 526-527,
    563
    protection realms, 526
SequenceInputStream,
    469-470, 565
ServerSocket, 358, 364-365,
    566
Socket, 358, 364-365, 566
SocketImpl, 566
Stack, 564
streams, I/O, 99
StreamTokenizer, 479, 565
String, 62, 563
    creating instances, 80
StringBuffer, 563
StringBufferInputStream,
    470-471, 565
StringTokenizer, 564
subclasses, 36, 128
subclassing, 42-47
superclasses, 36
System, 563
TextArea, 568
TextComponent, 304, 568
TextField, 568
Thread, 224, 440, 563
ThreadDeath, 563
ThreadGroup, 563
Throwable, 418, 563
Toolkit, 568
URL, 566
    creating instances, 358
URLConnection, 364, 566
URLEncoder, 566
URLStreamHandler, 566
utility, 99
Vector, 564
Window, 348-349, 568
wrapper, converting objects,
    138
see also objects
ClassLoader class, 562
CLASSPATH environment

variable
    classes, directories, 396
clauses
    catch, exception handling,
        421
    finally, exceptions, 425-426
clearing graphics, 207
clearRect( ) method, 207
client-side sockets, 365
clipping
    animation flicker, avoiding,
        236
    defining areas, 239
clipRect( ) method, 239
Clock2 applet, 49-50
    Web site, 51
Cloneable interface, 562
Close command (File menu),
    17
close( ) method
    input streams, 461
    output streams, 472
closing
    polygons, 200
    streams, 463
code, creating (Source Editor),
    16
CODE attribute (<APPLET>
    HTML tag), 178, 183-184
CODEBASE attribute
    (<APPLET> HTML tag),
    179, 183-184
color
    applets
        creating, 214-217
        creating arrays, 233
    backgrounds, 215
        setting with init( )
            method, 275
    color model, 214
    displaying, troubleshooting,
        242
    foreground, setting, 215
    methods, 215-216
    objects, creating, 214, 233
    selection, 214
    setting current, 215-216
    standard colors, 214

text, 130
troubleshooting, 218
Color class, 214, 567
instances, creating, 214
ColorBoxes applet, creating, 216-217
ColorControls class, 324
ColorModel class, 569
ColorSwirl applet, animation, 231-234
ColorTest applet, creating, 323-333
ColorTest class, 323
command toolbar, 14
buttons, Visual Java, 335
icons, Build Manager, 17
Portfolio Manager icon, 15
projects, creating, 15
command-line
applications, running, 144-145
parameters, passing to applications, 184
utilities, JDK, 578-581
commands
Build Manager, Build All Files, 34
File menu
Close, 17
Save, 17
Help, class library documentation, 99
new, *see* new operator
Portfolio Manager
Choose, 30
Create a New Project, 30
Remove the Selected Project, 30
comments, 32, 59-60, 539
* (asterisks), 60
documentation, 59, 163
HTML tags, 164
inserting, 164-165
multiline, 59
single line, 59
compaction (garbage collection), 517

comparison operators, 69
objects, 96-98
Compiler class, 562
compilers
C, GNU, 495
compiling
applets, 17-18
Build Manager, 34
bytecode
just-in-time, 513-514
platform independence, 8
errors
class names, 397
correcting, 18
importing packages, 44
method overloading, 166
exceptions, 418
images, loading, 246
just-in-time compilers, 488
methods, errors, 150
security considerations, 520
source code
Build Manager, 338
bytecode, 508
source files
selecting, 85
stub files, 498
Component class, 343, 567
components, 294-296
adding to panels, 297
canvases, 295
containers, 295
frames, adding, 348
hierarchies, 295
layout managers, 305
nesting, 314-316
panels
aligning, 306-307
creating nested, 314-315
grid layouts, 308
slide shows, creating, 310
user interfaces, 295-296
buttons, 298-299
canvases, 322
check boxes, 299-300
choice menus, 302-303
events, 297
handling actions/events,

311-313
labels, 297-298
radio buttons, 300-301
scrollbars, 319-321
scrolling lists, 318-319
sliders, 319-321
text areas, 316-317
text fields, 303-305
virtual machine, 507
window construction, 295
concatenation, strings, 73
conditional operators, 108-109
compared to if-else operators, 109
conditional statements, 543
conditionals
if, 107-108
nested, 109
switch, 109-110
configuration, troubleshooting, 584
connect( ) method, 364
constant pool, 511
constants, 129-130
declaring, 387
defining, 75, 129
constructors, 82, 154-158
buttons, creating, 298
calling, 156
check boxes, creating, 299
defining, 544-545
dialog boxes, creating, 353
frames, 348
labels, creating, 297
objects, creating, 80
overloading, 156-158
overriding, 159-162
scrollbars, creating, 320
scrolling lists, creating, 318
text areas, creating, 316
text fields, creating, 303
Container class, 343, 567
containers, 295
ContentHandler class, 566
ContentHandlerFactory interface, 566
continue keyword, 114-115
labels, 115-116

controlDown( ) method, 287
converting arguments, 143
    see also casting
coordinate system, graphics,
    194-195
copyArea( ) method, 207
copying graphics, 207
Countdown applet, 481
    Web site, 483
countItem( ) method, choice
    menus, 303
countItems( ) method,
    scrolling lists, 319
CrazyText applet, 528
    Web site, 531
Create a New Project command
    (Portfolio Manager), 30
CreateDate1 applet, creating,
    81-82
CreateDate2 applet, creating,
    83-85
createImage( ) method, 264
critical sections, 437
CropImageFilter class, 569

D

daemon threads, 440
data types, 573
    boolean, 31
    bytecode, 508
        security considerations,
            522-523
    casting, 93
    converting to strings, 73
    declaring, 58
    output streams, 475
    primitive, 8, 57
        arrays, 105
        char, 58
        converting to objects, 138
        floating-point, 58
        integers, 57
        returntype, 131
        switch conditionals, 110
    streams, 465-466
DatagramPacket class, 566

DatagramSocket class, 566
DataInput interface, 465-466,
    564
DataInputStream class,
    465-466, 564
DataOutput interface,
    475-477, 564
DataOutputStream class,
    475-477, 564
Date class, 224, 563
Date objects, creating, 81
date string, format, 82
deadlock (multithreading), 451
Debug/Browse dialog box
    (Project Manager), 85
Debugger, 12, 116-117
debugging, 116-117
    applets, 119-124
    breakpoints, 122-124
    jump-to-error icons, 116, 119
    line numbers, adding, 467
    mouse events, 287
    switch statement errors,
        121-122
    threads, 444
declaring
    class variables, 130
    classes
        final, 386
        protected, 379
        public, 377
    constants, 387
    data types, 58
    exceptions, 418
    interfaces, 402
    methods
        block statements, 107
        final, 387-388
        package access, 378
    variables, 55-56, 540
        arrays, 104
        final, 387
        types, 57-58
defining
    action( ) methods, 312
    class methods, 138
    class variables, 89
    classes, 31, 43, 128, 274, 543

default packages, 396
    threads, 227
constants, 75, 129
constructors, 544-545
instance variables, 128-129
methods, 131-132, 544-545
    object behavior, 28
    variable scope, 134-135
values, primitive data types, 8
design hierarchies (interfaces),
    compared to implementation,
    404-405
designing user interfaces,
    Visual Java, 334-335
destroy( ) method, 175-176
destroying applets, 175-176
Developer's Corner (JavaSoft)
    Web site, 13, 514
dialog boxes, 353-355
    Applet, 30
        creating projects, 15
    arguments, 354
    Build (Project Manager), 85
    creating, 353
    Debug/Browse (Project
        Manager), 85
    displaying, 354
    files, 369
        opening/saving, 355-356
    General (Project Manager),
        85
    modal, 353
    Portfolio (Project Manager),
        85
    projects, creating, 15
    Project Manager, 85
    Publish (Project Manager),
        85
    Run, 142
        Project Manager, 85
    Source Browser, 46
    Standalone Program,
        140-141
Dialog class, 348, 567
Dictionary class, 563
DigitalClock applet, 223-225
    threads, adding, 228-230
    troubleshooting, 226

DigitalThreads applet, creating, 228-230
Dimension class, 567
Dimension objects, 212
DirectColorModel class, 569
directories
    adding to paths, 396
    archiving, 409
    classes, hierarchies, 396
    creating homework directory, 13
    default, installing WorkShop, 13
    images, 247
disable( ) method, menus, 351
display resolution, 12
displaying
    color, troubleshooting, 242
    dialog boxes, 354
    information, applets, 366
    reports, applets, 163
    three-dimensional rectangles, 198
division operator, 64
do loops, 113-114
documentation
    class libraries, Help command, 99
    exceptions, 418
documentation comments, 59, 163
    HTML tags, 164
    inserting, 164-165
documentation tags, 164-165
documents
    HTML, creating, 177-180
dot notation
    class variables, assigning, 89
    instance variables, values, 87
    methods, calling, 89
Double class, 562
double quotes (") string literals, 62
double variable type, 61
double-buffering, 242, 263-267
    animation flicker, avoiding, 230
    applets, creating, 264-265

downloading WorkShop, 13
draw3DRect( ) method, 198
drawArc( ) method, 201
drawChars( ) method, 209
DrawDrink applet, creating, 248
DrawDrink2 applet, creating, 250-251
drawImage( ) method, 247-251
drawing, 195
    arcs, 201-205
    characters, 209-210
    clipping, 236
        defining areas, 239
    images, 247-251
    lines, 195
        changing thickness, 218
    ovals, 201
    polygons, 199-200
    rectangles, 196-198
    rounded rectangles, 197
    strings, 209-210
    three-dimensional rectangles, 197
    see also painting
drawLine( ) method, 195
drawOval( ) method, 201
drawPolygon( ) method, 199
drawRect( ) method, 196
drawRoundRect( ) method, 197
drawString( ) method, 66, 137, 209

E

EarthWeb Chat Web site, 4
echoCharIsSet( ) method, text fields, 305
elevators, scrollbars, 319
Eliza applet, 428
    Web site, 430
elliptical arcs, drawing, 204
else keyword, 107
enable( ) method, menus, 351
Enumeration interface, 563
Enumerator interface, 407-408

environment variables (CLASSPATH), class directories, 396
environments (execution), stack frame, 510
EOFException exceptions, input streams, 466
Eowyn4 applet, 219
    Web site, 220
equal comparison operator, 69
equals( ) method (strings), comparing characters, 97
Error class, 419
error messages
    exceptions, 422
    javac, troubleshooting, 585
    weblog file, troubleshooting, 585
errors
    arrays, subscripts, 106
    classes, importing, 397
    compared to exceptions, 427
    compiling
        correcting, 18
        importing packages, 44
        method overloading, 166
    exceptions, arrays, 106
    jump-to-error icons, 116
    methods, creating, 150
    switch statements, debugging, 121-122
    see also exceptions
escape codes, 62
evaluating expressions, 69
Event class, 567
event handling, handleEvent( ) method, 287-289
Event.DOWN, 283
Event.END, 283
Event.HOME, 283
Event.KEY ACTION, 288
Event.KEY ACTION RELEASE, 288
Event.KEY PRESS, 288
Event.KEY RELEASE, 288
Event.LEFT, 283
Event.MOUSE DOWN, 288
Event.MOUSE DRAG, 288

Event.MOUSE ENTER, 288
Event.MOUSE EXIT, 288
Event.MOUSE MOVE, 288
Event.MOUSE UP, 288
Event.PGDN, 283
Event.PGUP, 283
Event.RIGHT, 283
Event.UP, 283
events, 271-272
  ACTION EVENT (user
    interface components), 322
  applets, 174
  creating, overriding
    handleEvent( ) method, 287
  handling, 339-342
  IDs, 322
  instance variables, ID, 287
  KEY ACTION (text fields),
    322
  keyboard, 282-287
    modifier keys, 287
    non-alphanumeric key
      events, 283
  keyDown, casting into
    characters, 282
  LIST DESELECT (scrolling
    lists), 322
  LIST SELECT (scrolling
    lists), 322
  menu actions, 352
  mouse
    buttons, 290
    clicks, 272-277
    debugging, 287
    movement, 277-282
  mouseDown, 272-273
    methods, 272-273
    parameters, 273
  mouseUp, 272-273
    methods, 273
    parameters, 273
  options, 315-316
  panels, nested, 315-316
  return key, 290
  SCROLL ABSOLUTE
    (scrollbars), 322
  SCROLL LINE DOWN

    (scrollbars), 322
  SCROLL LINE UP
    (scrollbars), 323
  SCROLL PAGE DOWN
    (scrollbars), 323
  SCROLL PAGE UP
    (scrollbars), 323
  user interface components,
    297, 322-323
    handling, 311-313
  windows, 356
exception documentation tag,
165
exceptions, 417-420, 424, 546
  arrays, 106
  classes, 419-420
  compared to errors, 427
  compiling, 418
  declaring, 418
  documentation, 418
  EOFException, input
    streams, 466
  error messages, 422
  finally clause, 425-426
  handling, 420-423
  hierarchies, 419
  interfaces, 423
  IOException
    input streams, 456
    network connections, 361
  listing, throws clause, 419
  methods, 419
  nesting handlers, 421
  packages, 420
  programming, 424
  rethrowing, 421
  streams, resetting after
    marking, 460
  threads, determining thread
    death, 445
  URLs, creating, 358
  see also errors
exclamation point (!) not
logical operator, 70
exclusive check boxes, 299
exiting Source Editor, 17

explicit casting, 94
expressions, 54, 63-73
  arrays, accessing, 105
  conditional operators, 108
  evaluating, 69
    operator precedence,
      71-73
  variables
    accessing, 87
    assignment, 66
extends clause (interfaces),
inheritance, 403
extends keyword, 43, 128

F

false keyword, 61
Fan applet, 242
  Web site, 243
File class, 479, 564
file dialog boxes, 369
File menu commands
  Close, 17
  Save, 17
FileDescriptor class, 564
FileDialog class, 355-367
FileDialog( ) constructor
method, 355
FileInputStream class,
462-463, 564
FileNameFilter interface, 564
FileOutputStream class, 474,
565
files
  HotDrink.gif, 249
  input streams, 462
  opening, dialog boxes,
    355-356
  processing streams, 477
  retrieving
    applets, 361
    URLconnection class, 364
  saving, dialog boxes, 355-356
  source
    creating, 15-17
    saving, 17
    selecting when compiling,

85
weblog, 142
fill3DRect( ) method, 198
fillArc( ) method, 201
fillOval( ) method, 201
fillPolygon( ) method, 199
fillRect( ) method, 196
fillRoundRect( ) method, 197
FillText applet, creating, 313
FilteredimageSource class, 569
FilterOutputStream class, 474-475, 565
FilterInputStream class, 463-464, 565
filters
  output streams, 474-475
  streams, 456
    naming for line numbers, 467
    nesting, 463-464
final keyword, 129
final methods, compared to private, 388
final modifier, 386-388
final Pete applet (listing), 257-259
final source code of Guesser.java (listing), 340-342
finalize( ) method, 163
  compared to destroy( ) method, 175
  forcing, 528
finalizer methods, 162-163
finally clause, exceptions, 425-426
first part of the Lines applet (listing), 278
FirstPerson, 6
flicker (animation), 230
  avoiding, 230-231, 235-240
    clipping, 236
    double-buffering, 230, 263-267
flickering, double-buffering, 242
Float class, 562
float variable type, 61
floating-point

color values, 215
data types, 58
  casting from integers, 94
division, 64
literals, 61
flow control, 574
FlowLayout class, 306-307, 567
flush( ) method, output streams, 472
Font class, 208, 567
  instances, creating, 43
font metrics, Centered applet, 212-213
FontMetrics class, 208, 211, 567
fonts, 208
  creating, 208
  labels, 297
  methods, 211-212
  setting, init( ) method, 284
  setting current, 209
  troubleshooting, 218
for loops, 111-112, 144
  animations, 254
  statements, 111
foreground color, setting, 215
formats, date string, 82
formatting images, 247
forms
  applets, 369
  POST, 369
forward slash (/) division operator, 64
Frame class, 348, 567
frame register, 509
frames, 348-349
  animation, 223-225
  components, adding, 348
  creating, methods, 348
  dialog boxes, 354
  layout, default, 348
  painting, animation, 222
functions
  C, 496-497
  compared to methods, 48

G

Gamelan Web site, 191, 218
garbage collection, 83, 515-519
  compaction, 517
  disabling, 528
  marking and sweeping, 517
  object references, 517
  parallel, 518
  streams, 463
  threads, 228
General dialog box (Project Manager), 85
getAppletContext( ) method, 366-367
  SendMessage(), 367
getAppletInfo( ) method, 366
getApplets( ) method, 367
getAscent( ) method, 212
getAudioClip( ) method, 260
getCheckboxGroup( ) method, 301
getClass( ) method, 98
getCodeBase( ) method, 246
getColumns( ) method
  text areas, 317
  text fields, 305
getCurrent( ) method, checkboxes, 301
getDescent( ) method, 212
getDocumentBase( ) method, 246
getEchoChar( ) method, text fields, 305
getFont( ) method, 211
getFontList( ) method, 208
getFontMetrics( ) method, 211
getGraphics( ) method, 264
getHeight( ) method, 212
  images, scaling, 249
getHSBColor( ) method, 233
getImage( ) method, 246
getItem( ) method
  choice menus, 303
  scrolling lists, 319
getLabel( ) method, checkboxes, 300
getLeading( ) method, 212

getLineIncrement( ) method,
text areas, 317
getMaximum( ) method,
scrollbars, 321
getMinimum( ) method,
scrollbars, 321
getName( ) method, 98, 211
getOrientation( ) method,
scrollbars, 321
getPageIncrement( ) method,
text areas, 317
getParameter( ) method, 83,
184
GetRaven applet, creating,
362-364
GetRaven class (listing),
362-363
getRows( ) method, text areas,
317
getSelectedIndex( ) method
choice menus, 303
scrolling lists, 319
getSelectedIndexes( ) method,
scrolling lists, 319
getSelectedItem( ) method
choice menus, 303
scrolling lists, 319
getSize( ) method, 211
getState( ) method, checkboxes,
300
getStyle( ) method, 211
getText( ) method, 298
text fields, 304
getValue( ) method, scrollbars,
321
getWidth( ) method, scaling
images, 249
GIF, 247
global variables, 55
GNU C compiler Web site, 495
Go to Next Error icon, 116
Go to Previous Error icon, 116
Grader applet, 119-120
creating, 117-118
Graph applet, 191
Web site, 192
graphics, 194-195

clearing, 207
coordinate system, 194-195
copying, 207
fonts, setting current, 209
see also drawing
Graphics class, 194-195, 567
primitives, 195
greater than comparison
operator, 69
greater than or equal to
comparison operator, 69
GridBagConstraints class, 308,
567
GridBagLayout class, 308, 567
GridLayout class, 308, 567
grids (panel components),
layouts, 308
Guesser applet, creating,
334-342

H

handleEvent( ) method, 272,
287-289, 315, 322
overriding, calling event
handlers, 289
handlers (methods), actions,
313
HandleTo( ) macro, 492
handling
actions, 329
events, 339-342
Hashtable class, 563
header files, 492
creating, javah, 491
naming, packages, 491
heap
constant pool, 511
virtual machine, 511
HEIGHT attribute
(<APPLET> HTML tag), 179
Help command, class library
documentation, 99
help menus, creating, 350
hexadecimal integers, 60-61
hide( ) method, frames, 348
hierarchies

classes
diagrams, 547, 559
directories, 396
components, 295
exceptions, 419
interfaces, 402-406
design compared to
implementation,
404-405
packages, 395
hierarchy
classes, 36-37
creating, 37-39
homework directory, creating,
13
HotDrink.gif, 249
HotJava, 6, 20
Java compatibility, 4
threads, 432
HSPACE attribute (<APPLET>
HTML tag), 183
HTML
documents
creating, 177-180
returning URLs, 246
tags
<APPLET>, 5, 177-181,
184
embedding applets, 172
in documentation
comments, 164
<PARAM>, 83, 184
parameters, 83
HTML code for
BiggerPalindrome.html
(listing), 187
HTML code for
BigPalindrome.html (listing),
178

I

Iceblox applet, 391
Web site, 392
icons
applets, 30
Project Manager, 85

toolbars, viewing descriptions, 30
ID instance variables, events, **287**
IDEs (integrated development environments), 11
IDs (events), 322
if conditionals, 107-108
nested, 109
if keyword, 107
Image class, 246, 567
image observers, 251
ImageConsumer interface, 568
ImageFilter class, 569
ImageObserver interface, 569
ImageProducer interface, 569
images
animations
arrays, 253
creating, 252-259
bitmapped, drawing, 195
directories, 247
drawing, 247-251
formats, 247
loading, 246-247
image observers, 251
modifying, 251
Pete applet, 253
scaling, 249-251
implementation hierarchies (interfaces), compared to design, 404-405
implementing
interfaces, 128
methods, 132-133
implements keyword, 128
import statement, 17
classes, 397
programming style, 398
importing
classes, 397-400
* (asterisks), 409
multiple, 176
interfaces, 545
packages, 545
* (asterisks), 45
projects, 30
incrementing for loops, 111

indentation (programming), readability, 32
IndexColorModel class, 569
InetAddress class, 566
infinite.am Web site, 263
inheritance
class methods, 391
classes, 36-40
casting, 94
interfaces, 41
extends clause, 403
subclassing, 403-406
methods, 39
multiple, 40, 410
interfaces, 402
single, 40
init( ) method
applet parameters, 186
background color, setting, 275
fonts, setting, 284
images, loading, 268
overriding, 174
panel layouts, 325
parameters, retrieving, 184
initializers (variables), declaring, 56
initializing
applets, 174
creating layout managers, 306
arrays, 105
for loops, 111
instance variables, 151
objects, constructor methods, 162
input streams, 456-471
applets, file system, 462
EOFException exceptions, 466
file system, attaching, 462
IOException exceptions, 456
threads, 457
InputStream class, 457-461, 565
methods, 481
inserting, documentation comments, 164-165
insertText( ) method, text

areas, 317
Inset class, 310-311
insets, panels, 310-311
Insets class, 568
insets( ) method, overriding, 311
installing WorkShop, 13
troubleshooting, 584
instance methods, 28, 48, 138
instance variables, 27, 48, 54, 86
access modifiers, 381-382
accessor methods, 382-383
animations, 253
creating, 31, 128, 326
defining, 128-129
double-buffering, 264
ID, events, 287
initial values, 56
initializing, 151
length, testing arrays, 106
multithreading, 433
parameters, 186
threads, 227
values, accessing, 87
instanceof operator, 98
instances, 47
classes, 26
Color class, creating, 214
new operator, 82
String class, creating, 80
threads, creating, 440
URL class, creating, 358
int variable type, 60
Integer class, 562
argument arrays, converting, 144
integer data types, 57
integers, casting to floating-point values, 94
division, 64
hexadecimal, 60-61
literals, 60
octal, 60
read( ) method, casting to correct size, 458
integrated development environments (IDEs), 11

interfaces, 41, 48, 401-408, 545
  access modifiers, 403
  AppletContext, 570
  AppletStub, 570
  AudioClip, 570
  callbacks, 410
  casting, from objects, 95
  classes, 99
  Cloneable, 562
  compared to classes, 402
  ContentHandlerFactory, 566
  DataInput, 465-466, 564
  DataOutput, 475-477, 564
  declaring, 402
  Enumeration, 563
  Enumerator, 407-408
  exceptions, 423
  FileNameFilter, 564
  hierarchies, 402-406
    design compared to
      implementation,
      404-405
  ImageConsumer, 568
  ImageObserver, 569
  ImageProducer, 569
  implementing, 128
  inheritance
    extends clause, 403
    subclassing, 403-406
  LayoutManager, 566
  MenuContainer, 566
  methods, 402
  multiple inheritance, 402
  objects, networking, 481
  Observer, 563
  Runnable, 562
    adding to class definitions,
      228
    creating threads, 441
    testing, 441-443
    threads, 227
  SocketImplFactory, 566
  URLStreamHandlerFactory,
    566
  user
    designing with Visual
      Java, 334-335

    events, 322-323
    Visual Java, 334
  user components, 296-305
    creating with Visual Java,
      336-337
    handling actions/events,
      311-313
    placement limitations,
      343
    placing multiple, 337-338
  user components, 295
  variables, 402
Internet, Java, 4
**Internet Explorer, Java
  compatibility, 4**
interpreters, bytecode, 512-513
IOException exception
  input streams, 456
  network connections, 361
isBold( ) method, 211
**isEditable( ) method, text
  fields, 305**
isItalic( ) method, 211
isPlain( ) method, 211

J

Jabberwock class, creating, 29
JabberwockApplet
  creating, 30-34
  running, 35
**JabberwockApplet.java
  (listing), 33-34**
Java, 4, 504-505
  capabilities, 7
  compared to C++, 572-575
  development, 503-504
  ease of use, 10-11
  history, 6-7
  OOP, 10
  platform independence, 7-10
  security, 173, 520
  specification Web site, 538
java, 579-580
Java Developer's Kit (JDK), 7
java package, 42
  class libraries, 99-100
Java WorkShop, *see* **Workshop**

java.applet package, 99, 570
java.awt package, 99, 566-568
**java.awt.image package,
  568-569**
  images, modifying, 251
java.awt.peer package, 569
java.io package, 99, 564-565
  classes, 479
**java.lang package, 42, 99,
  562-563**
**java.net package, 99, 357,
  565-566**
java.util package, 99, 563-564
javac, 578-579
  error messages,
    troubleshooting, 585
JavaDoc, 580-581
javah, 581
  header files, creating, 491
  stub files, creating, 492
javap, 581
**JavaSoft API documentation
  Web site, 562**
JavaSoft Web site, 252, 496
JDK (Java Developer's Kit), 7
  applications, running from
    command-line, 144
  command-line utilities,
    578-581
  conflicts, installing
    WorkShop, 578
  Web site, 578
  Workshop compatibility, 13
jdk portfolio, 30
join( ) method, threads, 443
joined threads, 443
JPEG files, 247
jump-to-error icons, 116, 119
**just-in-time compiling, 488,
  513, 514**

K

Karl Hornell Web site, 259
KEY ACTION, text fields, 322
keyboard events, 282-287
  modifier keys, 287

variables, non-alphanumeric keys, 283
keyDown( ) method, 282, 285
Keys applet, creating, 283-286
keyUp( ) method, 283
keyword, this, 133-134
keywords
break, 114-115
labels, 115-116
class, 128
continue, 114-115
labels, 115-116
else, 107
extends, 43, 128
false, 61
final, 129
if, 107
implements, 128
public, 43
creating applets, 173
return, 132
static, 130, 138
class variables, 384
defining class variables, 89
super, calling methods, 160
synchronized, multithreading, 434
this, 151
omitting, 134
throws, 131
true, 61-62
while, 112

L

Label class, 568
methods, 298
Label( ) constructor method, 297
labeled loops, 115-116
labels (user interface components), 297-298
adjusting size, 337
buttons, 299
creating, 297
fonts, 297

text
aligning, 129-130
changing, 337
text fields, 303
Lamp applet
creating, 206-207
layout managers
AWT components, 305
BorderLayout class, 309-310
CardLayout class, 310
creating, 306
FlowLayout class, 306-307
GridBagLayout class, 308
GridLayout class, 308
LayoutManager interface, 566
layouts, 305-311
applets, creating, 324
components, adding to panels, 297
frames, default, 348
panels
creating, 324-325
default, 297
nested, 315
left shift assignment operator (<<=), 71
left shift operator (<<), 70
length instance variable, testing arrays, 106
less than comparison operator, 69
less than or equal to comparison operator, 69
libraries
classes, 8, 27, 562-570
java package, 99-100
packages, 42
native, creating, 498-499
LimeSweeper applet, 268
Web site, 269
line numbers, adding (debugging), 467
LineNumberInputStream class, 467, 565
lines
drawing, 195
thickness, 218
Lines applet, 166-167

creating, 278-282
Web site, 167
linking classes, 499
links, creating, 358
linkTo( ) method, 360
List class, 568
scrolling lists, creating, 318
LIST DESELECT, scrolling lists, 322
LIST SELECT, scrolling lists, 322
List( ) constructor method, 318
listings
alternative HTML code for BiggerPallindrome.html, 188
<APPLET> tag and HTML formatting for Calc, 77
<APPLET> tag and surrounding HTML tags for Countdown, 482
<APPLET> tag for Abacus, 345
<APPLET> tag for Eowyn4, 219
<APPLET> tag for BallDrop, 452
<APPLET> tag for Eliza, 429
<APPLET> tag for Fan, 243
<APPLET> tag for Graph, 192
<APPLET> tag for Iceblox, 392
<APPLET> tag for Lines, 167
<APPLET> tag for MktView, 500
<APPLET> tag for NeedleDemo, 147
<APPLET> tag for NowShowing, 371
<APPLET> tag for scroll, 291
<APPLET> tag for SharkLine, 126
<APPLET> tag for SmartMap, 412-414
<APPLET> tag for SparkleText on a simple

HTML page, 22
<APPLET> tag for StarField, 102
BiggerPalindrome class, 187
BigPalindrome applet, 177
BigPalindrome.java, 45
final Pete applet, 257-259
final source code of Guesser.java, 340-342
first part of the Lines applet, 278
GetRaven class, 362-363
HTML code for BiggerPalindrome.html, 187
HTML code for BigPalindrome.html, 178
JabberwockApplet.java, 33-34
Palindrome.java source code, 16
pop-up window example, 349
revised source code of Checkers1.java, 239-240
revised source code of Checkers2.java, 266-267
source code for Arithmetic.java, 65
source code for CreateDate1.java, 81
source code for CreateDate2.java, 84
source code for DigitalThreads.java, 229-230
source code for EchoArgs.java, 141
source code for Grader.java, 118
source code for SumAverage.java, 143
source code of AudioLoop.java, 262
source code of ButtonLink.java, 359-360
source code of Centered.java, 213
source code of Checkers1.java, 234-235

source code of ColorSwirl.java, 232
source code of ColorText.java, 332-333
source code of DigitalClock.java, 224
source code of DrawDrink.java, 248
source code of DrawDrink2.java, 250-251
source code of FillText.java, 313
source code of Keys.java, 286
source code of Lamp.java, 206
source code of Lines.java, 281-282
source code of ManyFonts.java, 210
source code of Passer.java, 136-137
source code of PersonApplet.java, 155
source code of PrePost.java, 68
source code of Range applet, 133
source code of RectApplet.java, 152-153
source code of RectApplet2, 157-158
source code of Spots.java, 276-277
source code of TestPoint.java, 88
source code of TestString.java, 90
lists, scrolling, 302
literals, 60, 539
    boolean, 61
    characters, 61
        creating objects, 80
    floating-point, 61
    integers, 60
    numbers, creating objects, 80
    strings, 63
loading
    applets, 173

audio files, URLs, 260
classes, 499
    security considerations, 524-525
images, 246-247
    init( ) method, 268
Visual Java, 335
local variables, 55
    block statements, 107
    values, assigning, 56
location( ) method, frames, 348
logical operators, 69-70
Long class, 562
long variable type, 60
loop( ) method, audio files, 261
loops, 543
    audio files, 261
    break keyword, 114-115
        labels, 115-116
    continue keyword, 114-115
        labels, 115-116
    debugging, breakpoints, 122, 124
    do, 112-114
    ending, 114-115
    for, 111-144
        animations, 254
        statements, 111
    labeled, 115-116
    optimizing code, 488
    threads, 451
    while, 112-113

M

macros, HandleTo( ), 492
main( ) method, 139
    applications, 173-174
    frames, 357
    signatures, 140
makeRange( ) method, 132
ManyFonts applet, creating, 209-210
mark( ) method, input streams, 460
marking and sweeping

(garbage collection), 517
markSupported( ) method,
    input streams, 460
Math class, 138, 562
MediaTracker class, 568
memory
    finalizer methods, 162-163
    garbage collection, 83,
        515-519
        compaction, 517
        disabling, 528
        marking and sweeping,
            517
        parallel, 518
    heaps, 511
    pointers, 93
    stack frame, 510
    variables, 54
    virtual machine,
        requirements, 507
memory management, 573
    objects, creating, 82-83
MemoryImageSource class, 569
menu bars
    creating, 350
    menus, adding, 350
Menu class, 568
MenuBar class, 568
MenuComponent class, 568
MenuContainer interface, 566
MenuItem class, 351, 568
menus
    action events, 352
    adding to menu bars, 350
    adding to windows, 352-353
    choice, creating, 302-303
    default, setting, 350
    disabling/enabling, 351
    help, creating, 350
    items
        adding, 351
        disabling/enabling, 351
    separator lines, adding, 351
    submenus, creating, 351
    windows, 350-353
messages (creating), browser
    status bars, 366
meta keys, 290

metaDown( ) method, 287
method area (virtual machine),
    511
methods
    abstract, 389-390
    abstract classes, 404, 410
    accept( ), sockets, 365
    accessor, 382-383
        speed considerations, 390
    action( )
        adding, 339
        defining, 312
        menus, 352
    actions, handlers, 313
    add( )
        adding components to
            panels, 297
        border layouts, 310
        frames, 348
        menu items, 351
    addItem( ), choice menus,
        302
    animation, 254-256
    applets, 174
        running, 223
    arguments, passing, 135-138
    arrays, 132
    available( ), 481
        input streams, 459-462
    buildRect( ), creating, 151
    Button( ), 298
    calling, 89-92, 160-161
    charWidth( ), 212
    Checkbox( ), 299
    class, 91-92, 138, 385
        defining, 138
        inheritance, 391
        naming, 92
    classes, comparing, 96
    clearRect( ), 207
    clipRect( ), 239
    close( ), output streams, 472
    color, 215-216
    close( ), input streams, 461
    compared to functions, 48
    connect( ), 364
    constants, 129-130
    constructors, 82, 154-158

    calling, 156
    creating objects, 80
    overloading, 156-158
    overriding, 159-162
controlDown( ), 287
copyArea( ), 207
countItem( )
    choice menus, 303
    scrolling lists, 319
createImage( ), 264
creating, 31-33, 150-151
DataInput interface, 465
DataOutput interface,
    475-476
declaring
    block statements, 107
    final, 387-388
    package access, 378
defining, 131-132, 544-545
    modifiers, 131
    object behavior, 28
    variable scope, 134-135
destroy( ), 175-176
disable( ), menus, 351
draw3DRect( ), 198
drawArc( ), 201
drawChars( ), 209
drawImage( ), 247-251
drawLine( ), 195
drawOval( ), 201
drawPolygon( ), 199
drawRect( ), 196
drawRoundRect( ), 197
drawString( ), 66, 137, 209
echoCharIsSet( ), text fields,
    305
enable( ), menus, 351
equals( ), comparing string
    characters, 97
events, boolean values, 315
exceptions, 419
FileDialog( ), 355
fill3DRect( ), 198
fillArc( ), 201
fillOval( ), 201
fillPolygon( ), 199
fillRect( ), 196
fillRoundRect( ), 197

final modifier, 386-388
finalize( ), 163
    compared to destroy( )
        method, 175
    forcing, 528
finalizers, 162-163
flush( ), output streams, 472
fonts, 211-212
getAppletContext( ), 366-367
getAppletInfo( ), 366
getApplets( ), 367
getAscent( ), 212
getAudioClip( ), 260
getCheckboxGroup( ), 301
getClass( ), 98
getCodeBase( ), 246
getColumns( )
    text areas, 317
    text fields, 305
getCurrent( ), checkboxes,
    301
getDescent( ), 212
getDocumentBase( ), 246
getEchoChar( ), text fields,
    305
getFont( ), 211
getFontList( ), 208
getFontMetrics( ), 211
getGraphics( ), 264
getHeight( ), 212
    scaling images, 249
getHSBColor( ), 233
getImage( ), 246
getItem( )
    choice menus, 303
    scrolling lists, 319
getLabel( ), checkboxes, 300
getLeading( ), 212
getLineIncrement( ), text
    areas, 317
getMaximum( ), scrollbars,
    321
getMinimum( ), scrollbars,
    321
getName( ), 98, 211
getOrientation( ), scrollbars,
    321

getPageIncrement( ), text
    areas, 317
getParameter( ), 83, 184
getRows( ), text areas, 317
getSelectedIndex( )
    choice menus, 303
    scrolling lists, 319
getSelectedIndexes( ),
    scrolling lists, 319
getSelectedItem( )
    choice menus, 303
    scrolling lists, 319
getSize( ), 211
getState( ), checkboxes, 300
getStyle( ), 211
getText( ), 298
    text fields, 304
getValue( ), scrollbars, 321
getWidth( ), scaling images,
    249
handleEvent( ), 272,
    287-289, 315, 322
hide( ), frames, 348
implementing, 132-133
inheritance, 39
init( )
    applet parameters, 186
    loading images, 268
    overriding, 174
    panel layouts, 325
    retrieving parameters, 184
    setting, 284
    setting background color,
        275
input streams read( ),
    457-459
InputStream class, 481
insertText( ), text areas, 317
insets( ), overriding, 311
instance, 28, 138
interfaces, 41, 402
isBold( ), 211
isEditable( ), text fields, 305
isItalic( ), 211
isPlain( ), 211
join( ), threads, 443
keyDown( ), 282, 285

keyUp( ), 283
Label( ), 297
linkTo( ), 360
List( ), 318
local variables, 55
location( ), frames, 348
loop( ), audio files, 261
main( ), 139
    applications, 173-174
    creating application
        frames, 357
    signature, 140
makeRange( ), 132
mark( ), input streams, 460
markSupported( ), input
    streams, 460
metaDown( ), 287
modifiers, 375-376
mouseDown events, 272-273
mouseDown( ), 275
mouseDrag( ), 277
mouseEnter( ), 277-278
mouseExit( ), 277-278
mouseMove( ), 277
mouseUp events, 273
move( ), frames, 348
multithreading, 434
    safe, 435-436
    synchronized statement,
        436-437
naming, 131, 383
native, 485-486
    applets, 486
    C code, 494-496
    classes, 489-491
    creating, 489-498
    limitations, 486-487
    platform independence,
        486
new Frame( ), 348
notify( ), multithreading, 451
oneToZero( ), 137
openStream( ), network
    connections, 361-364
optimizing code, 488
overloading, 100, 131, 150
    compile errors, 166
overriding, 40, 44, 159-160

final, 387
paint( ), 17, 275
    animation, 222
    animation flicker, 230
    creating fonts, 209
    Graphics objects, 194
    overriding, 44, 176-177
parameters, 132
play( ), audio files, 260
printMe( ), 159
PrintStream class, 478
private compared to final,
    388
read( ), troubleshooting, 480
readLine( ), input streams,
    468
repaint( ), 275
    animation, 222
    animation flicker, 230
replaceText( ), text areas, 317
reset( ), input streams,
    460-462
resize( ), frames, 348
RGBtoHSB( ), 328
run( ), 274
    animations, 254
    avoiding animation
        flicker, 237-239
    threads, 227
running, synchronized,
    437-438
Scrollbar( ), 320
scrolling lists, 319
select( )
    choice menus, 303
    scrolling lists, 319
    text fields, 305
selectAll( ), text fields, 305
setAlignment( ), 298
setBackground( ), 215
setCheckboxGroup( ), 301
setColor( ), 215
setCurrent( ), checkboxes,
    301
setEditable( ), text fields, 305
setFont( ), 209
setForeground( ), 215
setHelpMenu( ), 350

setLabel( ), checkboxes, 300
setLayout( ), creating layout
    managers, 306
setLineIncrement( ), text
    areas, 317
setLineNumber( ), input
    streams, 467
setMenuBar( ), 350
setPageIncrement( ), text
    areas, 317
setState( ), checkboxes, 300
setText( ), 298
    text fields, 304
setValue( ), scrollbars, 321
shiftDown( ), 287
show( ), frames, 348
showDocument( ), 366
showStatus( ), 366
    troubleshooting, 369
signatures, 131, 493
size( ), clearing applets, 207
skip( ), input streams, 459
sleep( ), threads, 224
start( ), 223
    overriding, 175
    threads, 227
stop( ), 223
    audio files, 261
    overriding, 175
    threads, 227
streams, 456
strings, 62
stringWidth( ), 212
synchronization, 435
TextArea( ), 316
TextField( ), 303
toString( ), 73
unread( ), input streams, 467
update( ), 329-331
    animation flicker, 230
    overriding to avoid
        animation flicker, 231
valueOf, 91
variables
    declaring, 55
    stack frame, 510
wait( ), multithreading, 451
write( ), output streams,

471-472
    yield( ), multithreading, 448
MIDDLE value, (<APPLET>
    HTML tag ALIGN attribute),
    182
minus sign (-) subtraction
    operator, 63
MktView applet, 500
    Web site, 501
modal dialog boxes, 353
modifier keys, keyboard events,
    287
modifiers, 375-376
    access, 376, 390
        classes, 401
        instance variables,
            381-382
        interfaces, 403
        package, 377-378
        private, 380-381
        protected, 378-380
        public, 377
    coding, readability, 377
    final, 386-388
    methods, defining, 131
    order, 376
    transient, 376
    volatile, 376
modulus operator, 64
mouse
    buttons, events, 290
    click events, 272-277
        arguments, 273
        parameters, 273
    events, debugging, 287
    movement events, 277-282
mouseDown events, 272-273
    methods, 272-273
    parameters, 273
mouseDown( ) method, 275
mouseDrag( ) method, 277
mouseEnter( ) method,
    277-278
mouseExit( ) method, 277-278
mouseMove( ) method, 277
mouseUp events, 272-273
    methods, 273
    parameters, 273

move() method, frames, **348**
multidimensional arrays, 106
multiline comments, 59
multiple inheritance, 40, 410
    interfaces, 402
multiplication operator, 64
multithreading, 225, 433-434
    critical sections, 437
    deadlock, 451
    methods, safe, 435-436
        synchronized statement,
            436-437
    scheduler, 451
    schedulers, testing, 447-448
    semaphores, 451
    synchronization, 435
MyRect applet, creating,
150-154

N

NAME attribute (<APPLET>
HTML tag), 191
NAME attribute (<PARAM>
HTML tag), 83, 184
naming
    applet parameters, 184
    class methods, 92
    class variables, 89
    classes, conventions, 397
    methods, 131, 383
    packages, 395
        conventions, 397
    states, objects, 129
    threads, 443-444
    variables, 56-57
        conventions, 57
native code, speed
considerations, 10
native libraries, creating,
498-499
native methods, 485-486
    applets, 486
    C code, 494-496
    C functions, 496-497
    classes, 489-491

    creating, 489-498
    limitations, 486-487
    platform independence, 486
    Web site, 489
navigation toolbar, 14
Needle class Web site, 147
NeedleDemo applet, 146-147
Neil/Fred's Gigantic List of
Palindromes Web site, 17
NervousText applet Web site,
531
nesting
    components, 314-316
    exception handlers, 421
    filters, streams, 463-464
    if conditionals, 109
    instance variable access, 87
    output streams, 474
    panels, 314-316
        events, 315-316
    streams, buffered, 464
Netscape Navigator 2.0, Java
compatibility, 4
networking, 357-365
    interfaces, objects, 481
networks
    classes, 99
    connections, opening,
        361-364
new command, *see* **new**
operator
new Frame() method, 348
new operator
    array instances, creating, 105
    objects, creating, 80-83
non-preemptive scheduling,
446
nonexclusive check boxes, 299
not equal comparison operator,
69
not logical operator, 70
notify() method,
multithreading, 451
NowShowing applet, 370
    Web site, 371
null parameters, 185
    troubleshooting, 191

Number class, 562
numbers (variables), naming,
56

O

Oak, 6
Object class, 37, 562
object references, garbage
collection, 517
object-oriented programming,
see **OOP**
objects, 24, 47, 542
    actions, testing, 312
    arrays, 104
        creating, 104-105
        references, 106
    attributes, 27-28
    behavior, 28
    casting, 94-95
        to primitive data types,
            95-96
    classes, 25-27
        determining, 98
    color
        creating, 214, 233
        setting current color,
            215-216
    compared to primitive data
        types, 100
    comparison operators, 96-98
    constants, 129-130
    converting to primitive data
        types, 138
    converting to strings, 73
    creating, 80-83
        arguments, 80
        memory management,
            82-83
        painting animations, 225
        parentheses, 80
        string literals, 63
    Date, creating, 81
    Dimension, 212
    fonts, creating, 208
    garbage collection, 528
    Graphics, paint() methods,
        194

initializing, constructor
    methods, 162
instances, 26
methods
    calling, 28
    defining, 131-132
networking, interfaces, 481
Point, 151
referencing, 92-93
    this keyword, 133-134
states, naming, 129
strings, 62
vending, 408
wrappers, 80
see also classes
Observable class, 563
Observer interface, 563
octal integers, 60
oneToZero( ) method, 137
online help, 12
OOP (object-oriented
    programming), 10, 23
    inheritance, 36-40
    objects, 24
        classes, 25-27
opcode, 508
opening
    files, dialog boxes, 355-356
    WWW connections, 361
openStream( ) method, 358
    network connections,
        361-364
operand stack, 510
operands, storage, 508
operating systems
    compatibility, 12
    threads, limitations, 432
operators, 63, 74-75, 541-542,
    574
    arithmetic, 63-66
    assignment, 66
        assigning variable values,
            87-88
        incrementing/
            decrementing, 67
    bitwise, 71
    comparison, 69
        objects, 96-98

conditional, 108-109
logical, 69-70
new
    creating array instances,
        105
    creating objects, 80-83
overloading, 96, 101
postfix, 67
precedence, 71-73
    parentheses, 72
prefix, 67
v, 98
optimizing programming code,
    488-489
optop register, 509
OR assignment operator (l=),
    71
or logical operator, 70
output streams, 471-479
    buffering, 475
    filters, 474-475
    nesting, 474
OutputStream class, 471-472,
    565
ovals, drawing, 201
overloading
    constructor methods,
        156-158
    methods, 100, 131, 150
    operators, 96, 101
overriding
    constructor methods,
        159-162
    handleEvent( ) method, 287
        calling event handlers, 289
    init( ) method, 174
    insets( ) method, 311
    methods, 40, 44, 159-160,
        174
    paint( ) method, 176-177
    start( ) method, 175
    stop( ) method, 175

P

package access modifier,
    377-378

package statement, naming
    packages, 394
packages, 42, 48, 394-401, 545
    archiving, 409
    classes
        accessing, 42
        importing, 397-400
    exceptions, 420
    hierarchies, 395
    importing, 44-46
        * (asterisks), 45
    java, 42
        class libraries, 99-100
    java.applet, 99, 570
    java.awt, 99, 566-568
    java.awt.image, 568-569
        modifying images, 251
    java.awt.peer, 569
    java.io, 99, 564-565
    java.lang, 42, 99, 562-563
    java.net, 99, 357, 565-566
    java.util, 99, 563-564
    naming, 395
        conventions, 397
    peer, 343
paint( ) method, 17, 275
    animation, 222
    animation flicker, 230
    fonts, creating, 209
    Graphics objects, 194
    overriding, 44, 176-177
painting, 241
    animation, 222
        creating objects, 225
    applets, 176
        importing Graphics class,
            194
    see also drawing
Palette toolbar, Visual Java,
    336-337
palindrome applet, creating,
    14-19
Palindrome.java source code
    (listing), 16
Panel class, 568
panel grids (Visual Java),
    modifying, 336

panels, 305-311
    components, grid layouts,
        308
    creating nested, 314-315
    insets, 310-311
    layouts
        adding components, 297
        creating, 324-325
        default, 297
    nesting, 314-316
        events, 315-316
    subpanels, creating, 326-328
    user interface components,
        adding to panels, 297
    see also windows
parallel garbage collection, 518
param documentation tag, 165
<PARAM> HTML tag, 83, 184
parameters
    <APPLET> HTML tag, 22
    applets
        case-sensitivity, 185
        changing, 188-189
        naming, 184
        passing, 184-189
        running, 83
    applications, passing, 184
    instance variables, 186
    methods, 132
    mouse click events, 273
    null, 185
    troubleshooting, 191
pararmeters
parentheses
    objects, creating, 80
    operator precedence, 72
Passer applet, creating,
    136-138
passing
    parameters to applets,
        184-189
    parameters to applications,
        184
    URLs, browsers, 358
passwords, text fields, 304
pc register, 509
peer package, 343

percent sign (%) modulus
    operator, 64
PersonApplet, creating,
    155-156
Pete applet, creating, 256-259
    images, 253
PipedInputStream class, 469,
    565
PipedOutputStream class, 479,
    565
pipes, 455
Pixel Pete, creating animations,
    252-259
PixelGrabber class, 569
platform independence, 7-10,
    505
    bytecodes, 8
    native methods, 486
play( ) method, audio files, 260
plus sign (+)
    addition operator, 63
    string concatenation, 73
Point class, 568
Point objects, 151
pointers, 93, 572
    soft, 518
Polygon class, 200, 568
polygons
    closing, 200
    drawing, 199-200
pop-up menus, 302
pop-up window example
    (listing), 349
Portfolio dialog box (Project
    Manager), 85
Portfolio Manager, 11
    classes, creating, 29-30
    commands
        Choose, 30
        Create a New Project, 30
        Remove the Selected
            Project, 30
    icon, 15
    projects, creating, 14
    toolbar, 15
portfolios
    awt, 30
    importing, 30
    jdk, 30

read-only, 30
POST forms, 369
postfix operators, 67
precedence, operators, 71-73
preemptive time-slicing, 446
prefix operators, 67
PrePost applet, creating, 67-69
primitive data types, 8, 57
    arrays, 105
    casting, 93
        to objects, 95-96
    char, 58
    compared to objects, 100
    converting to objects, 138
    floating-point, 58
    integers, 57
    returntype, 131
    switch conditionals, 110
PrintClass class, 159
printMe( ) method, 159
PrintStream class, 477-479,
    565
PrintSubClass class, 159
private access modifier,
    380-381
private methods, compared to
    final, 388
primitive data types,
Process class, 562
profiling, programming code,
    488
programming, 20, 393
    arrays, 104
    breakpoints, 116
    bytecodes, 8
    C compared to Java, 8
    case-sensitivity, 33, 57
    class hierarchies, limitations,
        402
    class libraries, 8
    comments, 32, 59-60, 165
    critical sections, 437
    debugging, 116-117
    development tools, IDEs, 11
    exceptions, 418-420, 424
    inheritance, 36-40
        multiple, 40
        single, 40

interfaces, 406-408
literals, 60
methods, overriding, 40
multithreading, 433-434
native code, speed
   considerations, 10
object-oriented, 23-24
objects, 24
   classes, 25-27
optimizing code, 488-489
primitive data types, 8
profiling code, 488
sockets, 364
Source Editor, creating source
   files, 15-17
speed considerations,
   optimizing code, 487
statements, 54
stub files, creating, 492-493
style
   import statements, 398
   readability, 32
threads, 431-432
   creating, 439-444
programming languages
   C
      compared to Java, 11
      composite data types
         compared to classes, 26
   Java, 4
   Oak, 6
Project Manager, 11, 85-86
   applets
      creating, 83-85
      testing, 179
   arguments, setting, 142-143
   dialog boxes, 85
Project Tester, 12, 18-19, 142
   applets
      running, 30, 35
      testing, 179
   applications, running, 586
   icon, 19
projects
   changing, 85
   compiling, Build Manager,

17
   creating, 14, 30-34
      dialog boxes, 15
   distributing, 85
   importing, 30
   testing, 18-19
Properties class, 563
**protected access modifier,
   378-380**
**protecting, class variables,
   438-439**
**protection realms,
   SecurityManager class, 526**
public access modifier, 377
public keyword, 43
   applets, creating, 173
**Publish dialog box (Project
   Manager), 85**
publishing applets, 180
pull-down menus, 302
**PushBackInputStream class,
   468-469, 565**

R

**radio buttons (user interface
   components), 300-301**
Random class, 564
**RandomAccessFile class, 479,
   565**
**Range applet, creating,
   132-133**
read( ) method
   input streams, 457-459
   troubleshooting, 480
**readLine( ) method, input
   streams, 468**
Rectangle class, 568
rectangles, drawing, 196-198
RectApplet, creating, 152-154
RectApplet2, creating, 156-158
referencing
   modifiers, 376
   objects, 92-93
      this keyword, 133-134
registers

arguments, 509
   virtual machine, 509
**Remove the Selected Project
   command, Portfolio
   Manager, 30**
repaint( ) method, 275
   animation, 222
   animation flicker, 230
**replaceText( ) method, text
   areas, 317**
reports
   applets, displaying, 163
   creating, Class Browser, 47
reserved words, 538
**reset( ) method, input streams,
   460-462**
resize( ) method, frames, 348
resuming, threads, 440
return documentation tag, 165
return key, events, 290
return keyword, 132
**returntype (primitive data
   type), 131**
**revised source code of
   Checkers1.java (listing),
   239-240**
**revised source code of
   Checkers2.java (listing),
   266-267**
RGBImageFilter class, 569
RGBtoHSB( ) method, 328
**right shift assignment operator
   (>>=), 71**
right shift operator (>>), 70
**rounded rectangles, drawing,
   197**
Run dialog box, 142
   Project Manager, 85
run( ) method, 274
   animation flicker, avoiding,
      237-239
   animation, 254
   threads, 227
**run-time systems, security
   considerations, 523**
Runnable interface, 562
   class definitions, adding, 228
   threads, 227
      creating, 441

Runnable interface, testing, 441-443
running
applets, 35, 174
as applications, 357
parameters, 83
Project Tester, 30, 35
running, 223
threads, 225
Visual Java, 586
applications, 142
command-line, 144-145
Project Tester, 586
JabberwockApplet, 35
methods, synchronized, 437-438
Symantec Cafe with WorkShop, 585
threads, 440
WorkShop, 13-14
troubleshooting, 584
Runtime class, 563
RuntimeException class, 419

S

Save command (File menu), 17
saving
files, dialog boxes, 355-356
source files, 17
work in progress, Visual Java, 338
scaling, images, 249-251
scheduler (multithreading), 451
testing, 447-448
scheduling, threads, 445-450
preemptive compared to non-preemptive, 446
scope (variables), defining methods, 134-135
SCROLL ABSOLUTE, scrollbars, 322
scroll applet, 291
Web site, 291
SCROLL LINE DOWN,

scrollbars, 322
SCROLL LINE UP, scrollbars, 323
SCROLL PAGE DOWN, scrollbars, 323
SCROLL PAGE UP, scrollbars, 323
Scrollbar class, 321, 568
Scrollbar( ) constructor method, 320
scrollbars (user interface components), 319-321
elevators, 319
event IDs
SCROLL ABSOLUTE, 322
SCROLL LINE DOWN, 322
SCROLL LINE UP, 323
SCROLL PAGE DOWN, 323
SCROLL PAGE UP, 323
thumbs, 319
scrolling lists (user interface components), 302, 318-319
compared to choice menus, 318
event IDs
LIST DESELECT, 322
LIST SELECT, 322
methods, 319
security, 20, 519-527
applets, 172, 190-191, 525
bytecode
data type information, 522-523
verifying, 520-523
class loader, 524-525
compiler, 520
Java, 173
language level, 520
run-time systems, 523
SecurityManager class, 526-527
warnings, 519
SecurityManager class, 526-527, 563
protection realms, 526
see documentation tag

select( ) method
choice menus, 303
scrolling lists, 319
text fields, 305
selectAll( ) method, text fields, 305
semaphores, multithreading, 451
semicolons (;)
for loops, 112
statements, 54
sendMessage( ) method, 367
separator lines (menus), adding, 351
SequenceInputStream class, 469-470, 565
server-side sockets, 365
servers, publishing applets, 180
ServerSocket class, 358, 364, 566
setAlignment( ) method, 298
setBackground( ) method, 215
setCheckboxGroup( ) method, 301
setColor( ) method, 215
setCurrent( ) method, checkboxes, 301
setEditable( ) method, text fields, 305
setFont( ) method, 209
setForeground( ) method, 215
setHelpMenu( ) method, 350
setLabel( ) method, checkboxes, 300
setLayout( ) method, creating layout managers, 306
setLineIncrement( ) method, text areas, 317
setLineNumber( ) method, input streams, 467
setMenuBar( ) method, 350
setPageIncrement( ) method, text areas, 317
setState( ) method, checkboxes, 300
setText( ) method, 298
text fields, 304
setValue( ) method, scrollbars, 321

SharkLine applet, 125-126
shiftDown( ) method, 287
show( ) method, frames, 348
showDocument( ) method, 358, 366
showStatus( ) method, 366
   troubleshooting, 369
signatures
   applets, 173
   main( ) method, 140
   methods, 131, 493
   mouseDown events, 272
single inheritance, 40
single line comments, 59
single quotes (') character literals, 61
size( ) method, clearing applets, 207
skip( ) method, input streams, 459
sleep( ) method, threads, 224
slide shows (creating), card layouts, 310
sliders (user interface components), 319-321
SmartMap applet, 411-413
   Web site, 415
Socket class, 358, 364-365, 566
SocketImpl class, 566
SocketImplFactory interface, 566
sockets
   applets, 365
   applications, networking, 364-365
   UDP, support, 370
soft pointers, 518
sound, 261-263
   background, 261
   loops, 261
   stopping, 268
   playing
      repeating, 260
      stopping, 261
Source Browser, 11, 46-47
   applets, displaying reports, 163-164
source code
   compiling, bytecode, 508

   creating, Visual Java, 338-339
source code for Arithmetic.java (listing), 65
source code for CreateDate1.java (listing), 81
source code for CreateDate2.java (listing), 84
source code for DigitalThreads.java (listing), 229-230
source code for EchoArgs.java (listing), 141
source code for Grader.java (listing), 118
source code for SumAverage.java (listing), 143
source code of AudioLoop.java (listing), 262
source code of ButtonLink.java (listing), 359-360
source code of Centered.java (listing), 213
source code of Checkers1.java (listing), 234-235
source code of ColorSwirl.java (listing), 232
source code of ColorText.java (listing), 332-333
source code of DigitalClock.java (listing), 224
source code of DrawDrink.java (listing), 248
source code of DrawDrink2.java (listing), 250-251
source code of FillText.java (listing), 313
source code of Keys.java (listing), 286
source code of Lamp.java (listing), 206
source code of Lines.java (listing), 281-282
source code of ManyFonts.java (listing), 210

source code of Passer.java (listing), 136-137
source code of PersonApplet.java (listing), 155
source code of PrePost.java (listing), 68
source code of Range applet (listing), 133
source code of RectApplet.java (listing), 152-153
source code of RectApplet2 (listing), 157-158
source code of Spots.java (listing), 276-277
source code of TestPoint.java (listing), 88
source code of TestString.java (listing), 90
Source Editor, 11
   applets, creating, 31
   debugging, 116
   exiting, 17
   HTML files, creating, 178
   source files, creating, 15-17
source files
   creating, 15-17
      text editors, 16
   sample programs, locations, 18
   saving, 17
   selecting, compiling, 85
SparkleText applet, 21
   Web site, 22
Spots applet
   creating, 273-277
   modifying, 290
Stack class, 564
stack frame, virtual machine, 510
Standalone Program dialog box, 140-141
StarField applet, 101
   Web site, 102
start( ) method, 223
   overriding, 175
   threads, 227

starting applets, 174
statements, 54
assignments, arrays, 106
block, 54
if-else conditionals, 108
blocks, 107
break, switch conditionals, 110
conditional, 543
empty, for loops, 112
expressions, 54, 63-73
accessing variables, 87
evaluating, 69
operator precedence, 71-73
variable assignment, 66
for loops, 111
import, 17
classes, 397
package, naming packages, 394
try, exception handling, 421
typedef, 58
states (objects)
attributes, 27
behavior, 28
naming, 129
static keyword, 130, 138
class variables, 384
defining, 89
status bars (browsers), creating messages, 366
stop( ) method, 223
audio files, 261
overriding, 175
threads, 227
stopping
applets, 175
audio files, 261, 268
streams, 455
applets, 474
arrays, 461-462
buffers, 457-458
caching, 464
classes, I/O, 99
closing, 463
combining, 469-470
data types, 465-466
exceptions, resetting after

marking, 460
files, processing, 477
filters, 456
naming for line numbers, 467
nesting, 463-464
garbage collection, 463
input, 456-471
applets, 462
attaching to file system, 462
EOFException exceptions, 466
IOException exception, 456
threads, 457
methods, 456
nesting, buffered, 464
output, 471-479
buffering, 475
data types, 475
filters, 474-475
nesting, 474
pipes, 455
StreamTokenizer class, 479, 565
String class, 62, 563
instances, creating, 80
StringBuffer class, 563
StringBufferInputStream class, 470-471, 565
strings, 573
arrays, 62
comparing characters, equals( ) method, 97
concatenation, 73
converting objects, 73
creating, 73
date, format, 82
drawing, 209-210
literals, 63
parameters, converting, 185
Unicode, creating, 473
URLs, creating, 358
StringTokenizer class, 564
stringWidth( ) method, 212
stub files, 493-494
compiling, 498

creating, 492-493
subclasses, 36, 48, 128
methods, overriding final, 387
protected access modifiers, 378
substituting for superclasses, 95
subclassing, 37, 42-47
Applet class, 173
extends keyword, 43
interfaces, inheritance, 403-406
threads, creating, 440
submenus, creating, 351
subpanels, creating, 326-328
subtraction operator, 63
subscripts, arrays, 105
SumAverage application
creating, 143-144
super keyword, calling methods, 160
superclasses, 36, 47
constructor methods, calling, 162
Object, 37
substituting subclasses, 95
suspending threads, 440
switch conditionals, 109-110
falling through, 110
switch statements, debugging errors, 121-122
Symantec Cafe, running with WorkShop, 585
synchronization, multithreading, 435
synchronized keyword, multithreading, 434
synchronized statement, multithreading methods, 436-437
System class, 563
system performance, troubleshooting, 585
system requirements, 12
long filenames, 12

T

tags
    documentation, 164-165
    HTML
        APPLET>, 5, 177-181,
            184
        embedding applets, 172
        in documentation
            comments, 164
        <PARAM>, 83, 184
        parameters, 83
Teach Yourself SunSoft Java
    WorkShop in 21 Days Web
    site, 584
ternary operators, *see*
    conditional operators
testing
    applets, 5, 179
    arrays, length, 106
    for loops, 111
    objects, actions, 312
    Runnable interface, 441-443
    schedulers (multithreading),
        447-448
    threads, priorities, 448-450
    variables, switch conditionals,
        110
TestPoint applet, creating,
    87-88
TestString applet, creating,
    90-91
text
    applet alternatives, 179
    color, 130
    creating, 208
    labels
        aligning, 129-130
        changing, 337
text areas (user interface
    components), 316-317
        compared to text fields, 304
text editors, creating source
    files, 16
text fields (user interface
    components), 303-305
        actions, 312
        event IDs, KEY ACTION,
            322

labels, 303
passwords, 304
TextArea class, 568
TextArea( ) constructor
    method, 316
TextComponent class, 304,
    568
TextField class, 568
TextField( ) constructor
    method, 303
TEXTTOP value (<APPLET>
    HTML tag ALIGN attribute),
    181
this keyword, 133-134, 151
    omitting, 134
Thread class, 224, 440, 563
ThreadDeath class, 563
ThreadGroup class, 563
threads, 225-226, 241,
    431-432
    animation, 254
    applets, creating, 226-228
    atomic operations, 433
    audio, stopping, 268
    communication, 469-479
    creating, 439-444
        applets, 450
        applications, 450
        Runnable interface, 441
    daemon, 440
    debugging, 444
    DigitalClock applet, adding,
        228-230
    garbage collection, 228
    grouping, 444
    input streams, 457
    instance variables, 227
    instances, creating, 440
    joined, 443
    loops, 451
    multithreading, 225, 433-434
    naming, 443-444
    operating systems,
        limitations, 432
    priorities
        assigning, 446
        default, 448
        testing, 448-450

problems, 443
run( ) method, 227
Runnable interface, 227
running, 440
scheduler, 451
scheduling, 445-450
    preemptive compared to
        non-preemptive, 446
sleep( ) method, 224
start( ) method, 227
stop( ) method, 227
stopping, 241
    determining thread death,
        444-445
suspending/resuming, 440
threadsafe variables, 434
three-dimensional rectangles,
    drawing, 197
three-dimensional rectangles,
    displaying, 198
Throwable class, 418, 563
throws clause
    circumventing, 427
    listing exceptions, 419
throws keyword, 131
thumbs, scrollbars, 319
toolbars, 14
    icons, viewing descriptions,
        30
    Portfolio Manager, 15
Toolkit class, 568
tools (development), IDEs, 11
TOP value (<APPLET> HTML
    tag ALIGN attribute), 181
toString( ) method, 73
transient modifiers, 376
troubleshooting
    color, 218
        displaying, 242
    configuration, 584
    DigitalClock applet, 226
    error messages, javac, 585
    fonts, 218
    null parameters, 191
    showStatus( ) method, 369
    system performance, 585
    three-dimensional rectangles,
        displaying, 198

variables, redefining, 135
Web site, 584
weblog file error messages, 585
WorkShop, 584-586
    installing, 584
    running, 584
true keyword, 61-62
try statement, exception handling, 421
type state (execution environment), 522
typedef statement, 58

U

UDP sockets, support, 370
Unicode character set, 56
    compatibility, 63
    strings, 62
        creating, 473
Uniform Resource Locators, *see* **URLs**
unread( ) method, input streams, 467
update( ) method, 329-331
    animation flicker, 230
    overriding, avoiding
        animation flicker, 231
updating applets, 329-331
URL class, 566
    instances, creating, 358
URLConnection class, 364, 566
URLEncoder class, 566
URLs (Uniform Resource Locators), 14
    applets, testing, 179
    audio files, loading, 260
    bookmarks, 360
    HTML documents, returning, 246
    images, loading, 246-247
    WWW connections, opening, 361
URLStreamHandler class, 566

URLStreamHandlerFactory interface, 566
user interface components, 295-305
    actions, handling, 311-313
    adding to panels, 297
    Attributes window, Visual Java, 337
    buttons, 298-299
    canvases, 322
    check boxes, 299-300
    choice menus, 302-303
    creating, Visual Java, 336-337
    event IDs, ACTION EVENT, 322
    events, 297
        handling, 311-313
    labels, 297-298
        adjusting size, 337
    layout managers, 305
    placement limitations, 343
    placing multiple shortcuts, 337-338
    radio buttons, 300-301
    scrollbars, 319-321
    scrolling lists, 318-319
    sliders, 319-321
    text areas, 316-317
    text fields, 303-305
utilities
    classes, 99
    command-line, JDK, 578-581

V

VALUE attribute (<PARAM> HTML tag), 83, 184
valueOf( ) method, 91
values
    ALIGN attribute (APPLET> HTML tag), 181-182
    boolean, event methods, 315
    color, RGB, 214
    parameters, 184
variables, 54-55

accessing, dot notation, 87
arrays, declaring, 104
assigning, 540
assignment, 66
class, 54, 88, 384
    accessing, 89
    creating, 128
    declaring, 130
    defining, 89
    naming, 89
    protecting, 438-439
class instances, 58
constants, 129-130
declaring, 55-56, 540
    final, 387
    initializers, 56
final modifer, 386-388
global, 55
instance, 27, 54
    access modifiers, 381-382
    accessor methods, 382-383
    animations, 253
    creating, 31, 128, 326
    defining, 128-129
    double-buffering, 264
    initializing, 151
    length, 106
    multithreading, 433
    parameters, 186
    threads, 227
interfaces, 402, 406
local, 55
    assigning values, 56
    block statements, 107
methods, stack frame, 510
modifiers, 375-376
naming, 56-57
    conventions, 57
objects, attributes, 27
overflow, 75
redefining, troubleshooting, 135
scope, defining methods, 134-135
testing, switch conditionals, 110
threadsafe, 434

types, 57-58
  determining, 75
values
  assigning, 59, 87-88
  defining, 8
  volatile, multithreading, 434
vars register, 509
Vector class, 564
vectors, 470
vending, objects, 408
version documentation tag, 164
vertical bar (|)
  bitwise OR operator, 70
  OR logical operator, 70
viewing icon descriptions, toolbars, 30
virtual machine, 505-512
  bytecode, 505
  components, 507
  heap, 511
  limitations, 512
  memory, requirements, 507
  method area, 511
  registers, 509
  specification, 506-507
  stack frame, 510
Visual Java, 11, 294
  applets, running, 586
  events, handling, 339-342
  Palette toolbar, 336-337
  panel grids, modifying, 336
  saving work in progress, 338
  source code, creating, 338-339
  user interface components, placing multiple, 337
  user interfaces, designing, 334-335
  windows, 335
Visual Java command button, 335
volatile modifiers, 376
volatile variables, multithreading, 434
VSPACE attribute (<APPLET> HTML tag), 183

W

wait( ) method, multithreading, 451
Web browsers, HotJava, 4, 20
Web pages (applets)
  adding, 177-180
  aligning, 181-182
Web servers, publishing applets, 180
Web sites
  Abacus applet, 345
  Animator applet, 263
  BallDrop applet, 453
  Calc applet, 77
  CarzyText applet, 531
  Clock2 applet, 51
  Countdown applet, 483
  Developer's Corner, 13, 514
  EarthWeb Chat, 4
  Eliza applet, 430
  Eowyn4, 220
  Fan applet, 243
  Gamelan, 191, 218
  GNU C compiler, 495
  Graph applet, 192
  Iceblox applet, 392
  infinite.am, 263
  Java language specification, 538
  JavaSoft, 252, 496
  JavaSoft API documentation, 562
  JDK, 578
  Karl Hornell, 259
  LimeSweeper applet, 269
  Lines applet, 167
  MktView applet, 501
  native methods, 489
  Needle class, 147
  Neil/Fred's Gigantic list of Palindromes, 17
  NervousText applet, 531
  NowShowing applet, 371
  scroll applet, 291
  Sharkline applet, 126
  SmartMap applet, 415
  SparkleText applet, 22
  StarField applet, 102
  Teach Yourself SunSoft Java WorkShop in 21 Days, 584
  troubleshooting, 584
  Workshop, 13
weblog file, 142
  error messages, troubleshooting, 585
while keyword, 112
WIDTH attribute (<APPLET> HTML tag), 179
wildcard characters * (asterisk)
  import statements, 398
  importing classes, 176
Window class, 348-349, 568
WINDOW DEICONIFY event, 356
WINDOW DESTROY event, 356
WINDOW EXPOSE event, 356
WINDOW ICONIFY event, 356
WINDOW MOVED event, 356
windows, 294-296
  applets, warnings, 368
  applications, 356-357
  Attributes, user interface components, 337
  creating, showing, 348
  events, 356
  menus, 350-353
    adding, 352-353
  Visual Java, 335
    Palette toolbar, 336
  see also panels
windows construction components, 295
WorkShop
  display resolution, 12
  downloading, 13
  features, 11-12
  installing, 13
    JDK conflicts, 578
    troubleshooting, 584

obtaining, 12-13
operating systems, 12
running, 13-14
    troubleshooting, 584
running with Symantec Cafe,
  585
system requirements, 12
troubleshooting, 584-586
versions, 12-13
Web site, 13
**wrapper classes, converting
  objects, 138**
wrappers, objects, 80
**write( ) method, output
  streams, 471-472**
WWW
applets, publishing, 180
connections, opening, 361

X-Y-Z

**XOR assignment operator (^=),
  71**
XOR logical operator, 70

**yield( ) method,
  multithreading, 448**

**zero fill right shift assignment
  operator (>>>=), 71**
**zero fill right shift operator
  (>>>), 70**

Java Developer's Guide

—Jamie Jaworski & Carie Jardean

Java is one of the major growth areas for developers on the World Wide Web. With Java, you can download and run small applications, called *applets*, from a Web server. *Java Developer's Guide* teaches developers everything they need to know to effectively develop Java applications.

The CD-ROM includes source code from the book and valuable utilities. *Java Developer's Guide* covers Java 1.1, and explains the Java interface, VRML extensions, security, and more. It also explores new technology and future trends of Java development.

$49.99 USA, $67.99 CDN,
ISBN 1-57521-069-x, 768 pp.

Laura Lemay's Web Workshop: 3D Graphics and VRML 2

—Laura Lemay, Kelly Murdock, & Justin Couch

This book is the easiest way for readers to learn how to add three-dimensional virtual worlds to Web pages. It describes the new VRML 2.0 specifications, explores the wide arrray of existing VRML sites on the Web, and steps the readers through the process of creating their own 3D Web environments.

The CD-ROM contains the book in HTML format, a hand-picked selection of the best VRML and 3D graphics tools, plus a collection of ready-to-use virtual worlds.

$39.99 USA, $56.95 CDN,
ISBN 1-57521-143-2, 504 pp.

Laura Lemay's Web Workshop: Graphics and Web Page Design

—Laura Lemay, Jon Duff & James Mohler

With the number of Web pages increasing daily, only the well-designed will stand out and grab the attention of those browsing the Web. This book illustrates, in classic Laura Lemay style, how to design attractive Web pages that will be visited over and over again.

The CD-ROM contains HTML editors, graphics software, and royalty-free graphics and sound files.

$55.00 USA, $77.95 CDN,
ISBN 1-57521-125-4, 408 pp.

Laura Lemay's Web Workshop: JavaScript

—Laura Lemay & Michael Moncur

Readers will explore various aspects of Web publishing—whether CGI scripting and interactivity or graphics design or Netscape Gold—in greater depth than the *Teach Yourself* books.

CD-ROM includes the complete book in HTML format, publishing tools, templates, graphics, backgrounds, and more. *Laura Lemay's Web Workshop: JavaScript* provides a clear, hands-on guide to creating sophisticated Web pages.

$39.99 USA, $56.95 CDN,
ISBN 1-57521-141-6, 432 pp.

Laura Lemay's Web Workshop: Microsoft FrontPage

—Laura Lemay & Denise Tyler

This book is a clear, hands-on guide to maintaining Web pages with Microsoft's FrontPage. Written in the clear, conversational style of Laura Lemay, it is packed with many interesting, colorful examples that demonstrate specific tasks of interest to the reader.

The included CD-ROM contains all the templates, backgrounds, and materials needed.

$39.99 USA, $56.95 CDN,
ISBN 1-57521-149-1, 672 pp.

Developing Professional Java Applets

—Casey Hopson, Stephen E. Ingram

Developing Professional Java Applets is a reference for the professional programmer who needs to develop real-world, business-oriented Java applets, not just animations and games. The book assumes a basic familiarity with Java and gets right down to the business of applying Java to professional development. This comprehensive guide to developing professional Java applets teaches how to create new Java applets for business, research, and education and is filled with extensive examples of real-world Java applets.

$49.99 USA, $67.99 CDN,
ISBN 1-57521-083-5, 560 pp.

Teach Yourself Web Publishing with HTML 3.2 in 14 Days, Professional Reference Edition

—Laura Lemay

This book is the updated edition of Lemay's previous bestseller, *Teach Yourself Web Publishing with HTML in 14 Days, Premier Edition*. In it, readers will find all the advanced topics and updates—including adding audio, video, and animation—to Web page creation.

This book includes a CD-ROM and explores the use of CGI scripts, tables, HTML 3.0, the Netscape and Internet Explorer extensions, Java applets and JavaScript, and VRML.

$59.99 USA, $81.95 CDN,
ISBN 1-57521-096-7, 1,104 pp.

Add to Your Sams.net Library Today
with the Best Books for Internet Technologies

ISBN	Quantity	Description of Item	Unit Cost	Total Cost
1-57521-069-X		Java Developer's Guide (Book/CD-ROM)	$49.99	
1-57521-030-4		Teach Yourself Java in 21 Days (Book/CD-ROM)	$39.99	
1-57521-143-2		Laura Lemay's Web Workshop: 3D Graphics and VRML 2 (Book/CD-ROM)	$39.99	
1-57521-125-4		Laura Lemay's Web Workshop: Graphics and Web Page Design (Book/CD-ROM)	$55.00	
1-57521-141-6		Laura Lemay's Web Workshop: JavaScript (Book/CD-ROM)	$39.99	
1-57521-149-1		Laura Lemay's Web Workshop: Microsoft FrontPage (Book/CD-ROM)	$39.99	
1-57521-083-5		Developing Professional Java Applets (Book/CD-ROM)	$49.99	
1-57521-096-7		Teach Yourself Web Publishing with HTML 3.2 in 14 Days, Professional Reference Edition (Book/CD-ROM)	$59.99	
		Shipping and Handling: See information below.		
		TOTAL		

Shipping and Handling: $4.00 for the first book, and $1.75 for each additional book. If you need to have it NOW, we can ship product to you in 24 hours for an additional charge of approximately $18.00, and you will receive your item overnight or in two days. Overseas shipping and handling adds $2.00. Prices subject to change. Call between 9:00 a.m. and 5:00 p.m. EST for availability and pricing information on latest editions.

201 W. 103rd Street, Indianapolis, Indiana 46290

1-800-428-5331 — Orders   1-800-835-3202 — FAX   1-800-858-7674 — Customer Service

Book ISBN 1-57521-159-9